# HIGH RISK

# HIGH RISK

The Politics of the Air

## Adam Thomson

SIDGWICK & JACKSON
LONDON

# ACKNOWLEDGEMENTS

Adam Thomson wishes to acknowledge the help, encouragement and support of his family and many friends and colleagues in the preparation of this book. Particularly he recognizes the special assistance of Tony Cocklin and Margaret Trett.

*High Risk* is dedicated to all those who worked with Adam Thomson in civil aviation, but especially to the people, at all levels, in British Caledonian who brought an independent UK enterprise to the forefront of world air transport.

First published in Great Britain in 1990 by Sidgwick & Jackson Limited

ISBN 0-283-99984-5

Typeset by Hewer Text Composition Services, Edinburgh
Printed in Great Britain by Billing & Sons Ltd, Worcester
for Sidgwick & Jackson Limited
1 Tavistock Chambers, Bloomsbury Way
London WC1A 2SG

# Foreword

Holborn Circus, on the western fringe of the financial centre of the City of London, is dominated by the great slab of offices constructed in the 1960s for one of Britain's newspaper and publishing empires. As the area forms a gateway to the City, so it also marks the northern extremity of that collection of streets, alleys and squares which informally takes the name of the area's most well-known thoroughfare, Fleet Street.

The road which links Fleet Street itself with Holborn Circus is Fetter Lane, extended by the premises of Mirror Group Newspapers to become New Fetter Lane. In this custom-made street, at the foot of the publishing factory, is a public house, the watering hole for the journalists, printers and office staff employed above and around. The pub, whose illuminated sign is the only indication of life in an otherwise bleak area, is the White Hart. Few who frequent it would, however, recognise its proper name. For reasons which can be imagined easily within the newspaper world of changing proprietors and circulation battles for the custom of a fickle public, the pub is known sardonically as The Stab in the Back.

It was in the incongruous setting of The Stab that I found myself on the evening of 9 December, 1987 in the company of one Leonard Bebchick, US attorney-at-law. Short in stature, balding, with hair trimmed short in that typically American way, Bebchick had been my friend, confidant, and US lawyer for something like twenty-five years. Born into an orthodox Jewish family, Leonard went to Yale Law School. After graduating began his career in aviation, joining the now-defunct Civil Aeronautics Board. He was subsequently to become the US lawyer for British Caledonian, a shareholder and joint company secretary for the company.

The congenial back bar of The Stab was, for Leonard, a long

way from Yale and his early career, as it was for me a lifetime away from my formative years in Scotland and my first encounter with aviation as a recruit in the Fleet Air Arm. We were there for a brief respite from a set of negotiations which created one of the biggest business events of 1987. It came to be known, by courtesy of newspaper headline writers, as The Battle for British Caledonian.

For on the opposite side of New Fetter Lane to the White Hart and its superstructure of ten storeys of offices is one of the London bases of the US investment bank, Goldman Sachs International Corporation, the merchant bank to British Caledonian Group plc. The day, like numerous others before, had been spent inside the bank's conference rooms with teams of financiers, lawyers and stockbrokers attempting to construct and negotiate a deal for the merger of British Caledonian Airways with another major airline.

Earlier in the year, my board of directors and I had agreed to a merger with British Airways, the recently denationalized state airline. A decision by Lord Young of Graffham, Secretary of State for Trade and Industry, to refer that proposal to the Monopolies and Mergers Commission had effectively crushed the deal originally confirmed in the height of summer by Lord King of Wartnaby, Chairman of British Airways, and myself. Reprieved in November by approval from Sir Godfray Le Quesne, Chairman of the Monopolies and Mergers Commission, the deal to merge the two airlines through the takeover of British Caledonian by British Airways entered a new phase. This was opened by a fresh bid to the shareholders of BCAL by the BA merchant bank, Lazard Brothers. From the original, recommended offer of £10.71 per share, which valued our airline at £237 million, BA's bid had plummeted to a derisory £5.75.

The new bid was not recommended to our shareholders. We moved away from BA and accelerated existing negotiations with another major airline interested in part ownership of and operational collaboration with BCAL – Scandinavian Airlines System, known universally as SAS.

Although we had signalled all along that there were other options to the takeover by BA, my belief is that BA and its advisers had assumed we were bluffing. That misinterpretation was to cost them dearly. By early December, we were in the final stages of tying up a complex package for the financial recapitalization of BCAL which included a major investment by SAS. Downstream was the plan for an effective merger between the airlines, giving BCAL the strength and stability of association with a major international airline and its complementary route structure, and SAS the benefit of a new hub of operations in the most important international air travel market in the world – London.

For us, SAS, airline competition and the consumer, the prospect of the BCAL/SAS tie up, focused on London's Gatwick Airport, was exciting. We were on the verge of pulling it off. For BA, however, the prospect presented a threat of monumental proportions which is why the full force of the airline's lavishly-funded lobby machine was arrayed against us.

At approximately 7 p.m. on 9 December, the deal with SAS was in sight. Our bankers, Goldman Sachs, were negotiating from one of the conference rooms in Strand House. The SAS bankers, Morgan Guaranty, had set up base in another, adjacent room. Legal and financial emissaries scuttled from one to the other, checking points of detail, reconfirming agreements, amending drafts and renegotiating. Sitting in the main Goldman Sachs boardroom a number of close colleagues and I were awaiting the final proposal from the bankers. It would be an hour away, we were told.

On the other side of London, in Portman Square, the President of SAS, Jan Carlzon, sat in his hotel suite, protected from the Press by a false name on the booking and a screened telephone. We both, no doubt, wondered whether we would get to meet that night to formalize a deal that would make history in the world of modern civil aviation: to achieve the first-ever major international airline merger.

Carlzon preferred to remain in his suite, conferring with his base in Stockholm and depending on the provisions of a room service menu. I opted for a breath of air and an environment less heady than the rarified atmosphere of a top-level financial negotiation.

So it was that Leonard Bebchick and I stepped onto the pavement of New Fetter Lane, dodged the traffic to cross the street and anonymously entered the saloon bar cheer of The Stab in the Back. The pint of bitter was refreshing, as was the ordinariness of the pub atmosphere. Giggling girls, probably secretaries, and jocular men, probably *Daily Mirror* journalists, taking a break between editions, jostled to and from the bar to replenish glasses.

Although my photograph had been across many papers over many years and especially in the last few months, I was not recognized. I wondered how the *Mirror* reporters would have reacted if they had known that in their midst, quietly supping a glass of ale, was one of the central characters of a top 'story'.

Bebchick and I talked not about our momentous negotiations, but about family – his back in Maryland and mine down in Sussex. We talked about boats and sailing, about mutual friends. We casually studied the framed originals of newspaper photographs adorning the walls.

My mind went to my own collection of photographs and souvenirs from a lifetime in aviation and, most especially, from the twenty-seven years my closest colleagues and I had devoted to the development of an airline that was to become British Caledonian. We had seen triumph and tragedy, laughter and drama. From virtually nothing, we had fought and clawed our way to the forefront of international civil aviation and, I felt without embarrassment, had left an indelible mark on a global industry.

From our base at Gatwick Airport, south of London, on the borders of Surrey and Sussex, our three fleets of aircraft flew to thirty-eight destinations in twenty-six countries, on four continents. We gave work to 7,500 people and carried approaching three million passengers a year. Right now, however, we were at a crossroads – a crucial period, in every respect. The stark and uncompromising truth was that British Caledonian was no longer able to survive on its own. As a board of directors, we had acknowledged that more than a year ago.

In truth, I had known so since late 1984, when the British Government turned down the proposals of the industry's governing body, the Civil Aviation Authority, for a radical reform and restructure of the industry in anticipation of the transfer of British Airways from State to private ownership. The CAA would have reduced BA in size, albeit marginally, and given strength to us and other independent airlines by a reallocation of route licences, the lifeblood of an airline.

That period, too, was marked by an intense lobbying campaign through Parliament and in the Press. Lord King was fighting to keep his State-owned inheritance intact for prospective investors. I was fighting for opportunities for growth and expansion, so far denied by the said State ownership. We were at an impasse.

At a meeting of MPs in the House of Commons, I had said in July 1984 that the Government had three options. These were to accept the CAA proposals for restructure; to allow us to move to London's Heathrow Airport to gain benefit from the bigger market there; or, if those two were not possible, to merge British Airways and British Caledonian to form one major airline for the UK.

The Government, in fact, did none of these things. Apart from some trading of a few routes, it let the status quo remain. The wounds of the industry were bandaged in a new White Paper, 'Airline Competition Policy'. This was always a cosmetic document, to my mind and, in fact, it turned out to be a hollow one. Thus, I felt that the road to Fetter Lane and the bar of the White Hart had begun during the autumn of 1984 in the Westminster building which houses the Department of Transport. In the office of the Secretary of State, then Nicholas Ridley, I had heard of the Government's decision that there would be no reform of the airline industry. British Airways was to be privatized with the full force of Government support, with no real regard for the existing independent airlines.

We were on our own. It was uncanny that three years later when preparing for the end of BCAL as we knew it, I should have wandered, quite by chance, into a place labelled by an industry as cynical as my own, The Stab in the Back.

# 1

'Doon the watter.' Mention of that phrase to a Glasgow schoolboy in the 1930s would bring a surge of excitement in anticipation of the great summer adventure.

What it meant was a trip on a Clyde steamer from Gourock, Wemyss Bay or from Glasgow's Broomielaw dockside. The cranes of the shipyards loomed over the Broomielaw on one side and the blind walls of the Victorian wharfs on the other. The boats steamed from the city centre to go on down the ever-widening river to the islands and seaside towns of the estuary.

For the ordinary people of Glasgow – the shipyard workers, factory hands, office clerks and their families – going 'doon the watter' on a Clyde steamer was the great travel adventure. To many, it was the only break from the monotony of a hand-to-mouth existence in the teeming tenements of the city.

For my elder sister, Evelyn, and I there was no greater adventure than to hang over the rails of a steamer, one of a fleet of perhaps five or six, racing each other from the islands to Wemyss Bay or Gourock. The boats were packed with families, all in festive mood, waving at other boats and cheering and jeering as one steamer overtook another.

If we could escape the sternly watchful eye of my mother, we would join in the irreverent Glasgow banter. But mother had no time for what she regarded as the ill-educated street slang of the Glasgow working class. A verbal slip on my part to acknowledge a question with the colloquial affirmative 'aye' instead of the formal English 'yes' would be met with a swift clip on the ear. Yet it was my mother who organized those Clyde steamer trips and brought us among the Glasgow crowds. It was one of her ways of opening our eyes to a bigger world and creating an urge to travel further, both physically and mentally.

She had brought me into the world on 7 July 1926 in Clarkston Road, Cathcart, a suburb of Glasgow. Here, I joined the family of Frank Thomson, railwayman; his wife, Jemima, shopkeeper; and their two-year-old daughter, Evelyn. My father was a shunter in the old London, Midland and Scottish Railway. He was in France during the First World War, but was invalided out after an attack of peritonitis in the trenches of Flanders. I was never sure whether this was really the truth or not, because those surgical scars, to an imaginative boy, looked remarkably like my idea of a bayonet wound, the result of an heroic encounter. Whatever the cause of the wounds, he was never a healthy man. The shift patterns of the railway in those days – eight-hour stints, either morning, daytime or night, plus overtime when necessary – meant that he did not seem to be in the house a great deal. When he was at home, he slept a great deal, sunk into an armchair alongside the coal fire in what we called the big room.

Whether or not the horrors of war had sickened his appetite for life I did not know, but he was a very quiet man, amiable, yet introspective with no apparent aspirations. He appeared reasonably content to plough on through his railway shifts, summer and winter, year after year, for an average pay packet of about £3 a week.

My mother, by contrast, was an active woman with plenty of ambition and drive. Her own humble background had denied her the level of education which her lively mind would have justified. She was later to make certain that neither Evelyn nor I would be shut out from opportunity, as she had been. My mother was a small woman, little more than five feet tall, but well proportioned. With dark brown hair and blue eyes, she seemed always to be dressed formally, either in a dark-coloured dress or a two-piece tweed suit. The glasses she had taken to wearing in middle age gave her the look of a school mistress and I now reflect that had circumstances been otherwise, that would be the role in life she might have chosen. She was born in 1888 in Gourock, on the banks of the Clyde. Her parents died young and Jemima – or Mina as she was sometimes called – lived with her elder married sister, Jean, who became her guardian. Jean Scott and her husband lived in King's Park with their young family which ultimately numbered twelve. As a child,

2

I remember many hours spent in the happy atmosphere of 'Auntie Jean's' large family.

After leaving school, my mother worked at the only respectable job available in those days for young ladies of small means: she went into domestic service. It was a few years before she met Frank Thomson, entered a courtship under the strict eye of sister Jean and subsequently married.

My mother was thirty-seven when I was born and I therefore only knew her as a middle-aged woman. She had a drive and energy which belied on her advancing years. Her preoccupation was with her family and her goal the betterment of our lives. When people of similar income around us found it hard to make ends meet, my mother somehow managed to scrimp and save to acquire goods to make our lives more elegant. In our three-room tenement flat, we had a new piano and a gramophone with what seemed a plentiful supply of records. There was always adequate food and, a rarity in such homes, always a bowl of fresh fruit on the kitchen table. Savagely constrained by a very low income, my mother nevertheless never gave up her drive for quality in our lives. As I write, this indomitable lady is 101 years old.

In those early days of my life, mother had a shop which sold a variety of products from confectionery to stationery. Although modest, the shop was a great local attraction as she kept a dog, a cat and a parrot there, with the result that local children would drag their weary resigned mothers to 'Mrs Thomson's'. It was my first early lesson in salesmanship.

But her mind was set on better things and better surroundings than the busy streets and flagstoned yards of Cathcart. In the early thirties, we packed up home and moved out to King's Park, a modern housing estate. We had a new home with a garden, a bathroom inside and open countryside surrounding us. The move out to the suburbs meant that my father had to sit and puzzle the permutations of bus services that would get him to the railway shunting yards at different times of day or night, depending on whatever shift he was working at the time. Despite the delights of our own patch of grassy garden, the fresh air and the luxury of the indoor bathroom, King's Park did not work out for father's job.

So it was that after a short while, the Thomson family, under the generalship of mother, made the return trek into town. We moved to a tenement apartment in Queen Street, Rutherglen. The building stood alongside the main railway line linking Glasgow with London and frequently cups would rattle in their saucers and ornaments shake on the mantelpiece as the trains steamed through.

By this time, I was six years old and receiving my first education at McDonald's School. It was some distance from Queen Street and the neighbourhood school. But McDonald's was generally considered to give a better standard of education, so I was bustled into this establishment by my ambitious mother. Her constant command was 'work hard and get on'. I, of course, never questioned what was to become a matter of family policy and my guiding principle for life.

Her own strategy for implementing the 'work hard and get on' policy was a job in another shop across the road. For my sister, having been propelled through the local schools, it meant enrolment at Skerrys College to learn shorthand and typing. She later became a nurse. In addition to schoolwork, I was encouraged to make my own pocket money from a newspaper delivery round, once in the morning, once in the evening; and an occasional milk round in the early dawn, before the first newspaper delivery. Father shunted and slept alternately and conferred his quiet approval on the industry of his family.

When I was about seven years of age, life and circumstances were taken largely for granted. Certainly we were aware of the rich folk with cars, big houses and membership of the golf club. The radio and the cinema brought visions of the glamorous and exotic, but for me, Rutherglen was the centre of the world and I was getting on fairly well.

As with most young boys, I used to move around with a group of friends, a gang, in the comradely sense of that word. Our collective mission was to explore, to share stories and adventures, and to discuss the ways of the world. One evening, in our usual forum, the corner of Queen Street and Rutherglen High Street, under the light of a street lamp, we got round to talking about class. With all the accumulated knowledge of seven-year-olds, we entered the debate profoundly.

My friend Archie declared that his family was not rich, but neither was it poor and that made them middle class. The other two of us nodded sagely and agreed that this was also true of our families. We were a middle class group and very satisfied to have this mutually confirmed. In fact, we all lived in three-storey tenement apartments – flats as they were known. Ours had two rooms, a hallway and kitchen. Archie's was similar. The other boy and his family lived in one room and a kitchen. The kitchens had just one cold water tap and the lavatory was shared with the two other families on each floor. Serious ablutions were undertaken at the nearby public baths. The three of us knew other children living in one-room apartments – single ends, as we called them. Viewing the circumstances of these people, we were surely middle class and glad to be so.

As a youngster the only time I was able to see what life was like away from the streets and tenements was literally by accident. One dark winter evening I was sent to a nearby shop on an errand for my mother. Leaving the shop I dashed across the road and was hit by a vehicle, which fortunately for me was an ambulance from nearby Victoria Hospital. A crowd gathered, I was identified, and someone went for my mother who came flying down the street, still with her kitchen apron on, followed closely by my sister. At least, that is what I was told. I was unconscious at the time and woke in the ambulance. Seeing blood on my arms and legs, I promptly passed out again. My mother's concern was not at all helped by one of the ambulancemen who told her in a matter-of-fact way, 'Picked him up for dead, I did, Missus.'

I was next fully conscious in a comfortable bed, surrounded by flowers, with the sun streaming through large windows. Injuries to my eyes meant that everything was in a kind of misty haze. Had I died and gone to heaven? A nurse lifted the gauze bandage from my eyes and I saw clearly. The ward was clean and bright, the domestic business of cleaning and serving patients their breakfast was going on around me. Some were wearing comfortable dressing gowns, sitting in armchairs in a bay window, reading papers.

The nurse looking after me was Nurse Love and I became infatuated with her. I had three weeks of hospital comfort, meals brought to me, books and comics on request, visits from Mother and Evelyn and the ever-welcome attention of Nurse Love. I was in heaven.

My next chance for hospital life came a few years later. A scarlet fever epidemic caught me again. (I had contracted this children's disease when I was five, but was nursed at home). This time, I was rushed to the Ruchill Hospital and placed in an isolation ward. Scarlet fever was extremely contageous. Once the fever had subsided, I started to enjoy the ordered, institutional life of the hospital again. I fell for another nurse and would have gladly stayed longer.

# 2

McDonald's School was an institution of meagre refinement. The curriculum was designed to provide a honest grounding in reading, writing and 'rithmetic, the formidable 'three Rs'. There were no sports, no clubs, no general interest groups, no art, no music. Pupils remained at McDonald's and the other primary schools until the age of eleven or twelve, before going on to a secondary school. The traditional path from McDonald's and the local school was to Gallowflat school where boys would stay to the age of fourteen or fifteen, to be prepared, as a matter of course, to join their fathers, elder brothers, uncles and cousins in the shipyards or the steelworks.

I, too, was an item on this educational production line. That is, until about a year or so before I was due to march with the rest over to Gallowflat and on to a factory floor. A new headmaster arrived at McDonald's. He was a progressive teacher, a man with vision who could see and encourage potential among the ill-assorted working class children in his charge. My mother saw her chance.

In best coat and bonnet and ever-present black umbrella, she swept across the school playground one wet, grey day and headed for the principal's study. She was there to petition him to allow me to attempt the entrance examination to Rutherglen Academy, an acknowledged higher seat of learning designed, like the public schools and grammar schools, to prepare students for university. This was the cradle for the professions, not the training ground for the factories.

Some of my friends and a number of the teachers at McDonald's were sceptical about this move to break from the ranks. But with 'work hard and get on' constantly in my ears at home, I passed the examination and was admitted to the academy. Along with one other boy from a similar background, I joined the Academy in 1939, aged twelve. I have no doubt that there were others from our humble local schools who were capable academically, but unless they had the drive of a parent like mine behind them, they stood little chance of being judged on their intellect, rather than their background.

Rutherglen Academy was a revelation, a transport to a world of broader horizons and deeper perspectives. Teachers took an enthusiastic interest in the process of learning. There were classes to learn and enjoy music. We were taught French and Latin and we had organised, competitive sports. Importantly, my enthusiasm for reading was harnessed and guided. I had always been keen on reading, but until I went to the Academy had received no guidance. Here, I was taught to discern and appreciate the beauty of language and literature. I filled every spare moment by reading and visiting the local library, becoming known as something of a bookworm.

My taste in literature was catholic. I waited avidly for the weekly boy's story paper, *Hotspur*, to arrive at the local news-agents. I devoured the novels of Alexandre Dumas and Edgar Rice Burroughs. *The Three Musketeers* and Tarzan appealed to my latent desire for adventure. The novels of Sir Walter Scott with their home-grown heroes never appealed to me half as much as more exotic stories. My reading habits matured with the discovery of George Bernard Shaw; his *Man and Superman*, as well as other plays, influence my perspective today as much as they did in the 1930s. The socialist writer, John Ruskin, gave me inspiration, not for politics, but for literature with his *Sesame and Lilies*. Joseph Conrad took over from *Hotspur*, Dumas and Burroughs in fuelling my appetite for adventure.

One of the teachers, known as 'Wee Mac', took a particular interest in me. Knowing my background, he, on a number of occasions, expressed his concern that I might have to give up my studies to go to work to help the family budget. His avuncular interest was a great source of encouragement.

Probably the greatest influence was exerted by Tony Shearer. He was an excellent French teacher who had been a journalist, and he was younger than most of the other teachers. It was easy to divert him from the conjugations of French verbs by asking about his experiences in Europe. The most fascinating of these centred on his work as a newspaper reporter in Germany, covering the great Nuremburg rallies of Hitler and the Nazi party. He described vividly the emotions generated by an impassioned Hitler. The raving oratory, he told us, reduced grown men to tears and tore a nation's heart to shreds.

Being closer to our age group than the other teachers, he felt at ease telling us about his experiences with the young ladies of the Continent, about the clubs and art galleries of Paris and the passionate violence of the Spanish Civil War. He loved music, particularly song. It was no great hardship to get him to demonstrate the versatility of the human voice by rendering songs in the style of the great Irish tenor, John McCormack. Nevertheless, he was not shy of discipline, being inclined to administer a dose of the strap when necessary. This was particularly so when our meandering French lessons resulted in a set of apallingly low marks from our class. I still hold a special affection for Tony Shearer as he taught me a great deal about life and the expectations and opportunities it could offer.

My fellow pupils at the Academy were, of course, from a much wider range of backgrounds than I had known previously. I talked with the sons of men who worked with their minds, rather than their hands, and began to learn the ways of the wealthier people who lived beyond the confines of the tenement flats.

My closest group of friends continued, however, to be the boys and girls I had grown up with around Queen Street. A social group of about twenty of us had evolved by the time I was thirteen or fourteen. Our main venue was a free church organization, the D.L. Roger Institute. D.L. Roger was a great evangelist and fully deserved the memorial of an institute. But at his eponymous premises, we gathered for social events in the evenings to be entertained by a local character and church member, Jimmy Fitch, and his accordion band. On Sundays, we attended church services, choir practice and took part in Bible classes.

The church was of the Protestant persuasion, as befitted our upbringing. There was intense bigotry in those days in Glasgow, as there is today elsewhere. Elders taught us not to trust Catholics who were mainly Irish immigrants who came to Glasgow for work. I had many Catholic friends and could see no difference between us. But the prejudice was ingrained in many Protestants and manifested

9

in public once a year on 12 July. This was Orangeman Day, when massed bands would march through Rutherglen, raising the decibels as they came close to the Catholic church. Years of tradition decreed that the bass drummer should strike hard enough to break the drumskin when abreast of the church. If he succeeded, the crowd on the streets roared its approval. For children this was great fun and part of the rich and colourful street life. On reflection many years later, it was a sad and misplaced kind of loyalty. Neither I, nor my friends, could ever imagine that one day in the future, I would actually meet the Pope himself.

My social life was beginning to take off. I had joined the Cub Scouts movement and then graduated to the Boy Scouts, where I became a Patrol Leader, one of five in charge of the other boys. This was exciting stuff and I was enjoying my standing among my contemporaries, so I sought other organisations to join. I discovered the Young Men's Christian Association and joined that. Its sister organisation for young women, the YWCA, had social activities in which boys could join. Naturally, I enrolled. The motivation for joining the YWCA was not only the close proximity of girls, but the fact that they offered classes in Japanese unarmed combat, jujitsu.

I was relatively short in stature and slight in build. At the same time, Glasgow was full of burly toughs, ready for a brawl at the drop of the Woodbine cigarette that they all seemed to smoke. Expertise in ju jitsu, I thought, would keep the Glasgow thugs at bay.

It was not long before my combat skills were called on. The taunting and shoving of a bully far bigger than myself led to the inevitable encounter. A little of the newly learned skill, helped by my lower centre of gravity plus a lot of luck, left him on the hard pavement. He was a well-known bully and a figure held in some awe around the neighbourhood streets. The result of the incident was that my reputation spread. I had a few other, more friendly, encounters with boys far stronger than me and each time was lucky enough to throw them or fix them with a potentially painful arm lock. The reputation I gained lifted my confidence and although more than once a bully threatened me with a good hiding they invariably added 'jujitsu or not'. But they never did come after me.

# 3

Shortly after my thirteenth birthday, war with Germany was once more declared. The onset of war heralded noticeable military activity around Glasgow and the shipyards. The most exciting of these, to teenage boys, was the launching of barrage balloons over the cranes and the construction docks. The news of the declaration of war came to me from people rushing out of their houses having heard the words of the Prime Minister, Neville Chamberlain, on their wireless sets.

The feeling of myself and my friends was not of fear or panic, but of excitement. Life among families in the tenements was already comradely, so there was no great hurdle for any of us to overcome in sheltering together, sometimes, all night in the communal air raid shelters that had been erected. Try as I might to peer out of the shelter entrance to witness the bombing, none ever dropped very close to our neighbourhood.

The nearest bombing I remember was across the Clyde. The Luftwaffe target had been a power station. They missed and brought down a tenement block instead. I can still recall the fire reflected in the river's murky waters.

The war took away older boys that I had known as playmates and returned them, on fleeting leave visits, fully grown-up, as soldiers. Sometimes, amid floods of communal grief, all that came back was a telegram from the War Ministry.

The blackout against air raids put a stop to our evening activities as surely as the blanket over its cage used to still my mother's parrot for the night. The war effort accelerated Glasgow's industrial production. There were never more naval vessels under construction, nor more ships arrayed along the dockside. My father continued to work shunting goods trains in the dockyards.

11

Occasionally, I went with him to stand on the footplate of his engine. Money became even more scarce and sometimes my trips to the dockyard railway were for the express purpose of racing home with my father's pay package, just as soon as he had received it. For some reason, defeated remnants from the French, Belgian and Polish armies found themselves based in Glasgow. One of their centres of recreation was the city's YMCA, where I and other members helped peel potatoes for their suppers. Other than blackout, rationing, scarcity of goods and the occasional air raid warning, war with Germany had remarkably little effect on my immediate circumstances.

The Boy Scouts continued to be a great source of interest and enjoyment. Meetings, games, parades, hikes into the country and competitions between patrols all helped slake a boy's thirst for excitement. More than anything, I looked forward to summer camps on the Isle of Arran. From there, on a clear day, we could see the aircraft landing and taking off from Prestwick Airport, on the mainland. It was, incidentally, in the Scouts that I learned to wear the kilt. It was part of our uniform, a warm practical garment and I wore it as normal dress for some time after.

While my father had little influence on our family development, the one great advantage he brought to us was the free passes and discount rail travel, a benefit from his job. Like every other windfall or opportunity that came her way, my mother took full advantage. In those hard-pressed days we had the diversion of the kind of travel and holidays denied other families. Mother would arrange to rent a cottage at one of the Clyde estuary resorts for three, four, or five weeks in the summertime and we would travel there as guests of the London, Midland and Scottish. Our favourite resort was Port Bannatyne on the Isle of Bute. There the sweeping beaches of Etterick Bay and the gentle fishing harbours were in stark contrast to the muscular activity of industrial Glasgow. We also had our summer outings on the Clyde steamers, at a railwayman's discount, sailing to Brodick, Campbeltown, Millport and other Clyde resorts.

My social life continued to flourish. My group of friends had matured with roughly the same number of boys and girls. Saturday was the highlight of the week, gathering in the afternoon to gossip and drink coffee in a local café and then generally larking around in the park before going to a dance hall. Our favourite dance hall, with mirrored walls and ten-piece orchestra, was, ironically, in King's Park where I had briefly lived several years before. On Sunday, we reverted to a more conservative mood, with church and Bible class.

One of the great freedoms of the times was brought to ordinary people by courtesy of the push-bike. To own a bicycle was a must for a teenager. During school holidays, I worked in Glasgow hotels or restaurants as a page boy or lift boy and saved up the grand sum of £15, five weeks' pay for my father, to buy the very latest Raleigh Lenton sports bike. It had drop handle bars, three-speed gears and a dynamo for the lights. Almost every weekend in the summer, a group of us, equipped with sandwich lunches, would set out from Rutherglen and ride through the damp, empty early-morning streets into the hills and countryside towards Gourock, Troon, Ayr, Maybole, even Edinburgh. Otherwise, we would cross the Clyde and head for Loch Lomond or Glen Coe to stay at one of the Scottish Youth Hostels.

Cycling became my passion. Sometimes we travelled in groups of about ten. At other times, there might be just two or three of us out on the open road. Occasionally, if the weather looked good on a Saturday or Sunday, I would pack my sandwiches and go off on my own. Millport on the Isle of Cumbrai became my favourite destination. So, too, was it the favourite of my friend and fellow cyclist, Johnny Banks. We decided to have our first grown up holiday at Millport, booking a room at a boarding house for two weeks. Here we met other boys and a group of girls with whom we swam, cycled and got involved in innocent romances. We went back to Millport for our two-week holiday for the next two years, meeting up with the same group of girls.

But flying was on my mind. The war had given us teenagers a set of new heroes, tank commanders, naval captains and, most of all, fighter pilots. I had joined the Air Training Corps, a voluntary cadet scheme designed to prepare boys for a career in the RAF. We learned about aeronautics, aircraft spotting, and underwent the quasi-military discipline and drill of the Corps. It was the ATC that was to give me an early, vivid perspective on my own life.

Knowing that I was a keen cyclist and that my bike was parked outside, one of the officers during an ATC meeting asked if I

13

would deliver a document to the home of the senior cadet. This was in Burnside, a wealthy district. It was a delightful summer's evening and I pedalled through the leafy avenues to the house, a self-contained, detached property, surrounded by gardens and lawns. The boy's mother answered the front door and asked me to go to the conservatory door at the side of the house. I went into a quiet, spacious and ordered home. The senior cadet, no more than sixteen, was in his own study revising homework. He was surrounded by books of the kind I had never seen. His study was a place I had never before imagined a boy could have to himself. I thought of my own cramped tenement home and the corner of the kitchen table on which I had to study. The contrast was dramatic. I was envious, but not angry. I felt a great sadness that such luxury and style were not available to me.

I left Rutherglen Academy at the age of fourteen in 1941, to enter Coatbridge Technical College. I chose Coatbridge for one reason – so I could become a pilot in the Royal Air Force. I had worked out, mistakenly as it happened, that a technical knowledge of engines and engineering would help me to be selected as a pilot. The college was interesting, but the drive towards science and technology meant that the arts were given second place. The English standard was not to the level of Rutherglen, and French and Latin tuition did not exist.

# 4

By 1943, the bombing blitzes on the Glasgow shipyards had become history, the conflict had reached global proportions and people in Britain, certainly in Glasgow, had settled down to a wartime existence. Glasgow had already earned a special place in World War II history when Winston Churchill met President Roosevelt's emissary, John Hopkins, at the old North British Hotel at the first negotiations aimed at getting the USA into the war alongside Britain. But in the days of 1943 when I would cross George Square from the Victorian Gothic City Chambers to the elegant façade of the North British, en route to the Central Station, I was unaware of the power politics that had taken place in ordinary Glasgow.

I was coming to the end of my time at Coatbridge College and was seeking a place at the Glasgow Royal Technical College. To the delight of the family, I was not only accepted, but awarded a small Carnegie Bursary to subsidise expenses. It was a necessary subsidy, as my father still earned just about £3 a week. Mother still needed to work to support the family. I still had to find part-time jobs to bring in spending money. Even with all the diversions available to me, my determination to become a pilot was unabated. The only thing holding me back was my age, a mere sixteen and a year too young.

My seventeenth birthday was marked by gifts which reflected this mature age – a new tie, smart collar, and gentlemen's hair cream. Thus it was that as a freshly scrubbed young man, at his sartorial best, with hair slicked back, I caught the tram into Glasgow and headed for the Royal Air Force recruitment office. 'I wish to volunteer to train as a pilot,' I told the recruiting officer who was sitting behind an entirely empty desk, wearing the uniform I coveted.

15

After some basic, standard questions, he looked up and said: 'I have to tell you that you are rather young and we have enough volunteers at the moment.' Sensing my disappointment, he added, grudgingly, 'I'll put your name down, though.'

Next door was the recruiting centre for the Royal Navy. Without hesitation, I made a smart left turn from the RAF, marched three or four paces and made another snappy left turn into the front door of His Majesty's Royal Navy. Again I told the officer that my business with him was about offering my services to train as a pilot. After another set of standard recruitment questions, I was informed that yes, I was accepted for interview. A few weeks later I was on the train from the Central Station to Edinburgh, where I was to meet the interview board. The rail journey, across the flat, central lowlands of Scotland, was spent putting the finishing touches to the revision of subjects I thought I might be questioned on. They were bound to drag me through engineering, trigonometry, maths and physics, I had assured myself.

After some time on a bench in the corridor, an orderly called my name and ushered me into what I would much later come to recognise as a board room. On the opposite side of the table sat a Commander, a Lieutenant Commander and a Lieutenant. As I entered, they each stood up, smiled warmly and shook me by the hand. A ramble of general conversation was followed by the first real question which threw me into utter confusion.

What, the Commander wanted to know, was the sine of theta in the diagram of a right-angled triangle he held before me. Having been immersed at Coatbridge College in advanced trigonometry and maths, I thought the question was somewhat basic and surely had to be a trick. For a few minutes, I looked alternately at the diagram and the expectant faces of my inquisitors. Eventually, I replied: 'Opposite over the hypotenuse . . . Sir!'

Nodding assent, they moved on to other general and equally basic questions before getting down to what they and I really wanted to discuss. We talked about flying and aeronautics, about pilot training and why I wanted to join them as a member of the Fleet Air Arm. I was accepted for assessment.

My admission as a pilot recruit had seemed so easy and uncomplicated that my extravagant plan of campaign, involving changing schools to obtain the engineering and technical qualifications, felt

16

unnecessary. In fact, I was very lucky to be accepted as, like the RAF, the Navy had more volunteers than it needed.

The assessment course involved about 200 young men. For two days we were put through tests and exercises to gauge aptitude, intellect, and physical ability. Only a quarter of us would be accepted and we were given the decision on the spot. It was 25 August 1943 when I was accepted, and I was deliriously happy.

Although proud of my success and supportive of my ambition, my mother was naturally apprehensive at the prospect of her only son going off to war, especially in an aeroplane. She knew that I could have legitimately applied for an exemption from military service by virtue of my status as an engineering student.

I was enrolled at the Royal Technical College and instructed to join the Glasgow University Naval Division. This was one of many similar university units created for young men deemed to have officer potential who had been recruited during their final year at school. They were seconded to universities for six-month academic courses before going in to the Royal Navy Volunteer Reserve for full-blown training as naval officers. Others like me were already at university or college and following a different course which was of a longer duration. Not many of us were pilot recruits.

By now, I was on my way to realizing my dream of flying and became far more interested in the activities of the Naval Division than the scholarly offerings of the Royal Technical College. Classrooms could not compare with the week-long exercise on a minesweeper, the HMS *Cerisio*. The weather was the worst the Irish Sea could throw at us, but my fellow cadet on board, John Donachy, and I slept in hammocks and listened to the tales of war and adventure from hardened sailors. It was the stuff of story books and we enjoyed every moment. Many years later, John Donachy and I met up once more when the lowly wartime cadet had become Chief Executive of the Scottish Council for Development and Industry.

Patience had never been a virtue and it was out of the question to waste any more time now. I set about angling for a place with the short-course students, or cadets, as we were known, rather than those who, like me, were on the long course. The difference was about six months. The short course was due to

17

leave Glasgow University in March 1944. A few weeks before I began my lobbying. It was not, as it turned out, too difficult. Our officer was First Lt Checketts, a great personality with a cavalier spirit. He had already seen action in motor torpedo boats and was admired by all the cadets. He must have identified with my quest for action. I pleaded that I had made so many friends among the Fleet Air Arm recruits and really did not want to wait for the long course to be called up. He said nothing, smiled as he searched for a document and deftly added my name to the short course list.

Checketts' simple, understanding gesture led to one of the most significant developments of my life. We went off for pilot training several weeks later. We could foresee, at that stage, that the war was drawing to a conclusion. By the time those cadets on the long course had started their flying training, the war was ending and their course cancelled. They never made it as pilots and neither would I have done, had it not been for the godfather figure of First Lt Checketts.

Fleet Air Arm 65th Pilots' Course took place over a one-month period at a station in Cosham, near Portsmouth, on the south coast of England, Britain's historic naval base. This was the furthest I had ever been from home and the rolling, soft downland of Hampshire was a vivid contrast to the more dramatic countryside of Scotland. Portsmouth naval dockyards and the whole coast along to Southampton formed a military area at 'action stations'. Ship movements at sea and troop movements on land were constant. You felt out of place in this part of the country without a military uniform and I was glad, at last to be issued with mine, especially as the white band around my cap indicated an officer cadet.

Our station was His Majesty's Ship *St Vincent*, it being a naval tradition that shore stations are classed as ships – and run like them. Our group of cadets from Glasgow joined colleagues from Naval Divisions of universities in England and Wales. The course was mainly indoctrination into the Navy. You had to be a sailor before you could become a flyer. We learned King's Rules and Regulations, the code of conduct and discipline that has ruled the Royal Navy from time immemorial. We were taught ship and aircraft recognition. We learned how to dismantle, put together and fire revolvers, rifles and machine guns. Most of all, we learned about Chief Petty Officer Wilmot. He was the naval equivalent of a Sergeant Major. The Navy belonged to him and we were intruders. His bearing was rigid, his dress immaculate. The sheer volume of his voice distorted the actual words he uttered. One came to learn his instructions on the parade ground simply by sound. His eyesight was uncanny, being able to spot a wink between cadets three rows back. CPO Wilmot was created for one role in life only – to instil discipline into those who dared consider themselves suitable to become officers and men in His Majesty's Royal Navy. His methods were tough but effective. Out of the drilling, kit cleaning and physical training came self-reliance. After six weeks with CPO Wilmot, boys were well on their way to becoming men. The last few days of the course found me confined to bed with a high fever. I was told that I would have to drop at least one course, perhaps two, before I would be fully fit to resume training. As the training ended, my colleagues left HMS *St Vincent* for leave before rejoining at Heaton Park, near Manchester. From there, arrangements would be made to begin flying training which we had learned, in a state of great excitement, would be undertaken in North America.

This was the cue for me to make a remarkable recovery. I pleaded with the Lt Commander to be allowed to cut down my leave to a few days, in order to catch up with my course at Heaton Park. He agreed, with the proviso that I was to report to the Heaton Park sick bay if the illness persisted. The prospect of flying combined with travel to North America was a great antidote for the fever and resulted in me staying with my many friends from Glasgow University – Gordon Walker, Peter Adamson, 'Purdie' Murdoch, 'Gabe' Dykes and others.

# 5

In late July 1944, I was preparing to go 'doon the watter' once more. But this time, it was no pleasure trip down the Clyde at holiday time. I was reporting for duty at the Greenock dockside, ready to board the Aquitania bound for Halifax, Nova Scotia.

Clydeside had taken a massive battering during the blitz. Bombsites were everywhere and the skeletons of blasted buildings formed eerie silhouettes as the sun dropped down into the horizon, somewhere in the grey Irish Sea. The docks themselves were hives of activity with supplies being unloaded from the transatlantic convoys and new convoys being prepared as cruiser escorts stood by at anchor.

The Aquitania stood out in the Firth of Clyde. In peace time she had held pride of place among the fleet of great transatlantic steamers. She was now, of course, given over to war service as a troopship, her staterooms, restaurants and ballroom dismantled, to make space for row upon row of four-tier bunks. She had been designed as a fast liner with all the fittings of luxury that were a hallmark of transatlantic travel in the 1920s and 1930s. I had seen these great ships being built on the Clyde, hardly imagining that one day, I would climb aboard as a passenger.

The Aquitania was to sail alone, not as part of a convoy, nor under the escort of a warship. She was considered too fast for the enemy submarines which lurked in the North Atlantic sea lanes. Most of the passengers were Canadian soldiers, casualties from the recent invasion of Normandy. Our group of recruits from HMS *St Vincent* formed the only Royal Navy contingent on board. We were regarded as sailors and given shipboard duties to perform. The quality of Chief Petty Officer Wilmot's training was now to be put to the test.

My area of responsibility was the boat deck, where the lifeboats hung on their davits, ever-ready for use in the dangerous Atlantic shoals. The Canadian soldiers were allowed to use the boat deck for relaxation, with one proviso: there would be no gambling. A monotonous sea journey with only packs of cards for collective entertainment made that a pretty unenforceable regulation.

My job, as a callow seventeen-year-old, was regularly to patrol the deck, and put an end to any gambling among these seasoned veteran soldiers, many of whom had been injured. With good grace on their part and relief on mine, we had an understanding that as I approached on regular patrol, they would cease the poker game and not restart until I was out of sight.

Although it was a momentous event for me, my recollection of the transatlantic crossing is sketchy, due, I am certain, to the overwhelming anticipation of arrival and pilot training. But I do recall the excitement of being on duty on the boat deck during the night watches, especially when the weather was foul – heady stuff for a lad from Rutherglen.

The five or six days at sea were, nevertheless, an important first step in the process of levelling among people of differing backgrounds and abilities. I became particularly close to a colleague from Glasgow University, Gordon Walker. He came from a comfortable home. His family would have been described by my mother as 'well-to-do'. Night-time chats with Gordon when he described his background and family experiences gave me valuable lessons in the nature of the society in which I was beginning to find myself. By this time I was known as 'Angus' as there were already too many Scots called Jock!

Jasper Hicks, another colleague from the University Naval Division, gave me my first real taste of classical music. A New Zealander, 'Sinner' Sinclair, took me to tne other end of the musical spectrum with his enthusiasm for jazz.

There was no noticeable discrimination between us. In the context of the Fleet Air Arm we were together as equals. The competition for a place as a pilot, the hardship of training, the adventure of the Atlantic crossing and the prospect of becoming fighter pilots conspired to bring us to the same level.

My first sight of North American land was disappointing. Whether or not the cinema and books had led me to expect

21

to see Mounties, cowboys, Indians and Rockies, the prairies, skyscrapers and wagon trains arrayed before me, I cannot be sure. Instead, I saw rocky headlands, very similar to the west coast of Scotland, and then a port with small, neat, single-storey houses scattered around. Again, just like some of the places I had known.

I reflected that not for nothing was this province named Nova Scotia, New Scotland, and thought about the earlier generations of emigrants who had fled the poverty or persecutions of their homeland and embarked on ships at Liverpool or Glasgow, to make the same journey my friends and I had just completed.

The mark of Scotland was as much a part of the landscape as it was a feature of the cheery welcome we received from officials as we progressed through the formalities of disembarking from the liner and being loaded on to transport for the 100-mile or so journey to Moncton, in the neighbouring province of New Brunswick. Moncton was a military transit camp, row upon row of barrack huts, interspersed with parade grounds and sports fields. Throughout the war, contingents of Royal Air Force and Fleet Air Arm recruits had paused at Moncton, en route to their actual training bases.

The first noticeable thing about Moncton was its food. Meat, vegetables, eggs, cheese and confectionery were available in what was to us an infinite variety and incredible quantity without the need of a ration book.

We were at Moncton for four weeks. We found our way around the sports facilities and games of football were continuously being struck up between the different groups. The evening social life centred on dances organised in the camp, with local girls brought in by coach. Priorities began to shift. Food, although important to us, dropped to third place on our list of priorities, after girls and sports.

The Fleet Air Arm contingent was split at Moncton and channelled to different training stations in North America. One half was directed to stations in Canada, the other to stations across the border in the USA. Perhaps because Canada was still too much like Britain, places in the United States were much sought after.

The selection process was dictated by a bizarre requirement. It had nothing to do with ability, but everything to do with the length of our legs. US fighter aircraft were, apparently, built like the cavalry horses of the previous century: for people with long legs. I wanted to join the training missions in the USA. There was a scheme for those who qualified as pilots in the USA to go to California and join an aircraft carrier bound for war in the Pacific, a prospect as glamorous as a young would-be pilot sitting on the bleak and windy shores of eastern Canada could wish for. So, I found myself as a candidate sitting upright, with my back to the wall, stretching my legs at right angles to my body, as far as I possibly could. Anybody who knows me would realize that my height of five feet six-and-a-half inches would never have made it.

From Moncton, therefore, we were transferred by train to Victoria, Quebec, for initial training, then on to St Eugene, Ontario, for the full flying course.

Bedecked in flying suit and leather helmet, I climbed into a second seat of a single-engine Fairchild Cornell on 24 October 1944. Just eleven days later, on 4 November, I completed my first solo flight, a short, exhilarating circuit around the airfield. In the jargon of flying training, I was 'in control'. By the time I had logged twenty-five hours flying time and had passed the test which came at that milestone, about ten students had been washed out. From Flying Officer Marshall, an excellent instructor who had brought me this far, I was handed over to an officer considerably older than the others. He must have been more than thirty. The fact that I have forgotten his name is a reflection of the amount of respect I held him in.

He was known as a heavy drinker and was not always on time for instruction flights. This was a bad omen to me. Having been brought up in a virtual teetotal household, I had learned the dangers of drink and, indeed, had witnessed the sickening sight of many a drunken brawl back in Glasgow. I was extremely apprehensive and quite unhappy about having to be sent to wake him up in the mornings. But he was generally docile, if bleary-eyed.

The most important thing in flying, he told me, was to cruise straight and level. No turns, spins or dives. We spent hours ensuring that I was the best straight and level flyer in 'A' flight. So concerned was I to maintain the straight and level attitude at all times, as it was drummed into me, that other flying exercises became difficult.

23

It was only after comparing notes with friends over glasses of beer in nearby Hawkesbury that the penny dropped. My careful instructor kept my flying as comfortable as possible in the interests of nursing his inevitable hangover. Panic started to set in. I had missed out on so much vital training while carting a drunk around the skies of Ontario, that my overall performance must be suffering badly. I couldn't tackle him on the subject, so my only course of action was to take a sneak look at the reports put in by other instructors with whom I flew occasionally.

They were locked in a filing cabinet, inside the equally locked instructors' offices. One morning, when the instructors were out flying with my trainee colleagues, I stole around the back of the office block, scrambled onto a windowsill and climbed in through the window. I hurriedly opened the cabinets, found my file and read the reports. Sure enough, my shortcomings on manoeuvres more complex than straight and level flying were duly noted.

I took every opportunity from that moment to talk through my progress and bring up the shortcomings with friends and the other instructors. I was able to practise the recommended exercises and, ultimately, to get through the flight tests. My sixtieth hour of flying was logged on 27 December 1944 and was my last flight at St Eugene. Of the forty trainee pilots who had started the course, twelve failed. The remainder was destined for No. 14 Service Flying Training School at Kingston, Ontario, with the knowledge that even more of us would fail to meet the requirements. In between, we were granted seven days' leave.

# 6

There was, of course, only one place to go: New York City. Gordon Walker, Jasper Hicks, Ray Vaughan and I boarded the train at Kingston and headed southeast. The journey took us across the Canadian border, into Buffalo, across the Adirondack Mountains and down the valley of the Hudson River, into Grand Central Station. The train ride was the stuff of countless Hollywood films – the club car, the sleeping car and the whistle blowing as we snaked around the mountain sides. Coming into New York by the 'back door' is not, as I later found out, quite as exciting as arriving by sea, past the Statue of Liberty and the Wall Street area to land on the West Side.

Nevertheless, we were excited as we caught our first glimpse of the city. The view was first there and then gone, as the train passed through tunnels and behind buildings. It was as though New York was some kind of temptress, dangling excitement before you and then taking it away.

The four of us set foot in New York on the concourse of Grand Central Station, a great marbled cathedral built as a monument to the railway age. It seemed to us that Grand Central was a city in itself, with shops, bars, restaurants, music and more people than I had ever seen in one place. We emerged from the subterranean rail station on to 42nd Street. It was like stepping into a Hollywood production. There were the bustling New York crowds, the hot-dog stands, the chestnut vendors and the steaming pavement grills. In the street, yellow cabs picked up fares and blasted their horns to clear a way through the traffic. It was cold but as bright as New York has ever been on one of those clear, crisp winter days. Above us towered the skyscrapers, built in tier after ornate tier, getting smaller as they reached the fiftieth and sixtieth storey like a series of awesome wedding cakes. Across Fifth Avenue was the familiar shape of the Empire State Building. In the other direction, the glinting top of the Chrysler Building. A police car siren wailed in the distance and the newsstands carried billboards about the war in Europe. It seemed unreal to imagine the war at home. Here was a city thriving, loud and noisy, no blackout, no shortages. The only real indication of war in New York was the number of men in uniform in transit on the railway.

Perched at the counter of a coffee shop, we were able to get drinks of hot coffee and to ask the woman serving for directions to the YMCA. The YMCA was, in those days, just off Park Avenue, on 34th or 35th Street, in the midtown centre of Manhattan. We shared a sparse but clean and warm room. After a wash and brush up, we could not wait to get back on the streets again. A taxi driver warned us of the perils of New York, particularly about getting mixed up with the wrong kind of girls. At that stage we were frankly not worried about what kind of girls we got mixed up with. But our taxi man insisted on driving us to a local USO dance.

After a while of sizing up the wallflowers we came across a group of four girls. Yes, they did want to dance. Yes, they did like the British. And, yes, they thought pilots were wonderful. We spent the rest of our leave in the company of these young ladies. We did the sights together – The Empire State, Central Park, the Statue of Liberty, Brooklyn Bridge, Battery Park, the Fifth Avenue shops, the Waldorf Astoria, the Plaza Hotel, Broadway and Times Square, a display of neon signs which amazed four British visitors used to the sombre blackout. The girl I became attached to was Margie. She took me home to visit her parents on Long Island. I was as astounded at the apparent luxury of their home, with its ice-box and washing machine, comfortable furnishings and, as always, food and drink aplenty. They in turn were friendly, courteous and interested in my training. But there was an underlying current of apprehension at the thought of their eighteen-year-old daughter getting mixed up with a British sailor.

We saw in the New Year – 1945 – in New York, at the Concourse Plaza Hotel. Beer after beer went down throats and we became so noisy that we were urged on to the stage to sing with the orchestra, and to end a medley of songs with 'America the Beautiful' led by a

26

well known opera singer. From the bottom of a glass of Budweiser, America was certainly beautiful. We nearly lost Gordon later that night when, for some obscure reason, he walked straight across a still busy road in Manhattan – looking neither to left nor right. His progress depended on the fast reaction from those trying to miss him. He stopped on the other sidewalk and we recovered him and guided him back to comparative safety.

At around eight in the morning 1 January 1945, we crept back into the YMCA. Thinking back to recent flying training, I hoped for a straight and level bed. Our departure from New York was delayed by the non-appearance of Ray Vaughan. He was eventually to be found slumped in an armchair in the YMCA lounge, facing the wall. As a result of our search for Ray we missed the train to Montreal, consequently failing to make the connection to St Eugene, and eventually arrived back two full days adrift.

Christmas and New Year probably had a lot to do with the fact that apart from a dressing down from the Commanding Officer and some fatigue duties, no more was said of the matter. I eventually lost touch with Margie, but have remained faithfully in love with New York City ever since.

# 7

The supercharged excitement of New York gave way to the quiet splendour of the country around Kingston, Ontario, where we were transferred to take on the challenge of the mighty, by our standards, Harvard aircraft.

Weekend leave would be spent hitch-hiking to Thousand Island Bridge to cross into the USA to visit Watertown and Syracuse, where the magnet was the co-eds, as we came to know them, from Syracuse University. It was a heady time, when the sight of a British uniform gave ordinary Americans the cue to launch a barrage of hospitality. Drinks were bought readily with a friendly slap on the back at any bar we cared to enter. Dinners at home were readily available from new acquaintances and daughters and sisters were introduced for youthful companionship.

At Kingston, the days were split half into flying and half into classroom work. I took immediately to the powerful, noisy Harvard and enjoyed the training. It was an aircraft which needed careful handling in the air, but responded generously to the right kind of piloting. The only accident I had, to my acute embarrassment, was on the ground.

Arriving at base from an evening sortie, I found the runways clear, but the rest of the airfield covered in snow. The sun was low on the winter horizon and I was landing to the west. One of the aeronautical aberrations feared by all pilots is a movement known as a 'ground loop'. This is when an aircraft running fast along the ground veers to one side and if not checked by brakes and rudder in time, can swing through 90 degrees to go sideways, or 180 degrees to find itself going in the opposite direction. On this particular quiet and lonely evening, the clear sky and the crisp new snow lit by a mellowing sun, I received my first experience of the ground

28

loop. I managed to check the dramatic lurch to starboard, but not before leaving the runway and ploughing into the banks of snow alongside. The Harvard nose-dived into the snow, the propeller acting like some demented snow-plough, cutting irregular swathes down to the grass below. The tail lifted high and fell back again. I cut the power as the aircraft settled to nestle comfortably in its soft and icy berth. We were safe, undamaged, but stranded.

My troubles, however, had only just begun. Only days before, a new firetruck had been delivered to the station, the pride and joy of the firecrew and the four men required to be on alert all the while the airfield was open. As I remained helpless in the wintry wastes, in full view of the control tower, I noticed movement from the fireshed. The new truck was on its way to my rescue. It arrived with just two men. 'Don't worry, we'll soon have you out of there,' said the driver. As an afterthought, he added: 'You're not hurt, by the way, are you?' It probably would not have mattered if I had been, for they were in deep concentration in the task of moving the aircraft. The driver attached a tow rope between the Harvard and the new firetruck, while the other man began shovelling snow away from the aircraft's wheels. With nothing better to do than watch, I jumped from the Harvard and used a spare shovel to help with the snow-clearing work. The engine of the firetruck was running at full revs in its attempt to inch the Harvard out of the drift. All of a sudden, the screaming tyres bit through the ice to find a firm grip on the grass. The truck leapt forward at a high speed, pulling the lurching Harvard with it, at the end of its tow rope. The fireman and I dived into the snow under the wings. The driver, by now on the hard surface of the runway, turned to the left and, unbelievably, stopped. Unfortunately, however, the Harvard did not stop, but came catapulting towards him. The port wing of the aircraft was the first thing to hit the truck, then, carrying even greater momentum, the starboard wing circled round and hit the truck from the other side, bending the Harvard's propellor en route! We ran on to the runway to find a shocked and mystified driver and two damaged vehicles, property of the Canadian Government. We stood there forlornly as the sun finally slipped beyond the horizon to draw the final curtain on this sorry drama.

Many years later, when I first heard the famous Gerald Hoffnung monologue about the bricklayer, it had a familiar ring. It reminded me of my recitation of the sequence of events of that winter's day to our Wing Commander. He was not, as I recall, particularly impressed. However, his wrath was directed primarily towards the firemen and their two colleagues who had seen fit to go off duty once I had landed. My punishment was the fatigue of washing three aircraft that night and three more the following day.

Spring came to the shores of Lake Ontario and melted away the danger of snowbound airfields. Like the young waterfowl on the lake shores, we were becoming more proficient at flying. The members on Course No. 126 passed the final air tests at the end of April 1944 and at last we qualified for our 'wings'. We were joined by course No. 127 for the celebration which took place a few days later. As the youngest member of the combined group, I was elected to propose the toast to His Majesty King George VI which I did with all the assumed maturity of a Royal Navy pilot.

From military formality the evening degenerated into military mayhem. Booze flowed, songs, both sentimental and sordid, were sung and in a drunken brawl the Commanding Officer was relieved of his trousers in the time-honoured ceremony known as de-bagging.

In the quiet, hungover gloom of the next morning, I lay on my bunk with my newly awarded 'wings' held in my cupped hands. I thought of the long journey I had taken from the cold streets of Cathcart to the warmth of the officers' mess at Royal Canadian Air Force Station, Kingston, Ontario. I thought of the sceptics who had scorned my flying ambition, especially the Royal Air Force recruiting officer by whom I had been shown the exit door. I thought of my mother, my sister and my father, lonely on the footplate of his shunting engine, somewhere on the bleak Clydeside docks. The melancholy of memory gave way to renewed self-satisfaction as I recognized the extent of my achievement. I wrote a letter home. It started: 'Dear Mother, I am a pilot. I received my wings last night and was asked to propose the toast to the King. I can now fight in the war . . .'

The course moved from Kingston to the Canadian Air Force bombing school at Gananoque. Here we were received and treated as pilots and set about learning formation flying and bombing tactics. The flying was free of the probationary restrictions I had become used to and we enjoyed ourselves. We were all, of course, preoccupied with the progress of the war which we learned from the radio, newspapers and service bulletins.

During the time were were at Gananoque, the Allied invasion under General Eisenhower had started, the German lines had been broken and Paris had fallen. Fighting was still fierce in the Pacific and the Americans were starting the reinvasion of the Philippines.

We returned to Moncton in May 1945, the month that the Allies entered Berlin and Germany surrendered. The US had recently seized Iwo Jima and Okinawa and the war with Japan was still at its height, and I was ready for it.

After formalities at Moncton and a good deal of socializing with the local girls, of whom we were not now so shy or ill-at-ease, Course No. 126 embarked on the converted liner, *Louis Pasteur*, to return to the UK. Our destination was Southampton, and as we entered the Solent and steamed up Southampton Water, the end of the hostilities was evident. Victory flags bedecked vessels small and large, as well as the dockside buildings. Military activity was still much in evidence, but the atmosphere of Britain was celebratory. I immediately started on the long rail journey back to Scotland. The trains were crowded and the whole nation seemed to be on the move.

# 8

The streets and tenement buildings of Rutherglen looked smaller than I remembered, but I was measuring them against the perspective of Canada. My parents and sister, Evelyn, were as delighted to see me as I was to be home again. They fussed around me and revelled in my stories of the training, the places I had seen and the people I had met. My homecoming was warm, but not flamboyant. My mother's way of celebrating was to be busy in the streets and the shops telling all and sundry of my graduation as a Navy pilot.

I met up with old friends and relived earlier times with a trip down the Clyde to Millport with Johnny Banks. But the Royal Navy had taken me from Glasgow mentally as well as physically. My heart was no longer in Glasgow and with the friends of yesterday. I was with Course No. 126 and the next stage of my flying career.

We went to Bootle, in Cumberland, where the Fleet Air Arm based its Officer Selection Board. Course No. 126 assembled for the interviews. In contrast with the little piece of honour it had brought me in Canada, my age was this time against me. I was judged to be too young for a commission, but like the others who were also turned down, we knew we would have another commission opportunity at the end of our operational training when we would be posted to our squadron. I was naturally disappointed, but not so much as some of the others who were shattered by this rejection. There was little else to do at the time but retire to the local pub where I offered to stand the first round of drinks. It was my nineteenth birthday.

Our advanced flying training was undertaken at Tern Hill, near Market Drayton. This was followed by a course at the Advanced Instrument Flying School at Hinstock. We were at Hinstock when the Atom bomb was dropped first on Hiroshima and then on

Nagasaki, to end the war with Japan. The general euphoria of the nation was in contrast to my own disappointment at the loss of my mission to be a fighter pilot on active service.

We returned to the base at Bootle before being found what was thought to be something useful to do. This was to attend the Royal Marine Commando training base at Aberystwyth in Wales. It was gruelling but fun, particularly the simulated battles, but it certainly was not aerial combat in the Pacific, or anywhere else.

The Commando course gave way to a two-month posting to Royal Naval Air Station Anthorn in Carlisle which in turn led to a posting to RNAS Abbotsinch, many years later to become Glasgow Airport. There I was put on Air Traffic Control duties and squeezed some flying in with a Tiger Moth bi-plane.

# 9

It was at Abbotsinch that a call went out for pilots to return to
flying, so long as they were prepared to sign on for a further two
years during what was called 'the present emergency', that is, the
mopping up operation after the war.

I found myself heading south, once again. This time to Lee-on-
Solent. It was spring 1946 and there at Lee were two old friends,
Peter Adamson and 'Mac' MacArthur. I was back in pilot's harness
again, flying Sea Otters and Harvards. We were all given the rank of
Chief Petty Officer, dreams of the King's Commission faded rapidly
once our training had been interrupted by the onset of peace.

Shortly after the transfer to Lee-on-Solent, the news came through
that a national day of celebration had been declared for 8 June 1946
– Victory Day. Its essential focus was a massed military parade,
of the kind not seen since Queen Victoria's Jubilee, before King
George and Queen Elizabeth at Buckingham Palace. It was also,
of course, the excuse for a great national binge, for the venting of
the pressure that years of constraint and hardship had built up
inside the British people. The atmosphere prior to Victory Day
was one of high excitement, as though every family in Britain was
preparing to celebrate, all at once, the six deprived Christmases of
wartime.

Gordon Walker and I vowed that we had to be at the centre
of things and planned to spend the few days of leave that the
Victory celebration brought us in London. We arranged to billet
at the family of Jasper Hicks, another Fleet Air Arm colleague, in
Southall, Middlesex, to the west of London and close to the site
of the present-day Heathrow Airport.

On Victory Day itself, we found standing room only on the
bus into central London. Pushing through good-humoured crowds,

34

using our pilots' uniforms as passports through the barriers of people, we aimed for The Mall, just in front of Buckingham Palace. To gain better viewing advantage, Gordon and I managed to scramble into the overhanging branches of one of the giant plane trees near the Victoria Memorial.

The parade of troops, airmen and sailors, representing every theatre of war, was stirring yet moving at the same time. As soldiers marched, bands played, crowds cheered and Spitfires roared overhead, the whole drama was drawn together by the centre-stage tableaux of the Royal Family on the balcony of Buckingham Palace.

As the last set of military boots crunched to the fading sound of the last military band, we set out for a tour of the pubs and bars of the West End of London, each of them offering shoulder-to-shoulder contact with fellow merrymakers and the occasional shower of beer as one group or another started to dance.

Eventually, seeking female company, we found our way to the famous Hammersmith Palais, one of London's biggest dance-halls. It was there, as we lounged with our backs to one of the many bars, that I spotted a group of girls talking among themselves, with no apparent male escorts. One of them was a blonde with wide blue eyes and a figure that in those days would have been described as 'petite'. I was attracted.

With beer-induced courage, I pulled my uniform jacket straight, ran a hand through my hair and dragged Gordon Walker over to the girls. 'Would anyone like to dance?' I asked the group while looking straight into the blue eyes of the petite blonde. After a few shy formalities of introduction, we found ourselves shuffling around the giant dance floor to the rhythm of a string of sentimental wartime songs.

This was the perfect end to the day, just as we had planned. See the parade, have some drinks and a bit of fun and find some girls. Her name, she whispered over my shoulder, was Dawn, Dawn Burt. Her home, she said, was in Surbiton in Surrey, the other side of the River Thames. She was a nurse living with her aunt and uncle. The latter, I was to learn, was a prominent doctor and a pillar of the local establishment. After a few more circuits of the dance floor, she accepted my offer to buy her a drink. In a shadowy corner, we talked more. This time she wanted to know about me,

35

about Scotland, about flying. Dawn was an avid listener. The more she laughed at my Fleet Air Arm stories, the more forthcoming and articulate I became. We were getting on fine and I felt she was enjoying my company as much as I was hers.

The test of her feeling came when I offered to see her home. I hit the jackpot. She agreed. We continued talking and laughing on the crowded bus over the river into the neat, surburban communities of northern Surrey. She took my arm as we stepped along the quiet avenues beyond the bus stop towards her home, a large, middle-class house with its own driveway. We swapped addresses and promised to keep in touch before she allowed me a chaste kiss on the cheek and then hurried to the front door. By this time, it was one o'clock in the morning and the busses had stopped. I was, therefore, left with the prospect of pounding the pavements all the way back to Southall which I reached two hours later. I had no regrets and probably would not have slept if I had been home earlier.

As all armed forces know, the energy of trained fighting men with no fighting to do is channelled into mischief. For some incomprehensible reason, Adamson, MacArthur and I took to digging holes in the road as practical jokes. We started 'roadworks' in Lee-on-Solent – complete with barriers and red oil lights – in places where most chaos would be caused. A favourite venue was outside the houses allocated to the WRNS in the local village. Shame and downfall came with the smuggling in of our illicit equipment to the base, where around midnight we proceeded to dig a trench across the main access road. We had been spotted, informed on, and soon the Military Police arrived. After a chase with whistles blowing in all directions we were nabbed and, later in the day, hauled up before the Commanding Officer. His sympathy with youthful high spirits must have been immense, for all the punishment received was a week of fatigue duties.

The incident was a reflection of our frustration at the situation we found ourselves in. We were war pilots in limbo, with no meaningful role to play except to ensure that the Fleet Air Arm was represented at as many London parties as possible. Demobilization came in March 1947.

I left the Fleet Air Arm with the sports jacket, grey flannel trousers and pork pie hat that made up my 'demob' suit, plus a cash gratuity of £35, several weeks' decent wages in those days. Adamson, MacArthur and I had earlier vowed to remain together and continue to fly as civilian pilots. Representations to Adamson's mother in London to provide board and lodging for me were successful. The objective was to attend the London School of Air Navigation, located somewhere close to Harley Street, to gain a civilian pilot's 'B' licence. That, as I recall, was achieved with little pain and much extramural enjoyment of the diversions available in the West End of London.

We set about looking for jobs with commercial airlines. We, of course, were aware that, unlike the big bomber pilots from the RAF, we had the disadvantage of only having operated single-engined equipment. Airlines wanted pilots with multi-engine experience.

Weeks of fruitless job hunting led us back to the only logical conclusion available, a conclusion we had often discussed before we left the Fleet Air Arm. If we wanted airline jobs, we would have to start our own airline.

A lot of argument, countless cigarettes and bottles of beer went into the formation of Amphibian Air Charter. Its one aircraft would be a Supermarine Walrus, an amphibious aircraft built between the wars for marine 'spotting' and communications. It was a bi-plane, with the wings mounted above the fuselage and one 'pusher' engine facing aft. The company's business would be based on providing 'joy-rides' from holiday beaches in the summer and flying mail out to the Arctic fishing grounds in the winter.

We somehow came across a man in a Fleet Street pub who pledged backing for the venture. We sought out an ex-Fleet Air Arm pilot by the name of Vivian Bellamy who was attempting to make his fortune by converting old Walrus aircraft into civilian aircraft down at Eastleigh Airport, near Southampton. I flew in a Puss Moth with Vivian to the Isle of Wight and we discussed some possibilities for Walrus operations with companies such as Somerton Flying Services and Saunders Roe. We spent an inordinate amount of time talking about the project before I returned to London.

A few weeks later, in fact the day after my twenty-first birthday, I hired a Miles Magister aircraft from Fairoaks Flying Club and flew it to Cowes Aerodrome on the Isle of Wight to meet the aerodrome owner who had passed messages indicating that he was interested in our plans. Chatting in the sunshine of Cowes, leaning on the wing of the Magister, he threw a job offer at me, in the same way that a poker player might throw a full house down on the table. He leaned back to check my reaction. The job would be as a demonstration pilot, selling Auster aircraft with a high commission for every sale. As the Walrus project was still a possibility I said I would think about it. 'Take your time, captain . . . but not too much,' he said.

We were also looking at other projects, one being leasing a Miles Aerovan for ferrying cars across the channel – but time and money were running out and with Amphibian Air making no tangible sign of progress, I packed my bags at Peter Adamson's house and made my way to Cowes.

The way of the world was dawning on me quickly. I found that there was in fact no such job as an Auster demonstration pilot. It was all part of a grand pipe dream on the aerodrome owner's part, not quite as tenuous as our own Amphibian Air Services.

# 10

My boats were burned, so to speak. I had left lodgings in London, abandoned Amphibian Air Services and stood on the airfield at Cowes, all my belongings in two suitcases and no job. To be frank I had already taken this possibility into account and was convinced that one way or another I would get a flying job.

We came to a compromise. I would be given a camp bed in the gatehouse, in return for general help around the airport. The owner operated a fleet of about six Auster aircraft and one Proctor and looked after some others for private owners. I was officially employed. I started work at £5 a week. I received a bonus payment of half-a-crown for every hour I flew on charters or joy rides.

The joy rides were the greatest fun of all. I was back in the cockpit, demonstrating my skills to excited holidaymakers who had never flown before. Little did we realise at the time that we were at the very forefront of the leisure industry which, forty years later, has assumed massive proportions.

After the war, people were ready to let themselves go in a celebration of fun and relaxation. They were the *Hi-de-hi* years. The holiday camps on the Isle of Weight had reopened and were full to overflowing. Optional excursions for the families from London and the industrial cities of the Midlands and North included flying trips.

Arrangements were made with the camp operators to bring people in by the coachload. They would line up for their turn on one of three or four aircraft which carried two passengers at a time. For their money – 7s 6d – they were taken on a circuit lasting five or six minutes. We churned out the joy rides at the rate of seven flights each hour. It was hard flying work, with so many takeoffs and landings, but the sheer excitement of ordinary people taking to the air for the first time brought a special kind of enjoyment to the pilots.

Our star attraction was the Aerobatic Joy Ride, costing the princely sum of 15 shillings. It took place in a Moth Minor, a low wing monoplane built, I believe, to replace the Tiger Moth, which in fact can still be seen today performing stunt flying at airshows around the country.

This took us into fairground showmanship. One of the airfield staff would act as the 'hustler', cajoling the crowd into pushing one of their number forward as the daring participant. I was, more often than not, the stunt pilot for the day. It was a well-rehearsed show. After take-off, the aircraft would be held just a few inches above the ground, before going into a 'split arse turn'; I climbed to about 2,500 feet and then I would fly one loop and then another with a roll from the top of the parabola. After completing one or two barrel rolls, I would put the Moth into stall turn, recover and go into a spin down to between 800 and 900 feet. I would follow this with a spiral dive – still one of the most interesting manoeuvres for pilots – which was straightened out above the heads of the crowd. The stunt would be completed by a steep turn round a very tight circuit and a slipping turn on the approach to land.

The customer was, naturally, well secured by a harness in the back tandem seat, but from my rear-view mirror, I could see him, or occasionally her, hold tightly to the side of the fuselage with their eyes firmly closed. But they were invariably exhilarated, going back to their friends, flushed and excited, urging someone else to have a go.

During these days, Amphibian Air Charter raised its head again briefly when the Fleet Street backer pitched up at Cowes, with another entrepreneur in tow who expressed interest in financing the Walrus venture. A demonstration of the seaplane confirmed its versatility: it could operate from the sea, inland water or land. It looked as though Amphibian might yet become a reality, until the two potential financiers disappeared from sight as abruptly and unexpectedly as they had arrived in Cowes. I later learned that the second businessman had actually bought the Walrus and had flown it to Tangiers, for what nefarious purpose I could only imagine, for these were the days of the burgeoning smuggling industry between North Africa and Europe.

I continued my fairly happy-go-lucky life, living now in digs in Cowes and operating pleasure flights and gradually building up a list of regular clients. One who was to become a regular 'charterer' made his first call in a remarkable fashion. A few of us were lounging in the clubhouse, drinking coffee and flicking through copies of *Aeroplane* and *Flight* when the peace was shattered by the sound of a powerful car engine, followed by the screeching of brakes and the spitting up of dust and gravel from the roadway. The car, a big, black, American Dodge, was highly evident. The driver, however, was nowhere to be seen. Investigation showed that an advanced state of intoxication had loosened his grip on the wheel and he had slumped across the seat and was feeling his way upwards to find the door handle and let himself out. The man was middle-aged, florid, with that alcohol-nourished facial appendage which we knew as a 'raspberry nose'. Having extricated himself from the car, he leaned on the bonnet, gently swaying, black homburg hat tipped back on his head, until he was helped into the clubhouse, where he demanded a flight, brandishing a clutch of white five pound notes. The other pilots knew this character well and had vanished to complete 'urgent' tasks. I was the only flyer immediately available and to whom the boss threw out an instruction to 'take the gentleman for a flight – a few loops and steep turns'. I pulled the airfield owner to one side: 'I can't do it,' I said. 'You know the Air Navigation Regulations about flying drunks.'

The boss looked me up and down before replying, tersely: 'Thomson, would you like to see the pile of applications for flying jobs I've received this week?' I grabbed my helmet and charts and invited the client to follow me to the aircraft. It was the beginning of a long relationship, known around the airfield as 'the Millionaire and the Tramp'. It was one of the millionaire's great pleasures in life to enjoy a drinking session in one of the local pubs and then go out for a spin, in much the same way that most people topped off a boozing session with a visit to the fish and chip shop.

He liked a degree of excitement in the air – high-speed runs and some aerobatics. So long as he behaved, I didn't mind. The only extra safety precaution I insisted on was that we went out in the Auster which had two seats side by side, so that I could keep an eye on him. We became great friends and I was always greeted with much warmth and back slapping. Except, that is, on the few occasions he arrived sober, when he would have nothing whatsoever to do with me. I was, however, to learn that the Air Navigation rules prohibiting drunken passengers were not written for nothing.

Unbeknown to me, he had brought along a half-bottle of whisky one morning, wrapped in brown paper. This he had placed on a ledge behind the two seats. We were on the runway, preparing for takeoff, with the aircraft speed just below that for becoming airborne. We were in the dual-control Auster, on which the second control column had been removed, but not the rudder pedals on the floor.

At this critical stage, the client turned round to his left to retrieve his whisky. It required a fair stretch to reach the bottle and, to do so, he braced his foot against the aircraft floor. Except that it was not the floor he pushed against, but the rudder pedal. He was changing the heading of the aircraft by about 50 degrees to port. Alarmed, I pushed with all my might on the right rudder to correct the heading, as we careered along towards a thick hedge and the pole holding the windsock. I thought of cutting the engine, but that would not have stopped us hitting the hedge. I thumped the client frantically until he realised something was wrong, swivelling back upright into his seat and taking his foot off the rudder pedal. He stared out of the window and cheered as I, sweating and cursing, steered the aircraft away from the hedge and the windsock, cleared the hangar by a few feet and ultimately took off about 30 degrees from the originally-planned direction. My mood was angry. The 'millionaire' got just a couple of loops for his money before we landed and I got him out of the aircraft. I headed straight for the clubhouse, confronted the boss and told him: 'Pilot glut, or not – I'm never flying him again when he's drunk.'

A few weeks later, I groaned as the big Dodge car pulled up outside the clubhouse. As usual, the driver was out of sight, slumped over the seat, fumbling with the door handle. But this time he had a passenger – a well-proportioned, auburn-haired beauty. There sitting beside him was a St Bernard dog.

I was greeted with bonhomie coupled with grovelling apology for the previous incident. I succumbed to the blandishments and agreed to give him one more chance.

'Oh no, you don't understand,' he said. 'I don't want a flight, it's for the dog.' I turned to the boss, sitting at a desk in the corner. 'You can both forget it. If you think I am going to fly a goddamn monster of a dog, you can think again,' I blazed.

By this time, I had acquired the nickname 'Tommy' among my close friends and the millionaire client was ever-obsequious. 'Come on, Tommy, my dear chap. He's a fine dog, with good manners and a lovely temperament. He's my best friend and I want to give him a treat. What difference does it make whether you have a human or a dog in with you, eh, Tommy, old boy?'

Reluctantly, I shifted my position. But only a little. 'All right,' I said, 'I'll take the dog in the aircraft, but I won't fly him. He can have a taxi ride round the airfield.'

Somehow, the great dog, looking soulful and bewildered, was humped and shoved into the right-hand front seat of the Auster. I sat beside him in the left-hand seat. he was so big that his head was pushed forward against the perspex top of the cockpit. The safety harness was somehow braced around his great shape.

I ran the Auster up and down the airfield. The dog sat placidly enough, so, on the next run, I got airborne and turned very gently. Halfway round at about 800 feet, going down wind, the St Bernard turned his head to look at me as if he thought I had gone quite raving mad. I comforted him with a few 'good boys' and he slowly turned his giant head back again. We landed softly, taxied to a standstill, whereupon the delighted owner unharnessed the dog, got him out and trotted him over to the car. I went to seek a refreshment or two.

The millionaire's next flying trip was a more ambitious, but less bizarre charter flight across to Jersey, in the Channel Islands. He had hired a Proctor with three passenger seats. His wife and daughter were going on the trip with him. I had volunteered for the flight, but he turned up entirely sober. He virtually ignored me, no doubt refusing to allow his wife and daughter to be placed in the hands of an idiot pilot, prone to dangerous aerobatics and taking pet dogs up with him.

He insisted on being flown by my friend 'Duff' Cooper, a steady, ex-RAF bomber pilot, not inclined towards aerobatics. However, the millionaire had not accounted for the technical contrariness of aircraft. The Proctor was found to have developed an engine snag and the operation was hurriedly switched to two replacement aircraft – one three-seat Auster Autocrat and a two-seat Auster. There being no other pilot available, I was to follow Cooper, the millionaire and wife, with the daughter.

The first leg of the journey was from Cowes to Southampton, where we would clear customs and obtain our cross-channel flight plan. Ready for the second stage, with passengers boarded, we found that no staff were available at Southampton's Eastleigh airport, to swing the propellers to start the engines. We were already behind schedule and the passengers were becoming impatient. Cooper had the most important and most vociferous cargo so I told him to jump in and I would swing his prop, then I would look for help with mine. He got underway and headed for the take-off point on the south side of the airport. Search as I might, I could find no help. In exasperation I decided to swing the propeller myself. I checked that the brakes were hard on and went round to the front to pull down with both hands on the prop blade. I had failed to take account of one major problem. At Cowes the field was grass which prevented an aircraft's wheels rolling easily. At Eastleigh, however, we were on smooth, hard concrete with little surface friction. The engine started, coughed into life and proceeded to carry the aircraft away, even with the brakes on.

Aghast, I threw myself to the right and grabbed hold of the wing strut and worked my way towards the door. As the Auster gathered speed, I knew that I had just one chance of thrusting my hand through the small window and knocking the switches off. The hysterical screams of the young lady passenger indicated that she was quite aware of the danger she now found herself in and that her father was entirely right not to prefer me as a pilot. I was almost airborne in the slipstream of the propeller as the aircraft speeded up, and my legs were pumping like pistons. Luck had it that I hit both switches in one and the aircraft came gradually to a halt. I looked up to see three faces from Cooper's aircraft peering at me as they taxied along. I also saw that poor old Duff was about to hit a large, three-feet high boundary marker board. I thought that he would be bound to look ahead now that he saw we were safe. Alas, he did not. His aircraft tilted up and bent the struts and the propeller, before falling back on its tail.

The millionaire, his wife and Duff trudged over to their tearful daughter in my Auster. The response to my nonchalant suggestion that we could easily try to get another aircraft over from Cowes and start again was not a civil one.

At twenty-one years of age, I remained entirely confident that this incident was nothing but a small setback and it was surprising to me that we never saw this client again.

Throughout this haphazard period, I kept my promise to Dawn Burt, the young lady from the Hammersmith Palais, and maintained a frequent, if irregular, correspondence. She responded and our romance flourished by courtesy of the Royal Mail. Whilst in London, I saw her frequently. We went to dances, parties or simply strolled the avenues of Surbiton, each becoming more forthcoming as our acquaintance grew. On occasions, Peter Adamson and his girlfriend would make up a foursome.

Inevitably, the day came when I was prompted to show this impressionable young lady the daring skills of a Navy pilot. I arranged to hire a two-seat (one behind the other) Miles Magister aircraft at Fairoaks airfield, just outside London. I made much of the pre-flight briefing with the flying club official. Dawn, I felt, was proudly excited as she took my arm to walk across the apron, in view of spectators, to the parked aircraft. I helped her into the cockpit and adjusted the safety harness before completing my external checks and then jumping into the front seat to go through the cockpit check list. I called out, 'Comfortable . . . all set?' She smiled and nodded as we revved up and taxied to the runway. The Magister took off. We proceeded straight and level, before turning to port to go on the downwind leg and climbing away from the airfield. Dawn was gazing out to starboard, clearly fascinated by the sight of the houses, farms and roads slowly receding.

'Enjoying it?' I shouted through the gosport tubes fitted to our flying helmets. She nodded.

But this was kid's stuff. I climbed to about 3,000 feet and went into a high speed series of rolls and loops. I was smiling in self-appreciation and turned to Dawn to smile at her. To my horror, she was sitting bolt upright, hands clasped to the side of her seat, face ashen and eyes closed. She opened them, looked at me with pursed lips to pass on the message by facial expression alone that she thought I must have gone completely mad and if

45

it didn't abolish her chances of getting back to earth, she would gladly have strangled me. In short, she was petrified.

She said not a word after landing and taxiing back to the parking area. 'Are you all right? It really wasn't dangerous . . . I thought you were enjoying it,' I mumbled, conscious of the fact that I had probably blown my burgeoning romance to smithereens.

Inside the flying club building she unfroze from her state of near-terror and said she needed a drink. After three or four sips of the brandy I rushed from the bar, she looked at me softly and whispered, 'Don't ever do that to me again.'

The more I saw of Dawn, the more I wanted to know about her. Her natural bright and vivacious personality, however, hid a sad and unhappy childhood. She was born, coincidentally, in the same year as myself, into a wealthy family whose fortune came from paper mills. They had property in Bournemouth, Reigate and Surbiton and a house in Kensington. Dawn's grandparents were local worthies in Bournemouth, her uncles mostly doctors or lawyers. She was born into the kind of comfort where, in contrast to my own childhood, nobody ever had to think about where the next penny might come from. Until, that is, a fateful day when Dawn was aged six and scandal of massive proportions for this worthy family broke out. Her father ran off to Australia with the children's nanny.

Dawn's mother, Gwen, was left to fend for herself and the children, being strangely cut off from the family as a consequence of the scandal. Although well-educated in England and Switzerland, she had no experience of work, professional or domestic. She simply could not cope. Dawn's aunt Freda had married a Dr Dourley and lived in Surbiton, at the very house I had escorted her to on our first meeting. Ultimately, she and the good Doctor adopted both Dawn and her sister Anne and both children were subsequently sent off to boarding school.

Dawn was to set her sights on a nursing career and on leaving school entered the Violet Melchett Nursing Home in Kent before obtaining a post with a nursing home near Surbiton. She was thus able to continue to live with the Dourley family, of whom she had become very fond.

As we had become more serious about each other, I took Dawn

46

to Glasgow to meet my mother and family. My relatives took to her brightness and approved of her profession as a nurse. Likewise, I had got to know the Dourleys and struck up a particularly good relationship with the doctor, which flourished as I became a frequent visitor to the household.

# 11

Summer seasons end in October and as seasonal airline and airport staff are still today laid off as autumn edges its way towards winter, so my flying job at Cowes came to end in the first week of October 1947.

I went away from the Isle of Wight, now strangely quiet with the holiday camps closed down, the funfairs and holiday shops boarded up, with assurances that I would be re-employed in the spring of 1948.

I caught the ferry across the Solent to Portsmouth Harbour to join the train to Waterloo Station in London, there to meet up again with Peter Adamson. Like me, he was temporarily out of work and we found a mutual objective in trying to find ways to raise cash.

The black market beckoned as a quick and easy way to make a profit. We decided to hire an Auster aircraft from Somerton Airways at Cowes, also hit by the winter trough. The plan was to fly to Guernsey, load up with duty-free cigarettes, brandy and perfume – as much as our legal allowances would cover – and bring it back for resale in London. The problem was seed money to finance the project. Adamson came up with a friend of his, a music student, Betty Dudley, whom, as I recall, played the cello. She somehow had the necessary funds to finance the venture, so this unlikely business partnership took shape.

It meant a return journey to Cowes to pick up the Auster aircraft to ferry it to Southampton for the customs clearance procedures which I remembered clearly from the summer. Adamson and Betty were waiting there to join me for the trip to Guernsey.

The reason why flying in light aircraft with no radio almost ceased in the winter was only too apparent. The weather was foul

– gusting winds, low scudding clouds and rain. The meteorologist at Eastleigh told us that the lowest cloud base was 300 feet. As Peter reminded me some years later, we nearly succeeded in flying into the Isle of Wight at about 200 feet!

Eastleigh's senior air traffic controller was horrified with this plan and put problems in our way when he refused to allow us to depart on the grounds that it was too dangerous at low level and on one engine over water. This was irony indeed for ex-Fleet Air Arm pilots.

Hasty consultation of the rules and regulations on our Ministry of Aviation documents showed that the controller, as well-meaning as he obviously was, had no authority over us. We took off and kept below the clouds, at a height of 150-200 feet all the way to Guernsey, where the weather had improved. We landed in time to hire a taxi and rode into St Peter Port for a late lunch on the harbour side.

The earlier omens should have told us that this was not entirely to be our day. For while we were lingering over apple pie with lavish helpings of Guernsey cream, the shops were busily pulling down the shutters and closing their doors. it was Wednesday, early closing day.

We could buy cigarettes and brandy, but perfume, the biggest potential profit earner, was not available. I was certainly not going to give up at this stage and persuaded Pete and Betty that Caen in France was only an easy two-hour flight away and was stocked full of perfumes.

Our only map was a small broadsheet of the whole of Europe, giving little local detail. It was also pre-war and, obviously, did not take account of features that had changed or even disappeared in the hostilities. We decided to follow the railway line to Caen, shown on the map. En route, the line suddenly came to an end, no doubt the result of the French post-war clean up of bomb sites.

It was by now getting dark and we droned on into the direction the rail lines had taken us. Out of the evening gloom the shape of a large airport appeared. We hoped this was Caen. A few minutes later we were thankful that it was. We landed on the taxi track as we saw bomb indentations on the main runway. The Customs official and the Gendarme who came out to meet the Auster were very friendly. We reciprocated their enthusiastic smiles, and shook hands, bowing stiffly, and responding to their greetings in halting French.

Cigarettes in France were still in short supply and black markets, operated by 'real' racketeers, flourished. So it was that smiles turned to sternness and we were bundled into a Citroen saloon, to be driven to the main police station in Caen, after the French officials had inspected our cargo of Players Navy Cut cigarettes. To make matters worse, we had no carnet for the aircraft. Indeed, never having operated internationally before, we had no idea what, in fact, a carnet – the equivalent of an aircraft passport – was.

Youth and inadequate French came to our rescue, as the Gendarmerie of La Ville de Caen slowly came to the conclusion that we were but three irresponsible young Brits rather than black marketeers. They charmingly escorted us to a lodging house, where the three of us were offered one room with two beds for the night. That was all that was available. The proprietor and the Gendarmes were clearly speculating on who was going to sleep with whom and this caused a great deal of amusement as they made gestures that left little to the imagination.

Another of the lodgers guided us to a local *auberge* and there we discovered that apples could produce more than pies and cider. They could produce Calvados; and this fiery spirit, after a day which we regarded as having been strenuous, was to our liking.

By the following morning, we felt as devastated as the war-torn city of Caen itself. The Calvados had taken its toll physically and financially. We were left with less than enough money to pay for the lodging, ten ounces of perfume each and the extra fuel we needed for the return flight. The compromise was to cut down the perfume to eight ounces each and to barter some of the cigarettes for extra fuel.

The auster took off from Caen and we cruised back across the Channel at 200 feet, not on account of the weather, but to save using more fuel than necessary by climbing to a greater altitude.

Arrival at Southampton found us once more in trouble on this fated trip. Although we had sent a signal to Somerton Airways to advise of our delayed return, we had advised no one else. Girlfriends and relatives who knew of the venture feared that we might have gone down in the Channel and there was quite a lot of explaining to do.

After returning the aircraft to Cowes, we scrambled to Southampton station to catch the 2 a.m. train, whereupon we opened one of the brandy bottles and swigged our way back to London. I recall that we only just managed to clear the costs of the journey by selling the goods to a man in the Civil Service Commission. This was ironic, as the next phase of my career was in the very same establishment.

The winter that year brought the country to a standstill. It was one of the fiercest on record with snow followed by a bitter chill and a total freeze. Coal was in short supply and deliveries uncertain. I have a clear memory of people flocking to the coal yards with prams, barrows, even sledges to collect fuel as soon as news of the arrival of a coal consignment was mentioned on the streets. In equally short supply were jobs for single-engine pilots. At the suggestion of Peter Adamson's parents, put as kindly as possible so as not to offend our pride, we postponed our quest for flying jobs. Instead we used their connections to apply for temporary jobs in the Civil Service Commission. We were admitted as TC IIs – Temporary Clerk, Grade Two.

Peter and I were assigned to an office where we joined eight other clerks under the supervision of a clerical officer. It was soon apparent that we did not altogether suit the style of the place. Our humour was alien to them and our arrogance, brought by the knowledge that we would at some stage leave to go back to aviation, did not, with a few exceptions, endear our presence to these lowly office workers.

After four days we were separated, as Peter was transferred to another office. The next week I was accused of working too hard. The average work rate was the completion of eight files each day. I was issuing twelve in the same period.

The principle of hard work inherited from my mother was under siege and so the following week I fought back by stepping up production to fifteen files a day. Retaliation from my superior came in the form of a posting to the File Registry, previously run by two clerks. I was delighted to find that I had replaced one and Peter Adamson had replaced the other.

With no major superiors breathing down our necks, we found the freedom to organize the work in a way that speeded up the process of filing – so much so that we found we could cover the work in the morning and do very little in the afternoon.

Matters came to a head one afternoon when a senior official found us floating paper aeroplanes down the central area of the quadrangular commission building. We explained, quite straightforwardly, that we had nothing better to do. Peter was promptly posted to another office. But instead of leaving me to do the work of two people, which I was happy to cope with, the Commission saw fit to assign another TC II to work alongside me. Job satisfaction took a turn for the better when I was later transferred to another office run by an official who had been in the Army and had seen action. He and his team – he had moulded his assortment of clerks into a sort of bureaucratic fighting machine – worked hard and effectively. However, there was still little work for me, so I was able to indulge in long lunchtimes spent window-shopping and the occasional afternoon being educated by the newsreels and entertained by the cartoon films at a nearby news theatre.

During all of this time, I was staying at a hostel for students in fashionable Lowndes Square, in Knightsbridge. My fellow residents were mostly similar to myself, young people from the provinces starting – or trying to start – careers in London. They were generally a lively group, always off to dances and parties at the weekend. But I was disturbed by an undercurrent of irreverence for the King and for the Government which I later learned to be fuelled by Communist Party recruiters.

I was still very much with the 'establishment', having joined, along with Peter Adamson, the Royal Air Force Voluntary Reserve, a sort of 'Home Guard of the Air' based at Panshanger Aerodrome, north of London. This activity, of course, gave us both the opportunity to continue flying and indulging in the heady talk of seasoned airmen. The RAFVR occupied most of my spare time during that bitter winter. When I was not at Panshanger, enthusiastically flying Tiger Moths, or shuffling papers in the Commission, I was writing off for flying jobs. I must have written to every air service in the UK and a good number overseas. Shortage of cash meant simply that I conducted my employment campaign from the deserted lunchtime offices of the Civil Service Commission, using their typewriters, stationery and postage stamps. It was like wearily fighting the tide, with too many pilots chasing too few jobs and me at the bottom of everybody's list of candidates with a shortage of flying hours and no experience on heavy aircraft.

Peter and I continued to plot ways of starting our own airline with ready-made plum jobs for ourselves. But our flight plans ended nowhere. After three months, I handed in my notice at the Civil Service Commission and set about looking for another, more rewarding form of work.

The Poplar Glass Company, of East London, was a flourishing concern involved in recycling glass for their various products. Demand for glass after the war was such that the Poplar Glass Company Ltd was recruiting collectors, men who would gather up broken glass and return it to their factory. Average pay, the advertisement said, would be about £5 a week.

I joined and was allocated the area of North and West London and found some success, but not much, at broken-glass gathering for the four weeks I worked for the firm. I found greater success in promoting the finished products of the Poplar Glass Company to a few of the factory managers I called on to collect the remnants. Back in the East End, they were impressed by my entrepreneurial attitude and offered a full-time position in the business.

In the meanwhile, an opportunity came along to work with the Pre-International Civil Aviation Organisation (PICAO) set up to prepare the regulatory framework for the developing international airline industry. It was another clerical job, but made palatable by the aviation context. Nevertheless, my restlessness at my inability to fly aeroplanes overcame the security of a steady job. After two weeks, I left.

I had received an encouraging note about another job at Cowes flying charters and joyrides. I returned to the Isle of Wight in reasonable style, at the controls of an RAF Tiger Moth bi-plane which I flew from Panshanger Aerodrome.

A redoubtable lady by the name of Audrey Morgan, a former Air Transport Auxiliary pilot, had started her own flying business and had taken over a concession at Cowes from Somerton Airways. I met her and after a few brisk questions and a withering visual inspection of my deportment, clothes and the whites of my eyes, she hired me. As a pilot for Morgan Aviation Ltd I spent the summer flying Auster and Percival Proctor aircraft on odds-and-sods charter flights and the increasingly popular joyrides, with aerobatic stunt flights thrown in for good measure – and good money.

Audrey was a great aviation enthusiast and a wonderful character, like so many of the ladies who flew for the ATA during the war. Later, I witnessed her crashing a Proctor on takeoff from Bembridge Aerodrome. She was an excellent pilot, but the fates were against her on this day when the soggy ground slowed the takeoff to the point where she just could not get the aircraft to clear the rising ground ahead. There were three passengers on board when the aircraft came to rest in a thick hedge. There were a few scratches and bruises for those on board but nothing serious – except for the fact that the aircraft was written off. The positive factor that emerged was that the insurance claim allowed our small airline business to survive for some months longer than we were anticipating at that time! In fact that was uppermost in Audrey's mind after she ascertained that there were no injuries to her passengers and whilst she was holding a dressing to staunch the blood from a cut on her neck.

# 12

With a new job and what I thought were reasonable prospects, it became obvious to Dawn and me that our romance had strengthened to the point where it was an unnecessary burden for me to keep shuttling up to Surbiton and for her to snatch the odd visit to the Isle of Wight.

After formal consultation with Dr Dourley and a laboriously-written letter to my mother, we set the date for our wedding. It was to take place on 17 July 1948 at St Andrew's Church in Surbiton, with the reception at the Dourleys' house. Gordon Walker was recruited to be best man and about eight other Fleet Air Arm friends attended the wedding, along with the traditional mix of family, friends and relatives, including my mother and sister Evelyn who had taken the long rail journey from Glasgow. It was moving for me to see her in her best tweed suit, in the midst of the Surrey stockbroker belt. But she was perfectly at home, mixing freely and referring to me as 'young Adam'. She made a particular hit with the Dourleys.

Our honeymoon was to be a few days on the Isle of Wight, getting together the home I had set up – two rented rooms in a house in Cowes. The only exotic part of the honeymoon was the journey to the Isle of Wight in an Auster aircraft I had hired from Croydon Airport. This time, the flight with a new bride as passenger was operated straight and level.

Dawn immediately took to the island, happy in the holiday atmosphere of the place and busying herself with making our rooms as comfortable as the budget would allow.

Audrey Morgan, with whom I was now well entrenched, moved her base of operation from Cowes to Bembridge in September 1948. Dawn experienced the first of the many upheavals and moves which attend a career in aviation. We moved to Ryde and re-established ourselves in a flat over a radio shop in the High Street. The holiday crowds were still abundant and the summer gaiety of the island resort softened the disruption of the move.

So far as Morgan Aviation was concerned, it was decided that, in addition to my charter flying, I should give flying lessons and to do so I should take an instructors' course at the RAF Voluntary Reserve station across the Solent at Hamble. With little further ado, I passed the course and was consequently appointed Chief Flying Instructor for Morgan Aviation Services. The fact was, I was the only flying instructor! The airfield was a grass strip in pastoral surroundings. It was an attractive destination for private pilots and in summer was kept busy with the comings and goings of groups of aircraft from flying clubs on the mainland, out for a flying trip, or 'flip', as contemporary jargon would have it.

One of the attractions of Bembridge was its flourishing car club at which young men of the kind that today would be labelled 'yuppies' showed off their Bentleys, Aston Martins, Rileys and Lagondas. For my part, I felt that I also cut a dash with the 1934 Frazer Nash TT replica which I had purchased for £150.

The flying was the usual seasonal mix of instruction, joyrides, charters and the occasional air show. Air show stunts ranged from the banal to the bizarre. One in the latter category concerned an air show along the sea front at Ryde. It involved dropping the Mayor of Ryde into the sea by parachute from a Tiger Moth, whereupon he would be picked up by a speedboat and be delivered onto the pier in front of a cheering crowd.

The parachute drop was to be made, of course, by a dummy tied to the lower wing and fitted out in mayoral robes. The 'live' major would be hidden in the speedboat, appearing once the dummy had been fished from the sea. We practised with the dummy at Bembridge, twice dropping a fast-falling dead weight on to the airfield when our home made rig of ropes failed to open the parachute. A different set of knots was tried and ultimately deemed to be effective.

On the day of the air show, I took off with an assistant, a man by the name of Bill, one of the airfield workers and, of course, the 'mayor'! At 2,000 feet above the Ryde seafront, to the faint sound of the public address commentator excitedly describing this death-defying stunt, I signalled to Bill to release the 'mayor'.

The dummy departed behind the aircraft with the parachute in tow. It would have pulled half the wing off if it had opened! The 'chute failed to open and the rope that should have gone out with it caught on the port wing strut. The Tiger Moth's speed decreased sharply with a series of shuddering thumps. Fearful of a stall or spin, I put on full power and pushed down the nose. The parachute was, by now, in the slipstream and gyrating in a maniacal pattern with the 'mayor' flailing its arms and legs uncontrollably. Bill, by now, was halfway out of the cockpit frantically trying to cut the rope with a large sheath knife.

Below us were several thousand townsfolk and holidaymakers, plus the real mayor concealed in his speedboat, watching this horrifying, lunatic performance. At about 600 feet, Bill severed the last strand of the rope and the 'mayor' glided gracefully down into the gentle waters of the Solent. We did not hang around to watch the next stage of the stunt which I was told later proceeded successfully, but headed back to the airfield and the nerve-calming remedy of two or three pints of the Isle of Wight's Burt bitter. It was, incidentally, a constant source of amusement to Dawn and I on our evening trips to country pubs, to try to work out whether the Burt's brewery at Ryde was a distant part of her estranged family's business empire. We never did find out, but I, at least, consumed an enjoyable amount of the brew in the meanwhile.

# 13

As in my previous spell on the Isle of Wight, the flying activities produced a good array of characters. One pupil introduced himself as a former officer with the Royal Tank Corps. A quiet and studious man, he diligently paid for his lessons, in advance, in cash. I had urged him to take a medical examination before he spent too much money and he was bitterly disappointed when he was turned down for flying by the civil aviation authority doctors – his training was almost complete. When he was almost forgotten at Bembridge, we were visited by the police who were on the trail of the criminal known as the 'Bristol Bank Robber', who had committed a series of robberies and killings in the West Country. Sure enough, it was my student who eventually turned his revolver on himself.

Another keen young student who also paid cash turned out to be a young delinquent who had escaped from the borstal institution on the Isle of Wight. He, like the Royal Tank Corps officer, financed his passion for flying by burglary. One cool autumn morning, the staff and I arrived at the airfield to find the hangar doors swinging open. One aircraft, a Percival Proctor, was stranded at the far end of the airfield and an Auster was missing altogether. After much head-scratching, we made the deduction that someone had attempted and failed to get the Proctor airborne, but had succeeded with the Auster. The fact that a certain young student whose attitude to flying aircraft was cavalier, to say the least, had not been seen for some days, focused my suspicions. The police were called in.

The story that unfolded was that the student was indeed the sought-after borstal escapee and, after learning the rudiments of flying, he had made his dash to freedom in the stolen Auster, landing at a small airfield near Cardiff. We proceeded to Cardiff to collect the aircraft. My assessment from its position and flying surface settings was that the borstal boy must have been on the point of stall and was very lucky to have landed safely. He was subsequently caught by the police and placed in custody. However, he escaped once more to steal another aircraft and fly to France – for some strange reason throwing the compass overboard en route.

Towards the end of October 1948, I came home to the flat over the radio shop to find Dawn in a state of cautious excitement. I was making myself a pot of tea and gazing out of the kitchen window to the High Street below, when she came close and said, in the time-honoured way: 'Tommy, I've got something to tell you.'

She was pregnant. We laughed with delight at each other. I abandoned the tea and raced to the off-licence for a bottle of sherry and a couple of quart-bottles of the famous Burt's beer.

I had serious responsibilities now and flying without radio and on one engine had great potential for problems. Getting caught in bad weather was not at all unusual. Neither was the loss of the engine.

Like every pilot, I experienced engine failures, having to make emergency landings, usually in fields. One unpleasant moment came when the propeller separated itself from the aircraft, an occurrence that would today be termed an 'Uncontained Engine Failure'. Another was when the prop fractured and virtually shook the aircraft to pieces. Both of these incidents required forced landings, needless to say.

My worst experience, fortunately, took place without passengers. I was operating an Auster between Portsmouth and Cowes. It was 19 April 1950. Halfway across the Solent, the engine spluttered, stopped, spluttered again and finally died. I was in for a swim. I had always prepared myself for a ditching by planning to drop the aircraft in the water tail first and with both doors unlocked. As the aircraft descended with only the eerie whistle of the wind on the fuselage, I held a shallow glide dive until I was a few feet above the waves, I then held the nose high until the aircraft stalled, with the tail going in first. The technique worked well, the aircraft floated and I climbed out of the port door onto the roof.

No ships were in sight and a strong tidal current was running. I decided that my best option with no rescue in sight and the Auster likely to sink at any time, was to swim for a large buoy. I swam for about ten minutes, but the current was taking me away. I looked back. The aircraft was still above the water, so I swam back successfully to gain hold of the tail section. I stood on the tail until eventually the aircraft sank completely. I had sighted another buoy and with earlier experience of the current, worked out the best navigational approach – about 60 degrees of deflection – and, alternating between a crawl and a breaststroke, swam in that direction. I had abandoned my best leather flying jacket and new pair of shoes. Some minutes later, I heard the pounding of an engine. I was in sight of the buoy, but intensely relieved to see a Royal Navy cutter come alongside. I was hauled aboard and amazed to discover that my legs would not work – I was feeling the initial effects of hypothermia and would not have lasted more than a few more minutes in the chill waters. I was carried below and set in front of a coal stove and given several tots of rum.

My soaking clothes were peeled off and I was kitted out in an ill-assorted selection of trousers, shirt and sweater, all too big, but wonderfully warm and dry. More rum was handed around on arrival at Gosport.

The rescue, which almost certainly saved my life, was due to an observant sailor in one of the Naval shore station buildings at Gosport who had seen the Auster plunge into the sea. An ambulance was summoned to take me to my old stamping ground, the Royal Naval Air Station at Lee on Solent, from where I was flown back to Cowes. Dawn was resting on a sofa, surrounded by women's magazines and listening to the wireless when I walked through the door. Her shock at my tramp-like appearance was relieved by my superficial description of the incident which became anecdotal by the time the whisky bottle I had opened was half-empty. She never knew how close a single-engined aircraft with no radio had brought her to widowhood.

But of course I flew on, ever more conscious of my breadwinning responsibility as Dawn grew larger. We had arranged that the baby should be born under the care of Dr Dourley in Surbiton, where Dawn would have access to more care and comfort than we could muster in Ryde.

The winter of 1948-9 brought more cold and darkness into our lives than we had bargained for. After a reasonable but marginal summer season of earning, Morgan Aviation was finding things difficult during the off-peak winter period. I was doing more hanging around than flying and the writing was clearly on the wall, or hangar door. With great reluctance and sadness, Audrey Morgan decided to close up the business to pay off the pressing creditors. There simply was not enough cash to provide a financial bridge into the next summer season. I kept my collection of pupils and transferred my flying instruction account to Bembridge Aero club. More secure employment came shortly afterwards when I gained a job at Cowes Airport managing a new Flying Training Administration Department, set up in response to new requirements for the training of pilots laid down by the Ministry of Aviation.

As the spring and early summer brought the holiday-makers back to the island, Dawn's pregnancy was nearing its end. In the middle of June, I took time off to pack up the flat and take Dawn on the train to London. In Surbiton, Dr Dourley took charge of the maternity arrangements and Dawn settled back into her old home. I was called from Cowes on 17 June and was with the Dourleys when our son was born in Kingston Hospital the following day.

After time with Dawn and the baby, whom we decided to name Scott, I raked out friends like Peter Adamson and Gordon Walker to celebrate. For two days my life alternated between the clean, quiet wards of the Kingston Hospital maternity section and the noisy pubs of the West End of London.

Several weeks later, I returned again to Surbiton to collect Dawn and Scott to bring them home to Ryde, where we settled into as normal a family life as a flying career would allow.

# 14

Towards the end of 1949, the opportunity came to join an airline, Newman Airways, at Ryde Airport. Newman's main base was at Croydon, then a main airport for London. I carried out much of my flying, mainly on a twin-engine De Havilland Rapide aircraft, from Croydon Airport. My boss was a man by the name of Stan Perrin, later to end up working for me at British Caledonian. The chief pilot was one Tommy Gunn, a larger-than-life character who had the status of a hero from his wartime exploits of flying Lysander missions into occupied Europe during the war. The radio officer was an Irishman, Tommy Carroll, with an irreverent sense of humour. I was the third flying crew member and known as 'Tommy' Thomson. The business was based on charter flights, but we had one regular scheduled service between Croydon and Ryde, catering for the more well-heeled of the Isle of Wight holiday visitors. Newman would have liked to have more scheduled routes, but opportunities were few and far between.

The company developed what it called 'club' flights from Croydon to the Channel Islands. To travel, passengers had to be members of a club which they joined for a small subscription fee before buying their tickets at the airport. The club technically chartered the aircraft for its members. This scheme and others like it were the first, early stirrings of a development that would later evolve into the package tour industry.

The airline had two Rapides, twin-engine bi-planes, carrying ten passengers and their baggage. One was extremely well-equipped with a full set of working radio facilities. This was Tommy Gunn's aircraft. The other, rather more poorly equipped with erratic radios, was mine. Weekdays we were assigned to ad hoc charters. At weekends, we operated the scheduled services and holiday club flights. On Friday evenings, I would operate the scheduled service from Ryde to Croydon. After an overnight stay at the old Airport Hotel on the Purley Way, I flew a Saturday programme of seven sectors: Croydon/Jersey; Jersey/Croydon; Croydon/Guernsey; Guernsey/Croydon; Croydon/Guernsey; Guernsey/Jersey; Jersey/Croydon. It was hard flying and the duty day would curl the hair of today's airline pilots, but it was manageable all the time there was good weather in the Channel.

I enjoyed Newman Airways, but two factors conspired to end my employment with that company. One was that the regulatory authorities of the day decided to clamp down on the club charters, so depriving the airline of important revenue and development prospects. The other was my ambition to attend an Air Service Training Course at Hamble to upgrade my Commercial Pilot's Licence to an Air Transport Pilot's Licence.

Despite the cost of supporting wife and child, I had managed to save money and this, plus the profit I made in selling my Fraser Nash, and a windfall Dawn received from her grandfather's will, was enough both to pay for the course and keep us in rent, food and clothes at the same time. It would be tight, very tight, but I felt we could manage. Therefore we moved to a rented home, close to Hamble, our fourth move since our marriage.

The course involved six months of study at Hamble, all class work with tough academic standards. This was the course which turned 'flyers' into serious commercial pilots, with its concentration on high operational and safety standards, air law and regulatory procedures. It was a sign of an emerging industry with heavy responsibilities towards the travelling public. It certainly changed my attitude to civil aviation.

My career sights were set on the major airline scene with my new 'ATPL' qualification. But out of the blue, came a wild card to upset my carefully prepared hand. I had always maintained interest in, if not allegiance to, the Fleet Air Arm. I read somewhere that the Admiralty was planning to introduce a scheme to encourage former Fleet Air Arm pilots, demobilised at the end of the war, to reapply for entry. In fact the Admiralty had picked out from the file correspondence from me about the possibility of rejoining, at the time that Morgan Aviation folded.

I had recently written to the two state air corporations, British

Overseas Airways Corporation and British European Airways but received little encouragement as the market was still glutted with pilots holding the kind of multi-engined experience the airlines were looking for. In the midst of this job searching, the Admiralty wrote back, inviting me to rejoin the Fleet Air Arm.

I was torn. The 'flyer' in me wanted to go back to the Navy. The career-man told me to go for the steady airline job with long-term prospects and security. Scott was now three years old and we still did not have our own home. The attractions of operating advanced naval aircraft, however, won the day. In May 1951 I accepted the King's Commission that had eluded me in wartime and rejoined the Fleet Air Arm as a Sub-Lieutenant.

I started my second service career with a small course at the Royal Naval Barracks in Portsmouth. It felt as if the years in between had barely existed and that I had never left. I was then transferred to RNAS Yeovilton, flying the advanced naval fighters, Firefly V and Griffin Engine Seafire, a development of the hallowed Spitfire. Shortly after, I moved to St Merryn, flying sea exercises for trainee observers, then went on to an operations training unit at RNAS Lossiemouth, in Scotland. The flying was varied and exciting, but the Navy was affecting my domestic life. Dawn, Scott and I found it difficult to find suitable accommodation as I moved up and down the country, from one station to another. But we did find a pleasant cottage in Lossiemouth owned by a very nice elderly Scottish lady. However, all of our savings had been spent on the ATPL course at Hamble and we were hard pressed.

After the happy-go-lucky, relatively undisciplined days of civil flying, I came to find the rules and regulations of the Navy irksome and found myself answering senior officers back. The worst situation came with Commander Air at Lossiemouth as I was standing by to lead a flight of three aircraft on a practice emergency scramble, the aviation equivalent of 'action stations'.

The scramble call came and we rushed from the pilots' hut to the aircraft. I found that my aircraft had been pushed back to the hangar. I swore at the ground crew, told them to push the aircraft out. I jumped in, started the engine, blasted the throttle, did a swift magneto check and taxied at high speed to the nearest runway. Shortly before becoming airborne I received a message on the radio to return to base. I replied, 'Negative, I am leading a scramble.'

The reply crackled over the airwaves: 'Commander Air orders you to return.' I returned.

Waiting for me was Commander Air, apoplectic with rage. I looked around the faces of the nervous officers standing slightly behind the CA and then glanced around the airfield. I saw the reason for his anger. Naval ratings were scurrying around the airport, collecting official paperwork which was blowing all over the place. In my haste to get airborne, I had set the engine on full throttle and as I had turned, my slipstream was pointed straight into his caravan which served as an office. I had blasted the Commander's papers straight out of the open windows!

Life in the Fleet Air Arm, second time around, was frustrating because of the civilian flying experience I had, in particular the leap forward I had taken with the ATPL course. I found that I was ahead in many respects of both the experience and knowledge of my service colleagues and found the course examinations elementary.

The course at Lossiemouth was due to finish in a few weeks and Dawn and Scott still had nowhere permanent to live. My family in Glasgow could help only for limited periods. I wrote to the Commanding Officer of the 899 Sea Hornet Squadron requesting a transfer to his unit after Lossiemouth. The Sea Hornet – a derivative of the wartime Mosquito – was the fastest piston-engine aircraft in the world and one that I wanted to fly.

At this crossroads, several letters arrived from airlines I had written to a year earlier, offering interviews for pilot positions. One was from BEA. Family circumstances and frustration in the Fleet Air Arm led me to consider resigning. My concerns were met with anger by Commander Air. I was lectured on duty to the service and loyalty to King and Country. I had never thought my principles and loyalty could be brought into question and the conversation became heated and unpleasant. I decided to leave the Fleet Air Arm and wrote a letter requesting release. They decided to post me back to Lee-on-Solent where I became Staff Officer (Air) to the Station Commander.

In the meanwhile, I took leave to attend an interview with BEA at Northolt and was offered a position. Within two months, I had left the Fleet Air Arm and joined BEA.

# 15

It was a misty autumn morning, with the weak sun low on the horizon, when I arrived at the complex of hangars and barrack-like offices at Northolt Airport, the headquarters of British European Airways. I gazed around at the buildings and beyond them on the tarmac apron of the airport the fleet of Douglas DC-3 twin-engined transport aircraft which formed the mainstay of BEA's scheduled operations. These were the famous Dakotas which had been operated valiantly as troop carriers and cargo transports during the war. I got my first feel of a major airline. Bembridge, Cowes and Ryde seemed like nurseries, compared with Northolt.

I went to BEA as a co-pilot on the DC-3 fleet. My uniform was issued, paperwork completed and I joined the DC-3 training course. It was the biggest aircraft I had ever flown, with a self-contained flight deck and a passenger cabin seating twenty-four people. The course, based on safe, straight and level transport flying and simulated emergencies, was in stark contrast to the antics I had been used to in the Navy as a fighter pilot. The key difference, however, was my role as the second pilot, taking instruction from a captain in the left-hand seat.

The course was completed comfortably and I was put down for a posting to Glasgow's Renfrew Airport, the hub of BEA's Highlands and Islands network. I was, at first, disappointed, not at the thought of going back to Scotland, but rather because I felt a posting away from the main base in London would hinder my progress towards conversion to larger aircraft.

Nevertheless, I was now in an airline as a qualified Air Transport Pilot, with a decent, secure salary and good allowances. Dawn, Scott and I moved into an attractive apartment in Park Terrace, Glasgow, overlooking Kelvin Park and close to the university. It was in the western end of the city and not far from Renfrew Airport.

Our DC-3 fleet served the Highlands and Islands network which has hardly changed to the present day. We flew to the Western Isles, to remote points on the northerly mainland and out as far as the Orkneys and Shetlands. It was good and satisfying flying, providing transport and mail service to remote communities. But the weather could be unpredictable and the radio aids were sparse. BEA pilots had a peculiar technique, fully-approved in the manual, at one particular airport. It was a manoeuvre I had never seen before and have never seen since. Stornoway, in the Hebrides, was prone to extremely strong westerly winds from the Atlantic and the runway headed out to the western shore. At times when heavy gales were blowing, the procedure was to land on the runway, stop, maintain the lock on the tail wheel, release the main brakes and select full flaps on the aircraft wings. The aircraft thus became a sailing ship and would be blown sedately backwards down to the beginning of the runway. A van would be waiting with passengers to the mainland and to take away those disembarking. As soon as the loading process was completed we would be in perfect position to take off straight down the runway.

The operation also took us to Ireland, Manchester and London. Highlight of the flying programme was the service from Glasgow to Paris, with a nightstop in the French capital after landing at the old Le Bourget Airport.

By and large, I settled into BEA at Renfrew very happily. The pilots and ground staff were a good team, most of them out of the Royal Air Force. But I was impatient for a command, to become a captain, which under the normal process would take about three years.

After a year of my plying the Scottish routes, BEA sent out for volunteers to be co-pilots for the new fleets of Ambassador and Viscount aircraft. I applied immediately, but was rejected, probably because of my limited time with the airline, or perhaps because of the difficulty in finding replacements to transfer to Scotland.

I was an avid reader of our 'trade' magazines, *Flight* and *The Aeroplane*, especially of the situations vacant columns. One evening, feet up on the sofa at Park Terrace, an advertisement jumped out of the page of *The Aeroplane* at me. It called for captains to fly Bristol

Wayfarers and De Havilland Doves in West Africa, based in Lagos, Nigeria. It was placed by West African Airways Corporation, operated by BOAC on behalf of the colonial governments of Nigeria, Ghana, Sierra Leone and Gambia. An application was made hastily and after a successful interview in London, I departed for Lagos in March 1953. I had arranged for Dawn and Scott to stay with relatives in London, before they came out to join me in the tropics, three months later.

# 16

Lagos, a city sprawled across a network of islands separated by saltwater lagoons, had the reputation in the old days as 'The White Man's Grave'. It was hot, sticky, and overcrowded. The airport, however, was located some twelve miles north of Lagos, in an area known as Ikeja. Life here was more pleasant, with open space and neat, colonial bungalows grouped in a series of small estates. There was also the Ikeja Arms Hotel, a haven for aircrew and passengers who travelled up to Ikeja the evening before their flight to avoid tedious delays on the dirt road from Lagos. The hotel was a bit of a frontier post, with wild parties almost every night. Its owner was an Englishman, an old 'Coaster', 'Chief' Joe Harrold. It was said that Chief Joe had won the hotel in a poker game from its previous owner.

Dawn and I settled down to a comfortable colonial life. We mixed mainly with the pilots and their wives and with the Nigerian ground workers, most of them gregarious, generous Yorubas or Ebus. This was to be the foundation of an association with Nigeria and Nigerians which exists to this day. I spent eighteen months with WAAC on the Wayfarers and Doves, operating up country to places such as Jos, Kaduna, Kano, Port Harcourt, Calabar; and across to Accra on the Gold Coast, as Ghana then was; Freetown, Sierra Leone; Bathurst, the Gambia; and Dakar, Senegal. The operation was inevitably less sophisticated than in the UK or Europe. Navigation was based on radio aids – non-directional beacons, mainly – which worked fine in good weather but failed when the heavy cumulus clouds of the tropics obscured the African airways. In other words, they were fine when you did not need them, but quite useless when you did.

Weather in the rainy season could be spectacular with equatorial thunderstorms going up to great heights and sometimes forming together to produce a line squall. The result of bad weather and poor radio aids was that a lot of the navigation had to be done by dead reckoning which depended on the pilots' experience of the routes and the landmarks along the way.

But WAAC and Nigeria did get me my coveted command position. My first flight as 'Captain' Thomson was on a Bristol Wayfarer. It lasted all of about seven minutes, as I was forced to return to the airport after the starboard engine failed shortly after we had become airborne. I was equally ill-fated on another flight, shortly after, from Lagos to Accra. My co-pilot and I experienced something that used to haunt flyers in those days of piston-engined aircraft. We had what was known as a 'run away propellor'. This occurs where parts of the drive mechanism fail and the propellor revolutions quickly exceed all limitations, setting up a high-pitched whine which gets louder and louder until a white-hot fire breaks out and the prop breaks off or the engine disintegrates. We went into the remedial drill prescribed for this alarming condition and frantically managed with much perspiration to close down the engine before the worst happened.

Apart from the regional and coastal services, we operated one long haul from Lagos to Khartoum in the Sudan, across the Sahara Desert, by way of Kano, Maiduguri, Geneina and El Fasher. It took a week to complete the round trip. Save for the season of the Hammatan wind which blows sand storms off the desert, the weather on this route across Africa was generally good.

Not so down the coast, which was subject to tropical rain storms off the South Atlantic. One flight up the coast from Accra to Freetown was in cloud and heavy rain almost all the way. My co-pilot and I took it in turns to fly the aircraft manually – conditions were too rough for autopilot. The cockpit leaked like a sieve, most notably over my left leg. It was like flying while sitting under a cold water tap.

If the passenger traffic formed a colourful mix of starchy colonial officials in white or khaki quasi-military gear and local chiefs in flowing robes, the cargo we were charged with was equally interesting. Livestock from the up-country areas to the markets of Lagos provided regular business.

At Kano, on one occasion, I was operating a Bristol 170, the cargo version of the Wayfarer, down to Lagos. My cargo was a consignment of birds, chickens, guinea fowl and ducks. The cackling, feather-flying cargo was contained in baskets, stacked one on top of the other in the aircraft's cargo bay whose access was through two front-loading doors. The cockpit of the Bristol 170 was above the main fuselage, in a style not unlike today's Boeing 747 jumbo jets. The co-pilot and I climbed aboard and closed the flight deck hatch as swiftly as we could. The smell was already powerful. We had inspected the loading operation and concluded that the wicker baskets would last out under the heavy mass of panicky birds for the time it would take to reach Lagos, about two-and-a-half hours. Thirty minutes into the flight, the starboard engine failed. It was the hot, dry season over the southern fringes of the Sahara. We were over high ground and the temperature of the port engine was beginning to rise. We diverted to the nearest airport, Kaduna, called base to report the problem and requested an engineer to be with us the next day, the soonest one could get to us.

'Right,' I said to the airline ground staff who had rushed out to meet our unscheduled arrival, 'get these birds off the aircraft – they'll roast alive.' But pushing his way through the throng of people was an imperious colonial, the local Health Officer. 'You can't do that,' he said. 'Regulations require that this livestock remain aboard the aircraft.' There was nothing our protestations could do to make him change his mind, either in the interests of the prevention of cruelty to birds or plain common sense. The fowl remained in their wicker crates for the rest of that day and most of the next.

The engineer duly arrived, replaced the broken magneto, cause of the engine failure, and we were on our way once more.

By this time, some of the birds had died. Others had broken out of the baskets and were hopping noisily and frantically around the aircraft. The smell had become indescribably putrid.

Ikeja at last came into our thankful view. We landed without incident, taxied, halted by the cargo shed and were shutting down the engine when I suddenly remembered the cargo unloading procedure. This was that a member of the ground crew would enter the aircraft from a hatch below, release the latches on the front loading doors and wind the doors back to open up

71

the cargo bay ready for the goods to be offloaded. My concern came too late.

As the bow doors swung open, those birds that had survived the nightmare journey saw the chance for freedom and bolted in a jumping, flapping cacophony out of the aircraft on to the airfield. When the eyes of the ground crew had gone back into their sockets and their limbs unfrozen from the shock of the scene, tthey set out chasing around the parked aircraft and the cargo sheds to catch the birds. The post mortem on the incident was conducted at several tables in the airport bar where pints of Star beer were downed amid gales of laughter from us and our Nigerian ground crew.

Dawn and Scott seemed to be enjoying life in our three-bedroom bungalow with its two bathrooms. There was no air conditioning, but the homes were built to catch as much of any prevailing breeze as possible. While I was away flying they were in the capable hands of our gardener-cum-watchman, Jonah. He was a giant of a man, formerly a sergeant in the King's West African Rifles, who was prone to patrol the garden with a wicked-looking sword. The sword and Jonah were out in a flash if anything unusual was heard at night. Burglaries happened, but there was little violence. Burglars who came in from the jungle outside our enclosure of bungalows were normally naked, except for a liberal coating of animal grease, so that they could slip easily away from any apprehending arm. Lack of air conditioning meant that windows had to remain open at nights and in the rainy season this was an open invitation for the insect world of Africa to come in. One of our pilots developed a taste for the 'sausage' fly, normally two to three inches long, with a fat, sausage-like body. His party piece, to the horror of the ladies, was to catch them and eat them.

Food supply was limited and illness not unusual. Scott contracted bulbous impetigo, and Dawn and I suffered an outbreak of unpleasant boils. I had a couple of feverish bouts of what was called malignant malaria.

It was in the bungalow at Ikeja that Dawn found she had 'something to tell me' once more. The fact that she was expecting our second child, combined with my realization from airmailed copies of *Flight* and *The Aeroplane* that there were major developments afoot in the British civil aviation industry, led to the decision not to sign on for a second tour of duty in Nigeria.

We returned to the UK in Summer 1954 with utter confidence in my market value, now that I had gained captain status. We leased a flat in a large house in Surbiton – not far away from the Dourleys, the doctor now being semi-retired.

# 17

I successfully applied for a captain's position with British Aviation Services, a conglomerate which included Silver City Airways, Aquila Airways – an operator of flying boats – and Britavia which specialised in long-haul charter operations. I started with Silver City on the Bristol 170 aircraft which I had flown in West Africa.

This was an outstanding venture led by Air Commodore 'Taffy' Powell, renowned for his wartime role as Senior Air Officer in charge of RAF Ferry Command operations. Silver City's business was based on high frequency cross-channel ferry services for passengers, freight and cars. The motoring tour of France was, in the early 1950s, a prime holiday pursuit for the well-to-do. The bow doors of the Bristol 170 through which I was used to seeing Nigerian livestock being loaded, now swung open to have Bentleys, Austins, Singers, Morrises and Morgans gently rolled on to the main cargo deck, underneath the cockpit. The passengers sat in a small compartment in the rear fuselage. I operated from Lydd and Lympne, two airports close to each other on the Kent coast. We flew several times a day to Le Touquet and Calais in France, and to Ostend, in Belgium. The channel crossing took about twenty minutes and we operated at 1,000 feet southbound, and 1500 feet on the return.

Lympne was a grass field which was no real problem in dry weather for these comparatively large aircraft. In the rain, however, the aircraft would skid on the mud. The runway, although legal, was short. The wet weather skid precaution was, however, extremely simple and effective. On murky wet days, the wide farm gate to the field adjoining the end of the runway was opened. If an aircraft skidded and needed more room to come to a halt than the runway length allowed, we would simply steer through the gate into the next field. A standard landing advice from Lympne tower would be: 'Surface wind northwesterly, 15 knots, cloud base 300 feet, field muddy and slippery . . . gate is open!'

I lived with some new-found friends in Hythe whilst Dawn stayed at Surbiton as the time for our new baby to be born drew close. Our second son was born on 12 July in Kingston Hospital. We named him Anthony Adam. With the baby joining our itinerant family, we moved to a house in Dymchurch before settling into a pleasant house in Hythe with a large garden.

I spent a year shuttling to and fro across the channel, but all the while my ambitions were focused on the long-haul operations of our sister company, Britavia, and its fleet of four-engined, Hermes aircraft.

The chance came unexpectedly when the airline wanted more pilots to operate trooping charters which Britavia had secured on contract from the War Ministry. I was accepted for the Hermes and transferred to Blackbushe Airport, near London. The family moved yet again. This time, however, a secure job for the present, and better opportunities in the uture, meant that we were able to buy a house. We chose, after much house hunting, No. 8 Froghall Drive in Wokingham, Surrey, within comfortable reach of Camberley where Blackbushe was located.

I now felt that I was in real transport flying. The Hermes was powered by four Bristol engines, carried about sixty-four passengers and had a non-stop range of about 1,500 miles. The flight deck was excellent: captain up front, on the left, first officer on the right. Behind was a radio officer, navigator and flight engineer. In the cabin, three hostesses took care of passengers.

It felt more like commanding a ship than an aircraft, at least the kind I had been used to. The captain was elevated to a position far more superior than simply 'pilot'. Procedures were carried out according to long check-lists. The role of the captain was to co-ordinate and supervise the operation from start to finish. For the first time, I had a 'staff' to carry out duties, such as the flight engineer adjusting the throttles when I called for power settings on the four engines. The Hermes was, for its weight, underpowered and an air-to-air sighting of another Hermes would show the aircraft in a 'tail down' attitude. But it was my favourite aircraft of all those I had flown.

Our trooping duties took us across the old British Empire. To Nairobi, via Benghazi; to Kano, via Malta; to Singapore, via Rome, Ankara, Bahrain, Karachi, Calcutta and Bangkok.

Many of the trips involved six, eight, ten or twelve days away from home. It must have been hard on Dawn with the new baby, but it was the kind of flying I came to enjoy most of all – and the overseas allowances were good. The captain was responsible not just for the flying, but for the overall management of the operation, including ground handling services en route and the care of passengers. Business initiative was expected in order to save unnecessary costs for the airline and decisions had to be taken on the spot. There was little chance to telephone head office for advice.

Perhaps these responsibilities sparked off a latent potential for business activities, for in the middle of the 1950s, an old friend from West Africa, Phil Daymon, and I got together to set up a car hire firm. Daymon and Thomson was formed to hire cars out to expatriates in the UK for periods of leave, on long-term lets of between one and four months. We appointed agents in Africa, the Middle East and the Far East and our competitive strength lay in personal service. Either Phil, his wife Edna, or myself would meet the client at the airport or seaport with one of the Ford Consul hire cars we had acquired. Likewise, we would meet the client at the end of the leave to take the vehicle back. We negotiated a special insurance deal from General Accident which recognised the unusually long period of hire. The business managed to finance two Armstrong Siddley Saphires for ourselves. Daymon and Thomson carried on for some years, being relatively successful in providing additional income, though never enough for either of us to live on.

# 18

Government policy towards the independent airlines which had emerged from the days of the Berlin Airlift was to encourage them into the field of trooping charter contracts. Scheduled services, with very few exceptions, were the exclusive province of State corporations. Names like Hunting Clan, Britavia, Eagle Airways, Skyways and Airwork led the independent field and trooped across the world to the outposts of empire. At the same time as the War Ministry was handing out charter contracts, the Foreign and Colonial Office was equally busy running down the empire and diminishing the need for strong garrisons of British troops. After a few years, most of the trooping business had disappeared and the airlines looked to other areas for work. Britavia transferred its base from Blackbushe to Manston, near Margate, in Kent.

The fine, long-haul Hermes aircraft were employed on short shops across the channel, with some ad hoc charters on inter-continental routes as and when these could be obtained. Charter work came from the brokers on London's Baltic Exchange which had devloped an aviation section as an extension of its traditional business of shipbroking. Work was unpredictable, with airlines having to respond almost instantly with quotations to the Baltic brokers who took five per cent commission from the overall charter price.

One such ad hoc charter was an assignment to carry groups of boy scouts and their leaders from Scandinavia, Holland and Greece to an international 'jamboree' in Manila, Philippines. I flew this job and was away for about a month. We had also started to pick up holiday charters for tour operators who were then beginning to integrate flights, hotels and ground excursions into what was to become known as the 'package inclusive tour'.

It was in the operation of one of these flights that I came close to a major, fatal accident. I was scheduled to fly a group of inclusive tour passengers from Manston to Pisa. I and the crew would then stay overnight at Pisa and return the following day with the group which had been on holiday the previous week.

Pisa was not a favoured airport. The radio aids were poor and its location in the Tuscan hills made radio contact with Rome or Milan difficult, especially if the weather was bad. Because of the possibilities of diversion if Pisa was weathered in, I ordered extra fuel at Manston. Preflight checks showed that the extra fuel had not been loaded. My two options were to insist on the extra fuel and delay the aircraft, or to depart on schedule. As standard fuel was sufficient in fine weather conditions – and the forecast was good – I had no positive reason to delay the departure.

The flight proceeded normally, the passengers were happy and the cabin staff were doing well with their sales of duty-free spirits and cigarettes. We had checked in with Marseilles control and received clearance to proceed along the airway to the northern tip of Corsica, from where we would make the Mediterranean crossing to Pisa.

As we left the Corsican coast at about 6,000 feet, flying smoothly at 180 knots, the sky darkened ahead of us. As we cruised along, the wind factor increased and the air became turbulent. I ordered the 'seat belt fasten' sign to be switched on and instructed the senior hostess to stop the tea and coffee service. I went on the public address system to apologise to the passengers and to assure them that the turbulence would not last long as our latest weather report from Pisa had indicated clear skies.

No sooner had I completed the message than we ran into heavy cumulus clouds and thunderstorms. Now buffeted by the storms, we could not contact Marseilles by radio, nor any other ground station we tried to call up. Our height of 6,000 feet was at the base of the storm and I had to get clearance from somewhere to move out of it. Eventually, we managed to get a message to Marseilles control via a nearby BEA aircraft and, in turn, received permission to turn northwards off the airways and reduce our height to 4,500 feet. Even at this level, below the cloud base, the air was still turbulent and the Hermes required to be flown by hand, rather than auto-pilot.

The turbulence caused by the storms was pretty well continuous across the Ligurian sea, under the western shoulder of Italy. The hostess reported that most of the passengers were being sick, but all were strapped in and everything was under control.

Under these weather conditions, the medium frequency, non-directional beacons were useless, so I navigated to intercept the Instrument Landing System, known as 'ILS', to the southwest of Pisa. The storms got progressively worse. We were clearly caught in freak weather conditions that couldn't have been forecast. Furthermore, we had consumed more fuel than normal and being out of radio contact, had no way of knowing the prevailing wind direction.

To play for absolute safety was the only option open to me. I chose a course that would, without fail, intersect the ILS beacon on the southwesterly approach, over the safety of the sea. It had to be at the expense of fuel. I could not risk running into high ground. With the aircraft pitching forwards and yawing sideways, I leaned back on my seat for a flight deck conference while the first officer wrestled with the controls. We were still not picking up the ILS signal. Regardless of the fact that we believed we could not possibly be to the north of Pisa, where the mountains are, I climbed to 8,000 feet, still out of contact with the ground control.

It was towards the end of the climb, through thick cloud, and darkness that we picked up the ILS. I turned the aircraft northeast on to the ILS beam which would guide us in. Astonishingly, the signal was getting weaker, meaning that we were flying away from Pisa airport, instead of towards it.

I told the first officer that we would complete a procedure turn. We implemented the standard drill for this manoeuvre – turn 45 degrees starboard for sixty seconds, then a rate 1 turn to port to get back on to the inbound heading for the airport.

As we were turning in, we broke out of the cloud to find ourselves surrounded by mountains as high as 7,000 feet. The first officer looked towards me, blowing out a long breath as he did so. We both knew that had we not climbed to 8,000 feet for no other reason than a gut feel for safety, the mountain range would have been our last resting place.

By now, fuel was becoming critical but we doggedly followed the ILS beacon towards Pisa and mercifully picked up the control tower by radio. We were told that a 30 knot wind was blowing across the runway. This was well in excess of the cross-wind landing limit for a Hermes, but we had to go in. There was no fuel to cover a diversion to another airport.

Our shaken passengers trudged quietly from the aircraft to the terminal building. We sat on the flight deck for a full five minutes after engine shutdown before completing our checks. Not a word was said until the senior hostess, a gangly brunette, appeared at the cockpit door and said, brightly: 'What kept you chaps?' Despite her brave smile, I noticed that her mascara was smudged with tears.

The following day, we heard from the Italian controllers that the storms had come from nowhere and the meteorologists had reported winds up to 150 knots at altitude. The Hermes cruised at 180 knots and we had been seriously blown off course.

# 19

In 1959 the future was looking extremely bleak for the independent airlines. The financial nourishment of War Ministry trooping contracts was drying up and many companies were going out of business, as there was no obvious replacement business.

My emerging interest in commerce, coupled with the dire necessity to keep a healthy salary going into the bank, with a wife, two children and a mortgage to support, led me to think about where Britavia's future business – and my wages – might come from.

With the base transferred to Manston, I had taken a share in a flat occupied by other pilots and flight crew in Broadstairs, rather than move Dawn again. Instead I went back to Wokingham during periods of rest and leave.

It was in the flat at Broadstairs as I lay on my camp bed that I thought of business schemes to take to the Britavia management. Some minor ideas that did not take too much vision or risk were accepted. Others, like a programme of holiday charter flights to the game reserves of East Africa, flights for German students coming to the UK for English course, or the unheard of idea of charter flights across the Atlantic, were rejected firmly. I could see little future for Britavia. The airline's owners were a British shipping company whose interests spanned vast areas of commerce and transport. Britavia was a very small part of their empire and did not appear to warrant much attention from the company's headquarters in the City of London.

'If they won't do it, I will,' I remember thinking to myself after another rejection of a business idea. I started to talk informally to my close friends in the airline. 'The way this place is going, none of us will have jobs before long,' was my sincerely-felt opening ploy. With airlines going 'belly up' around us, my primitive plans to go it alone began to strike chords with some colleagues. Pilots Bill Williams and Phil Bryant, Engineers Dennis 'Curly' Walter and Eric Goodyear and Senior Operations Officer 'Tosh' Parlane each confided seriously that they would join a new airline if I could get it started.

Almost every seaside town takes on an air of misery in wet, winter weather. Broadstairs was particularly depressing as I lay on the camp bed, listening to the rain sheeting against the windows. I mulled over the pros and cons of taking the enormous risk of throwing in my job, however poor I thought the company's prospects were, against the total uncertainty of a new airline. I had already discussed my restless ambition with Dawn. She was, naturally, worried about the risk. For the first time in our married lives we had some real security in the form of a steady job and a home. However, she promised that if I did decide to start my own business, she would be behind me.

I thought of my mother, still working in Glasgow. I decided that she would have encouraged me and would probably have answered my 'shall I, shan't I?' question dismissively with something like: 'For goodness sake, stop fussing – get on with it.'

As the rain lashed down on the grey slate roofs of Broadstairs, I slowly but firmly made my resolution. I would set about starting an airline. As I stared up at the ceiling, I felt a quiet elation. The burden of weeks of indecision had been lifted and I now had a path forward.

I first telephoned Dawn to tell her that I had made my decision to leave Britavia and go it alone into the airline business. We had some savings which would cushion her and the two boys for a reasonable period and I felt comfortable about that. However – rightly or wrongly – I had made up my mind that nothing would stop me now.

I next gathered my colleagues around at the flat – Williams, Daymon, Goodyear, Parlane, Walter and Bryant. 'I've decided to do it – start my own airline business,' I informed them. I asked them if they were still interested. A collective mumble of approval came from the assorted armchairs, sofas and camp beds on which they were sitting. I turned to each of them to obtain their personal commitment and to ensure that they knew what they were doing. Individual responses were the same. Affirmative. Only one person was missing from the group, a Britavia stewardess by the name of Jean Rodgie. Jean had flown with me many times and had become a good friend. I had confided my plans to her and I knew that she was interested. By the time of the meeting in the Broadstaris flat, however, Jean had left Britavia to work with some friends in New York.

In the city 3,000 miles away, Jean's new social circle brought her into contact with other airline people. Not unnaturally, she struck up a particular friendship with a couple whom she had worked with in BEA some years previously. This was John and Barbara de la Haye. John, a Jerseyman, had gone into aviation as a flight clerk on DC-3 services between the Channel Islands and London. He had won promotion as a flight steward on BEA's mainline operations from Heathrow. it was here that he met and married a BEA stewardess, Barbara Rough.

After flying the BEA routes across Europe and to the Middle East for some years, John felt the urge to become involved in the business of civil aviation, in much the same way that I had. He left BEA to join probably the premier independent of the day, Cunard Eagle Airways, as a commercial executive. Eagle, as it was known, was formed originally by Harold Bamberg, to operate converted bomber aircraft on the Berlin Airlift. Bamberg later succeeded in bringing in a shareholding from the Cunard Steamship Company to form Cunard Eagle.

John possessed a strong character and a capacity for forceful argument, which I was later to know well. With Eagle, he was allowed to go to New York and set up a Manhattan sales office for the airline, from which Eagle launched a transatlantic charter programme with DC-6B and Britannia aircraft.

Like me, de la Haye harboured the desire to put his own ideas into action for himself, if only he could find the way to do it. In an amazing coincidence, Jean Rodgie, in whom I had confided, was also the recipient of de la Haye's closely held ambitions. She wrote to me from New York to let me know about this mercurial airline character. His ideas for charter flights across the Atlantic matched some of my outline plans and I took this as affirmation that I was on the right track. I wrote to John immediately and suggested that we should meet and talk.

John de la Haye responded with a transatlantic telephone call, a dashing and expensive form of communication at the time, normally the privilege of big business tycoons. Through this initial telephone conversation and some follow-up correspondence, de la Haye affirmed his interest in the plans we outlined. At first glance, he saw the opportunity to operate his own agency in New York, selling, on an exclusive basis, our transatlantic capacity. He was impatient to know when we would start operations and what aircraft we could acquire.

The basic premise of my business plan, now shared with my Britavia colleagues, was that we would take our ideas to other airlines and sell them the operational and commercial 'package', with the manpower and expertise to go with it. A sort of franchise arrangement.

Initially, we did not contemplate the kind of investment entailed in acquiring aircraft and setting up the paraphernalia of an airline operation. One of our 'target' airlines was Overseas Aviation which operated a fleet of long-haul Argonaut aircraft, modified DC-4s. Their management was not receptive to our proposals and Overseas went on its own way until the company eventually folded in the 1961.

Another was Lloyd International, a British airline financed from Bolivia, which operated the original series of DC-4s. We talked at length with Lloyd, but apart from the possibility of joining as pilots, we found no meeting of the minds. With the franchise strategy blocked, we decided to look at the market for aircraft and assigned our engineer, 'Curly' Walter to do the scouting. His name was actually Dennis, but one glimpse of his shock of tightly sprung hair would tell you why he was universally known as 'Curly'.

We were looking at aircraft with an intercontinental range. On our 'shopping list' were the Douglas DC-6B, DC-7C, the Lockheed 1049H, known as the Constellation and the British-built Bristol Britannia, the so-called 'whispering giant'. The DC-7C, known in its scheduled service role as the 'Seven Seas', was a fine aircraft. Powered by four Wright Cyclone R-3350 engines, the aircraft could carry 104 passengers over non-stop sectors of about 3,500 miles. It carried a four-man flight deck crew – two pilots, navigator and engineer – and was fitted with the latest radio and navigation aids. It had been a front-line aircraft on the blue riband North Atlantic route with BOAC and had great appeal among passengers and a good reputation among the airline operators. No matter what other aircraft we assessed, our thoughts always came back to the DC-7C. A new DC-7C in 1960 would cost about £1 million from the Douglas Aircraft Company at Long Beach in California. It was far too much money for us to raise – we had no collateral of the kind that a bank would require and no business cash flow to service the debt, in any event. Clearly we had to find an airline with surplus DC-7Cs.

While Bill Williams, Curly Walter and I were busy with our aircraft evaluation exercises during the summer months of 1960, John de la Haye was busy with commercial schemes in New York. Our headquarters was my house at Froghall Drive, Wokingham and we set up our 'boardroom' around my dining room table. Dawn managed to keep the two boys in the kitchen or would take them or walks in the local park as we plotted our way into the airline business.

John de la Haye had also been considering which aircraft we should acquire and his choice was also the DC-7C. Our evaluation was originally handwritten on sheets of lined paper taken from a spring-bound reporter's notebook, a piece of stationery to be found in any schoolboy's satchel. It now seems extremely crude judged against modern, computerized methods – but the parameters of evaluation remain, by and large, the same as we used.

The North Atlantic charter market was in its infancy in the early 1960s. American non-scheduled airlines supplemented their military flights for the US Government with civilian group charter operations. These charters were mainly on the North Atlantic routes to various points in Europe. Our intention was to operate North Atlantic charters to the US and Canada. The latter presented no serious problem but the US restricted charter flights to a maximum of six return flights per annum. However, John de la Haye had had discussions with officials in the Civil Aeronautics Board which led him to believe that the restrictions on the number of flights could be changed through regulatory hearings at the CAB. If this was so it would certainly have far-reaching implications for charter operations on the North Atlantic.

John had developed strong relationships with expatriate Scottish, Irish and English societies in the northeastern USA, regularly attending dances, ceilidhs and Burns Night celebrations.

At the end of September 1960, I wrote to John from the flat in

Broadstairs with a very full status report on plans and preparations on our side of the Atlantic. It was in response to letters in which he had persuaded us against the East Africa safari tour flights which had been an original inspiration, and urged concentration on the transatlantic ethnic group charters. It was in this letter that I made the first firm offer to John de la Haye to come in on the venture with us.

In a section of the letter devoted to marketing, I wrote, rather pompously, 'This leads on to the function I had in mind for you and, quite honestly, this is completely open. I did mention to Jean [Rodgie] that you may be interested in coming in with us, with a similar position to the one you hold with your present company, but obviously with a direct interest in the running of the company and possibly more scope as the organization would be new and open to expansion.' This grand gesture was deflated later in the letter where I wrote: 'However, I suggest that we leave this for the moment as we are not really in the position to make any firm offer to you.'

I went on to press him to advise how much flying he could give us from the New York and Canadian club charters – we desperately needed to know how many hours he could provide and at what rate – to piece together the business plan. I brought him up to date on aircraft evaluation and talked about ways and means of obtaining traffic rights. I told de la Haye that we already had the possibility of 1,000 hours flying for the 1961 summer season and there were other opportunities.

John responded through telephone conversations and correspondence. He confirmed an interest in investing with us and coming to run the commercial and sales side of the airline.

In a telephone conversation towards the end of November 1960, de la Haye urged me to visit him in New York for a few days. I agreed. I was convinced that with myself and Bill Williams on the operations side, Walter looking after engineering and de la Haye taking care of commercial and sales, we had the three necessary ingredients for an airline.

On 29 November 1960 I wrote to Bill Williams to bring him up to date on discussions with John de la Haye and to tell him about the trip to New York. I wrote: 'In order to finance the visit to New York, I suggest that we all contribute £15.0s.0d. I am trying to get

86

a cheap seat across at present which would obviously cut down the expense. Would you please send a cheque for £15 to me at the above address [Broadstairs, as it happened] *BY RETURN OF POST.* If the cheap seat is obtained then it would not be necessary to use all of the £15.' With £15 from each of 10 of us, my transatlantic journey was budgeted at £150.

My excitement at the prospect of our airline becoming a reality was reflected in my further request to Bill Williams. I told him that I must know how much the group was prepared to invest before going to New York. I suggested between £500 and £1,000 per person as desirable, with a minimum investment of £300. I ended the letter with 'I am going to New York on Friday, therefore this is urgent'.

It turned out that the £15 whip-round for my visit to New York was not needed. I still hold the cheques today. In a phone call from John de la Haye, he told me not to come as he was due to be in London on Cunard Eagle business within the next two weeks. I was disappointed. I had been looking forward to seeing New York for the first time since my wartime training days in Canada.

De la Haye and I agreed to arrange a meeting at his hotel in London, the Skyway on the perimeter of Heathrow Airport. Bill Williams, Curly Walter and I climbed in to my Armstrong Siddley and set out from Manston for the two-hour journey.

We drove down the Bath Road, past the old Heston aerodrome towards Heathrow. The Skyway was one of the first of London's airport hotels. We parked to the noise of aircraft taking off on the other side of the Bath Road, pulled our briefcases and papers from the boot and walked into the main lobby. I went up to the reception desk and asked a young lady wearing her hair in a massive beehive style for Mr de la Haye. She called his room and ushered us to sit in the lobby. A few moments later, a young man, no more than 5 foot 6 inches tall, walked into the lobby. I noticed that his jaw jutted forward as he marched across to the receptionist. After some conversation unheard by us, the girl's arm pointed to where we were sitting. As the figure turned and came towards us, I got up and went towards him. 'Tommy Thomson,' I said. 'John de la Haye,' he replied. Introductions were quickly made and we bundled our bits and pieces together to set up our business conference in a quiet corner of the bar of the Skyway Hotel.

87

The first part of the meeting consisted of a dialogue between de la Haye and myself, with the others listening. We were feeling our way, going over our correspondence and testing each other to make sure that not only were our ideas in tandem, but that we were also equally serious. John went on to reveal the results of his sales activity in New York and to tell us that there was 'unlimited business' in Americans and Canadians of British origin wanting to get back cheaply to see friends and relations. We could tap the market through their ethnic clubs and associations. To emphasize the point, he waved a sheaf of papers in front of us. Each page listed about ten organizations. By the side of each name was the membership figure. I gave him my civil flying background and wove in the biographies of the others. De la Haye clearly understood aviation commerce. He knew about flying costs, direct and otherwise, and about the kind of revenue required to cover each flying hour. It was evident that we were in harmony. Not only did he fit our team personally, he offered valuable commercial experience and drive. We agreed there and then to go ahead with our business plans and shook hands on a new relationship that was to form the foundation of Caledonian Airways.

# 20

The vast potential of the undeveloped transatlantic charter market had come into sharp focus. Particularly interesting was the high incidence of Scottish groups and associations in the American ethnic mix. John de la Haye had opened my eyes to the scores of ethnic groups which, in the jargon of the aviation authorities, would be 'charterworthy'. The regulations demanded that such organizations could charter flights only if they could prove to have been formed for purposes other than air travel – and then seats could be sold only to members of at least six months' standing. The rules were, of course, designed to protect the expensive fare structure of the scheduled airlines; a stranglehold on the consumer market which we were eventually to break.

After talking earnestly with contacts and colleagues in both New York and Glasgow, de la Haye came up with the recommendation that the airline should adopt the mantle of Scottish identity and be registered in Scotland. The proposal made sound business sense and its appeal was magnetic to the Scots pride in me. Scotland, after all, had no 'national' airline to carry its name overseas. That name, we ambitiously decided, would be 'Scottish International Airways'.

The project had now assumed proportions far greater than the original primitive plans I had conjured up in Broadstairs. In the 1950s and early 1960s, conversation on charter airlines was inevitably tinged with scepticism about safety and reliability. We had decided that we would take our enterprise out of the traditional charter rut and present it as a professional, international airline. We wanted the company to have a solid financial base and be backed by the establishment in Scotland: the institutions, Members of Parliament, newspaper editors. The early intention was to operate from a London office, hopefully at Heathrow Airport, although the registered office would be in Scotland. Our association with the Scottish 'establishment' would be reinforced by a plan to operate from Edinburgh Turnhouse Airport, rather than Glasgow Renfrew, or Prestwick, out on the Ayr coast.

The financing activity went on in two different directions. John de la Haye had indicated at the meeting in the Skyway Hotel that he could probably find backing among the chartering agents he dealt with in New York. Apart from gaining capital, the attraction of this was that the agents would be committed to placing charter work with an airline they held a stake in.

The three key characters at the New York end were Murray Vidockler, Tom Garrity and George Martin. Vidockler was a travel agent whose business had begun with the operation of coach trips to Florida and had now developed into transatlantic charter flights. Martin, an expatriate Scot, was closely involved with ethnic groups and societies. Garrity was a lawyer. They would ultimately form a company called Scottish Air International to help fund the new airline.

My immediate job was to garner funds from the original 'Manston' group, in the first place, and seek investment from Scottish sources in the second. In a letter to Bill Williams, written on 1 December 1960, I proposed that the group raise about £13,700, in amounts varying from £300 to £1,000. Ideal investment would be £1,000 a head, with £500 up front in cash, to bring the Manston group's collective stake to £28,000 which would, as I indicated to Williams, put us in a strong negotiating position with John de la Haye and the New York investors who had proposed an initial investment of $200,000.

We were, of course, still employed by other airlines and the business development process was conducted through a patchy network of irregular meetings when time off duty coincided, messages left at home and snatched telephone calls.

I received a letter from Phil Daymon which typifies the style in which we were working:-

Dear Tommy,
No reply from Williams. Walters out on flight but message left for me to ring him. Ditto Martin; his secretary obviously knows something of what is going on, as I declined to give my reasons

for calling apart from that I was a colleague of yours which prompted her to say that she knew therefore what my business would be about . . .

Curly Walter, Flight Engineer and the group's technical expert, was assigned to scout for suitable aircraft, particularly the DC-7C which we all favoured. Phil Daymon, with whom I had been involved in the car hire business, was setting about the legal formation of the company. Phil took the project to a firm of accountants in Pinner, Middlesex. Initially, the mission was clouded in secrecy and the accountant concerned was asked to advise on a hypothetical case. After consultation with myself and Bill Williams, Damon confirmed in writing, on 6 December 1960, that 'I was again in contact with the group interested in forming an airline and I now confirm that it is the groups [sic] wish to go ahead immediately with the formation, as cheaply as possible, of a private limited company with a registered office in Scotland and with the name of (1) Scottish International Airways or (2) Air Scotland International or (3) Scotia International Airways.' He concluded the letter by revealing the names of Bill Williams and myself, with our agreement, of course.

As matters progressed, the Pinner accountancy firm guided us towards a firm of lawyers in Scotland, T. J. Addly Son & Company, of Young Street, Edinburgh. Work with Addly Son & Co began on 14 December 1960. This long-established Edinburgh firm must have been taken aback somewhat by Daymon's assertiveness as he wrote 'The group I represent wish to commence operation by 1/3/61 so the matter is somewhat urgent.' As the search for funds began to centre on contacts in Glasgow, we later transferred the legal activity away from Edinburgh to a Glasgow firm, Mackay McIntosh. There, our affairs were in the hands of Alex Donaldson, who was a great find for us, dependable and professional. He was ideal for our requirements and guided us through the many pitfalls in the arrangements we were proposing. 'No, you canna do that,' was one of his favourite sayings – but then he would tell us exactly what we could do without breaking the law!

The first step was to establish our name. In this matter, the pace at which we had planned to go forward was reduced substantially by the Registrar of Companies in Edinburgh and the 1948 Companies

Act. We received a note informing us that Scottish International Airways Limited was not available for the purposes of registration and our attention was drawn to a pamphlet on the regulations governing the use of the word 'Scottish'. The key paragraph of this had been marked with a tick by our solicitor and read: 'A name will not be allowed if it is misleading; for example, if it suggests that a company with small resources is trading on a great scale or over a wide field.' We considered three other options; Highland Airways, Scotia Airways or Caledonian Airways. Highland quickly fell away when we were astonished to learn, after a search within the Register of Companies, that such an airline already existed. Although not trading, Highland Airways 1939 Limited had become a part of British European Airways.

The process of choosing the right name proved to be no light task. The Registrar was not alone in doubting the ability of the applicants to create an international airline. He ruled out various names considered to be too ambitious and eventually refused point blank to allow the word 'international' to appear in the name.

On the finance side, I had made contact through John de la Haye with a travel agent based in the Pollockshaw suburb of Glasgow. His name was Jimmy McWilliam, a short wiry individual with immense energy who was later to become one of the UK travel industry's leading figures. Jimmy, who had introduced us to McKay McIntosh, was already involved in North Atlantic charters and he too saw the potential for a Scottish airline carrying ethnic charter groups across the Atlantic and wanted to invest. A respected businessman, he collected a string of local traders around him as potential investors – a printer, a baker, and a wine and spirit merchant. I was also making contact with some of the larger institutions, but the initial ground-breaking was tough.

Our entry into the New Year of 1961 was marked by the depressing news that the Registrar of Companies did not think that either Scotia or Caledonian were acceptable names. Nevertheless, the momentum was building for the formation of the new airline. Bill Williams, Jean Rodgiel and I were planning the operational side, trawling through the small details of cost accounting, crew patterns and the licensing procedure. We spent many hours in either written or verbal consultation with the Air Transport Licensing Board and the Ministry of Aviation.

One particular spectre which attended the birth of the airline was the same one which haunted us twenty-seven years later – the question of foreign investment. In 1961, our solicitor was concerned with the interpretation of that section of the Civil Aviation Act dealing with 'control' of British registered airlines. There was no specific guidelines and the definition of the phrase 'substantially controlled' could only be resolved in a court of law, should litigation arise for one reason or another. Our lawyer felt, however, that the Scottish Air International Investment of about 20 per cent would not take 'substantial control' away from citizens of the UK. We were by now, sufficiently enthusiastic to start the company running. The town of Windsor is renowned for two impressive features; the Royal Castle and Eton College, the traditional nursery for the British ruling class. There is also a well-known inn, the White Hart Hotel. It was in a room at the White Hart that the first formal meeting of our new airline's executive group took place. It was a Saturday morning, 11 March 1961.

Around the table were John de la Haye, Bernard Fisher, Frank Hope, Victor Surrage, Curly Walter, Bill Williams and myself. The discussion ranged over every conceivable aspect of starting an airline. We talked about approaching a number of prominent Scots to take on the role of Chairman of the company, including the Duke of Hamilton, our friend Lord Polwarth, Lord Boothby, the Marquis of Bute and the Earl of Tobermory.

We agreed that Curly Walter would let it be known around the aviation market that we were interested in DC-4 aircraft, to place a smokescreen around the real plan to operate DC-7Cs. The meeting resolved that John de la Haye and I should spend time in Scotland to drum up commercial support and finance. We talked about aircraft procurement, Ministry certification, licensing, offices in New York and at Gatwick Airport. We decided to buy a copying machine!

Importantly, we set 1 April 1961 as the target date for both the decision on aircraft and for the opening of the Gatwick office.

In due course the company would be formed as Caledonian Airways (Prestwick) Limited. It was only after the solicited intervention of the Scottish Council (Trade and Industry) and its Chairman, Lord Polwarth, whom I had lobbied sufficiently for him to become a staunch supporter, that the Registrar of Companies allowed the name to be used. US investment would be consolidated through Scottish Air International and Scottish investment through a company called Airways Interests (Thomson) Limited. AIT, as it became known, would, effectively, be the holding company for the airline.

It was agreed that the five directors would be myself, Curly Walter, Bill Williams, Frank Hope and John de la Haye. John would begin full time on the project immediately. We would start full-time work with the airline on 1 April 1961. Williams, Walter and myself planned to continue to fly on a freelance basis for other airlines during the peak summer and at weekends to help keep expenses down. The Caledonian Airways salary would be cut by the amount earned on freelance work and would not come to more than £1,000 a year. With the emphasis on piecing together the operating infrastructure and the commercial development, we agreed that John de la Haye would take on the role of managing director. I would be deputy managing director. Apart from anything else, once we were a going concern, I would be away on flying duties. The target date for the commencement of operations was December 1961.

The memorandum and Articles of Association for Airways Interests (Thomson) Limited and Caledonian Airways (Prestwick) Limited were filed with the Registrar of Companies in Edinburgh and the companies were legally incorporated on 27 April 1961.

A press reception at The George Hotel, Glasgow, was attended by a clutch of civic dignatories, travel agents, businessmen and press. It culminated in an invitation to take part in a television interview with the BBC's reporter, John Hossock. It was the first broadcast I ever did and then only after a stiff Scotch. A press release was issued:

### News from Caledonian Airways (Prestwick) Ltd

John de la Haye, Managing Director, has announced the formation of Caledonian Airways (Prestwick) Ltd, the new Scottish international airline.

Caledonian Airways will commence flying operations in December of this year, on World Wide Inclusive Tour and Group Charter Services with the emphasis on transatlantic flights. Offices will shortly be opened at Prestwick and a London Sales Office will be established in July. Negotiations are proceeding for offices at a London Airport.

Caledonian will have handling facilities available for other airlines at Prestwick starting in June of this year.

Sales Manager Bernard Fisher will commence an intensive sales drive immediately.

## First with DC-7C Equipment

Mr de la Haye said today that his company will be way ahead of its competitors in offering the modern dependable Douglas DC-7C 'Seven Seas' Aircraft for Inclusive Tour Services. He stressed the highly economical seat rates which will result from operation of this type of equipment.

Caledonian's first aircraft – the flagship 'Star O' Robbie Burns' will be delivered on 1 December 1961.

Caledonian's Deputy Managing Director is Glaswegian Captain Adam Thomson. A list of other executive personnel will be announced shortly.

Mr de la Haye said that the formation of a Scottish international airline is certain to excite interest not only in the Homeland, but also among pioneer Scots the world over.

In due course our aircraft would carry the name 'Caledonian Airways' with the tag 'The Scottish International Airline', no doubt raising the blood pressure of the Registrar of Companies a point or two.

# 21

For our colleagues in the airline business, both those who supported us and those who wanted to see us fall flat on our faces, the most significant part of our announcement on the formation of Caledonian Airways was the statement on the DC-7C. If sceptics could hardly believe that we had formed an airline company, they were ready to deride the plan to operate DC-7C equipment, still in front-line service with major airlines but, by now, beginning to be replaced by the new Boeing 707.

Curly Walter had scoured the world market for DC-7Cs, reporting back on what was available, how many hours each aircraft had clocked up and its state of maintenance. We came to the general conclusion that our best option was to take an aircraft on lease from one of the major carriers known to be meticulous about standards of appearance, engineering and safety.

British Overseas Airways Corporation had surplus DC-7Cs based at Heathrow, but they were not interested in a deal with us. Curly had, therefore, approached Sabena, the Belgian national airline, from whom he received a much warmer welcome. In particular, he forged a special relationship with one of the Sabena directors, Maurice Rose. Curly and I made many visits to the Sabena headquarters at Zaventem Airport, outside Brussels. Eventually, we concluded a contract for Caledonian, as our venture had become, to lease one DC-7C with 104 seats at the rate of £5,000 a month. All spare parts and overhauls would be covered by Sabena on a rate per flying hour. This effectively meant that if we did not fly, neither did we pay.

The 'Seven Seas' was, in 1961, the world's most modern piston-engined aircraft, designed for non-stop transatlantic flights. Its equipment included storm-warning radar and the aircraft cruised at 320 miles per hour at a height of 20,000 feet. The four Wright Turbo-Compound engines developed 13,600 horse power on take off.

Weeks of discussion over permutations of operating plans led to the conclusion that our main base of operation would be Gatwick Airport, thirty or so miles to the south of London. Gatwick had been redeveloped and opened as a major airport by Queen Elizabeth just three years earlier. It was the home of numerous charter airlines and the biggest single British independent airline, British United Airways, which had emerged as an amalgamation of a number of smaller airlines unable to survive successfully on their own. It was owned by a group known as Air Holdings which included British & Commonwealth, proprietors of my old airline, Britavia, now swallowed up into the amalgamation. The Managing Director of BUA was an air transport entrepreneur by the name of F.A. Laker.

John de la Haye and I found office premises in a market town close to Gatwick, Horley, in Surrey. We set up business in 2 Central Parade, above an estate agent. The symbol we had chosen was the Lion Rampant of Scotland, surmounted by a pair of wings. This was depicted in red, on a shield. The first letterhead announced us as 'Caledonian Airways, The Scottish International Airline,' Prestwick Airport, Ayrshire, Scotland. Principals were listed as J. de la Haye (Managing Director), A. Thomson (Deputy Managing Director), D. H. Walter (Technical Director).

By the time we had reached this stage, we had spent £10,000 of our capital on the process of company formation. Caledonian was formed with an initial working capital of £54,000 from John de la Haye's American investors the Manston group and Scottish sources.

We now set about putting a viable organization together. First we had to obtain the flying business and then we had to recruit and train staff. But, most important, we still had a massive task in raising sufficient finance to quite literally get the airline off the ground. Apart from anything else, we would be unable to obtain the necessary operating licence from the Air Transport Licensing Board, the basic operating permit to operate commercially for hire and reward.

The biggest single file in the new office was the one containing

97

correspondence relating to the licensing question and the biggest single subject in that file was the one of ownership. We were now running into a regulatory brick wall. The company had been set up with 49 per cent of the voting shareholding held by British investors, including staff employed by the airline; 31 per cent held by a British company, Airways Interests (Thomson) which would actually form the airline; and 20 per cent held by Scottish Air International, by now a US corporation.

Neither the ATLB, nor the Ministry of Aviation would give us the green light on the eligibility of the airline for British licenses, without us first going through a route licensing hearing. The dilemma was that more capital would have to be spent on getting the airline to the point of filing an application. If we were rejected, we would all be in personal financial trouble. We were meanwhile building up as steadily as we could. We needed an expert aircraft and route planner. Frank Hope, a former Royal Air Force navigator, was working in the London office of Eagle. He was approached by John de la Haye and recruited as one of the founding directors early in 1961. Bernard Fisher, also with Eagle, had been hired as sales manager, based in the UK. Jean Rodgie, who had been working tirelessly with de la Haye on the project in New York – both alongside their normal jobs – came to Horley to work full time.

The problems of additional investment from Scotland continued to rest on my shoulders. I was in the Horley office one day in the spring of 1961, when an insurance salesman called to sell his services. I noticed his Scottish accent and felt I recognised him. After some minutes of sales conversation, it dawned on me that he was a fellow recruit to the Glasgow University Naval Division. His name was Richard Marshall Gibson, known mostly as 'Marshall'. We had last met eighteen years previously. I did not buy any of his insurance services, but so interested did he become in the airline venture, that he agreed there and then to invest some money!

In Scotland, I did the rounds of the great and the good. I called on and was rejected by Sir Hugh Fraser. He told me that he had once travelled on a charter flight and did not think much of it.

Lord Polwarth of the Scottish Council remained a great supporter and provider of valuable advice, and put me in touch with numerous potential investors.

De la Haye and Fisher were busy building up the flying programme for 1962. We had built up a programme of more than 5,000 hours, made up of North Atlantic charters and commitments for European inclusive tour chaters. We were negotiating with Sabena for a second DC-7C on lease.

One of the great travel markets of the 1960s was formed by the migration of Commonwealth students and young people in general to Britain. For the purpose of low-cost travel, they were organised into clubs, in much the same ways as the transatlantic charter market worked. One of these was the South African Overseas Visitors Club, run by a controversial figure in the travel industry, Max Wilson. Wilson's scheme was to charter aircraft to operate from Lourenço Marques (now Maputo) in Mozambique to Luxembourg, two countries with 'open skies' policies on flight capacity and price.

The discussion with Wilson on selling him our DC-7C charters for the OVC broadened into the possibility of investment in the airline venture.

As well as this activity, I, along with other pilots, was flying freelance for an airline called Air Safaris. On one freelance flight between Tripoli, in Libya, and the Canary islands a Handley Page Hermes was contracted to carry cargo. The cargo was to be loaded at Tripoli overnight while we took crew rest. Only on checking the cargo the next morning did we realize that our shipment was, in face, a cache of arms. We certainly could not carry them, neither could we declare them to the Libyan authorities. Either move would have led to arrest. A flight-deck brainstorming session led to the solution. We would declare that we had a faulty engine which could only be repaired back at Gatwick. We could not carry the cargo load on three engines, so the freight would have to be off-loaded until we could return. The boxes of guns and grenades were laboriously off-loaded by a squad of Libyan loaders and stored in a hangar. We took off on three engines and started the fourth once airborne and out of sight of the Tripoli tower.

A couple of days later, the arms were discovered and the story broke in the British press. The pilots of the Hermes were hailed as heros for their part in breaking up an international gun-running operation!

# 22

It was ironic that while we were using freelance work from Air Safaris to subsidize our own entry into the airline business, that company was in the final throes of decline. A compulsory winding up order was made against Air Safaris on 18 December 1961. In the proceedings in the High Court, the airline was described as being as 'insolvent as it could be'. The petition was bought by the outfitters Alkit Ltd, presumably suppliers of crew uniforms, and included Esso Petroleum. Creditors claimed a total debt of £235,250.

In fact, the overall climate into which we were bringing an infant airline was extremely chill. Air Safaris became one of six independent airlines which had either gone out of business or had run off the financial runway in 1961. The others were Overseas Aviation, compulsorily wound up on 9 October; Falcon Airways which suspended operations and had its Air Operator's Certificate withdrawn on 21 September; Pegasus Airlines which ceased operations at the end of October; Tradair which went into receivership at the beginning of November; and BKS Air Transport which went into the hands of receiver managers in November. These six had followed the business collapse of Air Condor, Continental and Orion the previous year. If our many detractors, mainly former flying colleagues with safe jobs in the airline corporations, thought that the financial malaise among independent airlines would put us off, they were wrong. The situation simply firmed up our resolve. We were determined to learn lessons from the fallen. Our credo was simple: we were a business first and an airline second. Many of the independents which in aviation jargon had gone 'belly up' were under the management of people whose boyish enthusiasm for aeroplanes had overriden their commercial judgement.

In the autumn of 1961, we were nearing the launch of the airline. John de la Haye would, in addition to acting as managing director, run the commercial side of the business. I was to be deputy managing director. Frank Hope was the master planner. Curly Walter would be in charge of engineering; and Bill Williams was nominated flight operations director. The redoubtable Jean Rodgie became chief stewardess. We had recruited Dennis Standen to become head of administration and finance.

By now we had made a good impression on the Ministry of Civil Aviation who, we believed, recognized our serious, professional intent. Even so, we were still grappling with the problems of ownership and foreign investment. Our business plan was to take delivery of the first aircraft and operate our first commercial flight in November 1961, with a second DC-7C from Sabena following in the spring of 1962.

We were busily building up staff. Our advertisements for stewardesses were rewarded with a deluge of applications, mainly from Scots girls. The interview panel was headed by Jean Rodgie, but there was no shortage of volunteers from the male contingent of our management to sit in on a series of beauty parades. We wanted girls who were obviously attractive, but who had the more important characteristics of vitality and friendliness. We wanted an obvious level of intelligence but we were not concerned with academic qualifications. We wanted girls who would make flying fun for our passengers, who were not afraid of hard work and had the spirit to bear long absences from home. One girl whom we recruited and who went on to have a successful flying career, was a milkmaid from Ayrshire.

Our attention turned to uniforms for the aircrew we had recruited. One of my investment targets in Scotland was a wholesale tailor in Bridgetown. In spite of apparent enthusiasm, he never did invest. But he turned the tables by offering me the best quote I had so far received for aircrew uniforms. I accepted this rock-bottom offer, provided he accepted the work based on measurements taken at Gatwick. We could afford neither the time nor the fares for the men to go to Scotland for fittings.

By now, the crews who had joined were in Brussels, undergoing training on the DC-7C, garbed in an ill-assorted selection of 'civvies'. The uniforms duly arrived, but my bargain shopping

101

turned out to be a costly exercise. The shambles that occurred had to be seen to be believed as individual uniforms were found not to fit and pilots, navigators and engineers swopped jackets and trousers until a reasonable degree of suitability was achieved.

As 'the Scottish International Airline', we decided to establish an operating base at Prestwick, in addition to the main base at Gatwick. The move achieved the desired result of winning approval from the Scottish press to consolidate the Scottish image.

If we had earned respect and support from the Ministry, we were still not clear of the Air Transport Licensing Board hurdle. On 1 September we received a letter from the Board which stated that in their opinion, the company was not substantially owned and controlled by persons who were citizens of the United Kingdom. They were also not entirely satisfied with our financial structure.

In that ramshackle year of 1961, it was the ill wind of another airline's misfortune which was to blow us some good. The airline which had been operating Max Wilson's Overseas Visitors Club charters between Lourenco Marques and Luzembourg was the ill-fated Overseas Aviation. It was their failure in October that prompted Wilson to confirm his investment in Caledonian and to give us the contract for the African operation. The Wilson investment provided a balance to the US shareholding and boosted our finances at the same time. Our subsequent application to the ATLB was successful. An added bonus was that we were able to transfer our headquarters from the by now cramped accommodation above the estate agent's shop in Horley to the Overseas Aviation premises, just up the road; the grandly-named Imperial Buildings. Everything was beginning to fall into place. The Ministry of Aviation granted our Air Operator's Certificate and the Air Registration Board cleared the aircraft maintenance arrangements.

Alongside the heady matters of licensing and certification, were the nuts and bolts activities of putting an airline together. Not the least of these was organizing the aircraft livery and stewardess uniforms. This task fell mainly to John de la Haye. Clearly, the Scottish image was to be at the fore. We had already more or less designed the livery. This was depicted on the artist's impression of a Caledonian Airways DC-7C which, in the absence of a real aircraft to show off, we carted round to potential investors and charterers to represent the airline. We chose the red Lion Rampant of Scotland for the tail insignia. On the upper, forward fuselage was the name, CALEDONIAN, also in red, with the words 'The Scottish International Airline' running alongside in blue. The white of the upper fuselage and tail was separated from the plain metal of the belly by a strong blue 'cheat' line. Details were sent over to Sabena in Brussels who were preparing the aircraft. We obtained the registration for the aircraft, G-ARUD. As with every aircraft it became known by the phonetic alphabet version of the last two letters, 'Uniform Delta'.

We did, however, also decide on a policy of ship's names for the embryo fleet. In what, with hindsight, seems an exaggerated gesture towards Scottishness, Uniform Delta was named 'Star O' Robbie Burns'. This was painted on the nose, just underneath the flight deck window.

Stewardess' uniforms were somewhat more of a problem. We wanted tartan, but could clearly not opt for that of one clan. If we sported the Campbell, would the McDonalds fly with us? The agreed objective was to go for a neutral tartan and de la Haye spent days on end looking at tartans and designs for a jacket and kilted skirt.

In an inspired selection, John put forward the ancient Black Watch tartan, a soft pattern of blacks, greys and greens. It was elegant, not garish, unquestionably Scottish and undeniably neutral. A firm in Edinburgh produced the uniforms. Our first operational flight was contracted in November 1961. It was a charter for London Transport, bringing immigrants from Barbados coming to Britain to work on the capital's bus and underground transport systems. The ferry flight to Barbados would be used for inspection of our operation by the Ministry of Aviation. Some weeks before the first flight, John de la Haye and I flew to Brussels to check on progress with the aircraft. We were escorted to a hangar in the Sabena maintenance complex at Zaventem.

In absolute horror we viewed the DC-7C. Technically it was perfect, but the Belgians' attempt at interpreting our livery design was disatrous. The colours were wrong, the lion in the wrong position and the name on the side out of proportion. Heated words eventually led to an agreement by Sabena to strip the aircraft and complete a new paint job.

The aircraft was formally handed over to us on 4 November.

Aircrew training, involving our pilots operating as supernumerary crew members on Sabena scheduled transatlantic flights, had been completed. Stewardesses had been trained on the service procedures we had devised and checked out on the essential emergency procedures. The DC-7C was to be operated with four flight deck personnel and three stewardesses.

The crew for the first operation was headed by Bill Williams. Nine or ten of us travelled to Brussels on 26 November, staying at a local airport hotel for two days as we checked out the aircraft, now in the livery we had specified. To us, the Caledonian aircraft, parked alongside the Sabena fleet, was a momentous sight. We finally had our own, independent airline. To the airport personnel, going about their day to day business, it was nothing special, just another strange British airline and another Sabena lease deal. The first flight of Caledonian Airways left Brussels on 29 November 1961. It departed without any fuss or bother; in fact, a Sabena ground engineer and I were the only individuals who witnessed it.

# 23

Bill had decided to operate two sectors to Barbados, rather than attempting a non-stop operation on long-range cruise procedures, mainly because of the forecast 20/30 knot headwinds the other side of the Azores. The flight to Santa Maria, in the Azores, was uneventful. The transit cost £60, plus some money for additional fuel to cover a second climb out. Communications, once Williams was clear of Santa Maria FIR, were very poor. He received no weather information and was flying very much into the unknown. He told me later he was glad that he had not opted to stretch the operation on a direct flight. In addition to the operating crew, Williams had on the flight deck a Mr Luther from the Ministry of Aviation and a Captain Powell from Sabena, carrying out further training checks. It was extremely crowded. The transit operation at Bridgetown, Barbados, was not altogether smooth. Bill noted in his report that until loading manuals were given to our agents, captains would have to supervise loading and complete papers. 'Willing as they are, TCA [the handling agents] know nothing about 7C loading,' he wrote.

In spite of an early request, the crew received no weather forecast for the return flight to Europe. The landing forecast for Santa Maria eventually came just fifteen minutes before scheduled departure time – and this was only achieved by the handling agent telephoning Trinidad.

The passenger load was ninety-three men and two women. The payload was exceeded by about 500 kilograms. We had assumed an average passenger weight of 70 kilos, but the preponderance of males had pushed the weight up to an average per passenger of 75 kilos. After the trim and take-off parameters had been re-calculated, the aircraft left Bridgetown with our first revenue load. Elizabeth

Barrie, one of the training stewardesses, was travelling on the flight to observe and help with the passenger service operation. One of her observations led to a change in serving methods that airlines the world over use to this day:

> When serving coffee, I suggest that this be done as follows: stewardess should have a snack tray carrying extra sugar and milk jug – coffee pot in other hand. She should ask the passenger to place cup on tray and pour coffee into cup, making sure this is done in centre of aisle. This prevents having to reach across passengers and helps avoid such accidents as hot coffee dripping on to clothes, etc. It also looks more efficient from the passengers' point of view. I carried out this service and found it worked very satisfactorily.

The passengers were served with a separate meal on each flight sector. Captain Powell of Sabena commented that the cabin service was up to scheduled airline standard.

The next time I saw Uniform Delta was on its arrival at Gatwick. It was 1 December a cloudy and dismal morning in rural Surrey. The aircraft approached from the east, made its landing and taxied into a stand on the airport's old North Pier. Virtually every member of staff was with us at the airport to see the DC-7C and celebrate the fact that they were now part of an operating airline.

Our next operation was equally momentous, our first transatlantic crossing. I operated this flight with Bill Williams. We were flying from Prestwick, carrying a group of Scots, mostly first-time flyers, going to visit relations who had emigrated before the war. Our charter seat rate was about £40 for the round trip.

This was my first visit to New York since Fleet Air Arm days. This time I would be at the controls of a four-engined aircraft, operated by my own company. We marked the occasion with the issue of our second press release:

21 December 1961

### CALEDONIAN AIRWAYS FLY IN TO NEW YORK!

A DC-7C aircraft of Caledonian Airways landed today at New York International Airport, bringing members of the St

Margaret's Guild of Scotland to visit members of their sister organization in New York.

Glaswegian Captain Adam Thomson, deputy managing director of Caledonian, and Scottish-born Captain Bill Williams, also a director of the company, piloted the aircraft. Captain Thomson carried messages of greeting from the Provost of Glasgow, Mrs Jean Roberts, to the Mayor of the City of New York and to Scots-Americans in the United States.

Other Scots members of the crew were Captain Lockhart, Mr Strong, Stewardess Barrie and Stewardess Macpherson.

During the stopover in New York, festivities have been arranged for them by Scots-Americans on this memorable occasion of the first ever flight to the United States by Scotland's own International Airline.

On the return flight the aircraft will carry members of the Lennox Clan Albion from New York to celebrate Hogmanay with their friends and relatives in Scotland.

The flight was operated without problem and to schedule. We landed at the Idlewild Airport, later to become John F. Kennedy International. Everything seemed fine until we entered the customs and immigration hall in the International Arrivals Building with our passengers.

There was obvious commotion as the first group of passengers presented themselves at the immigration booths. Some of them turned round to point at myself and Bill. An immigration officer jumped off his stool and marched towards us. 'We have a serious problem here; are you the commander of this flight?' he asked. I promptly found myself in the office of the Chief Customs Officer being told that we had committed a string of offences against the US Immigration and Naturalization Act. The passengers did not hold I.94 forms and many of them had no entry visas, I was told. Matters were made worse when I asked what exactly an I.94 form was. The Chief Officer's demeanour was neither welcoming nor friendly towards the huddled mass which had just stepped off the Caledonian Airways flight, particularly the operating crew.

The fine, he said, would be $1,000 for each visa violation and $50 for each passenger without the mysterious I.94, which I soon learned was the immigration form required to be completed before

107

landing in the USA. It all added up to a sum of money which I certainly did not have in my possession and which the company, itself, would have been hard pressed to find in instant cash. I explained that this was the first time I had been to the USA since the War, when I entered as a serviceman, and that this was the first flight by Caledonian Airways, 'The Scottish International Airline'. Either he took pity on us or simply wanted to get us out of the way, because he eventually agreed to a nominal amount in fines, in return for a promise of 'getting this act together'.

John de la Haye was already in New York and waiting for us at a downtown hotel. As we drove in from Idlewild, through the suburb of Queens and into the tunnel to Manhattan, my mind went back to 1944. The look of New York had hardly changed in my eyes and the feel of the place was still one of excitement and anticipation. De la Haye had been carrying out a round of sales calls, firming up charter contracts and consolidating support from our US investors, Scottish Air International. It was only on reaching the hotel that Bill and I received the message that we were expected to attend a gathering of Scottish Air International investors that same evening in a hotel close to Idlewild Airport.

We piled all of the crew members into a small fleet of yellow cabs and headed off to the airport. We were met at the function by Murray Vidockler, George Martin and Jimmy McWilliam, over from Scotland. The one missing person was de la Haye, who had become unwell and stayed in the Manhattan hotel. We were in the ballroom of a large hotel, surrounded by a crowd of people I had never met before. Among them was a film actress, Wendy Hiller. She told me that she, too, was a pilot and was looking forward to my speech. Speech? Nobody has told me about making a speech and I was extremely nervous at the thought of being press-ganged into making one at this gathering. It turned out that all the people present had been sold shares in Scottish Air International, to found 'the first Scottish airline' and their enthusiasm for the project was boundless, in that special American way. My few words were greeted with cheers. After all, I was the manifestation of their investments. The event developed into a pretty wild evening and it was well after midnight that our cabs made the return journey through the cold streets of Manhattan.

The DC-7C carried 104 passengers. At the rear of the aircraft, mounted on the sidewalls, were four fold-down bunks. With Sabena, they were used for First Class passengers. We used them, however, as beds to meet legal flight time and crew rest requirements. The allowed operating times were 16 hours for a single crew and 24 hours for a double, or 'heavy' crew. The heavy crew, by taking turns to fly and rest, could keep an aircraft flying for the full 24-hour period. This was the way we operated the Overseas Visitors Club charter flights to and from Lourenço Marques. We flew non-stop overnight from Luxembourg to Khartoum, taking about 8 hours, 45 minutes. All of the passengers and all of the crew disembarked in the warmth of a Sudanese morning and sat down to breakfast in the airport restaurant. An hour or so later we would take off for Lourenço Marques arriving in the evening, about ten hours later.

After a day of relaxation in Lourenço Marques, then under Portugese control, we returned by way of Lagos, Lisbon and Brussels. One condition of the flight permit to operate into Lourenço Marques was that we should provide a stopover of two nights in Lisbon for the passengers, as a contribution towards the Portugese tourist industry.

I was thoroughly enjoying my job combination of deputy managing director and line captain. I took every opportunity available to fly. My own log book on Uniform Delta shows trips to New York, Nairobi, Georgetown, Gander, Santa Maria and Lagos.

The ethnic charter business flourished with operations to and from New York, Toronto and other North American points. Our rate was £245 per flying hour and working on a dollar conversion rate of $2.80 across a programme of 120 one-way flights, including 24 empty legs, we offered a seat rate in the USA of $203, round trip.

As we entered the second and third months our reputation began to be established. The Ministry of Aviation even relaxed its rule that an airline must have six to twelve months experience to gain trooping contracts on the Empire routes. John de la Haye's public relations programme was assisted by the recruitment on a part-time basis of Elizabeth 'Betty' Imrie, the wife of *Glasgow Herald* journalist Ian Imrie.

To say that we were immediately successful as airline operators is not high-blown fancy, merely a statement of fact. We had joined the list of airlines who had successfully passed the Ministry of

Aviation and the Air Transport Licensing Board's stringent test of competence and financial status to gain the coveted 'E' licence which allowed certain types of operation without restriction on origin or destination.

I still lived at Wokingham. Dawn was bringing up the two boys as I spent every possible hour in the office or flying the aircraft. We had had no holiday for a long while and even in the Christmas of 1961, I spent just Christmas Day at home. The important thing was that she had lived with the airline since its inception. She understood what I was doing and why I was doing it. It would have been unnatural for the strain on family life not to be vented in an occasional outburst of anger. But such disagreements were few and far between and, overall, she stood behind me 100 per cent.

# 24

My colleagues and I were in a buoyant mood as we continued to operate our one aircraft and we were already negotiating for a second aircraft when disaster occurred. At about 5 a.m. on 4 March 1962, John and I received calls from our operations manager, Tosh Parlane, advising us that G-ARUD had crashed in a swamp on take-off from Douala Airport in Cameroon. Our Operations Manager, Tosh Parlane, called me with the sad news.

I was stunned as I listened to the report of the aircraft having crashed on takeoff. The site of the crash was being combed, but initial indications were that all on board had perished. The aircraft had been carrying a crew of ten and 101 passengers. In command was my best friend, Bill Williams, and with him, Alan Frost, training captain; Gerry Wallman, first officer; 'Mac' McArthur, chief flight engineer; Peter Deane, flight engineer; George Legg, flight engineer; Douglas Strong, chief navigator; and Stewardesses Edith Tiplady, Elizabeth Barrie and Ruth Macpherson.

John de la Haye and I called an emergency management meeting, as calls began to mount up from the press. It was only the pressure of the situation which kept away our tears, although many of the girls on the staff sobbed at their desks as the news spread through our small company.

We agreed immediately that I should go to Douala as soon as possible accompanied by an official of the Overseas Visitors Club, the charterer, and Eric Goodyear, deputy chief flight engineer. De la Haye was left with the task of putting the crisis plan into action, informing the Ministry of Aviation, the Airworthiness Board and the ATLB. It was his task to commission the specialist undertaking firm, Kenyons. I rushed home to Wokingham, snatching my suitcase and leaving Dawn with the awesome task of informing

111

Bill Williams' wife, Ina, of the accident and preparing her for the news that he was probably dead.

I met the two others at Heathrow to catch the first flight to Rome and make a connection to Lagos, Nigeria. At Lagos we hired a private aircraft to fly to Douala.

On arrival at the Cameroon capital, we circled the crash site before landing. It was heart-rending to see the remains of Uniform Delta spread across the evil-looking mangrove swamp. The civil aviation officials who met us said there were definitely no survivors and bodies were still being recovered from the swamp. I was taken to see those bodies already recovered to see if I could make any identifications. I recognized nobody, but still retain the memory of the sight of a young man of about twenty-three, dressed in sports jacket and smart slacks. There was not a mark on him and it looked as if he had simply closed his eyes for a few moments.

After checking into the main hotel in Douala, I telephoned de la Haye to confirm our worst fears. The conversation was brisk, with no pleasantries on either side.

The crash site presented a view of devastation. The aircraft had hit some tall trees not far from the end of the runway. It had broken up and pieces had scattered in all directions as it plunged among the mangroves. There was little that I could do at the site, but Eric Goodyear remained for some days with the wreckage assisting investigators to find some form of explanation for the disaster.

Bodies were recovered and taken down-river by boats and canoes. As they came in to the landing area where a makeshift, tented mortuary had been set up, I attempted to recognise my friends. I saw none of them.

After a sleepless night, we started the gruesome task again in the morning. In the evening, I was faced with the stunning news that the local Medical Officer of health, a Chinese Doctor called Suen, had declared that there had been more people on board than were listed on the manifest. If the situation was not bad enough, this allegation was potentially ruinous and could lead to criminal charges. I knew with absolute certainty that Bill Williams and the rest of the crew would never, under any circumstances, have allowed the aircraft to be overloaded.

I raced for a telephone and called the UK to inform de la Haye. I wanted urgent help from British medical sources. Kenyons, the experienced undertakers, were already on their way and John managed to obtain Ministry of Aviation support with the dispatch on the next available flight of two pathologists.

Time was closing in on me. The devastating allegation against our airline could not be refuted without expert medical evidence. But while this help was on its way, the local authorities were demanding immediate burial of bodies and remains, the standard procedure in tropical areas. I stood fast and refused to allow burial until an accurate body count had been completed.

The Royal Air Force pathologists eventually arrived and, together with the men from Kenyons, set about the grim task of piecing bodies together and setting them in coffins. The work was carried out against the protest of Dr Suen, beside himself with indignation that his 24-hour burial rule had been broken. In the end, however, the British team was able to confirm that our passenger and crew list was correct. Part of the undertakers' work was to remove jewellery and personal effects from the bodies, eventually to be passed back to relatives.

I thanked God that Ken Mason and his RAF colleague were with us in Douala. I have rarely admired two men more highly than the two pathologists setting about their work with total professionalism.

A number of relations who had been contacted by the police in South Africa made the long and complicated journey to Douala to attend the funeral which took place on 11 May, seven days after the crash. Eric Goodyear and I stood in the stifling heat at the cemetery to witness the burial of our colleagues and our passengers. It was a moment of overwhelming sadness. I mumbled my own, personal farewell to Bill Williams and the others as a priest performed the litany of burial in French.

I had already contacted a Cameroon lawyer to guide me through the legal implications of our tragedy. Now I signed a contract with him for the maintenance of the graves and the memorial which we had arranged to be erected amid the lush, tropical vegetation of that cemetery on the outskirts of Douala. The job now, as with all aircraft accidents, was to piece together all available items of evidence to find out exactly what had happened. This work was done by a commission of inquiry set up by the Cameroon Director of Civil Aviation. He was assisted by Bill Tench, a senior Ministry of

Aviation accident inspector who had been assigned to the case from London. Tench, later to become Britain's chief accident inspector, and his colleague, John Novak, worked closely with the local authorities and French officials who had flown down from Paris. The French, in whose colony the accident had occurred, assumed authority. They arranged for the wreckage to be transported to a hangar at the airport and then to be flown to Paris.

I attended all of the investigation sessions and watched intently as the experts sifted through each item of wreckage, looking for clues. I was present when Tench and Novak held up an elevator spring balance tab and found unusual markings on it.

The elevator which, as the name suggests, controlled the up and down movement of the aircraft, was too heavy to be manoeuvred directly from the flight deck. To overcome this, a tab on the trailing edge of the elevator was activated by the control column movement. It moved in the opposite direction to the elevator, thus assisting the pilot to overcome the load on the flying surface. The marks indicated that the spring balance tab had jammed and that, in turn, would have left Bill Williams with an excessive load when he pulled the control column back.

Reconstruction of the situation found that the aircraft was 1,694 kilograms less than the maximum permitted takeoff weight. The wind was just five knots from the compass direction of 260 degrees. Williams made the takeoff from runway 12, which was 2,850 metres long. It was a night of darkness, with no moon and the takeoff direction was towards the jungle where there was no visual reference for the pilot, except a single light of low intensity, some 1,000 metres beyond the end of the runway. Bill would, therefore, have had to fly Uniform Delta by instruments from shortly after liftoff.

According to Tench's investigation, the Douala controllers witnessed a long takeoff run, about 2,400 metres, when it should normally have been only 1,500 metres. They reported that the aircraft gained height only with great difficulty and they watched the anti-collision light at low altitude and then saw it disappear behind trees. Something like five seconds later, a great fire lit up the African sky. The aircraft had crashed into the tidal creek of the River Wouri and the wreckage scattered over the banks. In his book *Safety Is No Accident*, Bill Tench reported that after several

114

months of investigation, it became clear that there had been nothing technically wrong with the aircraft except that a spring tab on the starboard elevator had become jammed and would not function. In order to assess the effect of a jammed spring tab, the Commission of Inquiry hired a DC-7C from a French airline and loaded it to the same weight as Uniform Delta and flew it with strain gauges fitted to the elevator circuit. I was on board as an observer.

Bill Tench wrote:

> The result was most significant. Instead of requiring a pull force of 14-16 kilograms and during flap retraction a force of 10-17 kilograms was necessary, instead of 5-10 kilograms. One can imagine the dilemma of the pilot who is way beyond Vi, the highest speed at which he can abort takeoff and come to a standstill within the length of the runway, and when he exerts the normal force on the controls, the aircraft does not lift off. From then on, he pulls ever harder, using up much more runway than usual and finally gets off the ground with such a heavy load on the controls that he dare not let go to trim the elevator and relieve the load. So he cannot achieve the necessary climb and finally hits the trees and crashes.

When the spring tab evidence first came to light and Tench described what had probably happened, I had a vivid mental picture of poor Bill, a pilot of immense experience, grappling frantically with a circumstance he could neither control nor understand. I imagined the nightmare of failing to gain height and the realization that a crash into the darkness was inevitable.

Tench took immediate action to advise other DC-7C operators of the spring tab problem. Operators of the aircraft type were subsequently required by the manufacturer, Douglas Aircraft Company, to make modifications and, so far as I know, no further accidents occurred from this cause.

# 25

Back at Horley, de la Haye and the others had very significant problems on the commercial side. Curly Walter had problems of another kind, in trying to arrange the lease of another DC-7C from Sabena. John was asked to attend a private meeting with the Air Transport Licensing Board on 20 March to discuss the financial liabilities arising from the accident and the situation regarding plans for the second, third and fourth aircraft.

Our plans to continue were virtually in place by the end of March. We were given great help and support from the Ministry and Sabena. One major blow was the withdrawal of a Ministry trooping contract. The key to our ability to continue was the definitive conclusion on the cause of the crash from Tench and Novak. If the cause had not been found, we would forever have been branded as an unsafe operator. As it was, we threw ourselves into the task of revitalization. Even in that dark period, not one member of our small team talked about the possibility of closing down, no one resigned and with one significant exception, none of our investors suggested we should close down the business.

The replacement DC-7C was delivered from Sabena on 5 April. It was registered G-ARYE, 'Yankee Echo', and named 'Flagship Bonnie Scotland'.

We battled with the Ministry of Aviation over the Air Operator's Certificate. They were, after all, aware that Douala had claimed our flight operations director, senior training captain, chief flight engineer and chief navigator. I had to take on the role of flight operations director and appointed other aircrew members into the management positions.

The worst threat we faced after the Douala tragedy came from

116

Max Wilson, charterer of the stricken aircraft and a major share-holder. The effect of the crash on him was profound – he wanted to get out of the airline business immediately. He wanted to be able to sell his shares; if not, he might have to take steps to fold the company. The dilemma was that, under the circumstances, it would be impossible to find a replacement investor. The four of us, myself, John de la Haye, Frank Hope and Curly Walter, did not have enough personal cash to buy out Wilson. There was money in the company, but, as directors, we could not take a loan.

After talking our way forwards and backwards through the problem, we came to a solution. Our operations manager was 'Tosh' Parlane, an old Britavia colleague and a trusted friend. We called him into John's office and sat him down. I explained the dilemma and emphasized that if we could not buy up all of Wilson's shares, the company would go under. The plan was that we would arrange for Parlane to borrow the necessary money from the company and with it, he would buy the Wilson shares. He had no way of paying the money back if things went wrong, so in a private understanding, away from the formal loan documents which made him liable for repayment, the four of us put our signatures to a statement which affirmed that we would pay him back personally. In a quasi-legal gesture, a twopenny stamp was affixed to the note and Parlane went back to his work clutching the paper which represented a financial safety belt.

For our first full summer operation, we retained the majority of the transatlantic charter flights planned and held on to the Lourenço Marques business. In association with a number of tour operators, we entered the Mediterranean inclusive tour holiday market. We endeavoured unsuccessfully to obtain rights to operate charter flights to South Africa and Australia. The main thrust was, however, on the North Atlantic. We wanted unrestricted charter rights to and from the USA.

The vital objective of penetrating the transatlantic charter market and mounting substantial numbers of flights from Scotland as well as England to both the east and west coasts of the United States and Canada required more than aircraft, marketing razzamatazz and tartan-clad cabin staff.

Over the winter of 1962-3, the aircraft operated War Ministry trooping flights to Germany and Cyprus, and also to Singapore.

In those days – and up until fairly recently – trooping flights had to be operated with rearward facing seats. The War Ministry had decided that this configuration was more likely to give a passenger the chance of survival in a crash.

All of us now felt we were really underway as an airline. De la Haye and his team of salesmen had given Frank Hope and his planning unit a programme of commercial operation for the following summer. It was of such size that it would have been impossible to cover with just one aircraft.

A board meeting approved the proposal to increase the fleet by three more DC-7Cs in 1963. Curly Walter and I went once again to Brussels to negotiate with Sabena. The plan was to take two more aircraft in April and a third in May. The negotiating technique adopted was one that we would use in many future aircraft deals. It was based on an arrangement to lease by the flying hour. If we did not fly, we did not pay. It made sound economic sense for us and for Sabena which would otherwise have had the aircraft standing on the tarmac, as their work was taken over by the new Boeing 707s.

In among these activities, we made a trip which was to become an annual ritual of the winter period. This was to take a team of directors, salesmen, pilots and stewardesses off to the USA and Canada to promote our flights for the coming summer season. It meant meeting the groups, throwing parties and getting down to contract negotiations with some of the most hard-headed businessmen I have ever known. Never mind that they were amateurs in commerce and were plumbers and clerks in their normal lives. Their feel for a good deal was acute. We were, at the same time, shuttling up and down to the ATLB in Glasshouse Yard, in the City of London, seeking licences for inclusive tour charters. Every single one of our applications and those of all other charter airlines was automatically objected to by BEA. The tour operators were under the constraint of the notorious 'Provision 1' of the Civil Aviation (Licensing) Act. This decreed that the cost of a package holiday could not be less than the lowest available public fare offered on BEA's European services.

Mindful of past airline failures, the Air Transport Licensing Board kept a wary eye on airlines' financial structures and took

118

precautions to ensure that companies did not overstretch themselves to the point of financial failure and resultant distress to charterers and passengers.

By this time, we had reformed the board of directors and John de la Haye had been elected chairman and I was elected as managing director. Earlier in the winter, James Barnes, the Board's secretary, had written to John to advise that decisions on our inclusive tour applications for Summer 1963 operations had been deferred on financial grounds.

The Issued Capital as at 24 October 1962 of the holder of this licence should, not later than 31 January 1963, be increased by not less than £40,000 of which not less than £20,000 shall be introduced not later than 30 November 1962. All the increase in capital shall be by way of cash.

We moved to raise the money in Scotland, through Airways Interests (Thomson) and succeeded in an arrangement whereby AIT placed an application for 2,000 'A' shares of £10 each to raise the £20,000. A board meeting on 29 November, chaired by John de la Haye and attended by myself, Frank Hope, Curly Walter and Dennis Standen, as company secretary, considered the AIT application. De la Haye made the proposal, I seconded it and it was unanimously agreed. A letter of confirmation of the increase in issued capital, together with a certified copy of the minutes of the directors meeting was sent to Barnes the same day.

The next step was to raise the remaining £20,000 by the January 31 deadline. This we did again through Airways Interests (Thomson), generating funds from existing and new shareholders, including £500 from Tom Garrity, the New York lawyer. It was the same formula – 2,000 'A' shares at £10 a piece. Again, we took the matter right to the deadline, with the formal directors' meeting taking place on 31 January.

If we were to grow – and that was obviously the plan – we would require more capital for the future. I heard through contacts in Scotland that Industrial and Commercial Finance Corporation, a Government-sponsored merchant bank, would consider an application. We took our accounts and business plan to Ron Hamilton, manager of the ICFC Glasgow branch. He was extremely interested

119

in the airline, but although I believe he put forward a recommendation, it was turned down. In the letter of rejection, however, he made it quite clear that we should reapply for funds later in the year. That was, when the 1963 fleet and operating plan had become reality.

# 26

What was essential was the securing of licences from governments on both sides of the Atlantic. For the United States, it meant that Caledonian had to secure a foreign air carrier permit for charter-only operations – a type of authorization which the US Government had never granted. Section 402 of the US Federal Aviation Act stipulated that foreign carriers possess a foreign air carrier permit as a prerequisite for conducting public operations.

Until Caledonian's entry onto the scene, transatlantic charter flights were being made principally by the scheduled airlines, both US and European. These charter services were authorized as an incidental addition to carriers' scheduled services. The governing charter regulations provided that a scheduled carrier could operate an unlimited number of charter flights between any two transatlantic route points over which it was operating authorized scheduled services flight (e.g. New York to London for BOAC, Pan American and TWA). In addition to such unlimited 'on route' charter authority, a carrier was permitted to operate 'off route' charter flights (e.g. New York – Birmingham, Louisville – London) subject to a capacity limitation. The combined mileage flown in 'off-route' charter flights in a calendar year could not exceed by more than ten percent the total mileage flown during that same period in the carrier's operation of its US scheduled services. The authority of US scheduled carriers to perform 'off-route' charter flights was limited in a comparable fashion.

It was only a small number of emerging US charter carriers, known as 'supplementals', who possessed the authority to operate an unlimited number of charter flights within the particular geographic areas for which each was licensed. The rules of the US regulatory regime served to favour, not surprisingly, the American airline industry. Given the large number of both domestic and overseas points to which the US scheduled carriers were licensed and the heavy volume of their operations, the US scheduled industry was able to reach the civil charter markets (the transatlantic market was the only one of significance) without any substantial constraint. In their wake followed the US supplemental carriers which had successfully won a spirited legislative and regulatory battle for authority to span the North Atlantic without limitation of the areas they could serve or the volume of their operations.

This imbalance of commercial opportunity provided both the economic and political opening for Caledonian's effort to secure the first 402 permit for a foreign 'charter-only' carrier. If that effort were to prove unsuccessful, Caledonian would be in difficult straits. Securing our commercial objective of becoming Britain's major long haul charter carrier required substantial access to the major transatlantic market. Without a 402 permit, Caledonian would be limited, under the strictures of US law, to operating no more than six *'deminimis'* charter flights annually, permits for which in effect exempted the airline from the need to hold a full 402 certificate.

Our timing was propitious in light of the action already taken by US authorities to scupper the efforts of a British carrier to undertake sizable transatlantic charter operations. Among the Eagle (later Cunard Eagle) group of companies were two which operated a low frequency of scheduled services between Bermuda and New York and between the Bahamas and Florida. Eagle had developed some interest in transatlantic charter business and had operated, through its Bermuda company, a small number of such flights in the late fifties, principally between New York and London via a stop in Bermuda. The routing via Bermuda qualified the charters as being 'on route' and thus subject to no volume limitation, but such circuitous 'one stop' services obviously could not compete effectively with non-stop transatlantic charters operated by route carriers such as the Pan American, TWA and BOAC on the New York – London route. An effort by the Bermuda company to secure CAB dispensation to operate a greater volume of transatlantic charter flights during 1960 was soundly rebuffed. The result was that Eagle was required to forego operating a considerable number of flights which it already had on the books.

Seeking a way out of the box, Eagle Aviation Ltd, the UK charter and IT operator member of the Eagle group, filed an application for a 402 permit to engage exclusively in charter operations between the United States and Europe as well as various Middle East and North African points. That application languished with no action being taken despite strenuous diplomatic efforts by the British Government. Fourteen months elapsed before the CAB at the end of June 1961 recognized Eagle's application. Rather than setting the application down for a hearing, the process suggested by the relevant legislation, CAB proceeded to issue an 'Order to Show Cause', asking Eagle to demonstrate why its application should not be summarily denied. The board gave as its 'tentative view' of disapproval, a reaffirmation of its position that a foreign carrier's off-route operations should not exceed ten percent of the mileage flown in US scheduled operations in the prior year.

The board observed that the award of off-route charter authority 'was designed to supplement in a limited fashion' a foreign carrier's right to conduct on-route services – services which the board stated should be promoted 'vigorously' with off-route charters being viewed as a supplementary facility available to accommodate occasional customer request.

As to the merits of Eagle's (by then Cunard-Eagle's) application for a charter-only 402 permit, the board noted that the Eagle group of companies operated in an integrated fashion and effectively constituted a single unit. CAB therefore concluded that the grant to one member of the group of a permit for unlimited 'charter only' transatlantic operations would be nothing more than a device permitting the Eagle companies providing US scheduled operations to wholly evade the ten percent 'off route' charter limitation. In somewhat righteous tones, the board announced that it would not treat Eagle's application other than as a request for an amplification of the off-route charter authority of the other Cunard Eagle Airways companies.

Both Eagle and the British Government were outraged with CAB's action, but the board had taken a firm public position from which it was hardly disposed to retreat. From the standpoint of US officials, however, an application by a British charter specialist, unaffiliated with any scheduled operator, for a charter-only, 402 permit would not be unwelcome. Such an application could enable the US Government to defuse the sour aftermath of the Eagle

'Show Cause Order' by demonstrating a willingness to reciprocate the British authorities' liberal award of traffic rights to the US 'charter only' supplemental carriers, while preserving its reaffirmed 'off-route' charter policy.

It was clearly becoming increasingly untenable for the Americans to insist that the charter authority held by a single British carrier (BOAC) for non-stop US–London flights effectively reciprocated the charter activities performed by two US route carriers as well as a growing number of US charter specialists. What was required was, in US terms, a new boy on the block – a British charter specialist wishing and equipped to develop long-haul transatlantic charter operations.

Hints to that effect had been dropped from time to time, and de la Haye on his soundings in Washington had been among the first to pick them up. But how, we wondered, could we bring it all off?

# 27

The first day of July 1961 was a balmy Sunday in Manhattan. At the Plaza, the elegant Fifth Avenue hotel, a lavish wedding reception was taking place to celebrate the coming together of two television producers, the groom of Italian background and the bride of solid Irish stock. In attendance were two friends of the bride, fellow colleagues from the international student movement. They were Tom Garrity, the lawyer involved in Scottish Air International, and Leonard Bebchick, who had recently taken the expertise gained from a six-month period on the CAB staff to a position with a small Washington law firm.

Within the small talk of their reunion, Garrity told Bebchick that he had helped organize a group of Scottish Americans to put some seed money in a Scottish charter airline that wanted to operate between Britain and the USA. The problem was, he said, that no carrier, let alone a foreign charter carrier, had ever obtained 402 authority to operate unlimited charters between the two countries.

Bebchick, who said later that he must have drunk too much champagne, replied, 'A charter-only 402? I can get it for them, Tom.'

Prior to this, de la Haye had met Jack Rosenthal of the CAB who was sensitive to the fact that American charter airlines were operating some charter flights into Britain as a sideline to their Military Air Transport Service contracts. Rosenthal was an enlightened public servant who couldn't say what the outcome would be but encouraged de la Haye to submit an application. This needed special legal expertise and a determination to win a new kind of battle. Acting on Garrity's recommendation, de la Haye wrote to Bebchick to ask if he would take on Caledonian as a client and endeavour to secure a 402.

Leonard's response was positive, and the race was on. A major issue to be resolved at the start was whether to seek authority to operate between all points in the two countries or whether to accommodate the concerns expressed in informal consultations with regulatory officials of both nations by going for a less ambitious plan. The notion of giving a foreign carrier authority to serve every airport in the United States was viewed as rather mind-boggling. Moreover, the Americans realized that their air travel market was substantially greater than all of Europe, including the United Kingdom, combined, and they (as well as the US majors) were not disposed to permit a foreign upstart to 'raid' the US charter market.

Constraint and restraint are concepts most congenial to the regulatory mind; indeed, if they are *sine qua non* of the regulatory process. We took the only obvious decision – to go for broke, to fight vigorously for unlimited US-UK charter authority, and to make practical accommodations only when the need to do so became irresistible. In short, and notwithstanding the whispered advice and knowing winks of the regulators, concessions were not to be made to avoid anticipated objections and difficulties. It was felt that the application for an unprecedented charter-only permit by an independent foreign charter specialist would generate a dynamism of its own, and that the course of events could not be predicted with assurance. In the event, what we finally received was very close to what we had been prepared to accept from the start.

The battle for the permit lasted well over twelve months. It involved countless submissions, rebuttals of statements of objections, hearings and behind the scenes lobbying. On 13 August 1963 President John F. Kennedy put his signature to a document: a 402 Foreign Air Carrier's Permit, in favour of Caledonian Airways. It was a piece of aviation history, the first such permit to be granted to a foreign airline. This development formed the breakthrough which led to the boom in low-cost transatlantic charter travel that became a feature of the air transport industry through the 1960s and into the 1970s.

In the summer of 1963, Caledonian had a fleet of four DC-7C aircraft, each leased from Sabena. We had decided to continue to push our ethnic identity forward by giving the new aircraft the names of the counties of Scotland. Thus G-ASHL 'Hotel Lima',

126

became County of Ayr, in which our Scottish base of Prestwick was located. G-ASID, 'India-Delta', was named County of Lanark; and G-ASIV 'India-Victor', took the title County of Midlothian.

Naturally, with this increase in fleet size, we required three times as many aircrew and cabin staff. Recruitment of flight deck personnel went on steadily. There were plenty of suitable people available, but many of them had bitter experiences, in terms of job security, with small independent airlines and so took a lot of convincing. Numbers swelled as the busy summer season drew closer and job offers from the state airlines and larger independents were not forthcoming. Stewardesses were another matter. Interview boards were set up in Scotland and at Gatwick Airport. Advertisements in local papers invited young ladies to come and talk to us.

As in the initial recruitment, we were swamped by applications. Our criteria were set more or less along earlier lines and our minimum age requirement of nineteen was two years below that of the state corporations. With youth, attractive looks, intelligence and personality the main basis of assessment, we recruited an enviable team. Along with the passenger service and safety and survival training, John de la Haye, Jean Rodgie and the senior cabin staff put into place the bones of a new dress code. Hair was to be neat and fashionable. Long hair should be tied in a pony-tail, off the face. Jewellery was limited to a discreet necklace and an engagement ring, where appropriate (air girls were not married, in those days). The kilted skirt could be worn at a fashionable length which, in 1963, meant above the knee. White gloves were to be worn at all times when not serving in the cabin.

The stewardesses who climbed aboard the DC-7Cs, sporting their Ancient Black Watch uniforms turned the heads of airport workers and passengers of all airlines everywhere we flew. They became a great asset, but it was not for a further twenty years that we would use their charm and style in a formal marketing campaign, when they became the 'Caledonian Girls'.

One of the new contracts negotiated early in 1963 was with Morris Perry, a travel agent who ran a company called Orientours specializing in pilgrim and tourist travel to the Holy Land. Although we were fully licensed by the UK authorities, the Israeli government, protective of its own airline, El-Al, and its pool partner on the

London to Tel Aviv route, BEA, was determined to keep out low-cost charter flights.

Their tactics were simple – they would ignore our requests for flight clearances. We received neither a 'yes' nor a 'no'. As the date for the first flight in the series came close, Frank Hope, John de la Haye and I decided we would try to call the Israelis' bluff. We had, after all, a binding contract with Morris Perry. We had his deposit in the bank and he, in turn, had sold seats to the public.

Captain Alan Limbert, in command of the first flight from Gatwick to Tel Aviv, was instructed by me to ignore the fact that he had no Israeli clearance and simply to proceed with his full load of 104 passengers to the border of the Tel Aviv Air Traffic Control Authority. Limbert was to maintain radio contact with our operations control room. I called Tel Aviv to tell them the aircraft was en route and said that I would report flight progress. They made no response.

I advised Tel Aviv of our aircraft's progress en route – but each time got no response. This game of 'chicken' continued until Limbert's aircraft was approaching the official line of Israeli air space, when they advised our Captain that he was refused permission to enter.

Plan B went into action. This was for Limbert to turn the aircraft around and head back for Nicosia where accommodation had been arranged for the passengers and crew. The next day, de la Haye and I, accompanied by Perry, arrived in Tel Aviv by scheduled flight. We had with us a press statement designed to attack the Israeli Government for refusing to allow bona fide pilgrims to enter the Holy Land. Through the journalists we had contacted, the government found us at our hotel. We were summoned to a meeting the following day. Those who confronted us included the Director of Civil Aviation with assistants and a representative from the Tourist Board.

They were adamant – no charters. We also stood firm – we would keep the pilgrims in Cyprus and the pressure of publicity going as long as necessary. De la Haye chivvied away at them. 'Have you considered,' he asked, 'how it is going to look to the rest of the world when we show – as we will, loud and clear – how Jordan allows us to fly Christian pilgrims into Jordan while Israel bars those same pilgrims from seeing the places most holy to them?' The Israelis seemed amused at John's mischievous negotiating tactics but the meeting reached no immediate conclusion.

In fact the story of the stranded pilgrims had, by now, generated its own momentum. Headline followed headline and we became minor celebrities. The saga had so much become part of Tel Aviv gossip, that one radio presenter wound up his recitation of the local football results with the remark: 'And the latest score for the game in the air is Caledonian 3, Israel 1.'

We then were invited to meet Teddy Kollek who ran Prime Minister Ben Gurion's office and who later became Mayor of Jerusalem. We also met Ygal Alon, the Minister of Labour, and a party and cabinet colleague of the Minister of Transport.

Within forty-eight hours of our arrival in Israel the pilgrims, none the worse for a brief all-expenses-paid sojurn in Cyprus, were in Nazareth. John and I went to our favourite night spot, the Omar Khayam in the old Arab town of Jaffa, where we had a ball to celebrate our success.

Through the summer of 1963, our fleet of four aircraft plied the charter routes across the Atlantic, the holiday routes to the Mediterranean and any other route on which we could operate one-off contracts, or 'ad-hoc' charters, as they were known.

In the May of that year we had presented ourselves publicly at the first of the Biggin Hill International Air Fairs, the brainchild of two aviation entrepreneurs, Ted Drewery and Squadron Leader 'Jock' Maitland. We had brought down from Scotland a contingent from the Glasgow Police Pipe Band which performed a daily display in front of the aircraft on exhibition to the public. Special flights on which the girls served champagne cocktails were laid on for guests – the travel agents and tour operators to whom we were selling and members of the press. One young journalist with whom we made our first face-to-face acquaintance was Tony Cocklin, who covered aviation for the main travel industry newspaper, *Travel Trade Gazette*.

Armed with the new 402 permit, we were in full swing with the North Atlantic flights. By the end of that summer, we had clocked up a total of more then 100,000 passengers and £2.5 million in charter revenues.

The arrangements with Sabena proceeded well. As the Belgians took care of all major maintenance on the DC-7Cs, we had need only for a small team of engineers at Gatwick and Prestwick. The operational side had settled down with new men in the senior positions left vacant by the Douala tragedy. Sales staff concentrated on the opportunities made available by the 402 permit, but also looked for flying work from every conceivable source.

One of our ideas was to set up a charter-based package tour from the USA to Scotland, the very first of its kind. It was a two-week arrangement which included flights to and from Prestwick, hotel accommodation and golf on each of five famous Scottish courses. The inclusive price would be £175. To test the market, I led a team of six, including pilots turned salesmen for the winter, on a sales drive to New York. The travel agents and golf club professionals we contacted gave us a positive response, especially when we revealed the price which included ten per cent commission for them. We knew that we would have to seek special licences from the ATLB in London and the CAB in Washington. These flights would, after all, be sold openly to the public, not through the closed groups of the ethnic associations. We knew also that we would face stiff objections from the scheduled carriers, especially BOAC. Indications from the market were, nevertheless, promising and we felt that if we could prove a market existed, we would be halfway to winning the licences.

Several days into the sales drive, the six of us had come in from our various sales calls to meet for lunch in a restaurant at the foot of Manhattan's Pan Am building. It was during the course of that meal that the mind-numbing news of the assassination of President Kennedy, in Dallas, came through. America went into the shock and depression that comes with the state of bereavement. Business virtually closed down and we abandoned our sales activity and, indeed, never resurrected the plan for golf tours to Scotland. Everybody in the airline felt especially touched by the hand of fate on that dismal November day as they did, of course, throughout the world. The signature of approval on our 402 permit, the key to our success so far, was that of the stricken President himself.

We decided to return to the UK by way of Toronto where I signed contracts for thirty-two charter flights to be operated the following summer.

130

# 28

I continued to operate as a line pilot, in between sales and administrative duties which were becoming more and more intense as our activity grew.

One flight I operated was a British government charter to Moscow. The schedule was to operate from Gatwick to Copenhagen where we would take on board two Soviet pilots who would oversee the navigation through USSR airspace and then proceed to Moscow. The flight was known to be part cargo, part passenger, but it was not until reporting for duty at Gatwick that I saw the cargo was not the sophisticated scientific equipment I had imagined, but building materials, planks, cement, shovels and picks. I also saw that the passengers were not high-ranking diplomats, but ordinary British building workers. I was flying them to Moscow so that they could carry out work on the British Embassy building. The Foreign Office had decided that security considerations favoured the use of British men and materials. Inevitably, the newspapers got hold of the story and the following day Caledonian found itself at the centre of a major piece of news.

Another government charter was to the West Indies. For this flight we were briefed well in advance. The purpose was to return immigrants and visitors under deportation orders to their countries of origin. Among them were hardened criminals, including some awaiting murder charges. I was not happy about the safety and security in the cabin during the flight. Instead of operating with the normal crew of three stewardesses, I rustled together a group of hefty male stewards from Britavia to carry out a freelance operation. The passengers arrived at Gatwick under police guard, complete with motorcycle escort. They were marched up the steps to the aircraft, and seated by the police who then promptly left us to it.

It was a midnight departure on a miserable night with rain driven by a westerly wind lashing the tarmac.

The four engines of the DC-7C powered us along the runway and up into the low scudding clouds. It was bumpy and uncomfortable, but this had the effect of keeping the passengers docile in their seats. Well into the cruise stage of the flight en route to the refuelling stop in the Azores, the stewards reported that all was quite, with most of the passengers asleep. About four hours later, I handed the controls to the First Officer to look into the passenger cabin. Incredibly, the passengers were wandering about the cabin, talking and laughing with each other. It was their first taste of any kind of freedom for some length of time and they might just as well have been tourists on their way to a Caribbean holiday. The burly stewards I had hired to act as airborne warders were, on the other hand, fast asleep in empty seats at the rear of the aircraft. They were awakened rudely and told to remain on their feet for the rest of the flight.

Through this kind of ad hoc flying, Caledonian began to gain a reputation for the handling of unusual or difficult flights. We were asked to put forward a proposal and a quotation for taking the first British team to the Paraplegic Olympic Games in Australia. For these brave people we constructed a special boarding ramp, four times as long as normal aircraft steps, and perfected a procedure where the staff pushed the passengers in their wheelchairs up the ramp to the rear door and then along the centre aisle where they were lifted into their seats. The wheelchairs were passed up to the front of the aircraft, handed through the forward door, folded down and stowed in the holds. The disembarkation procedure was the same thing in reverse. Caledonian was contracted to carry out many such flights for the paraplegics, to the extent that many of the competitors and officials became firm friends of the aircrew and cabin staff. Our aircrew, particularly Captain Phil Bryant, developed an ongoing association with the paraplegics from Stoke Mandeville. Our main growth area was the North Atlantic, followed by European inclusive tour operations. We were making steady inroads in North America and our operations spread from New York and Toronto to such places as Boston, Syracuse, Chicago, Detroit and Miami. The pioneering work achieved with the breaking of the regulatory deadlock to gain the 402 permit had given us an instantaneous high status within the travel and air transport industries and we played on the perception that Caledonian was a bigger and more experienced airline than it actually was.

For 1964, we planned further fleet expansion. The four DC-7Cs were fully committed to the North Atlantic for the summer. In fact, we needed a fifth aircraft for this work. At the same time, the European inclusive tour business was growing and additional equipment was required to fulfil the contracts concluded with tour operators.

Sabena had no further DC-7Cs available, so we went once again to Heathrow to talk to BOAC. This time we were successful and agreed a deal to acquire a DC-7C from the state corporation. The arrangement was for delivery on 29 April 1964. The aircraft was registered as G-AOIE, 'India Echo', and we gave it the name, County of Perth.

What Sabena did have available, however, were two DC-6B aircraft powered by four Pratt & Whitney 2800 engines. They were designed as medium-range aircraft and they were ideal for inclusive tour charter flights. Contracts were negotiated to lease the two aircraft for delivery in April and May, respectively. This was another deal with Sabena whereby if we did not fly we did not pay and it worked well for both airlines.

By midsummer, 1964, the Caledonian fleet numbered seven aircraft. On one momentous day, we managed the tricky logistical task of getting all of the aircraft lined up on the North Park at Gatwick. John de la Haye and I took our proud turns to be photographed in front of the fleet.

The summer programme took off and proceeded normally. Delays because of weather or technical problems caused frantic moments at the Horley headquarters, mainly in Frank Hope's planning room, where he and his team would study the boards, rearranging schedules and substituting one aircraft for another to get the programme back on track.

The biggest single problem came in September, on the 28th, to be exact. We had continued to bid successfully for War Ministry trooping flights and were in the process of operating a series between the UK and Singapore. Captain Barry Damon was operating such a flight with 'India Delta'. En route back to Gatwick, Damon, a highly experienced pilot, prepared to land at Yesilkoy Airport, Istanbul, for refuelling before the final, homeward leg. Although there were heavy storms in the area, the landing was in daylight.

On the final approach, Damon was lower than he should have been by several feet. Instead of clearing the threshold to make his landing, the pilot undershot and planted the undercarriage in a steep ridge just before the runway. The result was that the landing gear crumpled under the impact and the aircraft screamed and scraped its injured way along the runway under the force of its momentum, with wheels, engines and parts of the main airframe falling off as it rolled from side to side on its belly.

As the DC-7C ground to a halt, the crew took firm control and went automatically into the emergency drill. The fact that the passenger load comprised servicemen used to operating to orders must have helped the emergency evacuation to be completed in a minute or two. There were no apparent casualties, but Damon ran back on board to check. He was confronted by the senior stewardess, Sally Parton, calmly pulling on her white gloves and reporting: 'All clear, Captain, everybody evacuated.' Damon threw himself to her, grabbed her by the waist and pulled her to the doorway, screaming, 'Get the hell off the aircraft – she's about to blow!' The two of them got out and away from the wreckage as the DC-7C burst into flames to become a total write-off.

It was inexplicable to me that a pilot as experienced as Damon could have made such an elementary mistake. He was unsure of what actually happened in the final seconds before the crash and was convinced that he had sufficient power on to take him over the runway threshhold. In those days, there was a theory that downdrafts flattened out before hitting the ground, although it proved to be invalid in many subsequent accidents. It was to take a further twenty-two years before the microburst effect was fully acknowledged and then only after the 'mysterious' crash of a Delta Air Lines Lockheed 1011 at Dallas Fort Worth Airport on 2 August 1985. I remain convinced that Damon and 'India Delta' were victims of such a microburst, long before the phenomenon was scientifically discovered.

# 29

1964 turned out to be something of a watershed for our evolving business. Due to the timing of the start of Caledonian, our financial year ran from 1 October to 30 September. At the end of September 1964, we had earned a profit of £90,614 on a turnover of £2,310,585. This compared with a profit of £28,118, on revenues of £966,947 in the previous twelve months, our first full year of operation. Passenger carryings had grown from 46,781 to 110,730; and staff numbers from 120 to 185. Business had, in fact, boomed.

On the North Atlantic charters, we had carried 17,304 passengers, a rise of 122 per cent. Holiday inclusive tour charters had risen by 180 per cent to 56,885 passengers. Trooping contracts had grown by a massive 530 per cent, to provide 17,207 passenger; and the general ad hoc charters had brought in 24 per cent more passengers.

We had applied to the Air Transport Licensing Board for no less than fifty separate inclusive tour 'B' licences that year, in association with a range of tour operators, the household names of the day, such as Pontinental, Gaytours, Wallace Arnold, Rentavilla, Lord Bros, Hickie Borman and Spain Only. The destinations included Barcelona, for the Costa Brava; Perpignan, for the South of France; Malaga, for the Costa del Sol; Rimini, for the Italian Adriatic; Palma and Ibiza, for the Balearic island resorts; Dubrovnik, for the Yugoslav Adriatic; and Genoa, for the resorts of Liguria. We operated the IT flights in a varying summer series which could be as many as fifty round trips to Alghero, or as few as nine to Lisbon. A typical flight-time in the piston-engined equipment to Palma, for instance, was 6 hours, 30 minutes for the round trip. Our rate, per hour, for such a journey was £255.

The majority of services were operated from Gatwick, but inclusive tour charter programmes were also flown from Prestwick and

135

Manchester. The package tour business in general was well on its way to becoming the major industry that it is today. In 1964, 592,000 Britons travelled on holiday by charter flights, 397,000 of them by British airlines and 195,000 by foreign charter airlines such as Spain's Spantax and Italy's Societa Aerea Mediterranea (SAM). British airline carryings had increased by 52 per cent over 1963 which, in turn, had shown an increase of 18 per cent over 1962.

In the middle of the year, we had plotted a bold plan for the immediate future. Although there was plenty of European flying, the big money was in the longer routes. Quite simply, the longer the route, the higher the aircraft utilisation, the lower the costs, and the higher the profit. So long, of course, that you could achieve a good load factor and an adequate seat rate. The inroads we had made on the Atlantic routes meant that the Europe to North America business was ripe for development. Although the North Atlantic was in the grip of the scheduled airlines and protectionist agreements between the British and US governments, our earlier breakthrough with the 402 permit provided the spur to be daring.

It had not passed our notice that the incumbent flag carrier, BOAC, was not in favour with the recently elected Labour Government, under Harold Wilson. The previous November, a House of Commons Select Committee had been appointed to examine the Report and Accounts of the nationalized industries. In June, 1964, the Committee's Report on BOAC was published. The report was made against the background of the airline's accumulated deficit of £80 million at 31 March 1963. Even though an operating surplus of £7 million was forecast for the 1963/4 financial year, BOAC's interest charges were likely to be as much as £8 million and there was, therefore, very little chance of reducing the deficit. One of the economic problems cited by BOAC was sharpening competition on the North Atlantic routes. Central to the inquiry was the financial fiasco which had occurred involving the aircraft manufacturer Vickers over orders and costs for the new VC-10 aircraft. It was a damning report and the committee had little option but to recommend that BOAC should be compensated by the government for the additional costs of the VC-10, so that the corporation's new board would be able to make a fresh start. This was the sort of financial feather-bedding for the state corporations that we were to see more of in the future.

At the time, however, we wanted some security of tenure on the North Atlantic. We also wanted to bring the burgeoning European inclusive tour business to the North American routes. At a special board meeting during the summer of 1964 we agreed to the plan to apply for low-cost scheduled services between London and New York, plus inclusive tour 'B' licences, one to New York, the other to Toronto. The tour licences would be in association with one of our shareholders, Donaldson Line, the Scottish shipping and travel group. Donaldson would involve other tour operators in a consortium to produce and promote all-inclusive holiday packages based on the Caledonian charter flights.

All of our dealings with the ATLB had been involved investigations into our financial standing. While the board recognized our commercial success, the members harboured concerns about the company over money matters. I believe some of the old gentlemen of Glasshouse Yard felt that they had to curb our enthusiasm. The fact was that we had been expanding and were planning to expand further than was prudent for our current capital base.

Control of Caledonian was in the hands of Airways Interests (Thomson), our 'holding' company, with 50.75 per cent of the voting shares. Donaldson Line held 28.83 of the voting shares, Marshall Gibson 14.94 per cent, Ian Raynard 4.28 per cent, and Duncan McLeod, our auditor, 1.20 per cent. Scottish Air International held 12.13 per cent of the overall shareholding, but they carried no voting rights.

We decided that the North Atlantic applications had to be backed by further capitalization. Our budget for the new operation, drafted over hours of meetings long into the summer nights, indicated that the start up costs of the venture would be £77,200. We therefore set about raising an additional £80,000.

It was achieved through agreements with Donaldson to put in a further £24,625 for shares and for the AIT investors to increase their stake by £25,375. The remaining £30,000 would be obtained from the bank in the form of a medium-term loan or short-term revolving credit. The reason for this was that AIT could raise no more than the additional £25,000. Any more investment around that sum from Donaldson would upset the balance of the existing

137

shareholding and affect control of the company. The result of this change was to give Caledonian an issued capital of £176,000 and loans of credit of £30,000. It provided a reasonable gearing, or debt/equity ratio.

The haste with which we worked on the project was prompted to a large extent by intelligence from the USA that some of the US supplemental airlines were moving towards plans for transatlantic inclusive tours. The applications were duly filed with the board.

We called on Leonard Bebchick who had, so expertly, fought and won the battle for the elusive 402 permit, to present the case and prepare the submissions. He in turn, called in a leading Washington aviation economist, Sol Colker, to back up the Caledonian case as an expert witness.

The hearing itself took place in the quasi-judicial environment of the Air Transport Licensing Board's meeting room at Glasshouse Yard. Our application was to operate up to fourteen inclusive tour flights annually, in each direction, between April and October. British holidaymakers would embark on an all-in, two-week package covering Boston, Niagara, New York and Washington. In the USA, a two-week tour offering seven days in Scotland and seven days in England would be marketed. As previously planned, the tour operator would be Donaldson Line.

The bid was opposed bitterly by BOAC whose objection rested on the claim that Caledonian's inclusive tour operation would cause 'material diversion' of traffic and provide only 'wasteful duplication' of its own services.

Bebchick was fired up for this case and entered the hearing with all legal guns blazing. Neither the ATLB, nor BOAC had ever before encountered such spirited advocacy and fierce cross-examination in the context of the normally dull process of a British air licence hearing. Leonard's performance led one of the elderly gentlemen of the board, sitting in judgement, to lean forward and remark at one particular point of cross-examination, 'Mr Bebchick, we'd prefer less of the Perry Mason tactics, and would you please stop walking up and down when addressing the board and questioning witnesses.'

In that pregnant period between the end of the hearing and the publication of the decision, Caledonian once again came under financial scrutiny from the ATLB. A request for fifteen copies of the current balance sheet was coupled with a summons to an investigative meeting. The meeting was scheduled for 4 September.

Among the commuters at Horley railway station that morning was the Caledonian delegation. Led by John de la Haye, it included Leonard Bebchick, Pat Holt, a pilot and shareholder who had become director of special projects; Alan Bartlett, our planning manager; Dennis Standen, company secretary and financial director; and Len Donovan, the chief accountant.

The meeting was tough, more like an inquisition, de la Haye told me later. In the post mortem session, however, we came round to the conclusion that if the board was preparing to turn our applications down, they would hardly have gone to the trouble of making a thorough examination of the accounts and budgets. In actual fact, we were in pretty good financial shape.

Within two weeks of the post-hearing meeting with the members of the ATLB, the board published its decision. The licences were granted as applied for, but for a limited, three-year period, 1965-7.

The protectionist policies of BOAC were exposed and derided publicly in the board's decision. 'A sense of proportion is necessary. Within the modest limits of these applications, we think it extravagant to talk in terms of wasteful duplication of and material diversion from the transatlantic services operated by BOAC.'

The board had, however, rejected the Caledonian application for full-scale scheduled service licences and, in contrasting this decision with the approval for the inclusive tour series, it wrote: 'the inauguration of inclusive tours on a particular route is bound to generate some entirely new traffic and to that extent, have a lesser impact on scheduled services.'

While the independent airlines had built up a formidable operation of holiday charter flights to the Mediterranean, this was the first time that the concept had been applied to the transatlantic routes, dominated by major airlines under restrictive international agreements and protected by the fare-fixing cartel of the International Air Transport Association (IATA). The ATLB decision was hailed by the press as a 'sensation in the travel world', according to one headline. In the BOAC boardroom at Heathrow they must have been rather upset! The state airline took the immediate decision to call foul and appeal against the ATLB decision to the Minister of Aviation, then Roy Jenkins. BOAC charged that the board had wrongfully been imbued with what it called the 'Palma-Rimini' complex and that, if sustained, the decision would threaten to wreck the entire 'delicate' IATA fares structure. An appeal hearing was set up under a Commissioner and took place in December at Burlington House, a government building behind Piccadilly which today, curiously enough, is the location for the Museum of Mankind. We were to wait a full six months for the outcome of the hearing.

# 30

In November 1964 John de la Haye suddenly tendered his resignation and severed all ties with the airline. He announced that the 'highly satisfactory development and profitability of Caledonian now enabled him to concentrate on a new project in which he had been interested for some time'. John indeed was coming to feel that the company had matured sufficiently so as not to require his full attention and he felt that his creative drive was being stifled by the – often, to him, humdrum – requirements of management on the broad scale.

But the 'pursuit of other interests' rationale, here as in most cases, did not tell the full story. In fact, John's voluntary departure was an act of great personal sacrifice taken to save the airline from possibly disastrous consequences. What follows has been sheltered from public view for a quarter of a century, and John and I both feel that the time has come to disclose what really happened.

The seeds for John's departure were planted at his 'command performance' appearance at the CAB hearing on Caledonian's 402 application in August 1962. John was closely questioned about the financial involvement of US individuals and concerns in Caledonian as well as his personal dealings with both the US investors and other Americans. Both UK and US regulatory authorities had initially been concerned at the extent of the US holding in the airline – £15,000 which represented 28 per cent of the share capital held as non-voting shares. That concern abated as investment from Scotland grew over the next two years and the US percentage holding was halved.

But the financial picture given to the CAB when John appeared did not tell the full story which he had kept to himself. In the dark days following the Douala accident and the withdrawal of Max

Wilson as a principal shareholder, John, in order to help maintain the appearance of British control of the airline, registered in his own name shares beneficially owned by a US citizen.

Caledonian's relationship with the American investors, and particularly those involved in SAI, was marked by occasional discord. The problems arose from the clash and jealousies of strong-willed personalities, each of whom sought preferential commercial relations with the airline and all of whom became discontented when John and I made it clear that Caledonian would deal only on a business-like basis.

In the autumn of 1964, John learned that one of the Americans with knowledge of the share-deal had, in a fit of pique, reported the matter to Pan American officials who had passed the information on to a CAB staffer. Pan American had vigorously opposed Caledonian's 402 application and had candidly told Bebchick that it was determined to use the regulatory process to smother the company in the cradle so it could never become a serious competitive challenge.

Several weeks later, Bebchick rendered a troubling report following one of his periodic briefing sessions with a senior CAB official. Leonard was told that Pan American was looking closely into the question of Caledonian's ownership and control, that the airline should be prepared for an exhaustive probing of this question at the upcoming hearing for the renewal of its permit, and that we would be advised to review the testimony of Caledonian's witnesses in the 402 proceeding as Pan American would be going over this past testimony with great care.

Leonard was briefed by John about what had occurred, and he was asked to provide his best counsel – what were the risks and what should be done? Wishing to leave nothing to chance, Leonard consulted with the most eminent of Washington's aviation lawyers – L. Welch Pogue who had served as the CAB's first chairman and was a US representative in the negotiations which had produced the historic US-UK Bermuda Air Services Agreement. What Leonard sought was an informed insider's view. Pogue's advice supported the conclusion that Leonard already reached. The CAB, egged on by the US scheduled carriers, were likely to react strongly.

The fact was that a concealment had been perpetrated under oath on a subject of regulatory importance – the nationality of a carrier's ownership and control. That view had been echoed in a recent Federal appeal court decision, ironically written by Leonard's former employer and mentor, which upheld the government's refusal to renew a radio station's broadcast licence on closely analogous facts. In the view of Pogue and Bebchick, the very continuance of Caledonian's transatlantic permit would be placed in jeopardy, and the company surely would be delayed in securing an enlargement or renewal of its permit rights at a time when the North Atlantic market was Caledonian's life blood. Also, it was likely that the airline would be subjected to financial penalties.

The end came on 10 November 1964 at a meeting called by John to air the entire matter. Frank, Curly, Leonard and I were present. John quickly outlined the problem, asked Leonard to put his personal feelings and their close relationship aside and to give him the answers to two questions. 'Are we in serious danger of losing the transatlantic licence?' Leonard replied, 'Yes'. To the second question, 'Is there a reasonable chance of it all blowing over if I go?' Leonard replied, 'Yes'. The questions were for our benefit because John had already put them to Leonard in private and knew the answers only too well.

Before the rest of us fully could assimilate what was happening, John responded, 'Right, that's it!' and announced that he had decided to make the ultimate sacrifice.

Curly, Frank and I certainly would have fought the battle in support of John had the option been presented. As it was, we had to accept the loss of our leader, a man we both liked and respected and whose foresight and imaginative drive had achieved so much. John surrendered his directorship, stock holdings and all employment arrangements and departed. It was a sad occasion for all.

John had been the airline's leading light. His departure was not only a blow to the Caledonian team, but potentially damaging in terms of public and trade perception. I now knuckled down to solving such problems, for immediately following John's resignation, I was elected to take on the role of chairman and chief executive of both Caledonian Airways and Airways Interests (Thomson) Ltd.

My feelings were a mixture of both sadness and great excitement. On one hand, my flying duties would have to be curtailed; on the other, I would be completely at the helm, and following John's success story would be no easy task. I took over John's office at Imperial Buildings in Horley, and along with it the company's senior secretary, a young lady by the name of Margaret Trett. Margaret, whose experience and training was in high-powered commerce, had joined Caledonian as a stop-gap job, after returning from working in France. She is still with me to this day.

Over the summer of 1964, we had operated a fleet of six aircraft, four DC-7Cs and two DC-6Bs. The business strategy, for which I now took full responsibility, was to add three long-range Britannia aircraft in 1965 and release one of the DC-6Bs. The expanded operation would mean an extra 100 staff added to the 185 people we now employed.

The pace of change in aviation is rapid. Our once envied fleet of DC-7Cs were now becoming obsolete and we were forced to turn our attention to modernization. Curly Walter once more scoured the market, this time for the Bristol Britannia aircraft on which we set our sights for the immediate future. Ironically, it was BOAC, still fighting bitterly to curtail our commercial expansion, which had three Britannia aircraft available for sale, because of their own re-equipment programme involving VC-10s and Boeing 707s.

In December 1964 we agreed the purchase terms for the three aircraft and arranged for maintenance checks and refurbishment work to be carried out at Southend by the Aviation Traders company, run by Berlin Airlift veteran Bob Batt. The aircraft were scheduled to come into service the following summer. British-built, the Britannia was powered by four Proteus 300 series turbine engines, carried 131 passengers and had a non-stop range which comfortably met our requirements for flights to the eastern seaboard of the United States. It was a popular, quiet and steady aircraft, known universally as 'the Whispering Giant'.

Along with the expansion programme, it was decided that Caledonian needed a fresh new image. Inspired by the Burns poem which ends with the lines 'It's guid tae support Caledonian's cause, And bide by the buff and the blue,' I called in a young commercial artist I had known back in Broadstairs when flying for Britavia. His name was Don Fuller and he set about producing impressions for a new livery based on the colours blue and gold. Gathered around our boardroom table, our management team sifted through Don's drawings and eventually selected one which featured the lion rampant in gold, against a dark blue background. The top of the fuselage was white and separated from the plain metal of the belly by a gold and blue cheat line. It was this livery which was to take Caledonian into its next phase of development and be carried on by successor airlines.

As we planned our way into the future, the airline was in the throes of a typical winter operation. The main European inclusive tour services and transatlantic charters operated predominantly in the summer season, April to October. For the intervening months, charter airlines were forced to seek out other forms of work to at least cover the overheads and minimize the inevitable winter losses. Some airlines simply put their fleets on the ad hoc charter market, through the Baltic Exchange, and waited for the phone to ring. Although the Baltic could be a welcome source of ad hoc business, it was too unpredictable. We set about finding our own winter markets.

We launched into round-the-world charter tours, the first of which we operated for the tour operator, Wings Ltd, at the end of 1964. The aircraft, under the command of Captain Hugh Dennison, simply carried a group of ninety-three well-heeled tourists on a seven-week itinerary around the world. We carried out trooping contracts for the Ministry of Defence and continued the programme of flying pilgrims to the Holy Land at Christmas time. Ad hoc work included carrying football supporters to international matches, ferrying ships' crews from one port to another and the occasional freight flight.

But the most interesting winter work centred on the annual pilgrimage undertaken by Moslems throughout the world to Mecca – the Haj. The Haj is concentrated over a designated period of time each year in the late winter. The consequence is that there is unprecedented demand for transport from every country in which there is a significant Moslem population. Air transport is usually co-ordinated by the respective national airline which, in turn, sub-contracts other carriers to provide capacity.

Our inroad to the Haj market was made initially by one of our commercially-minded pilots, Pat Holt, and consolidated by an energetic sales manager, John Hughes. Hughes spent weeks at a time travelling in the Middle East and Africa for negotiations

145

with the airlines and the boards which controlled the conduct of the Haj.

The method of operation was to transfer aircraft, crews, engineers and ground support staff to the major departure points for the Haj – for example, Tripoli, Kano, Kabul, Kuala Lumpur and Teheran. For several weeks the aircraft would perform shuttle services between these places and Jedda in Saudi Arabia, carrying the pilgrims, many of them people who had perhaps never seen an aircraft before, let alone travelled on one. I can recall, in particular, the scene at Haj time in Kano, Northern Nigeria. Whole families would come to the airport from the outlying areas with the person chosen to make the Holy Pilgrimage. Rather than return to their villages, some would remain, camped, at the airport until the pilgrims returned. The operations to Jeddah covered about three weeks' flying. The return started after the Pilgrimage and covered about another three weeks, returning to a large number of destinations.

Our cabin staff became expert in meeting the requirements of the pilgrims, including their need to face eastwards during the five daily prayers and the necessity to wash before saying them, even when in flight. Many senior Moslems I have met since, mostly in West Africa, have told me that they carry the venerable title 'Al Haji', by courtesy of a flight with Caledonian. Eventually one year we flew more pilgrims to Jeddah than all of the other airlines combined.

The very first of our Britannia aircraft was delivered to us at Gatwick on 13 March 1965, and immediately positioned to Rabat, Morocco, to operate Haj services on behalf of Royal Air Maroc. This aircraft was G-AOVH, 'Victor Hotel'. It took the fleet name County of Angus. It was followed on 13 April by the second Britannia, G-AOVI, 'Victor India', which took the name 'County of Argyll'. Fifteen days later, the third aircraft, G-AOVJ, 'Victor Juliet', arrived at Gatwick with the name 'County of Aberdeen'.

These new aircraft which carried more passengers at faster speeds than the DC-7Cs and DC-6Bs operated a flying programme on which the airline carried more than 30 per cent more transatlantic charter passengers; more than 50 per cent more passengers on trooping flights and more than 30 per cent more passengers on

146

general charters. Holidaymakers on inclusive tour flights increased by just 2.5 per cent.

With an increase in staff of more than 50 per cent, we opened a sales office in central London, with three full-time salesmen, and added an office in Toronto to the existing sales headquarters in New York. Demand was increasing in Scotland and this led to the poaching of British Eagle International Airlines' manager for Scotland and Northern Ireland, J.M. 'Ian' Ritchie. British Eagle was the new airline formed by Harold Bamberg after his Cunard Eagle Airways had been merged into BOAC and was mounting head-to-head scheduled service competition against BEA on the routes between Scotland and London and in other areas.

Even with more resources, it is fair to say that, in 1965, the organization was just barely managing to cope with the work. Staff in every department, from accounts to flight operations, were just about keeping their heads above water. Our offices in Horley were becoming cramped and, therefore, inefficient. We began to look around for new and roomier premises.

In May we learned of the long-awaited outcome of the appeal hearing against the transatlantic tour licences. The Minister, Roy Jenkins, issued his decision, saying that he had accepted the recommendations of the Commissioner, Sir John Lang, to uphold the ATLB decision. He dismissed the BOAC appeal. This was ten months after we had first applied and, now, too late to market a programme for the forthcoming summer period. In addition, without the British license, we had been unable to seek reciprocal authority from the US Government.

The US situation was complicated. A major licensing procedure was under way involving all of the US long-haul charter airlines, or 'supplementals' as they were known. These carriers operated under specific legislation as operators who were designed literally to supplement the activities of the major scheduled carriers and the military transport operation of the USAF. Controversy surrounded the question of whether or not the CAB was authorized to allow them inclusive tour rights. Under these circumstances, we felt it hardly likely that the US government would license a foreign charter carrier for services not yet sanctioned for their own charter companies.

The issue was not legal, but political. An investment made a year earlier was about to mature in our favour. In addition to lobbying the United States Travel Service, Leonard Bebchick and John de la Haye had paid a visit to Senator Edward Kennedy during which they had laid out the original plans for the inclusive tour services. Caledonian's proposal was that the US terminal for the tour flights would be Boston, an aspect that appealed to the Senator for Massachussetts. Kennedy recollected that he had learned at the knee of his grandfather, 'Honey Fitz' Fitzgerald, that Boston was America's closest gateway to Europe, and had been unfairly displaced by New York in the era of the steamers. Kennedy was also an advocate of competition and lower air fares. He saw that the licensing of a British airline for tour services would quickly tip the scales for the authorization by the Civil Aeronautics Board of the supplemental airlines. Bebchick, who also happened to be a Massachussetts Democrat, paid a return visit to Kennedy. The operating proposal was reduced to a plan for fourteen flights for the summer of 1966 only. Kennedy took on the Caledonian cause and began to lobby the Department of Commerce.

The outcome was that in August, Caledonian and Donaldson Line placed applications with the CAB for the fourteen flights. The bid was supported by a letter from the Secretary of State for Commerce. The reaction was remarkable. The CAB responded by ordering an expedited proceeding to authorize the flights by granting an amendment to Caledonian's 402 permit. The board ordered that the normal, mandatory structure of such proceedings be stripped down to the barest essentials. An oral hearing took place on 18 October and the board came out with a favourable decision on 5 November. We had received this new authority in just a single month. In comparison, the process of obtaining the 402 permit had taken sixteen months.

Thus it was that the first-ever charter-based inclusive tour programme to the USA appeared on the British market at the end of 1965. Donaldson had brought three other travel companies into a consortium. These were Hickie Borman, Lord Brothers and Wings. An eight-page brochure was produced quickly. Only the front page featured colour. The tour, covering the flight to and from Boston and an itinerary which included pullman coach travel and first class hotels in Boston, Binghampton, Niagara Falls, Williamsport,

Washington and New York, was offered for '115 Guineas' or £120.15s.

In the event, not a single 115-guinea tour was sold. The Donaldson programme ran into difficulties and was never operated. It was down to the protracted proceedings for the necessary permits and licences and although the CAB's expedited process was unprecedented, final authority came too late for the tour programme to be effectively marketed for the 1966 season.

What we lost in flying hours and revenue, however, we gained many times over in publicity. Caledonian became renowned on both sides of the Atlantic for innovation and competitive pricing, at a time when international air transport was conducted for the benefit of the operators, rather than the consumers. Additionally, the Caledonian proceeding in the USA assisted the CAB in taking the regulatory plunge and licensing the US supplemental airlines to operate inclusive tour charters. That move heightened even further the controversy as Pan American World Airways (today's Pan Am) and Trans World Airlines took the CAB to court. The court reversed the CAB decision, but within six weeks Congress intervened and enacted legislation specifically authorizing IT rights for the US charter airlines. The supplementals had won decisively in an historic American expansion of charter rights.

I firmly believe that this action in the mid-sixties was the thin end of the wedge which was ultimately to open the door of protectionism by the IATA airlines and bring a liberal, competitive, consumer-oriented regime to the prime North Atlantic air routes.

# 31

At the Gatwick base, I was settling and taking hold of the reins of the business. Dawn and I had not long before decided to move from Wokingham to be nearer the office and the airport.

Just south of Gatwick, the Sussex market town of Crawley was beginning to mature as a 'new town' created after the Second World War to rehouse Londoners whose homes had been lost in the blitz. Crawley was a pleasant place in 1965 with the old, picturesque High Street sitting comfortably alongside a modern shopping centre and office complex. The new housing constructed by the borough council and the New Towns Commission was well-designed in spacious estates, broken up by open spaces and woodland areas. Around the town was open countryside, mostly farmland, interspersed with ancient Sussex villages and hamlets. To the south were the Downs and the Sussex coast. Yet Crawley was less than an hour by train from Victoria Station on the main London-Brighton line.

Private property was beginning to be developed around the outskirts of the town and it was these houses that Dawn and I inspected over a series of weekends. We eventually settled in an area known as Gossops Green which lies between Crawley and Horsham. For the two boys, now sixteen and twelve it was ideal, with at that time, plenty of open space and good schools. I was now living virtually over the shop, being able to get to the office in fifteen minutes or the airport in ten.

One of my first priorities was in the area of staff communication. The growing number of employees meant that the kind of 'kitchen table' communication we had enjoyed previously was no longer possible. In particular, the aircrew and cabin staff were an absentee workforce, spending their time either flying or resting at home and rarely coming into the office. I decided that we needed a staff newsletter to be written and produced occasionally, probably quarterly. I consulted Ian Imrie, husband of our public relations representative in Scotland, Betty Imrie. Ian was air correspondent for the *Glasgow Herald*. Both Ian and Betty had given us valuable help and advice from the very beginning. Ian took on the task of writing and producing a house newspaper which became known as *Caledonian International*. The first edition appeared in spring 1965 with a 'Chairman's Message' from me on the front page. I was thirty-nine and, in those days, still extremely young for a company chairman. Therefore I was photographed in a sombre business suit, with a grim facial expression, holding a pipe. This was designed to imbue me with maturity and wisdom and the company with strength and stability! Behind the scenes, however, the airline was suffering the effects of expansion and the extent of the operation outstripped our financial control mechanisms. During the year, Tom Garrity, the US lawyer representing the American shareholding, resigned from the board. My old friend and shareholder, Marshall Gibson, came in as a director, bringing much-needed commercial expertise from his world of insurance and finance.

The accounts for that year showed a profit of £86,883, a small reduction on the previous year, despite an increase in revenue of close to £1 million. I had been concerned for some time with the accounts department. It clearly needed to be reorganized and required more staff of a higher calibre. We had recently recruited an able young chartered accountant, Trevor Boud. I asked him to put forward plans for a reorganization. In the annual audit, surprisingly low results were produced, inconsistent with various management accounts and estimates. Trevor began to investigate. He went back to the beginnings of the airline and found debits of £45,000 against 1963 and £54,000 against 1964 which had not been brought into account. The conclusion was that simple inefficiency had occurred through high workload and pressure. I put Trevor in charge of the accounts department from that moment. Shortly after, he was appointed financial director, at the tender age of twenty-seven, and remained at the financial helm of the airline throughout its career.

It is fair to say that Caledonian was now taking shape as a

significant airline. The inclusive tour programme in 1965 served seventeen destinations in Europe. The North Atlantic charter programme was, by now, substantial enough for us to invest in our own ground handling unit at John F. Kennedy International Airport, New York. Assigned to the job of station manager, New York, was a fellow Scot, a former colleague with West African Airways in Nigeria, Alan Stronach. We really had two operational points, one was Alan's at the airport, the other was under the control of Janet, his wife, operating from their home at all hours of the day and night. Our aircrews experiencing problems would call either base for instructions. This was quite typical for Caledonian. Alan was to remain with the airline for the length of its history. At Prestwick, in Scotland, we had a staff of twenty under station manager, Jimmy Hislop, whose proud innovation in the summer of 1965 was the introduction of walkie-talkie radios to give instant contact between the staff in the terminal and those on the airport tarmac.

One piece of new business planned was a series of fortnightly inclusive tour charter flights to the Bahamas, operated in conjunction with a company called Bahamas Holidays Ltd. The two-week holidays were planned to retail for £162.10s.

I was concerned with both short and long-term planning. The jet age was now firmly with us and aircraft like the Boeing 707 was carrying, on scheduled services, many more passengers, over longer non-stop sectors, at almost twice the speed of the Britannias. To compete in the future, Caledonian needed to fly jets. In the meanwhile, we had decided to consolidate on an all-Britannia fleet for the 1966 operation.

Across the Atlantic, in Canada, Canadian Pacific Airlines was moving rapidly into jet equipment and had three Britannias available. We could justify buying only two of the aircraft, but so keen was 'CP' to dispose of the three, that a third aircraft was acquired at a knock-down price, on the back of the main purchase arrangement. The total cost was almost £1 million. Again, these aircraft were scheduled for maintenance and refitting at Southend and planned for delivery to us at Gatwick in January and February 1966. The three remaining DC-7Cs were to be phased out.

The longer term, I felt, required deep and careful analysis. The question which faced the company was whether to remain as we were, operating on a small scale, with second-hand equipment, or to take the quantum leap into front-line jet operations. If the latter course was correct, could we retain control of the company, with the need for major financing arrangements?

I had already sought studies on jet aircraft from an aviation economics expert and former Eagle executive, Maurice 'Guy' Guinane, to help the other directors and myself through the conundrum. I articulated my thoughts in a memorandum written in New York in September. I headed it 'Where do We Go From Here?' On 23 and 24 October I called the directors together at a hotel in Brighton for a two-day think-tank tỏ discuss my paper. Gathered on the south Coast were Frank Hope, now deputy managing director; Dennis Standen, company secretary; Curly Walter; Marshall Gibson; Pat Holt; and Captain Stewart Calder, our flight operations director. I had also asked John de la Haye to join the meeting.

We wrestled with the problems of growth and finance associated with the possible introduction of jet aircraft and reviewed a plan to launch scheduled services from Glasgow to a range of European points. Overall, the meeting judged that the risks of maintaining the airline as it was were far greater than the risk of expansion. John de la Haye pointed out that two of our main competitors in the transatlantic charter market, the US airlines World Airways and Capitol Airlines, already had jets. The competitive arguments were overwhelming.

We studied the possibilities of the Super VC-10, being built by British Aircraft Corporation the Douglas DC-8 family of aircraft, and the Boeing 707. Entry into the jet age for Caledonian we knew would be extremely expensive, but it was vital that we chose an aircraft that could meet our requirements for long-haul as well as medium-haul operations. Selection began to focus on the Boeing 707-320C, the latest version of the 707, capable of long-range operations – non-stop between London and Los Angeles, for example – and conversion to all-cargo operations. The total cost of acquiring one 320C, including two spare engines and duty, would be £3,366,000.

Attention now concentrated on the financial structure of the company. Even without the burden of financing jet aircraft, we were already undercapitalized and we needed to increase our capital to £500,000, particularly in view of the fact that we always had

153

problems with cash flow in the winter period. In the past Sabena had allowed extra time for payment of maintenance bills on the DC-7Cs and DC-6Bs and Shell had been lenient on the payment of fuel bills. We felt that British United Airways which, through its parent company, Air Holdings Ltd, owned Aviation Traders, would be stringent with credit on the maintenance contract for the Britannia fleet. We calculated that by obtaining more share capital from existing institutional stockholders and increasing our own shareholdings, we could push the capital up to £400,000 without losing any degree of control.

Frank Hope put through a telephone call to Boeing in Seattle, where he spoke to a Hal Young, who we had been working with for some time. Frank was told that for delivery of a Boeing 707-320C by 1 May 1967, it would be necessary to place an order by the end of December 1965. The terms were that a deposit of £18,000 was required on placing the firm order and a further £150,000 (five per cent) on signing the contract. During the first six months after the order was placed, 281/3 per cent would have to be paid, spread over monthly instalments. The remaining 662/3 per cent would be demanded on delivery. Young had pressed Frank to send over to Seattle a letter of intent, dependent on Caledonian obtaining adequate finance.

We looked at Boeing's figures and concluded that an initial increase in capital to £400,000 would be sufficient for the present, but it was required instantly. It meant that we had to raise £190,000 to add to the existing capital of £210,000. Phase two of the capital reconstruction would happen in spring 1966, when £125,000 would be required for the deposit on an aircraft.

By spring 1967, the target date for jet introduction, we estimated we would need capital of £1 million. On top of the existing £525,000, the airline would require £250,000 of working capital, £100,000 for pre-operating costs, £50,000 for interest on loans and a further top-up of £75,000.

Frank Hope who had always kept his feet firmly on the ground to err on the side of caution, suggested that we delay the jet introduction until 1968. The rest of us insisted that competitive pressures forced us to act sooner, rather than later. The final conclusion was that, provided the increases in capital could be arranged, under acceptable terms, and that further financing could

154

be acquired, again under acceptable terms, the airline should purchase one Boeing 707-320C for delivery in May 1967.

On the question of the scheduled services from Scotland, we had agreed to set up a study group comprising Pat Holt, 'Guy' Guinane, Ian Ritchie, and Marshall Gibson. If their recommendations were positive, applications would be made to the ATLB as soon as possible, with a view to starting operations in 1967.

This proposal led to another confusing debate. Marshall Gibson was to make the first stand in a minor crusade he kept going for the next twenty-three years. In my 'Where Do We Go From Here?' memo I had listed as an option a plan to move the base of the airline to Glasgow to concentrate on the development of scheduled services from Scotland. He leapt on the idea of 'The Scottish International Airline' becoming absolutely Scottish and basing its headquarters in Glasgow. There was no doubt that we were Scottish, with the vast majority of our ownership held north of the border, a registered office in Glasgow and a substantial operating base at Prestwick. But Marshall wanted to go further. In reality, there was no question but that we had to remain in the London area, at the centre of the UK aviation market and close to the government bodies which regulated the industry. We talked of splitting the activity and headquarters between Scotland and England, but the consequential extra costs and inefficiencies cancelled that proposal out.

Nevertheless, we did agree that we needed some form of corporate office in Glasgow which we would use as a base when working in Scotland. But our major concern was that, whatever happened, we would soon have to move from Imperial Buildings in Horley. We had outgrown them. Therefore, we resolved to seek new headquarters in the immediate vicinity of Gatwick.

Perhaps the most important development from that Brighton meeting was my plan for a radical change to the management structure of the airline. If we were to go forward with the ambitions we harboured, I wanted to see a fast transition from the somewhat cavalier style we had grown up with to a more mature and serious management formation. Above all, I felt it essential that the directors freed themselves from the 'hands on' airline tasks to concentrate on policy and strategy. I wanted accountability to be laid on heads of departments and supervisory staff, rather than being passed up to the board of directors, and for middle management to be responsible for taking decisions.

The proposal was to put in place an executive management, responsible directly to the board. It would comprise a general manager/administrator; a commercial manager; a financial adviser; and an economic study group. So far as the economic study group was concerned, I knew that we now needed proper research and development capability to deal with statistics, route studies, cost studies and licence applications. We agreed to employ Guy Guinane on a temporary basis to set up this unit, with a view to him joining us full time later.

# 32

Air transport has always been vulnerable to unpredictable changes in political circumstances. Mostly the effects are adverse, occasionally they bring good fortune. It has gone down in aviation lore, for instance, that the post-war British independent airline sector owes its foundation to the emergency of the Berlin Airlift. At the end of 1965 a similar situation, on a much smaller scale, however, emerged in Africa.

The British colony of Southern Rhodesia, led by its Prime Minister, Ian Smith, made its infamous Unilateral Declaration of Independence against the British Government of Harold Wilson. Enraged, Wilson and his Cabinet imposed sanctions against Southern Rhodesia, attempting to cut off supplies which had traditionally come from the port of Dar-es-Salaam in Tanzania. One unwitting victim of the situation was the newly-independent state of Zambia, formerly Northern Rhodesia, led by Kenneth Kaunda. The British colonial trade routes had been structured so that the Zambian territory was, in turn, supplied from the Southern Rhodesian capital of Salisbury. Sanctions against Rhodesia meant that Zambia was cut off, especially from that most vital commodity, oil.

The British Government planned an airlift of oil to Zambia from Tanzania. One of our Britannias was contracted for the work. Victor Hotel left Gatwick on 28 December and after refuelling at Khartoum, arrived in Dar-es-Salaam the following day. Although the aircraft had no freight door or heavy duty floor, it went into immediate service, shuttling loads of 45-gallon oil drums to the Zambian capital of Lusaka and, occasionally, to the copperbelt town of N'dola. We arranged for an engineering team from Aviation Traders to go to Tanzania to support the operation. As demand grew, one of the ex-Canadian Pacific Britannias was drafted into service earlier than planned and dispatched to Tanzania on 7 January. In February, a second ex-CP aircraft flew out on airlift work to relieve Victor Hotel which returned to Gatwick, having suffered damage when a load of oil drums shifted on take-off.

Two Caledonian Britannias remained on the Zambian Airlift until spring 1966. Operating a schedule of two flights daily between Dar-es-Salaam and Zambia, the aircraft transported about one million gallons of oil. Most of the work was straightforward routine, but ground engineers working on an aircraft one night were surprised by a leopard, his mate and three cubs which wandered out of the bush and on to the airfield where they were working.

These airlift flights were treated with great importance by the British Government and I received a letter from the Minister of Aviation, Fred Mulley, expressing his thanks to the airline and the personnel taking part in the operation. The ill wind of Africa had blown some good in Caledonian's direction, by taking up all of our ad hoc charter capacity for the winter period.

For the generation to which I belong, 1966 was a year of great moment. The liberated, free-for-all of the sixties was in full swing, with British popular music and fashion setting the pace for the rest of the world. The charismatic, avuncular figure of Harold Wilson led the Government. England beat West Germany at soccer by four goals to two to win the World Cup. At our Horley headquarters, things were equally momentous for Caledonian Airways. It was our fourth year in business and, with the help of the Britannia aircraft, we were clocking up our most successful year to date.

So successful had the original three Britannias proved to be on the previous year's operation, that we had taken the decision to acquire three more for 1966. These were the aircraft from Canadian Pacific which were rushed into service on the Zambian Airlift. With the existing three DC-7Cs, Caledonian's total fleet numbered nine aircraft. Staff had increased to 370 people, predominantly aircrew and cabin staff. The most significant effect for our business of the faster, more productive Britannias was on the North Atlantic charter flights, where our traffic increased by 61.7 per cent, to a total of 36,786 passengers. Traffic on Mediterranean holiday flights rose by a healthy 11.3 per cent. Trooping and general charter business actually declined because of the deployment of Britannia capacity on the Zambian Airlift.

For the very first time, cargo statistics entered Caledonian's table of results. The shuttling of oil drums between Dar-es-Salaam and Lusaka translated itself, in the traffic figures, as 10,366,191 lbs of freight. Most importantly, the profit we earned that year virtually equalled the sum of the first three years' profits put together. It amounted to a figure of £205,085.

The airline had pressed ahead with its plan for scheduled services from Glasgow. We won two of the five routes applied for and were now licensed as a scheduled service operator on the Glasgow-Barcelona and Glasgow-Ibiza routes. (An appeal against the rejection of these licences was dismissed.) Plans for the operation of these services was deferred for two years, due to delays in obtaining reciprocal permission from the Spanish authorities.

In Washington, Leonard Bebchick had not only successfully obtained renewal of our Foreign Air Carrier Permit – the 402 – but had won extensions of its validity for five instead of the usual three years. He had also gained approval for a number of significant new benefits. This included a blanket authority for inclusive tour charters between any point in the UK and any point in the US. Significantly for the future and the anticipated operation of larger aircraft, we won approval for 'split' charters. That is, we would be able to contract two different charterers for the same flight.

The new permit also included authority to operate up to ten one-way cargo charter flights annually; and it gave us the ability to operate charters from a total of twenty-one British-governed points throughout the world to the USA. A sixth new operational category was for 'circle tours' allowing us to add any other country to the USA to make up an itinerary. We were, however, refused permission to operate inclusive tour charters from the USA to the UK, clearly the area with the most potential. Neither were we allowed to operate group charter flights from countries in continental Europe to the USA.

The company itself was now more buoyant than ever. By the end of September 1966, Marshall Gibson, Trevor Boud and I had negotiated deals to increase the capital to £861,772. We had taken up the offer of Industrial and Commercial Finance Corporation to 'come back another time', when they initially refused to invest in the airline. This time, they agreed to invest as shareholders. Along with ICFC – later to become 3i – came an Edinburgh investment bank, National Commercial and Schroders, a subsidiary of our main bank, then called The National Commercial Bank. We struck up an excellent relationship with John Burke, the Bank's manager in Glasgow. He later became managing director of the (renamed) Royal Bank of Scotland and was a good friend and colleague. Sadly he lost his life in a climbing accident in on 12 November 1983.

Our faithful supporters at Donaldson Line agreed to increase their shareholding. The total amount of the new investment was £400,000. The new shareholding arrangements were due to be ratified at an extraordinary general meeting of existing shareholders.

The problems of office space had dogged us all year and we had scoured the property market around Gatwick. We came, at last, to select a new building in the High Street of Crawley, Sussex House. I suppose it was a sign of the sixties that the several floors of offices were built over the Starlight Ballroom and Casino at one end and a bowling alley at the other.

On a personal level, I was delighted to welcome John de la Haye back to the company. After two years of being out of the airline, involved in various business schemes which ranged from airline catering to a holiday village in Spain, John returned on a full-time basis and was re-elected a director.

Weeks of study had been consumed in analyzing the economics of the jet aircraft. It formed a massive investment for our small company and it needed only a small slip of business planning or a degree of misjudgement to bring financial disaster. Maurice Guinane and his economic planning team had evaluated both the British Super VC-10 and the Boeing equipment. It became clear early on that the VC-10 fell far short of the Boeing both in range and payload capability. As fine an aircraft as it was and already in service with BOAC and British United Airways, the VC-10 could not operate non-stop between Europe and the West Coast of North America. Neither was the VC-10 a fully-convertible passenger/freight aircraft. Significantly, British Aircraft Corporation was unable to guarantee delivery of a Super VC-10 until at least one year later than Boeing could provide a 707-320C. The limited production of the VC-10 type meant that the aircraft lagged behind the 707 in amortization, re-sale value and availability of finance. As much as we would have preferred to buy British, the prospect for a VC-10 was far too risky. There was no question in our minds, but that the 707-320C and the VC-10 were two altogether differend kinds of aircraft. Our Boeing 707-320C was due for delivery in May 1967 and we obtained an option for a second aircraft in 1968.

The competition we faced from the US supplemental carriers was fierce. These airlines were not slow to see the potential of a market we had largely pioneered and were now competing with a vengeance. Between them, they were offering ten jet aircraft in the transatlantic charter market in 1966. By 1967 airlines like American Flyers, Capitol Airways, Overseas National Airlines, Saturn Airways, Trans International Airlines and World Airways would be deploying a collective fleet of twenty-three long-range jets. The American carriers had a significant advantage over us with the amount of military traffic they could obtain from US government sources.

The 707-320C, by virtue of its speed, capacity and range, unmatched by any current aircraft, would provide Caledonian with a competitive edge. The aircraft's seat-mile costs were substantially lower than the Britannia's, it had 50 per cent more capacity and its cruising speed was just about double. One of our calculations showed that the 707 matched against a DC-7C would produce 3.31 times the amount of work, at less cost. We had already talked with our old friends at Sabena and were confident that an arrangement for the 707 to be maintained in Brussels would be easily negotiated. The firm order was placed with Boeing in June. The aircraft was going to cost us $7.5 million. Part of the financial process was the routine task of applying to the Board of Trade for a licence to import the aircraft free of duty. Had there been a comparable British aircraft import duty would have been levied. Our straightforward request was to land me in the first of a long series of controversies with politicians. The Board of Trade wrote to me on 1 June to deny our application to import the 707 free of duty. Their position was based on the fact that they believed the Super VC-10 to be an equivalent aircraft and we were to be penalized for not buying the home-grown product.

The VC-10 project had been fraught with problems and the enforced purchase by BOAC of a larger fleet of these aircraft than it required had almost brought the state airline to its knees financially. Whitehall's support for the manufacturer, BAC, was understandable. But I was angered by the reaction of a bunch of

161

civil servants who could have no knowledge of our business, let alone the operational parameters of different aircraft types.

On 7 June I wrote to the President of the Board of Trade, Douglas Jay. In this I outlined the nature of our business, illustrated why the two aircraft were different and declared that his imposition of duty on a 707 would in no case lead Caledonian to buy a Super VC-10, if the aircraft could not be commercially justified for our kind of work. 'I think it does not overstate the case to say that the real decision before Her Majesty's Government is whether British charter operators will be permitted effectively to compete with foreign carriers, or whether they will be compelled to withdraw from a substantial portion of the international charter market, with the attendant loss of foreign earnings, specifically dollars, to the Exchequer,' I wrote. The letter concluded by requesting a meeting.

# 33

In the meanwhile, our sales people in the USA had been laying the groundwork for the 707 operations. The maximum profit from the 707 was made when operating over the longest sectors. We sought, therefore, to extend our North American markets to the West Coast of both the USA and Canada. I had personally made a visit to California, after seeing the giant Boeing plant at Seattle. I had been impressed with Boeing who had treated myself, Leonard Bebchick and Curly Walter with our one insignificant aircraft order as though we were one of the biggest and most important airlines in the world.

In Los Angeles I had been given introductions to one Tony Stute, a debonair emigrant Englishman. Stute ran a travel company, Continental Express, which had entered the charter market by acting as agent for the numerous expatriate British clubs and societies which flourished within the immigrant communities. He and I met at a restaurant on Sunset Strip, Sneaky Pete's, famous for spare ribs and modern jazz. Adorned in that theatrical way with signed photographs of film stars, singers and musicians, Sneaky Pete's was to become a favourite eating place for the Caledonian team as our West Coast business developed.

Stute revealed that he organized between sixty and eighty charters each year between Los Angeles and Europe, by a mix of carriers. He was willing to place all of the business with Caledonian, on the obvious proviso that our prices were right. He also indicated a willingness to invest in the airline. I was confident that our 707-320C rates on the highly-productive, 6,000-mile flight from Los Angeles would be unbeatable. I made arrangements for Frank Hope and Ian Ritchie to follow up with a final negotiating visit to Stute's company in South Beverly Drive.

163

Ritchie's appointment in Scotland had proved to be inspired. He was more than a cut above the average airline sales manager, with an all-round knowledge of operations as well as commerce. He very quickly outgrew the small, but important, market in Scotland and was brought down to Gatwick as general sales manager, filling one of the key appointments in my new management structure.

In Northern California, we had become aware of a group of British clubs, similar to those to which Stute had access in Los Angeles. A large community of expatriates existed in and around the town of San Jose. The various clubs had been consolidated into an organization known as the British American Club which was effectively managed by its secretary, Pat Shasby. Shasby came from Portsmouth, in England, and had emigrated to California as a toothbrush salesman. He had dabbled in the organization of charter flights for his expatriate members to make low-cost visits to Britain. But I do not believe he realized the full potential of charter activities until we visited him. Shortly afterwards, Shasby formed a special travel agency, Anglo California Travel Service, to organize programmes of charter flights with us from the airport to Oakland, just across the bay from San Francisco.

Charter flights were operated under very rigid rules. The charter airlines, the groups and their agents were under constant surveillance by the scheduled, IATA airlines. We were taking a significant share of the overall transatlantic air travel market at fares at least 50 per cent below the scheduled service prices. In 1958, charter travel represented just 6.5 per cent of the total market. By 1966, it had grown to represent 15 per cent. In 1966, of the total passenger journeys across the Atlantic to and from the USA, 438,000 took place on charter services. Although much was to be made in later years of low-cost airlines entering the transatlantic market, there is no doubt that the charter activities by Caledonian and others formed the real pioneering spearhead towards lower fares. It was, after all, the charter flights which opened up vast new markets of consumers who would otherwise not have been able to travel.

Cheap charter travel was open only to bona fide clubs or organizations formed for purposes other than travel. They included the expatriate clubs, so-called social and fraternal organizations, student groups, and professional associations. The method was that the chartering organization booked and paid for a whole flight, or series of flights. Seats were then sold to members on a pro-rata basis, calculated simply by dividing the charter rate by the number of seats on the aircraft. To qualify to travel, individuals had to be members of the organization for a minimum of six months. The charterer was responsible for paying the full aircraft price, whether or not all of the seats were filled. There was, therefore, a great temptation to replace people who cancelled with people not eligible under the regulations. Breaches of the rules placed our operating permits at risk and, therefore, we adopted a system of policing every operation. In those early days of mass air travel, a cut-price ticket was even more a desirable commodity than it is today and the charter market attracted the attention of individuals and organizations whom I can best describe as less than desirable. It was not unknown for our sales managers in the USA and Canada to be offered bribed and threatened by those who wanted to offload capacity for illegal sale.

Such was the need to retain our valuable permits that I do not believe we ever knowingly committed a serious breach of the regulations and, by and large, the charter flights were happy, straightforward operations. For UK return flights we charged from £50 a seat to New York and Toronto, £100 to San Francisco and £104 to Los Angeles. Meals on board were complimentary, of course. From the UK we carried such groups as the Paisley Buddies Club from Scotland. In the USA we flew the Scots American Club of New Jersey; The Bluebell Social Club of Ontario, Canada; Michigan University; and the Knickerbocker Educators Club of New York, a group of school teachers. They paid from £50 a seat to New York and Toronto, £100 to San Francisco and £104 to Los Angeles. Meals on board were complimentary, of course.

The planning and sales team, led by Frank Hope and Ian Ritchie, had put together a good programme of charter flights for the Beoing 707 which we expected to begin operating in May 1967. Plans were set back, however, when the Boeing Company informed us that delivery could not be made until July. It meant that with crew training requirements, we could not economically operate the aircraft for 1967. Charters were cancelled, the 707 introduction deferred until 1968 and the aircraft leased, in the interim, to the US cargo airline, Flying Tigers. This was a real body blow – the circumstance meant a sharp drop in planned

165

revenue and a corresponding effect on profitability. Over 1967, we struggled on with a fleet of six Britannias. The last of the DC-7Cs was sold in September, 1966, and its passing was marked by a great deal of sadness. The 'Seven Seas' was the manifestation of my early dreams of forming an airline. It had served us well and left memories of great triumph and great tragedy.

The pace of our business and the industry, in general, was accelerating rapidly in 1967. The residual fleet of six Britannias had carried 187,588 passengers, 41,000 more than in the previous year. The reduction in fleet caused by the passing of the DC-7C and the non-appearance of the 707 had reduced staff numbers by eighteen. Revenue dropped by about £1 million and the profit plummeted to £124,658, a little more than half of the 1966 figure.

We were momentarily rocked by the news that Donaldson Line, the prominent shareholder in Caledonian, had decided to go into voluntary liquidation. We had enjoyed a good relationship with the Donaldson Line and were very sorry, not only to lose a shareholder, but to see the end of an old established Scottish shippingh company whose ships I well remembered as a boy as they left the Clyde with hopeful emigrants aboard, bound for Canada. However, we had already been in financial negotiation with the Great Universal Stores organization of Sir Isaac Wolfson over a loan to finance the acquisition of a second Boeing 707-320C. The dilemma caused by the Donaldson liquidation was very quickly resolved by the agreement of GUS to take on that shareholding through its subsidiary company, Commercial Credit Trust (Leeds) Ltd. This arrangement brought with it the appointment of GUS's Sydney Robin, and later Lawrence Rose to our board of directors. Later in the year, the Scottish company, Lyle Shipping, joined us as a shareholder and our capital reserves figure stood at £1,040,143.

Trevor Boud, our chief accountant, had been promoted to the board as financial director. The interests of Scottish Air International were represented by Murray Vidockler, the Brooklyn-based coach operator, travel agent and tourism entrepreneur who we had first met as we were forming the company in 1961 and 1962.

John de la Haye was back in full swing with us as marketing director. With an instinct for public relations and promotions, de la Haye put to us a proposal for the employment of a full-time press officer. We met and brought into the team Tony Cocklin, aviation correspondent and deputy editor of the prime travel industry newspaper, *Travel Trade Gazette*. With a break in the mid-seventies he was to remain with us until the British Airways takeover of BCAL.

We were busy with two main development projects, both of which would require major public relations effort from the new department. The first of these was a renewed bid, on a much larger scale than before, to operate scheduled services on transatlantic routes, in competition with the major airlines, BOAC, Pan American and TWA. Maurice Guinane and his planning team had conducted a worldwide freight study and a North Atlantic passenger study. With our large investment in intercontinental jet aircraft and we could not, for much longer, rely on the season-by-season existence of the charter market. We required long-term security of tenure in a market we had helped to develop.

Unknown to us at the time, both Harold Bamberg and his team at British Eagle, and Freddie Laker at British United were formulating similar plans. Just days after we had met in the third-floor boardroom at our new Sussex House headquarters in Crawley to finally agree to pursue scheduled licences, Eagle and BUA filed bids with the Air Transport Licensing Board for similar operations.

We moved very quickly indeed to collate our proposals and translate them into a formal application. For this licensing procedure, we had already consulted a young solicitor who specialized in aviation, by the name of David Beety. The offices of this family business, Beety & Co, in Covent Garden, were dominated by the Caledonian project as myself and the other directors came and went.

In a move which caught the imagination of our staff, shareholders and the press, we filed with the ATLB applications for a comprehensive range of routes from any of the three London airports – Heathrow, Gatwick or Stansted – and from Manchester and Birmingham to the USA and Canada.

British Eagle sought to win licences for flights from Heathrow or Stansted, Liverpool, Manchester, and Prestwick to New York. They also wanted to operate from Heathrow or Stansted to Bermuda, Nassau and Chicago.

British United, in a surprise move, withdrew its own applications, but lodged objects to us and Eagle. BOAC, needless to say, objected to all of the applications. The stage was set for the biggest air licensing showdown yet seen in British civil aviation. Public hearings were scheduled to take place at the ATLB's new headquarters in Great Peter Street, in the ominous shadow of the Houses of Parliament, over sixteen separate dates starting on 16 January 1968. Our abiding task was now the painstaking preparation of the Caledonian case and the compilation of formal submissions.

Operationally, we still had not taken delivery of the first 707, but we had littered photographs of it in Caledonian livery across the press, and promoted the aircraft so that an average member of the public – or indeed a politician – might be forgiven for believing that we already possessed a sizeable long-range jet fleet. The fact was that we were plodding along with the trusty but obsolescent Britannia. As we planned its replacement on the long-range routes, so we looked at the future of the short-range European inclusive tour charters. The DC-7Cs, DC-6Bs and Britannias were capable of operating both intercontinental and European flights economically, giving a flexibility that was crucial in the early days. By no stretch of the imagination, however, could we operate 707s on the holiday flights to Palma, Rimini, Barcelona and other Mediterranean resort areas. Evaluations of short-haul aircraft took place and, again, the aircraft best suited to Caledonian, in terms of performance and economics, came from the Boeing stable – the 737. Negotiations had been completed with the Boeing Company and we were posed to confirm an order for three 737s. I had gone so far as to approve Tony Cocklin's press release and he was finalizing a special advertisement for the trade press.

# 34

Arrangements for the duty-free import of the 707 had been the subject of tough and tricky negotiations with the Board of Trade following my lengthy correspondence with its president, Douglas Jay, the previous year. New applications to import 737s were met by fits of frenzy from the civil servants and politicians. British Aircraft Corporation and the government were looking for customers for the longer-range version of its twin-engine jet, the BAC 1-11. The new version was labelled BAC 1-11/500. The aircraft was inferior to the 737 in both its non-stop range and the number of passengers it could carry, although technically it was extremeley sound.

The ultimatum placed on us by the Board of Trade was that if we persisted with an order for 737s, they would be the subject of full duty levies, and we were also advised verbally that the concession on the 707s may be withdrawn. The financial implications for Caledonian were severe.

Frank Hope, John de la Haye and I had offices adjacent to each other at one end of the third floor of Sussex House. As it happened, it was the end of the building over the Starlight Casino, where the workers of Crawley fluttered their weekly wage packets against the spin of the roulette wheel, the turn of a blackjack card or the numbered ping-pong balls of the bingo game.

It was our habit at the end of the working day to gather in one of the offices, usually mine or Frank's, open the cocktail cabinet and weigh up the ever-fluctuating odds of the airline business. On one such evening we reluctantly agreed that, on the aircraft duty deal, the odds were stacked very firmly against us. It was left to me to call the board together the next day, to obtain the formal agreement to abandon the 737 proposal and begin negotiations with BAC for a fleet of 1-11/500 aircraft.

The enthusiasm I felt for this turn of events was reflected in my report for the 1966/7 financial year. After writing, almost lyrically, about the transatlantic scheduled service applications and the new shareholdings, I wrote rather tersely: 'We have ordered three BAC 1-11/500 series aircraft and have an option on a fourth aircraft. These aircraft will be used on our European Inclusive Tour Services.'

But the biggest gamble we had so far undertaken came, quite literally, home to roost at the end of 1967. The delayed delivery of the first Boeing 707-320C was due to occur in November, but the row with the Board of Trade over import duty took us to the brink and beyond. We required the aircraft at Gatwick for as much as the winter period as possible, to complete aircrew and ground support training for the first jet aircraft Caledonian had ever operated, in time for the next summer season.

Our delivery deadline came and went as the details of a compromise deal were being worked out. We stuck to our contention that there was no comparable British aircraft available. The Board of Trade was equally obstinate in its view. Our immediate dilemma was solved by a plan to bring the aircraft to Shannon in the Republic of Ireland, outside the Board of Trade's jurisdiction, but close enough for us to be able to send teams of captains, first officers, flights engineers and navigators to complete training.

In the early days of December, the breakthrough came at one of what had seemed an endless series of meetings at the Board of Trade's offices. A piece of paper was pushed across the table towards Trevor Boud and myself. It represented a face-saving deal for the government, by allowing us to import the Boeing 707-320C aircraft free of duty, provided a major percentage of its operations with us were operated on the kind of non-stop sectors which the Super VC-10 was incapable of achieving. We agreed instantly to the arrangement and returned to Gatwick to make arrangements for the 707 to be delivered. This was what we had been pushing for all along and we had already abandoned the 737 for the BAC 7-11. Had the Board of Trade not moved in this direction, we would certainly have disclosed the reason for abandoning the 737.

I was shortly to receive another blow, this time a personal one. Towards the end of 1967, I began to experience a worsening of pain from the duodenal ulcer I had had for many years. I came home unusually early one afternoon, weak and in great pain. I collapsed on the bed. Dawn, although quite frantic with worry at my pale, drawn and pained face, maintained the calm she had learned to display as a nurse and promptly called in the local doctor. After the usual prodding, temperature-taking and pulse-reading, he appeared not to be too worried. Dawn sensed otherwise and insisted on a specialist consultant being brought in. This turned out to be a surgeon by the name of Mr Pitt. After his first examination, he declared that the ulcer had burst and I had lost a great deal of blood. He immediately called for an ambulance to take me to the private hospital at which he practised in Reigate, Surrey, to the north of Gatwick Airport. Mr Pitt set out for the hospital in his own car, Dawn and a close neighbour set off in another. It was a dismal, rainy evening and the ambulance drivers, only used to driving to the main town hospitals, got lost on the way to Reigate. I had no idea where we were and try as they might, they could get no directional sense from their patient.

The surgeon and Dawn were beside themselves with concern when the ambulance at last turned into the leafy driveway of the private hospital, some thirty minutes behind them. I knew that I was ill, but didn't realize the seriousness of my condition until I was rushed into a bed and prepared for a blood transfusion. It was nearing midnight and only nursing staff were on duty. The whole occasion became something of a farce as Mr Pitt was unable to insert the needle into my vein. Another doctor was called in and left his bed for the hospital. After 'feeling' the bumps and swellings, (his eyesight wasn't very good) made by Mr Pitt in my left hand, he switched over to the right hand and had the needle in and blood flowing within seconds.

The next morning, after a hazy awakening, I felt normal again. In fact I felt so good that I sat up in bed and began to compose a letter to the chairman of the British Airports Authority, Sir Peter Masefield. The BAA, then, as now, owned and operated the three main London airports, along with Glasgow's Abbotsinch, Edinburgh's Turnhouse and Belfast's Aldergrove. I had been seeking additional airport facilities at Gatwick for Caledonian. At a recent meeting with the Gatwick management, I had been curtly dismissed by being told that I was 'asking for the moon and offering sixpence'. Sir Peter was an awesome figure in British aviation. He had been involved in manufacturing, had been aviation attaché with the British Embassy in Washington DC, a Chief Executive of British European Airways and was now Chairman of the recently formed BAA. I was an upstart by comparison.

Literally buoyed up by new blood and whatever drugs I had been given, I penned a missive to the great man laying down the claim that his officials were wrong and that I was right in the matter of airport facilities. I headed the letter 'The Moon and Sixpence'. When we met a few months later Sir Peter certainly agreed that we should have the facilities we were requesting.

Having completed the last flourish of the pen on my pad of lined paper, I felt fit enough to get dressed and return home. I told Mr Pitt so when he arrived shortly afterwards. He clearly did not intend to enter a discussion on the matter, but said simply that the staff were having to keep infusing new blood at a faster rate than I was losing it and that he wanted me in the operating theatre in one hour and forty-five minutes' time.

The subsequent operation removed about two thirds of my stomach and it took some time and great skill from Mr Pitt's nurses to get me back to health. Depression settled on me after I left the hospital. I was told this was normal after major surgery, but felt a great need to get away by myself. I am sure Dawn must have been hurt by this, but she appeared to understand. I flew to Los Angeles, hired a car and drove off across the desert to Palm Springs. A week of driving in the warmth and clear air of the California desert gradually lifted my depression.

Tony Stute of Continental Express drove out in his Lincoln convertible to visit me. We ended up negotiating a deal for a substantial programme of charter flights from Los Angeles for the following year. A scheme through which Tony, Pat Shasby of San Jose and a man called Jim Lockett of the Council of British Societies of Southern California could acquire a stake in Caledonian Airways was suggested but this never materialized. The outline agreement between Stute and I was formalized in a document typed by a friendly nurse in a local hospital which I had visited as part of the aftercare prescribed by Mr Pitt.

I returned home fitter, slimmer, clear of depression and wanting to get back into the office, where significant events were about to unfold.

The competitive nature of British air transport in the late 1960s is authentically reflected in the basis of the BOAC objection to the transatlantic route applications of Caledonian and British Eagle. It was simply that for the ATLB to grant the licence would be contrary to UK government policy, whereby BOAC was the so-called 'single chosen instrument' to operate scheduled flag services across the Atlantic and throughout the world. British European Airways was similarly protected on European routes.

A number of the independent airlines had entered the scheduled service field on a string of minor routes. The main anomaly was, however, British United Airways, the amalgamation of a number of smaller airlines, which had built up a considerable scheduled network of services from its Gatwick base to continental Europe, East, West and Central Africa and within the UK. The feather in BUA's cap was the flag routes to Brazil, Uruguay, Argentina and Chile which the independent had picked up after BOAC had decided to abandon these services as uneconomic. Nevertheless, the two state corporations still accounted for more than 90 per cent of total British output on international scheduled services and dominated the industry by any measurement.

But the independent airlines, like Caledonian, were growing, becoming ever-more ambitious about the scope of operations they wished to provide and more and more critical of a regime that owed considerably less to competition and consumer choice than it did to the need to protect the corporations.

# 35

The industry was growing at a rapid rate – an average of 17 per cent per annum over the previous ten years. British scheduled output – the amount of capacity deployed on a route or route network – had been doubling every five years, while inclusive tour charters had grown twenty times in ten years.

The industry was on the brink of a capacity explosion with the imminent introduction of the giant Boeing 747, labelled by an incredulous British journalist as the 'Jumbo Jet'. The Concorde supersonic aircraft, produced by the Anglo-French consortium comprising British Aircraft Corporation ad Aerospatiale, had made its first flight at Toulouse, France, on 2 March 1969 and would be coming into service in the 1970s.

It was against this complex background that the government commissioned, in July 1967, a Committee of Inquiry into Civil Air Transport. It was chaired by Professor Ronald Edwards and its terms of reference were:

> To inquire into the economic and financial situation and prospects of the British civil aviation industry and into the methods of regulating competition and of transport in this country, what changes may be desirable to enable the industry to make its full contribution to the development of the economy and to the service and safety of the travelling public.

Between the lines of those words from Whitehall, we saw the chance to achieve the first major reform of the airline industry since the end of the Second World War. The strength of our arguments to Edwards would be crucial for the future which he and his committee were charged with mapping out.

Caledonians's ambitions for growth and expansion were out-growing the opportunities available in the restricted commercial world of charter operations, where airlines sold and counter-sold against each other for a bigger share of available contracts from tour operators, charter groups and the Ministry of Defence. Only changes in policy could open up new areas of competition.

John de la Haye, an avid student of aviation politics, and I readily saw that 'Edwards' formed the first real opportunity to restructure the industry and create new policies since the Cadman Committee of the late 1930s created BOAC as the 'chosen instrument' of UK overseas aviation from the old Imperial Airways.

I decided to create an 'Edwards' working group and charged it with putting together a case for the defence of independent aviation in every way as forceful as if we were on trial for our lives. The truth was that, in commercial terms, we were.

The work on Edwards was to be co-ordinated by Hugh Brilliant who had recently joined the company as joint company secretary, working in tandem with Leonard Bebchick. Hugh, a former civil servant with responsibilities for aviation with the colonial goverment of Nigeria, had more recently been secretary-general of the British Independent Air Transport Association, a body comprising of the small airlines in the UK. In 1967, Caledonian, British Eagle and British United were distancing themselves from the rough and tumble, cavalier image of the traditional charter airlines and had each, separately, decided to withdraw from BIATA. These moves led to the collapse of the association and the redundancy of Hugh Brilliant. He possessed, however, just the kind of 'establishment' background and experience we felt we required as we began to dabble in the new science which became to be known as 'aeropolitics'.

For the immediate future, our minds were engrossed on fighting for the kind of opportunities which we hoped Edwards would ultimately bring freely, through the traditional channel of the licensing process.

Submissions to the Air Transport Licensing Board were normally sober documents, prepared by lawyers. John de la Haye saw the chance to make a political statement with the issue of our document in support of the application for the transatlantic scheduled routes. It took much of his considerable power of persuasion to convince the rest of the board and the lawyers, but he eventually forced through a front cover in the art style of the sixties which depicted two plants, each in a pot decorated with the union flag. They were meant to depict the state of British civil aviation. The pot to the left – the status quo – contained a dry, withered plant. The pot to the right showed a vigorous, flourishing plant being liberally sprayed by a watering can meant to represent an enlightened licensing authority. The document became known as the flower power document. No doubt it was received with a certain amount of derision in the BOAC boardroom, but we had made a point.

The hand of government came to feel our collars even before the formal hearing began. In a directive from the Board of Trade, the ATLB was required to prejudge some parts of the applications from ourselves and British Eagle. Effectively knocked out of contention was Eagle's plan for services to Jamacia, and for Chicago as an intermediate point between London and Bermuda or Nassau. We were precluded from proceeding with bids to serve Los Angeles or San Francisco from Manchester, Birmingham or Prestwick, or from carrying passengers and cargo between Chicago and the west coast points. Neither could we plan to serve both Los Angeles and San Francisco, just one or the other. The applications we were left with were from the UK points to New York, with Boston, Philadelphia, Baltimore and Washington as options; to Toronto and Montreal; and to Los Angeles or San Francisco.

For weeks, the boardroom at Sussex House was turned into a replica of the ATLB's courtroom. With the lawyers, Leonard Bebchick and David Beety, we rehearsed the hearing, putting ourselves on the stand and undergoing the kind of cross-examination we could expect from the board and from BOAC. As part of our public relations programme, Tony Cocklin had invited Philip Clarke, editor of the *Sunday Times* business news section to Crawley. He wrote in a subsequent article: 'Airline executives are not normally given to play acting. But down at Crawley, the top men of Caledonian Airways are in a deadly efficient and earnest way. They are learning their lines for a drama called the North Atlantic hearing on which the curtain goes up on 9 January [1968] in the offices of the Air Transport Licensing Board, the body which says yea or nay to British airline applications to operate the routes they want.'

In fact, the 'play acting' was the culmination of a critical path

176

analysis set out by Maurice Guinane to prepare thoroughly the countdown to the hearing. The hearing actually started on 16 January, a week later than originally expected. The hearing room at the ATLB headquarters in Gaywood House, behind Westminster Abbey and a few steps from the Houses of Parliament, had been prepared with a table and set of chairs for each of the main participants in the centre of the room. In front, separated by a waist-high partition, was the platform on which sat the members of the board. To one side was the witness stand, to the other, the press table. In the centre, between the advocates an the board, was a chair for the official stenographer. To the rear of the room were several rows of theatre-style seats for any member of the public who wished to eavesdrop on the proceedings.

Leonard Bebchick had flown in from Washington several days earlier and travelled with myself and the rest of the team by train from Crawley, along with the rush of morning commuters. We had arranged to meet David Beety in a cafe in Marsham Street, close to Gaywood House and opposite the present-day headquarters of the Department of Transport. Behind steamy windows, we went through some final details and fortified ourselves with than mugs of strong tea. Most of us were fairly calm. Bebchick, on the other hand, was excitable, constantly moving from one chair to another as he talked. He was like a terrier, having seen the rabbit and waiting to be unleashed.

The Caledonian group filed into the hearing room, to find Peter Webster, QC, counsel for British Eagle, quietly laying out his papers. Bob Forrest, secretary and solicitor for BOAC, was conferring with colleagues to one side of the room. Polite acknowledgements were made and Bebchick in the tradition of the legal profession went across to shake hands and talk with his adversaries.

At 10.00 a.m. promptly, a door to the rear of the room opened and the Air Transport Licensing Board, led by its chairman, Professor D. T. Jack, and with its secretary, Cyril Lark, at the rear, entered the room. We all stood and sat down again as the venerable gentlemen took their seats.

That procedure was to take place on fifteen further mornings until the hearing closed. Thousands upon thousands of words were taken down by the relay of stenographers, pages of exhibits

177

presented, analyzed and questioned and a four-cornered web of cross-examination woven across those sixteen days.

Our case for a second British carrier on the tansatlantic routes hinged on the fact that BOAC on its own was failing to maintain Britain's rightful share of the UK/USA air travel market. The best available statistics showed that the UK share had dropped to 28 per cent, when it should rightly have been at least 50 per cent. We set out to prove that Caledonian was best suited, in terms of experience and competitive equipment – the 707s – to become the second British scheduled carrier across the Atlantic. After all, by virtue of charter carryings, we were already bigger in this market than any other British airline, except BOAC.

Evidence was produced to show the cost of mounting the operation and we submitted our revenue projections. Under the scrutiny of the board, I took the stand to provide evidence that our main shareholders were behind us, philosophically and financially, in the venture. We played on the marketing advantages we felt we had. This centred on the airline's clear Scottish image and its appeal to large sections of the US consumer market. We pointed up the success of airlines like Aer Lingus and El Al, with their distinct ethnic appeals.

Our plan was to start the London-New York, London-Montreal-Toronto and Brimingham-Prestwick-New York services in the 1969/70 period. The routes from London to Chicago and Los Angeles and from Birmingham and Prestwick to Toronto would follow in 1970/71. By 1972/73 we projected that Caledonian would be carrying more than 400,000 passengers a year on the network of routes at load factors – percentage of seats filled – of up to 60 per cent. Revenue generated in the 1972/73 financial year would be in excess of £10 million. The evidence supporting these claims was comprehensive and intricate. A total of seventy-four different exhibits was presented. The one difference between this and subsequent attempts by us and other airlines to gain entry to the Atlantic market was the absence of new, low fares. At that time, fares were fixed by the incumbent airlines through the machinery of the so-called traffic conferences of IATA and enshrined in the bilateral Air Services Agreements between respective governments. We had no room to manoeuvre on price. The objective was to get more British capacity and consumer choice into the existing market.

An interesting part of our case was the proposal, should Caledonian become an established scheduled, transatlantic carrier, to build an engineering and maintenance base at Prestwick Airport.

British Eagle's case was broadly similar to our own, but it was tinged with what was to my mind a degree of obsequiousness towards the state airline. Eagle's proposals were invariably prefaced with the suggestion that the airline would serve to complement and support, rather than compete with, the services of BOAC.

For its part, BOAC stood firm on its 'chosen instrument' platform. Sir Giles Guthrie, the banker who had been brought in as chairman to resolve the Corporation's financial muddle, was called as a witness. In arguing against BOAC's retrenchment and its waning share of the market, he said that the airline's policy, on his explicit direction, had been to build what he described as a 'sound financial springboard, before taking the next leap forward'.

He told the board what we, from the rough school of private enterprise, knew only too well: 'There is no better way of losing money than to have even one aircraft unemployed, or a fleet of aircraft underemployed to an equivalent extent.'

Sir Giles told the hearing that in the following summer, BOAC would be mounting nine extra services a week and had the capacity to repeat this increase in 1969. I quietly wondered whether the state airline would have made this extra commitment to the transatlantic market had not we independents been at its heels. Sir Giles went on to talk about the introduction by BOAC of the Boeing 747 aircraft – more than twice the size of the 707 – in 1970 and the estimate that by 1971, the airline's annual capacity on the UK-New York routes would double to a total of 957,000 seats. Guthrie's strategem of throwing taxpayer's money – in the form of expensive aircraft capacity – at the problem posed by the independent airlines, carried weight with the ATLB.

In its decision, published on 22 May 1968, the board trawled through the argument in a forty-three-page summary.

The ATLB appeared to be overawed by the operations of transatlantic scheduled services which, in the fundamental areas of passenger service, reliability and punctuality, differed hardly at all from the busy programme of charter operations we had mounted successfully over five years. It doubted whether we could compete

179

with the big airlines in terms of performance and whether our aircraft maintenance arrangements were capable of sustaining a scheduled Atlantic network. Caledonian's technical operating ability did not come to question, but the board was doubtful of either our, or Eagle's ability to provide adequate financial muscle.

The board commented on the political situation:

> We have been conscious throughout these proceedings that behind all the argument and evidence lay a fundamental issue of national aviation policy. On the one hand, it was argued by Sir Giles Guthrie that since 1945 it has been the considered policy of governments of all political complexions that BOAC should be 'the chosen instrument' of this country and should have a monopoly of schedled services on these routes. This policy should not be reversed without powerful reasons. On the other hand, it was argued by Mr Bebchick of Caledonian that these proceedings provided, in all probability, the last opportunity for changing this policy, if a change seemed desirable. He forecast that by 1972 or 1973, it would be impossible to enter this market without supersonic equipment and no privately-financed newcomer would be able to launch an operation with these aircraft. But the next three or four years can provide a financial and operational run-in for expansion of this kind. Both arguments are substantial.

Overall the ATLB was persuaded that BOAC did intend to bid for a substantially larger share of the market over the next three years and that it could match the two-pronged US competition from Pan American and TWA. After months of preparation, sixteen days of hearing and about £25,000 in costs, our North Atlantic bid was turned down. So was British Eagle's.

As the Board said: 'Our decision means, nonetheless, that the nation's civil aviation destiny in the North Atlantic area will depend on BOAC's readiness to use, as Sir Giles Guthrie said, their present strong position as a springboard for a determined effort to secure a much greater share of this lucrative market and, we would add, on consistent government support for BOAC in the pursuit of that policy.'

Politics had, on the face of things, condemned our legitimate,

British enterprise to a limited role in civil aviation, with restricted opportunity for the future.

As angry as I was with this, there was one other part of the board's decision which really rankled and made me determined, more than ever, to keep up the challenge to the political establishment. In discussing commercial abilities, our much-vaunted and authentic Scottish background and image had been described as a 'gimmick'. But, Leonard Bebchick had argued in the hearing, gimmicks attracted business. Concluded the board: 'We go some way with him in his claim that gimmicks attract customers. But in a market such as this, a gimmick will not build an airline.'

# 36

After the build-up of a considerable wave of excitement over the North Atlantic project, an air of despondency settled for a short while over Sussex House. I was particularly concerned over the interpretation that the ATLB's legislative phrase describing us and British Eagle as not a 'competent and fit and proper person' to operate the services might give rise to. Accordingly I spent several days after publication of the report telephoning and writing to shareholders, customers and, of course, staff.

It turned out that in early June, we were visited by a group of officials from the Board of Trade, led by Robbie Burns. It was one of a regular series of field visits undertaken by the officials who governed the industry to look at airline operations from the grass roots level. It would be these same officials who would be involved in the consideration of any appeal that might be lodged against the ATLB decision and I had told the shareholders we would certainly appeal against the decision.

In an off-the-record conversation with Burns, I was told that because of the current inquiry being undertaken by Sir Ronald Edwards and his committee, the ATLB could hardly have come to any other decision. They were, in short, forced to maintain the status quo pending the outcome of the inquiry. The wink was tipped that we should wait and see what Edwards came out with before once again pursuing the Atlantic bid.

Day-to-day activities in the airline were continuing at a brisk pace. Despite the growth in the number of employees to 450, Caledonian retained a family atmosphere. Ian Ritchie had been promoted to the board as executive director (Sales) and had collected around him an effervescent team of salesmen who styled themselves 'The Dirty Dozen', after a contemporary film of that name which featured a group of rogues and criminals turned-war-heroes. It was a reflection of the way many of the staff in general thought about themselves. They might be under-privileged underdogs, from the wrong side of the air transport tracks, but they were determined to take on my competition and win.

Among the 'Dozen' was a gregarious young Scotsman, Gordon Mason. He had been dragged to the south by Ritchie, from his job with the Glasgow tour operator, Mercury Air Holidays. Gordon had more than a touch of show business in his personality and looked after the transatlantic charter business, charming the group organizers and the agents with his laugh-a-minute personality. John Warren, who joined from a major air broking firm, was more serious, but a deadly earnest sales manager, looking after general charters and Far East contracts. The new cargo sales unit, formed to take advantage of the 707-320C came under a genial Londoner, David Gerrard, whose superficial, barrow-boy techniques which went down well in the cargo market disguised a shrewd commercial mind. Another Londoner, Derek Magowan, had joined from British United to head up the inclusive tour charter sales department.

In contrast to these was Maurice Cleaver, a scholarly bachelor who might well have become a schoolteacher, had the war not taken him into the Royal Air Force and from there into air transport. Behind Cleaver's nonchalant exterior lay a mathematical mind. While others struggled with slide rules to analyze routings and payloads to respond to a telephone inquiry for a charter quote, he would pick up a piece of string from his desk, stroll to a world globe, lay the string between the two points of a particular route to assess the mileage, and work out the costs and the quote while ambling back to his desk and picking up the phone to offer a price.

Cleaver's close friend was Reg Farrell, a quiet, dapper individual. It was Farrell who we selected, in November 1967, to go to Los Angeles to open Caledonian's first west coast office to develop the charter market we had recently opened up. Soon after, we assigned Cleaver to open a sales office in Frankfurt to carve out a share of the burgeoning European charter market.

It is a cliché, but the management and staff did operate on a 'work hard, play hard' basis. The stewardesses who joined us in

183

increasing numbers from all parts of the UK usually got together in twos, threes and fours to rent accommodation in the areas around Gatwick. Hardly an evening went by in those heady days when there was not a party at one place or another. For a while, the centre of the party scene seemed to be John de la Haye's picturesque cottage in the village of Ifield. Another venue was a house near Horley rented by a group of the girls. Its name, The Wick, gave rise to much ribald comment.

The club and bar of the bowling alley underneath Sussex House became the company canteen, where the manager, Peter Field, and his wife kept the Caledonian army marching on stomachs full of pie, chips and beans.

The heart of the airline was the seventh floor, where the aircraft planning boards were kept alongside the operations control room, manned twenty-four hours a day. Before the days of computers, the entire operation for a year in advance was plotted on a series of boards which ran for most of the length of the building. Whenever a problem occurred or a new development was being assessed, we would assemble around 'the boards'.

Alan Bartlett, a dedicated operations man, was in charge of the planning boards on the top floor of Sussex House. This was long before computers took over and it was a task that needed continuous dedication and application as he switched flights around to achieve the maximum return. Sadly Alan was killed in a flying accident and was greatly missed by all in Caledonian.

It was 30 December 1967, a fairly bright winter's day. The wind from the north east brought chilly blue skies. All of those staff who could get away from their work took up vantage points around the maintenance buildings and terminal area of Gatwick. Some of the ground staff were in touch with the operations control room on the seventh floor at Sussex House. Shortly after the buzz went round that Boeing 707-320C G-AVTW, 'Tango Whisky' was on its final approach, the aircraft appeared in the westerly sky. It looked immaculate with its fresh gold and blue livery above the clean, bright metal of the underbelly. It made a perfect landing and taxied over to our small maintenance hangar on the southern side of the airport. It was a proud and moving moment for all of us.

People from other airlines were also watching our piece of history unfold. One of them was Freddie Laker, looking out across the runway from the window of his office. Later in the day I received a telegram from him. It congratulated us on taking delivery of our 'beautiful' new Boeing 707. He concluded, profoundly, 'At last the independents have come into their own.' Three years earlier, Laker had taken the industry by surprise with a sudden resignation from his post as managing director of British United Airways. He re-emerged, shortly after, with his plans for the formation of a small charter airline operating BAC 1-11s on holiday charter flights. He called it, simply, Laker Airways.

# 37

The area known as Los Angeles is not a single city, defined by specific boundaries, but a collection of suburbs which starts somewhere around Anaheim to the south, home of Disneyland, and spills over the Santa Monica hills into the San Fernando valley, in the north. The locations that might be described as central are downtown LA, the business district, Hollywood and Beverly Hills. The whole suburban complex is strung together by a system of freeways. Los Angeles International Airport is south of Beverly Hills, on the Pacific coast, just off the main north-south San Diego freeway. It was here that I, Frank Hope and Ian Ritchie had created the bare bones of a new market for the long-range 707 equipment. It was a lucrative market and therefore a tough one with plenty of intense competition from the US charter airlines.

We had decided from the beginning that we would get a grip on the business so tight that the competitors would find it difficult, if not impossible, to break in. In collaboration with Tony Stute of Continental Express, a promotional programme was mapped out. We would visit Southern California and give a series of parties and dinners, not for the booking agents, but for the chartering clubs' officials and members. We would get to the heart of the market – the individual expatriate family working in some factory tucked away in the suburbs behind the freeways. It was a repeat of the methods we had used years before in New York and Toronto.

The first of these exercises took place in 1967 and the scheme was repeated each year after. They took place either at the end or at the beginning of the year, when the clubs were planning their charter programmes for the following summer. In Southern California, the numerous British clubs and organiztions were consolidated under the umbrella organization, the Council of British Societies, run by one George Fitzpatrick. Stute was the main agent involved, but also in the business was an expatriate Scot, Bobby Logan, who ran an outfit called Siyor Travel Agent. Pan American's advertising at the time was signed off with the line 'Call Pan Am or see your travel agent'. Logan traded off Pan Am's advertising budget for many years.

The team that went out on these trips included myself, Frank Hope, occasionally John de la Haye, Ian Ritchie, Tony Cocklin, Margaret Trett and a squad of air hostesses. The idea was to promote ourselves as big, successful and professional with a great play on the Scottish image. At one end of this promotional spectrum was the search for bagpipers to play at our functions. At the other, was a carefully arranged series of meetings with the Mayor, business leaders and the British Consul General.

On the first of these visits, our budget was so slim that we could only afford one suite at a top hotel. I was installed at the glitzy Century Plaza in Beverly Hills. The rest of the team put up at the Hacienda Motel, down on Sepulveda Boulevard in the nether regions of the airport complex. It turned out that the sales manager for the Hacienda was a former London policeman. So well did we get on with him and so well did the staff look after everybody that we ended up giving them our crew contract. This was economic for us and valuable business for the Hacienda.

A typical evening for the Council of British Societies would begin with cocktails in a private suite at the Century Plaza, or on later occasions at the Beverly Hilton Hotel. Guests would be met at the door by two uniformed hostesses. The men would be given a sprig of white heather, decorated in tartan ribbon, for their lapels, the ladies would receive a gardenia to be pinned to their dresses. The instruction to the Caledonian executives was to circulate and talk to stoke up the gathering into a good party. At the appropriate time, the press-ganged piper would lead the group to the hotel ballroom for a formal banquet at which I and the senior guest made laudatory speeches about each other. For most of these ordinary people, the Caledonian team from Crawley, Sussex, brought them into the glamour of a big Holywood occasion.

It was a poor event that did not end up in my suite with most of the guests joining in an impromptu ceilidh led and conducted by a be-kilted Gordon Mason. It was at these times that I thought about the Air Transport Licensing Board back in London telling us that the 'gimmick' of a Scottish image would not build an airline.

From Los Angeles, the Calendonian circus travelled on, up to San Francisco or San Jose to meet and entertain Pat Shasby and his British American Club. It was a little less formal in Northern California and the parties and dinners more riotous. I remember being threatened with eviction from one hotel after our bibulous efforts at Scottish dancing had woken up the people on the floor below. There was also the occasion when Ian Ritchie went missing. We had gone along to the opening of a shop selling Scottish products. Ian had dutifully donned his kilt and full Highland regalia. At the sight of this, the owners insisted that he stand in the window among the displays of whisky, porridge oats, claymores and tartan to be photographed. Fortified by the malt whisky, which was being distributed liberally, Ian stood in the window as camera after camera snapped away at him. The whole party moved on to a lunch function and it was only when we got to the venue that Ian was missed. He had been locked in the window as the proprietors closed the shop. When they arrived back at the shopping mall, there was Ian, trying to mouth messages from behind plate glass to the highly-amused crowd of shoppers gathered round this odd sight.

The expatriates of Northern California were, by virtue of geography if nothing else, more close knit than the 'Brits' of Los Angeles. They were a jovial bunch and were highly amused at their achievement in getting funds together to purchase a church to turn it into a pub and meeting place in the centre of San Jose. On one occasion, at a formal dinner in the grand St Francis Hotel, San Francisco, a woman member of the British American Club stood up to make a solemn presentation to me, 'in recognition of services to the British community'. Under the gaze of Her Majesty's Consul General and assembled civic dignitaries, I opened the package to reveal a pair of skimpy tartan underpants.

The club even re-scheduled its annual weekend trip to the winter sports resort and gambling centre of Lake Tahoe, a town which straddles the border dividing California and Nevada, so that the Caledonian team could join them, as their guests, at their expense.

We were to meet our customers at Lake Tahoe many times, but the effort to get close to tyhis major source of airline business wasn't always easy. It all went wrong on one Tahoe trip when the bus encountered blizzards and we took eighteen hours to reach our destination through perilous icy mountain roads.

All the while we were away on these sales and promotional trips, we kept in constant touch with the operation back at Gatwick. Frank Hope, in particular, made at least two calls a day back to Crawley to check the operation and give guidance on problems of delays or diversions that occurred.

That summer on 1 June the second 707-320C – G-AVKA, 'Kilo Alpha' – was delivered to join Tango Whisky in operating a series of charters from Oakland and Los Angeles to the UK on which we carried 15,000 passengers. The following year, with the addition of the third 707, we planned to more than double the size of the west coast market.

The total fleet of two 707s and four Britannias generated revenues of more than £6 million for 1968, to give a record profit of £220,000. The new freight sales department, marketed as 'Caledonian Jetcargo' brought in 6 million lbs of business which ranged from crates of tomatoes from Spain to the shipment of a railway to Pakistan. One of the 707Ss more bizarre ad hoc assignments was the carriage of a flying fashion show around Europe for the Reid & Taylor textile company.

Total passenger carryings were 220,163. The inclusive tour charter market was still buoyant – Caledonian had increased traffic to more than 83,000 passengers – but some dark clouds had appeared the previous year, with economic recession bringing devaluation of sterling and the introduction of a £50 overseas travel allowance. At home, one of the industry's major social events of the year was the British Airlines Ball, a charity event staged at London's vast Albert Hall. The ball was run by a committee comprising representatives from the five major UK airlines, BOAC, BEA, British United, British Eagle and Caledonian. The combined purchasing power of the airlines was pressed into service to obtain prizes as grand as boats and cars from suppliers. It was a great and glamorous occasion, when the industry let its collective hair down and raised thousands of pounds for charity at the same time.

The tradition was that the airline sponsors took boxes around the first floor of the Albert Hall to entertain corporate guests.

The Caledonian guest list for the ball usually mixed our senior government contacts with business contacts. It was during the afternoon preparations for the Airlines Ball in 1968 that the shattering news came through that British Eagle had collapsed. It turned out that Harold Bamberg's airline had been hard-pressed financially for some while. The peak summer season with a good cash flow had enabled Eagle to keep going through the year, but its fate was finally sealed in the dark winter months, when the flying programme slowed down, yet staff and overheads still had to be paid.

There had been strong industry rumours that one of Bamberg's survival plans was to seek a merger with British United and that talks had taken place between him and the BUA Chairman, Sir Myles Wyatt. In every likelihood that was true, but any form of agreement that might have existed was too late for the tragic Eagle. If this was not bad enough for the independent side of the industry, the Eagle failure was followed shortly by the collapse of another charter airline, Transglobe Airways.

Ironically, I was in the final throes of negotiations to increase Caledonian's share capital by £800,000 to bring capital and reserves to more than £2 billion. The bulk of the new capital was being subscribed by existing shareholders, Industrial and Commercial Finance Corporation, Great Universal Stores (through its NC George St Nominee subsidiary), Lyle Shipping Co. and National Commercial and Schroeders. Marshall Gibson had been successful in attracting a new shareholder, Hogarth Shipping Ltd of Scotland, which invested £150,000.

The increased capital base was necessary to underwrite the expansion programme brought about by the plan for a fourth Boeing 707-320C and the fleet of four BAC 1-11/500s, the first three of which were due to begin operations in the summer of 1969.

The introduction of the 1-11 brought us our first contact with the tour operator, Global of London, later to become Global Tours. They were owned by the Great Universal Stores organization and it was logical that they would want to see their two major travel investments benefit from each other.

With the high capital cost of modern jet aircraft on one hand, and the increasingly competitive nature of the tour business on the other, a scheme known as the time charter had evolved. It meant, simply, that rather than charter a series of separate flights from an airline, the tour operators contracted a quantity of hours for its flights. Obviously, the higher the number of hours, the cheaper the rate. The airline was rewarded with contract security and the tour operator with competitive seat rates.

After a number of meetings, Global contracted to time charter one of our 1-11s for two years and also made an agreement for a series of flights for the summer season of 1969. It was worth £2 million to us.

Another of the main inclusive tour operators who come in to charter Caledonian 1-11 aircraft was Blue Cars Ltd, the traditional continental coach tour operator which had launched into the holiday flight market under the brand name Blue Sky.

The 1-11s, we had decided, would be named after Scottish islands. All previous aircraft had been given the names of the counties of Scotland. The first would be *Isle of Skye* and arrangements were made for an elaborate ceremony to be conducted at Prestwick by the Laird of Skye, Lord McDonald of McDonald. John de la Haye had another corporate image trick up his sleeve to be launced at the same time, a new uniform for the air hostesses. Ancient Black Watch had served us well, but the time had come for something bright and new.

Again, we were faced with the problem that if we selected one tartan we would delight the chosen clan, but upset all the others. The answer was to choose a range of different tartans, nine in all. The uniforms would, of course, be tailored in exactly the same way, but the air hostesses and ground staff would be able to choose the colour which suited them individually. After arduous consultation with the Museum of Scottish Tartans in Scotland and the respective clan chieftains, de la Haye unveiled his selection: Dress Black Watch, Kennedy, Red Macduff, Hunting Macrae, Mackellar, Graham of Monteith, Macnab, Macinnes and Hunting Ogilvie. The result was astonishing. The girls took immediately to the uniform which was not uniform and created bright splashes of fashionable colour on the aircraft and in airports, in sharp contrast to the traditional military styles of most of the other airlines.

The new tartan entered service with the new 1-11/500s. *Isle of Skye* was delivered on 29 March 1969. *Isle of Iona* came two

191

days later, and *Isle of Eriskay* completed the initial 1-11 fleet on its delivery at the end of April.

With the operation of four Boeing 707-320Cs and four Britannias, in addition to the three 1-11, Caledonian doubled its passenger carryings in 1969 to 430,000 and profits rocketed to a record £641,513, more than twice as much as the previous year. Shareholders received a dividend of ten per cent.

The year of 1969 was, however, to mean much more to me and our 650 staff than a hard but successful flying operation. The industry was working in a political vacuum. Neither the Board of Trade, nor the Air Transport Licensing Board wanted to make any significant moves which would create long-term effects while the report from the Edwards Committee was still awaited.

One of the Board of Trade officials at the time was Ray Colegate, later to achieve a position of supreme importance in the regulation of British air transport. Early in 1969, Colegate was tinkering with the rules surrounding inclusive tour prices. The prices that people paid for their holidays in the Mediterranean were governed by a piece of air transport legislation known as 'Provision 1'. This said that the price of an inclusive tour operated by charter aircraft could not be less than the lowest-available public fare offered on the same route by BEA. Thus, if a holiday to, say, Majorca, could be marketed by a tour operator for £100, but the lowest public far available from BEA was £150, the public ended up paying £50 more than necessary. The Board of Trade, under lobby from the charter industry, had agreed an experimental tariff, with Provision 1 lifted, for the 1968/9 winter season.

The result was that our operators, increasingly competitive with one another, in an expanding market, were passing on the Provision 1 profits to their customers in the form of extras, such as free drinks, champagne dinners and free sightseeing excursions. I had, in fact, insisted on a call for the relaxation of the tour price rules being included in our Edwards submission.

The Board of Trade proposals being articulated by Ray Colegate were controversial. Freddie Laker especially, was frightened of a price war and the driving down of charter rates. He had written to Anthony Crosland, President of the Board of Trade, pressing for capacity regulation and the maintenance of price controls. Further, Laker wanted controls over the charter seat rate. His formula was that the tour operator should buy the charter seat for the price of the lowest-available fare on an equivalent scheduled service, less 14 per cent. And he wished to do away with 'giveaways' on holiday flights – the only 'extra' would be the in-flight meal.

This reactionary and protectionist stance went against most of the rest of the inclusive tour operators, both airlines and travel firms. Laker knew this. He said in his letter to Crosland: 'I regret to say I am a lone wolf in these views, but I do feel strongly enough to put them on paper . . . I honestly believe that the private operators at the present time are unable to agree amongst themselves and are also unwilling to impose restraint and unless something is done as a matter of urgency I am afraid that more private operators will go to the wall . . .'

Nevertheless, the artificial constraint was eventually lifted, initially for short-stay winter breaks. The aggressive British travel industry responded with throw-away packages offering a weekend in Majorca for £10, designed as loss leaders to win brand loyalty for the main summer tours.

I was, however, much more concerned with aeropolitical turbulence building up over the Atlantic. One controversy centred on a porposal for a Canadian airline, Pacific Western, being contracted to carry Rolls Royce engines for the new Lockheed 1011 'Tristar' aircraft from Northern Ireland to the Lockheed plant in California. With the Board of Trade, through its official Ray Le Goy, we fought this move on the basis of Canadian Government restrictions against British airlines. Another row involved a deal that emerged for the US cargo carrier, Seaboard World Airlines, to be a founding partner in a new British cargo airline to be called Tradewinds Airways.

Mindful of the earlier battles we had gone through over the thorny question of foreign investment, I was not prepared to stand by and see a deal take place, whereby a US carrier could unload spare aircraft capacity on the British market through an ownership arrangement. It was, to my mind, the thin end of a dangerous wedge. I wrote to William Rodgers at the Board of Trade objecting to the proposal. John Sauvage, managing director of Britannia Airways at Luton, felt the same way and wrote to Rodgers expressing similar concern.

But the most chilling wind sweeping in across the Atlantic was the US Government's proposals to impose uplift restrictions against foreign charter operators. This move would restrict the number of charter services we could operate and seriously affect Caledonian's plans for the immediate and long-term future. Our investment in Boeing 707-320C aircraft was considerable and we were planning substantial growth, particularly in the west coast market.

The issue was complex, involving the ratio of British groups carried by US charter airlines against US groups uplifted by UK airlines. I wrote to Robbie Burns at the Board of Trade demanding a solution to the immediate problem and a long-term resolution of the whole matter. If the government was unable to achieve a lasting agreement on charter uplifts with the Americans, I proposed that Britain should restrict the UK/USA services by airlines foreign to both countries, known as 'fifth freedom' rights. Such carriers included Air India, El Al, and Japan Airlines. Fortunately the majority of these threats came to nothing.

But by far the biggest game in town among the aviation and travel community was the one labelled 'Waiting for Edwards'.

# 38

The Edwards Committee had been formed in the summer of 1967 and its first consultations with the airlines had taken place before Christmas. The government had anticipated getting its report by spring 1968. In the interim, diaries of most of the key figures in the industry had been filled with Edwards meetings and consultations and with the field trips that the Professor and his team had undertaken.

Submissions had been drafted, discussed, rewritten and presented to the committee's office at Millbank. Requests for supplementary information had been fulfilled diligently. Spring, summer, autumn and winter 1968 had passed with no Edwards report. The industry had been in a frenzy of expectation for many months and was becoming increasingly impatient. I had earlier warned my colleagues about the dangers of pressing for a fast inquiry and urged the government to let Edwards take its time. The future well-being of civil aviation deserved far more than a superficial review, followed by a string of hasty conclusions. But the collapse of British Eagle and Transglobe highlighted the delicate economic fabric of the industry. Some of the other airlines collected together in an industry lobby to pressure Edwards into producing the report quickly or, at least, publishing an interim report.

I distanced Caledonian from the independent lobby and set about conducting a political lobbying and PR campaign of our own. It was, of course, based on the issues we had taken up with Edwards and those centred on the proposal that the restrictive policies which protected the air corporations as 'chosen instruments' should be abolished, with equal opportunity among all British airlines, at least those who could prove themselves to be operationally, commercially and financially capable. The new-look structure would be regulated by an autonomous new authority, based on the US Civil Aeronautics Board, and built on the existing base of the Air Transport Licensing Board.

Specifically, we promoted the case for a second British scheduled carrier on the Atlantic routes, our prime charter market. In a particular lobbying document I wrote:

> We are not asking for special treatment. Merely equality of opportunity and obligation. We at Caledonian are proud of the airline we have built. All we ask for is an environment in which we can demonstrate how Caledonian can grow to greater heights than we have already achieved. The Edwards Committee, we hope, will lay the foundations for this. That is why we prefer to wait for its coolly considered judgement.

The 'Waiting for Edwards' issue reached the House of Lords in December 1968, when a short debate on independent airlines was promoted by a question from Lord Kinnoull. William Kinnoull was then and is today a great supporter of competitive air transport. Against the failure of British Eagle and Transglobe, Lord Kinnoull wanted to know what action Her Majesty's Government was taking beyond 'just waiting for the Edwards Committee to report next year'. The debate ranged over the whole area of air transport.

I knew that our lobby machine was working well when Lord Beswick, pressed for an expedited Edwards, told the Upper House: 'I could go to the Caledonian company for support, because I notice that in their news sheet which my noble and learned friend on the Woolsack was glancing at recently they said: "Nothing could be more harmful for the airline industry as a whole than for Professor Edwards and his colleagues to be stampeded into producing a hasty, stop-gap report." ' The debate was, inevitably, inconclusive. It ended optimistically, however, with Lord Beswick quoting the Chairman of BEA, Sir Anthony Milward, who had recently said: 'We are likely to have a mixed economy in the air transport industry.'

Of course, a large part of my argument not to rock the Edwards boat was that John de la Haye, Frank Hope, Maurice Guinane and I had gained the distinct feeling that we were winning. In every conversation and every piece of correspondence we had with Edwards,

196

we became more and more sure that the committee was impressed with Caledonian as a model of contemporary British independent aviation and that our arguments were getting through.

While we were thrusting to break into the big time scheduled service league, British United, the largest by far of the independent carriers, was fighting to maintain its scheduled base and gain opportunities for expansion. In 1969, BUA operated a fleet of three VC-10s, ten BAC 1-11/200s, five BAC 1-11/500s and three Viscounts. A total of 42 per cent of its business was from scheduled service operations, 56.2 per cent from charter work and 1.8 per cent from trooping flights.

The airline was attempting to recover from operating losses incurred in 1966 and 1967 with stringent cost-saving schemes. Alan Bristow, the buccaneering helicopter pioneer, had been pulled across from his Bristow Helicopters company at Redhill (owned by the BUA parent company) to take control of the airline as managing director. A number of 'special directors' were being appointed as a sort of task force to revive the company. One of these was the former general manager, planning, Alastair Pugh. Chairman of BUA was the Hon Anthony Cayzer, deputy chairman of British and Commonwealth Group which had taken over control of BUA.

Because of its structural changes, BUA filed its submissions and financial statements later than Edwards would have liked. Although always totally discreet in their dealings, I certainly detected an air of impatience with BUA among the Edwards group, especially its secretary, Gordon Manzie. Without being pompous in any way, I believe that Caledonian was regarded by the professor as his favourite pupil. We had pursued our objective of making a career for Caledonian out of the Edwards inquiry. BUA was frustrated with its scheduled services being constrained in the number of flights it was allowed on respective routes, as the 'chosen instrument' policies formed a leash on its neck. The much-publicized takeover of the abandoned BOAC South American routes had resulted in four years of substantial losses on those operations, adding up to a cumulative total of more than £800,000.

BUA came to the conclusion that its survival depended on a reallocation of air routes and that it should take over some of BOAC's existing operations. In particular, the airline proposed

197

to Edwards that it should take over all of BOAC's African routes by 1973.

BUA's financial dilemma was reflected in a letter from Anthony Cayzer to Sir Ronald Edwards, just before Christmas 1968. 'There is really no alternative to BUA taking over some of BOAC's present business. We are well aware that this is an unpalatable conclusion, but after a careful and lengthy examination of the problem, we see no other practical solution if BUA is to exist at all as an independent airline with responsibilities for scheduled services,' wrote Cayzer. He based his conclusion on the fact that his airline could not remain competitive by acquiring the new-generation, wide-body aircraft such as the Boeing 747, DC-10 and Lockheed 1011, if it did not have an adequate route structure. He continued, 'I think it is necessary that I should underline the view I expressed, both as chairman of BUA and representative of its major shareholder, that we can see no future at all for the airline if it does not have a stake in British scheduled services or if it is to be forced out of this business because it is unable to compete with the equipment available to it.'

The opposition Conservatives were, naturally, concerned with Edwards and its implications. One of their key players was the MP Fred (now Sir Frederick) Corfield, who set about what can only be described as a 'mini Edwards' review by investigating the industry and gathering around him a group of industry advisers in an attempt to formulate Conservative policy towards the future of civil aviation. Already a faction within the party wanted denationalization of the state corporations right away. (The word privatization had not yet crept into the party political lexicon.) Fred, a kindly man, and a lawyer by profession, saw right away that denationalization would preclude any route restructuring. Investors would want the airlines intact.

Fred was involved in the setting up of a Tory sub-committee to consider the effects of denationalisation. The chairman of this group was the Opposition Front Bench spokesman on Trade and Technology, Nicholas Ridley, MP. We were to revisit the denationalisation argument and Mr Ridley in the future.

# 39

On 28 April 1969, I received a letter from the Board of Trade. It was marked 'Personal and Strictly Confidential'. Signed by the Second Permanent Secretary, C.M.P. Brown, the letter advised me that the Edwards Report was due to be published on 2 May. Enclosed were copies of two draft chapters dealing with opportunities for independents. I read, for the first time, a phrase that would haunt the rest of my aviation career, Edwards talked about the creation of a 'Second Force' in British air transport.

We would receive an advance copy, at the same time as Edwards was released to the press. No doubt all of the other airline bosses received a similar letter, but I felt that I was in possession of a state secret.

Margaret Trett was instructed to get de la Haye, Hope, Guinane and Brilliant to my office immediately. They sat on various chairs and sofas, as I lit a cigar, went and closed the door behind them and returned to my desk. I puffed at my cigar and announced, 'Edwards will be out in three days' time.'

We plotted our campaign for reaction to the report. All meetings away from the office were scrapped for 1 and 2 May. We would concentrate on devouring and analyzing the report and getting the Caledonian reaction out on the streets as quickly as possible.

It was with a certain amount of smugness, therefore, that I heard the report from the House of Commons that Anthony Crosland had made public the date of 2 May, in response to questions from Conservative MP Neil Marten and Labour MP Robert Howarth, who was a great supporter of Caledonian. 'I shall urgently consider the committee's recommendations and I hope all interested parties who wish to put their views to me will do so as reasonably possible after publication.' He could be sure of that.

Neil Marten asked if Crosland would take steps to leak the contents to the House before they appeared in the press. No doubt with a wry smile, the president replied that leaks never emerged from the Board of Trade. He added seriously, after further questions from MPs, among them Cranley Onslow, that he hoped to issue a White Paper during the course of the summer which would form the basis of Parliamentary debate.

After almost two years of inquiry, the Edwards report emerged under the title 'British Air Transport in the Seventies'. It was, inevitably, a weighty document, covering some 394 pages. Among its major recommendations was the setting up of a Civil Aviation Authority to be responsible for the economic and safety regulation of commercial aviation, including the air traffic control services. It proposed that BOAC and BEA retain their separate identities, but be managed by an overall holding board.

But the vein of gold that lay buried in the Edwards mine of painstaking reports and endless tables of statistics, was unearthed in the Chapters 8 and 11 that the Board of Trade had so confidentially given me in advance. Chapter 8 dealt with the future size and shape of the British airline industry and looked at projected growth trends up to 1980. Edwards predicted that, by 1980, passenger traffic would have grown to five times the level of 1966 and that UK airlines would need almost twice as many aircraft to cope with it.

The different airlines' views reported by Edwards were entirely predictable: BOAC tended in the long term to favour monopoly, BEA wanted to preserve its position as a short-haul specialist, and most independents wanted access to more and better routes, recognizing that there would have to be some rationalization to bring this about.

The report trawled through the case for monopoly, citing the Transport and General Workers Union as one of its proponents, and the case against monopoly. It finally came down against creating one, overall air transport monolith, with the words: 'We conclude that a monolithic structure for the UK airline industry, though not impracticable, would create more problems than it would solve and we recommend against it.'

What, then, would Edwards recommend? The committee decided that on the prime, long-haul scheduled service networks, it would

200

be valuable to have more than one 'source of expertise, judgement, experience and enterprise, including commercial innovation', and went on to propose the creation of what it called a 'second force' airline to both complement and compete with the state corporations.

Its estimate was that the second force airline would, by 1975, require a long-haul fleet comprising three supersonic aircraft, three large tri-jets and eight contemporary jet aircraft, producing at least 4,000 million seat-miles a year to be economically viable.

Chapter 11 came swiftly to the point. 'Although it is not our task to nominate specific private airlines for any future licences, it is obviously necessary to consider what they have to offer. When we contemplate the catalogue of requirements for the second force airline . . . including the ability to raise large sums, we find it impossible to resist the conclusion that, although some of the smaller airlines have excellent qualifications in particular activities, there are few which approximate the qualifications which are necessary to provide a substantial part of the new second force airline.'

At the end of 1968, after the collapse of British Eagle and Transglobe, the UK had a total of nineteen private airlines. This excluded BKS Air Transport, based in the North East and Cumbria Airways of Wales, which had been rolled up by BEA into a regional subsidiary called British Air Services. Of those nineteen, six were very small operators, leaving thirteen of any significant size.

Edwards, however, considered only two airlines for its second force concept. The first to be mentioned was BUA which it saw as the only independent with the kind of basic facilities on which the second force could be built. The committee was impressed with BUA's technical engineering base at Gatwick. The other airline to be brought into the Edwards equation for the future shape of UK air transport was Caledonian.

'Another airline which, as we see it, could provide a useful contribution is Caledonian Airways whose gross revenue last year was £6 million on an average capital of £6 million . . . It thinks of itself as "the Scottish International Airline" . . . We have been particularly impressed with the results it has achieved in the development of North Atlantic charter operations . . . Nevertheless, despite the favourable impressions, the vigour of its management and the additional capital now being injected, Caledonian alone could not provide the experience and resources to sustain by itself the role of the second UK carrier on major inter-continental routes . . . There are, however, various aspects of Caledonian's organization and operations, particularly in its North Atlantic charter marketing experience, which we think would be valuable to the second force airline.'

My initial reaction was one of jubilation. In just six years, our airline had come from nowhere to leapfrog over some famous independent airlines like Channel Airways, Euravia (now renamed Britannia Airways), Skyways Coach Air, Autair International (later to become Court Line), Dan-Air, Air Ferry, Tradair, British Midland (the renamed Derby Airways) and Lloyd International, to be counted by Edwards among the elite, alongside BOAC, BEA and BUA.

Edwards saw the second force being owned partly by the state, through the National Air Holdings Board which it proposed to control BOAC and BEA, partly by the participating airlines and partly by the public, through a flotation of shares. The report did, however, make it clear that the committee had not asked any of the airlines whether and on what terms they would join together, but it did make the fundamental recommendation that 'to make room for a really viable second operation must involve some sacrifice of corporation territory'. Edwards' wording was cautious, but it was announcing clearly that the new second force airline would have to be endowed with routes transferred from the state corporations. 'We think that it would be possible to mount the second force on acceptable terms, but we would not expect BOAC to welcome it,' the committee noted drily.

The report's final paragraph was No. 1090. It said:

To sum up, we recommend a better integrated but flexibly organizsed public sector, a second force, mainly privately owned; a mixed ownership group of small regional airlines; a private sector of inclusive tour and charter (including freight) operators; an industrial and financial structure conducive to competitive efficiency, safe operations and good human relations; and a semi-autonomous authority devoted to holding and strengthening Britain's place in world aviation. These recommendations

202

should, to quote our terms of reference, 'enable the industry to make its full contribution to the development of the economy and to the service and safety of the travelling public'.

The importance of the Edwards inquiry and report cannot be overestimated. It formed the first comprehensive review of the industry since the 1930s and was the blueprint on which modern British civil aviation was to be constructed and governed. Such an exercise was not to be repeated for a further fifteen years. For those of us in the independent sector in 1969, Edwards represented a Magna Carta. We needed only to persuade the government to endorse it.

Although its words had been chosen judiciously, the Edwards report was immediately interpreted as recommending some form of merger between Caledonian and BUA for the second force. Writing in the *Financial Times* on the day the report was published, Michael Donne, one of the most diligent aviation correspondents and a shrewd observer of the airline scene, wrote, 'The Committee believes British United and Caledonian Airways should merge to form the first "second force" airline, although it is not suggesting a "shotgun" marriage.' Donne's comment was echoed by his Fleet Street colleagues, thus linking us, in the public's perception, to the new second force and the political upheaval which followed.

Despite the success we had achieved in the Edwards exercise, my overall excitement at prospects for the future was tinged with some disappointment. If we were to take full advantage of the kind of opportunity unveiled by Edwards, Caledonian would no longer be able to stand alone, run independently by a team which operated almost as a large family. We would have to join forces with others, presumably BUA, to continue the crusade for big airline opportunity we had started several years before. The alternative – to relegate ourselves to the confined backwaters of charter-only operations – was unthinkable and unacceptable.

BUA's immediate reaction was to congratulate the Edwards Committee on its 'thoroughness and foresight' and promised to give active consideration to its proposals.

I admitted to journalists that we were disappointed that the report could not see an independent role for us, but said we would adopt a realistic and constructive attitude towards any forthcoming negotiations.

Leading articles in both *The Times* and *Financial Times* welcomed the Edwards recommendations.

# 40

In contrast with the fresh views for the future brought by the independent airlines, through the Edwards report, the major news from the corporations was of continuing industrial unrest. The day prior to the report's publication, Anthony Crosland had stood in the House of Commons to report that a strike by BOAC pilots the previous month had cost the airline a loss of revenue of about £5 million and a loss of profits of about £4 million. Among the BOAC pilot body at the time was one Norman Tebbit. Five days later, it was reported that BEA's 1,100 pilots were threatening to work-to-rule in protest against call-outs for flights at too short notice. Apparently they were unable to plan their home life properly.

Political reaction to the report was muted. Edwards had manifestly cleared the report with Crosland and William Rodgers, his Minister of State at the Board of Trade, and the anomaly of a Labour government favouring the private sector was apparent in comment at all levels. The Conservatives were judged to be pleased, as their policy planners were concerned over the question of the denationalisation of the corporations.

Labour backbenchers, however, were unsettled at the curious doctrine emerging. Trade union leaders, to put it bluntly, were in a rage. Clive Jenkins, joint general secretary of the Association of Scientific, Technical and Managerial Staffs, put a motion to a mass meeting of about 3,000 BOAC and BEA staff at Heathrow. The motion expressed the meeting's 'strong disapproval of the suggestions in the report for the hiving off of air corporations' services to a privately owned second force'. It was approved.

In his harsh Welsh lilt, Jenkins had told the workers that the Edwards proposals would be 'the recipe for the making of millionaires'. He threatened that attempts to reallocate routes would be met by political activity and, if necessary, by national action.

He was backed by Mark Young, then secretary of the trade union side of the National Joint Council for Civil Aviation, a sort of arbitration and consultative body which brought together union representatives with airline management. 'We cannot allow BOAC and BEA to be broken up in any way and handed on a plate to big business,' he said.

Young later went on to become general secretary of the British Airline Pilots Association. In the longer term he became a trusted confidant and good friend of mine.

Jenkins and Young were joined in their attack on Edwards by *The Guardian* newspaper which in a leading article on the subject said that the Edwards proposals did not make sense.

A good deal of opposition had been fired up by the view of BUA which wanted to create spheres of influence. That is, BUA, or the second force, would operate all British routes to Africa, the Caribbean and South America, thus becoming the British 'north-south' airline, leaving BOAC to operate routes to the west and to the east. Edwards had had some sympathy with the proposal, but in reality had only recommended a second British operator on the North Atlantic and a second British service to Paris from Gatwick, in competition with existing flights from Heathrow to the French capital. The irrational combination of the two proposals led opposers to see a wholesale plundering of the corporation's routes.

Mark Young's colleagues on the trade union side of the National Joint Council published a pamphlet with screaming headlines, printed in blood red ink. 'Professor Edwards' Committee has produced a doctrinaire document aimed at creating wasteful competition and the squandering of public money. Its basic proposals all must be rejected,' it said.

For its part, the Government said nothing, at least not in public. Neither did it intend to until the publication of a White Paper. In the meanwhile, the airlines were invited to provide reactions to the Board of Trade.

There was one development causing concern to the independent airlines which grew in importance following the publication of the

206

Edwards report. BEA in January had formed a new subsidiary, Airtours, to operate inclusive tour charter flights, with aircraft no longer used on scheduled services, in direct competition with us and our independent colleagues. The concern was, of course, that the state corporation could, at will, muscle in on our bread and butter business, while we were precluded from competing with BEA on scheduled services. At the same time, there was no doubt in any intelligent person's mind that BEA's foray into charters would be subsidizsed, one way or another, so giving an unfair advantage.

Edwards had recommended that BEA should be allowed to operate inclusive tour charters and so, in June 1969, BEA Airtours announced that it had sold £12 million of inclusive tour charter flights on a fleet of nine Comet 4B aircraft which would begin operations from a Gatwick base in March 1970. Announcing the development, Gerry Draper, BEA's market development manager and a member of the Airtours board of directors, incited anger among the independents, with a comment reported by *The Times* that was regarded as insulting if not libellous to the people who had built up a sector of the business carrying more than three million people in the year, many on new jet aircraft, superior to the obsolescent Comets. He said in the context of claiming a rush of interest from tour operators, 'We think it is because the public is still uneasy about charter operations and the tour companies it sees BEA's name as synonymous with reliability.' I think that the first time I ever heard the phrase 'the arrogance of monopoly' was in the angry retorts from independent airline people to Draper's remark.

In any event, reaction against the BEA Airtours development was swift and hard. BUA announced that it was making the strongest possible representations to the authorities and that it was consulting with other airlines. A fellow Scot, Tom Geekie, who had recently formed a new charter company, Donaldson Airways, summed the situation up by saying, 'BEA cannot have the best of both worlds. I do not think that this is in the best interests of British civil aviation.'

I wrote to William Rodgers at the Board of Trade to protest. We still had not seen the White Paper emanating from Edwards. 'We are particularly concerned at the implications of BEA Airtours' entry into a traditional charter market wholly developed by British private enterprise,' I wrote. We did not mind competition, but wanted a fair deal! 'In direct practical terms, we see a real danger that the long-term stability of our industry may be jeopardizsed unless entry by the corporations into the charter market on a large scale is accompanied by some counterbalancing opportunity for the private sector.' I asked Rodgers to take this consideration into account in the formulation of policy.

As things turned out, BEA Airtours, later restyled British Airtours, continued to operate as a charter subsidiary of the state corporation. In the light of subsequent history, however, the creation of Airtours at the time we were contemplating taking Caledonian into the ranks of the major scheduled airlines was a supreme irony.

# 41

The truth was that BEA had every reason to be concerned at the growing competitive threat from the independents. By the time of the Edwards inquiry and the formation of BEA Airtours, inclusive tour charters were carrying two million passengers in a year to the Mediterranean resort areas. The state corporation had sat and watched this business double in volume over the previous four years. The big difference now was that while in the early days, the charter airlines operated cast-off aircraft, they were now competing with the very latest equipment, with high passenger service standards. In the same way, BOAC's marketing people no doubt viewed the transatlantic charter business with a mixture of anger and envy.

As if to justify the Edwards Committee's faith in Caledonian, the airline was progressing from strength to strength. While the post-Edwards debate simmered in the corridors of Whitehall and the lobbies of Westminster, the airline was carrying three times as many passengers on the North Atlantic and four times more passengers on holiday charters than in the previous year. Two additional Boeing 707-320Cs had been introduced, together with three BAC 1-11s.

From the very beginning, John de la Haye and I had laid an almost obsessive emphasis on passenger service. We were stringent in the selection of cabin staff. Only after a series of interviews and examinations were applicants considered for employment. And then the offer was for a six-month period only. If those six months were completed successfully, the young lady or young man – most of them young ladies, though – were given full-time employment. We had, by now, established our own training centre, in a building adjacent to Sussex House. Here, cabin staff recruits underwent a one-month period of initial training, followed by a regular series of refresher courses. Cabin staff management and training was, in fact, under the control of two former corporation men, Colin Williams, formerly with BOAC; and Malcolm James, ex-BEA. The reason for their employment was that although Caledonian operated only charter services, we had wanted full scheduled service style and standards. In fact, Caledonian's standards were much more exacting because, while scheduled services rarely operated full, our charter flights were always at a load factor of 100 per cent, or very close to it.

To the base of full international standards of service and safety, we added the ingredient of flair, brought about by the quality and character of cabin staff we selected, coupled with the style and training and the airline's overall *esprit de corps*. My motto, constantly rammed down the throats of everybody in the airline, was 'Best personal service – of any airline in the world'! The emphasis was on the word 'personal' which put the onus on the individual staff member. It did not matter that passengers were brought to us as groups and organizations. We had to treat each one as an individual and provide service that was efficient and polished, yet friendly and caring. The cup of tea for the grandmother from Scotland on her way to see her family in Canada had to be just as much a service priority as the bottles of champagne sold to the businessmen on their way to golfing holidays in the South of Spain. I wanted everybody in the airline, especially those dealing directly with the customers, to be able to walk away from their flights, from their desks or from a sales meeting feeling pride in the job they had done.

Ian Imrie of the *Glasgow Herald* produced an article for our *Caledonian International* newspaper. He wrote: 'Caledonian's record is a proud one . . . proud because while carrying out research, I found that everyone, from chairman to office girl, had pride in their airline.' He went on:

> For passengers, Caledonian's integrity ensures that aircraft will not be allowed to fly unless they have been proved to be in perfect operating condition; that the in-flight meals will be of top quality and served with the utmost charm and courtesy; and, perhaps most important, that the stewardesses and flying crew will have been trained and retrained to standards well above those recommended by government authorities.

Caledonian's service standards were applied vigorously through-out the operation. On the transatlantic flights, each group had its own specially printed in-flight menu. A Boeing 707 charter flight would begin, once seat-belt signs came off, with free cocktails from the drinks trolley which came to each row of seats. The main meal began with a separately served hors d'oeuvres, followed by a main course of fillet of beef, Tournedos, lamb or a chicken dish. This was accompanied by a selection of complimentary wines. A dessert course was followed by choice from a cheese tray and a basket of fresh fruit. Tea or coffee came with complimentary brandies and liqueurs and free cigarettes for those who smoked. Ours was a service far and away better than anything a passenger could obtain in the economy class of a scheduled transatlantic airline.

It prompted Ian Ritchie, executive director, sales, to write in a report on future business: 'There is little doubt that the Atlantic programme and the volume of future business being offered to us must be directly attributed to the standard of cabin service.'

In that year of Edwards, the airline doubled its turnover to £12 million and improved the profit by almost three times, to £646,000. My prime concentration was, however, on the future. The immediate future. We had, in fact, prejudged the Edwards recommendation for the second force airline and as early as September 1968 had outlined plans for the possible merger of Caledonian and BUA. At a meeting at the GUS headquarters, Universal House, in London's Tottenham Court Road, Sydney Robin, who represented the Great Universal Stores interest in Caledonian, had put together a paper which proposed a new company in which we would hold 51 per cent of the shareholding, with BUA holding the remaining 49 per cent. We called the new airline Caledonian International.

Two months before the publications of the Edwards Report, I drove the short distance from Crawley to the BUA operations and maintenance base at Gatwick. In those days, the entrance to the BUA complex of offices and hangars was marked by the wingless fuselage of an old Hermes aircraft, on permanent display. It was maintained in immaculate condition and served both as a museum piece and as a practical training unit for cabin staff. In its heyday, the Hermes had been one of my favourite aircraft to fly. By this time, I had acquired a Jaguar and a driver, a Caledonian employee by the name of Ken Woolley. Ken swung the car through the gate

211

on the Gatwick perimeter road and into the BUA complex. I gazed wistfully at the Hermes as we cruised along to the headquarters building, known as the 'ops block'.

The Directors of BUA were installed on the third floor of the building in a suite of offices labelled by their staff as 'rosewood alley', after the style of furniture they had chosen. In the biggest of these offices, at the northern end of the building, I was to meet Alan Bristow, the helicopter pioneer who had been chosen by BUA's owners to take over as managing director of the airline and to use his buccaneering style of management to kick the operation into financial shape. Bristow was a tough but jolly individual with whom I could identify. He was a flyer, had come up the hard way and had little time for the politicians and civil servants who regulated the industry. Surrounded by the bureaucratic trappings of a larger company, I am sure that Bristow's heart was really with his helicopter company, several miles north of Gatwick at Redhill Aerodrome. In any event, we talked about the state of the industry, of the inclusive tour market and of the impending Edwards report, before getting to discussion about the merging of our two airlines. Bristow, I believe, was in favour of the proposal, but he had to keep from me the views expressed in the BUA Edwards submission for the takeover of BOAC routes to Africa, the Caribbean and South America. The meeting was inconclusive and I went away, mildly mystified by Bristow's reticence to get down to some 'nuts and bolts' discussion.

# 42

With the political lobbying, meeting with ministers and consulta- •
tions with major shareholders and bankers, I was spending more
and more time in central London. The journey to and from Crawley
was making the days even longer than normal. On many occasions
I got home after Dawn and the boys had gone to bed and left again
before they were up the next morning. She was constantly concerned
with my health and the strain that the pressure of work was placing
on me. But she, who had lived with the airline from those restless
days when Caledonian was just an idea in my head or a doodle
on the back of an envelope, knew what the airline meant and
supported my strained lifestyle. To meet our team's requirements
for a London base, we settled on a flat in the Dolphin Square, a
complex of apartments which lies on the north embankment of the
Thames between Chelsea Bridge and Vauxhall Bridge. Being close
to Whitehall and Westminster, it was an address highly favoured
by diplomats and politicians.

Having progressed very little with Bristow, I had decided to
contact the Chairman of BUA, Anthony Cayzer. He was, of course,
a senior member of the family which owned British and Commonwealth, the shipping firm which was BUA's major shareholder. As
soon as I had received advance information on the outcome of the
Edwards inquiry, I contacted Cayzer through his aide in B&C's
city headquarters, Peter Gordon-Potts. A meeting was arranged
for 1 May, the evening before the publication of the report, in the
Dolphin Square apartment.

The Hon. Anthony Cayzer displayed all the hallmarks of his
background. His manner was crisp, yet courteous, he was an
interested listener, but mildly condescending in his response. He
was born just six years before me, had been educated at Eton

213

College and the Royal Military College, Sandhurst, was commissioned in the Royal Scots Greys and served in the Second World War. From war service he entered the family shipping business and by the time our paths crossed, had become deputy chairman of the giant British & Commonwealth Shipping Co. and chairman of its subsidiary, British United Airways. The head of the Cayzer dynasty, the chairman of British and Commonwealth, was his elder relative, Sir Nicholas Cayzer.

The contrast between our backgrounds was remarkable: de la Haye and I from the back streets of Jersey and Glasgow respectively, Anthony Cayzer and his family came from the stately thoroughfares of power and privilege. Yet here we were, meeting like mediaeval barons, plotting to merge our manorial estates.

The basis of the discussion was, of course, whether we could, between us, seize the opportunity of creating the 'second force' conjured up by Professor Sir Ronald Edwards. The conclusion of the Dolphin Square meeting was an agreement to pursue the proposal. My liaison was to be Peter Gordon-Potts. But even if we could eventually come to financial agreement for the merger of Caledonian and BUA, the prospect would flounder if the political will was not there.

We were still awaiting the publication of the White Paper on civil aviation following the Edwards Report, but in May I sought a meeting with the President of the Board of Trade, Anthony Crosland, and his Minister of State, William Rodgers. I met them in the government offices at Victoria Street and outlined the second force plans, telling them of the confidential meeting with Cayzer. They were generally in support of the proposal but were wary of the antagonism from the unions.

It was, therefore, agreed that the meeting would be followed up by a further discussion with Rodgers, but this time he would bring along one of the Labour MPs with a trades union background, Ray Dobson. Dobson had been general secretary of the Post Office Workers Union before winning the parliamentary seat for Bristol northeast. He was an assistant government whip and Minister of Technology at the Board of Trade.

I invited them both for lunch at the Belfry, a private dining club in Belgravia. Bill Rodgers and I had already had a very friendly association and on meeting Ray Dobson I took to him

214

immediately. He was bright and warm in his greeting, with a smiling, open, honest face. In modern vernacular, his attitude was what might be termed 'laid-back' and his company was genial. Ray Dobson appeared to be genuinely interested in aviation and hung on every word I uttered. He was not an ideological unionist, but one who saw the logic of harmonious development between capital and labour. His thinking was far ahead of its time in the broad political spectrum, but it was just the kind of philosophy that a privately owned second force airline needed from the ranks of Labour politicians. All of those who had stood against this concept, particularly Clive Jenkins and Mark Young, were of course close colleagues and friends of Dobson. His help and guidance would be invaluable and we adopted him for the moment as an industrial relations consultant.

The summer of 1969 was consumed by a tangle of meetings with British & Commonwealth as we pursued the merger proposal. They were of necessity kept extremely confidential and took place in a succession of obscure locations owned one way or another by the shipping group. The basement of St Mary Axe building in the City saw one meeting take place. Another was in the Bond Street office of Union Castle Line. On a further occasion, I was aked to be in the foyer of the House in Park Lane to meet Cayzer. The only meeting open to public gaze, albeit very select, was a lunch at the Savoy Grill.

In the shadow of the Caledonian-BUA project was the possibility of another merger, between Caledonian and Britannia Airways, the rapidly developing charter airline based at Luton. It had been formed on the back of the earlier Euravia, an airline founded by the aviation entrepreneur, J.E.D. 'Jed' Williams. I met Britannia's chairman, Hilary Scott, on several occasions, but the talks came to no real conclusion.

With excitement mounting in the airline industry at the imminent prospect of the aviation White Paper, a Government reshuffle took place in October 1969. It was a crucial time for us and relationships at the Board of Trade had been carefully developed. We were, however, to lose both Crosland and Rodgers. In their place came Roy Mason, as president of the Board of Trade; and Goronwy Roberts as Minister of State. It was important to waste as little time as possible in establishing contact with our new

215

political masters and on 16 October I wrote to both Mason and Roberts, seeking early meetings. To illustrate Caledonian's achievements, thereby encouraging the ministers to provide political nourishment, I enclosed statistics to show that our transatlantic charter carryings were now greater than the scheduled service volumes of such airlines as Swissair, Sabena, Aer Lingus and El Al, Israeli Airlines. Although we were preparing the ground for possible merger, BUA and Caledonian were publicly pursuing their own, separate campaigns. BUA's was based on substantial route transfers from the state airlines to give instant growth. Ours focused on providing licensing opportunities to provide scope for organic development. In both letters I referred to the prized North Atlantic routes. 'BUA deems to become the second British carrier. But Caledonian is already in that position,' I wrote.

Of foremost concern is the mounting sense of disappointment and frustration we are experiencing because of the continued delay in any expression of the government's views on the future of the British transport industry . . . I have no doubt that the White Paper will have something to say about the second force concept, whether or not perpetuating the association by name of this company with British United Airways. The prominence given to recent statements by the latter, quite apart from initiatives they have taken under the existing licensing system, make it essential that I should leave you in no doubt where Caledonian stands. Whereas BUA seeks extensive guarantees to warrant long-term investment in future generation aircraft and thus become the so-called second force airline, especially on the North Atlantic, Caledonian neither seeks nor requires any guarantees whatsoever, other than the security of tenure which we would expect any reasonable licensing system to offer and upon which we could build a sound economic future. Whereas, prima facie, BUA regard access to BOAC routes on a large scale as essential to the fulfilment of their aspirations, Caledonian simply wishes to complement existing, albeit limited, British participation in a commercial market of great potential.

BUA's strategy was being driven, behind the scenes, by Alastair Pugh and was becoming more and more firmly based on route

216

transfers. The airline had come to regard itself as the air transport messiah, foretold by the Old Testament of the Edwards Report. The airline prejudged the politics, taking on the mantle of the second force, and, in a controversial move, lodged applications with the Air Transport Licensing Board for the entire BOAC network of routes to Africa.

The first two weeks of November 1969 were busy with activity. On the last Saturday of October, we had staged the Caledonian staff party in the Starlight Ballroom, below the Sussex House offices, to celebrate the end of another busy summer season. It was then back to the continuing grind of political meetings with Ray Dobson, further discussions with British & Commonwealth and, of course, normal airline activities. These ranged from future planning, with presentations on the Boeing 747 aircraft from the Boeing Aircraft Company, to current operational problems, through meetings of the airline's aircrew council.

Political activity was kept up at a lively, determined pace. I had established sound contact with Fred Corfield, a shadow trade minister for the Conservative opposition. In early November, I had a lengthy meeting with the Conservative leader, Edward Heath, at the House of Commons.

On November 12, I was called to a meeting with Goronwy Roberts at the Board of Trade to be briefed on the aviation White Paper to be presented to the House later that afternoon. The White Paper broadly endorsed the Edwards findings and, particularly, supported the formation of the second force airline, formed as it said 'by the amalgamation of two or more existing independent carriers'.

However, the presumptuous attitude of BUA was slapped down by the government's statement that it could not accept that the formation of a second force should be made conditional upon the transfer to it of a significant part of the air corporations' route networks. It did not, however, rule out some reallocation or readjustment of routes, but emphasized that a second force airline must evolve progressively, proving itself at each stage.

# 43

To counter the BUA attempt to dominate the second force arena, the Caledonian team had worked on a public relations campaign to build up awareness of the airline and its activity. This was led by John de la Haye and Tony Cocklin. It had been extremely successful and the result of the White Paper publication was intense publicity, focused on us, anticipating the next moves to form the second force.

Talks with Cayzer and his executives continued. We were taking on the aura, within the industry, of a promising challenger for a championship boxing match. We were greeted as such at the Airlines Ball of that year. Our star stunt had, however, failed to come off. We decided to invite Sir Ronald Edwards and his wife as our guests to the Ball. The sight of the architect of the future of British civil aviation in the Caledonian box at the Albert Hall would have a profound effect on our airline and travel industry colleagues. Sir Ronald, however, had to decline the invitation because of weekend engagements in the country.

John de la Haye, Trevor Boud, Marshall Gibson and I had already laid the financial ground for merger with BUA through lobbying meetings with our institutional investors. After publication of the White Paper, I made a further round of the finance houses in Edinburgh and had no qualms about our ability to raise money.

In December, I accelerated the negotiations with British & Commonwealth by writing to Anthony Cayzer.

I said that the White Paper, plus the separate and joint discussions with Board of Trade officials, led me to conclude that little additional opportunity would be available to either Caledonian or BUA on their own. If, on the other hand, some way could

218

be found to merge the airlines, showing the right financial base, a good management structure and modern fleet and maintenance facilities, then reasonable extra opportunity would be probable. I mentioned additional opportunities in Africa and entry to the North Atlantic scheduled market. I also pointed out that a merging of the maintenance programmes would save at least £400,000 a year between us. I had gone along with Cayzer's earlier proposal that shares in the merged company should be held by a consortium of strong individual investors, so long as the Caledonian interest was not swamped.

I had become frustrated with the British & Commonwealth/BUA instransigence on the matter of route transfers. It is certain that they preferred a go-it-alone policy to become a major scheduled carrier, rather than become more involved than they were in the business of charter flying. I told Cayzer, 'I see a distinct possibility that the second force may not be formed in the near future because of a failure on our part to overcome our potential problems and in my opinion this would not only result in a great loss to the British airline industry, but also the loss of a potential benefit to our joint shareholders.'

I felt that we had done everything reasonably possible to advance the merger. Much earlier I had briefed the Board of Trade at a meeting with Max (later, Sir Max) Brown and Ray Colegate and given Cayzer a confidential report of the meeting. John de la Haye had written confidentially to Colegate about a possible merger. All along, I had pressed Cayzer for the mutual protection device of a Heads of Agreement document so that we could continue negotiating and trading confidential information about the respective businesses in a safe environment. He dragged his heels on this and stuck on the issue of the BUA shareholders (effectively his own British & Commonwealth) being cautious about the North Atlantic, the major strength of Caledonian. We even offered to stage a North Atlantic 'teach in' for the British & Commonwealth directors in order that they could understand the economic potential of the market.

I had become exasperated. After all, the initial merger approach had come from British & Commonwealth, but after that, all the running was made by Caledonian. If there were to be no merger, we had to get on with our own development plans which centred on

219

the acquisition of new, wide-bodied aircraft and a further attempt to gain a North Atlantic scheduled licence.

I had maintained discussions with Alan Bristow, the BUA managing director, and he, in turn, had expressed interest in becoming involved in any consortium which might be set up to finance and own a merged airline. I mention this because something had clearly occurred between Bristow and his British & Commonwealth owners. On 30 December, after my continued pressuring, Anthony Cayzer wrote to inform me that Sir Nicholas Cayzer and some of the other shareholders had discussed the merger proposals and agreed to proceed with studies, on the firm understanding that neither British & Commonwealth nor Caledonian would seek to create a consortium with Alan Bristow, or any other party, and that the merger study be carried out in the strictest confidence.

The next formal meeting took place at the Grosvenor House Hotel in London on 23 January 1970. Trevor Boud and I had travelled from Gatwick for the negotiation and British & Commonwealth was represented by A.E. Lemon and Peter Gordon-Potts. This was what might be termed an enabling meeting, where we identified a number of items of financial and commercial importance to be prepared prior to a comprehensive meeting.

About one month later, I drew up in a taxi at the main door of Cayzer House in St Mary Axe in the City of London. There, in the board room, I met Anthony Cayzer, Lemon and Pots. This session produced more progress than any previous meeting. We agreed to form a merger study task force. From BUA, it would comprise Frank Nickalls, the finance director; Alistair Pugh, planning director; and Bill Richardson, engineering director. The Caledonian side would be made up of Frank Hope or Maurice Guinance and Trevor Boud.

We discussed the financial structure of the proposed new company. I had assessed the net asset value of BUA at £7 million and Caledonian at £3 million. Because of the imbalance in size, I put before Cayzer a phased financial programme. Initially, British & Commonwealth would hold 40 per cent, Caledonian shareholders 40 per cent and IRC 20 per cent. We were already in discussion with the chairman of the IRC who had expressed an interest in participating. Through this, B&C would gain £3 million for the shares sold to the other parties. In the second stage, B&C's stake would be reduced to 20 per cent by the introduction of another investor, possibly GUS. The third and final stage, in three or four years' time was a flotation to sell 45 per cent of the stock to the public, leaving Caledonian as the major shareholder with 25 per cent and B&C and the other main investor with 15 per cent each.

Of all of the B&C executives, Peter Gordon-Potts came across as in favour of the merger. He constantly fell towards our side of the arguments and offered encouraging co-operation both inside and outside the formal meetings.

I continued to press for a legal Heads of Agreement to cover the negotiations. Ultimately , this was agreed to, with some reluctance. A draft would be prepared prior to our next scheduled meeting in early March. In fact, some rough Heads of Agreement had been prepared before the end of the previous year, but they were, by now, out-dated.

On 3 March, Peter Gordon-Potts wrote to me. It was a hand-written note, on private heading. He enclosed the draft Heads of Agreement. However, he did query whether I really wanted 'all the formality' of Heads of Agreement. Would not an exchange of letters between 'A.C.' and myself mean just as much? His reasoning was that an exchange of letters could be very quickly prepared, whereas Heads of Agreement would take longer, adding cryptically, 'by the time the work will be done!'

I was very soon to realize the full meaning of Potts' message. I doubt if he knew that all the while our talks were proceeding, B&C was quietly perpetrating a double-cross. The draft Heads of Agreement would shortly become the most valuable asset of Caledonian Airways.

Remaining obsessed with the status and scope of network it believed it should have for BUA, British & Commonwealth, in the form of Sir Nicholas Cayzer, its chairman, made an approach to BOAC just before Christmas 1969. They ranked themselves alongside the state corporation and sought to negotiate an agreement for the pooling of aircraft equipment and route net-works.

An assessment of the situation is that these discussions were inconclusive, but they did lead to BOAC becoming interested in buying BUA. The details of those negotiations, proceeding all the while B&C were meeting with us, are, no doubt, locked away in the archives of Cayzer House. Early in the New Year, the BOAC/BUA proposition was taken to the President of the Board of Trade. On the basis that discussions between Caledonian and B&C were alleged to have broken down, Mason gave his approval for the BOAC deal to go ahead.

Just three days after Potts had forwarded the Heads of Agreement, the story of the BOAC/BUA sale leaked in a dramatic way. Appropriately, it was Chapman Pincher, the renowned correspondent and author specializing in defence and espionage, who broke the news. On 5 March, he called the Board of Trade and asked for confirmation of the fact that BOAC was about to acquire BUA. The response was a statement from Roy Mason confirming the matter and saying that he had approved the deal in principle.

The story broke in the *Daily Express* on Friday 6 March. Immediately after publication of the newspaper's first edition, Roy Mason issued a statement to confirm that he had approved the deal, in principle. Pincher's story was splashed across the front page of the *Express*. Inside the newspaper carried a leader which effectively articulated the view of the independent airlines and their supporters in the Conservative ranks. It said: 'This is a wretched affair, to be deplored by all who value the spur of competition and a resolute check against the encroachment of the state octopus.'

Freddie Laker entered the debate, with a hastily-issued press release in which he claimed that the BOAC/BUA deal was part of an overall plan to nationalize air travel in the UK. He said that the air corporations between them had already lost over £150 million of taxpayers' money since the war, concluding 'the death knell of British independent aircraft operators is now being rung unless this BOAC/BUA takeover is stopped in its tracks.'

To say that I was shocked and angry was an understatement. I was stunned by the news. I had led the talks with B&C in all seriousness, had been diligent in keeping shareholders informed on progress. It was now apparent to all that I had been taken for a long and tortuous ride.

I called in de la Haye, Guinane, Hope and the lawyer, David Beety, to analyze the situation and plan whatever move might now be possible. It was clear that the swallowing up of BUA by the state corporation would mean an end to aspirations by the independent airlines for any meaningful scheduled service opportunities. Whatever BOAC might say about maintaining BUA as a separate company, with its own identity, there was no doubt that within a relatively short period, BUA's routes, staff, aircraft and network would disappear to become part of BOAC. The Edwards report and the subsequent White Paper would, to all intents and purposes, be dead.

# 44

Our concern was to buy ourselves time by delaying the deal. The trump card laid in the hand of the Air Transport Licensing Board was an immediate application for the revocation of all BUA's scheduled licences and for Caledonian to be licensed on every sector instead. Effectively, we would wipe out BUA's most valuable asset, its route network. At the same time, we outlined the plan to mount a takeover bid for BUA.

The following day was a Saturday, but a telephone ring-round by Margaret Trett brought all of the relevant executives into the office within about an hour. The licensing bid, with associated PR and political lobbying strategies was put together, and we were ready to go into action at the start of the following week.

The key fact that had been kept well hidden from us was that BUA's airline trading position was weak. The airline had built up a cost base reflecting that of a major scheduled carrier, yet its revenue was based substantially on low-yield charter traffic. The capital costs of its fleets of VC-10s and BAC 1-11s were high and the scheduled services were simply not bringing in an adequate return.

The company shortly suffered a further, major blow with the loss to the new BEA Airtours of one of its principal inclusive tour charterers, the old established travel firm, Hickie Borman.

Our campaign team was, however, set to turh up the fire under BUA and its owners at British & Commonwealth. The story of the bid to transfer the BUA route licences to Caledonian and snatch the airline from under BOAC's nose was rushed up to Fleet Street. The Press notice was followed up with hard, personal contact with individual journalists by de la Haye and Cocklin. They played on the implications of a double cross, of the plight of Caledonian's

224

'David' against the 'Goliath' conspiracy of a nationalized industry in collusion with the establishment of the City of London.

Similarly, we took our story to Westminster to raise the temperature of the aviation debate among MPs of all parties, in both Houses. John de la Haye and I came to know the lobbies and committee rooms of the Houses of Parliament very well, as we took our indignation to the highest debating forum in the land. We had both always got along very well with many of the Labour MPs, probably because we came from the kind of background in which post-war socialism flourished, even though we were involved in a capitalist enterprise, with a mission to achieve equality of opportunity with the nationalized airlines.

The initial objective, however, was to force a debate on the issue, and for this we required the active support of the Opposition. Our secret weapon in the campaign was, of course, the draft Heads of Agreement which proved beyond any shadow of doubt that British & Commonwealth was in serious merger negotiations with us. We did not intend to maintain the document's secrecy.

Paragraph 1 of the Agreement comprised a statement confirming that the shareholders – of both sides – agreed in principle that the proposed merger would appear to be in the best interests of the two airlines and their staffs. The second paragraph formed much more of an indictment against the Cayzers of St Mary Axe. It read, 'The Shareholders agree that detailed work should be put in hand . . . with a view to the production of a document for consideration by the Shareholders, prior to the execution of the merger. This work, which it is hoped will be completed by mid-April, will be co-ordinated by Mr Anthony Cayzer and Mr Adam Thomson.' We were now in March, only a few weeks away from that stated deadline.

I had taken copies to the Board of Trade, to Goronwy Roberts and his officials, Ray Colegate and Sir Max Brown. Colegate had been briefed on second force possibilities through the merger of Caledonian and BUA, but along with his Minister, was astounded at the evidence of the extent of our discussions, against the background of the BOAC deal. Colegate's quick deduction was that despite the enthusiasm of the airline itself for the second force concept to bring a true, mixed economy in British civil aviation, British & Commonwealth, with 92 per cent of the stock, had simply given up for the cash deal.

The Central Lobby of the House of Commons is reached through the St Stephen's entrance, opposite St Margaret's Church, and alongside the statue of Oliver Cromwell. It is where the queues form to gain entrance to the public gallery. Those with special business with MPs bypass the queue to go through the main doors. After a check by the police force attached to Parliament, one walks through a vast, echoing corridor, lined with the statues of eminent parliamentarians of the past. At the end of the corridor is the circular Central Lobby. It is the busy crossroads of Parliament, linking the Commons to the east with the Lords, to the west, and providing access to the complex of committee rooms, restaurants, bars and offices to the south. High on the Lobby's domed ceilings are stained-glass representations of the British patron saints, St George for England, St Patrick for Ireland, St David for Wales and St Andrew for Scotland.

I sat on one of the green-coloured benches, amid the railway station-like bustle of the Lobby, gazing at the patriarchal figure of St Andrew. I had put in a card – the time honoured custom for lobbying MPs – for Fred Corfield, the Conservative shadow Trade Minister. Over cups of tea in the Members' lounge, Corfield studied the documents I laid on the table and listened intently to my methodical catalogue of events. I could sense the anger building up inside him and knew that we had secured a powerful ally. He went to work. As Fred prepared to bring the Parliamentary machinery grinding into action, we kept up the pressure in the Press and through the political and financial network formed by Caledonian's institutional shareholders.

None of us could remember when the airline business had ever enjoyed such a high public profile as it did in the spring of 1970. I was becoming a practised hand at radio and television interviews, though I had needed a stiff Scotch before making my first TV appearance. Press photographers were constantly toing and froing at Gatwick, getting shots of myself and the other Caledonian directors and pictures of the aircraft, not just for instant news coverage, but also to establish a Caledonian 'library' to illustrate what the news editors of Fleet Street, aroused by our own PR activities, sensed would be an important and long-running story.

Interwoven with the second force development and the new political battle, was the business of running an airline and taking on a fresh business venture, in the form of a tour operator. Blue Sky Holidays was one of our main charterers for the BAC 1-11 fleet and committed to Caledonian for a significant amount of revenue and flying hours. The company was run by a young entrepreneur, Andrew Gordon. Towards the end of the 1969 season, we noticed that payments from Gordon were becoming more and more delayed. Ian Ritchie began to sound commercial alarm bells and after a series of tough meetings with Gordon and his accountants, we negotiated to prop up the travel group with a cash loan of £1,379,410 and took control of 40 per cent of the travel firm's equity share capital. This ensured the continuance of the Blue Sky programme and, most importantly, the security of the BAC 1-11 charter work.

Frank Hope, Ian Ritchie and our Crawley management team concentrated on running our airline whilst those of us in London battled with politicians – both those in support and those against us – and civil servants.

At the end of January, our normal sales promotional junket with the group charter organizations on the west coast of North America took on a more serious tone than usual. The market had been sent into a spin by a complaint made against us and four other airlines by the Bureau of Enforcement of the US Civil Aviation Bureau. It alleged that our arrangements with 'umbrella' organizations representing a number of individual clubs and affinity associations were illegal and said that we should 'cease and desist' from such activity, and if we did not comply, our permit should be withdrawn. The CAB was getting at organizations like the Council of British Societies of Southern California. This was made up from a range of different clubs, but it was COBS which actually contracted the charter flights and sold the seats to individual members through its body of clubs. Leonard Bebchick set about tackling the case in Washington and we ultimately won the argument, with no penalties. But so delicate was the situation among individual charter members through the publicity generated by the CAB complaint, that for the west coast tour, we took Leonard along to address every group we met to settle the market down for the busy summer season.

As we rushed around California, Frank Hope and I maintained a constant contact with London and Crawley to oversee the political situation. John de la Haye and Maurice Guinane had stayed behind and were maintaining the pressure on the Cayzers, on one hand, and the Government, on the other. Nevertheless, we still found time to make the weekend trip to Lake Tahoe with Pat Shasby and his British American Club of Northern California colleagues. This time, the weather stayed calm and the mountainous coach journey took place without delay or mishap.

# 45

In the afternoon of 18 March 1970, I was again in the House of Commons to see Fred Corfield. This time, John de la Haye and I had a seat in the box under the gallery, virtually on the floor of the chamber. Fred Corfield was in his place in the Opposition benches on the floor of the chamber and Ray Dobson, a Government whip and our sponsor for the day, was on the front bench.

The Conservatives had brought in a Censure Motion against the government on the current events in the saga of the second force. At twenty minutes past four, the speaker called Fred Corfield. He stood up, looked towards the Speaker's chair and said: 'I beg to move . . . that this House deplores the approval in principle by Her Majesty's Government of the proposals by the British Overseas Airways Corporation to take over British United Airways, thereby undermining their own policy for civil air transport as stated in Command Paper No.4213, and urges Her Majesty's Government to ensure that the establishment of a second force independent airline is not frustrated either by the implementation of this proposal or by surrender to threats of industrial action.'

Caledonian had had the humblest of beginnings; now its future was the subject of Parliamentary debate. The industrial action which Fred Corfield referred to was the crude counter to our campaign to preserve BUA for the independent second force from the union leader, Clive Jenkins. He had threatened that if the BOAC deal was not allowed to proceed, he would bring the state corporation to a standstill by strike action.

Corfield now turned his attention to the President of the Board of Trade, Roy Mason, sitting opposite on the Government Front Bench. He trawled through the background of the Edwards committee and its report and into the political promises of the subsequent

229

White Paper. 'In these circumstances,' he said, 'and even with this Government, with their dismal record of broken promises and reversed policies, the House, the industry and the country are entitled to assume that those proposals set forth in the White Paper represented the genuine policies of the Government, on which they could rely.' He castigated the Government for having refused to allow previous debates either on the Edwards Report of the White Paper.

Corfield quoted back to the Government their own White Paper phrase that a key objective was to place the minimum of restraint on competition or innovation. What greater constraints on competition could there be than a monopoly? he asked. He went on to argue eloquently the case for competitive choice in air transport, the second force airline against the state corporations.

Eric Lubbock, the Liberal MP for Orpington, attempted to interject several times, as did Leslie Huckfield, the Labour MP from Nuneaton. Fred steamed on like a battleship at full speed. Lubbock's point was to bring attention to a sentence in the Edwards Report which said that it was for the airlines to decide, in the exercise of their commercial judgement and the light of market forces, whether and in what ways to come together. In his view this exonerated the BUA deal with BOAC. Fred blew this out of the Parliamentary water by proving that it was written in the context of an independent second force, not a state takeover. He offered to read to Lubbock the whole of the Edwards Report. Huckfield in his first attempt to interject did not get beyond rising from his seat. Fred spotted him preparing to speak and called across the Chamber, 'I shall not give way, I still have a lot to say.' What Fred had to say became more and more interesting to a packed Chamber.

> As the House remembers, the news of this proposal [the BOAC/BUA deal] and that it was to be accepted in principle by the Right Honorable Gentleman [Roy Mason] was made public on Friday 6 March. It has generally been described as a leak and I believe it was a leak. If it was a leak, one can only assume – and perhaps the Right Honorable Gentleman will be in a position to confirm or deny this – that the intention had been to tie up this deal completely and present it to the House

and to the country as a *fait accompli* without any opportunity for debate. But whether it is true or not, it is curious that the announcement was made that the deal had been approved in principle. We should ask the Right Honorable Gentleman what exactly that means.

As I understand it, the actual figures had been agreed between the two negotiating parties and therefore, I imagine that they must have been available to the Board of Trade for detailed analysis. But I could not believe even of this Government that, had they known that parallel to the British & Commonwealth negotiations with BOAC, there was also negotiation with Caledonian with a view to a merger which would have been very close to what the Edwards Committee and, as we thought, the Government had in mind, they would have allowed this deal to proceed.

The Minister of State assured me – and I want to make it absolutely clear that I am not for one moment suggesting that he was not telling me the complete truth – that the Board of Trade was wholly unaware of this possibility. I have no doubt that the Board of Trade was not aware of it. My impression was that the Board of Trade was not only unaware of it, but had the definite impression – and I am not sure that I was specifically told this, and I would not like to say it if it is not correct – that such a possibility was utterly and wholly non-existent as far as BUA was concerned. It is only fair to say that there are different views of the discussions held by BUA on the one hand and Caledonian on the other.

Having seen some of the documents which were prepared and agreed, I have not the slightest doubt that had it not been for the bid by BOAC, the further discussions which should have started on the following Tuesday would have opened up a very real possibility of the merger which Edwards and others had in mind. There was at that time no question of a takeover of BUA by Caledonian; that came later when Caledonian heard of the BOAC takeover proposal. But I have no doubt now that the report that Caledonian is willing and able to make a takeover offer is genuine and I have even been given to understand that it is prepared to top the BOAC offer, provided that it can be substantiated as a sound offer on the basis of the financial figures.

# 46

Corfield went on to note that other independent airlines had also shown an interest in taking over BUA. Notably, Freddie Laker had announced his intention to make a bid. In association with him was Alan Bristow, the existing BUA managing director. Squadron Leader Jack Jones who ran Channel Airways from Southend Airport had also announced a BUA takeover plan. This barrage continued during every stage of the saga, including a denouncement of the industrial sabotage threatened by Clive Jenkins.

Corfield now attempted to back the Government into a corner:

I remind the Right Honorable Gentleman that, if he does not reverse the deal, he lays himself open – let us forget Mr Jenkins for the moment – to be charged that behind the facade of the Edwards Committee there has been a determined effort to eliminate the independents. For months, we have had the Edwards Report regarded as the excuse for inaction . . .

Before that, we had the pronouncement . . . that no scheduled routes would henceforth be given to the independents in competition with the Corporations. We have had the Government subsidizing BEA to operate an aircraft which other airlines are quite happily operating profitably and without subsidy. We have had the nationalization of an important sector of the air tour market. We have had the establishment of BEA Airtours, which is clearly operating on a subsidized basis in competition. We have had the attempt by the President of the Board of Trade to restrict the inclusive tour traffic across the North Atlantic . . .

Now the Government proposes, or was about to propose, or has approved in principle, a merger which would shatter all hope of the emergence of a viable independent scheduled operator and put a question mark over the whole future of the independents, even in the inclusive tour and charter sector. And all this behind a smokescreen of lip service to a mixed economy, competition and service to the public.

Corfield paused, glanced around the Chamber and, I felt, looked towards John and me in our box before delivering his final, rapier thrust. 'Our motion states our views. To it I add a charge of ineptitude, insincerity and cynicism.'

Fred had started speaking at twenty minutes past four. As he sat down forty highly-charged minutes later, the cheers and cries of 'hear hear' from the Tory benches rang out. He had delivered a virtuoso performance.

The House quietened as Roy Mason, President of the Board of Trade, moved towards the Dispatch Box. He started his response quietly and methodically, in the confident knowledge that he had surprises in store, by stating that the White Paper which followed Edwards was the first comprehensive statement of civil aviation policy to be made by any Government since 1945. Edwards and the White Paper, he said, were 'major landmarks' in the industry's history.

He followed with a few retaliatory thrusts against Fred Corfield, wrapped up in an accusation that the Tories had set up the Air Transport Licensing Board in 1960, but had given it no policy guidance. Mason claimed that the Tories were 'mealy mouthed' when they talked about standing up and championing the cause of independent civil aviation.

I had always felt that Roy Mason was an honest and sincere man and had some sympathy with him as he diligently painted in the historical and political background to the civil aviation issue. Mason defended the ATLB decision to refuse North Atlantic licences to us and British Eagle. The decision, he said, was wise, as events had shown, because one airline had since collapsed and the other had, 'pleasingly', as he put it, considerably strengthened its position. That was Caledonian. He emphasised that despite Fred Corfield's accusations, the Government was quite sincere in its 'second force' proposals.

"We think that the best national advantage would flow from an

233

amalgamation that would result in an independent airline strong enough to compete on the North Atlantic. If it can hold its own there, it can hold its own anywhere. But at the same time we have to be satisfied that it is strong enough."

In what I took to be a knock at the Cayzers and BUA, Mason went on to say that the Government was not attracted to the proposition that any existing airline by itself be labelled the second force. 'Experience in running scheduled services is not enough. Successful experience of the United States market is also needed, and, incidentally, so is the right attitude towards industrial relations.'

Mason continued with an attempt to clarify the thorny question of route transfers from the state corporations to the independent sector. 'As the White Paper says, we do not rule out the rationalisation of airlines' route networks under the supervision of the Civil Aviation Authority where this is in the national interest . . . But the tidying up of route networks is a very different thing from taking a large block of routes away from one airline and giving it to another, such as the whole of BOAC's African network, which is what BUA originally asked for. That is ridiculous in the extreme.'

After further policy background delivered in his unflustered, reasoned manner, Mason turned abruptly to what he called 'the events which have occasioned this debate.' He told the House that at the Board of Trade, after publication of Edwards and again after the White Paper, discussion had taken place between myself and Anthony Cayzer on the possibility of a merger. He confirmed that just before Christmas, Goronwy Roberts had met Cayzer and myself and noted that the BUA side had demanded assurances that substantial transfers of BOAC routes would be granted. Subsequently, he told them, he was approached in late January by BOAC, seeking approval for its purchase of BUA. He emphasized firmly that the initiative had come from British & Commonwealth Shipping Company and he, therefore, had invited its chairman, Sir Nicholas Cayzer, to see him in early February.

John and I stared at each other in amazement when Mason said: "The clear impression that he then gave me was that there was no real possibility that a merger between BUA and Caledonian would take place. As I understood him, this was because he saw BUA as predominantly an operator of scheduled services and so in a different category from the other independent airlines which are mainly in charter and bulk travel. For this reason, he saw nothing worthwhile resulting from a merger with any other group of independents. He wished BUA to expand as an operator of scheduled services and he did not think that the idea of a second force airline was practical because achieving it would involve depriving BOAC of routes it already had. He thought that the sale of BUA to BOAC was therefore the course that would best serve the national interest. In reply to a direct question from me as to what he would do if BOAC were not allowed to buy BUA, he did not mention a merger with Caledonian as an alternative course."

It was incredible that Sir Nicholas Cayzer could have been blindly unaware of the discussions between his deputy chairman and myself. I had to conclude that in that cozy interview with the President of the Board of Trade, Sir Nicholas had metaphorically stabbed Caledonian in the back.

Mason said that he had concluded that the prospect of a combination of airlines emerging as the second force no longer existed, so far as BUA was concerned, and there was no reason of policy why he should prevent the BOAC takeover of BUA taking place. The fact that BOAC had said that it intended – for a period – to run BUA as a going concern had assured him that the jobs of BUA's 3,000 employees would not be put at risk. Mason then revealed that after his 5 March statement, confirming Chapman Pincher's story, it was brought to his knowledge that, despite the impression he had been given to the contrary, British & Commonwealth had been in real and close discussion with Caledonian right up to the time of the announcement by his department.

'Evidently,' he said, with indignation now emerging in his voice, 'I had been seriously misled in supposing that there was no prospect that a merger could take place.' The House was stunned at this statement, carrying as it did serious allegations against the Cayzers. I knew that our move to block the deal had paid off when Mason remarked that the applications we had made with the ATLB for the entire BUA route network materially affected the appraisal of any investment by BOAC. He also acknowledged our intention to mount a rival bid for BUA.

He said the words I was waiting for: 'In these new circumstances, it is clear that my proper course is to withhold approval from the investment proposal put to me by BOAC until the situation has been clarified.'

Mason went on to say that it remained Government policy to encourage the formation of an independent second force, by amalgamation, whether by merger or purchase. He continued: 'I want to allow ample opportunity for BUA and Caledonian, which are the two airlines named in the Edwards Report as forming the most likely nucleus of an appropriate combination, to resume their negotiations and take them to a conclusion . . . Accordingly I have asked the chairmen of British & Commonwealth and of Caledonian to resume their negotiations on the basis of merger, or failing that, of takeover, and to pursue them with all possible speed and sincerity.'

Mason had taken the wind out of the Conservatives' sails. They had clearly expected a socialist carve up of the airline industry. Michael McNair Wilson, who was to respond to Mason for the Opposition, admitted that he was in the unfortunate position of having to revise what he was going to say and, instead of his planned blistering attack, he ended up by commending the President of the Board of Trade.

But the heat of the debate was turned up by three Labour MPs, Russell Kerr, Leslie Huckfield and Eric Heffer, who turned their faces firmly against Roy Mason's policy. Kerr, who had been absent for the early stages of the debate, was in a state of anger. He brought into the Chamber a telegram he had received from Clive Jenkins, said to be on behalf of 3,000 BUA staff at Gatwick, and which supported the BOAC deal. Kerr was a member of Jenkins' ASTMS union and repeated Jenkins' colourful description of those of us in independent aviation seeking greater opportunity in competition with the state corporations as 'freebooting mercantile adventurers', in other words, pirates. Kerr rhetorically questioned whether Freddie Laker, Jack Jones or I were the successors to the legendary figures of pioneering, risk-taking aviation . . . the Lindbergs, the Kingsford Smiths (Kerr was an Australian), the Amy Johnsons and the rest.

I became bemused when he went on to say that what the House was talking about was 'some very well-heeled gentlemen who probably at this moment are drinking themselves silly in their City clubs and other places celebrating the great news they

236

have had this afternoon . . . We are certainly not talking in this context about the workers in the industry. We are talking about people who know a "quick buck" when they see one.'

As much as I, by now, felt like a drink, I was far from any 'City club'. Freddie Laker was probably down at Gatwick in his office in the corner of a hangar and, no doubt, Jack Jones was luxuriating in the surroundings of his work-a-day base at Southend. Kerr was clearly becoming totally irrational and proceeded with the allegation that the safety standards of the Corporations were far ahead of those of the independents.

Sir Keith Joseph called Kerr's remarks 'intemperate rubbish'.

Labour's Leslie Huckfield, like McNair-Wilson before him, found himself in an awkward position. The speech he had prepared to use against the Tory front bench would now have to be used against his own Front Bench. Nevertheless, he proceeded to point up the trade union case for parity of pay between the state corporations and BUA which Kerr had mentioned earlier. He finished off by stating the hope that the BUA-Caledonian deal did not come off, against his leaders' wishes.

The debate rolled on, ranging over numerous aviation issues, including the length of the runways at various provincial airports and the No. 727 bus which runs between Gatwick and Heathrow.

The fact was that we had a curious situation in which the policies of the Labour Government were supported by the conservatives and the Liberals, through Eric Lubbock, their aviation spokesman, and opposed fiercely by a number of their own MPs. Kerr had, in fact, stormed out of the Chamber. Eric Heffer articulated the Labour back bench view. 'I believe that my Right Honorable Friend must recognise that many of us are bitterly disappointed at his announcement today.'

It took Cranley Onslow, whom Heffer had earlier called 'an objectionable and obnoxious anomaly', after telling another Tory MP, Freddie Burden, that he regarded 'him and his Honorable Friends as a row of extinct volcanoes', to put it all into perspective. 'This has been a funny old day, really,' said Onslow. He went on to get to the heart of the controversy and the thing that had whipped up the anger – BUA's demands for wholesale route transfers.

'BUA must also take its share of the blame in many respects, not least for the extravagant demands that it made when it initially came forward and claimed to take over the whole of BOAC's African service. That was not a helpful approach and must have represented a considerable exaggeration of its needs.'

The debate went on until close to ten o'clock at night, veering off the second force to discuss the problems of industrial disruption at Heathrow. But Roy Mason's stance had turned the tables on the Conservatives, whose Censure Motion was withdrawn.

John and I left the House to take a taxi to the flat in Dolphin Square where we intended to make a few phone calls and start drinking ourselves silly, in Russell Kerr's words, with several cups of strong tea, accompanied by the ultimate capitalist extravagance of a cheese sandwich each.

# 47

The banner headline over the lead story on the front page of the *Daily Express* on 19 March 1970 read: BUA – I WAS MISLED. A sub heading alongside declared: 'Defiant Mason halts take over.' The British civil aviation issue had assumed massive importance and Caledonian, the small airline over the bowling alley in Crawley, was at the centre of things. Every newspaper and broadcasting outlet was covering the saga for both its aviation and business interest and because of the political implications of the split in the governing Labour Party.

The story had, of course, been fuelled by Clive Jenkins' attempt to halt the second force concept and any arrangement which would prevent BUA going into the hands of BOAC with industrial action. He had made direct threats against Caledonian prior to the debate, as a frantic response to our successful PR and lobby campaign and the political battle waged by Fred Corfield and the Tories. Any independent which successfully put in a counter bid for BUA could face strike action, Jenkins had warned in a public statement. What he was saying was that if the democratic process of Parliament and legitimate business negotiations brought about a situation not to his liking, he would have his way through anarchy by bringing the new airline to a standstill.

'If an independent airline were to bid for BUA, it would run into industrial trouble. This is a warning – don't bid. I don't think Caledonian is capable of making a bid. If it does, we'll take steps to block it,' he told the *Financial Times*.

I told the same newspaper: 'If the intemperate statements of Mr Clive Jenkins are to be believed and his threats implemented, the result would be anarchy. No country can be run in this manner.'

Jenkins' hysterical stance became the subject of a leading article

239

in the *Daily Telegraph*. It was headed "Government By Clive" and accused him of attempting to usurp the responsibilities of Government and the functions of Parliament. Jenkins inspired a telling cartoon in which he was depicted hijacking a BUA aircraft at gunpoint and telling the pilots "Take us to BOAC", while shop stewards toting machine guns lean out of the open aircraft door bouncing bullets off a Caledonian aircraft and a Laker aircraft.

Lord Shawcross was prompted to write to *The Times* in an angry response to Jenkins and I have no doubt that the ugly display by the union leader was noted carefully by the Conservative MP for Finchley, one Margaret Thatcher.

The evening after the great debate, Roy Mason faced a turbulent meeting of the Parliamentary Labour Party at Westminster. Leslie Huckfield accused him of adopting Tory policies, implying that he had betrayed Labour doctrine. The truth was that Mason had bravely and honestly remained dedicated to the policies developed by the Edwards Report and enshrined in his White Paper. Earlier in the day, amid further Parliamentary discussion on the subject, Mason's statement was described by Labour MP John Lee as an 'aeronautical Munich'. Huckfield called it a 'caving in to private enterprise'. Kerr weighed in with his comment, 'a kick in the teeth for public enterprise'.

The Prime Minister, Harold Wilson, however, stood firmly behind his Cabinet colleague, affirming that Mason had the full support of the Government and himself.

As for Sir Nicholas Cayzer, accused in Parliament of misleading the Government, he was away in the warmth of Cape Town, South Africa. In press statements from those sunny shores, Cayzer denied this and said there would be little point in reopening talks with Caledonian, as British & Commonwealth had decided to sell BUA to BOAC. Cayzer clung to the BUA dogma of route transfers and had authorized a statement to be issued to BUA staff by Alan Bristow: 'I thought I had made it clear to the President of the Board of Trade that, in my view, the idea of a second force without additional scheduled routes was stillborn. As no promises of greater opportunity in this sphere have been forthcoming at any time, I thought that only in association with BOAC could BUA fulfil its destiny as a long and short haul service airline. Certainly talks with Caledonian were taking place but, within my philosophy,

240

were not relevant unless a merged company was to be granted a viable route network. When asked by the President of the Board of Trade what I would do in the event of approval to the BOAC deal being withheld, I replied that I should have to come back asking for additional licences. Had this happened, a new situation would have arisen and the talks with Caledonian would have been relevant.'

The day after the debate, John de la Haye and myself arrived back at Sussex House and called an urgent meeting of the main directors. We decided to resume talks with British & Commonwealth immediately and after a ring-round of the principal shareholders, I put in a call to Anthony Cayzer asking for a resumption of our negotiations. I was told that nothing could be done until Sir Nicholas had returned to London the following Monday. Nevertheless, we told the press, now phoning constantly for news of developments, that we had resumed contact with British & Commonwealth and planned to go ahead as quickly as possible with takeover negotiations.

In fact, no meeting with British & Commonwealth took place in the immediate aftermath of Roy Mason's statement. Once Sir Nicholas Cayzer had returned from Cape Town, the situation was carefully studied by the British & Commonwealth board and their partners in BUA, Eagle Star Insurance Company. The outcome was the appointment of Baring Brothers, the merchant bankers, to conduct negotiations with parties interested in acquiring BUA.

On 23 April a full two months after Mason's announcement, Barings announced that information relating to BUA had been completed and had been disclosed to us. Caledonian was invited to make an offer at a minimum price of £7.5 million. It was to be submitted within twenty-eight days and on condition that we withdrew applications already made to the ATLB for BUA licences. It was also a condition that if our bid was not successful, we would make no similar applications for one year.

In turn, we had appointed the merchant bankers, Industrial and Commercial Finance Corporation (ICFC) and Kleinwort Benson, as our financial advisers in the negotiation. ICFC was already a major shareholder.

The information on BUA was duly received and analyzed by Trevor Boud and the Kleinwort bankers. Astonishingly, we found the figures deficient, especially in regard to the trading position of

BUA. Kleinwort's request for more information was met with a refusal. This was becoming sinister, as we understood that the same information had previously been supplied to BOAC.

We had completed the rounds of existing shareholders and potential new investors for funds to finance the acquisition of BUA and, thereby, the creation of the second force. Response had been encouraging. But against the background of a refusal to provide all the financial information we required to make sound judgements, we could not put a value on BUA and could not justify the case for investment.

We were also irritated by the licensing condition. I certainly did not think that it was proper, by private agreement, to erode the jurisdiction of the ATLB by withdrawing the applications.

We remained committed to the second force concept and our potential role in it, but we were ready to pull out of negotiations with British & Commonwealth if they were not going to play fair and square with us. I wrote to British & Commonwealth asking them to reconsider their attitude and affirming that we were ready to resume negotiations at any time. In any event, I urged for a meeting with Anthony Cayzer.

I also sought and obtained a meeting with Roy Mason and Goronwy Roberts to brief them on the situation and a press release was issued, making public the impossible position we were in. It was, by now, 15 May.

# 48

The setbacks and frustrations which kept the prize of the second force just out of reach simply served to strengthen our determination to snatch BUA away from the jaws of BOAC. The political lobbying, the PR campaigns and the financial planning continued at a furious pace. At the same time, we still had an airline to run.

The six- and even seven-day week became normal. Leave was forsaken and long hours were worked almost every day. My forty-fourth birthday – 7 July 1970 – was a minor exception, as I left the office at about 7 p.m. to join Dawn and the boys for a family supper.

The intensity of our campaigns on several different fronts, the polarization of opinion in Parliament and the reaction of the trade unions to our plans had produced a supercharged atmosphere. Rarely was Caledonian out of the press and the staff at Sussex House became used to the journalists, radio reporters and TV crews who came down to interview us. de la Haye and Cocklin formed an unofficial squad of hostesses to be used for publicity. Needless to say, they were the most attractive and photogenic among our girls. Ian Ritchie's sales executives were drilled into a code of smart appearance, with none of the long hair which was the style of those days. Offices were kept in an immaculate condition. The switchboard ladies, under the long-serving supervisor, Judy Laverick, were trained to deal with calls quickly, but with friendliness. Any visitor was in the care of the elegant, uniformed Sylvia Morant. We entertained with style either in the boardroom, in London or at the many travel industry events that took place annually. An invitation to the Caledonian party or hospitality suite became a sought-after commodity. My public-speaking ability improved as we picked up and sought out any suitable platform to project the company.

Above all, we insisted on rigorous standards of passenger service at the airports and in flight. We mixed the need for efficiency with encouragement for staff to be friendly to the passengers, to treat them as though they were guests in their own homes. The new fleets of boeing 707s and BAC 1-11s gave us a modern, technologically-advanced image.

And, of course, we boosted our Scottishness. Guests at our functions were greeted by one of our 'publicity' girls who pinned a sprig of heather to their lapel. Pipers were used in all kinds of publicity activities, whether leading guests into a dinner party or giving a salute to special groups at the foot of an aircraft's steps. We drew our pipers from the surprisingly large number of expatriate Scots in the Gatwick area who had kept up their piping – and drumming – from their days in the bands of the Scottish regiments or one of the Scottish police forces.

In the summer of 1970 Gordon Mason and Tony Cocklin came up with the idea that a full-scale band would be an ideal vehicle to symbolize the near-military way in which we were waging our battles on the commercial and political fronts. With the help of a local Scot, Jimmy Hamilton, the Pipes and Drums of Caledonian was formed to march and beat its skirling way through carnivals, fetes and industry events.

The overall result was that Caledonian people seemed to walk somewhat taller than their colleagues and competitors in other airlines and virtually without exception, every outside contact, at all levels, was left with the impression that this airline knew what it wanted and knew how to get it. Both de la Haye and I believed that if you wanted to win, you had to look and act like winners.

Down in his second floor office, or maybe in some Fleet Street pub in the company of journalists, Cocklin had dreamed up two mischievous paraphrases which he successfully drip fed around the media. BOAC became 'Better Off At Caledonian', and BUA changed from British United Airways to 'Better Under Adam'. They were designed to get across to the BUA workforce, by now in a dilemma of confusion and waning self-confidence.

All of the PR and image-building would have meant little without the base of genuine commercial success. The truth was that the airline was going from strength to strength. An additional BAC 1-11 and three further Boeing 707-320Cs were added to the fleet.

Trevor Boud and Curly Walter had secured the 1-11 and two of the Boeings on a long-term leasing arrangement. The third Boeing was on a eighteen-month lease, with the shrewd condition that it would be returned to the US lessor for four months in the off-peak winter period. North Atlantic charter traffic increased, as did European inclusive tours and freight services.

In a momentous sales coup, Frank Hope and Ian Ritchie pulled off a deal with the Australian airline, Qantas, to operate immigrant charter flights from a range of points in Europe to Australia. We provided the aircraft and crews, Qantas financed the fuel uplifts and line maintenance. Hope and Ritchie made numerous visits to Sydney in pursuit of the deal. In the end, while other airline bidders toed and froed, Ritchie simply set up camp in the city's Wentworth Hotel, refusing to go away until the contract was signed.

Normal charter flights to Australia were prohibited by the authorities in Canberra, supported, naturally, by BOAC in the UK. Yet there was a vast demand from Australians – mostly young people – for cheap travel to Europe. In the main they came by tedious sea voyages or by rugged overland journeys. Gilbert Brown was a travel entrepreneur specializing in Australian traffic through his company, Far East Travel Centre. He already chartered Caledonian to the Far East, but in one inspired session, he and Ian Ritchie came up with the idea of operating low-cost charter flights to Kuala Lumpur, Malaysia, which had an 'open skies' policy to attract business to its magnificent new airport, and then carrying the passengers by sea to Fremantle and Sydney. For this, Gilbert chartered a Soviet vessel and launched his 'Jet-Ship' programme to and from Australia. The hub moved to Singapore shortly after as Ritchie, helped by his experience of the East gained with a trading company in Borneo, negotiated his way through officialdom to achieve an 'exempt' permit. That is, we were exempt from the pricing and charter conditions of the Air Services Agreement between the UK and the Republic of Singapore. The only problem was that the permit was valid for just three months at a time, so four times a year, Ritchie would travel down to Singapore to meet up with the Australian we had appointed as Far East Manager, Graham Broadbridge, for the next round of negotiations to keep the service running.

The weight of the established airlines was firmly stacked against us, but one way of smoothing the tricky path was to give Singapore's former Director General of Civil Aviation the job of managing Far East Travel Centre's operation in the city republic. The service developed to the extent where it ceased to be a charter operation and we sold individual seats through a specially formed subsidiary, Golden Lion Travel.

The investment in Blue Cars, the tour operator, was proving an exacting proposition and Trevor Boud and I, together with our main shareholders, were contemplating a move to increase the company's share capital. Blue Cars was run by its Chairman, Andrew Gordon, a young business opportunist who the popular press would have labelled a 'whizkid'. Describing himself as 'an industrialist', he drove around in a maroon Rolls Royce and dressed in the latest fashions. His lieutenants in the business seemed to style themselves on their boss. The flamboyant arrival of the Rolls, from which the Blue Sky team scrambled out to attend frequent meetings at Sussex House, did not fail to catch the attention of the staff. Gordon and his men soon became known within Caledonian as the 'Quality Street Gang' after a TV commercial which used exaggerated gangster characters to promote confectionery.

Gordon based himself in Palma, Majorca, for long spells in the summer months, he said to take care of the busy operation in the holiday island. We thought that it might be an idea to inspect the Blue Sky activity at the resorts and so de la Haye, Boud and myself jumped on one of our BAC 1-11 charter flights to meet Gordon in Majorca.

During the tour of the main resort areas, Arenal, Cala Mayor and Ca'n Picafort, we noticed Blue Cars' signage on some of the hotels. Gordon explained that this represented a great promotional coup he had brought off with the hotels' owners. We took that for granted for the moment. Deeper investigation, however, revealed that Gordon was involved in developing a string of hotels.

We brought in the lawyer, David Beety, and he and Boud moved very swiftly. We had, after all, made substantial cash advances to Blue Cars to protect the charter business. £1.37 million, to be precise. Blue Cars' books showed net assets – excluding goodwill – of only £1.22 million. Confronted by the Caledonian demands,

Gordon and his advisers agreed to hand over a further 40% of the equity share capital at no cost to us. With control of Blue Cars in Caledonian's hand, we then arranged for further advances to enable the company to acquire 100% of the Majorca hotel company. To our fleets of aircraft and a tour company, we added two Spanish hotels, the Bali and the Java, with a further nine under construction or being planned. The operating company was CHM, Compania Hotelera del Mediterraneo.

Another operation on which we depended and which was becoming increasingly dependent on Caledonian was NAS Airport Services (Gatwick) Ltd, the in-flight caterer. de la Haye had become a director of NAS during his absence from the airline and assisted the company's development at Gatwick. NAS stood for Nairobi Air Services – the firm had originated in Kenya. John proposed that we take an interest in NAS for sound economic and operational reasons. Board agreement led to the successful negotiation with Robert Seaman, NAS's founder and owner, for Caledonian to take a 50% shareholding. In fact, airline catering became the centre of some controversy. The Air Transport Licensing Board had investigated whether in-flight meals on domestic routes were really necessary, out of concern for airline finances. The cost of airline meals on UK internal routes was estimated by the board to amount to £800,000 – money which it felt could be better used in helping carriers to become more efficient. The airlines were, however, entirely reluctant to abandon one of the ways to achieve a competitive edge over the opposition.

Pressure on airlines to reduce charter seat rates affected catering. Desperation to trim prices led Global to demand that we abandon the traditional meal layout on holiday charter flights and simply give the passengers a slice of pie. 'Global Pie' it became known as. Continuing price pressure led to the disastrous experiment known as 'seat back catering'. In what, on reflection, can only be described as an aberration, the charter airlines, including Caledonian, adapted seats to incorporate a two-shelf compartment. In the top compartment, was the meal – or snack – for the outbound passengers, and in the lower section, the one for those returning home. As the food for the return trip would be sitting in the small compartment for several hours, a refrigeration technique was adopted – a pellet of dry ice was placed under the plastic food container. It became necessary to employ a further piece of technology when it was found that hungry outgoing passengers were eating both meals. We installed locks on the lower compartment, to be opened by the cabin staff during the turn-round of the aircraft at its destination.

I was always against this lowering of service standards and continually railed against the tour operators who were placing unrealistic demands on the airline, in terms of both catering and the number of passengers they wanted to cram into the aircraft to reduce the individual seat rate. I saw the total irony of one particular meeting with two of our main charterers, Vladimir Raitz of Horizon Holidays and Sydney Perez of Global. We met, to listen to their demands for minimal catering and tighter seating arrangements, in the hallowed luxury of Pall Mall's Reform Club. As we sat in considerable comfort around the dining room table, going through three courses apiece, the conversation became rough. I told them they were destroying the business and were it not for being tied to existing contracts, Caledonian would have had nothing to do with it. I argued against the ridiculous seat-back catering idea and the cramming of passengers to the extent that anyone more than 5ft 7ins tall had to squirm sideways to get their legs in the seat row. Their argument was that competition was forcing down the rates and they had to offer lower and lower prices to hold on to their market shares. Our heated words caught the attention of other diners who responded with disapproving stares.

Not only were we at the mercy of a helter-skelter market as an airline, but also our new hotel venture was suffering the same kind of cost-paring by the same tour operators. Compania Hotelera del Meditteraneo was turning out to be a can full of worms. David Beety, assigned to review the business, reported back the alarming news that Andrew Gordon had allowed funds to be transferred to Spain. If that was not enough to set us worrying, he also discovered that no planning applications had been made for construction work already started. I ordered that the best men in Majorca be hired to get us out of the immediate mess and set the company on a straight and profitable path for the future. They came in the unlikely form of Pedro Prats de Vera, a Spanish hotelier with an elegant manner and aristocratic bearing, and Bill Brown, a short, portly expatriate Scottish accountant. Their advice was to make a clean breast of events to the appropriate Ministry in Madrid, to gain their support in setting the record straight. We had no real option but to agree. Although the case of CHM was received with courtesy and sympathy, the ponderous wheels of Spanish bureaucracy took a full two years to grind out a conclusion.

The economic fact of life was that the inclusive tour market was undergoing forced growth. BEA Airtours had entered the market with an additional 245,000 seats and the Clarksons company had emerged as a shark in hitherto gentle waters. Clarksons was playing the numbers game – building up market share at almost any cost. Their airline was Court Line, based at Luton. It had been formed from the former Autair, an operator of obscure scheduled services – Luton to Blackpool, for instance – which had become uneconomic. It was Court Line who invented the seat-back catering, which was taken up by the other operators involved in Inclusive Tours. Similarly, Jack Jones at Channel Airways decided to abandon his network of scheduled routes to concentrate on charters.

Together, UK airlines had planned to operate a total of 2,700,000 seats on holiday charter flights, almost a million more than provided the previous year. The capacity race had its effect in the resort areas, mainly Spain, where hotels were overbooked and hotels under construction but featured in brochures were simply not ready when the holidaymakers arrived. It was not unknown for builders to be sweeping rubbish out of the back doors of hotels when customers were coming in the front. A travel trade anecdote at the time concerned Tom Gullick, the head of Clarksons. He was said to have been refused entry into Spain on account of the fact that there was no photograph in his passport, just an artist's impression.

Caledonian carried 750,000 passengers in 1970, more than half of them on inclusive tour charters. The advent of the jet fleets saw our performance, in terms of revenue passenger miles, triple in two years. In short, we were carrying three times the number of people over three times the number of miles.

We continued to hold our own on the North Atlantic, but rates were becoming depressed as the scheduled airlines moved into the jumbo age with Boeing 747 aircraft, releasing older aircraft for the charter market. The US supplemental airlines, experiencing a downturn in military flights between the USA and Vietnam, pushed more capacity on to the Atlantic charter market. We increased our turnover to £16.7 million (from £12.3 million), but due to higher costs and keener rates in the two key markets, our profit dropped from £641,513 to £549,544.

# 49

Very little that occurred in the industry that summer of 1970 could have diminished the importance of my consuming preoccupation, the take over of BUA to form Edwards' second force.

We had arranged with Tony Stute of Continental Express, the Los Angeles charterer, to rent an office at his London headquarters in Pall Mall, cheek by jowl with the clubs of the establishment figures of politics, the civil service and big industry.

In June, we lost the redoubtable Roy Mason, whose steadfast honesty and sense of fair play had so far saved BUA from the clutches of BOAC, in the General Election which swept the Wilson government out of power and ushered in the Edward Heath administration. Michael Noble had become President of the Board of Trade and our champion, Fred Corfield, his Minister of State. The key civil servants, Ray Colegate and Robbie Burns, had not changed.

I had set our team the task of preparing a prospectus for the second force and clearing the way for as smooth a takeover of BUA as possible. One of our biggest obstacles was the trade unions, so to the core team of myself, John de la Haye, Maurice Guinane, Frank Hope and the lawyer, David Beety, we drafted in Ray Dobson, as the industrial relations expert. Happily for us, although he was not best pleased at the time, Ray lost his Parliamentary seat in the election and was free to become a more or less full-time consultant. It was Ray who organized a meeting, at the Pall Mall office, of union leaders, including Clive Jenkins and Mark Young. We were committed to accepting union representation through the strength and influence of national officers and union members in BUA. Having done so we were constructive in our discussions with Clive Jenkins, Mark Young and a whole clutch of senior union officials.

251

We had no intention of accepting a 'closed shop' regime, but the fact that we agreed to recognize the unions concerned helped to iron out the various matters raised. The fact that Ray Dobson was to join us as our Personnel and Industrial Relations Director was very helpful indeed in reaching a reasonable understanding on both sides.

In earlier meetings with the Conservatives, then in opposition, they had outlined their own aviation policy. In a meeting in Edward Heath's room at the House of Commons, the Tory leader, supported by Corfield, had said that they were basically in line with Edwards – private capital in BOAC and BEA, an independent second force with guaranteed routes, greater competition on domestic routes and subsidized expansion of operations serving development areas in the UK. Crucially, the Conservatives had accepted that to create a viable second force, the corporations would have to lose some routes in a transfer arrangement.

The success of the second force concept depended – as does any venture – on the willingness of investors to subscribe capital. In the first place, we required cash to acquire BUA. We and our advisers, ICFC and Kleinwort Benson, estimated the purchase price at between £8 and £10 million. Secondly, the merged airline would require overall re-financing for future development.

The backroom team of analysts and economists led by Maurice Guinane set about drafting the 'prospectus'. Their first task was to assess likely profitability for 1971 and then to project forward to 1975. The year, 1975, was an important milestone as Edwards' parameter for the second force was that it should achieve a long-haul operation of at least 4,000 million seat miles by that date. Our prospectus estimated that in 1971, the second force could earn a revenue of £15.4 million on scheduled services, £27.2 million on charter operations and finish up with a profit of £3.85 million.

Vital to the plan was the long sought for access to North Atlantic scheduled services, the ability to compete on the important London-Paris route, a freeing up of restrictions against BUA on the UK domestic trunk routes and a small degree of route rationalization between us and the corporations. The prospectus went into minute detail on operational and financial performance, including an analysis of each aircraft type in the combined fleet. Having argued the case for the viability of the venture, we wrote our final conclusions: 'In short, the ultimate profitability of a company is a direct reflection of the skill, expertise and enthusiasm of those who control and operate the firm. Caledonian's record to date provides objective evidence that the future profitable developments . . . are likely to be achieved.'

And so we entered yet another phase of unrelieved pressure and as time went on our sleeping quarters more and more became the Grosvenor House Hotel. At this excellent institution the cheerful response of the staff, despite our invariably seeking dinner around 11 p.m., is well remembered and indeed was exemplary.

During the year we made numerous approaches to the Scottish business community and rarely met with anything less than a courteous and sympathetic consideration; this was also true of the City institutions where the response was equally encouraging.

ICFC (later to become the 3i so well known today) together with Kleinwort Benson became our most valuable allies and the former's Paul Hildesley and latter's Charles Ball played such key roles that the second force airline might not have become a reality without their participation. Although from different camps they made a superb team, which was to be seen at its very best during the prolonged and tortuous negotiations that were to follow.

The breakthrough came from Whitehall on 3 August. The new Conservative Government announced its policy for the airlines. Although they had been in office for just two months, such was the heightened atmosphere in the industry their announcement was regarded as 'long-awaited'. To put things in racing parlance, we had gone through the card.

Essentially, Michael Noble announced the government's endorsement of the second force concept and pledged support to the extent of promising that it would be endowed with some routes taken from the corporations. Although, the routes were not specified, Noble did say that the transfer would be 'exceptional'. That is, having been launched, we would in future fight for our place alone. The new routes, he said, should be operational by summer 1971, less than seven months away.

The statement said that the new second force airline could provide a new source of management and innovation. Its existence would permit the licensing of a second British airline on the North Atlantic. It could serve domestic routes to offer the public a choice of airline. The new airline should be given preference over other operators in the licensing of new scheduled routes. It would also be given preference in the licensing of a second carrier on existing routes, or in any other sector of the market.

To say that the news surprised us would be a display of contrived modesty. The fact was that our mission had by now become a crusade and we expected nothing less.

Roy Mason, from the Opposition front bench, challenged the policy, but only on the question of route transfers. The Government had forestalled any possibility of being persuaded otherwise by BOAC, BEA and their supporters by announcing that transfers would be mandatory, through its powers in the Civil Aviation (Licensing) Act of 1960. There was to be no argument and neither Sir Keith Granville, Chairman of BOAC, or Sir Anthony Milward, Chairman of BEA, could but any buts!

Clive Jenkins' reaction was predictable. I could hear his Welsh sing-song voice ringing out when I read his comment about 'an affair which is bound to harm public interests and produce huge copper-bottom profits for the faceless men behind these negotiations'.

My face was set firmly forward. I announced that I would seek immediate discussions with British & Commonwealth. Battle with the Cayzers would commence once more. This time, we were not so naïve. The political odds were stacked in our favour and the financial artillery was arranged in readiness. The prospectus and hard talking had conscripted powerful second force investors with enough cash to take the shipping magnates out of aviation.

# 50

Along with all Channel Islanders that I had ever met, John de la Haye had a special affinity with the sea. As a boy in the Merchant Navy he had been involved in the liberation of Jersey. Indeed, he was the youngest member of the liberation forces. He has an abiding passion for naval history, especially the adventures of Nelson. It was, therefore, with a great amount of glee, in appreciation of an extraordinary coincidence, that he announced our victory over the Cayzer empire on Trafalgar Day, 1970.

Months of agonizing negotiation with British & Commonwealth had moved us from high summer to a damp and misty autumn. Our prospectus had been hawked around the major institutions to solicit new investment for the second force. The trump card in our hand was the government's pledge to provide the new airline with an additional annual revenue of £6 million, through routes transferred from the state corporation, although those routes had, so far, not been specified. The response from BOAC and BEA had been bitter, but they were helpless against a determined government, their sole shareholder. We came face to face with our main enemies, the union leaders, at a meeting in the office at Pall Mall. Clive Jenkins, who had labelled me a pirate and whom I had, in turn, accused of being a purveyor of anarchy, sat square in the middle of the table. Alongside him was Mark Young. On our side was their fellow unionist and former Labour MP, Ray Dobson. The talks were tough, but we made it clear that the private enterprise force was going ahead. We rejected demands for a closed shop deal, but made it clear that we would deal with them and recognize their negotiating rights on behalf of staff. The key part of the peace-making process was our agreement to consider comparability pay with the state corporations. Behind

255

this reasonably relaxed meeting, however, had lain weeks of hard persuasion and guidance on the part of Ray Dobson. His part in bringing the unions into the second force was invaluable. But Clive Jenkins never reconciled himself to our plans – at this meeting he referred to his determination to prevent 'the rape of BOAC' – he looked daggers when John de la Haye said, 'What Clive, not even a little kiss?' It was the first time that I had seen Clive lost for words.

Numerous discussions had taken place at the Board of Trade, when permutations of routes, revenue analyses and profitability levels – 'operating ratios', as they are known in the industry – were examined in a bid to come to a grand total of £6 million. To date, however, no direct talks between us, BOAC and BEA had been allowed.

It was around a table in the offices of Kleinwort Benson, our joint financial advisers, that we faced British & Commonwealth formally for the last time. Anthony Cayzer was with his lieutenants, R L Cumming, A E Lemon and my namesake, J A Thomson. On my side were Trevor Boud and Maurice Guinane. de la Haye had returned to Crawley.

After the long campaign of fierce PR battles and political uproar, the fight for the second force came down to a dry, legal document. With barely a word passed between us, I signed first, before passing the papers to Cayzer. Those two signatures represented an agreement for us to purchase the whole of the ordinary share capital of British United for £6.9 million. We were to pay £1 million within eight days and the balance on 30 November, St Andrew's Day, which I took to be a good omen.

We emerged with the deal on 20 October. After telephone calls to the main shareholders, to Leonard Bebchick and Murray Vidockler in the USA, I called de la Haye in Crawley. By the time Trevor Boud, Maurice Guinane and I arrived in the car park at the rear of Sussex House, the office workers were vacating their parking places for the night-time patrons of the Starlight Ballroom.

Those who had been running the airline at Sussex appeared to be subdued as we gathered for a board meeting. I was astonished when Frank Hope declared that, in his opinion, we had made a mistake of monumental proportions. Frank, who had been party to all that had occurred, suddenly voiced his view that we should not have dealt ourselves into the second force poker game, but remained as we were, a successful charter airline. Frank indicated that he was speaking on behalf of those who had managed the business while we had stalked the corridors of Whitehall and Westminster and pounded the streets of the City. The others, however, remained silent. Disagreement in the board room was nothing new for Caledonian, but I had never seen anything quite so bitter as Frank's argument. He was implacably opposed to the second force. It was, however, too late. The die was cast. Frank did not appear to be able to see my point – that while our main business on the North Atlantic was buoyant and growing for the present, the introduction of massive capacity increases by the scheduled operators with Boeing 747 aircraft would wipe out the charter market. Frank, in the end, was out-voted, and in any event, his stand was too late.

De la Haye had organized a night shift of volunteers to print and collate the announcement to go out the following morning. Plans were made to speak to mass meetings of the Caledonian and BUA staffs. A good twenty or thirty people worked through the night in the open-plan office in Trevor Boud's accounts department. Sandwiches were ferried in from the NAS flight catering kitchens and the drinks cabinet thrown open. In spite of our board room row such was the heady air of victory that I do not believe any one of us wanted to break the spell by going home that night.

The three urgent actions on the following morning, 21 October, were: to brief the Caledonian staff; to meet the BUA staff en masse; and to get out our news release. Our own Caledonian people were organized to be in the hastily hired Starlight Ballroom on the ground floor of Sussex House. I told them the details of the deal.

The agreement with the Cayzers involved the acquisition of BUA and all of its subsidiaries, with the exception of British Island Airways, the contemporary successor to the old Jersey Airlines which Cayzer clung on to. We had also agreed to buy, from a British & Commonwealth subsidiary, three new BAC 1-11 aircraft at a cost of £5 million. In turn, B & C agreed to continue various aircraft loan and leasing arrangements they had had with BUA.

The financial arrangements centred on a rights issue to existing shareholders of 2,150,000 Ordinary £1 shares at £2 per share and

257

£4 million of 101/2 per cent Convertible Unsecured Loan Stock, convertible up to the end of 1980 into Ordinary shares at £2.5s. per share. The £8.3 million raised covered the purchase price and provided working capital for the new airline.

I went on to tell the staff that Cayzer, Alan Bristow, Robert Cumming and A E Lemon were resigning immediately from the BUA Board. In the interim, J A Thomson would become chairman of BUA and I was to be elected as a director. On completion of the takeover, we would announce a full reconstruction of the board. The total capital and reserves would amount to £12 million.

To our existing list of shareholders, we had added nineteen new institutional investors, including major City names like Kleinwort Benson, General Accident, Standard Life Assurance, and General Scottish Trust.

Airways Interests (Thomson) Ltd, the original investment company formed at the beginning of the venture, was to be renamed Caledonian Airways Ltd into which the new shareholdings would be taken. Under this parent company, scheduled services would be operated by BUA and charter by Caledonian Airways (Prestwick) Ltd. The purpose of this was to differentiate between the IATA activities of BUA and the non-IATA operations of Caledonian's charter work. The combined airline would have a workforce of 4,400 staff, including 450 flight deck personnel, 800 cabin staff, 1000 engineers and 700 ground operations people.

Excitement was clearly high as I recited the facts of the takeover. Spontaneous applause broke out among the several hundred Caledonian people, as I announced that the merged fleet of thirty-one aircraft would all carry their Golden Lion symbol and the name on the side would be 'Caledonian/BUA'. With an estimated 2,750,000 passengers in 1971, the new airline would, I said, be bigger or comparable with such national carriers as Swissair, Qantas, Aer Lingus and Sabena, the airline which had given the unknown Caledonian its 'leg up' on to the world stage in 1961.

I was by now feeling the pangs of emotion as I looked at the rows of faces, mostly friends and dedicated colleagues, as I said: 'It fell to Caledonian to attempt to form the second force airline recommended by the Edwards committee – a recommendation endorsed by the Labour Government and actively encouraged by the present Government. I am delighted that we have been able to bring this project to fruition. The new airline will provide an alternative source of stable employment in the airline industry and will contribute significantly to the national economy.'

The applause was somewhat muted as I remarked that we were moving into a new era which would affect each and every one of us. The Caledonian directors and I then proceeded to Gatwick. I entered the gates of the BUA complex, past the old Hermes, once more. This time reporters, photographers and television crews crowded the entrance. We swept through and entered BUA's Hangar No.1. There, in place of the usual 1-11 aircraft undergoing maintenance, stood the massed ranks of a several-thousand-strong workforce, in sharp contrast to the small band of Caledonian people in the ballroom. Before them was a specially constructed platform, dressed with a microphone and amplifier.

I gave them the same outline, but instead of feeling among warm and admiring friends, I felt an atmosphere that was at worst hostility, at best indifference. I chose my words carefully, emphasizing not the phrase 'takeover' but the word 'merger'.

The people of BUA quite naturally and commendably had a great amount of pride in their airline. Over the last two years, they had been buffeted by the gusting winds of politics and been the subject of a series of takeover battles which they were helpless to influence, one way or another. Dotted among the overalls of the engineers and the suits of the office staff, was the bright blue of the stewardess' uniforms. For those girls, the prospect of throwing that away to take on the tartan of what they regarded as just a charter airline, was an indignity.

Coming to the end of my 25-minute speech, I reassured them that this was not just a cynical commercial takeover, but an aviation development supported and encouraged by two successive governments. I pledged that there would be no redundancies.

'I am sure we can make it a success. There will be no need for redundancy and we aim to pay wages that will reflect our position in the industry', I said. At that, a trickle of applause began in one corner of the echoing hangar and very soon built up into a reassuring swell.

The rest of that 'Trafalgar Day' was taken up in a whirlwind of interviews, television broadcasts and photo-sessions. The following morning's press coverage was predictably massive. '£6m BUA takeover establishes Britain's second force airline,' said the headline in *The Times*. The *Daily Express* enthused: 'Better Than BOAC Bid by New Airline.' The Brighton-based *Evening Argus* blazed across its front page: 'Tartan takeover: £7m BUA deal.' In New York, the *New York Times* reported: 'Top 2 Private Airlines Are Merging in Britain.' 'Now It's Hail Caledonian' said the *Scottish Daily Express*.

A special leading article in the *Glasgow Herald* began: 'There can be special Scottish satisfaction that Caledonian Airways, a Scottish company, largely backed by Scottish finance, should have taken over British United Airways to form Britain's second force airline . . .' In fact, editorials up and down the country supported our success. It was, after all, the first move towards real competition in scheduled service air transport and leader writers licked their lips at the prospect.

City pages majored on our stated intention that the new company should go public – float shares on the Stock Exchange – as soon as we possibly could. But opposition also featured in the coverage, as union leaders and left wing Labour MPs attacked the government proposal for route transfers.

Tudor Thomas, chairman of the union side of the National Joint Council for Civil Aviation, made plain his opposition to any transfer of services from the public sector. Clive Jenkins went further and threatened to take the President of the Board of Trade to court. 'We think the Secretary for Trade and Industry cannot do it legally,' he railed. If Jenkins remained firmly against route transfers, he was no longer against the second force as such. The delicate negotiation and persuasion of Ray Dobson in particular had paid off as Jenkins qualified his threat of litigation with a welcome for 'the emergence of a bigger private airline which would be more capable of paying higher salaries'.

The man who effectively started the process which led to the formation of Caledonian/BUA, Roy Mason, came out with ideological opposition to route transfers. He accused the Government of 'connivance' with us private airlines behind the back of BOAC. 'This operation on the basis of taking BOAC routes is morally wrong. It is legally doubtful and I hope BOAC, BEA, the unions and the Labour Party challenge its validity,' Mason said from his constituency in Barnsley.

The press reported, analyzed and commented upon every aspect of the takeover from the power politics and high finance to the nitty-gritty of putting two sets of people together. The *Evening Argus* contacted BUA stewardesses and sought their views on the change of uniform. Said one: 'Ours is much smarter and more flattering to the body. With the Caledonian uniform, you're in trouble if you have a big bottom.' The fact was we intended that there would be no 'big bottoms' physically or metaphorically in the new airline. If anyone was not prepared to fit the tartan, they did not suit us.

For those who were giving up more than just a uniform, things were different. Alan Bristow had cleared his desk at the BUA headquarters and had returned to his helicopter company at Redhill. After a year of trial and uncertainty, he made the comment: 'I feel like I have been born again. I am now back being full-time chairman of Bristow Helicopters and loving every minute of it.'

Sir Nicholas Cayzer's statement read: 'The sale of BUA to Caledonian heralds the advent of the second force airline. As Chairman of B & C, I was asked by Roy Mason, at that time President of the Board of Trade, to use my best endeavours to sell BUA to an independent airline. When the present Government came to power, they were also anxious to see BUA purchased by an independent. Thus what Government and Opposition desired has been achieved. It remains for me to wish the new group and the second force all good fortune in the challenging future that lies before them.'

# 51

The crucial issue now was the one of route transfers, politically charged and a test of the new Conservative Government's resolve. The raising of finance to acquire BUA to form the second force had been achieved partly by the government pledge to strengthen the scheduled service network of the new airline by no later than the summer of 1971. Before the finalization of the deal with B & C, we had sought a firm assurance on the matter from the Board of Trade. On 2 October, Michael Noble, President of the Board of Trade, had written me a letter which confirmed his intention and advised that he intended to use existing, valid, powers to effect the transfers, but should he be challenged by legal action causing an unacceptable delay to the plan, the Government would introduce legislation to ensure that the transfer was effected speedily. Armed with this piece of paper, all of us in the airline, our shareholders and backers, remained entirely confident in the face of Clive Jenkins' subsequent threats.

The truth was that we had been studying the options for route transfers with the officials of the Board of Trade for some time. They had laid open many of BOAC's route performance figures for our experts, under Maurice Guinane, to study. We had come up with two options, the transfer of BOAC's Caribbean and South American routes, or the transfer of the corporation's West African trunk services to Nigeria and Ghana. West Africa very quickly emerged as the favoured major transfer as the network could easily be isolated from the BOAC structure, with no impact on other routes, and it fitted in with the existing BUA 'Safari' route, a BAC 1-11 'bus-stop' operation which trailed through the Canary Islands to Bathurst, Freetown, Accra and Lagos. The trunk routes serving Lagos, Kano and Accra, operated by VC-10s, were estimated to be worth between £4 and £4.5 million. The deal with the Board of Trade was agreed in October, after we had made assurances that we would continue the pooling arrangements with Nigeria Airways and Ghana Airways if the governments of the two countries wished us to do so; and that we would continue the employment of local Nigerian and Ghanaian staff. With West Africa agreed, we were left to haggle over what other routes might be transferred to make up the remainder of the £6 million revenue target.

We declared a preference for taking over the twice-weekly BOAC operation to Lusaka in Zambia. It would fit comfortably into the BUA East African network serving Uganda and Kenya. However, Lusaka's revenue value was, according to BOAC, more than £2 million and this would take the deal over the £6 million ceiling. However, we were prepared, albeit reluctantly, to forsake one of the BUA frequencies to Nairobi. A whole permutation of possibilities was worked out and discussed. In the meantime, the Board of Trade underwent its own form of takeover when its activities were swallowed up into the newly-created Department of Trade and Industry. Secretary of State was John Davis.

The haggle over route transfers continued well into the next springtime. The problem was that, after the West Africa transfers, BOAC and BEA were simply offering bits and pieces of unprofitable routes for the second force. Our first choice remained Zambia. Failing that we wanted Mauritius, in the Indian Ocean. If those two were not possible, we sought the route to Lisbon.

Route offers were discarded only after deep and detailed analysis showed that these would be of nil or doubtful advantage to the new airline. Other factors were coming into play and I put these to Michael Noble, Minister of State at the Department of Trade and Industry. It had been our plan to introduce a programme of phased salary increases in the process of bringing Caledonian/BUA pay in to line with the corporations'. However, on takeover, it became clear that BUA had already committed itself to comparability from the start. Our wage bill was much higher than budgeted. The year of uncertainty over BUA's position had led to a weakening of the airline's position in the market and the scheduled service revenue had fallen. The third element in the financial jigsaw was a result of the spate of hijackings in the Middle East, when insurers raised premiums on aircraft considerably; certainly by much more than we expected. Looming on the horizon was a crisis in the oil industry and we could see fuel costs rising substantially. For these reasons, I told Michael Noble that it was pointless, if the second force was to get off the ground, to endow it with anything other than profitable routes.

At our next Department of Trade and Industry meeting, Noble laid his latest offer on the table. We could take the Tripoli route from BOAC, with services beginning that summer, and the BEA services to Paris Le Bourget later in the year. There was to be no discussion, this was the final offer. Noble had had enough of the pressure from the corporations and the chivvying from us. Our choice was stark and clear: take it or leave it. BOAC's and BEA's power and influence had won the day – a portent of what was to follow over subsequent years.

Revelation of the route transfers did not, however, emerge for a little while afterwards. In the Starlight Ballroom, underneath the Caledonian offices in Crawley's High Street, midnight on 30 November 1970 was marked by the skirl of the bagpipes and uncontained merriment. Three separate events had exploded into an enormous celebration. For a start, it was time for the annual end of season party which would normally have taken place in September, but had been deferred because of the takeover battle. Second, it was St Andrew's Day and the anniversary of Caledonian's first flight. Third – and most important – it was the birth of the new airline. The deal had been completed and the sale price paid earlier in the day. From the stroke of midnight we owned BUA and the second force was a reality. Each one of the 1,000 or so staff present were given a bottle of champagne and as the pipers played, the uncorking of the bottles gave out a noisy salute.

One of the main preoccupations of the intervening period had, naturally, been the selection of a board of directors for the airline and the appointment of managers. My criterion was simple: the best man gets the job, from whatever side he or she comes. Several weeks of intense review of all the people involved took place before the management structure was announced on 1 December. I recognized that our new joint board was too large; my dilemma was that I had no idea of the capabilities of the BUA working board. They were more experienced in running scheduled service operations than we were in Caledonian. I decided, with a few exceptions, to

264

merge both working boards and review the situation after about a year's operation. We needed the skills connected with running scheduled services as well as charters – as we were the largest charter airline operator in the world at this time.

The management structure was myself as chairman and managing director and alongside me were three deputy managing directors, John de la Haye, Maurice Guinane, and Frank Hope. Trevor Boud was director of finance and administration, Curly Walter was director of special projects, Stewart Calder was director of flight operations, and Hugh Brilliant was director of external affairs. Ian Ritchie was placed alongside BUA's Ted Bates as joint commerical director. In addition to Bates, we retained from BUA, W A 'Bill' Richardson, engineering director, Alastair Pugh as director, research and development, Frank Bentley as chief accountant and J R 'Mick' Sidebotham as director, operations and customer services. From outside, we brought in two key people, our legal adviser, David Beety, as company secretary and solicitor; and Ray Dobson, our industrial relations consultant, as executive director, industrial relations.

It was with a certain amount of irony that I unpacked the paraphernalia of my Sussex House office into the suite vacated at the BUA base by Alan Bristow – the very room in which I had visited him on many occasions. The other Caledonian directors were moving into offices along BUA's 'rosewood alley'. The whole process of merger was now beginning to take shape, with respective departments and activities being consolidated and arrangements for the repainting of aircraft and the issuing of new uniforms to BUA staff being made. For the moment, the Caledonian and BUA staffs kept their own uniforms, but were consolidated onto one roster. The result was that an aircraft crew on the 1-11 fleet, common to both airlines, would have some crew in tartan and others in BUA blue.

The one major problem was the inverse nature of the takeover. BUA was much bigger than Caledonian, with the result that our people and their characteristics were in danger of being swallowed up by BUA. The whole idea was that the BUA infrastructure was required as the basis for the second force, but that it would be shaped and guided by Caledonian's go-ahead spirit. The scale of the job of turning BUA hearts and minds came home to me when interviewing one senior executive. He told me that he had found the best way to solve a problem was to get out of the office and play a round of golf while thinking it over. He was not invited to stay.

John de la Haye was frustrated by the fact that some of the people saw the airline as some kind of extension of the military service, rather than a hard-going commercial concern. He never forgave the manager who invited him for a tour of 'the camp'.

But the single biggest headache was the merging of the pilots. Pilots, being groups of people on the same level – captains, co-pilots, or first officers – are ranked according to seniority. Simply putting them all together on their individual years of service would mean that some Caledonian captains would come behind BUA first officers in the ranking, and vice-versa. This problem consumed many hours of discussion with the pilots' union, BALPA. The problem was that most of the BUA pilots had been with their airline for a lot longer than our pilots had been with Caledonian. Stewart Calder's first proposal that we should take the number 1 from Caledonian, the number 1 from BUA, the number 2 from Caledonian, the number 2 from BUA and so on. Another proposal was to halve the seniority of the BUA pilots.

The solution that eventually evolved in the form of a resolution from BALPA's central board was that, on the captains' list, one Caledonian captain would be slotted in for every two BUA captains: and the ratio of co-pilots should be three Caledonian for four BUA. In the end this system worked, but only after a good deal of concern and argument among the aircrew. In fact the two factions were still poles apart and it was necessary for me to say that the decision was final and there was no point in further discussion.

# 52

In mid-December 1970, the problems of financing the three additional 1-11s we had taken from British & Commonwealth, together with finance plans for future equipment, took me to New York for meetings with bankers, notably Fred Bradley of the First National City Bank, probably the world expert on aircraft financing. Margaret Trett accompanied me, as she did on many business trips, to carry the weight of secretarial duties. It was in New York that the Government announced news of the West African route transfers.

A conference with Guinane and de la Haye over the transatlantic telephone very quickly concluded that I should go immediately to West Africa to talk with and reassure the British High Commissioners in Accra and Lagos and the Governments of Ghana and Nigeria of our intentions to maintain full British flag services.

The blitz of meetings with British diplomats, Government ministers and officials, representatives of the expatriate community and the press in Accra was followed by a similar programme in Lagos. I met the local BOAC managers who were courteous and formally welcoming. But none of them could hide their underlying resentment at the prospect of losing their routes to Caledonian/BUA. For me, it was a sentimental return to Nigeria. I had not been there since my days flying aircraft for West African Airways Corporation as a captain. Here I was, staying at the city's top Federal Palace Hotel, at the head of the airline which would soon be operating the British flag service from Lagos and Kano to London. It was a far cry from the rest of the events of that year and on the BOAC flight back to London, where a round of Christmas celebrations lay ahead, I reflected on them.

As I gazed out of the aircraft window over the areas that I had flown years before, trying to recognize landmarks, I thought of the cabinet ministers, senior civil servants and the journalists I had met. I thought of the Cayzers. I had had interviews with two successive Prime Ministers, Harold Wilson and Edward Heath. We had succeeded in bringing the vision of Professor Sir Ronald Edwards to reality, despite the opposition of some Labour MPs.

Political support was only one half of the equation. We could not have succeeded without support from the City of London, from Industrial and Commercial Finance Corporation and Kleinwort Benson who led the investment campaign. Neither would we have got very far without the continued support of our Scottish institutional shareholders. I recalled that Lyle & Hogarth Shipping had broken the tradition of over 150 years by calling an unscheduled board meeting on a Sunday morning at the home of their chairman, Percy Agnew, to agree increased investment in the new airline.

My thoughts turned to the great support, encouragement and guidance from GUS who never failed to offer the benefit of their vast experience. I remember the demands from Kleinwort Benson for the letter of reassurance on the West African route transfers that I had pressed out of Michael Noble against strong resistance from Board of Trade officials. 'If I don't get a letter, you don't get a second force,' I had told them.

Finally, succumbing to the offer of a whisky and soda from the BOAC steward, I thought of my colleagues waiting for news of the visit to West Africa, of the loyal Caledonian staff, now grappling with the frustrations and excitements of building a new airline with their colleagues from BUA, and of Dawn and the two boys who had seen more of me in newspapers and on television during the year than they had in the flesh.

I felt now like dictating some reports, but Margaret Trett had fallen asleep. Instead of waking her, I turned back to the window and the sight of the endless barrenness of the Sahara Desert slipping away beneath the VC-10.

Towards the end of November 1970 my wife and I were invited to attend the first 'Business Man of the Year Award luncheon' at the Savoy Hotel. Jocelyn Hambro was mainly responsible for this event which was also a fund raising enterprise for National Cancer Day Society. Naturally I was delighted to hear later that I was to receive the award. This was a great boost for all of our staff, coming as it did seven days after our takeover of BUA. We took a couple of tables for those who had been deeply involved with the negotiations, including John de la Haye, Marshall Gibson, Frank Hope, Margaret Trett and others.

# 53

The *New York Times* of 1 April 1973 carried among its voluminous broadsheet pages an advertisement which carried little more than a list of names.

At the head of the list was Earl Mountbatten of Burma. Within it were such names as Lord Boyd Carpenter, chairman of the Civil Aviation Authority, Lord Harlech, the former British Ambassador to the US, Lord Redmayne, chairman of the North American Advisory Committee of the British Overseas Trade Board, and Lord Beswick. There were 100 names in all, representing Government, Parliament, the Press and the travel industry. It was, in fact, the list of passengers on our inaugural scheduled service between London and New York – our way of announcing to the sophisticated New York market that we had arrived, in competition with the other nineteen major airlines plying the North Atlantic.

We had filled the Boeing 707 with the great and the good, including five former Ministers of Transport, the high and the mighty and as big a Press corps as we could muster. After ten years of trying, our airline was at last joining the ranks of the transatlantic scheduled operators. The aircraft was 'Whisky Delta' and had been specially fitted out for scheduled services, along with four other Boeing 707s. The planners and engineers had converted the aircraft to what was known as the 'wide-body' look, an attempt to compete with the 747s, DC-10s and Lockheed 1011s entering the market. It was largely a trick of remodelling and lighting. In-flight entertainment systems were fitted and a new seating arrangement installed which allowed the centre seat in a row of three to be folded down when not in use, providing a degree of space and comfort not previously available in the economy-class cabin. That first week of April formed the momentous climax to a year of intense hard

270

work and planning. Not only were we inaugurating a service to New York, but also to Los Angeles – and not only from London, but also, in June, from Manchester and Prestwick.

The flight deck crew and the cabin staff for the inaugural had undergone meticulous training and briefing. The aircraft was under the command of our Caledonian chief pilot, Roy Hermes. The whole show had been put together under a blaze of publicity. A section of the pipe band played on the tarmac at Gatwick as the VIP passengers mounted the steps to board the aircraft, but not before they were handed the traditional sprig of heather by two hostesses. Another section of the band was positioned in New York. The inaugural flight was ready to depart on schedule at 13.15 and arrive at New York's JFK International at 16:05, local time.

The golden lion on the tail of Whisky Delta surveyed the scene. It was the same lion with which we had started Caledonian and which had remained dominant in the formation of the second force, Caledonian/BUA takeover battle. But now the lion surmounted a new and different name, British Caledonian Airways. After several months of wrestling with the cumbersome nature of the utility title, Caledonian-BUA, we had sought to carve out a more solid identity and image with our advertising agents, Hobson Bates. 'British Caledonian' emerged as the natural and obvious choice and we adopted it in November 1971, just a year after the takeover. As with most airlines, we took on a short-form acronym. The ranks of BOAC, BEA, Pan Am, KLM, TWA, Qantas, Sabena, SAS and the rest were soon joined by 'BCAL'.

The news of the success of our final attempt to gain the Atlantic scheduled licences came on Friday 18 February 1972, the morning after that year's dinner of the Scottish Passenger Agents' Association, probably the most bibulous event in the travel trade calendar. Our hospitality suite had continued in the business of after-dinner entertainment until the early hours, but the weariness of myself, Ian Ritchie and those who had been in Glasgow with us gave way to euphoria as the news was broken by way of a telephone call from John de la Haye.

We had already been through a frantic fifteen months. The West African services to Lagos, Kano and Accra were opened with VC-10 aircraft in April 1971. The market among the British expatriates was resentful at the changeover from an airline they had known well, to this hybrid second force. But we set about creating dialogues, through lunches and receptions and becoming deeply involved in the community. Special efforts were made to establish ourselves with the Nigerians, the Military Government, under President Yakubu Gowon, and the traditional rulers, such as the Emir of Kano at his desert palace in the old city of Kano, and the Obah of Lagos, down on the coast. We went on to become part and parcel of the commercial community, to the extent that some years later I and the President of the West African Chamber of Commerce, Mines, Industry and Agriculture, the late Chief Henry Fajemirokum, laid the foundations for the formation of the Nigerian-British Chamber of Commerce. I encountered resistance from government officials who wished to use existing channels — in fact I recall a blazing argument with them at a reception in London.

Henry and I celebrated the formation of the new Chamber late into the night in London at the Europa Hotel. We formed a UK Chamber as well as the Nigerian Chamber and both were used effectively over many years. I remember our Chamber healing a Nigerian rift with the UK when we quietly involved our new High Commissioner at one of our Chamber luncheons in Lagos — he had been ignored by the local establishment after an incident with the previous High Commissioner. Our association with the Chamber and Henry Fajemirokum continued for many years. Sadly Henry died on 16 February 1978. Without Henry's drive and with my own concentration in other parts of the world, the Chamber gradually ran down. But there is no doubt that during its best years it was an effective association for business and commerce.

The route to Tripoli in Libya, oil-rich but under the reforming zeal of Colonel Muammar Gaddafi who had deposed King Idris, was opened in July with less publicity than we would normally have generated. Three months later, BCAL 1-11s began operations on the route between Gatwick and Le Bourget, replacing BEA which now concentrated on the Heathrow-Orly route. For the first time, after hours of practice with a tape recorder and the guidance of our manager in France, Michel Camhi, I made a speech in a foreign language. It was at a reception in the Hotel Grand, draped from ceiling to floor with gigantic strips of tartan. The inaugural delegation from Gatwick stayed at the Hotel Meurice, the wartime headquarters of the German High Command. It was in a telephone call to his generals made to this hotel that Adolf Hitler asked the infamous question, 'Is Paris burning?' It may not have been burning, in those early November days of the BCAL inaugural, but it was most certainly fog-bound, holding us and our passengers in France until late afternoon.

In addition to effecting the route transfers, we had stepped up the pace of the scheduled service operation. Frequencies were increased on the domestic trunk routes to Scotland and Northern Ireland, where we concentrated on promoting full in-flight service, including hot meals, of which the star was a full English breakfast, to put competitive pressure on BEA which offered only the barest passenger service.

First Class service was introduced on the flights to East and Central Africa, on the West African 'safari' service and on the Genoa route. We experimented with a first class cabin on the London-Edinburgh route for the commuting financiers and politicians who sought higher standards. Tunis was added as a stop on the flights to and from Zambia; and the Seychelles Islands were served as an extension to the Nairobi route. Casablanca was introduced as an en route stop on the South American service to Brazil, Argentina and Chile – acquired with the take-over of British United Airways.

One of the problems we had encountered, which was the basis for one of our final battles with the Air Transport Licensing Board, was the viability of the UK domestic routes. Costs were increasing heavily and both BCAL and BEA applied for fare increases of 10 per cent, to be achieved in two separate steps of 5 per cent. We were allowed 5 per cent only. But we did seek to innovate to improve the economy of the domestic routes. One of our sales managers, Andrew Hamilton, in consultation with a planning manager, Ranald Noel-Paton, came up with a plan for a low-fare late night service between Scotland and London. Fares could be brought down through the marginal costing achieved by extending the operating day and positioning aircraft at either end of the route, ready for the following morning's early departures. The result was 'Moonjet' flights at a fare of £5. These were 'no frills' operations, with no in-flight service, but 'Moonjet' became extremely popular and placed great competitive pressure on BEA.

1971 was the last year of the ATLB. It was to be replaced by the new Civil Aviation Authority on 1 April 1972. After eleven years the board which had sat in judgement over the entire commercial development of British civil aviation was coming to end. But its last year was far from a period of decline. In among the 4,513 applications it had received and decided upon, two were applications for transatlantic scheduled service. One was our own, duly granted, and on which the board said: 'The decision . . . was the board's last word on a topic which had been prominent throughout its existence.' The other bid was from Laker Airways for a standby service, that is a first-come, first-served, no reservations arrangement, between Gatwick and New York labelled by Freddie Laker as 'Skytrain'. This was refused by the board and, on subsequent appeal, by the Department of Trade and Industry.

The board, generally regarded as a crusty and dusty organization, indulged in a degree of whimsy in its final report. In among the usual quasi-legal reviews of the industry and its affairs was a short section, headed 'Envoi'. It said:

This is the Last Will and Testament of the Air Transport Licensing Board. It bequeaths:

To the Civil Aviation Authority a portfolio of problems that include those already mentioned.

To the air transport companies in trust the licences already granted to them and the hope that the licensing system evolved during the past twelve years is fair and orderly enough for them to build upon it successfully in the future.

The demise of the ATLB and emergence of the CAA brought us, once more, under the Parliamentary scrutiny. The CAA was created by the Civil Aviation Act of 1971. In 1972, John Davies, Secretary of State for Trade and Industry, and Lord Carrington, Secretary of State for Defence, presented a joint White Paper to Parliament, 'Civil Aviation Policy Guidance'. The paper necessarily covered the whole range of the CAA's responsibilities. However, in the Air Transport Licensing section, the Government reaffirmed established policy by stating that the British Airways Board airlines (BOAC and BEA) should remain 'the principal providers' of scheduled services. British Caledonian should continue to be the principal independent scheduled airline. In order to ensure that we and the corporations would be able to compete effectively in international markets, the White Paper said that other operators should have only limited access to international scheduled services.

This increased the discontent of a group of independents, Britannia, Court Line, Dan Air, Laker, Lloyd International, Transmeridian and Donaldson, who prepared a memorandum on the subject. They had a number of champions in the House of Commons who believed that BCAL, the second force, should not have precedence in licensing. The debate, in the evening of 13 March 1972, ranged backward and forward over the old policy issue of route transfers. During the proceedings the Labour MP, Russell Kerr, regretted that it was not possible to put the Minister, Michael Noble, in the dock for 'grand larceny'. At a later stage, Charles Loughlin, Member for Gloucestershire West, was suspended over a dispute with the Deputy Speaker after he had called Kenneth Lewis, Member for Rutland and Stamford, a fool. I believe that this debate raised the first, primitive soundings of a Conservative policy which was to emerge much later, under the label 'privatization'. BCAL was the means of privatising part of the activities of the state corporations, through the route transfers and the method of bringing competition on a more comprehensive scale than ever before.

The Labour Party, however, saw the moves already made and the pledge of preference for the second force as a giveaway of taxpayers' assets. To the casual observer, it might have seemed as if we were being given the carcass of the state corporations to pick over, rather than the crumbs from a rich table. It took Robert Adley, MP for Bristol Northeast, to point out that the effect of the transfers to BCAL was far less, in revenue terms, than the effect on BEA of the electification of the London to Manchester railway line. This was said to have cost the airline £10.5 million in traffic diverted to the new, fast, train services.

In the Chamber, listening, was John Boyd-Carpenter, a former aviation minister and MP for Kingston-upon-Thames. He was shortly to take up the position as Chairman of the CAA. In the Division which followed sometime after ten o'clock in the evening, the policy guidance to the new Authority was passed by 305 votes to 268. Among those Parliamentary 'Ayes' were some figures who would have a major influence on future events. They included Margaret Thatcher, Norman Tebbit, Nicholas Ridley, Paul Channon, Sir Geoffrey Howe, Cecil Parkinson, William Whitelaw and George Younger.

BCAL continued to be the centre of controversy. In the high summer of 1972, BOAC announced its first deficit for eight years, blaming the loss of some of its African routes. Lloyd International, the charter airline, went into liquidation, complaining that its failure was due to Government policy in favouring the second force.

The same summer saw controversy of a different kind in the heart of Africa when President Idi Amin of Uganda expelled virtually the entire Asian community. A massive airlift ensued using every aircraft available from a busy summer schedule. Work in Uganda went on tirelessly among the BCAL staff for which our manager, David Brooksband, was nominated for an MBE.

The airline industry in general was experiencing turbulence, though hardly as disturbing as the tragic events in far-off Uganda. We had ended 1971 with a profit of £1.722 million, a result that I judged satisfactory after we had accounted for £600,000 losses by BUA, a loss of £580,000 for the Blue Cars tour-operating subsidiary and foreign exchange losses of £458,000 caused by devaluation of the Argentinian peso.

Overcapacity in the market, particularly on the North Atlantic, had led to airlines spilling into other markets not traditionally their own and going for traffic at almost any cost. North Atlantic charters were a prime target and not only did more airlines than ever enter the fray with lower and lower rates, many of them also blatantly disregarded the fragile affinity-group rules which governed charter traffic. The inevitable regulatory crackdown led to officials being present at airports, questioning passengers and turning away those who did not meet the rules and had purchased their cheap flights from the 'bucket shop' agents to whom tickets were siphoned off for sale on the streets. So desperate was the rush to unload capacity on the North Atlantic that charter rates were now as much as $50 below the level we had obtained five years previously.

The situation was a mess, an unreasonable free for all in pricing, capacity and rule-bending. The key commercial directors, Frank Hope, Maurice Guinane, John de la Haye, Ian Ritchie and myself, laid a plan to reduce our risk on the North Atlantic charter market. The fact was that the more we flew, the more money were we in danger of losing. The response of the regulators on both sides of the Atlantic was to clean up the market by effectively doing away with the rules. The CAA, through Ray Colegate who had moved across from the Department of Trade and Industry, revealed plans for a new scheme of publicly-available Advance Booking Charters (ABCs). These flights could be organized by a travel firm holding a new kind of licence, Air Travel Organizers' Licence, or ATOL. An ATOL holder would charter the flights and market the seats at any rate he chose either direct to the public or through travel agents. The ABC scheme was to give birth to such new mass travel firms as Jetsave, formed by Reg Pycroft, who had been in independent aviation for many years; Airplan, set up by former BOAC man, George Clay; and our own Golden Lion Travel. The European inclusive tour market was no better. The lemming-like rush for market share at any price had produced a collective loss among UK tour operators of £8.7 million and they still pressed for lower and lower charter rates from the airlines. We were in a dilemma – we lost money if we flew for the tour firms, but we would lose more if we did not, simply because there was no other place to immediately redeploy the aircraft.

By the end of the financial year, 30 September 1972, our slim profit had deteriorated to a loss of £194,000, due almost entirely to the sorry state of the charter markets. We actually lost a contract from one of the major tour operators for refusing to fly at the kind of unacceptable rates the firm was being offered by other airlines, including the BEA subsidiary, Airtours.

On the other hand, scheduled services were beginning to perform well and profitably. I began to promote the strategy that BCAL should begin to move away from the volatile and uneconomic North Atlantic charter market towards the more stable and profitable scheduled service market, although the latter required more skill, more competitive innovation and more investment. In addition, it was inevitable that the new 747s, DC-10s and Tristar aircraft would lead to lower fares, diverting passengers from charter aircraft. Our prime preoccupation, therefore, was the development of the transatlantic scheduled flights. We had earmarked a £3 million investment for the start up. Although we knew the North American market, scheduled services were quite different from the charters we were used to. Ian Ritchie consequently masterminded what I am sure was, and still is, the biggest airline sales blitz ever mounted. In a frenetic period, he and his team of salesmen toured every one of the mainland States visiting more than 5,000 travel agents in the process. This was backed by a public relations and promotional campaign in every major city. Ian called his exercise 'The BCAL Roar-In' and not one stone of potential business was left unturned from New England to California, and from Mississippi to Michigan.

Concentrating on the Atlantic market did not mean, however, that our minds were closed to other opportunities. One notable venture came in the form of a request during 1871 for participation in an hotel development at Gatwick. It had been instigated by Pat Shasby, the charterer from Northern California. He had wanted to develop a relatively modest guest house, of about fifteen rooms, from a farm house up for sale in the vicinity of the airport. Along the way, he brought in the London pub and restaurant firm, Goodhews Ltd. Between them they saw that a much bigger operation was needed for the project to become viable. But an airport hotel needed a ready source of airline business. After a meeting with Shasby and the head of the Goodhew company, Don Goodhew, we agreed on a 25 per cent stake, worth £37,500, in the project. On 18 April 1972, the Copthorne Hotel at Copthorne, a few miles east of Gatwick, opened its doors. Ian Ritchie and John de la Haye represented the BCAL Group on the board.

As we had streamlined the name and image of the airline itself, so my attention was drawn to the need for a streamlining of a cumbersome management structure, necessary for the immediate merger process, but now too awkward. Since the airline was formed, I had carried on the dual role of chairman and managing director. I decided to separate these and appoint a managing director to take care of the running of the airline, while I concentrated on the broad strategic responsibilities of a chairman. Proposals were

Left: Adam Thomson in 1952.

Right: With the Fleet Air Arm. Sub Lt.
Thomson is first left, front row. Below: Outside
Buckingham Palace with Scott, Dawn and
Anthony after being knighted by Queen
Elizabeth. (Financial Times)

Above: The Board meets in 1968. Below: And twelve years later. (Financial Times)

Above: 1961, and the start of Caledonian. (Behr Photography). Right: Delivery of the first Boeing 707 in 1968. (Boeing Company)

HRH Prince Charles visits Gatwick Airport. (Financial Times)

Above: A picnic with President Kenneth Kaunda after a round of golf. (Financial Times Photography)
Below: In chieftain's robes with the Ooni of Ife at his palace in Nigeria (Financial Times).

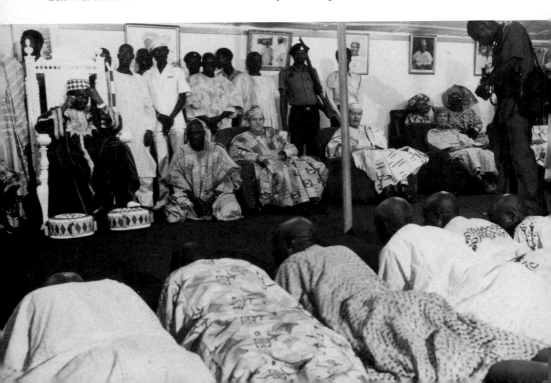

Left: The Queen and Prince Philip are greeted at Gatwick after a royal tour, (Financial Times Photography). Below: The Earl of Mountbatten is given a Caledonian send-off on B-Cal's inaugural flight to New York in 1973). (J C Watts & Partners)

Right: The Rt. Hon. Edward Heath, Sir John Junor and other friends at Hamble, 1979, (Sunday Express). Above: With General Yakubu Gowon, Nigerian Head of State, in 1972.

With Jomo Kenyatta in Kenya in 1972.
(Bob Dewar Publicity, Nairobi)

And with Michael Heseltine at Gatwick
Airport. (J C Watts & Partners)

Below: And with Prince Philip in 1980 at
the official opening of the Caledonian
Airmotive engine plant at Prestwick.
(Financial Times)

Above: In Los Angeles, 1973. B-Cal's inaugural flight is celebrated, indeed lionised. Left: 'I wish they all could be Caledonian . . .' The unforgettable stewardess style. (Financial Times)

Right: Back to basics, 1984,
(Financial Times). Below: In
1971 we were preoccupied
with the BUA takeover.
(J C Watts & Partners)

The glamour and beauty of
flying is exemplified by the
airborne sight of a DC-10-30.
(Financial Times/Glyn
Genin)

Right: 1983: I celebrate my knightood with John de la Haye, Dennis Walter and Frank Hope. Below: It was always our style at B-Cal and Gatwick to keep the whole team informed of developments. (Financial Times)

With George Younger, Secretary of State for Scotland, in 1986. (Financial Times)

Left: Happy days. The Guild of Airpilots and Navigators, (Francis-Thompson Studios Ltd). Below: John Brizendene of McDonnell Douglas snips 'Mac' Mackenzie's tie on the day we received our first DC10. (Financial Times)

We returned from a successful Tokyo launch of the first non-stop service to Japan. (Financial Times/ Glyn Genin)

Our first Jumbo. My little outfit really meant business.
(Financial Times)

Left: Lord King. (Press Association)

Below: Lord King and I announce the deal to merge B-Cal with
BA to an incredulous press on 16 July 1987. (Financial Times/
Alan Harper)

Gatwick Airport in 1965. (Gatwick Airports Ltd)

Gatwick in 1989. (Gatwick Airports Ltd)

put to a meeting of our holding board. The plan was endorsed and Maurice Guinane named as managing director for the airline. His two fellow deputy managing directors, John de la Haye and Frank Hope, remained in those positions but with new responsibilities for policy planning and forward development. Ian Ritchie had proved his expertise was considerable and was named overall marketing director. Alastair Pugh moved from research and development to become production director, responsible for engineering, operations and flight operations.

The change to the top management structure coincided with my own election, in October 1972, to the council of the Institute of Directors. This placed me in the heart of the business establishment through which I felt I could do much to help influence the development of British trade and industry in general as well as represent civil aviation in particular. I was to become much more closely involved in the Institute's affairs in the years to come.

# 54

On 1 April 1973, in the first class cabin of the Boeing 707, Whisky Delta, Lord Mountbatten took an avid interest in the development of the airline as I described the events which had led up to this day of inauguration of transatlantic scheduled services. Mountbatten was, of course, a legend, and I would have been proud to fight under him as a trainee pilot in the Royal Navy – had I been given the chance. In those days of barrack-room daydreaming in Canada, I could never have imagined that, one day, Mountbatten would be my guest on our airline, opening services across the Atlantic.

I very much enjoyed talking with him as Whisky Delta crossed the Scottish coast towards Northern Ireland to head out into the same Atlantic Ocean on which I had voyaged to Canada thirty years earlier. As we talked, champagne was served, followed by a lavish first class lunch. Mountbatten had, in fact, agreed to join our inaugural as it fitted in with his plans for a holiday visit to the Bahamas. But not only had he agreed to travel on the service, he had also assented to speak at the inaugural banquet we had planned at the Plaza Hotel, New York the following day.

In New York, the publicity team had laid on an arrival ceremony at JFK International, where the pipe band would salute us before we were greeted by an array of New York officials. A very different welcoming party awaited us, however. As we flew closer to the North American mainland, one of the stewardesses whispered a message that Roy Hermes would like to see me on the flight deck. Hermes turned in his seat to tell me that weather reports from the USA were not good. Tornadoes were sweeping up the East Coast and threatened to reach the New York area. It looked as though the aircraft might have to divert, but Hermes affirmed that he would continue towards JFK to 'see what it's like'. I told him to pull my other leg as it had bells on it – until he showed me the log confirming tornadoes at New York. If the reported brutal cross winds were not dangerous enough, the lack of adequate visibility certainly would be. As the aircraft bumped and lurched in the worsening weather conditions, Hermes made his announcement to the passengers, strapped firmly in their seats. As uncomfortable as he must have felt, Mountbatten did not complain but calmly read some correspondence. Hermes explained that the weather conditions at New York were well below our normal minimum and he had no alternative but to divert to Boston.

An unscheduled diversion is a complex problem under any circumstances, but with an aircraft load of VIPs and a member of the Royal Family, the situation assumed nightmare proportions. As we made our way north to Boston, the airline's ground staff in New York began frantically to lay on arrangements. Boston was already congested with other diverted flights. We were not previously expected and nothing, so far, had been prepared. Among the welcoming party at JFK was Murray Vidockler, the travel agent and coach tour operator who had been one of the original Caledonian shareholders. He went into action immediately to assist our JFK Airport Manager, Alan Stronach, in arranging bus transport and hotel accommodation in Boston. Given the pressure that the city was under for transport and accommodation for hundreds of diverted passengers, it was something of a miracle that three coaches and 112 rooms at Boston's Hilton Hotel were obtained. We had no handling agent at the Boston Logan airport and those that were there, were busy with their client airlines. The only answer was for the BCAL executives on the flight to take off their jackets and get down to the task of moving baggage from the customs hall on to the coaches, in a tropical downpour, and ensuring that no bag went astray. In the midst of this chaotic scene, I noticed the figure of Lord Mountbatten. He was sitting erect on a public bench in the arrivals hall, his trilby on his head and his raincoat neatly folded over one arm. He was a truly vice-regal figure amid the confused bustle as crowds of airline passengers milled around not knowing what they were supposed to do next. Mountbatten's holiday in the Bahamas was, apparently, a result of medical advice requiring him to slow down his activities. We agreed with his private secretary who had travelled with him that the strain of an unscheduled night stop in Boston, followed by another flight the following morning, would be too much for him, so a chauffeur-driven limousine was arranged to take him directly to New York to the home of the friends he was scheduled to stay with. The rest of us shuttled over to the Hilton which had probably never before seen a Sunday evening quite like this.

Of course, the story of the diverted inaugural was filed back to London by members of the Press corps on board. Our staff back in the UK must have been amazed to wake up to headlines on Monday morning such as: 'Gatwick Jet in Tornado Drama'; and 'Maiden Flight Blown Off Course'. The irony was that the second inaugural flight which departed behind us to operate via Prestwick, had arrived in New York during a lull in the weather and landed normally, on schedule. Some inaugural guests were on board that service, including the actor Jack Hawkins, to whom we had given the ride to New York for an urgent medical consultation. Cancer of the throat had led to the removal of his vocal chords and that famous voice was reduced to an echo of its former self. Hawkins had arranged to see a New York doctor who had developed a mechanical voice box.

The one thing missing from our inaugural banquet was the star attraction, Lord Mountbatten. He was under strict medical instruction to rest for a full twenty-four hours before proceeding to Nassau. The Boston diversion had eroded that rest period, forcing him to forego the banquet. Instead he made a tape recording of his speech which we played to the several hundred guests in the ballroom of the stately Plaza Hotel. The ballroom took on the reverential air of a British family sitting around the radio after Christmas lunch to hear the Queen's speech. Mountbatten's rich and authoritative voice demanded, and received, the attention of even the most hardened New Yorkers.

He started: 'I'm terribly sorry that I can't be with you all tonight to celebrate the inaugural flight of British Caledonian Airways to New York.' He went to explain his medical orders. Mountbatten remembered our in-flight conversation, mentioning that I had started my aviation career in the Royal Navy as a Fleet Air Arm Pilot. He said he was delighted but not surprised to discover that.

'Those of you who travelled out on the flight yesterday will, I am sure, agree that it was an excellent one. And the standard of service throughout the flight, second to none. I particularly liked the mini-kilts of the pretty air hostesses. I felt everyone appeared to receive real personal attention all the way through. Even the bad weather in New York might have been arranged by British Caledonian to demonstrate the wonderful emergency arrangements they could make at a moment's notice to take care of their passengers.'

To the delight of the audience, Mountbatten recalled his first flight at the age of six when he was watching the departure of a Parseval airship and unexpectedly was picked up by the scruff of his neck to be thrown into the gondola to act as ballast. He concluded: "If the inaugural flight yesterday was a foretaste of British Caledonian's standards, then I have no doubt they're on to a winner. And I wish them all good luck in their new venture." The dinner, as well as the rest of the meetings, receptions and functions during the week, was very effective indeed.

From New York I took a small team to Los Angeles to link up for the inaugural celebrations of the next part of the new venture – the simultaneous opening of the Los Angeles route. Guests on this flight included members of the Institute of Travel Managers, those people, usually former travel agents, who run the travel departments of the major companies. The ITM, as it is known, forms a powerful lobby in the industry and is responsible for placing the vast majority of business travel bookings.

This time the flight did arrive at the right place at the right time. The welcome was laid on once again by the itinerant pipe band with an addition: a live lion by the name of Major. The lion had been press-ganged into service by a publicist we had hired in the USA, Al Kaplan. Kaplan is a typical New Yorker with a fast and irreverent wit born simply out of trying to get along and make things work in that hard-nosed city. He could draw crazy ideas out of the air and, faced with competing for publicity in Hollywood, he dreamed up the idea of getting a live lion to be on the tarmac of Los Angeles International Airport to meet the BCAL lion on the tail of the aircraft. From somewhere, Kaplan found a man who owned a fully-grown lion and who was prepared to let us have the animal on loan for the price of a ticket to East Africa, where he could view more lions to his heart's content. That bit, Kaplan admitted later, was easy. The hard part was to persuade the airport authorities to allow the lion on to the tarmac. The story of a lion on the loose at a major airport equalled anything that Hollywood could have dreamed up and there was total disbelief as Kaplan explained to assembled customs, immigration and security officials that he was really serious and that there would be no problem. He allayed their fears by swearing that the lion would be drugged.

Sure enough, as the aircraft taxied in, there on the tarmac, sitting on top of a specially-made plinth, was Major the lion and from somewhere appeared a scantily clad beauty queen. In a ceremony by the aircraft, I was required to stand alongisde the lion which looked as if, any minute, it might casually turn round and chew off one of my arms. Sheriff Peter Pitchess of Los Angeles County was there too, to welcome the new service and made me an honorary deputy sheriff. Pitchess had fewer qualms about the lion than I did, as he patted the beast's mane while posing for photographs.

The lion earned his keep that week, as the story and pictures made most of the Los Angeles area newspapers and TV news bulletins. As our pipe band went into a full programme of appearances in and around the city, the Mayor, Sam Yorty, declared the period of the inaugural visit 'British Caledonian Week' and was our guest of honour at the special banquet in the Beverly Hilton Hotel.

The launch of the transatlantic services and the marketing programmes which backed them up had been immensely successful. By this time we had switched our advertising account to Garland Compton, though it was later to be taken over by the brothers Charles and Maurice Saatchi. In the USA we contracted the agency's North American counterpart, Cadwell Compton, led by a formidable Madison Avenue lady by the name of Frankie Cadwell. The underlying theme used by Garland Compton in the UK was to pick up the real momentum of the growing airline and translate that into a slogan: 'Let's Go British Caledonian'. A driving TV commercial jingle exhorted viewers: 'Let's Go, Let's Go, Let's Go British Caledonian; Let's Go British Caledonian!'

For the transatlantic launch, the copywriters, creative directors and our own publicity people created a new country, Nyandla – New York and Los Angeles. One commercial featured the late Roy Kinnear demanding a ticket to Nyandla from a confused travel agent. Inevitably the story line explained through the characters that New York and Los Angeles formed the latest BCAL destinations.

In the USA, Frankie Cadwell and her team in close co-operation with John de la Haye came up with a campaign based on the slogan 'The Airline Other Airlines Hate'. The line was that because we were dedicated to personal service and looked after passengers well, with better in-flight service, better schedules, better service on the ground, the other carriers could not compete and, therefore, 'hated' us. The campaign, costing more than £400,000, worked well and ended up being voted one of the year's 'Top Ten' in the New York trade journal, *Advertising Age*.

But that tornado into which we had flown on the inaugural service to New York was to prove to be a portent of commercial stormy weather to follow. Overcapacity on the North Atlantic with the increasing introduction of Boeing 747 aircraft led to serious undercutting in the market place, depressing the rate of return below the cost of providing the product. At the same time, a crisis in the supply and pricing of oil began to develop. It had its foundations back in 1970, at an OPEC meeting in Caracas, Venezuela. In short, the oil producing countries had taken it into their own hands to constrain the supply of oil and therefore drive prices up to reap bigger profits. There was little immediate reaction from the oil-consuming countries and industries, including air transport. The problem was compounded in the course of 1973 when the USA, unable to meet the demand for fuel from its domestic petro-chemical industry, became an importer of foreign oil. The result was that the going rate for internationally-traded oil increased by between 300-400 per cent over a three-year period.

In the UK, the first full commercial effect of the merger of BOAC and BEA, under the British Airways Board, was seen in the market place. This was the formation of a consolidated sales and marketing operation under the title, British Airways Travel Division. Its acronym was BATL, pronounced 'battle'.

In turn, we had opened a new battle front in the bid for further route expansion. This time it was in the hearing room of the new Civil Aviation Authority. While we were planning and implementing the new Atlantic routes, Maurice Guinane had led a team on the development of a set of what became known as

285

'cannonball' routes, a network of long-range operations to three continents.

The applications covered four routes: London–Bahrain–Singapore; London–Boston–Atlanta–Houston; London–Toronto–Vancouver; and London–Seychelles–Perth–Sydney. Needless to say, the wrath of BOAC descended on us once more with formal objections and a counter bid from them to return their old licences to Lagos, Kano and Accra. BOAC claimed in the hearing, which carried on throughout the month of July 1973, that it stood to lose almost £213 million in revenue if the BCAL bid was granted. This would virtually double the revenue we had projected for 1975. David Beety, who handled the hearing, told the CAA that this was a gross overestimation and that the true effect on BOAC would be about 2.5 per cent in retrenchment. The plan was that the Singapore route would begin in January 1974, followed by the Canadian services in April, Australian flights in November and the new USA routes in 1975.

The cannonball applications were a manifestation of our developing policy to move away from the uneconomic charter market and develop scheduled services. The dilemma was where to look for opportunity, as I told the CAA on the last day of the hearing. 'If we move in one direction, we run into British Airways BEA; in the other direction, we run into British Airways BOAC; if we walk straight ahead, we run slap into both.'

I asked the members of the authority whether the basic second force policy was to be changed or nullified. 'Our re-examination today, is British civil aviation to be strengthened or weakened by our now very real presence in the industry? Or does new thinking bow to the implacable hostility of British Airways, arguing from an entrenched position.'

As we waited for the CAA decision on the cannonball case, we emphasized our determination to achieve scheduled service expansion with further applications, this time for the routes to Brussels, Frankfurt and Algiers. The inevitable objections came from BEA to the two European applications. Algiers was left alone as the state carrier did hold a licence but was not operating the route.

The CAA Chairman, by now elevated to the Peerage as Lord Boyd-Carpenter, called a private meeting with myself, Maurice

Guinane and Trevor Boud. Over two-and-a-quarter hours we faced Lord B-C, as we labelled him, and eleven of his officials. Their purpose was to probe BCAL's financial situation before making up their minds on the licensing issue. Their main concern was with our debt-equity ratio. It stood at about 1:1.2 and we regarded that as reasonable. In any event it met the requirements of the banks. Lord B-C was particularly concerned about the increase in fuel prices and he noted that the free, or 'spot' market price in Rotterdam had increased by 50 per cent. After discussions which ranged across the new Atlantic services, the proposed cannonball routes, our hotel interests and the state of Blue Cars, Lord B-C wanted reassurance from our bankers as to the extent of financial support they would provide if, as he put it, 'things are going to go wrong'.

I replied, 'We can get letters, sure. Now I don't think they are exactly useless, but they won't say that the overdraft will go on for two years.'

'Wouldn't they give you one year?' asked Lord B-C.

'The banks are well covered,' interjected Trevor Boud.

'Will you get letters from them?' Lord B-C demanded.

'Yes,' I replied.

The letters from the banks were duly presented to the CAA and on 21 August the authority announced that it had awarded us licences to Boston-Atlanta, Houston, Bahrain and Singapore; and to Toronto. Vancouver was refused and so was Australia, on the basis that the Australian government had indicated its refusal to allow a second British carrier.

In rejecting BOAC's objections and also its bid to duplicate the West African trunk network, the CAA said that it did not accept BOAC's estimate of their potential losses of revenue. 'Unless some chances of this kind are taken, British civil aviation will become static and lose the taste and capacity for adventurous expansion,' the CAA said.

In a Press statement, I said: 'Until today, we have been only an embryo of the second force that was envisaged. Now we are moving towards establishing ourselves to give the country the full benefit of having a viable and efficient private enterprise airline.'

287

# 55

In reality, the bright skies of hope and confidence in the future under which British Caledonian was formed and nurtured, were becoming darkened by the grey clouds of economic depression.

The new transatlantic routes operated well in their first summer, achieving good loads of tourist traffic in the peak months. Inevitably, rates had to be discounted for the major US tour wholesalers who found themselves in a buyer's market, with the extra capacity flooding on to the North Atlantic routes.

The situation for the industry was not at all a happy one. Costs were higher than revenues, yet still airlines went on to put more seats on more routes, adding to the glut. Over a three-year period, airline capacity had grown by 50 per cent, while traffic had increased by only 40 per cent. These topsy-turvy economics led me to come to the firm conviction that if the airlines were not going to look after themselves, then the regulators should do so. I believed that there should be capacity restraints imposed and also that pricing – minimum fares and charter rates – should be established and enforced.

Along with a range of eminent airline leaders, I flew to Auckland, New Zealand, in November 1973 to attend a special meeting of the International Air Transport Association and put my views forward in a special paper. The overriding need, I told my colleagues, was for stability; capacity therefore must be related to demand and price to cost. We should, of course, recognize legitimate consumer needs, but this should not mean acceptance of a 'seats at any price' philosophy. I was backed up by the intelligent and articulate chairman of Canadian Pacific Airlines, Ian Sinclair. He used Lewis Carroll's words from *Alice Through the Looking Glass*, to summarize the plight of air transport: 'A slow sort of country . . . it takes all the running you can do to keep in the same place. If you want to get somewhere else, you must run at least twice as fast as that.'

For British Caledonian, events were conspiring not just to keep us running on the spot, but to drag us backwards. The whole of Britain was flying headlong into the infamous Winter of Discontent precipitated by the oil crisis and confrontation between Edward Heath's government and the miners. At Gatwick, we had at least the comfort of being able to work a full week, with lighted offices, as the rest of the country, in a crisis measure to conserve fuel, suffered the three-day week, unlit and unheated homes, unlit streets and petrol rationing. Air transport was considered an essential strategic service and benefited accordingly. The constraints on energy led to sparse heating arrangements. But staff carried on working, more often than not with overcoats on.

In addition to all our other problems in 1973, John de la Haye was taken seriously ill and spent twelve months in and out of hospital. John tried repeatedly to return to full time work but although he continued to use his experience and ability to the great benefit of the group, he was never again able to take a front-line role in the airline.

John resigned from the airline board in 1974 and from the group holding board in August 1975, but I'm glad to say was able to accept my invitation to become a part-time consultant advising Ian Ritchie and myself on external affairs. He continued to represent the group on the board of Copthorne Hotel.

For 1973, the combination of our decision to reduce activities in the uneconomic charter markets, increasing costs and the investment in new routes, led to a loss of £1.5 million on air transport activities. The impact of the fuel crisis came in the form of higher costs and in rationing. Michael Heseltine, Minister for Aerospace and Shipping, had imposed fuel allocations and we were required to operate within the limit of the fuel supplied. It meant the cancelling of many flights with poor loads which did not justify using valuable fuel and the consolidation of two flights into one in order to economize. Things were not to get any better.

1974, the year we were stumbling into through the darkness of economic recession, came to be described by the Civil Aviation Authority as 'the worst year in living memory – both for civil aviation and air travel industries'.

Inflation in most of the major markets had sent prices soaring by up to 25 per cent, and world trade was depressed. The effect of the fuel price crisis was estimated to be costing Britain an additional £2,500 million. For British Caledonian, the price of aviation fuel more than doubled from 15 US cents a gallon, to more than 30 US cents. It meant an additional fuel bill of £11 million. As a proportion of total costs, fuel had increased from 12 per cent to around 25 per cent. Holiday travel, both in Europe and across the Atlantic, was hit particularly badly, as people simply could not afford the cost of their holiday trips.

As well as managing the airline on a day-to-day, almost hand-to-mouth, basis, we were concerned with the long-term future. Although we had the additional new cannonball routes in our pockets, they would be immensely expensive to introduce and would not give a profitable return for several years. Against the economic background, British Caledonian remained vulnerable. The charter business was falling away and the scheduled network was too small to withstand being bowled over by the harsh winds of recession.

Maurice Guinane and Alastair Pugh met the CAA regularly, at least once a month. The authority had an obligation to maintain a financial monitor on the development of the second force and, in turn, we required constant consultation with the regulators of our industry. In the course of our own discussions and these meetings with the CAA, we steadily developed a strategy for what we termed 'route rationalization' between British Caledonian and British Airways – BOAC and BEA were now fully consolidated. Under the existing scheme of things, with tightly-controlled inter-national agreements designed to protect national airlines, there was sparse opportunity for major route development. Transfers of more routes from British Airways was unthinkable and so we came to the conclusion that the most effective solution, in the interests of both airlines and the stability of British civil aviation, would be to rationalize our respective intercontinental route structures so that we would not compete head to head with each other on individual routes. We would have our routes on which British Caledonian was the UK flag airline, and British Airways would have theirs.

The CAA, primarily Ray Colegate, saw the sense in this plan and encouraged a series of quiet and confidential discussions between the two airlines, led from our side by Alastair Pugh.

The early part of the year heaved us, once again, into political turmoil. After the disastrous winter, Edward Heath faced a General Election in March which his government had every likelihood of losing. There had been threats from the Labour side of Parliament that, if they gained power, steps could be taken to return to British Airways the routes transferred to BCAL by the Conservatives, or our airline could be fully nationalized and incorporated into the state machine.

Five of us – myself, Maurice Guinane, John de la Haye, Ray Dobson and Hugh Brilliant – sat around the board room table to assess the position. The current make-up of the House of Commons meant that it was likely that whoever won the election would operate as a minority government. In turn that meant that at sometime in the future, we estimated about a year, the administration in power would seek to strengthen its position by going to the country once again.

In the event of a Labour minority government, we agreed that our priority should be the protection of the routes transferred in 1971. Possibilities for route rationalization would, we determined, depend on discussions with various official bodies and political groups.

The return of a Conservative minority government would mean that the route transfers would not be called into question. Our priority would be to continue the rationalization discussions already under way and we would consider further licensing applications.

Plans were laid out for the British Caledonian political lobby to step up its activities. The campaign was outlined for the short-term – the period up to the Queen's Speech; medium term – the period after the Queen's Speech; and long-term – the period before another election. I took on the assignment to contact Sir Peter Thornton, Permanent Secretary at the Department of Trade, and Lord Boyd-Carpenter at the CAA. Guinane would tackle the next most senior officials in both organizations. For the CAA, this meant Ray Colegate, whom we had first known in the sixties at the old Board of Trade. Hugh Brilliant would take on the lobbying of the Liberals; David Steel, its aviation spokesman, and Lord Avebury, the elevated Eric Lubbock. We extended the network of lobbying to Scotland, in particular Winnie Ewing, the first Scottish Nationalist MP. We would bring in the Confederation of British Industries, Chambers of Commerce and the Unions. The long term aims were simply survival, if we faced a Labour government; and route rationalization, if Conservative.

We felt particularly vulnerable on the newly-licensed cannonball routes. There are two important regulatory stages to the implementation of a new air route. The gaining of the licence to operate is just the first step and only half of the story. Once the licence has been issued, it remains the perrogative of the responsible Ministry, at that time the Department of Trade, to 'designate' the airline with the respective foreign government as an authorized British flag carrier under the terms of the bilateral air services agreement. Only after designation has taken place and been accepted by the foreign authorities can air services begin.

Our fears were that, under pressure from the state corporation, a new Labour Government might deny us the designation of the clutch of important new routes, so halting BCAL's development. If we could persuade the existing Conservative administration to make those designations before the election, the new routes would be safe. Once enshrined within the terms of the international agreements, it would be extremely difficult for rights to be withdrawn. I therefore sought an urgent meeting with Michael Heseltine. Sadly, he took no action, with the result that our hard-won new routes sure enough ended up in the regulatory wilderness of non-designation.

Several years later, Heseltine confided that, at the time, he was disposed to effect the designations, but that his civil servants had persuaded him otherwise, on the hunch that BCAL was unstable financially and could face collapse.

The second Wilson Government swept in in March 1974 and in place of Michael Heseltine, the slim and lanquid Peter Shore took over as Secretary of State for Trade to govern our affairs. My first task was to write to Shore, requesting a meeting. The second political duty was to write to Edward Heath to acknowledge his Government's work in enabling the second force to come about.

Our concern was that the new Labour administration would make policy moves on the civil aviation issue before we had a chance to get the rationalization strategy in place. However, in his first press conference, the new Secretary of State told journalists pressing for his reaction to the Conservatives' route transfers that, 'I would not wish to pretend that I have yet been able to give this whole question the serious attention it deserves.'

That indicated that we were safe from an immediate move, but Shore nevertheless did not waste time. On 2 April his Parliamentary Under Secretary of State, Stanley Clinton-Davis, and two officials called a meeting with Lord Boyd-Carpenter, his deputy Robin Goodison, and Ray Colegate. The route rationalization plan had come to be known between us and the CAA by the cryptic label 'Big R'. An initial paper on the subject had been given to Clinton-Davis by Boyd-Carpenter. A second paper was placed on the table for discussion. The original rationalization plan had, in the course of refinement, gained the added element of a possible part ownership in British Caledonian by British Airways. An outline of the drift of the meeting was confidentially reported back to Maurice Guinane. Clinton-Davis' political dilemma had been made obvious. To accede to Labour demands for a return of transferred routes would have serious adverse effects on the second force which the same party had conceived. He wanted the time of the forthcoming Easter holiday to read the papers before him. Those in the meeting obtained the impression that Clinton-Davis would recommend to Peter Shore either to take on the 'Big R' strategy to solve the situation, or to undertake a further wholesale review of civil aviation.

Yet again, on 10 April, the instruction to the cab driver at Victoria Station was to take myself, Guinane and Pugh to the nondescript office block which houses the Department of Trade at No 1 Victoria Street. Once again, we sat in the anteroom to the Secretary of State's office before being called in. I took immediately to Shore. He displayed a highly analytical mind yet had the warmth and ordinariness that must have come from his Liverpool background and his current constituency of Stepney and Poplar, in the working class East End of London. Although approaching fifty, he had a youthful and athletic look about him, accentuated by a flop of hair which, every so often, he would push back from his face. In addition to a file of papers about the politics and commerce of British civil aviation in general and the second force in particular, I had prepared a verbal brief. I sat before him and read my speech ending with a paragraph which I hoped would underpin the recommendation we believed Clinton-Davis had put to the Secretary of State.

'We believe that the best course for the British airline industry is to continue with the Edwards' Committee second force concept, as well as the massive state airline. But we believe improvements could be made that would result in a better position for both airlines than that which exists at the moment. Ideas have already been floated as to how this may be achieved and, while the all-important details have to be worked out, some of these would retain the many advantages that Edwards saw in the creation of a second force airline and the comments on its relationship with British Airways. We think that some of these ideas which have come from those with intimate contact with the industry, should be recommended to you for further investigation.'

Operationally, the ill winds of the winter of 1973/74 followed us into the spring and summer. Reductions in traffic and the decision to cut down on charter activities reduced the long-haul fleet by two Boeing 707s, to a total fleet of eight. Similarly, the short-haul 1-11 complement was cut by two aircraft, placed out on overseas leases, to provide a total of twelve aircraft.

To shore up equity, Trevor Boud masterminded a share rights issue to raise £3 million and arranged loans against leasehold property at Gatwick to provide an additional £4 million in cash.

The European inclusive tour industry, already weakened by the price wars was, by now, beginning to reel under the economic squeeze. The downturn in the market was further exacerbated by increasing fuel costs. Holidaymakers who had booked or were planning to book inclusive tours were now being pressed for fuel surcharges as the airlines passed on the extra costs to the tour operators who, in turn, passed on the charges to the customers.

Something had to happen – and in February 1974 it did, with the collapse of Horizon Holidays, one of the longest-established and most respected names in the travel business. Founded and run by two characters, Vladimir Raitz and Len Koven, Horizon succumbed to the squeeze and announced its intentions to cease operations and go into liquidation. British Caledonian was one of Horizon's main charter operators and in a year which was bad enough in any event, the loss of this business – amounting to £1 million in revenue which could not be quickly replaced –

was a body blow. In fact, the Horizon collapse left us with three 1-11s idle.

No doubt the scene of Horizon spreadeagled on the financial floor brought glee to the Court Line company, whose tour operator, Clarksons, had, to my mind, precipitated the vicious rates war. Certainly, Court Line moved quickly to acquire the remnants of Horizon and its forward business.

Our minds were now firmly on survival as the future for British Caledonian looked very shaky indeed. The new North Atlantic services, which had begun to look promising, began to lose more than had been budgeted for as traffic declined dramatically in the summer. The result for IATA carriers on North Atlantic services was a collective loss of US$300 million in 1974. We were not alone with the problems, but we neither had the strength of the big US airlines or the subsidized support of the state-owned carriers of Europe and elsewhere. The effect on BCAL was, therefore, more pronounced.

We had been careful with planning and budgeting and, indeed, had met or improved on the revenue budgets until June. It was during the peak summer months, when revenues were traditionally at their highest, that the serious shortfall came about.

It was not an auspicious time to open a new route, but we did so in June with the introduction of the recently-licensed Gatwick-Brussels service. The African routes were, by contrast, proceeding reasonably well. I made visits to Nigeria and Kenya to help consolidate our position in these markets, having talks with the respective heads of state, President Yakubu Gowon of Nigeria and President Jomo Kenyatta of Kenya.

Towards the end of June I made the acquaintance of another African Head of State, President Sir Dawda Jawara of the Gambia and began a friendship which persists to this day. Sir Dawda was invited to pay a state visit to the UK and as head of the flag airline serving his tiny country on the West Coast of Africa, Dawn and I were invited to official banquets with The Queen at Buckingham Palace and with the Prime Minister at 10 Downing Street.

The glitter of these occasions was, however, in stark contrast to the mood at Gatwick. Whenever I was congratulated on the achievements of the airline, I outwardly accepted the compliment with pleasure, but inwardly I thought of the awesome prospect of

295

collapse. The strain had already begun to tell in the board room. Frank Hope had fought long and hard against our scheduled service development policies. Unable to rationalize his feelings with the path the airline had been taking, Frank resigned, to my great sadness, in December 1973.

# 56

During that fateful summer, the plans and strategies for expansion were put away, as desks and minds were cleared to concentrate on one task – survival. The overriding preoccupation was on the revenue we could earn next week and next month. Never mind, for the moment, the next five years.

Sales staff were shaken away from the tasks of putting together future plans and sent out on the road. Ian Ritchie's blunt, but descriptive, order to them was, 'Get out and shake the trees.' Ritchie, in fact, set up a sales programme for the UK to emulate his famous 'Roar-In' in the USA. He and his team came up with a plan for a hard-selling travelling roadshow covering every major area in Britain. We called it 'Expo '74' and took it to a national audience of about 1,500 travel agents.

In the third-floor executive suite at Gatwick, the mood was sombre. Meetings among myself and the hard core of six or seven directors continued until late in the evenings. We were developing a plan labelled 'S' for survival. At a BCAL board meeting we discussed the crisis we were facing. Passenger and cargo revenues were down – fuel and other costs were rising. The whole industry was suffering and we were no exception. My position was to take a 'zero base', take our best routes first and progress to the point where any additional operations were endangering the objective of survival. This exercise was followed through and resulted in our redundancy plan.

I had become particularly close to two of our main board members. One was Paul Hildesley, tall and distinguished, who represented the ICFC investment. The other was a highly-regarded accountant, Stuart Young, who sat on our board on behalf of GUS. Young was an elegant person who fitted the description of 'dapper'.

297

He came from a hard-working Jewish family which had encouraged him and his brother, David, to work for the rich prizes of life. Stuart went on to become chairman of the board of governors of the BBC, before his untimely death. David became better known as Lord Young of Graffham, Margaret Thatcher's Secretary of State for Trade and Industry.

I consulted informally with Stuart, seeking his views on the 'S' plan and the future for BCAL. His wise advice, obviously in the interests of the investments represented, confirmed my own feelings.

Hildesley's recommendation was that a staff and organization review, with the aim of cutting costs, should be carried out objectively, by an outside consultancy. He introduced me to a colleague, Gerry Richardson, head of ICFC's management services organization, ICFC-NUMAS. Richardson, a genial, scholarly man, and his team began the work of auditing the BCAL management and workforce in June. Maurice Guinane and Alastair Pugh concentrated on an audit of routes and performance. The yardstick of measurement used was the level of contribution to profit, or otherwise, per flying hour, by aircraft type. The picture emerged in the form of a league table based on the ratio mix of revenue to expenditure on each of the routes. In this, only eight routes, headed by West Africa and including South America, remained profitable in the worsening economic climate.

The one, immediate way out of the need to invoke the 'S' plan was the route rationalization strategy between BCAL and British Airways. Talks with the state airline had been going on since April and, we felt, were progressing steadily. The discussions were held under agreed terms of reference which called for the development of a stable relationship between the two airlines. Initially drafted by Stephen Wheatcroft, British Airways' Deputy Managing Director, the reference document went so far as to include studies on technical co-operation between the two airlines in areas such as aircraft overhaul, communications, computer services, traffic handling, interline arrangements and sales representation.

So far as the routes themselves were concerned, we had come to the point where BCAL would relinquish, in favour of British Airways, the services to New York, Los Angeles, Tunis, Gibraltar, Malaga, Ibiza, Palma, Glasgow, Belfast; routes from Glasgow to

Amsterdam and Southampton; and the so far unused licence for Toronto. In exchange, we would acquire all British rights into Central Africa and take over the British Airways routes to Miami and Mexico. We would be secure in our existing areas, notably West Africa and South America, and British Airways would agree to keep their US activities north of the Mason/Dixon line, leaving us clear to develop the new services to Houston and Atlanta and to seek other opportunities, as they came along, in the southern States.

This route rationalization plan, relinquishing routes which were unprofitable for BCAL, but which had distinct benefits to British Airways on one hand, and the addition of established routes which fitted into our existing network on the other, would make a substantial difference. Above all, it would mean that the existing structure of workforce and aircraft could be justified.

In the midst of these negotiations with British Airways, the industry was rocked with the news of the collapse of the Court Line empire in August, the peak holiday month. The holiday group which included Court Line, the airline, Clarksons Holidays and the recently-acquired Horizon, floundered spectacularly as its costs and debts outweighed its income and the banks decided they would take no more. Warnings about the imprudence of Court Line's policies of market share at any price had been coming hard and fast from the CAA and other observers, including myself. They went unheeded and the result was tragically inevitable. To those warnings, Clarksons had earlier responded, 'If you can't stand the heat, stay out of the kitchen.' With our cutting back on uneconomic charter flights, we had, indeed, kept out of the kitchen. Now it was not only hot, it was on fire!

Court Line left thousands of passengers stranded in Mediterranean resort areas. In an airlift organized by the club of holiday firms known as the Tour Operators' Study Group, BCAL alone carried home nearly 2,000 holidaymakers, at no charge to them, in the first few days after the crash. Our tour operating subsidiary, Blue Sky, doubled its reservations staff at its headquarters in East Grinstead, to the east of Gatwick, and set about organizing an extra 7,000 Mediterranean holidays to go on to the market to fill the vacuum left by Court Line. Perversely, for the airline, it meant a boost to revenues of £500,000

299

as we picked up Court Line's business with a number of tour operators.

The airline received a further windfall the following month as official carrier for the British Industrial Exhibition in Sao Paulo, a major shop window for Britain's businessmen and their freight to the exhibition totalled £100,000. Princess Alexandra and Angus Ogilvy travelled down to Brazil to perform the official opening of the show. The next most senior British visitor was none other than Peter Shore. I assigned Ray Dobson to travel with him to take every political advantage of having the Secretary of State for Trade in our hands.

But these events were mere sideshows to the action taking place on the centre stage of our business. Route rationalization was now the only way out of our own financial dilemma if the airline was to remain intact. At a board meeting on 6 September I proposed – and it was agreed – that we should waste no further time but go to the Government with the plan. We wanted two key agreements from Peter Shore – first that the route rationalization plan was acceptable to the Government, and second that to avoid further swinging losses during the commercially sterile period of implementation, the Government would provide stand-by finance, in the form of guarantees to be used as necessary.

At his office in Kingsway, I told Lord Boyd-Carpenter of our decision to bite the bullet with the Government on the route rationalization issue. We talked over the pros and cons and, against the background of our situation, Lord B-C agreed that we had no real alternative but to put the scheme to the Secretary of State.

On 10 September 1974 I wrote to Peter Shore. I told him that our discussions with British Airways had progressed to a point where certain preferences had been indicated and that talks were continuing. But, I said, in the circumstances, we believed that the proper course was to take the initiative, giving consideration to British Airways' preferences for BCAL routes in a rationalised route structure. I explained that, initially, a disadvantageous revenue imbalance would occur and that was why government financial guarantees were necessary.

My letter concluded: 'If I may be quite blunt on this issue, there is need for an urgent decision on these proposals, for otherwise we are left with little alternative but to introduce from next month the modified operational programme which we regard as essential to our survival, notwithstanding the large measure of redundancy which will inevitably result.'

In addition to Lord Boyd-Carpenter, I had also briefed our union leaders on the problems. We had always been frank with union representatives whose members depended on a successful BCAL for their livelihood. We would certainly require their co-operation to plan and effect redundancies, but they might also press Peter Shore to act on the route rationalisation plan if that meant saving jobs.

Sir Peter Thornton, Shore's Permanent Secretary, called me to a meeting with the Secretary of State immediately on receipt of my letter. Two days after sending the correspondence, I was again sitting with Shore at No. 1, Victoria Street. He listened intently as I redrew the scene already outlined in my letter, but made no significant comment, other than a wish to be kept advised of talks with British Airways.

Under cover of an IATA meeting, those talks resumed in Montreal on 18 September but did little more than keep the route rationalization ball rolling. They were scheduled to continue in London a week later. Despite the months of talks and rearrangement of the possible permutations of route exchanges, the British Airways side deflated any optimism we had at the prospect of pulling off the deal, with their lethargic attitude. They rejected outright the first proposal placed on the table and were lukewarm about a second, more advantageous plan. In order to extract a fast decision from the state airline, we had further eroded our network by offering to withdraw from East and Central Africa, but even this carrot failed to move the British Airways donkey any further along the road to a solution. Whether or not the Department of Trade had briefed British Airways on the full extent of the BCAL plight and the airline was simply holding out to see if we went under, I do not know. It remains, however, a lingering suspicion.

Activity at Gatwick became frenetic. With no route rationalization and no government financial guarantees, we had no option but to implement the 'S' plan. Secrecy was crucial both within the airline and certainly within the market place. Any hint of major cut-backs, with the implication of financial instability, could cause a squeeze with creditors, particularly the oil companies, withdrawing credit and the travel industry holding off bookings.

301

Only the directors and a small team of specialist managers knew of the plan. In early October, I wrote to Peter Shore once more to tell him that since our last meeting, little progress had been made on the route rationalization strategy. We had timed the implementation of the 'S' plan for 1 November, the beginning of the airline winter season. Staff and union representatives would have to be told a few weeks earlier.

This was my last stand and I pressed Shore hard with every argument I could muster. I warned that unless route rationalization was achieved, the problems of internecine conflict between British scheduled airlines would only be perpetuated. The time to act was now. I threatened that, in a few weeks' time, when staff and union officials were advised of the need for reduced operations, I should have to tell them every alternative avenue had been explored.

'I shall have to advise them that route rationalisation talks have failed and I have no doubt whatsoever that I shall be asked to approach the Government for assistance. I shall have to say very firmly that the request has already been made and that the Government felt unable to assist. I would be surprised if the Government was not approached by the Unions direct,' I wrote.

I offered three possible solutions: implementation of the 'S' plan; that Government or CAA or both took on the task of achieving a fair route rationalization plan, with some form of financial assistance; or that the Government made a straightforward financial investment in the second force. I wound the letter up: 'I am deeply concerned for those staff, including colleagues and friends throughout the organization who will be made redundant in a few weeks' time. Accordingly, in my approach to you, I must ensure that I have left no stone unturned that may avoid this situation coming about. Further, if you confirm that you are unable to assist, then in the interests of the remaining staff, your answer on this point has to be crystal clear.'

# 57

At the end of 1974 we were facing a loss on airline operations of £4.3 million, as the crash in the inclusive tour market, decline on the Atlantic, spiralling fuel costs and rampant inflation bit deeply into our profit and loss account.

Some remedies had been taken, primarily in the form of the setting of minimum wholesale and retail prices for the CAA's new Advance Booking Charters on transatlantic routes for the summer of 1975. By shoring up the charter market which had declined by 20 per cent, the scheduled carriers would have an economic base-line for the setting of their fares. Talks between airlines, under the auspices of IATA, eventually led to a new kind of low fare, the Advance Purchase Excursion (APEX), being formulated and introduced. The aim was to act on straightforward commonsense by putting in place the kind of fare which the public was demanding, so avoiding uncontrollable illegal discounting.

But some of the problems were worsening. In the vicious economic circle of the times, the oil-producing members of OPEC, meeting in Vienna in mid-September, decided that to meet inflation in industrialized countries, they would increase the cost of crude oil by 3.5 per cent. Only Saudi Arabia abstained from this course. The OPEC members stipulated, however, that the increase should be absorbed by the royalties and taxes levied by Governments on the oil companies and not passed on to the consumer. On behalf of the air transport industry, the Swedish Director General of IATA, Knut Hammarskjold, telexed each of the Transport Ministers in the principal oil-consuming countries, urging them to ensure that increases were not passed on to airlines.

The oil companies themselves took a different view and announced publicly that the 3.5 per cent increase would be passed on to consumers. I wrote yet again to Peter Shore asking for his intervention in this gloomy situation.

But the BCAL die was cast. No positive word from either Shore or British Airways on route rationalization led to a unanimous Board decision to invoke the 'S' plan. The ICFC-NUMAS work by Gerry Richardson and his team had produced a more streamlined organization involving the redundancy of more than 800 people, including a number of directors. The study had begun as a long-term strategy; it was now to be realized as an expediency.

Operational cutbacks had been arrived at by taking the organization down to zero and gradually building up a structure of the most profitable routes, to the point where we broke even with the minimum cut in people. 'A phoenix rising from the ashes,' Alastair Pugh said sardonically. As we had originally planned, the cutbacks would be enforced from 1 November; 17 October was set as the date for announcement.

It was sad and tiring work to pare away the routes and aircraft we had fought so hard to acquire. Most of all, my thoughts turned to the people we would have to send away through the airport security gates. It was inevitable that I would feel especially sad about those directors – close friends, in fact – who would suffer the 'S' plan axe. Among them were Maurice Guinane and Hugh Brilliant. Also leaving were sales director Ted Bates and customer services director Leonard Crosbie. The agonizing thing was that none of them knew of their impending redundancy and would not be informed until the day before the public announcement.

Support from the members of our holding board at this difficult and trying time was immense. Ironically this main board had recently been strengthened with the appointments on a non-executive basis of two eminent men. The first was Sir Iain Stewart, the Scottish industrialist, whom I had first encountered as a member of the board of our shareholder, Lyle Shipping. He had, at first, been against Lyle's investment in BCAL, believing that the shipping firm had its own problems to deal with, without chancing the aviation industry. Iain was also a Board member of BEA but resigned in protest at the move to merge the airline with BOAC. I sought him out, through Marshall Gibson in Scotland, with the invitation to join our board. His experience, I felt, would be invaluable to us. The second was one of the most famous and respected names in civil aviation, Sir Peter Masefield. A former aviation attaché with the British Embassy in Washington, Peter Masefield had been a chief executive of BEA and was the first chairman of the British Airports Authority. He had willingly accepted the invitation to join our board and we were delighted to catch this prize.

A key part of the 'S' plan was that the airline should do away with the structure of a separate full time chairman and a managing director. My own plan was to take on the role of managing director, stepping down as chairman in favour of either Stewart or Masefield. I felt that I could not carry these two responsibilities effectively. After I confided this plan to Iain Stewart and Peter Masefield, they would hear none of it. They both saw the strategic danger of me being perceived as having been demoted and the effect this would have on both shareholders and the market place. The compromise turned out to be simple. I would remain as chairman and managing director, with Stewart becoming deputy chairman to take on some of the work load.

Work on the route cutbacks went ahead with increased pace. The first to go would be the new services to New York and Los Angeles. After ten years of fighting for the Atlantic and just eighteen months of operation, their loss was a tragedy for the airline. Also to be discontinued were services linking Gatwick with Belfast, Le Touquet, Gibraltar, Palma, Ibiza, Malaga, Tunis and the West African 1-11 coastal service which tramped from London, through the Canary Islands to Lagos, by way of a number of stops.

The reduced operation on the short-range routes led, of course, to a surplus in aircraft capacity and plans were laid to sell or lease out up to seven 1-11s. On the other hand, we planned to increase the long-haul fleet by replacing the VC-10s with further Boeing 707s to increase activity on North Atlantic charters, now that minimum seat rates had been imposed. A cautious re-entry into the European inclusive tour market was planned.

Working long into the evening we carved out and discarded no fewer than sixty-eight different plans to find ways of surviving intact. We found, however, no way of continuing to operate the existing total network that did not result in a substantial loss for the forward year.

The evening of 16 October, like many evenings before, saw me bent over my desk, hard by a window which looked out over the Gatwick runway threshold and across to the airport terminal area where our aircraft were coming and going and staff were busy with boarding and disembarking passengers, loading and unloading baggage, filling up with catering supplies, refuelling and undertaking the myriad other pieces of logistics which go into every single arrival and departure. Instead of running over the latest plan, I was putting the finishing touches to a letter to all staff which, the following morning, would announce the drastic 'S' plan. In turn, the words of my letter were to be redrafted to form a press announcement and a letter to politicians. Earlier in the day I had met the airline directors to advise them of the redundancies, including their own where applicable – until now a secret guarded closely within the confines of the holding board. If the pill of redundancy was a bitter one to swallow, it was even harder for me to prescribe, especially to men I had worked with closely and who had become friends. In fact the basis of redundancy was not emotional, but rational. We had set out to reduce the layers of management and staff. We determined that the spread of redundancy should be throughout the company, starting with the board. In percentage terms, the board took the hardest blow, with a loss of 33 per cent. Manager ranks lost 15 per cent; supervisors, 14 per cent; flight deck crew, 9 per cent; cabin staff, 14 per cent; overseas staff, 27 per cent; and others, 14 per cent.

In the letter I was preparing for staff, I filled in the background to our crisis, detailing the events and circumstances which had conspired to bring the airline to its current impasse. Aircraft landed and took off as I wrote:

There is no doubt that disaster would have overtaken us during next year if we had tried to continue a full-scale operation. Alternatives were studied: we consulted with Government and the Civil Aviation Authority and we came to a final conclusion which is the only viable alternative open to us. That solution involves operating the most profitable parts of our airline, concentrating on these and ceasing operations on other routes and activities. This means selling or leasing certain aircraft and these will be BAC 1-11 500s. This results in the fact that we cannot afford to maintain our present level of staff if we are to survive. Therefore, redundancies are, regrettably, necessary.

Our plan includes an expansion of certain long-haul activities, including freight and passenger charters. This does not compensate for the reduction in other areas, but it does lessen the consequences with regard to redundancy and realistically improves our projected results for 1974/75.

I can assure you of this – our plan is workable, our plan is viable, our plan will ensure the airline's survival.

I came to the most crucial part of the plan and wrote, bluntly:

827 colleagues and friends will be leaving the airline. Those remaining will total 4,846. Of those leaving, some 27 per cent will be staff based overseas. Some of those leaving are new to the company, others have been with us for a considerable time. The redundancy includes a number of directors, senior managers and managers, as well as staff of other grades throughout the whole company. Redundancies inevitably result in hardship and the redundancy decision is the most difficult decision any management has to take, but the realities are stark, clear and unavoidable. We can only ignore them at our peril and I have no doubt that if we had done this, the result would have eventually led us to a 'Court Line' situation. The difference for British Caledonian is that we do have all the facts and figures and forecasts necessary for a decision to be taken with regard to our future. This decision will not only allow us to continue, but also allow us to lay down the basis for a gradual profitable expansion after our period of consolidation.

The news broke at Gatwick on the morning of 17 October and within hours its reverberations were felt throughout the industry, within politics, and the trades union movement. Left-wing Labour MPs called for BCAL to be immediately nationalized. The union view, as articulated by Clive Jenkins, was that the airline's assets should be sold to British Airways, or the profitable West African routes should be confiscated in a mutilating move to bring us finally to our knees.

British Airways, which announced the following day that it was fearing losses of £12 million for the year, agreed to take over bookings on the North Atlantic services after 1 November. The announcement of our intention to re-enter the European inclusive tour market led Dan Air to complain publicly that it stood to lose the £2 million in revenue it expected to obtain from our own tour operator, Blue Sky.

Freddie Laker had at last secured his licence for the proposed no-frills, low-cost, Skytrain operation between London and New York. But the designation of the service at the UK end and the permit from the US was held back as regulators saw great folly in allowing a fifth operator on the New York route, alongside BOAC, Pan Am, TWA and ourselves at a time of economic crisis and declining traffic. On the Friday of that fateful week, he called a press conference to announce his intention to sue the four incumbent airlines in the US courts over the agreement to restrict North Atlantic capacity, which he alleged prevented the start of his Skytrain operation.

Peter Shore stood firm against the pressure being heaped upon him by his own left wing, the union leaders and other airlines. Refusing to consider any form of nationalization for BCAL, he instead promised a full review of British civil aviation. Effectively, he was stepping in to take control of the route rationalization talks between us and British Airways.

In the meanwhile, the sad work of nominating those to be made redundant was going on at Gatwick under Ray Dobson's personnel department. It was, ironically, another Trafalgar Day, 21 October 1974, that I announced the new management structure. One of the saddest losses was Maurice Guinane who, having helped mastermind the whole 'S' plan, told staff that, being an architect of a scheme in which so many lost their jobs, he had no alternative but to walk away from the airline with them.

I formally took on the new role of chairman and chief executive and brought two new faces on to the smaller board. Duncan Haws, who had spent his entire career in the travel industry, had earlier been recruited as managing director of Blue Sky. I now moved him into the airline as sales director. Colin Smith, a finance expert, was brought in from outside as the airline's financial director, to beef up that side of the business, leaving Trevor Boud free to concentrate on group financial strategies. Of the existing people, Ian Ritchie

308

moved from sales to set up a new external affairs division which welded public relations, government affairs and industry affairs into one unit. Alastair Pugh was planning director; Bill Richardson engineering director; J.R. 'Mick' Sidebotham operations director; Captain P.A. 'Mac' Mackenzie special director, Flight Operations; and Ray Dobson industrial relations and personnel director.

The new board met for the first time on the day of its announcement. It contemplated the future, looking at a sadly depleted route map on one hand and the prospect of expansion in the charter markets on the other. One of the first moves in this direction was the signing of a £2 million contract for transatlantic charter flights with our old friend and customer, Pat Shasby, whose dealings in charters for the British American Club of Northern California had led him to form the travel company, Anglo-California Travel Service, which was now venturing into the new advance booking charter market.

The mess of the implementation of the 'S' plan was still around us, with departments reforming and redundant staff sorting out the process of their departures, but the atmosphere in the board room was of confidence. There was some consolation in the fact that airlines around the world were in deep financial trouble and we were not alone. Estimated losses now included £15 million from British Airways, £35 million from Pan Am; £20 million from TWA; £20 million from Alitalia; and £40 million from Air France.

At the annual general meeting of IATA in Montreal, the director general, Knut Hammarskjold, told members that the collective estimated loss on North Atlantic routes was £125 million. Fuel costs had increased by 225 per cent, other costs by £60 million and transatlantic traffic had fallen by 20 per cent. It all prompted Hammarskjold to say: 'This year presents a worsening picture on all routes. Skyrocketing oil prices have fuelled an inflationary spiral in airline operating costs with a resultant forecast industry operating loss.'

But the greatest consolation was that we were the only carrier of any size to have grasped the nettle of economic crisis to ensure survival. As I said in a letter to *The Times*: 'We have had to administer a dose of preventative medicine not yet taken by many other airlines experiencing the same industry problems.'

In Whitehall, Peter Shore was preparing to get together the

309

ingredients to formulate his own brand of preventative medicine for the industry. On 5 December he announced his intention to conduct a review of civil aviation policy, with specific terms of reference: 'To consider what changes may be desirable to UK civil aviation policy . . . in the light of the present economic and financial position and prospects of the British civil air transport industry.'

There is little doubt in my mind that an agreement with British Airways on route rationalization would have prevented the redundancies at BCAL.

In an interview on the Sunday after our cutback announcement, British Airways' director of planning, Alec Finlay, said that the rationalization proposals were not that important to the airline. 'We're not sitting back waiting for events to take their course, hopefully in our favour, but we are very much preoccupied with the really major problems which face us over the next five years. If we let our attention wander to other, more speculative things, then our eye would leave the target.' (Many years later, the former head of BOAC, Sir Keith Granville, told me that, with hindsight, he wished he had gone along with our rationalization proposals!)

In the same article in the *Sunday Telegraph*, another, unidentified, British Airways source was quoted as saying that the solution would be for BCAL to become a division of BA operating West African and South American routes. BCAL could then come off Central Africa and Singapore where, in BA's view there was 'too jolly much' competition. It was left for Henry Marking, BA managing director, to spell the BA philosophy out loud. 'We all like to be monopolists,' he said. 'Monopoly is only a bad thing if you haven't got it.'

In fact, despite its drive to improve its standards and its image, British Airways itself was beginning to get closer to a major financial pitfall.

At the end of 1974, the corporation was committed to a £200 million expenditure on new aircraft, including five Concordes, scheduled to enter service in 1976 and whose cost had escalated from the original £115 million to as much as £140 million. The airline was overmanned, with 58,000 staff, and management was trying feebly to reduce numbers by 4 per cent through natural wastage. Their ideal target, to match the efficiency of the big US carriers, would have been a workforce of about 40,000. But the scale of redundancy that would entail was unthinkable under a Labour government.

310

# 58

I came to learn by hard experience that the only way to fly as a passenger is asleep – especially if you have immediately on landing to step straight into a programme of meetings and business activities. As 'the boss' I was entitled, along with other directors and senior managers, to the privilege of a first class seat when I travelled on my frequent visits to points on the BCAL network and, indeed, on other airlines when going to areas we did not serve. But, even for me, that first class seat was only available so long as it had not been sold to a fare-paying customer.

On most routes, however, a first class seat was usually found. On daylight flights, I would spend the first few hours catching up with correspondence with Margaret Trett who necessarily accompanied me on business trips. I would eat only one or two courses of the usually-lavish lunch and drink water – no wine or spirits – before trying to get some rest.

So-called jet lag is caused by a combination of a rare atmosphere and dehydration. It is profoundly increased with too much alcohol and smoking. To veteran travellers, if the syndrome seems less marked now than it did in earlier years, this is because modern aircraft are pressurized to a lower height. A Boeing 747 or DC-10 is, for instance, pressurised to 5,000 feet, whereas the earlier jets like the Boeing 707 and DC-8 were pressurised to 7,500 or even 10,000 feet.

On the night flights which are a feature of travel to Africa, the Far East and from North America to Europe, my method is to ask, immediately after takeoff for a snack from the aircraft's dry stores larder – usually a glass of milk and a cheese roll. With the milk, I take a mild sleeping pill, originally prescribed for me by the BCAL chief medical officer, Dr Peter Chapman. As other passengers are beginning to enjoy their second cocktail, I cover myself with a blanket, take the sleeping pill and sleep soundly for the duration of the flight. The result is a clear mind and a fresh body when stepping into the airport gate on arrival.

In the months after the cutback I did a great deal of travelling, especially to the USA to speak personally to staff and authorities during the unhappy process of closing down the routes. I travelled to east, west and central Africa to ensure that our remaining staff, our customers and government officials retained confidence in the airline. It was a very busy period, but it was also the time that I came to take up the game of golf. It was curious to many that, as a Scotsman, I had never learned the game and it was consistent prompting from a group of professional golfers that led me to begin lessons at Walton Heath Golf Club in Surrey, not far from Gatwick. These were the BCAL Golfing Lions, whose manager was Derrick Pillage. His team of professionals, whom we sponsored with the provision of tickets to tournaments in Africa, South America and Europe in return for promoting the airline, included the likes of Brian Barnes, Malcolm Gregson, Tommy Horton, Sandy Lyle, Ewan Murray, Martin Poxon and others. In the various areas, especially Africa, the Golfing Lions formed a powerful and unique promotional medium when they gave 'clinics' or played special matches with our commercial guests. They were indeed the entré to golf-loving President Kenneth Kaunda of Zambia with whom I established a sound relationship to the benefit of the airline and our hotel interests over many years. So keen on golf was 'KK' that he had a course laid out in the grounds of State House, Lusaka. An enduring feature at the time of the Zambia open golf tournament was a special match played between the BCAL Golfing Lions and the President's team at State House.

In any event, I took up golf and found the game to be not only relaxing – at my modest level at least – but also an incredible door-opener to important people who might find it difficult to make time for a business appointment, but who would turn out for a game of golf, weekdays and weekends, at the drop of a hat. Through golf, I met senior people in the business community in the various cities on the BCAL route network; negotiations with aircraft manufacturers and engine makers have been helped along considerably by a stroll round an adjacent golf course. The attraction of this simple but expensive and infuriating game to otherwise sane men with important positions, led me and the Golfing Lions to set up an annual Pro-Am invitation event to which we invited the very key contacts, political and commercial, from every major market on the network. They took place throughout the rest of the history of BCAL, alternating between Gleneagles in Scotland and Walton Heath or another famous golf club. There cannot have been another golf tournament in the world quite like it, where for instance President Sir Dawda Jawara of The Gambia could be seen strolling down the fairway with Admiral Alan Shepard, or Neil Armstrong, the US astronaut; and the professional, Brian Barnes, would take to the stage at the prize-giving dinner to give a bawdy rendition of 'Swing Low, Sweet Chariot' accompanied by Senator Shad Tubman of Liberia.

I have often thought that the analogy between the game of golf and the airline business is an appropriate one. In both, the start-up capital costs are high, both require a large degree of training and skill, both take up a lot of land, both keep you away from home a great deal and both offer very slim margins for mistakes.

The period after the 'S' plan cutbacks was spent, metaphorically, digging ourselves out of the rough to get back on to the financial fairway. The loss we eventually recorded for the disastrous year of 1974 was £5.6 million. We were engrossed in recovering as much as we possibly could by a combination of cutting costs right back and earning as much revenue as we could. By September 1975 we were able to get the loss down to a figure of £366,000, by improving our revenue performance by 23.9 per cent. In fact, the airline actually achieved a trading profit, but we were hit by a devaluation of the Argentine peso which cost £1.2 million.

Behind the scenes of the airline operation itself, Alastair Pugh's planners were busy preparing submissions for Peter Shore's review. It was just like Edwards all over again. This time, however, we were not fighting for opportunity. We were battling for our very existence. Attached to our formal submission which analyzed every aspect of the route structure, was a ten-point memorandum, headed 'Reasons for Retaining a Second Force Airline'.

It made points about previous aviation policy, about competition, about profit motivation in a private company and about the proposal that two international airlines could do more to boost

Britain's share of the world market than just one. It wound up with two key points:

As an alternative source of management, no single management can have a monopoly of innovation or ideas about the way in which airlines should best be run or the policies the industry should develop. With a monopoly, the actual situation becomes the norm, whereas comparison can demonstrate where management skill can be exercised. Labour relations provides one example; tariff policy is another.

Because of the need to develop services from Gatwick, the second airline, based at Gatwick, has an interest in such development to a greater extent than can ever be the case with British Airways, which would have to divide activity between Gatwick and Heathrow.

Focus shifted, inevitably, towards the House of Commons in the summer of 1975. The review had been completed with the deep involvement of the CAA. In seeking ways out of the BCAL/British Airways dilemma, most of the minds concentrating on the aviation review looked to two classic examples overseas. They looked at France, where two major international airlines, Air France and Union de Transports Aeriens (UTA) operated their own separate route structures in tandem. They looked also to Canada where a similar arrangement worked between Air Canada, the state airline, and Canadian Pacific Airways, CP Air, as it was known, the independent. The earlier route rationalization talks had led to the general conclusion that an 'areas of interest' policy was the most logical solution. But we did not want it to be so rigid as to preclude valuable opportunity for route development. Neither did we want to be boxed into a structure of second rate routes.

Perversity ruled the day on 29 July when Peter Shore announced in the Commons the first results of the review. His announcement overturned the entire base of our long-term plans without stating what replacement opportunities would be available. Shore declared his intention to end the practice of allowing two British airlines to operate on the same route, known in the jargon of aviation policy as 'dual designation'. Our forward growth plans centred on dual

314

designation on the routes we had won from the CAA – the new cannonball routes to Bahrain, Singapore, Toronto, Boston, Atlanta and Houston. Had Michael Heseltine designated us on these routes when he was Minister for Aerospace, then we would have been in a much better bargaining position. Shore also required us to give up the licences for the New York and Los Angeles services, routes which we regarded as only temporarily suspended as a result of economic crisis.

He declared:

> Nevertheless I want BCAL to continue as a second carrier on major routes. I accept that BCAL has made a valuable contribution to the UK aviation effort in the past few years, that it is valued by many consumers for providing a choice of British airlines on a number of domestic and European routes and that it is the main operator from Gatwick, where traffic must be expanded progressively as part of our national strategy.
>
> I am anxious to retain BCAL as a second centre of airline expertise in the UK and to do what I can to make more secure jobs for the substantial number of workers who depend on BCAL for their livelihood.
>
> I have therefore decided that British Caledonian should have a sphere of influence for its long-haul scheduled activities. This will be based upon its West African and South American services and I envisage a limited exchange with British Airways which would consolidate the two airlines' respective spheres of interest and be of benefit to both.

As much as I was encouraged by Shore's confirmation of BCAL's role in the political scheme of things and the prospect of stability for Africa and South America, I was deeply concerned at the thought of the new route expansion plan being tossed out of the window of No. 1 Victoria Street. Especially, it was intolerable to be excluded from the important North Atlantic routes.

# 59

The negotiations between ourselves and British Airways had been completed under the guidance of the Department of Trade and the CAA. The dark winter days saw Peter Shore's Second Secretary, David Hubback, putting together the draft of the White Paper containing the outcome of the inter-airline negotiations, and one or two surprises.

It was 11 February when Peter Shore came to present his White Paper, 'Future Civil Aviation Policy', to Parliament. The House was told largely what it had come to expect, so far as BCAL and BA were concerned. We would withdraw from East Africa, ceasing operations to Uganda, Kenya and the Seychelles, enabling BA to become the sole operator in this area. Similarly, we would halt the Singapore 'exempt' charter operation. In turn, BA would withdraw from Zambia, giving us sole British rights on the London-Lusaka route. They would withdraw from the South American countries of Venezuela, Colombia and Peru and BCAL would take over these routes. We would lose our licences to New York, Los Angeles, Toronto, Bahrain and Singapore – but we would retain the Atlanta and Houston licences and be cleared to operate these new transatlantic services once the cities were included in the bilateral agreement between the two countries. The European and domestic routes would remain entirely unchanged.

Our respective spheres of influence were clearly defined. In Africa, ours was to the west of a line which followed the eastern boundaries of Libya, Chad, the Central African Republic, Zaire and Zambia, and to the north of a line which followed the borders of Zambia and Angola. The only exception was Morocco which sat as a BA island in the BCAL sea. In South America, everything was ours, apart from Guyana which remained BA territory, as it

316

was served as part of their Caribbean network. Each airline had preference for charters operated in its own sphere of influence. In all other areas, opportunity would be available on an equal basis for all British airlines.

Arrangements for the route changes were required to be completed by 1 April 1976. One of BA's top priorities was in selecting routes for the Concorde operation which would begin in 1976. Their plans so far were for supersonic service to New York, Washington, Melbourne via Bahrain and Singapore, and Tokyo. However, they had also studied a service to South Africa which would operate via Lagos, inside our sphere of interest. Shore made a special exception for Concorde, leaving open the possibility that Concorde service in our area might take place. His White Paper suggested that we might, ourselves, provide a Concorde operation in an arrangement with BA. More ominously, Shore ruled that the policy to end dual designation on long-haul routes would not apply to Concorde services. That meant that if BA wished to introduce supersonic flights on our route to, say, Rio de Janeiro, it would be permissible, while we were precluded from attempting to fly on any of their existing routes.

But the biggest shock of all came for Freddie Laker. Shore's paper argued that if Laker's proposed Skytrain was allowed to go ahead, it would certainly be reciprocated by a US airline. The fact that the new transatlantic advance booking charters had been developed (Laker was, in fact, a major operator of these flights) and that low promotional fares had been introduced on scheduled services, meant that, in the Government's view, there was less scope for a Skytrain style of operation. Shore's officials had estimated that BA would incur losses of about £6 million a year if the Laker operation and a corresponding US service were to be operated.

In one swoop, he therefore ordered the cancellation of Laker's designation as a scheduled service operator to the USA and announced that the CAA would take steps to revoke the Skytrain licence under the terms of the new policy. Laker's reaction was dramatic. I learned later from journalists that he had gatecrashed Peter Shore's press conference at which he announced the new policy and, in an emotional state close to tears, demanded to have his say. He called the decision 'shabby and immoral' and promised

317

to go on fighting, despite Shore's confirmation that there would be no appeal against his decision.

The act that put paid to Laker's Skytrain plan was to set off a train of events which would have a profound effect on the industry. Laker retreated momentarily to consult with lawyers. One month later, he reappeared with a writ served on Peter Shore, alleging that the Secretary of State had acted beyond his legal powers in giving guidance to the CAA to revoke the Skytrain licence. The day after the Shore announcement I was delighted to find in my mail a warm and encouraging letter from Lord Boyd-Carpenter, the CAA Chairman.

My dear Adam,
Now that the great operation is over, I do want to tell you how much I have admired the way in which you fought your corner. No one could have done more; and most people would have effected far less. I know, of course, that you did not get all you wanted. It is, of course, very rare for any of us to do that. But it is a very considerable achievement for you to have obtained, under a Labour Government, an increase in the routes actually to be operated. Those of us whose memories go back to 1971 realise very well both the amount of success which you have had and the degree of courage which the 'S of S' has shown. I personally, am particularly pleased that it has been possible to save Atlanta/Houston . . .

After the months of uncertainty and political infighting, we had reached a period of respite. Over the last weekend of February, I took the BCAL board away from Gatwick to Scotland to discuss policies for the future.

I wrote in reply to Lord Boyd-Carpenter, 'The tranquil Scottish countryside proved a pleasant aspect and, for once, we were able to talk about the future without the uncertainties which surrounded us over the past few years. Naturally, we still have a great deal of work to do before putting our corporate plan to bed including finalising the selection of wide-body aircraft and its date of acquisition.' I concluded: 'As always with BCAL, charters continue to give some cause for concern, but to end on a happier note, barring coups, strikes, national disasters and other such occurrences, we should achieve our target profit for this year.'

My optimism was well-founded. 1976, which had begun so uncertainly, turned out to be the year of great turnround. Arrangements were made to end the East African and Singapore services and to inaugurate the new routes to Caracas, Bogota and Lima, in South America. Passenger traffic was growing again, as was cargo. We had introduced a new route to Algiers and resumed services to Tunis, suspended in the 1974 cutback. The Spanish hotel company, using its association with the airline, picked up its first overseas management contracts – for a new hotel in Zambia, ultimately to become Lusaka's prestigious Pamodzi and the Bintumani hotel and conference complex in Sierra Leone. Revenue increased from £86.3 million to £117.1 million. The previous year's loss turned round to a £5.6 million profit and we were well on the way to eliminating all of the accumulated deficit.

The stability which Peter Shore's White Paper brought enabled us, a couple of months after his announcement, to firm up our plans to bring new, wide-body aircraft into the fleet. In June we announced our decision to place a $70-million order with McDonnell Douglas for two DC-10-30 aircraft and to take options on a further two. They were scheduled for delivery over the following winter and for entry into service on routes to West Africa, South America and on transatlantic charter flights in the summer of 1977.

In a gesture that I accepted as an honour for the airline, I was nominated for the award of a CBE in the New Year Honours. In a rare family outing, Dawn and my sons, Scott and Anthony, joined me in the trip to Buckingham Palace on 22 March 1976, when the award was presented by Queen Elizabeth.

In a message to staff, I said of the events of 1976, 'We can stop worrying about politicians putting us out of business and, by our own efforts, make our future secure.'

# 60

Until one memorable weekend in California my only golfing involvements were the lessons at Walter Heath and the presentation of prizes at our annual Pro-Am, but doing so without any understanding of what the participants were talking about. Later I was to play courses from Gleneagles to Lagos, Houston to Hong Kong and Bel-Air to Banjul. Now here we were, Trevor Boud knowing as little if not less than I did, becoming acquainted with those magnificent lush green fairways, comfortably shaded from the burning sun in a motorized buggy. That we were not despatched from the course immediately after the first divets soared skywards was perhaps due to the influence of our host, Charlie Forsyth.

The executive vice president of McDonnell Douglas, Charlie Forsyth was a stoutish silver-haired man brimming with good humour. He and his lady, Becky, had a delightful home in Palm Springs and it was to their house and, of course, Charlie's golf club that I was invited with a clutch of colleagues one weekend in May 1976. It was Charlie (and the influence of our Golfing Lions Team) who for better or worse, as far as the game is concerned, gave me an abiding passion for this most frustrating and yet exhilarating of sports.

We were in the final stages of planning for the introduction of wide-body aircraft and had been with the McDonnell Douglas people at their headquarters in Long Beach, California. Charlie had suggested that we wind up the week with informal talks at his home, with perhaps the chance of a round of golf; it was a clever sales ploy, I didn't mind. The chance for our team to relax in the near-perfect climate of Palm Springs was a welcome respite from the hours of analysis and negotiation that goes into an aircraft purchase. We flew down in some strength with Bill

Richardson, engineering director; Alister Pugh, planning director; Ian Ritchie, and Mike Carter.

The airline had been studying the relative merits of wide-body aircraft – the Boeing 747, the Lockheed 1011 and the DC-10 – throughout the early 1970s. We knew clearly that wide bodies would be required for competitive reasons if nothing else. There was only so much time for the Boeing 707s. Against the wide-bodies, the 707s were uneconomic and increasingly unattractive for the passenger. If adequate traffic could be generated for aircraft that carried upwards of 260 passengers, the efficiency would translate into profitability at a handsome level. If not, the overheads and costs of such aircraft would be crippling. Until 1976, the time for BCAL to operate wide-bodies was not right. Now, however, we were in the throes of an intensive selection process. Aircraft evaluation is complex, involving the close study of route traffic forecasts and operating capacities. Some of the BCAL routes were long-range, like Rio or non-stop charters to the US West Coast. Others, like Lagos, were medium range. We required an aircraft that could handle shorter flights economically and the longer routes without payload penalty. It also had to have a passenger capacity to suit the market, neither too small nor too big and good capability for carrying cargo.

Executives and technical experts from each of the three US manufacturers visited us at Gatwick, complete with their own studies based on the BCAL route network. Equally, our own planners, analysts and engineers travelled out to Seattle to visit Boeing; Palmdale, California, to visit Lockheed; and Long Beach, California, to negotiate with McDonnell Douglas. I insisted to all of those involved in this evaluation that there was *no* favourite aircraft and that *no* decision would be taken until *all* negotiations had been completed and the final figures were on the table.

It was now time to begin the hard bargaining with the manufacturers and Trevor Boud, with Bill Richardson, and some others, including myself, took off to do the rounds of the manufacturers. We were joined by Curly Walter who now headed up a subsidiary company we had formed to deal with aircraft purchase and sale, British Caledonian Aircraft Trading.

We started in Seattle with Boeing to discuss the 747-200 series and the new short-body, 747 SP. The letters after the type number stood for Special Performance and the aircraft was a 747 variant designed to carry smaller payloads over greater distances non-stop.

Aircraft manufacturers with the prospect of orders worth tens of millions of dollars have a renowned capacity for immense and generous hospitality. To round off the several days in presentations and negotiations with Boeing, our host, Clancy Wilde, laid on a trip to Vancouver from where we would enjoy two days' sailing on a luxury yacht. Clancy wanted the two days to cover discussions but as much as I liked the boat I felt that one day's cruising was sufficient. Thus, Boeing flew us back to Seattle from British Columbia a day earlier than they had planned. We were going on to Los Angeles to meet the Lockheed team led by Larry Kitchen, who was later to be chairman and chief executive of the organization. After the same round of sales pitches and bargaining sessions, interspersed with elegant lunches and dinners, we travelled down the Californian coast to Long Beach.

It is fair to say that we found ourselves in a buyers' market with all three manufacturers. The economic situation had meant that airlines were not falling over themselves to boost capacities. The worst hit of the manufacturers was McDonnell Douglas. They were sitting on three aircraft already built which remained unsold. In our industry, such aircraft with no purchaser and therefore no airline insignia to paint on the fin are known as 'white tails'.

After our time with McDonnell Douglas, including the retreat to Palm Springs, our team repaired to a hotel close to Los Angeles International Airport. Our strategy was to go back to the three manufacturers to say that we felt each of their prices was too high and that they should come back with revised figures. This they did, to a greater, or lesser extent. We then decided to close in on McDonnell Douglas by making an offer to them, which blatantly took advantage of the fact that they had three unsold DC-10s on their hands. In fact we felt, at that time, the 747 was too large for our requirements and the Tristar was not as flexible as the DC-10.

I telephoned Charlie Forsyth with our 'shopping list' which effectively cut his first bid to ribbons. For part of the long telephone conversation, I thought he was either having a nervous breakdown or a heart attack at the shock of our bargaining audacity. Nevertheless, he agreed to talk, which we did into the early hours, and the following day we clinched the deal and set up a new relationship with McDonnell Douglas which was to last for many years in a spirit of genuine friendship and co-operation. We subsequently concluded many more purchases of this aircraft, but we never again repeated such an advantageous deal.

On a Saturday evening in July, just a month after the announcement of the DC-10 order, the Copthorne hotel, which had grown from its humble beginning to become an international four-star operation, was host to a transatlantic gathering. Its specially-named Caledonian Suite, an elegant room with French windows leading out to cultivated lawns and shrubberies, echoed with the noise of a group of men in high spirits. The occasion was a celebratory dinner laid on by Sanford McDonnell, president and chief executive officer of McDonnell Douglas and nephew of its founder, James S. McDonnell, a Scot who had emigrated to the USA to found one of America's greatest business empires. Sanford, known by all and sundry as 'Sandy', was proud of his Scots heritage and nothing could have pleased him more that evening than to be in a room called Caledonian, celebrating the sale of his aircraft to a Scottish airline.

His guests included myself, Peter Masefield, Iain Stewart, Curly Walter, Trevor Boud, Alister Pugh and all the senior managers of the team which had evaluated the DC-10 and negotiated its acquisition. Sandy's fellow hosts from McDonnell Douglas numbered among them the Apollo astronaut, Pete Conrad, who now worked for Sandy McDonnell, and their senior team mates on the 'BCAL Project'.

The evening was spent in jocular conversation, much of it pointing to the hard bargain we had driven on the aircraft. Sandy couldn't let this go when he had the opportunity to make an informal speech. There was a joke, he said, obviously of English origin. It asked how you make a mile of copper wire and the answer was that you drop a penny between two Scotsmen. 'I think, Adam, that you and I have proved that story wrong. We had slightly more than a penny between us and, far from reducing it to copper wire, we have come up with something I believe is very attractive for both sides.'

He said he knew his team was dealing with a man who had won the Hambros Bank Businessman of the Year Award in 1971 and who was awarded a CBE in the New Year's Honours. What I didn't realize they knew at the time was that I had also received the Scottish Free Enterprise Award just the day before, but he surprised me when he continued. With a man with these two awards, he said, you approached negotiations with respect, but someone with a special Scottish award you took cover from. To merriment from his team, he referred to the deal we had put forward and won, in an understated way as 'a short but exhilarating period of final bargaining'. Before sitting down he presented me with a gold pen, with the remark that there was now no way that I would be getting out of signing the contract.

I was not at Long Beach on 12 March 1977 when the first DC-10 was handed over to us. Instead, the BCAL delegation was headed by Sir Peter Masefield and Sir Iain Stewart. Along with them were other holding board members, Stuart Young and Jimmy McWilliam, together with Trevor Boud, Alister Pugh, Bill Richardson and Mick Sidebotham.

McDonnell Douglas had a ceremony for first delivery aircraft – this involved cutting the customer's neckties just below the knot. Those who were briefed sought out their oldest ties – those who weren't just had to have a sense of humour, like it or not. They all received a DC-10 tie in place of the mutilated one.

After a rousing ceremony hosted by the McDonnell Douglas President, John Brizendine, the aircraft, G-BEBM – 'Bravo Mike' was scheduled to fly non-stop from the US West Coast to Prestwick in Scotland. It was there that I would meet the aircraft to participate in one of our traditional naming ceremonies. For the new fleet we had decided that the aircraft would carry the names of famous Scots. Looking back over my shoulder to our very first Douglas DC-7C, 'Star o' Robbie Burns', I had proposed that the first DC-10 should be named 'Robert Burns – the Scottish Poet'.

We did once come very close to equalling our earlier bargain when seeking a further three DC-10s and their General Electric engines. It was during one of our British Caledonian Pro-Am golf tournaments at Gleneagles. After a day on the fairways and a good Gleneagles dinner, Charlie Forsyth and Neil Burgess of General Electric sat around a table with Trevor Boud and I. Whether they were so relaxed with the golf, the fresh air, the food and the wine that they were amenable to any suggestion, I don't know. I do know we obtained an informal agreement on an especially advantageous deal before setting off in the early hours for our beds and another day's golf. The next morning at breakfast, though, Charlie asked Burgess: "Neil, what the hell did I agree to last night?"

We never regretted ordering our fleet of DC-10-30 aircraft. The aircraft served us well and the fleet with General Electric engines was in operation with British Caledonian up to the time of the British Airways takeover at the end of 1987.

# 61

The unlikely figure at the speaking podium in a specially-decorated gate lounge of the Houston Intercontinental Airport was none other than His Royal Highness, the Prince of Wales. Prince Charles, who was in Texas on an official visit, had consented to go the airport to greet the first BCAL service between London and Houston. The date was 24 October 1977.

It was during this visit, at a dinner in the city, that the Prince made a remark still repeated at Texan dinner parties. Like most British people, Prince Charles' natural inclination was to pronounce the name of the city 'Hooston'. He was good-humouredly rebuked by a Texan lady who said, ' "You should say "Hewston", not "Hooston".' Prince Charles retorted; 'Madam, when you start saying "Barkley" instead of "Burkley" Square, I'll start saying "Hewston"!'

In publicity terms, it could not possibly have been a better week for us to resume transatlantic scheduled services with the opening of the Houston route which, at times, had seemed to be slipping from our grasp. To coincide with the pro-British fervour of a Royal visit was one thing, but to have the heir to the throne waiting to meet the aircraft and its passengers at the airport was quite another. Among those inaugural guests met by Prince Charles were two men who had been key figures in the struggle to get the new service off the ground. They were Stanley Clinton Davis, the Aviation and Shipping Minister, and Lord Boyd Carpenter, who had recently retired as first chairman of the Civil Aviation Authority, handing over to Nigel Foulkes.

The high emotion of the occasion masked the backroom drama surrounding this service, which opened in October, instead of the following spring as we had planned, and with Boeing 707 aircraft, instead of the DC-10-30. But Prince Charles was briefed and ready to help us sell the new British service to the Texas market. To an audience headed by Houston Mayor Fred Hofheinz and Louie Welch, our great friend and President of the Houston Chamber of Commerce, and including every civic dignitary who could drive, cycle, run or walk to the Royal occasion, he said; 'I'm delighted to be able to have this opportunity of doing something for British Caledonian. It is very nice and appropriate that this flight coincides with the Queen's Silver Jubilee in 1977.'

He went on to say that Texans not experienced in flying to London might be alarmed at thoughts of having to arrive at a place called Gatwick. 'In fact,' he said, 'it takes only forty minutes to go by train to London. If you get held up on the road to Heathrow, it takes a damned sight longer.'

The road to Houston itself had, for us, been one of hold ups and frustrations. Three months to the very day of our inaugural flight a new air services agreement had been signed between the US and UK governments on 23 July. The agreement was known in the industry and among the politicians and government officials as 'Bermuda II'. The original treaty which laid down the provisions for the conduct of air services between the two countries had been known as the Bermuda Treaty, having been negotiated in that British colony in 1946. One of the original negotiators had been Sir Peter Masefield.

In the spring of 1976, the Secretary of State for Trade, Peter Shore, was succeeded by Edmund Dell, whose political leanings were more to the right of the ruling party. Dell decided to terminate the thirty-year-old treaty and, accordingly, our Ambassador in Washington, Peter Ramsbotham, was to write to the US Secretary of State, Henry Kissinger. In his diplomatic note of 22 June 1976 the Ambassador expressed the British view that the existing Bermuda Agreement conferred benefits upon the United States which were not equal to the United Kingdom's. Capacity provisions were seen as too lax and being in part responsible for the over capacity problems that the industry experienced in the early 1970s; in addition its system for the establishment of fares was unworkable.

In London, Edmund Dell announced the termination of the Bermuda Agreement to the House of Commons. The objective of this move was to obtain an increased share of North Atlantic traffic for British carriers through greater access to the US market and to constrain US carriers who were operating with full traffic rights beyond London. Even today, Pan American, for example, may operate services between London and Germany but on the other hand, British airlines still do not have similar rights in the USA.

In August, prior to the first full round of negotiations with the Americans, the Department of Trade held a briefing meeting in London with the airlines involved in transatlantic services. Our representative was Charles Powell, the manager responsible for dealing with the Department of Trade and foreign authorities in traffic rights and operating permits. We termed the job 'international relations'. In charge of negotiations was the Department Under Secretary, George Rogers. As in all such negotiations where British Airways was involved as a carrier, the Department found it hard to reconcile its responsibility for British civil aviation in general with its position as the sole 'shareholder' in the state airline. In other words, except in negotiations with governments of countries where we were the sole UK airline, I was never sure that the British objectives were not being dictated by the demands of British Airways.

In any event, Rogers' aim in the negotiations with the Americans was to impose more restrictions on the North Atlantic routes. He wanted a regime of just one airline from either side on each UK-USA route – so called 'single designation' – with pre-determined capacity and fares fixed through IATA.

Our own objective was to gain agreement allowing us to open the routes to Houston and Atlanta, the licences we had won and which Peter Shore had upheld in his policy of the previous year. The civil servants at the Department of Trade were not happy with this. They could not see the potential of the southern states and a requirement for Houston and Atlanta complicated their negotiating stance.

As it was, Rogers was running headlong into the blast of liberalism blowing from President Jimmy Carter's Washington. Along with Houston and Atlanta, there were many cities in the USA clamouring for direct transatlantic services and an equal number of US airlines eager to break into the transatlantic scheduled market, so far dominated by two airlines, Pan Am and TWA. None of us in BCAL had any doubt about the long-term viability of the two 'Sunbelt' services, but we were aware that, initially, they would be thin in traffic and would need careful nurturing. We estimated that each would take three years to recover all of the start-up costs and begin to make overall profits. They were entirely new transatlantic routes without even any history of charter services to Europe.

We believed that the development task should be left to a single carrier, with a direct competitor being introduced as soon as an adequate market was created. The plan was for a three-year moratorium on competition for new gateway services, an arrangement that made good business sense for all concerned. However, we felt that the Americans would buck against a move which appeared to be anti-competitive. Leonard Bebchick in Washington was consulted. He felt otherwise and reminded me in a long telephone conversation that the Americans were, first and foremost, pragmatic and that in the end ideology would bow to commercial logic. They just needed to be sold on the idea, he said.

We therefore took our proposal to the Department of Trade. They agreed to push hard with the Americans for its acceptance. There was, however, one proviso – that we would leave all the negotiating to them and not attempt to undertake direct dealings with the US negotiators. It was against our inclination and past practice not to fend for ourselves, but we agreed.

The early rounds of the Bermuda II negotiations seemed to be tedious and made little or no progress because of the restrictionist nature of the British position. The Americans wanted less restriction and more competition. The talks went through the autumn of 1976 and over into the New Year. The Americans were becoming frustrated and an industry observer at the time commented that the US side seemed to have a growing feeling that 'we have listened, we have been nice guys and now it's time for the British to listen to us'.

Washington stepped up the pace by upgrading their negotiating team with the appointment of Alan Boyd, a former Secretary of State for Transportation, as a 'Special Ambassador' at its head.

In London, George Rogers had become unwell, and the British also moved in a new chief negotiator, a more senior Under Secretary, Patrick Shovelton. Early talks with Shovelton indicated that he felt that our scheme for the Houston and Atlanta routes

329

was unrealistic. I therefore arranged a small dinner party at the Caledonian Club in Halkin Street, just off Belgrave Square. The idea was to convince Shovelton that the three-year 'solus' plan for Houston and Atlanta was workable and negotiable. It would, of course, be on a quid pro quo basis. With Houston our priority, we would have the first three years on that route, with a US airline enjoying similar status on Atlanta.

Within the confines of the private dining room of the Caledonian Club, Shovelton could not contain his enmity towards BCAL. He did not want to know about our proposal and as the discussion became more and more heated, he burst out, 'Why don't you go back to running charters?' Needless to say the dinner party broke up earlier than expected, but we knew where we stood – on our own. To the civil servants in the Department of Trade, BCAL was a nuisance and its objectives fell into the 'too hard' category. Every indication was that the Houston and Atlanta proposal had not been put to the Americans. It seemed that our effort to return to the USA by opening services to the cities in the rapidly-developing southern states, spurned by British Airways, was to be scuttled by civil servants with pedestrian mentalities.

It was with bitterness and anger that I called Leonard Bebchick to tell him of this latest kick in the pants. 'What can we do now?' I asked. His reply was simple. 'Unleash me,' he said, referring to our earlier agreement not to become involved in dealing with the Americans directly. What was there to lose? I told him to get on with it.

His first move was to arrange a lunch date with Stephen Piper, Alan Boyd's special assistant for the Bermuda II negotiations and an old acquaintance. In a private booth at Washington's Jockey Club, Bebchick learned what we already suspected – that the British negotiators had made no effort to seek US acceptance of our proposals. Bebchick proceeded to make the case, using all the political persuasion he could muster. Not the least piece of this was that a three-year moratorium would see a second carrier on the new routes by the time of the next Presidential election in November 1980. Bebchick asked Piper if he would take the proposal to Alan Boyd. He agreed to do so.

Piper called Bebchick two days later. The message was short,

Boyd had agreed and would respond positively to the suggestion if the British raised the subject.

The obvious airline to open the Atlanta-London route was Delta, based in Georgia. They wanted a transatlantic link and were keen to get their home city on the transatlantic schedule. Charles Powell flew down to Atlanta for talks with the Delta management. After careful presentation they, too, accepted the logic of the moratorium arrangement for the sensible development of new gateways.

We had very swiftly achieved what the British civil servants had failed to do – bring the Americans in on the BCAL proposal. But our work meant nothing unless it was formally agreed at inter-governmental level and enshrined in a new Air Services Treaty.

The next step, therefore, was to talk with Shovelton and tell him that far from going back to charters, the ground was now well and truly laid for new scheduled services to Houston and Atlanta. He took the news with stern-faced diplomacy, but I have no doubt that anger and resentment were boiling away under the enigmatic, civil service veneer.

Shovelton, however, had another preoccupation by this time. A wild card had entered the pack, in the form of Laker Airways. As the talks dragged into their fourth round, in London in February 1977, Peter Shore's move to take away the Skytrain licence to New York was overturned in the courts of law. The Prime Minister, James Callaghan, and Edmund Dell decided that the Government would fight the case no longer and elected not to appeal. The consequence was that the Government now swung behind this member of the airline flock which a year earlier had been cast out as a black sheep and pressed for the Laker Airways service to be negotiated within the Bermuda II talks.

Negotiations continued right up to and over the 22 June deadline. Fears that no agreement would be reached and UK/USA airline services would cease resulted in contingency plans being drawn up by the airlines. The fears had, in fact, been fuelled by hawkish US Transportation Secretary, Brock Adams, who threatened to pull his team out of the talks in an effort to place pressure on the British. British Airways planned to feed traffic for the USA through its Canadian points. Pan Am would focus on Amsterdam and arrange for Laker Airways to operate connecting services to the UK. TWA proposed to divert its London services to Paris and asked us to lay on the connections to and from London. There was top-level intervention between President Carter and Prime Minister Callaghan. Callaghan made a plea for 'fairer treatment' for the UK. Carter's reply was that he wanted competition on all routes and had hoped that the two sides would have become closer by now, the middle of June. He would not budge on points of principle, but some new concessions might be made by the USA and he would be giving fresh instructions to Alan Boyd.

In addition to the Atlanta and Houston routes and the new requirement for Laker Airways, the talks were floundering over capacity demanded by the Americans and proposals for the charter market and entry on to the Seattle route for British Airways. At the last minute, Boyd came in with a new proposal. The Americans wanted Dallas/Fort Worth in Texas brought into the agreement, with a US carrier to start service to London. We were not happy with this, as Dallas/Fort Worth was too close to Houston. The talks went on in London through the night of 21 June 1977. Just after six o'clock on the morning of 22 June Charles Powell called me from London to tell me that the agreement had been signed, ten minutes after the old treaty had expired.

The news was that we had won the deal for Houston and Atlanta, but Dallas was in, with a US carrier operating non-stop services exclusively for three years. The new services would operate from Gatwick and this, in turn, meant that the Laker Skytrain operation, originally licensed to go from Stansted, would move to Gatwick. All-cargo services to Houston were immediately available to both sides. A capacity control formula was brought in and dual designation was permitted for New York and Los Angeles only. British Airways received approval for Seattle. 'There is general confusion in the building – the place is awash with papers,' said Powell.

For BCAL, the fruit of months of negotiations was bittersweet. Houston was approved, but hedged in with the new service from Dallas/Fort Worth and competing all-cargo flights. We would be able to begin flights to Atlanta three years down the line. However, the entry of Laker on to the scene meant that our designation for New York, a route we had intended to restart, was taken away to facilitate the Skytrain service. Nothing was said about a second

332

British carrier for Los Angeles, for which we remained licensed and designated. I wrote to Edmund Dell, asking for clarification, but he refused to confirm that we would remain designated for Los Angeles.

The Government hailed the signing of the Bermuda II agreement as a massive victory, worth 'tens of millions of pounds for Britain.' So it might have been for British Airways, which gained non-stop rights to San Francisco and Seattle, and Laker, with its Skytrain, but certainly not for BCAL. The irony was that it was us who had fought for three years to open new gateways to the USA to give more competition and choice, yet the expediency of covering the Government's embarrassment over the Laker court case brought us a bodged treaty and financial disadvantage.

I wrote the same day to Edmund Dell telling him so. I also wrote to the Opposition Leader, Margaret Thatcher. The Conservatives' response came from the shadow trade spokesman, John Knott. He echoed my view with a statement which, in the midst of Government euphoria, described the outcome as 'an obvious failure for Britain'.

Plans for the Houston route were hastily re-examined. The last-minute US demand for a US cargo service reduced our estimated first-year revenue for the route by something like £750,000. The impact of a competing service out of Dallas/Fort Worth would cut estimated revenues by £5.3 million.

Several days later, we came to our conclusion. We would bring the start date for Houston forward from the spring of 1978 to October 1977. But instead of the high-capacity DC-10-30, we would begin with the smaller Boeing 707. I cabled Mayor Hofheinz: 'Delighted to advise that British Caledonian will commence daily services between London and Houston on 23 October stop hope to see you in Houston soon stop best wishes Adam Thomson.' In fact, I was to see Hofheinz again in London. In July he travelled over with Louie Welch and to emphasise the importance of the new air service encouraged Texas Governor John B. Connally, the former Secretary of the US Treasury, to come and meet this new airline.

My other move was to immediately apply for a licence to serve Dallas/Fort Worth, by including the airport on the existing Atlanta licence, although under the moratorium arrangement we would not be able to operate for another three years.

The scramble to get the route underway started immediately. Duncan Haws was dispatched with a team to go and camp in Houston until all the bits and pieces required to begin service on 23 October had been put into place.

While the Bermuda II negotiations were going on, another front was opening up. In April the Government had issued a policy statement on the roles of London's two airports, Heathrow and Gatwick. Edmund Dell directed that Gatwick, where a £70 million expansion and modernisation programme was nearing completion, should be given preference over Heathrow in the development of international scheduled services. This was sweet music, as we had battled to compete from an airport with a sparse network of feeder services against the biggest interline point in the world. In accordance with this policy, we applied for and were licensed to operate to four Scandinavian points from Gatwick. In turn, British Airways was confirmed as the operator to serve Dublin, Dusseldorf, Frankfurt and Zurich from Gatwick.

In a move which was to prove futile, Edmund Dell initiated discussions with Canadian, Portuguese and Spanish governments aimed at forcing their national airlines to transfer from Heathrow to Gatwick. All three ultimately resisted the move and won.

But Dell had written into the Bermuda II agreement the clause that all new transatlantic services should operate into Gatwick. Whilst this would bring revenue to the airport, now geared to handle up to 16 million passengers a year, it did not help the requirement for European connections which would enable us to establish a bigger market base for intercontinental services.

Our bid to expand this Gatwick 'feed' by taking up the licences granted by our Government to serve Scandinavia met with a negative response from the governments of Norway, Sweden and Denmark. They simply tore up the air services agreement with Britain thus putting an end to any early hope of establishing these routes.

The main spotlight, however, remained on Houston. The city became something of a rallying point for the airline and all who worked with it. Although we had made a quantum leap into the wide-body era with the new DC-10s, the Atlantic still retained some extra special mystical pull. The winning of the Houston licence in the first place, the years of planning to make the route

334

a reality, and the intense pressure of Bermuda II all combined to make the announcement of the start date a very special event which symbolised a resurgence after the bitter disappointment of 1974. Although we had continued with our charter operations throughout the intervening years, Houston was to see British Caledonian back on the Atlantic, firmly entrenched as a major scheduled operator.

To confirm our confidence in ourselves and to demonstrate the commitment we had to the job of providing that extra bit of service, in the air and on the ground, we had a new advertising slogan created. It became our credo, completely synonymous with British Caledonian from then on. It said simply, 'We never forget you have a choice.' First appearing in the press the month before the Houston start-up, the slogan became a rallying point around which we built a programme of dedication to customer service.

Our attitude and corporate philosophy was summed up in the text of the very first of the new advertisements. Over a headline in which the letters of the slogan were composed of pen drawings of people representing the staff of BCAL, was the text:

Here at British Caledonian, our 5441 people have to do everything a little better than other national airlines.

We have to reserve your ticket a little faster. Serve your meal a little better. Be a little more helpful.

Because, unlike most other national airlines, we're an independent business.

Your travel agent has details of our forty routes. On thirty-nine of them, we're in direct competition with other airlines.

If we didn't run a better business, we wouldn't have a business to run.

So it was, armed with the confidence and vigour of the early Caledonian days, that we landed in Houston to a Royal welcome.

Four days after that inauguration, we brought the city of Houston to London to mark the start of eastbound services. In fact, we brought six Texan cities to London, for in our inaugural party, in addition to Houston's Fred Hofheinz and Louie Welch were the Mayors of Galveston, Corpus Christi, San Antonio, El Paso

335

and Harlington. Representing the state was Lt Governor William Hobby. We took them on the most glittering tour of London we could lay on. They mixed with MPs at the Houses of Parliament, were addressed by Edmund Dell at a celebration dinner in the Middle Temple, met the Lord Mayor of London, Sir Robin Gillett, at the Mansion House and rubbed shoulders with the City of London establishment at a luncheon in the Merchant Taylors' Livery Hall. I also wanted them to see my home country and the place where BCAL originated. We arranged a trip to Edinburgh, where they were entertained by the Lord Provost, Kenneth Borthwick.

Bowled over by the tradition and history of London and Edinburgh, Louie Welch said at the Mansion House, 'A number of us have got together and we are dedicated to building an old building as soon as we get back to Houston.' But, as so often, it was left to Peter Masefield to catch the mood of the day when he said, in proposing a toast; 'St George for England; St Andrew for Scotland; Gatwick for Texas, and Houston for British Caledonian.'

# 62

'Air transport history is strewn with the carcasses of defunct airlines, bankrupt travel agencies and tour operators, stranded passengers and unpaid creditors. I have seen it all before and I do not want to see it again.'

I was speaking in Madrid, at the 1977 annual general meeting of the International Airlines' Trade Association. IATA annual meetings – unlike most of its other working conferences – were traditionally relaxed affairs, when airline chiefs and their wives got together for a few days in a selected city. The work of the meeting was usually minimal and of a rubber-stamping nature. While the men conferred in the meeting hall, usually the most prestigious conference venue which the respective cities offered, the ladies took part in a social programme of tours and fashion shows. The evenings were filled with lavish hospitality from the host airline, the host city and the airline manufacturers, eager to get to this annual audience of a hundred or more of the airline industry's decision-makers.

Ian Ritchie, responsible for industry affairs, and his wife Jane usually accompanied us to the IATA meetings. It formed a rare treat for Dawn and Jane to travel with their husbands, normally away from home in some corner of the BCAL network or another.

But there was a seriousness about this meeting in Madrid. Having barely recovered from the crisis-strewn path of a few years before, the industry was facing a new phenomenon, the emergence of the deregulation policies of Alfred Kahn, at the helm of the US Civil Aeronautics Board. In short, Kahn was promoting a free for all philosophy in which any airline could fly any routes it wanted at any price it chose to offer. That was fine for the USA where there was a domestic market big enough to sustain large numbers of airlines, but the export of deregulation on the North Atlantic routes to Europe was another matter. Here, the airlines were all, apart from BCAL and UTA, the French carrier, the charter airlines and the large US airlines, state-owned and used to a tightly-regulated regime. I gave no support to the old system – after all, it was restrictionism and protectionism which had held back our North Atlantic and other ambitions for so long. But it was clear that an established order of things could not be changed overnight. Free competition was right, so long as it was fair.

And to be fair, all airlines had to be on an equal footing, with equal access to the markets. In Europe and the rest of the world, this was simply not the case. Most of the state-owned carriers could soak up loss-making competitive response through government subsidy, using taxpayers' money, and indeed did so. It was Alitalia's Chairman, the urbane Umberto Nordio who told the Americans that he would, if necessary, go on selling fares at $10 a time for as long as it took to break US competition. At the same time, the web of inter-governmental agreements which controlled air transport were restrictive, with constraints on competition designed to protect and stabilise the state airlines.

Caledonian had begun life as a rebel, but as we graduated into the bigger, more complex world of front-line aviation, it had become clear that the political strategy which would achieve change and more opportunity for ourselves and other developing carriers, was to work within the system. Revolution would not work: evolution would.

That is why we had purposefully taken the decision to participate in IATA. Against the background of Alfred Kahn's regime in the USA, IATA was coming under increasing attack as a cartel, serving only to protect its members and keep fares high, against the consumer's interest. It is true that for many years, IATA's traffic conferences had set fare levels across the world and that decisions were subject to unanimous agreement, rather than a simple ballot. But in the past it was governments, notably in the US, which had delegated their own responsibility for setting international air fares to the airlines. Indeed, any proposal that IATA made was not valid until ratified by the governments involved. IATA and its Director General, Knut Hammarskjold, was, I believe, treated unfairly by press and public opinion. The issues were perhaps too deep and complex for the average member of the public to understand or even care about. But the fact was that with disparate and differing national aviation policies and, in many cases, no real policies at all, it was left to the airlines themselves, through the forum of IATA, to keep international air transport running. Similarly, BCAL had become a member of the Association of European Airlines and in 1977 I was its chairman.

The cause for my concern at that IATA meeting in Madrid was the situation which had developed with the introduction of Freddie Laker's Skytrain operation between Gatwick and New York. British Airways and the US airlines naturally responded to the Laker fare of £59 with a range of drastic counter offers – budget fares and standby rates. I had visions in my mind of the crazy price wars in the UK inclusive tour industry three years earlier and remembered clearly the wounds that had been inflicted.

I told the assembled delegates that I was convinced that the new fares rat race on the east coast USA routes was suicidal for the industry and against the long-term interests of the consumer, as it would produce instability within the airlines. It was not as if there were no low fares on the Atlantic. Apart from the charter market in which both BCAL and Laker were major participants, about 75 per cent of scheduled passengers were already travelling on promotional rates. I pointed out that North Atlantic services had brought losses for IATA carriers over the past seven years of $2.5 billion.

'To those who criticise IATA as an international cartel, I would say that, if it is, then it must be the most unsuccessful cartel in history,' I told the meeting. 'There is no doubt that the price war on the North Atlantic is just beginning. I am quite convinced that charter operators on both sides of the Atlantic will undercut the lowest fares being charged at the moment. I am also convinced that this will lead to unprofitability for them and that their services will either have to be subsidised by some other activity or their shareholders will have to accept the losses. Some airlines, like BCAL, may decide that anything other than limited participation is unjustified,' I told my airline colleagues.

As it was, we had seen the way things were going much earlier in the year. For the first time in our short, frenetic history as

British Caledonian, the summer of 1977 gave us a chance to stop, take stock and draw breath. I decided that the board of directors should once again get right away from the day to day pressures of the airline and so, at the beginning of June, we flew to Jersey and checked into the Atlantic Hotel, near St Helier, for a weekend of relaxed discussion. The idea was to plot an up to date five-year plan for the development of the airline. Three key issues came into focus as we sat, in casual clothes, around the conference table or strolled in the colourful, summertime gardens.

The first was the worsening economics of Atlantic charters. We took the decision to withdraw from this market to concentrate on scheduled services. The wide body aircraft – 747s, DC-10s and Tristars – were providing low fares in the aft cabin which could compete with charters.

The second was the problem of the airline's dependence on politically and economically unstable markets in Africa and South America. We were beset with the problems of currency devaluation in some countries and the inability to remit earnings to the UK in others whose foreign currency coffers were empty. The airline was saddled with a useless fortune in Ghanaian cedis, Sierra Leone leones, and Nigerian pounds. Our solution was to place emphasis on developing services to more stable areas, North America and the Far East, as and when opportunities arose. In network terms, BCAL needed to become an East-West airline as well as a North-South one.

The third main issue was the one of our base itself, Gatwick. The airport still had a charter image and was not acknowledged as a serious scheduled service alternative to Heathrow. After a major redevelopment programme, which included improved passenger terminal facilities, Gatwick still did not have a sufficiently large network of scheduled operations. Neither did it have adequate 'interline' links with Heathrow, nor totally satisfactory communications with the centre of London. We recognised that as competitive as our own BCAL services might be, against any competition, Gatwick itself was a handicap. We resolved to find practical and promotional solutions for the Gatwick problem.

The company overall was now healthy and well on the way to complete recovery from the losses incurred in those disastrous years of the early 1970s. In 1976, we had achieved a profit of £5.6

million against the loss of £366,000 for 1975. The two DC-10s were performing well, providing more passenger and cargo capacity on services to West Africa and South America. Revenue was coming in at a faster rate and higher volume than ever before.

After the expedient redundancies of 1974, when Maurice Guinane left the company and I took over the twin role of chairman and managing director, the airline was expanding. It was becoming increasingly difficult for me to be responsible for long-term business and political strategy for the group overall which now included an expanding tour operation and hotel company, as well as for the day to day running of the airline.

We had other plans in store. For the DC-10 we had selected a new engine type, the big fan CF-6, manufactured by General Electric of the USA. With plans for a large fleet of DC-10s, we would also have a need for the overhaul and maintenance of the CF-6s, a highly specialist function which could not easily be carried out at our own maintenance base.

I began to formulate plans for some key restructuring of the main managerial team at head office. But before that was ready to be implemented, we made one key appointment that was to have a significant effect on the airline's development of strategies to build up North Atlantic services. The Houston route had been launched in the USA by a team seconded from the UK under our sales director, Duncan Haws. With him had been some of the US-based staff we had retained following the closure of the New York and Los Angeles routes in 1974. One was Alan Stronach, the operations specialist, who managed the continuing charter activity. Another was Gerry Swift, who had remained in New York to take care of the sales to be generated from transatlantic airlines feeding on to the BCAL network at London – 'off-line' or 'inter-line' sales, as they were known.

But we needed a permanent head man for the USA. Somebody immersed in the US air transport industry who not only knew how to run and market air services, but could also grasp the commercial implications of the new policies emerging in Washington DC.

Thus we came across an archetypal tall and rangy Texan by the name of H W 'Rocky' Cox. His actual first name was Horace, but somewhere along the line he had adopted the tough-sounding sobriquet 'Rocky', more suited to a man of the rough, outdoor world of the western rancher, not to mention the cut-throat business of air transport. We poached Cox from Trans World Airlines where he was in charge of their New York operation. Whether it was the prospect of taking on something entirely new or the fact that he would be returning to his home state, I am not sure. Probably it was a combination of both, but I was pleased with the appointment. There was nothing flamboyant about Rocky Cox. He was a man of few words, but those he spoke were straight. There was no waffle with him. His responses to ideas and questions were black and white. It was either a 'Yep' or a 'Nope' delivered in a distinctive Texan drawl. He was a man of high principles, believing in the self-reliance embodied in the old 'code of the west'.

I was to come to value Cox's insight and advice over the years. Many executives try to cover up realities by telling a company chairman what he wants to hear. Cox would have none of this. He gave me information straight, even though it might be painful to both of us. He was exactly the man we needed in the USA and he joined the airline as executive vice president, Houston, on 1 January 1978.

I recall a meeting I had with Rocky and one of the newspaper barons in Houston. This gentleman was similar to Cox – he didn't say a lot! In fact he hardly said anything – I gradually dried up as I was getting nowhere fast. Rocky and the baron conducted the conversation with a series of yups and nopes. When we left the office I said how painful the conversation had been. Rocky said, 'Nope – he's my kind of guy!' In fact with the passage of time we became good friends.

# 63

Just a few hundred miles up the Interstate Highway from Houston, the twin cities of Dallas and Fort Worth, combined in a piece of urban planning known as the 'Metroplex', were preparing to take advantage of their last minute designation as a transatlantic gateway in the Bermuda II negotiations.

It was up to Alfred Kahn's Civil Aeronautics Board to decide which of the US carriers would pick up the right to fly from Dallas/Fort Worth – known for short as 'DFW'. Contenders included the DFW-based Braniff. The airline operated internal US services and a network to South America. It was headed by one Harding Lawrence who was married to a Madison Avenue advertising executive, Mary Wells. It was the Lawrence/Wells team which had brought notoriety to Braniff with a new image for the airline which included painting the aircraft each in a different colour and giving hostesses a selection of uniforms which were changed at different stages of the flight. Braniff had a reputation for looking somewhat outrageous. And no better was the Braniff style manifested than in their Boeing 747 which was painted all over in a vivid, bright orange. The aircraft was known as 'Big Orange' and was soon to squirt juice into the face of the British Government.

By now, the basic qualification for winning an air route licence in the USA was simply to offer the lowest fares, in the free for all started by Kahn. The British plan for low fares was, however, more cautious. As part of the Bermuda II agreement, it had been decided by both sides that the experiment with Laker's low-cost, standby service would be watched for a period of twelve months, the results analysed and a fares policy drafted from the experience.

Kahn was working to policy orders laid down by President

Jimmy Carter who, in a letter dated 21 July 1977, told the Civil Aeronautics Board chairman, 'I am requesting that you submit a recommendation to me by early October designating a carrier to begin service to the Atlanta-London market and a carrier to begin service to the Dallas/Fort Worth-London market. I hope to make designations by 1 November 1977. Service could then begin shortly thereafter.'

Carter continued: 'The services you recommend should enhance the competitiveness of the US flag air system and be economically viable. I would also urge you to take into account the fact that a US carrier may provide non-stop Houston-London service after 23 July 1980, and US carriers may provide one-stop service in this market upon signing of the Agreement.' He was, of course, referring to the Bermuda II agreement.

Delta Air Lines of Atlanta, won the route and began service into Gatwick in the spring of 1978, as we were preparing for our first summer period on the London-Houston route. But as we had predicted, the threat from a DFW-London service and a US airline operating from Houston with one stop on the way to London was boxing us in and giving the British side a severe handicap.

At home, we were preparing to engage in yet another battle with British Airways for the DFW route which would become available to a UK carrier after the same kind of moratorium period. I had also written to Edmund Dell, seeking re-designation for BCAL on the Los Angeles route, suspended by both ourselves and Pan Am in the oil crisis of 1974, but Laker, now flexing the piece of muscle it had in the scheduled service market through the Skytrain operation to New York, also wanted the Los Angeles route. Freddie Laker made his move by applying to the CAA to have our licence revoked so that he could take it over.

Despite some misgivings within the US Civil Aeronautics Board at the anomaly between Braniff's gung-ho low fares policy for the Atlantic route and its conservative, high-fare stragegy on the protected South American network, the DFW carrier duly received designation to operate the US flag service to London. The trouble began when Braniff announced its fares. There were the expected low fares on the point-to-point DFW-London sector, but the CAA in London reacted mostly against Braniff's filing for fares on connecting services to and from other cities. In a bid to suck away most of the traffic from our Houston market, they were simply giving them away. A passenger in, say, Lubbock, West Texas, to whom it was irrelevant whether he went through Houston or DFW to London, had no real choice but to travel with Braniff because his internal flight was free. We, of course, having no internal US flights, could not compete.

The result was that Braniff's fares were rejected by the CAA in London. The Americans retaliated. Alfred Kahn at the CAB put up an order to the White House for Jimmy Carter's approval. It called for the suspension of all BCAL approved tariffs between Houston and London. During the suspension BCAL would have to charge, on Houston-London, the same fares which the CAB had approved for Braniff. Further, it proposed to order that if Braniff was blocked from beginning its service, then the Americans would bring our Houston flights to a halt.

The Americans were completely out of line, although they believed that the Bermuda II clause covering fares did not apply to a new route. Bilateral agreements such as Bermuda II allow for consultation between the respective governments in the case of a dispute. The Americans had not called for talks with the British authorities, nor did they intend to. It was a move typical of the cavalier style of Alfred Kahn and his cohort, another academic recruited to the CAB, Mike Levine.

The line between Gatwick and Leonard Bebchick's office in Washington was once again kept busy. Bebchick's response was that the USA had certainly acted in breach of the treaty with the UK and that, if it came to it, we would happily go before a Federal Court.

On 3 March 1978 I put together an 18-paragraph telex to be sent to Edmund Dell and Patrick Shovelton, the British Bermuda II negotiator. It was copied to other politicians, Margaret Thatcher, leader of the Conservative Party, David Steel of the Liberals and Donald Stewart of the Scottish Nationalists. In addition to the giveaways proposed by Braniff, the issue was whether the new budget and standby fares on the New York market should be extended to other gateways, or whether the tariffs experiment should be reviewed in August 1978 to see how it had fared in practice before the policy was applied to other routes.

The former was clearly the American position the British preferred the latter option. So, in my telex I said: 'I believe it to be essential that we do not succumb to American might and bullying tactics.'

The BCAL Houston route was in its early days and quite fragile as we carefully built up the market. A suspension of operations, causing a diversion of traffic to other services, probably via New York, could prove to be disastrous. I said to Dell that we intended to fly the daily 707 service regardless of any CAB order; we would continue to charge only those fares approved by the British CAA and if the Americans wanted to take us to court they could. I stated that the CAB's action was 'unlawful, unconstitutional and contrary to an international agreement of the United States.'

Dell telexed back immediately in full support of the BCAL view and took steps to contact the US State Department in Washington. The next two weeks were frantic with diplomatic activity and it was understood that the impasse on air fares, centred on a place called Dallas/Fort Worth, which most British people knew nothing about save for the Kennedy assassination years before, was the subject of urgent telephone conversations between the Prime Minister, James Callaghan, and Jimmy Carter.

Seventeen days after my telex, Edmund Dell published an answer to a parliamentary question placed by the MP for Tynemouth, Neville Trotter. He told the House of Commons that negotiations on the issue had been concluded in Washington on 17 March and that an agreement had been reached with the Americans. Inevitably, it was a compromise. The US got its way with the extension of new, low fares to points other than New York. However, the fares would still be regarded as an experiment and, in conjunction with other European governments and the Canadian government, the US and the UK would get together in the autumn, in Ottawa, to review the situation. On the British side, we got the Americans to agree that Braniff would withdraw its trivial add-ons from points behind Dallas.

In his answer, Dell said, 'The new fares arrangements . . . will increase travel between our two countries. Total traffic last year was roughly 4 million passengers, both scheduled and charter; we estimate that this will rise to over 4½ million this year and the

346

importance of London as the premier European gateway from the US had been maintained.'

His last few words referred to the Americans' ploy of attempting to undermine the UK position by negotiating liberal agreements in favour of US carriers with smaller European countries, such as the Netherlands. The plan was simply that if Britain would not come to heel, they would focus transatlantic activity on airports like Amsterdam's Schiphol, to the detriment of London.

The way was clear for Braniff to begin its service into London. Gatwick soon became used to the 'Big Orange' Boeing 747 plying to and from the airport. Among airport staff, the aircraft was dubbed 'the flying carrot'. This unusual machine to me became the vivid manifestation of the export of American deregulation policies and, with the later financial failure of Braniff, how harmful those policies could be.

During the Braniff fares affair, one or two other matters also drew our management's attention. One was the introduction of BCAL's smallest operation, a regular feeder service between Birmingham and Gatwick using a Piper Navajo Chieftain, a twin-engined aircraft, in order to tap business traffic from the Midlands. But our main preoccupation was now the battle for the Los Angeles route. Laker's application to fly the route with a Skytrain all-standby service, and to revoke the BCAL licence was matched by our objection and bid to retain the licence, with plans for a new service.

Our aviation law specialist, David Beety, and Alastair Pugh, in charge of planning, put the case together. Members of the team they gathered around them were Peter Smith, a young man we had recruited as our North Atlantic product manager and from Cranfield Institute, where he was a lecturer. Also, by this time, John de la Haye, now partially recovered from illness, rejoined us on a part-time basis as a consultant. Tony Cocklin, who had spent the previous four years outside the airline on freelance public relations and journalism work, came back to head up the PR team. With de la Haye and Cocklin back working together in Ian Ritchie's external affairs division, we were once again beginning to sharpen our public relations edge which, although it had never been entirely blunt, now needed to be razor-keen in the new competitive world of air transport.

We believed that while the Laker standby service might be

347

justified for the vast New York market, it was inadequate for Los Angeles. The West Coast of the USA required services that catered for all types of traffic. We had good experience of the market from the early charter days and from the short period of scheduled services, when the BCAL operation had the effect of increasing the British share of the market from 12.9 per cent when we began in 1972 to 28.5 per cent when the oil crisis forced us to suspend the operation.

At the same time, we proposed a non-stop schedule with the long-range DC-10-30 aircraft. Laker could only manage a service which had to stop to refuel at Bangor, Maine, with his DC-10-10s.

Our trump card, we believed, was the innovation in style of service and fares which we created for re-entry into Los Angeles. The planners, crunching numbers on the floor below my own office in the Gatwick 'Ops Block', analysed the market carefully. Things were changing in air travel, especially on the Atlantic. The proliferation of low fares had meant that in the economy cabin of aircraft a businessman paying the full rate in order to have total flexibility, including the ability to change flights to a different date or even to another airline without penalty, could be sitting next to a passenger paying only half as much for a fare restricted by different terms and conditions.

It caused some amount of resentment within the key business travel market – and it was key because these were the people who travelled frequently throughout the year, providing regular business, unlike the leisure traveller who flew mostly in the peak periods, during summer and at Christmas.

By early 1978, the North Atlantic market analysis showed that 5.7 per cent of passengers travelled first class and 25.8 per cent travelled on full-fare economy tickets – that is, they were business travellers or business-related travellers, like wives and family joining husbands posted overseas. Of the remainder, 25.2 per cent of the market flew on excursion fares and 43.3 per cent on special promotional offers.

We concluded that there were six different categories of passengers who each had their own priorities and required fares and service standards tailored to their specific needs. The fundamental difference was between the business passenger, paying full fare and who wanted a high standard of service, and the leisure traveller

348

whose principal priority was price and was not so much bothered by the detail of service, so long as it was adequate, caring and professional.

The idea came to us to divide the economy cabin into two separate units, one for the full-fare payer, the other for the low-fare traveller. Because of the nature of the full-fare passengers, we elected to call the new section of the aircraft 'Executive'. First Class would remain as it was, but the low-fare end would be called 'Thrift Class'.

The next step was to put fare types into place. For the new executive cabin, we would have two fares. The first was the fully-flexible tariff, allowing 'interlining' on to other carriers and change of flight. The second was an optional point-to-point fare at a lower rate, for customers who would be going only from London to Los Angeles and back, with no side trips and who did not envisage itinerary changes. In the thrift cabin, where meals would be charged extra, would be people travelling on very low advance purchase fares and a 24-hour, last-minute purchase fare at the same level. In addition, there would be a cut-price standby fare, available only two hours prior to flight departure. We called this the 'Eleventh Hour' fare. It was set at £69 one-way and it was easily, mile for mile, the lowest scheduled fare on the North Atlantic routes. It was £14 lower than Laker's proposed flat rate fare for his Los Angeles standby service.

We called our package the 'Six Lane Skyway' and took it, with extreme confidence, to the route hearing at the CAA's headquarters in Kingsway.

Against Laker's one-stop operation, putting several hours on the flight time to and from Los Angeles and its service which catered for only one section of the market, plus his higher standby fare, we felt that we had won the case. David Beety had put up a fine performance.

In May, however, the CAA came out with its decision. To my anger and disgust, they revoked the BCAL licence in favour of a Laker Skytrain operation. The grounds were that we would be at a disadvantage against US competition, whereas the novelty of a Laker service might not be. I can hardly recall being more angry than when I heard of the decision in a phone call from David Beety. If Laker had put up a better case and a better deal for the consumer than we had done, I would have understood. As it was, we had beaten the Laker team comprehensively at the hearing. I could only conclude that this was further illogical appeasement for Laker following the Labour government's climb-down after the airline had taken Peter Shore to court after the Civil Aviation Review of 1976.

I told Beety to appeal against the CAA decision to the Secretary of State for Trade, Edmund Dell. But it was to no avail. Dell upheld the CAA decision with an announcement in August and Laker began flying what I regarded as 'our' route the following month. But I was determined to watch Laker like a hawk on the Los Angeles run and take advantage of any opportunity that came along to get their licence revoked so that BCAL could return to the West Coast.

Our plan for the Los Angeles 'Six Lane Skyway' was not, however, lost. The scheme had been thought out and was in place at the time when the US and UK governments were wrestling over the Braniff fares proposal.

On its conclusion, with a fares free-for-all now agreed to routes other than New York, we decided immediately to switch the 'Six Lane Skyway' plan to Houston. We announced the Houston fares scheme just two days before the official talks in Washington concluded, saying that, subject to final government approval, they would be introduced the following month.

On 14 April, along with the £69 standby, still the lowest fare mile for mile across the Atlantic, the BCAL Boeing 707 setting out or its daily run to Texas, proudly featured a major innovation – the first business class ever to be seen on the transatlantic air routes, British Caledonian 'Executive'. The industry reacted with scepticism to the special business class. Both Pan Am and TWA said that it would never work, yet within twelve months most of the transatlantic airlines were following our lead.

In the midst of the transatlantic wrangle, a call came through from Lagos. It was the airline's general manager for Nigeria, Ranald Noel-Paton, with a sad message. My good friend and colleague in the Nigerian British Chamber of Commerce, Chief Henry Fajemarokum, had died after becoming ill during a Lagos Chamber of Commerce mission to the Ivory Coast. The news came as a shock. I had known Henry as a larger-than-life, fit and jolly

350

man. He was a shrewd businessman and a good human being. His abiding mission was to cement trading and cultural relationships between Nigeria and the UK, for which he had a great love and admiration. We shared the view that Britain should be Nigeria's major trading partner and the formation of the NBCC was our attempt to realise our mutual ambition.

I dropped everything to attend Henry's funeral at Ile Oluji in Ondo State, Nigeria. Noel-Paton met me at Lagos Airport where we took a chartered light aircraft. The funeral was a massive affair, with crowds of people pressing to get into the church and milling around the church grounds. Such was the throng that Noel-Paton was forced to carry our floral tribute above his head in order to squeeze through the press of bodies to the church. Perspiring under a blazing sun, his arms thrust skywards with no hope of getting them down to his side, Noel-Paton had no chance against the young pickpocket who calmly reached into his jacket, took his wallet and dodged under the legs of the crowd to get completely out of sight. Henry, I felt, would have been furious on one hand, at the robbing of a guest in Nigeria, but on the other, he would have roared with laughter at the sight of a helpless European, in full business suit, at the mercy of a cheeky Nigerian urchin.

# 64

With the battles of Bermuda II and the start of the Houston service behind us, in the early months of 1978 I concentrated on some re-organisation at the top level of the company. The changing nature of the industry demanded that I spend time on helping to shape industry strategy and policies for the benefit of BCAL, and on other business developments.

Alastair Pugh, our planning chief, who had recently returned from a course at the Harvard School of Business Administration, had already assumed the mantle of deputy chief executive. I proposed that he should be appointed managing director and also that he should take a seat on the board of the BCAL parent company, Caledonian Airways Ltd. Alastair would become totally responsible for the running of the airline. In another move, I wanted Sir Peter Masefield to join Sir Iain Steward as joint deputy chairman. Some of the other directors raised their eyebrows at this suggestion. Iain Stewart had performed an invaluable service deputising for me on important overseas visits, as well as at functions in the UK. But his time, too, was stretched. I could think of no better person to assist with work of representation at very high level than the eminent Peter Masefield. The moves were, in the end, amicably agreed and both Peter Masefield and Alastair Pugh were to have crucial influence on the further development of BCAL and of British air transport in general.

Activities for BCAL were beginning to move at an even greater pace than before. Just before Christmas, Leonard Bebchick and Trevor Boud flew to Long Beach in California to meet Charles Forsyth of McDonnell Douglas. Their mission was to sign an order for two further DC-10-30 aircraft, doubling the DC-10 fleet and bringing our total investment in the aircraft to £83 million. The new DC-10s were scheduled for delivery in the autumn of that year and in spring 1980.

These additional new aircraft with their General Electric CF6-50C turbo fan engines also increased our requirement for major engine overhaul services. Thus in January, we announced the formation of Caledonian Airmotive Ltd and, with substantial financial assistance from the Scottish Development Agency, the creation of an engine overhaul and maintenance plant at Prestwick, Ayrshire.

At the same time a new shape was beginning to change the Gatwick skyline. This was the new hangar under construction for the DC-10 fleet. Unlike the existing hangars at the airport, the DC-10 facility would be large enough to take the wide-body aircraft. It also had a special tail dock fitted, to enable the engineers to work under cover on the third engine and the tail assembly, which was taller than that of any other aircraft in the fleet. The result was a huge, space-age building. The hangar, with a new block of engineering offices alongside, quickly came to dominate the south side of the airport.

'Gatwick's a really nice place.' The words came from Prince Charles. Less than a year after the Royal launch of the Houston route, HRH was again personally involved in a piece of BCAL's history.

The morning of 9 June 1978 saw me at the Gatwick railway station in an official reception line which included the chairman of the British Airports Authority, Norman Payne, the airport director, John Mulkern, Freddie Laker, by now knighted, and others. We were awaiting the arrival of one of British Rail's new 'Rapid City Link' trains which would soon be operating a fast and frequent service between Gatwick and Victoria.

On board was Prince Charles, coming to inspect the completion of the airport's £100 million, seven-year development programme. The improved, expanded facilities were designed to boost Gatwick's capacity to 16 million passengers a year. The programme, masterminded by Norman Payne, involved the total replacement of existing facilities to provide a brand new international gateway for London. There were suggestions, which I supported fully, that Gatwick's development should be marked by giving the airport a new name. 'Winston Churchill International' was the favourite,

353

but the great man's name never did more than grace Gatwick's VIP suite.

Nevertheless, Gatwick was in the ascendancy. Our own scheduled service development, combined with the new US airline services by Braniff and Delta, Laker's Skytrain flights, and scheduled development by airlines like Dan-Air was shifting Gatwick's image from that of a 'bucket and spade' charter terminal to a full-blown international gateway. British Airways, although its Airtours charter subsidiary was based at Gatwick, had only elected to offer a token service from Gatwick. Likewise, a number of foreign carriers – Iberia, TAP of Portugal and Air Canada – were resisting British Government pressure to move from Heathrow to Gatwick.

Government policy, laid down in a White Paper, was for the development of scheduled services at Gatwick. This was a great day for the BAA, for BCAL and for British Rail. Some years earlier, Norman Payne, Bob Reid, the BR chairman, and I had got together to affirm our mutual commitment to the development of Gatwick, I with my aircraft and routes, Payne with his infrastructure of facilities, and services and Reid with his all-important rail link. We met regularly four times a year, and created a framework of working groups in which our three organisations could find collective solutions to the problems of developing the airport. Now we were about to see a Royal preview of the results of our endeavours for Gatwick.

Proposals for the airport's development had gained momentum in 1974 when the project to construct a major new airport for London on the Essex coast at Maplin was scrapped by the Government. The Maplin airport, scheduled to open in 1982, was beset with disputes throughout the 1960s and early 1970s. It was finally killed off, not by environmentalist objectors, but by the very same recession which forced our own cutbacks in 1974. The cancellation of Maplin meant that future air traffic in London would have to be accommodated at the existing airports. Maplin's loss was Gatwick's gain.

But to be a fully-fledged international gateway, Gatwick's services desperately needed to be built up. That did not just mean more scheduled flights to more destinations, especially Continental Europe, but also better access and an efficient link with Heathrow, the dominant London airport which Gatwick was supposed to operate in tandem with.

The M23 motorway now fed road traffic to and from the airport, but only so far as a place called Hooley, south of Croydon. Planning problems had forced the abandonment of the original plan to run the motorway right into Central London. To the south, the motorway spilled into a regular, two-lane highway at the aptly-named Sussex village of Pease Pottage. Gatwick's road link to the city centre of London was, indeed, a mess of pottage. The M23 became known as the freeway which ran from nowhere to nowhere.

All the more reason to press for the evolution of the existing rail link between Gatwick and Victoria, run on standard Southern Region rolling stock, travelling by way of Redhill and East Croydon.

Prince Charles arrived at Gatwick from Victoria on board one of the new Rapid City Link trains in just 30 minutes. This new, fast, non-stop journey time was to become the norm for Gatwick passengers as the rail service evolved into the efficient Gatwick Express service.

But the main focus of his visit was something much more exciting than a railway. After a tour of the terminal facilities, Prince Charles would leave Gatwick on the inaugural flight of the new helicopter service between Gatwick and Heathrow, 'Airlink'. This was a major step forward for the airport. At last, London's two main airports could operate in tandem. The 15-minute helicopter flight, operating at high frequency, would effectively link the two airports' respective flight networks. We could offer our passengers in Houston or Lagos, for example, easy connections to virtually anywhere in the world. And, of course, Heathrow airlines could feed passengers on to Gatwick flights.

The Airlink service was a curious and unique operation, involving three partners: The British Airports Authority, which acquired the Sikorsky S-61N helicopter; British Airways, whose helicopter subsidiary operated and maintained the aircraft; and us, who managed and marketed the service and provided the single cabin staff member. We had started moves for the Airlink operation a year previously. Talks with BAA and BA led to an agreement to go ahead and this, in turn, led to an application for a licence to the CAA. Announcement of the plans brought out the protesters in full force. We faced objections from the so-called Gatwick Area Conservation Campaign at one end of the route, and from the Federation of Heathrow Anti-noise Groups at the other. The Sikorsky, they said, would cause noise pollution.

At the public hearing which ensued, we found ourselves for once on the same side as British Airways, presenting a joint case. Together we argued for the benefits of the helicopter link, emphasising the government policy which regarded Gatwick and Heathrow as a single London gateway. Between us, we estimated that the service would carry 64,000 connecting passengers a year. On the assumption that each of the passengers would be connecting to a British airline and the resulting yield would be on average £150, the service would benefit the UK balance of payments by about £10 million. The helicopter service would weld the two airports together to create the biggest and best international gateway in the world, winning traffic away from the developing airport hubs at Amsterdam's Schiphol and Paris's Charles de Gaulle.

The licence was granted on a compromise arrangement. The CAA said that we would operate for an initial 18-month experimental period. Frequency was limited to ten flights daily – we had originally asked for an unlimited frequency – and our operating day was restricted to the hours between 06.45 and 22.00. The protesters were furious with the CAA's statement that the incremental nuisance would not be sufficient in the existing noise climate, along the route taken as a whole, to outweigh the benefits conveyed by a viable air link between London's two major airports.

In fact our planners had worked hard to create a route at height levels which would have the least-possible impact over the shady avenues of the stockbroker belt which lay between the two airports. The CAA acknowledged that in its decision.

So it was that on the morning of 9 June 1978, Prince Charles and I climbed aboard the 28-seat Sikorsky to fly the 30-odd miles to Heathrow. One of his questions as we swung across the green Surrey hills was about the progress of the Houston route which he had launched for us eight months earlier. I told him that the service was going well and business was booming.

In fact, on top of the normal daily flights, we were about to launch one of the strangest airline services ever seen. Our promotions in the Houston area had created an unexpected demand for low cost travel to the UK. The same was true in the other direction. The daily 707 simply could not cope. Rocky Cox in Houston came up with the idea of running a series of weekend specials for the summer period. Designed primarily for younger travellers, the flights would be one class, with 147 seats on a Boeing 707. There would be no frills, but a lot of fun.

Latching on to the Western image, all the rage at the time, Cox called the service out of Houston the 'Saturday Night Special'. In London, we called it the 'Texas Special'. Eastbound passengers would get a main meal of chilli and beans with a free can of Texas Lone Star Beer. Breakfast would be flapjacks and syrup. For those going to Texas, lunch would be shepherd's pie and beans and the afternoon snack a 'Hero' sandwich. There would be no traditional bar service, just beer and soft drinks. The aircraft's audio channels would be turned over to country and western music and the in-flight films were to be westerns. At Houston, live country and western bands were recruited to send off departing passengers and welcome those arriving. Fares on the 'Saturday Night Specials' were $434 return eastbound; and £238 return westbound.

The stories that came back from the crews were legion. Every flight became a party, with many passengers bringing along their own musical instruments to accompany airborne sing-alongs. Something like 600 cans of beer were consumed on every trip.

'Saturday Nigh Specials' operated every weekend between July and mid-September and were mostly booked solid. The whole mood of the strange service was summed up in a US advertising poster. It showed a cowgirl riding astride a Boeing 707, reins in one hand, her stetson in the other. The engines of the aircraft were four bottles of Lone Star beer.

But the battle for Texas took on a new and serious tone back in London. Again we were before a panel of the CAA and again we had British Airways as our opponent. The target for both of us was the route to Dallas/Fort Worth. Under the Bermuda II 'moratorium' arrangement, DFW would become available to a British airline in the summer of 1980. Both BCAL and British Airways wanted the route.

The issue was clouded by BA's stated intention that, before direct non-stop flights could be operated, it would run a one-stop service. This would be a Concorde operation, an extension of its

London-Washington flights. We attempted to head this off by offering to co-operate with BA in the joint operation of a Concorde service, as an ancillary to a main, daily non-stop operation.

BA claimed that they were entitled to the DFW route as the city did not fall within the BCAL sphere of influence. We argued that if the original DFW licence had been approved in 1973, along with Houston and Atlanta, it would have been incorporated into Peter Shore's policy review.

The fact was that it was vital for us to have DFW alongside Houston. The two places were too close together and the markets intertwined. BA on DFW would put Houston at great risk. Also, we were at the same time negotiating to acquire two more DC-10s. The commitment for their purchase was largely dependent on the winning of the DFW route.

There was also another important consideration in the case, on the question of airport policy. Although British policy was geared to ensure that all new services to London used Gatwick rather than Heathrow, there was a side letter to the Bermuda II treaty that required Braniff to have the ability to operate from Heathrow if the British airline serving DFW was a Heathrow operator. On this point we gained the support of the BAA. They said at the hearing that if the outcome of the hearing was to the detriment of the development of Gatwick, they would be prepared to take the matter to court. This was strong stuff and the CAA took due note.

After three days of hearings at the end of June, the CAA was in a dilemma. It considered being even handed, allowing us the main non-stop service and giving BA rights for a Concorde operation. But this would mean seeking designation for two British airlines for DFW. The authority also looked at the possibility of a joint BCAL/BA Concorde operation. But that would mean seeking the same kind of double designation for us at Washington. The CAA was also wary of the Gatwick/Heathrow situation and the BAA's legal threat. After waiting through the whole month of July for an answer, the CAA came out with its decision on 11 August. After recounting the case and the opposing arguments, the CAA said: 'BCAL's present route network is profitable but is exposed to particularly high risks. It is clearly desirable that BCAL should be enabled, for its long-term profitability, to diversify its present network, at least to a small extent.' That was all I needed to read as my eyes raced through the 18-page document. It was barely necessary to go to the final, terse paragraph which said simply that the BCAL application was granted as applied for; and the BA bid was refused.

That decision sparked a mood of euphoria within the airline. Only two days before its publication by the CAA, an extraordinary general meeting of the company had approved a plan I had long been promoting for an employee profit sharing scheme. I wanted our staff at all levels to have the opportunity of a stake in their organisation and we would do this with the allocation of free shares. The scheme allowed the directors to allocate up to five per cent of profits for this purpose. The money would be handed to a board of trustees to purchase shares to be allocated to individuals in quantities related to salary level and length of service. The winning of the DFW route immediately after the shares announcement was a major boost to staff morale and their longer term prospects.

The decision came through on the eve of a trip to Houston. I had just signed at Gatwick a contract with McDonnell Douglas for not two, but three further DC-10 aircraft. It was a package worth £65 million and the aircraft would be delivered in 1980 and 1981, to bring the total DC-10 fleet to seven aircraft.

At the same time, we had also completed an agreement to boost the fleet, albeit temporarily, with a Boeing 747, the first ever to be operated by a British independent airline. The background to this deal was that in starting the Houston service earlier than originally planned with the Boeing 707, I had assured the Houstonians that we would bring on wide-body aircraft as soon as possible, certainly no later than the 1978/79 winter period. Industrial problems at the McDonnell Douglas plant at Long Beach, California, had, however, slowed down production and the aircraft destined for the Houston route would not be delivered until the following spring. In order to fulfil my commitment to Houston, Curly Walter was dispatched to find a wide-body aircraft which we could lease for the interim period. He came up with a 747, call-sign 'Paddy Zulu', from Aer Lingus. The Irish airline, however, had no spare crews – they could offer only a 'dry' lease, that is, the aircraft without a crew. BCAL, of course, had no 747-trained pilots, so we would have to find them from somewhere else. We eventually did a deal with

359

British Airways for the loan of pilots to operate the aircraft. The cabin crew would be our traditional, tartan-clad stewardesses.

So Paddy Zulu, repainted in BCAL livery, owned by Aer Lingus, and flown by British Airways, was scheduled to operate between Gatwick and Houston five times weekly between November and mid-February, when our own, new DC-10 would be delivered. To mark the introduction of this hybrid operation, we agreed to offer a special fare of just £50 one way on each flight in Paddy Zulu's first week on the route.

I was travelling to Houston to announce the wide-body development. I very quickly got Margaret Trett to telephone Rocky Cox to make arrangements to extend the trip to Dallas and Fort Worth so that we could begin laying the ground for the new service among civic leaders and the business community.

The atmosphere was good for the planning of the new service into Texas. Houston was achieving results beyond our expectations. We had planned for 47,000 passengers in the first year. By the time of my August visit, we had carried 50,000 and the first full year still had three months to run. We estimated that would be 20,000 passengers above target. First year revenue, we reckoned, would be £11 million and to date we had carried six million pounds of cargo.

Our sights were set on even more expansion in the USA with the opening of direct flights to three other cities which, so far, had no transatlantic service. They were St Louis, New Orleans and Denver. Applications were filed with the CAA.

Back in Europe, not all events were going our way. The award of licences to serve the Scandinavian cities of Stockholm, Gothenburg, Oslo and Copenhagen the previous year had resulted in the Scandinavian governments calling for a renegotiation of their air services agreement with the UK. After a tortuous series of negotiations the Department of Trade allowed the Scandinavians to force an agreement which prohibited dual designation. This effectively cut us out. Our response was to re-file immediately for a licence between Gatwick and Sweden, as the sole British operator. Alongside the application was a bid to revoke British Airways' licence.

Closer to home, at Gatwick, the airline was suffering from the result of the fast growth that had occurred over the previous few

360

years. The airline accommodation was spread over a collection of offices, hangars and portable buildings at the airport and in Crawley. We had recently been forced to fragment even further by taking office space in the Sussex market town of Haywards Heath to house the growing sales division. Accommodation became a priority and plans were put together for the construction of a brand new headquarters building. We acquired the site of a former bus depot at County Oak in Crawley, just a few miles south of Gatwick. We required it to house all of the staff, other than those who needed to be on the airport itself. Trevor Boud and I had admired the new, efficient glass and steel buildings in places like Houston and Dallas and insisted that was what we wanted. Plans were filed with the local planning officials for a nine-storey building with twin towers. An immediate objection came from the CAA which claimed that the building was too high to be so close to the airport. It would affect the radar surveillance. Plans were amended to reduce the building by two storeys to seven, and to expand it laterally. Approval for the new plans came through at the end of the year and work proceeded on selecting contractors. Our requirement was for the building, to be named 'Caledonian House', to be ready in 1981.

# 65

Sunday morning golf at Walton Heath Golf Club, near Reigate, in Surrey, came to be a welcome relaxation from the hurly burly of the airline business. As often as overseas travel permitted, I would leave home on Sundays at around 9 a.m. to get to the club by 9.30, in order to tee off and fight my way around the heather-clad heathland for the next three or four hours. One of the other club members to whom I was introduced early on in my golfing career was a fellow scot, John Junor, then editor of the *Sunday Express* and famous for his acerbic 'JJ' column. John and Bill Martin, the picture editor of the *Sunday Express*, became my regular Sunday morning partners.

John's other great passion, apart from his newspaper and his golf, was sailing. My great passion, aside from the airline and golf, was also sailing. We had a good deal in common, became very good friends and enjoyed each other's company a great deal.

It was to Junor's huge delight that one of the main promotional activities of Express Newspapers was the sponsorship of the annual Boat Show in London. He took great pleasure in hosting a special lunch on the occasion of the Boat Show, to which he invited a selected list of eminent people. At the luncheon in early 1979, I found myself sitting next to the Leader of the Opposition, Margaret Thatcher. I had met her before and lobbied her on aviation issues. But this time I was able to talk about the problems of the industry, about the frustrations of the private sector and the role that independent aviation could play in the future. I felt that she was receptive. After all, Iain Stewart, our deputy chairman, who knew Mrs Thatcher well, had marked my card by telling me she was a keen admirer of BCAL's.

I followed up the lunch meeting with a letter to her at her private office. I suggested that the lunch discussion be extended in a visit to Gatwick to see our operation. This she declined due to heavy commitments. But she wanted me to meet John Nott, the shadow trade minister.

Three months later, after the General Election of May 1979, my Boat Show lunch partner had become Britain's first woman Prime Minister. John Nott had moved from opposition spokesman to become the new Secretary for State for Trade, our industry's minister. His Parliamentary Under Secretary was Norman Tebbit.

A Conservative government, committed to free enterprise and the relaxation of the grip of government regulation on commerce and industry, seemed to be exactly the kind of administration we needed. The one cloud nudging its way across the horizon was the rumoured prospect that the new government would at some stage seek to sell off part of British Airways to the public. Our fears were that unless some balance was brought to the industry, British Airways, with its superior route network and Heathrow operating base, would attract the cream of investment to the detriment of the independent sector. But no indication of the government's plans in this area was forthcoming.

Our immediate priority was to focus attention on our own development and the development of Gatwick. Our method was to produce a booklet and promote it hard through every possible political and business channel. We called it *British Caledonian and Gatwick Airport in The Eighties*. Though scheduled services now accounted for the majority of the business, we faced something of a brick wall on the path to future development. New licences were hard to come by, at least any that were worth operating and offered positive growth. BCAL was only about 13 per cent of the size of British Airways. In an industry growing at between 10 and 15 per cent each year, this meant that every year BA increased in size by an amount equal to the total size of BCAL.

Our political booklet set out two major objectives for the 1980s. The first was that we would seek to develop for ourselves a more stable and less vulnerable route network so as to strengthen ourselves against the regular economic crises which afflict the airline industry. The second was to progressively work for the acceptance of Gatwick as one of the world's major international airports. The booklet was distributed throughout Whitehall and

Westminster. We met politicians and civil servants. Our message was that both our objectives could be attained by allowing BCAL to enter new and growing markets, through a clear and more flexible policy which would encourage enterprise and place emphasis on consumer benefits.

# 66

One of the pieces of financial news in the spring of 1979 which caught the attention of the press and, I hoped, the politicians, was our announcement of a £644,000 distribution of shares among the staff of BCAL. From the pre-tax profit of £12.2 million earned in the previous financial year, we had allocated money so that shares could be purchased for members of staff. The cash was, in fact, handed over to a board of trustees under the chairmanship of Stuart Young.

The airline was riding high and the first tangible sign of the profit-sharing scheme appeared to give the staff an even greater motivational lift than they possessed naturally.

In a message in a specially-prepared financial report for employees, I told them: 'Profits don't just happen – they are made. Human beings are the determining force. Not everyone dedicates themselves full-time, all the time. But that is what we must have because the simple fact of life is that a group company, division, department or section does not succeed or fail just because it is there.'

BCAL now employed 5,994 people. The aircraft fleet numbered 29 and carried 1.9 million passengers and 50,000 tonnes of freight over a network serving 40 destinations in 28 countries. The balance of the airline's business had shifted to 70 per cent from scheduled services and 30 per cent from charters. The Gatwick-Heathrow Airlink helicopter service had carried more than 50,000 passengers and was well on its way to reaching the target of 64,000 set for the first year's operation.

We were not short of problems. Of major concern was currency devaluations in certain countries in South America which depleted revenues, and the hold up in remittances from Africa. One serious problem, which had emerged over the previous two years and continues to dog the industry, became a matter for major concern. This was the increasing number of flight delays caused by the inadequacy of the air traffic control systems in Europe.

In the area of route development, we had been disappointed by the frustrating outcome of the plan to open a network to Scandinavia. We failed to obtain rights to introduce a service to Bologna, in Italy, and the Brazilian government had prevaricated over an application for more frequencies.

The slow progress of the UK government's airports policy, designed to bring more services into Gatwick, worried me. In a move which I can only describe as cack-handed, the Labour administration had simply issued instructions that a few designated carriers would move from Heathrow to Gatwick. Among them was Iberia, the Spanish carrier. The Spaniards retaliated by suspending the BCAL rights through Madrid to Argentina. We negotiated a new temporary arrangement with the Portuguese to operate through Lisbon, but the problem still cost us a good deal of money.

Perhaps our main frustration at the time, however, was the stalemate on European services. The few we had were insufficient to build a true hub at Gatwick and British Airways did not appear to be interested in moving some of its operation from the congested terminals at Heathrow. Our move to develop a network of services to Scandinavia had been blocked and we were at an impasse.

But the mood in Europe was changing. Consumers were beginning to turn their attention to air travel and questioning the old, restrictive order of things. European air transport had been developed on protectionist lines whereby the respective national carriers operated in 'pool partnership' with each other. That is, the airlines controlled capacities and frequencies of flights on the respective routes, working out a mutual timetable, controlling the level of air fares and sharing out the collective revenue, usually on a 50/50 basis at the end of the day. It meant that fares remained high on the one hand and that there were very few opportunities for new market entrants on the other.

The emerging dissatisfaction in the market place was manifested in a special report, prepared for presentation to the Parliamentary Assembly of the Council of Europe, by a Swedish member of

366

the European Parliament, Anders Bjorck. His thesis soon became known universally as the 'Bjorck Report'. Bjorck urged more competition in Europe: doing away with 'excessively rigid intra-European tariffs' to the benefit of the consumer and the economy as a whole. He went on to call for new policies to eliminate monopoly, or duopoly as it correctly was, and to cut prices. He wanted the development of competition, flexibility and increased airline efficiency.

Against the background of the Bjorck Report on the Continent and the failure of the airports policy in the UK, a major think-tank was set up at BCAL under Alastair Pugh. What eventually emerged after a great deal of study, discussion, analysis and computation was a plan which combined the innovation of the BCAL pricing developments on the North Atlantic with the ambition for a larger European network.

The plan was called 'Mini-Prix', a phrase which crossed the European language barrier to signify low cost. It was a simple scheme which by operating at off-peak times would cut the cost of European air travel by an overall 40 per cent. In some cases, by using stand-by fares, prices would drop by as much as 80 per cent.

In a flurry of licensing and public relations activity, the Mini-Prix campaign was launched in April. Simultaneous press conferences were staged in London, Brussels, Paris and Bonn. The news release material and an accompanying brochure was translated into the main European languages and disseminated throughout the Continent.

The crux of the strategy was the bid to operate to twenty new points in Europe. We sought licences to serve Frankfurt, Dusseldorf, Hamburg, Hanover, Cologne-Bonn, Stuttgart, Vienna, Copenhagen, Helsinki, Marseilles, Athens, Rome, Milan, Turin, Oslo, Lisbon, Madrid, Barcelona, Zurich and Geneva. At the time, BCAL had only four routes into Europe from Gatwick – to Paris, Brussels, Amsterdam and Genoa. Copenhagen was served from Edinburgh and Newcastle; Amsterdam from Glasgow and Newcastle. We wanted the Mini-Prix fares on the existing routes and similar new fares on domestic trunk services to Scotland, Manchester and the Channel Islands.

The prospect of Mini-Prix fares like £15.50 to Paris and £27.50

to Vienna caught the imagination of the press throughout Europe and the result was massive publicity, with Alastair Pugh and myself constantly on the phone to journalists or speaking into tape recorders or to television cameras.

The Mini-Prix announcement was coupled with a statement of intention to acquire a new aircraft fleet for Europe, either the A.310 from the European Airbus Industrie consortium or the planned Boeing 767. Both aircraft were highly-efficient, advanced-technology aircraft, the new generation jets.

The momentum was stepped up a few months after the Mini-Prix announcement when, in July, in the wake of the Bjorck Report, the EEC Commission issued from its Brussels headquarters a discussion document, *Contribution of the European Communities to the development of air transport services*. Its first and main objective fitted the BCAL Mini-Prix concept and philosphy perfectly. 'A total network, unhampered by national barriers with efficient services beneficial to the different user groups, at prices as low as possible, without discrimination.'

The Commission's memorandum had, in turn, been heralded by the publication of the new Government's *Conservative Manifesto for Europe 1979*. It stated, 'The principles of competition which govern other industries in the community should also be applied to air travel.' It called for more competition with the state airlines by private carriers, leading to a more varied structure of fares and a reduction in their costs.

The political bandwagon had begun to roll, but in doing so it gathered some other followers on the way, each with their eye on a main chance in Europe. Freddie Laker didn't sit still for long and came out with an unrealistic proposal for a free-for-all network of 660 routes based on 34 European cities. Laker envisaged a pattern of routes criss-crossing Europe, ignoring national boundaries and existing bilateral agreements. The airline would operate this network with a fleet of Airbus A.300 aircraft in which it would invest £250 million.

Britannia Airways weighed in with a bid to carry scheduled service passengers on its range of inclusive tour charter flights. From Air UK – the new name for the old British Island Airways – came a bid for licences to serve Geneva, Milan and Hamburg.

The CAA drew the whole thing together in a public hearing,

scheduled to take place in several sessions between October and January the following year. The chairman of the hearing was Ray Colegate whom we had known since our very earliest days when he was at the old Board of Trade. It was a complex hearing. Laker's application was objected to by British Airways, Air Anglia, Air UK and ourselves. In turn, our Mini-Prix bid was opposed by British Airways and Laker. Objectors to Air UK were British Airways, ourselves and Laker, and to Britannia, British Airways, ourselves, Dan-Air and Laker.

Before the hearing began, the Scandinavian issue raised its head, with John Nott, the Tory Secretary of State for Trade, instructing the CAA not to hear any applications which involved services to Denmark, Norway and Sweden. This was because of the new bilateral agreement with the UK which, prompted by our previous application, specifically precluded dual designation.

David Beety, backed by a team of witnesses which was headed by Alastair Pugh, was assigned to take our case. Beety, Pugh and the airline's planners had put together an extremely thorough submission, where each route in the application was analysed and supported by financial and operational data. Colegate was later to commend this, in contrast to the Laker bid, largely unsupported, but which was based on an interpretation of the Treaty of Rome, the agreement which effectively forms the constitution of the European Community.

The hearing started with the usual opening statements before the real meat of such occasions was reached: the cross-examinations.

After three days there was an adjournment, but we had a significant PR project up our sleeves. The morning of 29 October found a group of us – myself, Alastair Pugh, John Prothero-Thomas, Ian Ritchie and Tony Cocklin – waiting at Gatwick for an executive HS 125 jet to arrive from Toulouse. It was bringing Bernard Lathiere, President of Airbus Industrie, to Gatwick to join me for a press conference in London. We were announcing a £136 million deal for three Airbus A.310 aircraft, with a further three on option. In fact, Lathiere and I were actually to sign the contract on a table at the London Press Club, with photographers and TV cameras present. The A.310s were destined for the European Mini-Prix routes and I wanted to harden up our claim currently before the CAA.

The morning was fraught. In the first place, the aircraft didn't arrive at Gatwick on schedule. When we chased it up through the aviation communications system, we found that it was circling Heathrow. On arriving at Gatwick, Lathiere and his team disembarked to go to the small General Aviation terminal on the north side of the airport. There we found, to our horror, that Lathiere had forgotten his passport and might be refused entry. After some urgent words with the immigration officials, however, he was allowed in on the strength of his driving licence. So we were on the road to the Press Club, when the next hiccough occurred. My Jaguar, with driver Les Smith at the wheel, incomprehensibly came to a halt on the motorway spur out of the airport. The following two cars, each with BCAL drivers, were bringing other members of the BCAL and Airbus teams. As they came up the spur road, they were amazed to find myself and Lathiere strolling down the hard shoulder back towards the airport and the Jaguar sitting with its bonnet raised and Les Smith sprawled over the engine. Roadside re-adjustments were quickly made with the two other cars and we were on our frustrated way to London. Lathiere couldn't resist saying you should buy a Peugeot!

In any event, the announcement of the A.310 order had the desired effect – a splash of publicity, with headlines like 'Airline plumps for Euro-jets' and 'Airline flies the flag' plus pictures of myself and the ebullient Lathiere signing the purchase contract in the newspapers just before the hearings were set to resume.

If the timing of the announcement had signs of a PR stunt about it, the reality was quite different. Evaluation of the two aircraft contending for the BCAL order, the A.310 and the Boeing 767, had been an arduous task. Both were extremely fine aircraft and the order could very easily have swung in Boeing's direction, but for the A.310's better economic levels on shorter distances.

The aircraft was designed for a flexible operation. Its two engines could efficiently handle medium range or short routes, carrying 206 passengers. Delivery of the three aircraft was scheduled for February, March and April 1984. As it was, I was delighted to place the very first British order with the European manufacturing consortium in which British Aerospace was a partner and whose Hatfield-Chester Division would make the wings for the new aircraft. Initially, we planned to operate the A.310 on the

370

West African Coastal service and to points in North Africa and on high-volume routes in Europe.

I said at the news conference, 'The drive towards a freer European air transport system, spearheaded by our low-fare Mini-Prix plans, will allow us eventually to operate more routes in Europe with stage distances of between 300 and 1,500 miles. The A.310 is very suitable indeed for this job.'

After concluding the European route hearing on 24 January 1980, Ray Colegate's panel came out with its decision on 13 March. The Laker bid was rejected. Of that bid the CAA wrote, 'Laker Airways was, in effect, offering a map of uncharted territory in support of an application for a carte blanche.' It did leave the door somewhat ajar by inviting Laker to make new applications for specific routes, 'fully supported on the lines followed by British Caledonian . . .' The Air UK and the Britannia applications were refused.

As for Mini-Prix, we came out with six of the twenty routes we had applied for. The CAA licensed us for the Helsinki, Vienna, Cologne, Hamburg, Hanover and Stuttgart routes which it deduced were important to the development of Gatwick and which could sustain competition from existing services at Heathrow. The CAA did say: 'the grant of some of the routes was in line with the evolutionary approach it was felt was right for European development and clearly constituted a beginning upon which further development could be based.'

That further development would turn out to be a painful, frustrating process in which British political and commercial aspirations would be held back by the barriers of European protectionism.

371

# 67

Nowhere is the news of aircraft accidents more profoundly received than in the offices, airports and operational centres of the industry itself. May 25 1979 was no different. It was with shock and sympathy that we in BCAL heard the news of an accident to a DC-10-10 aircraft at the O'Hare International Airport in Chicago.

Tragically, all 273 people on board were killed and the circumstances were mystifying. The aircraft, bound for the West Coast, had started its take-off run and begun to lift off when one of its wing-mounted engines separated from the aircraft. This caused the DC-10 to flip on to its back and crash back on to the runway. It was an horrific accident and the shocking photographic evidence was very soon placed before a worldwide audience. All of us in BCAL felt for the management and staff of American Airlines and for the relatives of the victims. But we were not prepared for the saga which was to follow.

The DC-10 was – and still is – a very fine aircraft. It is technically reliable, economically efficient and comfortable for passengers. However, there had been previous accidents involving a latch on a cargo hold door and this had, at the time, given the DC-10 a poor image for a while. Now the response to the Chicago crash was one of hysteria. Almost before the officials of the US Federal Aviation Administration and the National Transportation Safety Board had begun to piece together the evidence, accusations were made about the DC-10's design with the implication that the aircraft was inherently unsafe. It was alleged that the pylon which holds the engines on to the wing was badly designed and the bolt which locks the engine on to the pylon was held up as the guilty piece of machinery.

The US authorities ordered the grounding of all DC-10s. The

British CAA followed suit immediately. For BCAL and Laker, the other main DC-10 operator, the Chicago accident had sparked a situation which was potentially disastrous. It was the beginning of the summer season, the year's peak period for travel, and our fleet of three DC-10s was scheduled to operate services to West Africa, South America and to Houston.

The grounding meant the redeployment of our own Boeing 707s onto the DC-10 routes and hurried arrangements to lease in aircraft from other airlines. During a thirteen-day period all British-registered DC-10s were checked by airline engineers, McDonnell Douglas technical experts, and the CAA. Similar checks were being made across Europe. By the end of the period, the British and European authorities reissued Certificates of Airworthiness, permitting the DC-10 to fly again, provided special inspection procedures were followed. However, the FAA in Washington kept the DC-10s grounded for a further thirty-eight days and refused to recognise foreign Airworthiness Certificates for the DC-10. It was an outrageous situation which ended up costing us £2.5 million of profit. The FAA's stance was in breach of the Bermuda II Air Services Agreement which required each country to recognise the other's airworthiness certificates and, on this premise, I ultimately ordered the BCAL lawyers to take action against the US FAA to reclaim £1 million.

It was in the middle of July that the head of the FAA, Langhorne Bond, announced the decision to let the DC-10s fly again in US territory. His statement vindicated the innocent McDonnell Douglas company and its aircraft from safety allegations – but the image of both had been badly bruised.

Bond said that the investigation following the crash had been the most intensive, exhaustive and thorough in aviation history. 'That effort has been a success. We have resolved to my satisfaction the safety questions raised by the tragic crash and we have worked out strict measures to ensure that such a crash will not happen again.' He went on to say that there was a possibility of some re-design of the pylon to make the thrust link more easily inspected and of the aft pylon bulkhead which, he said, had failed in the Chicago crash because of 'maintenance abuse'.

The fact which came out in the official FAA investigation report

373

was that American Airlines had not followed maintenance procedures laid down by McDonnell Douglas. The company was then and still is a very sound airline, highly respected in the industry, with a proud history. Engines are regularly taken off aircraft for maintenance and overhaul and replaced. It is a routine affair, but a delicate process. The normal method is for the engine to be placed in a mechanical 'sling' which is carefully and slowly lifted into position, to be 'mated' with the fitments of the wing pylon. However, in order to speed up the process of engine change, American had adopted what turned out to be a less precise manoeuvre of lifting engines to wings by fork-lift truck. So far as the Chicago DC-10 was concerned this had weakened the pylon fittings and the tragic accident was the appalling consequence.

Our own DC-10-30 returned to the Houston route on 14 July, almost two months after the crash at O'Hare. For us, the DC-10 was performing well, achieving an average daily utilisation of twelve to thirteen hours. Despite some misgivings about the effect of the Chicago crash on the market, especially in the USA, the aircraft achieved a 45 per cent increase in passenger kilometres and a 326 per cent increase in freight tonne kilometres on the Houston route in the full year of 1979, compared to the previous twelve months. At the time of the crash, three DC-10-30s operated in the BCAL livery. A fourth was due for delivery in August.

The emergency of the DC-10 grounding took place against a much broader battle for the airline; a political one. The new Conservative government had indicated two specific intentions for the airline industry. The first was amendment to the 1971 Civil Aviation Act and the policy guidance procedure provided to the CAA. The intention was, in the style of the Thatcher government, to lessen the hand of government on the industry and to give the CAA a blanket guidance to conduct the route licensing process. Effectively, the CAA was to be given a free hand within certain loose parameters. This, when it came to the sternest test several years later, would prove to be an irony. The second move was an indicated intention to sell off part of the shareholding of British Airways to the public, a matter of great concern to us at BCAL.

On 24 July I made my way to Victoria Street for a meeting with John Nott, the new Secretary of State for Trade, his Parliamentary Under Secretary, Norman Tebbit, and some of the senior civil servants. I told Nott that it was important to me that he heard the BCAL view before the new CAA guidance took shape. I handed over a copy of our booklet, *BCAL and Gatwick Airport in the 1980s*. It set out our plans for route network development and how we saw the development of Gatwick. Naturally, it was designed to give BCAL a sound position now and for the long-term future.

I outlined recent history particularly the review under Peter Shore through which we were locked into areas that were unstable or had little development potential. I suppose I was playing for another wholesale review as I told Nott that the new guidance could, if the Government wished, redress the balance and provide BCAL with a meaningful network, allowing us to play a full role as an international airline. Nott dismissed this by saying he had not been around in the past, and was only interested in what should happen in the future. He had not been connected with the airline business until now, and really did not want to get involved with it. He wanted to leave all that to the CAA.

I pressed on – I had to take the chance to get points home. BCAL, I said was locked into South America and Africa, while British Airways held the worldwide network of routes from Britain outside our licence area. There was little opportunity for double designation – very few foreign governments would allow two British airlines on a route – and unless some hard policy guidance was to come from Government, there was little opportunity for development into stable areas.

In fact behind my words to John Nott was a larger political lobbying campaign being run by Ian Ritchie and John Prothero-Thomas designed to build up pressure in the Government for a fresh review of air transport and, ultimately, a situation where routes could be re-allocated, some of the routes controlled by the state corporation being made available to the independents.

Nott asked about my concern over the possibility of part of British Airways being sold off to the public. I told him that I welcomed it and, indeed, would like to see him selling the lot off to private enterprise. However, my concern was two fold. On one hand, the Conservative Party might regard this move as covering the requirement for private enterprise in civil aviation and ignore the existing independents. On the other, British Airways might take up all of the capital investment that the financial

375

institutions were prepared to put into the airline business, to our detriment.

At this point Norman Tebbit entered the meeting. In that brash manner which the nation was to know so well and which the Labour politician Dennis Healey was to describe as belonging to 'a semi-house-trained polecat', Tebbit said as far as he was concerned, it was up to the CAA to award licences – his only interest was that the British airline industry developed and he had no interest whatsoever which airline or airlines led this development. There was a bit of cross talk about free market forces. I told the politicians this was fair enough if there was an equitable distribution of licences. Otherwise their ideology was meaningless.

We went on to talk about Gatwick. Nott knew I was not keen on British Airways operating from the airport, especially since BCAL was barred from flying out of Heathrow. I explained that the development of Gatwick should be left to those with a vested interest in the place – only then would meaningful results be obtained. I said that our view was that the airport had a potential capacity of 19 or 20 million passengers a year, but even with one runway, it was necessary to have a second terminal. Nott agreed on this.

The Secretary of State then turned and said he was going to say something which would, no doubt, annoy me. 'Why,' he said, 'are your people – British Airways, Laker and all the others – always around at the Department of Trade? Why are you all so nervous about the guidance? Why are Pugh and Ritchie and you and all the others always here?'

The answer, I told him, was very simple. It was because he and his department dictated our future. Furthermore, the guidance that he was now writing for the CAA would be vital to our future prospects.

We talked a little about how consultation with the industry should take place. Nott gave no indication of how he thought it would occur, but said there would be consultation. The White Paper should be ready to go to Parliament for the next session.

The meeting had lasted an hour and fifteen minutes. In closing I thanked Nott for his time and asked him to please be sure to read our nine-page document when he was on holiday in Cornwall the following week. He promised to do so not in Cornwall, but immediately after the meeting.

Despite his lack of knowledge of the industry and lack of interest in knowing of its evolution so far, which I found inexplicable for the responsible Minister, I took to John Nott. He was impressive and clearly very able and I felt he should be cultivated as much as possible in the future. As for Norman Tebbit, he had been a good listener and friendly to the independents' view as an opposition MP. I was not at all sure of his leanings now that he was in power.

If John Nott thought that we were simply hanging around his office waiting for him to hand out routes, he was wrong. We were prepared to fight for expansion. Had he been close to industry activities, it would not have been necessary for me to tell him that we had applications in for a number of new routes to the USA, and a number of points in the Middle East, and to that bastion of British Airways monopoly, Hong Kong.

# 68

The view from the windows of the Tamar Suite in Hong Kong's illustrious Mandarin Hotel looks down towards the harbour and across to the Kowloon peninsula and the runway of Kai Tak airport. This was the target I was aiming for and the reason I had flown across the Pacific with Margaret Trett from meetings with Boeing in Seattle.

Joining us in Hong Kong were Ian Ritchie and Tony Cocklin who had travelled the long way round, with Japan Airlines, via Tokyo. The reason: to avoid being noticed by British Airways which operated the only direct service from London. Also linking up with us was an English journalist based in Singapore, Alwyne 'Bob' Taylor. He had carried out some public relations and political contact work in Singapore in the days we were operating there. Now we needed his help in Hong Kong.

We were in the luxury surroundings of the Mandarin to pursue a bid which to many seemed impossible, to break the British Airways monopoly on Hong Kong and open up a route to the colony from Gatwick. The venture had started from a chance remark after a meeting with the CAA in London. We had been talking about our network aspirations in general. As a few of us walked down the corridor on the way out, one particular CAA official turned and looked me straight in the eyes and said, 'Take a look at Hong Kong.'

As a British crown colony, Hong Kong counted virtually as a UK domestic route – or as it is known in the industry, a 'cabotage' route. British Airways and its predecessor, BOAC, had monopolised the route from the very beginnings of intercontinental air travel. We and other independents had, in the past, operated passenger and freight charters to Hong Kong, but the route had been protected from scheduled service competition.

We picked up the throw-away line from the CAA and set about studying Hong Kong. We also had to review the Middle East, as an en-route stop was vital. Eventually we chose Dubai which had an 'open skies' policy to attract business to its lavish new airport. British Airways' services to and from Hong Kong were, to say the least, not popular. Especially with the market in the colony. Delays seemed to be frequent, service was alleged to be sloppy and, in short, there was great dissatisfaction. The state airline was going through a very bad patch in almost every area of operation. In Hong Kong, its initials were parodied into 'Bloody Awful' and one commentator was heard to say, 'it's not a national airline, it's a national disgrace.'

Unless the UK/Hong Kong market was prepared to travel by circuitous routes with foreign airlines, they had no choice but to travel with British Airways. On top of all this the fares were high. In short, the scene was set for the kind of competitive bid which was previously unthinkable. The result was that we filed an application with the CAA in London for a licence to serve Hong Kong. However, although a colony, Hong Kong had its own autonomous government and its own Air Transport Licensing Authority, until now only concerned with charters and the regional operations of the locally-based airline, Cathay Pacific, in which British Airways held a stake.

To operate the route we required a licence both from the CAA in London and the ATLA in Hong Kong. We knew we would face fierce opposition from Cathay Pacific and its shareholder, British Airways, so a careful battle plan had to be drawn up.

The Tamar Suite began to resemble the boardroom back at Gatwick, as we discussed plans. Representatives of our local general sales agent were wheeled in to give advice about local market conditions and politics. The press was monitored, especially the radio phone-in programmes which invariably included complaints about British Airways.

Ian Ritchie visited the offices of the licensing authority to obtain the necessary forms for a licence application. The one thing we needed was as much publicity as we could possibly muster. We needed a high profile so that the entrenched interests could not easily sweep us under the political carpet and out of sight. We focussed on fares, a matter of resentment among the Hong Kong air travel market, and brought the transatlantic formula into play. In our package, we would launch the first-ever stand-by fare between Hong Kong and London. Its price: £100, or 990 Hong Kong dollars.

Cocklin and Taylor rustled up the press, English language and Chinese, to bring them in relays to the Tamar Suite. The story of our bid to fly the route and the low stand-by fare broke the morning that Ritchie took a cab to the Air Transport Licensing Authority to formally hand in the application. Our plan was for a daily service with DC-10-30 aircraft, offering three classes of travel, starting from April 1980. The publicity machine went into overdrive as radio, television and newspapers beseiged the stately lobby of the Mandarin to obtain interviews which we were only too pleased to grant.

The expected backlash from Cathay Pacific came swiftly. I believe we caught them entirely off guard initially, but they responded with an announcement of their own plans to operate to London and this served only to increase the pace and depth of the press coverage in a story where BCAL held the lead position. The activity in Hong Kong did not escape the attention of Freddie Laker who subsequently entered the battle with his own licence bid. The London-Hong Kong route, he said, would be part of a round-the-world Skytrain operation.

The scene was set for probably the most curious and elaborate air licensing procedures ever to take place. We first had to fight for a licence from the Hong Kong authorities and then repeat the same process in London before the CAA. Hong Kong, we believed, was a case for Leonard Bebchick. Backed up by Peter Smith and his planning team, Leonard set about preparing our case.

Judge Ross Penlington set up a makeshift courtroom in one of the commercial buildings in the Victoria business district of Hong Kong Island. Into it on the morning of 12 November 1979, trooped the competing lawyers: Leonard Bebchick for BCAL; his fellow American, Bob Beckman, for Laker; Peter Martin for Cathay; and Trevor Philipson for British Airways. Each had prepared a weighty submission backed by an array of statistical and financial exhibits. Alongside them were their team of witnesses and technical experts, ready to fight attacks in their respective areas and to seize on any mistake made or loophole left open in the competitive case.

The Hong Kong Government, represented by the Attorney General, John Griffiths, was formerly in support of Cathay. The Hong Kong faction believed firmly that the colony should be treated as a foreign country. That is, that Cathay, as the local airline, should have the reciprocal rights to British Airways. We knew that the Hong Kong lobby might be an awesome, perhaps insurmountable, obstacle and therefore conjured a plan that, if necessary, would involve a joint operation with Cathay Pacific. This would get us on to the route and satisfy Hong Kong at the same time. Bebchick put this proposition forward on the opening day, after first lambasting British Airways.

BA was to come in for a drubbing from day one. Bebchick told the hearing that their service was third class, with dirty aircraft, unsympathetic cabin service and unhelpful attitudes. In the last 31 months, he said, 53 per cent of British Airways flights had been delayed at Kai Tak airport and BA had ignored the requirements of the market. John Griffiths also attacked the BA service in his statement supporting the Cathay case.

The BA counsel, Trevor Philipson, attempted to smooth over the tirade against his airline, but in the main his initial task was to warn the applicants that they had each over-estimated the market and that our economics were wildly wrong. Clearly, however, BA realised that the end of their Hong Kong monopoly was in sight. Philipson told the hearing that, yes, there was room for improvement – and another carrier if the capacity of the service was related sensibly to demand.

Freddie Laker himself turned up in Hong Kong as Beckman's star witness, only to receive a mauling from Leonard Bebchick on the inadequacy of the airline's traffic projections. Laker's response was typically unscientific. He said he believed passionately that there was a vast, untapped market and pointed out that all previous market projections were based on old, established figures and there were no statistics which talked about the people who had not flown, or who would like to fly. Laker, said Freddie, would beat the bushes to find them. With his usual display of showmanship, Laker dismissed the careful market research and statistical analysis undertaken by BCAL, BA and Cathay as pure unadulterated rubbish.

381

The facts of the case, behind the rhetoric of cross-examination and the analysis of complex statistics, were simple. We wanted a high frequency, daily DC-10-30 service, catering for all classes of traveller, First, Executive and Economy.

Cathay wanted a similar operation, but with the larger Boeing 747 aircraft operating three days each week. Laker wanted a daily Skytrain-type service designed purely for the low-fare traveller and the tourist.

Of the fares, however, our stand-by remained the lowest on offer. Laker's Skytrain fare was 40 HK dollars above our stand-by and Cathay's lowest fare was 25 dollars above Laker.

British Airways, fighting the rearguard action, knowing in their hearts that they would have to concede the monopoly, claimed they would lose about 100 million HK dollars with another carrier on the route.

Bebchick, who kept in constant touch with me at all kinds of odd hours, because of the time difference between Hong Kong and London, focused the final BCAL position on the political compromise we had earlier worked out. In his closing submission, he re-affirmed our proposal for a three-carrier regime – BA, BCAL and Cathay. He went so far as to promise that if the Hong Kong authority licensed both us and Cathay, we would support that decision with the CAA in London. Cathay's fear of the London hearing was that they were not classified as a British airline and the CAA could only licence a carrier which was wholly or substantially owned in the UK.

'We don't mind you conditioning our licence or Cathay's licence if you want. You can impose, I am sure the Attorney General realises, whatever conditions you want. You can stipulate that our licence is granted on the condition that Cathay also is licensed by the CAA to operate the route. I don't mind that,' said Bebchick.

The hearing in Hong Kong closed on 18 November. Many weeks later Ross Penlington announced his decision. Bebchick had won – the political ploy worked. BCAL was licensed to operate four services a week and Cathay three, against the seven provided by British Airways. Laker was rejected and BA dejected.

There was little time for celebration as the lawyers, planners and analysts packed their bags and files, preparing to move on to London where a re-run of the hearing, this time before the CAA, was due to begin before Christmas. The proceedings would go on to the end of January. In the main, the hearing covered much the same ground as the sessions in Hong Kong. Perhaps because of the less exotic location, the proceedings were less lively.

The eventual CAA decision, which came out towards the end of March 1980, dropped like a bombshell. We were given the sole rights to compete with British Airways on the Hong Kong route. It was a monumental coup for the airline and for Leonard Bebchick in particular. Both Cathay and Laker were refused their applications.

The CAA said it had accepted the evidence of the Hong Kong Government that the service provided by British Airways had not been adequate and that the spur of competition from another carrier was needed. It came to the conclusion that the Boeing 747s proposed for the route by Cathay would be inappropriate for a route demanding rapid build up of frequency. The DC-10 was better fitted. The Laker application, said the CAA, was aimed specifically at the bottom end of the market, without offering convincing evidence as to its size.

'Taking account of both aircraft type and marketability of service, the Authority has concluded that British Caledonian's proposals are best suited for the route,' the CAA stated.

I immediately made an announcement that we would start the Hong Kong service with four flights weekly in August 1980, increasing to a daily frequency in November. Three new DC-10-30s were due to be delivered in 1980. On the strength of the Hong Kong win, we took up an option on a fourth new aircraft, to be delivered in April the following year, to bring the total fleet to eight aircraft. In fact, two of the additional DC-10s, worth £50 million, had to be earmarked for the Hong Kong route, in order to operate daily in each direction over the long distance. During the process of the London hearing, we had devised a plan to expand service in East Asia and had applied for licences to serve Taiwan and Manila as extensions to the Hong Kong route.

The mood in BCAL was euphoric. At last we were breaking out to become a true East to West airline, instead of just a North to South one. Within a few days of the CAA announcement, I was en route to Hong Kong. Less than a year after we had, as an unknown quantity, revealed our plans to a sceptical Hong Kong

383

market, I would be back to announce the route start-up plans and meet government ministers and officials, the travel industry and the airport authority for the new service.

As I sat in the First Class cabin of the British Airways 747 I reflected on the tumultuous year behind us. We had increased flights to our single most important market, Nigeria, to ten each week. For the first time, four services a week were operated to South America; new services to Quito and Guayaquil in Ecuador were started to make this our seventh South American country. Frequencies to Morocco, Tunisia and Algeria were all increased and a new operation to Oran started. A major staff party had taken place in the new £5.5 million DC-10 hangar to celebrate its completion. We called it the Bill Richardson Hangar, in honour of our long-serving engineering director. Work on our new head-quarters building was well advanced and due to be completed later in the year. We had won the licence to add St Louis to the North American network and as I travelled to Hong Kong a team under our operations director, J R 'Mick' Sidebotham was in the city preparing for a start with Boeing 707 aircraft, later to be replaced by DC-10s on 29 April.

Similarly, our people were hard at work in Atlanta, preparing to start competitive operations against Delta from 1 June. Atlanta was part of the Bermuda II deal of 1977. St Louis became possible through a new agreement between the US and the UK – known in the business at 'Bermuda 2½' – reached the previous month. In addition to our St Louis route, the agreement allowed Laker to fly to Miami and British Airways to serve New Orleans the following year. On the other side, US airlines were allowed to begin new services from Boston, Denver and Miami. Crucially, the agreement brought good news for Gatwick, in that both sides agreed that services on the new routes to London would not use Heathrow.

As the Boeing 747 ploughed on across the Middle East and headed towards the Indian subcontinent, I thought of events at Heathrow. In November, as we were embroiled in the Hong Kong hearing, John Nott brought in his Civil Aviation Act (1980), giving the CAA greater powers, and announced plans for the part-privatisation of British Airways.

My thoughts went back to the summer when on 4 August

BCAL undertook its first Royal flight, carrying Her Majesty The Queen, Prince Andrew and the Royal entourage from Lusaka to London in a specially fitted Boeing 707 after she had opened the Commonwealth Prime Ministers' Conference in Zambia.

Just before leaving London, I had announced the latest financial results – a trading profit for the group of £7.4 million. Passenger carryings topped the two million mark and scheduled service activities increased to account for more than 75 per cent of total passengers. It would have been higher if not for the DC-10 groundings and sharply rising costs, now becoming a matter for serious concern.

Massive increases in landing charges, security fees and navigation costs would give us an additional bill of £2.7 million in 1980. At the same time, demand was increasing for lower and lower fares and more airlines were bringing more capacity into markets. A vicious circle was in the making.

My reception in Hong Kong was mixed. On the one hand, the news of the breaking of the British Airways monopoly was welcomed. On the other, however, many factions of the British expatriate community regarded the CAA's refusal of Cathay as a snub to Hong Kong. I sensed the resentment towards us at many meetings. Cathay was largely owned by the powerful Hong Kong trading empire, the Swire Group. Their power and influence was reflected in an old Hong Kong anecdote. To the question, 'Who runs Hong Kong?' the answer would come back, 'The Jockey Club, the Swire Group and the Governor, in that order.'

The nature of the fierce lobby which developed against us in Hong Kong and London became unpleasant. Stories began to spread around the colony questioning the safety of the DC-10. Our people became so angry that I had to restrain them from leaking the story about a 'haunted' Cathay Lockheed 1011 – one that had crashed in the USA, killing crew members. After being patched up and put back in service, other crews claimed that the ghosts of their dead colleagues had been seen on board. With the superstitious Chinese, news that this aircraft was operating in Hong Kong would give Cathay a difficult time.

The Hong Kong lobby focused its attention on London and on John Nott to whom both Cathay and Laker had appealed against the CAA decision. By early June, political soundings, indicated

385

that Nott might reverse the CAA decision and throw the Hong Kong route open for a free-for-all, despite his recent decision to devolve all licensing policy to the CAA. We had been willing to share the new competitive role with Cathay, but were now committed to extra DC-10s to operate daily. An aircraft on our hands with no immediate opportunity for route expansion could be disastrous. Nothing demonstrates more clearly than this how the financial fortunes of BCAL were constantly at the mercy of endlessly changing ministerial policies.

Hong Kong represented a great watershed in BCAL's development. After years of pushing and pressing for opportunities for expansion, this was the major breakthrough. Everybody, from the board members to engineering apprentices, knew so. When serving Hong Kong, which we had won fairly and squarely at two successive hearings, came under threat because of political expediency, hackles were raised among our staff. A small delegation came to see me to ask if I would allow the staff of BCAL to mount a political demonstration. To my look of enquiry, they said they wanted to march to the Houses of Parliament, protest to MPs and hand in a petition to John Nott. Who was I to refuse?

So it was on 16 June that the streets of Westminster echoed to the sound of the airline's pipe band and witnessed the sight of 350 staff, many of them off-duty stewardesses and pilots in uniform, carrying banners carrying statements demanding protection for the Hong Kong licence. At risk, their spokesman told MPs and journalists, were two DC-10s and £40 million of revenue with all the implications that had on jobs and the general economic development at Gatwick.

Peter Hordern, MP for Horsham and Crawley, which covers the Gatwick area, told the BCAL marchers that he supported them and had made his views known to the Secretary of State. 'I fully support your cause. A lot of money has been spent by BCAL building up its fleet on the expectation that the route would be secure for many years.'

A spokesman for the CAA told the press that in the eight years of the CAA's existence no appeal had been successful in overturning a decision. The following day, in the House of Commons, the CAA's eight-year record was broken. John Nott, under pressure from all sides, went for a decision which in my view was the easy political compromise. He decided that everybody should have a licence. The careful analysis and judgements of competent authorities in Hong Kong and London was thrown into the common garbage can.

After a preamble, he told the House that he concluded that 'substantial new traffic' likely to be generated by a wider variety of services would offer a reasonable prospect that four operators could, over a period, achieve an economic return on the route. 'I have accordingly upheld the CAA's decision to licence British Caledonian but in addition have directed it to reverse its decisions on the other two applications and issue licences in the same terms to Cathay Pacific and Laker,' said Nott.

Effectively, we were back to the Hong Kong decision. Both we and Cathay now had – or would have – licences from both ends of the route. Laker would have only a UK licence and would need to go once more to a hearing in Hong Kong.

Our reaction was to confirm our plans to begin a four times weekly service on 1 August. We would, however, re-assess the proposal to step up to daily flights in November. The future of the seventh DC-10, due for delivery in October to go on the Hong Kong route, was in doubt and might have to be sold or leased. As much as we would have liked to start Hong Kong as quickly as possible, the route was dependent on the DC-10 delivery in July. Cathay had aircraft available earlier and announced a 17 July start.

The Hong Kong outcome was more dismal than we had expected, but we set about getting the service up and running with enthusiasm. A special sales drive was extended to the owners and staff of Chinese restaurants up and down the country.

In Hong Kong, we set up shop under the management of Ranald Noel-Paton, our former in Nigeria, whom I persuaded back to the airline from his new private business in Scotland. One good portent for Hong Kong was that the lion was regarded as a lucky symbol. Our golden lion emblem was, therefore, welcomed by the Chinese community. Borrowing some lore from the traditional dragon dance in which a black pupil is painted on the eyeball to make it come alive, Alastair Pugh, who took the inaugural flight out accompanied by the British aviation press corps, staged a ceremony in which he

387

was hoisted by a 'cherry picker' machine to dot the eye of the lion on the tail of our DC-10 at Kai Tak airport. Little more than a year after I had gazed out of the windows of the Mandarin Hotel to the lights of Kai Tak with nothing more than a wish, the BCAL lion had come alive in Hong Kong.

# 69

In the summer of 1981 a visitor to the conference hall of the European Free Trade Association in Geneva would have encountered a meeting of grim-faced men, in earnest discussion on ways to avert a major international disaster. This was no political summit, but the chief executives of the world's major airlines called hurriedly together in the face of an economic disease which, if not averted, might paralyse the international transport system.

They were in Geneva under the auspices of the International Air Transport Association at a time described as the peak of negative achievement in the history of the airline industry. I write with some authority about the occasion. It was my unfortunate lot to have been asked by Knut Hammarskjold, the IATA Director-General, to be chairman of their crisis conference.

Based on the results of the first four months of 1981, I had to tell the industry that estimates for the year showed that collective revenue on international scheduled services would amount to $37.2 billion. Costs would come to $38.9 million to give an operating loss of $1.7 billion. But with interest charges forecast at $900 million, the loss would escalate to $2.6 billion and the industry would end up with a negative cash flow of $700 million.

In short, the airline industry was virtually bankrupt. It was said that 1980 had been the worst year in the industry's history. Now 1981 was going to be even worse than that.

The reasons for the sorry state of financial affiars were the worldwide economic recession affecting traffic, the massive increase in costs and interest charges, uneconomic passenger fares and cargo rates, and currency fluctuations. Added to this the airlines were deploying excessive capacity on many of the world's major air

389

routes – or, to quote an old aviation cliche, too many seats were chasing too few bottoms.

The industry's cumulative loss since 1979 totalled $6.2 billion. Manifestations of the economic illness were only too vivid. Carriers like Pan Am, Eastern, American, Japan Air Lines, and Delta were recording losses in huge sums.

BCAL itself made its only loss in the past eight years. From a profit of £9.7 for the group in 1980, after investing in major routes starts like St Louis, Hong Kong, Atlanta, and Dallas/Fort Worth which came into the network as an extension of the St Louis service, we slumped to a loss of £6.2 million in 1981.

British Airways had in February acquired a new Chairman, recruited from the ranks of private industry. His name was Sir John King. Over that year, King was to preside over one of the biggest airline losses of all time – £544.8 million. By 1982, the British state airline was technically bankrupt.

The mood of that conference in Geneva was to set in motion a course of crisis management. Costs were reduced, capacity cut back, uneconomic pricing was tackled. Management philosophy went into reverse gear. Instead of planning for development, the industry was concerned with pruning back to reduce the loss. This was indeed a tough conference because the vast majority of airlines – world wide – were still owned by their governments. Under these circumstances their priorities were to include matters of principle outside of the profit and loss accounts and these were uppermost in the minds of a number of airlines.

However, Ian Ritchie and I hammered away over the two-day period of continuous concentration until we had the opposition down to about five carriers. The last man was a European and he was the toughest, he was determined to hold out even if it meant a conference failure. He finally collapsed when I insisted that I wished to speak directly to his chairman so that I could advise him that his senior delegate was about to be responsible for the massive losses continuing and that he was the only objector.

Agreement reached in Geneva was for an overall five per cent increase in passenger fares and cargo rates. We also established an organisation known as the Fare Deal Monitoring Group. Ian Ritchie was nominated as its chairman with the objective of wiping out, or at least containing, the epidemic of illegal discounting which had become rife in the industry as airlines desperately sought to fill excesses of seats at any price. The worry of discounting was that the illegal prices could not be offered through legitimate, licensed travel agents, they had to go through non-recognised outlets – consolidators who handled large volumes of traffic, especially among ethnic markets. They became better known as 'bucket shops'.

That year of 1981 went on to be bleaker than we first imagined. Many carriers were experiencing severe financial difficulties. National carriers were backed by their governments, others were supported by banks. Some were bolstered by aircraft manufacturers. The market in secondhand aircraft was severely depressed and banks with heavy investment in the hardware could not afford to let airlines fail.

Many costs outside our control continued to rise at alarming rates even beyond the UK inflation rate of 12 per cent. Fuel prices rose in sterling terms by 42 per cent and now accounted for 42 per cent of total costs. An industrial dispute involving UK air traffic controllers disrupted operations and cost us £2 million. Air traffic control costs themselves surged by 52 per cent.

Against a background of depression BCAL was fighting to get its new routes established. Hong Kong was doing well in terms of traffic, but the fight for market share between Cathay, BA and ourselves was having its effect on the financial side. On the transatlantic routes, the main difficulties of over capacity and discounted, unprofitable fares was largely contained in the major market.* In smaller markets off the beaten track, Houston, Atlanta, Dallas/Fort Worth and St Louis were less affected. Nevertheless, we were expanding on the North Atlantic at a time when the combined losses of the IATA airlines on the North Atlantic were reaching $650 million.

In contrast to the depressing financial situation, however, BCAL was growing rapidly. The first full year of operation on the four new routes, coupled with the expanded fleet of DC-10s, gave us a

---

* Various US airlines commenced new services to Gatwick, but in this bleak year flights from Boston, Pittsburgh, Denver, Anchorage and Honolulu were suspended and others operated at reduced frequencies.

32.5 per cent increase in production, easily the largest growth rate of any airline. Productivity increased by a large percentage and revenue per employee rose by 22 per cent. Another achievement was the 13.2 hours average daily utilisation on the DC-10 fleet, the highest for any airline operating these aircraft.

# 70

Despite the enormous growth of the airline and the group companies associated with it, I still liked to retain a close, family relationship among the 6,000 staff, much as we had done in the early days of the original Caledonian.

One of the ways I tried to do this, apart from being freely available to staff at all levels and walking the shop floor from time to time, was by way of a special annual report in which the complexities of accounts and balance sheets were fully explained to employees in easy language. Another way was through a New Year message, circulated on the first working day of every year.

In January 1982, looking back on the previous twelve months, I told the BCAL staff, in a parody of the Chinese calendar where years are named after animals, that 1981 had been 'the year of the lemming'. I wrote that 1982 was not going to be easy. The general recession was still with us and even if we started climbing out in the second half of the year, it was doubtful whether this would lead to substantial improvements before the year end. 'For one thing, I am afraid the lemmings are still rushing recklessly, particularly on the North Atlantic, where the objective seems to be market share at any price.' The 'lemmings' were, of course, the airlines, undercutting like crazy on the prime transatlantic routes.

'Lessons are being learned the hard way, but for political regulatory and marketing reasons, changes towards a more viable fares structure will undoubtedly take time. Accordingly, 1982 will be another hard year,' I wrote. I did not know at the time how hard those lessons would be or how swiftly they would be taught to the industry.

The economic depression of 1981 followed us into the New Year. The serious overcapacity, with demand for travel at a very

393

low point, led to severe cut-backs and the grounding of fleets of aircraft. More than 100 wide body aircraft were mothballed in the Arizona desert, where the warm, dry air reduced the risk of corrosion. Reduced values meant that in the case of some older equipment, the value of the aircraft had fallen below the amount of loans extended by the banks to cover the original purchase.

In the UK the effect on BCAL was worrying. But far worse was the effect on British Airways and Laker. Rumours flew thick and fast about Laker's financial standing. Towards the end of the previous summer, Laker had started moves to refinance his airline. In his typically cavalier way he announced to the press: 'I said to myself, Laker, you are an innovator. You have innovated the airline business. Now you must innovate the banking business.'

His battle for survival went on for the next five months. On Christmas Eve, the press reported that a rescue plan had been agreed – one which would meet the demands of the CAA, seriously concerned at the state of Laker's finances. It rested on an additional £5 million which the CAA said it wanted on top of the existing refinancing to give what it called head room. This £5 million was to come from McDonnell Douglas and the engine manufacturer, General Electric, which had vested interest in the Laker DC-10 fleet.

To those of us following the Laker saga from the top floor of Caledonian House, this news was unthinkable. Here was our most important aircraft supplier preparing to prop up a competitor with cash. Further, McDonnell Douglas said that it would turn its part of the Laker loan on its DC-10 fleet into shares in the company. I simply could not understand what was happening. How could McDonnell Douglas conduct business with other carriers, sharing their commercial secrets and operating plans in the process of negotiating aircraft supply, when it was a shareholder in a competitor?

I summoned Ian Ritchie and told him to send a telex to John Brizendine, President of the Douglas Aircraft Division of McDonnell Douglas saying that if his company became a substantial shareholder in Laker, we would no longer be prepared to do business with him. I told Ritchie to copy that telex to all of the other DC-10 operators in Europe, including such airlines as Lufthansa, Swissair and Scandinavian Airlines System. The McDonnell Douglas deal never came off, not so much because of my protest, but because no package of financial salvage measures was able to save Laker in the end.

But Laker carried on attempting to patch up the finances, making statements that all was well in public, while wrestling with bankers in private. Things reached a head on the evening of 4 February. The date coincided with BCAL's annual marketing conference, when sales and marketing people from around the network came to Gatwick to discuss forward strategies. As the BCAL delegates were relaxing at dinner in the ballroom of the Hilton Hotel at Gatwick, more earnest discussion were taking place in a suite upstairs. It was the suite of Harry Goodman, boss of the International Leisure Group. In desperation, Freddie Laker, recently returned from a visit to New York, sought out Goodman in an attempt to hatch a deal which would help save Laker Airways. The talks were reported as going on deep into the night, but with no successful outcome.

The following day, the industry was shattered by the news that Freddie Laker had been forced to give up the fight and call in the receivers. Laker Airways had gone to the wall. The announcement came after a final board meeting in Laker's Gatwick headquarters, just a stone's throw away from our own offices. A statement was issued which said:

It was announced on 24 December 1981 that agreement had been reached in principle on the restructuring of Laker's financial affairs, with a view to securing its long-term viability.

On Monday night it was firmly believed that the most stringent of these conditions had been met and the way forward was clear. However, on Wednesday, events took a sudden and dramatic turn.

Yesterday, the facilities available to the company from its bank, Clydesdale, and the arrangements reached with McDonnell Douglas seem, unhappily, not considered adequate by others to meet the anticipated requirements of the company over the next few months, although Laker strongly disagrees with this view.

However, as the holiday season approaches, Laker are vitally concerned that there is no risk whatsoever that passengers are stranded as a result of the airline's collapse in the summer months.

Laker are mindful of the views of others and recognise that they must act in a totally responsible way. Accordingly, it is with the deepest regret that Laker has requested Clydesdale Bank to appoint a receiver and manager.

By 'others' Laker meant the CAA, which had refused to accept that the rescue plan was strong enough to see the company through the summer season.

By the following day, the entire Laker fleet of three Airbus A.300s and eleven DC-10s was back in Britain. One of the DC-10s was impounded at Gatwick by the British Airports Authority as security against money owed.

It was a sad end to Laker Airways and I sympathised with the airline's 2,500 staff, now facing bleak prospects. However, I believed firmly that Freddie had brought the crash on himself. He had not only led the 'lemming' rush, but had also been on the other side, pushing the cliff towards the advancing horde, with commitments for expansion into opportunities which simply did not exist in reality, such as his sixty routes plan for Europe.

As the latest aviation minister, Iain Sproat, said many months later in a radio interview on the subject of deregulation in Europe: 'Well, Laker went bankrupt, but not because of anything to do with deregulation or liberalisation, Freddie Laker went bankrupt because he borrowed far too much money at far too high a rate of interest to buy far too many aeroplanes which he didn't need . . . I'm afraid this company just wasn't very well managed financially and that is why he went down, nothing to do with what government allowed him or did not allow him to do.'

The Laker story veered off into other highly-publicised directions, but our job was to look at the immediate aftermath of the Laker collapse. Our first task was to help Laker passengers stranded overseas, mainly in the USA. This we did at no charge whatsoever, bringing in our partners Eastern Airlines to carry the Laker people from places such as Florida to our gateways so that we could carry them to London.

The next thing we looked at was the Los Angeles route – our route that Laker had been allowed to hijack several years earlier. With Laker going down, the slot for a second British carrier was empty and would remain so until another airline could obtain a licence and start operations. The licensing process would be lengthy. We had aircraft available and could start Los Angeles quickly, so we approached the CAA to grant us a temporary exemption so that a BCAL service could be mounted while the normal licensing procedures ensued.

The second major development to come out of the Laker collapse concerned the British tour operators holding contracts with the airline for the operation of European inclusive tour charters. The tour operators were devastated by the Laker collapse. Their programmes for the summer were out and they were in the middle of the peak holiday booking season. But now they had no way of operating their holiday flights. The proposal, which came from Peter Drew of Rank, was that BCAL should take over the operation of two of the Laker DC-10 aircraft and fly on behalf of a mixed consortium of holiday firms, the biggest of which was Rank Travel, parent company for Wings and Owners Services.

Alastair Pugh and Trevor Boud took on this project and brought it to a successful conclusion after arranging to take over the lease of the two aircraft from the owners, Mitsubishi. The result was the formation of a separate subsidiary, British Caledonian (Charter) Ltd., in equal partnership with Rank. A joint board was set up with each side providing a chairman who would be in control for every other year. The new operation needed, however, a full-time managing director. Alastair and I conferred and came up with the name of Frank Hope. Frank had resigned from the board of BCAL in 1973 but had continued working for us in Monrovia on a management contract we had secured from Air Liberia, the national carrier. Frank came in from his home in Crawley to be confronted with the offer of running his own charter airline. He had resigned in protest against the BCAL strategy for scheduled service development, preferring to stay in the charter market. His enthusiasm for the project was immediate and he accepted the job. Trevor Boud, Curly Walter, John de la Haye and I were delighted that one of our original Caledonian colleagues was back in the fold to do what he did probably better than anyone else in the industry: the plotting, planning and running of complex charter schedules.

In order to differentiate between the scheduled and charter operation, Frank's company later changed its name to Cal-Air

International. Much later, for reasons to be explained, the airline became Novair, the name it holds today.

The Laker demise brought us other opportunities. We were able to acquire the Laker hangar and offices at Gatwick to expand our own engineering facilities and to house the new charter company. We also took over four Laker BAC1-11-300 series aircraft to boost the short-haul fleet.

But the biggest prize of all was the Los Angeles route. In March, the Secretary of State for Trade, John Biffen, was preparing to appoint a new Chairman for the CAA. Nigel Foulkes was due to retire and the new man would take over at the beginning of April, the start of the new financial year. Biffen selected a person entirely unknown to the airline industry, John Dent, a gritty industrialist who had previously been managing director of the Dunlop company. In early March the CAA, having considered our request to gain the temporary exemption, came back with a flat refusal. Their reasoning was that they did not want to let another carrier on the route while there was still a possibility of a direct successor to Laker emerging, an extremely unlikely outcome.

In anger and frustration, I took the matter directly to John Biffen and Iain Sproat, warning that unless a new carrier was allowed to fill the Laker hole quickly, Britain's share of the market would decline rapidly. The politicians moved quickly and just a week after the CAA refusal, John Biffen gave a direction to the CAA to grant us the exemption and allow us to return to Los Angeles. Within days, Rocky Cox from Houston, with his marketing chief, Gerry Swift, were at Gatwick to plan the route start-up. A completely new infrastructure had to be put in place – offices, staff, airport facilities and ground handling equipment. The target date for the BCAL return to the west coast of the USA was 21 May.

While we planned for a triumphant return to Los Angeles after an absence of seven years, the airline was on the move in other directions. We had applied to expand European services with the addition of the route between Gatwick and Geneva which we had already been operating for some time as a regular charter flight.

In Scotland, a retired insurance agent by the name of Peter Park and his wife Lily received, out of the blue, an invitation to come down south for a meeting with an array of Nigerian dignitaries, Alhaji Ado Bayero, the Emir of Kano, Adeyinka Oyekan, the Oba of Lagos and Alhaji Shehu Awak, the Nigerian High Commissioner in the UK.

The reason for Peter and Lily Park's trip to Gatwick was the naming ceremony of BCAL's first Boeing 747, at least the first to enter the fleet on a permanent basis. We had acquired the aircraft for exclusive operation on the Nigerian route: among the Nigerian leaders and the senior expatriate businessman there was more demand for first class seats than we could normally supply. The quandary led us to the decision to acquire a 747 and fit in as many first class seats as the aircraft galleys and equipment stowage facilities would allow. We ended up with a total of fifty-two first class seats on the aircraft, more than twice the number on the DC-10. Along with the other wide-body aircraft, the DC-10, we would give the 747 the name of a famous Scot. As the aircraft would concentrate on Nigeria, I selected the name Mungo Park. On hearing this decision, my colleagues in the airline went scrabbling for their reference books. Very few had ever heard of him. But to Scots and Nigerians alike, the name Mungo Park was familiar from their schooldays when the story of his exploits in search of the River Niger in the early days of the previous century was taught in history lessons. Peter Park, the great-great-great grandson of one of Mungo Park's brothers, was the explorer's sole surviving relation and, as I recall, enjoyed his day immensely in the incongruous company of men whose ancestors would have met his own ancestor's brother face to face. 'Mungo Park – the Scottish Explorer' made his return to Nigeria in the form of a BCAL Boeing 747 on 16 May.

But as it always seems in the perverse business of air transport, when things are beginning to go in a forward direction, something occurs to create a setback. The South American services had been built up steadily since 1964 when the former British United Airways took them over after they were abandoned by BOAC. The civil aviation review of 1976 had added Venezuela, Colombia and Peru to the existing network which served Rio de Janeiro, Recife and São Paulo in Brazil, Santiago in Chile and Buenos Aires in Argentina. We had recently added Guayaquil and Quito in Ecuador to bring the South American network to its present level of operations with DC-10 and Boeing 707 aircraft.

The main part of the network, in the southern part of the continent, was pinned together by Buenos Aires. Not only did we have rights between London and the Argentinian capital, but also had the ability to carry traffic between Buenos Aires and Madrid, the Brazilian cities and Santiago. Argentina was, therefore, extremely important in the economic scheme of things so far as South America was concerned.

War in the South Atlantic broke out in April, when after much political acrimony, the Argentinian government ordered the invasion of the Falkland islands, or Las Malvinas, which they regarded as their own sovereign territory. Margaret Thatcher, determined to safeguard the islands and their British colonial inhabitants, mustered the military and sent forth the invasion task force.

Air services to Buenos Aires ceased at the beginning of the month placing our South Atlantic network in disarray. In addition to being unable to serve Buenos Aires, we could not cross Argentinian airspace. This meant that we had not only lost important traffic between Argentina and Chile, but also that we had to make an expensive 1,000-mile detour around the borders of Argentina to get to Santiago.

The airline pressed on with this uneconomic, fragmented operation for several months, but as trade and air travel between other countries and Britain began to tail off as a consequence of the war with Argentina, we were forced at the end of the day to cease services to Chile, Ecuador and Peru. The direct consequence of the Falklands war was a shortfall in earnings of some £6 million and this, in turn, was directly responsible for a loss in a year when we had been confidently predicting a return to profitability.

It was an immense blow to the company and to the staff who, in willingly picking up collective responsibility for getting the airline back to profitability, had accepted a wage freeze to form a substantial part of the package of measures to cut costs, increase efficiency and improve profitability.

But there were still successes to score and none more satisfying than the return to Los Angeles. Rocky Cox had placed a special team in the city he irreverently called 'Tinseltown' and they had worked what seemed like twenty-four hours each day to get the infrastructure into place. On 21 May, as the team in Los Angeles were in their beds after the final day of preparation, I was at Gatwick welcoming guests joining me and other airline directors on the inaugural flight. There was the Hon Angus Ogilvy, with

400

who I had become acquainted over the previous few years; Ray Colegate of the CAA; Lord Kinnoull and Lord Campbell of Croy, two of staunchest supporters in the House of Lords; Sir Patrick Meaney, managing director of the Thomas Tilling group; Howard McDonald, group treasurer for Shell; John Caines of the British Overseas Trade Board; Hamish Morrison, chief executive of the Scottish Council; Norman Chumley of the Scottish Tourist Board; and my golfing friend and good contact, John Junor.

Already in Los Angeles, literally drumming up publicity, was the pipe band. On the aircraft with us was a Scottish singer, Helen McArthur. Our plan was to mark our return to the West Coast with a dinner and a Scots ceilidh at the Beverly Wilshire Hotel in Beverley Hills. The programme we had laid on for our guests from the UK included a weekend in Palm Springs, trips to Disneyland and a tour of the McDonnell Douglas plant at Long Beach. But the highlight was to be the ceilidh where we would be entertaining about 300 business and civic leaders.

I can do no better than to quote from the column in the *Sunday Express*, written by John Junor on his return from Los Angeles. Under his usual weekly title, 'Current Events', Junor wrote:

The time was last Monday night. The place the banqueting room of Hollywood's plush Beverly Wilshire Hotel.

The dinner audience consisted of some of the wealthiest and most influential citizens of the West Coast of the US. In this sophisticated venue, a most unlikely and unsophisticated cabaret was being presented. The pipe band of British Caledonian Airways was playing and tartaned Scots lassie Helen McArthur was singing all the sad, haunting, martial and patriotic tunes of . my native heath.

I expected restlessness among the natives. Yet for thirty minutes, so enraptured was the audience, there was not even the sound of a coffee spoon stirring.

When it was over, the 200 dinner guests headed by Mr Donald Douglas, boss of McDonnell Douglas Aircraft, rose to their feet and cheered and cheered and cheered and cheered.

BCAL was back.

# 71

In the afternoon of 2 June 1982 anyone calling my office would have been told: 'I'm sorry, he's gone to see off the Pope.' The story of the airline's association with the Vatican began about a year before, when a request for a meeting came from Monsignor Ralph Brown, Vicar, General Diocese of Westminster.

Sitting on a sofa in my office, he said he wanted to speak in the strictest confidence, before revealing that plans were being made for a pastoral visit to the UK by Pope John Paul II. It was to be an event of great historical importance – the first time a Pope had ever visited the British Isles. It was also a matter of great security, hence the confidentiality at this stage.

The reason Ralph Brown had come down to Gatwick was to discuss the vital travel arrangements for a six-day tour in which the Pope and an entourage of Cardinals and Vatican officials were to cover England, Scotland and Wales. In particular, for reasons of speed and security, helicopters would be necessary for a large part of the tour.

Incredulously, I listened to my guest as he told me that he had come to BCAL after being rebuffed by British Airways. BA, which had helicopters operating in the North Sea, had told him that the aircraft were too busy working on the oil rigs and none could be released for the papal tour. I couldn't believe the opportunity the state airline had thrown in our direction. Didn't they see that the first visit to Britain by any Pope would attract massive publicity and kudos?

I didn't hesitate. After talking through the outline programme, I told him that we would lay on the helicopters required, two Sikorsky S-61Ns. We would also provide a BAC 1-11 for the longer sectors; and we would provide a Boeing 707 to take the Papal party home

402

to Rome. I told him we would carry out the operation at cost, not making a penny profit. I was not going to let BA have a second chance at this contract, nor was I going to let anybody else in. My offer was designed to be a shut-out bid which nobody else could match.

I called in Mick Sidebotham, former operations director, now working closely with me on strategy matters. I explained the project and told him he was in charge of arrangements. Working with Monsignor Brown, the police's Special Branch, our helicopter people and the airline's operational experts, Sidebotham set about the task with great enthusiasm. It was a logistical and security nightmare, but painstakingly Sidebotham and his colleagues steadily developed a programme.

The giant task of planning and cross checking every single detail meant inspecting proposed helicopter landing sites and obtaining CAA permission for their use. It involved deploying ground staff, engineers and relief pilots at every stage of the way, co-ordinating with nine different police forces and the different airport authorities. Sidebotham's team went so far as to seek out Polish speakers among our staff to make the Pope feel at home with BCAL.

After the news of the Papal visit was announced, the event attracted great publicity and assumed massive proportions. Pope John Paul arrived at Gatwick on 28 May on an Alitalia flight from Rome and travelled by train to London. Our first helicopter flight took place the following day when we carried the Pope from Wimbledon to Canterbury to meet the Anglican Archbishop. That afternoon he was flown to Wembley to officiate at an open air Mass in the sports stadium. On 30 May, the Papal party flew with us from Wimbledon to Crystal Palace, where John Paul II met members of the Polish community, before going on to Coventry airport for another open air Mass. Next stop was Liverpool for a further Mass at the Roman Catholic Cathedral. The following day, the Pope, evidently tireless, flew to Manchester and then on to York. At RAF Leeming, near York, the Papal party boarded a BCAL 1-11 for Edinburgh, which would take the Pope on his tour of Scotland including visits to Holyrood House, Rosewell, Bearsden in Glasgow and on to Bellahouston Park for a further open air Mass. Reflecting on the Pope in Glasgow, my thoughts turned to childhood memories of the Orangemen's march, heavily anti-Catholic, which drummed its way through the streets of Rutherglen every 12 July. I thought of the irony between now and then when I, brought up Presbyterian, would, innocent of the religious history, cheer on the Protestant marchers.

From Glasgow, we took the Pope to his final stop in Britain, Cardiff. While he was celebrating his final open air Mass on British soil, at Ninian Park, I was boarding the specially-fitted Boeing 707 at Gatwick. The aircraft was positioning to Cardiff's Rhoose Airport in readiness to carry the Pope and his entourage back to Rome and the Vatican City.

As everywhere, crowds upon crowds had thronged the approaches to the airport and filled to capacity the public viewing areas, to catch a glimpse of John Paul II. Cheering became louder as his special vehicle, constructed so that he would stand behind bullet-proof glass and be seen by the crowds and dubbed by the Press as the 'Pope-mobile', slowly approached the airport.

The airport was beseiged by photographers and television crews as the Pope took his special farewell of the Cardinals and Bishops. I was standing by the steps of the aircraft and was the last person he spoke to on British soil. His words of thanks were gentle and sincere and he shook my hand and turned to walk up the steps of the forward doorway of the 707. On reaching the top step he turned to offer both hands upwards for what seemed like an eternity before he finally disappeared inside the aircraft.

The tour had been conducted under a bombardment of coverage from television and radio and the press. Every TV news bulletin throughout every day of his visit followed the Pope's movements. Every newspaper carried pictures. In the centre of that coverage were the BCAL helicopters and fixed-wing aircraft – and, of course, our uniformed staff. The coverage was transmitted around the world and, at Gatwick, we were inundated with telexes from overseas managers excitedly describing the extent of coverage of the Pope and BCAL on their TV screens.

Against the crashing disappointment of the effect on the airline of the Falklands War, the airline's starring role in the Papal visit to Britain was an immense boost.

404

In reply to a request for a statement from a journalist at Cardiff, as the Pope's Boeing 707 climbed away towards the west, I said: 'This was the first time that a Pope had visited Britain and the event is of great historical importance. BCAL is proud to have been able to play a significant part.'

# 72

The Thatcher government had nowhere near made its selection of the person to take on the chairmanship of British Airways. It had listed some likely names, among them Sir John King, chairman of the Babcock International company and deputy chairman of the National Enterprise Board. The story goes that at an informal occasion in 10 Downing Street, the Prime Minister casually inquired as to whether he would be interested in being a contender for the job. Needing no further encouragement, King went the next day to the office of the Trade Secretary, John Nott, and to the politician's bewilderment, stood before him and said; 'Right, I'll take the job!' It is, clearly, an apocryphal tale, but it serves to illustrate the forthright, even buccaneering style of the man who did, of course, become Chairman of British Airways, taking over from the airline professional, Ross Stainton, in 1981.

King was put in charge to clean up the airline, in preparation for some form of denationalisation on which the Thatcher government was so keen. The early plans centred on selling off only part of the shareholding to the public, with the government retaining a majority holding.

King took over chairmanship of British Airways in February 1981. He inherited a shaky empire, no doubt surveying it with some misgiving and disbelief from the office he took over on the fourth floor of Speedbird House at the airline's Heathrow headquarters. Six months later, his was the signature on the set of accounts for the year. He had to report that the airline had lost £141 million, before tax. Borrowings had reached virtually £800 million, more than double the amount of equity capital. The statutory financial target set by Government for British Airways over this period was a 6 per cent real rate of return on average net assets. The real rate of return in 1980/81 was minus 9.7 per cent. The airline was clearly in a mess and the Government plan for a part-privatisation in 1981 was optimistic in the extreme.

Bringing in fresh business brains to the ailing British Airways in the form of Alex Dibbs, deputy chairman of the National Westminster Bank and a colleague on the National Enterprise Board, and RA 'Bobby' Henderson, chairman of the merchant bankers Kleinwort Benson (BCAL's own financial advisers), King set about the task of knocking British Airways into shape. His plan was based on an investigation and recommendations from the accountancy firm Price Waterhouse and involved massive cost-cutting, including redundancies on a major scale, the selling off of assets and a redrawing of the balance sheets.

In BCAL, we were watching the events at British Airways with a mixture of fascination and concern. Commercially, the state airline had taken a course of action which placed quantity before quality. They were playing the numbers game, going for as much traffic as possible, whatever the effect on quality of service. In contrast, we had embarked on a strategy designed to capture the premium business travel market, by providing very high standards of passenger service, both in the air and on the ground.

It is fair to be self-congratulatory and state that while British Airways' standards were faltering, BCAL was being held up as the shining example of the best of British air transport. As somebody said in an informal luncheon speech some time later, 'At a time when the national airline was a national disgrace, it fell to British Caledonian to hold up British standards in airline service.'

The Laker collapse, which the Government was, rightly, unable to avert with financial assistance, pointed up the irony of the British Airways privatisation plan. As the sole shareholder, the Government was effectively piling cash into the state corporation's bank balances, in order to prepare the organisation to be floated off to private investors. There can be little doubt that after the Laker episode, the Government saw that it should hive off British Airways totally and have no residual involvement in the airline which could lead to embarrassments at a later stage. This played into King's hands: he wanted a full, rather than partial privatisation. It also meshed with my philosophy that British Airways should be wholly privately-owned, subject to the same commercial disciplines as ourselves, with no fairy godmother in Downing Street able to wave a financial magic wand every time the bad wolf of economic misfortune appeared at the door.

In February 1982, shortly after the Laker demise, it emerged that the Government now had a strategy for a 100 per cent privatisation. King's proposals to ready the company for a Stock Exchange flotation were accepted in Whitehall. The British Airways vehicle was pointed on the road towards a flotation at the back end of 1983. The Government wanted a successful conclusion before the next election. The political steering wheel was put in the hands of the Parliamentary Under Secretary for Trade responsible for civil aviation, Iain Sproat.

While the general policy of the State to divesting itself of responsibility for funding an airline was correct, the implications for BCAL and the other independent airlines of this radical shift were enormous. I had confidently assumed that hand in hand with the proposals for the privatisation of British Airways would come a new civil aviation policy which would take into account the achievements of private enterprise in civil aviation and safeguard the interests of fair opportunity and fair competition for the future.

It seemed to me that those who had invested in independent air transport for many trying years already had as much, if not more, right to a share of the State's divestment of its aviation interests than the potential new investors. More importantly, the disposal by the State of British Airways, with its vast route network, was a golden opportunity to restructure the British airline industry, in order to achieve more balance and stability among the airlines, more opportunity for the future, and therefore more competitive ability in the world market place.

To the amazement of myself and colleagues such as Alastair Pugh and Peter Masefield, no cohesive plan for the future of the airline industry was apparent. Masefield, by this time, had been appointed chairman of London Transport and was in a unique position to view government thinking. It was clear to all of us that the Government was running headlong at privatisation with no real regard for the effect on the existing independent sector.

This policy raised two fundamental problems of serious concern for our own future. The first was that, if the sale of the state airline was successful, we would have much more difficulty in raising additional capital as the sources of finance would be similar and the financial institutions, in particular, would tend to limit their investment in the airline industry. The second was that, if British Airways was sold with its inherited route network intact, there would never again be any chance of a route review. The Government would be unable to reallocate any asset which it had sold to private investors in good faith. We therefore had to implement a strategy for the protection of our own business against the threat posed by a government eager to satisfy its privatisation policy at any cost.

On 25 June 1982, I put my signature to two letters which Margaret Trett had placed in a correspondence folder on my desk. One was to the Secretary of State for Trade, the other to his Parliamentary Under Secretary, Iain Sproat. The letter to Arthur Cockfield was ostensibly to confirm a lunch appointment for Alastair Pugh and me to meet him and his senior civil servant, William Knighton. I told him that I wanted to bring him up to date with the BCAL position following the Falklands War and the downturn in trade in Nigeria. I also said that I wished to make suggestions regarding the British Airways privatisation plans.

Despite a repeated number of telephone calls to Sproat's office to follow up the letter, I received no response from him. In the event, however, it was through the offices of a mutual friend, Robert Sowter, managing director of Airlease International Management, a consortium of banks and finance companies, that a dinner with Sproat was arranged on the evening of 12 August 1982.

Over the table I detailed our concerns about the privatisation process and how this could adversely affect BCAL. He said that he took my points very well indeed and asked what he could do. I zeroed in on the target, telling him that balance and fairness could be achieved through route adjustments between British Airways and BCAL and mentioned a number of possibilities. Sproat appeared to be very receptive and suggested that the best move was for a meeting between myself and John King to explore possibilities which might be mutually beneficial. He wanted the meeting to take place in August. I said that he should first contact King and then I would arrange to meet him.

In fact, Alastair Pugh and I had already had some exploratory route adjustment talks earlier in the year with Roy Watts, British Airways' deputy chairman and chief executive, and Stephen Wheatcroft, director of economic development. The talks had been abortive.

On Friday 20 August 1982 I spoke to John King by telephone. We agreed that we should meet and as he was due to be away for three weeks from the following Sunday, the meeting was fixed for the next morning, Saturday 21 August. The venue was to be his home at Wartnaby in Leicestershire and he arranged to send a light aircraft to Gatwick to transport me to and from Leicestershire.

John King greeted me in a friendly fashion and gave me a tour of his estate. We then met in a smallish but very pleasant study. King started off the discussion with disarming frankness, telling me of the 'astonishing' situations he had found at British Airways, some of the problems he was grappling with and the actions he was taking. He was clearly fascinated by the airline business and surprised at how complicated it was. I told him, with equal frankness, that as a result of the Falklands War, we would be struggling to make a profit for 1982. In any event, our result would be better than last year and better than most in the industry. Assuming that the industry's recovery from its current critical situation would take some time, I suggested that, together, we could take some action which could improve the result for both airlines. I told him of the earlier inconclusive talks with Watts and Wheatcroft.

King said that he would be very interested in any such schemes provided they improved his prospects and, after some scathing remarks about the attitudes of others, said he was just not interested in operating routes unless they were profitable.

I described to him some of the tentative route adjustment ideas we had in mind and emphasized that there could be a significant disparity in revenues on any specific route swap between British Airways and BCAL. I suggested that, in the past, too much emphasis had been put on this, when the main factor was the effect such changes had on the last figures in the profit and loss account – the bottom line.

We then tried to find the best way to carry the talks forward. I asked if he could nominate one or two individuals from the British Airways management who could meet with us during his absence. I said that this should be at a high level and kept extremely confidential. He replied that he could not nominate others and expect the talks to remain confidential. I, too, was due to be away for a while in the USA, so we agreed that we should meet again after we had both returned. I would bring with me Alastair Pugh. He would bring his recently-appointed new chief financial officer, Gordon Dunlop, a former chief executive of the Commercial Union Insurance Company, recruited from the Inchcape Group in Singapore.

I travelled back to Gatwick in the small aircraft, making notes for circulation to our members of our holding board. I noted that while we waited for the next round of talks with British Airways, we should not stand still. We should, I said, continue to press the line that were it not for the Falklands War, we would be confidently forecasting a profit, but the loss on the South Atlantic of £5 million was making this a struggle. One of the reasons for this was that if the markets, especially the travel agents, believed that the airline was inherently unprofitable, rather than going through a difficult phase, business would fall away, with disastrous results.

We should also, I said, continue to express concern in political and financial circles about the possible negative effect on BCAL of the Government preparing to pump between £600 and £800 million cash into British Airways in order to prop it up for sale.

The implications for BCAL of the privatisation were now becoming a preoccupation within the company. A focus group had developed comprising myself, Peter Masefield, Iain Stewart, Alastair Pugh and Ian Ritchie. Between us, we had launched on an informal programme of lobbying politicians and senior civil servants, among them Norman Tebbit, Cecil Parkinson, at that time Conservative Party chairman, and George Younger, Secretary of State for Scotland.

As our concerns came more sharply into focus, I decided that we should go right to the heart of Government and approach the Prime Minister herself.

I wrote to Margaret Thatcher on 26 August 1982. I wrote about the Falklands' effect on BCAL's profitability and expressed concern about the indications that her Government was proposing to inject massive amounts of cash into British Airways, in preparation for a sale of shares. I explained that other British airlines operating either short-haul scheduled flights or charter services might be

411

unaffected, but not BCAL, which served predominantly long-haul routes and was in competition with British Airways.

We now see one of our main competitors about to receive massive government support, on a scale never before contemplated, without any apparent regard for the effect this will undoubtedly have on the British private enterprise carrier that has kept the flag flying, in spite of all opposition, for the last twelve years. My suggestion is that, instead of the Government simply endeavouring to find a solution for British Airways, it should be considering what steps should be taken in the interests of the British airline industry as a whole and that means including British Caledonian.

I told the Prime Minister about the problems of the industry, about regulation on a national and international scale, about the hard process of route licensing, the protective policies of overseas government and the problems of overseas remittance. Overall, I wrote, we are in a business that is simply more dependent than most on government policies at home and abroad.

There are a number of actions that can be taken between British Airways and British Caledonian that could result in improvement for both. In the past, we have been rebuffed by the British Airways management when we have put these forward. I have recently put such proposals to Iain Sproat and John King and received more positive responses and a willingness to give them consideration. I expect serious discussions to take place on this subject during September.

Why, then, am I writing to you? Simply because the Government's objective seems to be singular – turn British Airways into an efficient, effective operating unit and privatise it. I would like to see British Caledonian's own efforts in creating an international airline, operating to forty-eight cities in thirty-one countries, recognised through an objective which is designed to take consideration of our industry crisis. I would suggest that an appropriate strategy would be, 'encourage the profitable development of the two British international airlines through the privatisation of British Airways and an allocation of routes to both which will allow them to compete effectively in the international market place.'

I believe that right now, with the enormous financial difficulties of the US airlines, we have a unique opportunity to lead the world in air transportation and I think it would be ironic indeed if this government's constructive plans for British Airways excluded consideration of the significant part the existing British, wholly private enterprise flag carrier has played in the past and could play in the future. British Caledonian has a good track record and I would suggest deserved better than being excluded from current Government policy.

Certainly, I am talking constructively to Iain Sproat and John King and they are being as constructive as they can be under the present policy – but right now it seems to me that they must be severely limited as they are working to a directive which they are determined to fulfil – 'Privatise British Airways' – Regardless? Beyond that, shouldn't the Government's clear objective be to encourage the development of a strong profitable air transport industry of which the nation can be proud?'

It took a full fourteen days for the Prime Minister to reply. In the meanwhile, we judiciously copied my letter to a group of selected individuals. In addition to three Cabinet members, they were Iain Sproat, Michael Colvin, chairman of the Conservative Parliamentary Aviation Committee, Robert McCrindle, another MP with strong aviation interests and Peter Hordern, MP for Horsham and Crawley, a constituency which covered Gatwick Airport. We told each of them that we were contacting only a limited number of people, were not asking them to do anything, but would consult further when we had heard from Margaret Thatcher. In general, response from the individual politicians was favourable towards my arguments and they each expressed an interest in discussing the Prime Minister's reply.

The letter headed simply '10 Downing Street – The Prime Minister' arrived at Gatwick on 11 September. Acknowledging my concern, Margaret Thatcher wrote:

I can assure you that we are most anxious to see a thriving and healthy airline industry in this country and are very concerned

413

that our airlines should recover as quickly as they can from the problems which have been created for them by the economic recession. Indeed, it is because we have confidence in their ability to do so that we believe British Airways will be more successful in the private than in the public sector.

In your letter, you speculate about various changes which may be made to pave the way for privatisation. While some reorganisation of British Airways' finances may be necessary, the Government have not yet received nor approved any specific proposals.

You suggest that some reallocation of routes might be of benefit to British Airways as well as to your own company, and I understand that you have recently given some specific examples to Iain Sproat of route exchanges between your two airlines which you have proposed to Sir John King. I am sure this is the most constructive and fruitful way to proceed and if you are able to agree on some mutually acceptable proposals to put to the CAA, I have no doubt they will respond helpfully.

The next, penultimate paragraph of the letter turned out to carry an ironic twist.

John Biffen, in his reply to your letter of August 1981, explained why he did not think the Government should initiate such a redistribution, and I am sure you will appreciate that that would be quite contrary to the change which we brought about in the Civil Aviation Act 1980; which made the Authority [the CAA] rather than the Secretary of State responsible for policy on route licensing.

Margaret Thatcher finally thanked me for words of support I had given on the Falkland policy and said she was sorry that 'those events' had made life difficult for us. By hand she wrote 'Every good wish' before signing off.

One of the other people to whom I had given a copy of my letter to Thatcher was John Dent, CAA Chairman. I had liked Dent from the moment I had first met him earlier in the summer. His background was commerce and industry. He was open and direct. Alastair Pugh and I met him shortly after the letter had gone to Downing Street. Dent analysed the possible outcomes of British Airways' privatisation: either BCAL would be 'brushed off' with a minor route exchange, or the Government might embrace BCAL in BA's capital reorganisation and industry restructure.

He was concerned that the latter option might be regarded as anti-competitive and referred to a recent appeal decision by Lord Cockfield to uphold the grant of licences on domestic routes from Heathrow to British Midland Airways.

A discussion flowed back and forth across the whole subject of the BA privatisation and the future of the industry. Dent said that he thought, perhaps, the CAA could mount a study on what was best for the UK airline industry. Both Alastair and I welcomed this suggestion and agreed with Dent that the timing would depend on the Prime Minister and Iain Sproat's reaction and also on how Sproat would tackle the problem if he were asked to do so.

Effectively, events as they so often do in the air transport industry had turned full circle. We were back to the situation of the early 1970s where British Airways and ourselves were preparing for a round of negotiations to see where routes could be traded off against each other. The BCAL planners and analysts were embarked on a process of detailed evaluation of every single route operated by both airlines to study the possibilities which might exist for route swapping.

A follow up meeting with John King had been set for 5 October and, on the British Airways side, was to involve only himself and Gordon Dunlop. None of the BA 'establishment' figures – Roy Watts, Gerry Draper, Stephen Wheatcroft – were invited to attend and, indeed, probably knew nothing of the planned meeting.

At the time, BCAL was caught between two stools. On the one hand, we were struggling to stem the losses caused by the Falklands War; and, on the other, we were fighting to bolster our financial situation against the background of the BA privatisation. By September of 1982, we were forced to consider more drastic measures than we had previously contemplated. These involved the axing of a string of uneconomic or marginally economic routes: Santiago, Quito, Guayaquil and Lima, in South America; Algiers, Oran, Casablanca, Tangiers and Dakar in Africa. They were in addition to those services already dropped on routes to Argentina, the Canary Islands, Lisbon, Madrid and Benghazi. At the same

415

time, BA's heavy cost cutting exercise had involved the termination of about fifteen routes and the odds were that another batch was planned to go. There would, no doubt, be a great deal of hedging, as the moment that either airline was suspected of wanting to drop a route, its trading value would be negligible.

Our route trading plan eventually took shape. We would be prepared to hand over Dallas, the mid-Atlantic routes covering San Juan, Caracas and Bogota; the depleted South Atlantic routes to South America; the West African coastal service; and Lusaka. In addition, we were prepared to withdraw from the hard-won Hong Kong route which, because of John Nott's decision to allow a free for all and overturn the CAA decision, was now overserved and uneconomic.

In return, we proposed that BCAL should take over from BA Mexico and the Western Caribbean, Central Africa, Calcutta and Dacca, Bologna and Naples, and their three routes from Gatwick to points in Germany and Scandinavia.

British Airways' management headquarters and operational nerve centre is at Heathrow. Yet John King preferred to operate from the centre of London, presumably to be close to Whitehall and the City of London, keeping the day-to-day airline activity at arm's length. He continued to base himself in the heart of the West End's clubland, in the appropriately-named King Street. As Alastair Pugh and I were driven down King Street on our way to the meeting, it amused me to see that, along the same thoroughfare, was a pub named The Golden Lion.

King, with Gordon Dunlop, was waiting for us in his corner office which looked over into the gardens of St James's Square. I had sent John King a copy of my letter to Margaret Thatcher. In view of the straightforward way he had entered confidential discussion with us, I believed that it was only fair and honest to let him know of the correspondence with the Prime Minister on issues which directly concerned him and his airline. King and Dunlop presented a curious duo: the big, bluff industrialist-farmer from Yorkshire, and the dark, Scottish accountant.

The meeting lasted for almost two hours and the conversation occasionally drifted off in some peculiar directions. Alastair and I outlined two possible approaches for co-operation between our airlines. The first was a widespread policy approach covering the long-haul routes with a spheres of interest policy. BA would remain by far the larger airline, but both would have networks that would be profitable. Bearing in mind the bad economic situation in the world airline industry, the scheme would have to exclude any other British airline for a period of, perhaps, five years. Government and CAA agreement would have to be obtained and such a policy would require renegotiation with the Americans to achieve a policy of single designation on UK-USA routes – that is, only one British and one US airline would serve each route between the two countries. The second approach was a programme of route adjustment between us on a basis that would be beneficial to both, but of no great significance to either. The examples contained in the route analysis were quoted.

I then put it squarely to King that we at BCAL were not prepared to accept the Government's plans to prop up BA with massive financial assistance without having regard to the effect this could have on our airline.

King said that he was interested in only one thing – making BA a profitable airline so that it could be sold to the private sector. He favoured 100 per cent privatisation. He said he was very willing to work with us, if it was to our mutual advantage. He had no inbuilt prejudice against giving up routes. He favoured pursuing the second approach, however.

I argued for the first scheme, on the ground that if we began with a much wider objective, we would have a better chance of achieving some success. I called it the 'shoot for the moon, and be content with a star' approach.

Both King and Dunlop recognised that they would have to pull in some technical expertise from the airline and mentioned Keith Wilkins, a senior planning manager. The meeting concluded with an agreement that a further working meeting would take place between Dunlop and Wilkins for BA and Alastair Pugh and our own senior planning manager, Peter Smith.

As we left King Street for the Department of Trade, Alastair and I reflected on the meeting. We agreed that we should continue our gentle political pressure with the close group of contacts we had already involved, until we could establish whether or not any serious attempt would be made by BA to meet our requirements. If not, then the ground work would be in place for a hard political push against the Government's BA privatisation policy which we did not oppose, in principle. We did object, however, to their lack of consideration of the serious effect this would have on BCAL.

The small entrance and forecourt of the Department of Trade's offices at 1, Victoria Street were as familiar to my driver, Les Smith, as his own backyard. He swept the Daimler expertly through the narrow entrance to pull up in front of the drab foyer, bristling with security guards. We had arrived for a meeting with Iain Sproat and his senior civil servant, Christopher Roberts. The purpose was to warn them of our plans to stem losses with the closure of routes.

I opened by telling Sproat that BCAL would be fairly close to a break-even position at the end of the current financial year, in October. The Caledonian Aviation Group, encompassing the other subsidiary companies, would be profitable – not by much, but at least the group would be in the black.

I told him that many different plans had been studied for the next financial year and the one chosen involved some route closures and redundancies overseas. So far as the UK was concerned, we hoped that redeployment of people whose jobs were displaced by the route closures would take place and redundancies avoided.

I told the Minister that our latest estimated loss, as a result of the Falklands War, was now more than £6 million.

Sproat then turned the conversation by asking if there was any development with British Airways. I said that we had, in fact, just come from a meeting with King and Dunlop and that further meetings would be taking place. If the Minister seemed to me not to have his mind totally on the issues I was bringing to his attention, there turned out to be a very good reason.

As British Airways was undergoing what can only be described as revolution under King and Dunlop, the old guard of former BOAC and BEA officials threw up from within their ranks a team of moles – men or women who either out of some sense of duty to the past, or for the purpose of making damaging mischief for their new masters, leaked confidential information and sent out to the press and the industry lampoons on the way things were going inside the airline. One of these moles was assigned to BCAL and he regularly came through on the telephone to a selection of our managers, announcing himself as 'Mr Hong Kong'. We and, I believe, BA never established the identity of the moles, but in mid-October 1982 they were hard at work, leaking information about the airline's financial situation, shortly to be published in the annual report for the year up to 31 March 1982.

There had, in any event, been plenty of rumour and speculation about how BA was to be cleaned up for privatisation in the press and in Parliament. Now there were rumours abounding that to prop up a British Airways floundering in a sea of debt and inefficiency, the Government had thrown in a financial lifebelt of £1.5 billion. *The Guardian* commented that £1.5 billion was more than the Government gave each year to the railways, or agriculture, or the arts and was roughly the same amount it invested in housing.

The facts came home to an incredulous public on 19 October. At a London press conference, John King announced a deficit for 1981-2 of an astounding £544 million. This was more than the airline's net worth and meant that, technically, British Airways was bankrupt. Scrutiny of the report showed that BA's regular account showed a deficit of £18 million. It was boosted to £545 million by what were termed a number of 'extraordinary' charges. Two of these charges were the write down in value of 'certain aircraft types' and 'certain specialist buildings' by £208 million; and additional interest on borrowings of £38 million.

The third extraordinary charge was £199 million allocated to a drastic programme of staff cuts taking place in the year under review and into the new financial year. BA's staff numbers had already been cut from around 59,000 in 1979 to the current level of 41,000 and King's plan was to reduce staff numbers by a further 6,000 by March 1983.

The stark and uncompromising truth was that the Government was using taxpayers' money to wipe out BA's debts, accelerate depreciation on aircraft and fund the costs involved in shedding a total of 20,000 staff, more than the total employed in the whole of the independent sector. One of BCAL's accountants worked out that the BA clean up amounted to a public subsidy of £32.54 for each of the airline's 16.9 million passengers.

At his press conference, King made few apologies, but he did say that overmanning was on a prodigious scale and was now coming under control. 'The airline has been conducted in past years as though money grew on trees. No longer,' he said. He could not resist a dig at one of the things that had rankled when he first stepped

419

through the doors of Speedbird House at Heathrow. This was the lifestyle of the executive directors. Each had substantial personal staff and each enjoyed the luxury of chauffeur driven limousines. It was one of the things he told me about at our meeting at Wartnaby. King told the press that money had also been saved in small but significant ways. 'Costly limousines have been replaced by family cars. We no longer cushion our administrators with lavish staff numbers.'

The telling paragraph in King's annual report was written by the auditors, Ernst & Whinney. 'The accounts have been prepared on a going concern basis on the strength of your [the Secretary of State's] assurance to the British Airways board that HM Government will ensure the availability of adequate financial resources to meet the Board's obligations as they fall due.'

The first broadside against what became to be termed 'financial plastic surgery' was launched by John Smith MP, the Labour spokesman on aviation. The tough, gritty, highly articulate Scot said:

As is evident from BA's accounts, the finances of the airline are being manipulated for the political purposes of the Government. Last year's loss has been deliberately exaggerated by adding in redundancy payments for the future. The sole objective of this shabby manoeuvre is to make the airline seem currently more profitable than it is and to assist the selling off of shares in the coming year.

The result is that the taxpayer will have to bear the full cost of these deliberately-inflated past losses while future profits will go to the private investor . . . this Government now intends to use taxpayers' money to write off hundreds of millions of pounds of BA debt before any shares are put on the market.

These shabby and dishonest manoeuvres are designed for one purpose only – to indulge Mr Sproat's personal obsession to sell off shares before the next election, regardless of the cost to the taxpayer, the airline, its employees or the public.

For BCAL, our fears and concerns were turning out to be well-founded. In fact, prior to the release of the BA accounts Ian Ritchie had confronted an embarrassed Conservative MP, Michael Colvin, at a meeting in the Savoy Hotel. A product of Eton, Sandhurst and the Grenadier Guards, Colvin was a safe-seat, archetypal Tory. In one of those curious twists of coincidence he had married into the Cayzer family with whom we had battled to create the second force airline in the first place. Colvin had recently taken over chairmanship of the Conservative Aviation Committee, a group of backbenchers interested in aviation. The committee held no constitutional power, but it did form a powerful and influential lobby.

Ritchie was, on the face of it, meeting Colvin to finalise plans for a forthcoming visit to the USA by himself and his colleagues, Robert Atkins and Graham Bright. In particular, they would be returning by way of our new service from St Louis to London. The opportunity was taken by Ian to hand over a copy of the Margaret Thatcher letter, once the niceties of the travel plans had been discussed. Ritchie reported to me afterwards that Colvin was immediately defensive about the Government's plans for BA. Ian told Colvin that it was now past the stage of debating justification of the privatisation plan. The point now was to position BCAL in a positive way in the administration's aviation policy. According to Ritchie, Colvin continued to press on with justifying plans for BA, until he was asked, point blank, where BCAL figured in his, or his Committee's plans. Colvin was forced to reply that we did not figure anywhere.

Ian told me: 'As a fairly recent Chairman of the Aviation Committee, he [Colvin] feels particularly vulnerable to the argument that they are so hell-bent on the privatisation of BA that they totally overlooked the existence of the private sector flag carrier.'

On St Andrew's Day, 30 November 1982, I wrote to Iain Sproat. I first congratulated him on the progress that was being made within British Airways, with a view to privatisation. I continued:

However, as I anticipated, recent actions confirm that I was right to express concern for British Caledonian's position if this was not taken into consideration at the same time as the necessary steps were to make British Airways attractive for the market . . . A £545 million airline loss is impressive, even in an industry that is experiencing troubled times. Obviously, this has been accepted by the Government as assurances to Ernst

& Whinney were necessary, but in giving these assurances, you are already effectively assisting British Airways to compete with British Caledonian – and other private airlines.

Writing off a redundancy of about £100 million that occurs this year into last year's accounts is, I know, arguable, but a luxury that few airlines could afford. Naturally, if an aircraft type is being put up for scrap, then a write off is necessary, but if they are continuing in operation, that is another matter.

I asked Sproat to make the appropriate figures available, including which type and mark of aircraft were involved, with the amounts being written off and the new applicable periods for depreciation. The Lockheed 1011 Tristar, Trident, Boeing 707, BAC 1-11 and Sikorsky S-61N and Boeing Chinook helicopters were mentioned in the BAA annual report. We were competing with all of these types in the scheduled service and charter markets. We were also competing with the helicopters for North Sea oil industry support contracts.

I reminded Sproat of his response to a question put to him by Robert Atkins in the House of Commons three weeks previously. Sproat had said: 'I share the concern that the private sector should be put at no competitive disadvantage by what we do over British Airways. I have therefore decided that, over the coming few weeks and months, I should give every opportunity to the management of private sector airlines to come and tell me what they feel about this matter.'

I was picking up his offer and told him that in view of our previous discussions, I was just a little surprised that action had been taken and that we now faced a fait accompli, even though I did understand his zeal to privatise British Airways.

Detailed discussions with British Airways, following up my meeting with King and Dunlop, were taking place and there was a possibility that they could lead to proposals that would slightly improve the prospects for both airlines. However, the sheer size of British Airways compared with BCAL militated against anything really meaningful for us. My view of any equitable outcome was pessimistic. The government had to become involved. I said to Sproat that without somebody like himself sitting in the middle to consider what was best for the British airline industry as a whole, there would be little chance of success. I reaffirmed our support for the privatisation policy. I wrote:

My concern remains that if you continue your present course of action with British Airways, regardless of British Caledonian, you will most certainly damage British Caledonian. Furthermore, if British Airways is not privatised before the next election (this must be a real possibility) and if, by chance, a Labour government comes to power, we shall be facing a British Airways that will remain nationalised but, in the meantime, significantly strengthened by the taxpayer as a result of the Conservative Government's actions.

Of the three British long-haul scheduled airlines in 1982, Laker went bust, British Airways lost £545 million and has had to be propped up by Government and only British Caledonian is standing by itself. The industry is facing the worst crisis in its history and it would appear that your one real concern is to sell half of British Airways to the private sector. When such a fundamental change is being made, I would have thought that the Government and the CAA would, at least, be giving serious consideration to the effect this will have in the British airline industry and what steps should be taken to ensure that the greatest possible benefit for the country is achieved.

Having failed to achieve any meaningful degree of under-standing with the Government as to our concerns regarding the dangers to British Caledonian as a result of the Government's plan to privatise British Airways, we shall now prepare a detailed document on the whole subject, with a view to formally submitting it to the Government and the CAA.

In short, I was telling Sproat that if the Government itself either could not or would not prepare a cohesive policy for civil aviation, then we would write one.

# 73

Events in the UK were something of a sideshow within the world aviation circus. The industry was in deep financial crisis. A measure of the depth of the problem was seen in the decision by IATA, the International Air Transport Association, to forego the traditional, lavish annual general meeting in some exotic part of the world, replacing it with a no-frills, utility event at its home base in Geneva.

The BCAL delegation, accompanied by a group of British air correspondents, travelled to Geneva on our 1-11 service.

Knut Hammarskjold, the IATA Director General, delivered his state of the industry message. His terse words, delivered to the chairmen and chief executives of each of the world's major carriers, were damning in the extreme. The industry, he said, was in trouble. That trouble was to amount to a combined deficit of some 2 billion US dollars.

It fell to me to respond to Hammarskhold's address and to propose the acceptance of his report. I walked slowly from the table assigned to BCAL, where Alastair Pugh and Ian Ritchie were sitting alongside me, up to the rostrum in the cavernous Geneva conference centre. I surveyed the delegates assembled from every conceivable corner of the earth. They represented the so-called IATA 'cartel', yet unlike any other cartel in history, they had conspired to achieve a hideous collective loss, rather than fat profits.

I told them that the picture painted by Hammarskjold was a dark one indeed and while the figures reported were bad enough, the problem was even deeper. The fact was that in order to finance the necessary investment in new equipment, a minimum level of profitability of 7.5 per cent was required. To maintain a healthy balance sheet, a return of ten per cent was probably necessary. I said:

424

Accordingly, the true reflection of the state of the air transport industry is a very much blacker picture indeed than the losses indicate.

Taking into account the quite modest business requirements to provide for future investment and keep the books respectable, our real shortfall for 1982 is between $5-$6 billion, based on a 7.5 per cent return.

In 1983, applying what we really need – a ten per cent return on revenue – the true shortfall would be more than $6 billion, a figure three times worse than shown.

Our approach to the business of air transport differs considerably and, I would suggest, we fall into four groups, all experiencing severe problems at the moment.

First, we have the US carriers, experiencing a blood bath which inevitably had to follow their deregulation policy. Perhaps, as some say, at the end of the day, those who survive will be fewer, stronger, more efficient and robust – and looking for expansion throughout the world. The deregulation policy has had a spin-off effect on the Atlantic, in particular. Consumer organisations can, of course, still point to the benefits this has brought – in selected cases – the travelling public, but at a cost to the airline stockholders.

This leads me to the second group, airlines of the developed world outside the USA. These airlines are mainly owned by governments and the losses are, consequently, borne by the taxpayer, creating the situation whereby the taxpayer who does not fly is subsidising the one who does.

I thought of the zealous and idealogical Iain Sproat, as I said:

In spite of this, we still have pressure for complete deregulation coming from enthusiastic amateurs who know nothing about our business: politicians seeking the popular, uninformed vote; and consumer groups, looking for short-run benefits, all favouring an expansion of deregulation.

Sproat, along with the mission to privatise British Airways, was clamouring for deregulation in Europe, with the objective of free-for-all competition to achieve lower and lower fares. He and the Conservatives did not appear to take account of reality, of the

425

protection built into air service agreements by the State proprietors of most of Europe's airlines. Wholesale deregulation in Europe, of the kind that had occurred in the federated USA, was impossible. He needed only to look at our Mini-Prix low fares scheme of 1979 to see that restrictionism in Europe was entrenched. Free competition in Europe could be achieved only by a concerted political will among the Governments. I spoke on:

> Many of us have said, for very valid reasons, that our international business just will not fit into a deregulation environment. Free market forces in international aviation are a myth. What greater example could you have of this than that applicable to the UK at the moment, where the nationalised airline has announced a loss of \$925 million which will be absorbed by the taxpayer – and this under a government which can reasonably be described as Conservative.
>
> British Caledonian is the only wholly privately-owned European airline operating to the USA and I can assure you that the last thing we want is a price war with Air France, British Airways, Sabena and the other European airlines, because this means a price war with their governments. Confident as we might be of our own efficiency and resources, we are not so naive as to believe that we can withstand the mighty resources of European governments.

I went on to say that the third general group of carriers was that of developing nations who wished to establish their own air trading links with the rest of the world. They are inevitably involved in significant development costs and, of course, affected by the world airline situation. This resulted, in most cases, in losses that must be borne by their taxpayers.

> Then there is the handful of non-US, privately-owned airlines like British Caledonian. Our four groups may all have a profit motive as a high or low priority. But our differing strategies are certainly not conducive towards solving the massive problems that we face.

I drew a parallel with the shipping industry with its enormous problems. The shipping companies were in the doldrums in large part because they had lost their business to the airlines. But unlike sea transport, nobody was threatening to take over our business and nobody in the foreseeable future could. The enemy was within.

> Even through this depression, our business is not reducing. In fact in some areas it is still expanding, albeit at a very low rate. We still have the demand. We shall have the supply – too much supply – and we are controlling our costs. But we are not covering the other basic business ingredient, our prices. A simple, back-of-the-envelope calculation involving published fares mix and likely load factor can, on many routes, illustrate vividly the likely loss.

My general outlook was not optimistic and I doubted the forecasts of the industry economists than an improvement in the business climate was on its way.

> I hope that the glasses of ourselves and some of our economic advisers are not becoming rose-coloured. Most of us expected an upturn this year which did not materialise. We talk about recession in world economies. But there is very little doubt – certainly among many elder statesmen – that we are in the throes of economic depression and we must not delude ourselves by believing that the problem is any less serious . . . We can no longer rely on expansion solving our massive capital requirements and there are no new technological breakthroughs in sight.
> We have three options: to suffer a total collapse; to be held in permanent bondage to the banks and financial institutions; or to work towards salvation by real and meaningful industry consolidation and concentration.
> If we can sublimate our own short term objectives in the interests of a viable industry, surely we must all gain in the long run. I do not believe that anybody except ourselves has the will or the ability to lead us out of this catastrophic situation.

I realized that my words, against the background of calls for more competition and lower and lower fares, especially in the UK, would not be popular. But the industry was in a hopeless economic state and had to get back to a reasonable level of profitability if it was going to be able to continue serving its worldwide marketplace on the scale that was demanded. In the first place, this meant tackling the fundamental problem of fares and yields. It was sheer lunacy to continue selling seats for less than the cost of production. The industry would have to eliminate illegal discounting and bring fares, in general, to a level that related to costs and build in a reasonable margin – yield as the airlines call it – for profit. If a route for one particular airline was uneconomic, then it should cut its costs and cease operations. Bucket shop deals would only serve to destroy the total market for that airline and its competitors. It has to be said that viewing civil aviation from a strictly commercial stance, as any privately-owned carrier had to, there were many countries around the world who had no right to be in the airline business at all.

The industry's problems and a denunciation of its self-deluding practices became the subject of many speeches and lectures I gave around the world. It was to the World Affairs Council in Los Angeles that I gave an address titled Conflict and Crisis in Air Transport. I cracked a small joke in the address which came to be quoted and requoted many times over within the industry. I said that recession was when you had to tighten your belt. Depression was when you had no belt to tighten. When you had lost your trousers, you were in the airline business.

# 74

My wife, Dawn, continued to take as much interest in the business of BCAL as she had done in the very early days of struggle and hardship to get our airline off the ground. However, as the years passed, Dawn experienced severe problems with her joints, particularly in her spine. She had already had fusion in her toes, but the really serious problem was spondylitis in the lower spine. A major operation had to be done and Dawn spent six weeks in hospital. Concern was evident from the consultant who carried out the operation. Dawn gradually recovered but inevitably she found long flights were a great discomfort and, indeed, this also prevented her from joining me on the punishing schedule of receptions and dinners in London and overseas that I attended.

It was in anticipation of her pleasure that I carried from the office in November 1982 a letter from Downing Street. The contents were to remain entirely confidential, but I was asked whether, if nominated, I would accept the honour of being created a Knight Batchelor. Dawn was enthralled, not so much at the prospect of becoming Lady Thomson, but at the fact that my work had been recognised at the top level. I also told Margaret Trett, my personal assistant, of the honour – she, as much as anyone, deserved to know, for her skill in running my office and dealing so effectively with the high and the mighty in our industry. The knighthood was announced in the New Year Honours list of 1983. It was bestowed for services to commercial aviation, on the recommendation of Margaret Thatcher.

The citation said that I was, 'an international personality, widely recognised for abilities, not only for running a respected airline profitably, but also providing a quality of excellence which brings great credit to the UK at a time when standards are falling.' It would be ridiculously modest not to say that the Knighthood was a grand honour for me personally and one that I enjoyed receiving. I did feel, however, that it was a tribute to everybody in BCAL for what we had jointly achieved over the years. I hoped that staff at every level would feel that part of the knighthood belonged to them and that we could share and enjoy it together.

To anybody in line for a knighthood, I would warn them to be prepared for an absolute avalanche of congratulatory letters. In the early days of January, I received no fewer than 600 letters, each of which had, of course, to be answered personally. Margaret Trett, with assistance from some other secretaries, and I spent hours each day and into the evenings, dictating, typing and signing responses from colleagues, business associates, members of staff and unknown, well-wishing passengers and members of the public.

News of the honour came at the end of a year of trial in which our measures to cut costs and stem losses resulting from the Falklands War brought home a loss on airline activities of £655,000. Profits from the other activities of hotel operations, inclusive tour holidays and engine overhaul at the new plant in Prestwick, produced, however, an overall group profit of £1.54 million. It was a dramatic improvement on the loss of £6.22 million in the previous financial year. As we entered the new financial year in November 1982, deep recession still prevailed, although there were some signs of improvement in trading conditions.

Nevertheless, BCAL was now leaner, fitter, more efficient and more flexible than at any time in the past. Our productivity, calculated by measuring the number of employees against air transport production, had increased by 8.3 per cent. Revenue earned per employee rose by 23 per cent. The DC-10-30 fleet of eight aircraft, the mainstay of the intercontinental operations, achieved an average daily utilisation of 12.66 hours, a very satisfactory figure. The Boeing 747 used on the Nigerian services operated six days every week and had achieved the notable technical dispatch reliability figure of 94 per cent. The three Boeing 707s were busy supplementing DC-10-30s on long-haul routes and the 16 BAC 1-11s plied the high-frequency Continental European and UK domestic routes. The two DC-10-10 aircraft, acquired from Laker after the firm's collapse, had successfully operated an inclusive tour charter programme, carrying a total of 368,000 passengers. Had

430

we not been able to complete arrangements to fly these aircraft on behalf of the tour firms, it is fair to say that a large number of those passengers would not have been able to travel on holiday.

We had, of course, effected route cutbacks in South America, North Africa and some other areas. More cutbacks came in early November, when we were forced to reduce the frequency of services linking Glasgow and Edinburgh with England.

This came about as a result of Michael Bishop's British Midland Airways winning licences to compete with British Airways to fly to the Scottish cities from Heathrow. A year earlier, Bishop had been refused licences by the CAA. The authority had said in its decision that the introduction of a third airline on the Anglo-Scottish trunk routes would not only damage the viability of existing services, but also put the new entrant at risk. British Midland refused to accept the decision and took the matter, on appeal, to the Secretary of State for Transport. Lord Cockfield overturned the CAA's judgement and ordered that Bishop's airline be licensed to operate up to six round-trip services a day on each of the two routes.

The effect was that substantially more seats were available from the more powerful hub at Heathrow and the British Midland flights drew traffic away from our Gatwick operation. The domestic services had traditionally lost money in their own right and were justified economically only by their ability to feed traffic from the regions on to intercontinental services from Gatwick. Our remedy was to reduce frequencies and gear those flights that remained to connect with the long-haul operation, especially to transatlantic services.

We were, however, far from pulling away from domestic operations. In an innovatory development, under the planning expertise of John Prothero Thomas, we formed an organisation called British Caledonian Commuter. This was an umbrella organisation to provide top class handling and marketing assistance to the growing number of commuter airlines which were now serving Gatwick from such places as Humberside, Norwich, Plymouth, Leeds/Bradford and Birmingham. They used small-capacity aircraft such as the Embraer Bandirante, the de Havilland Twin Otter and the Shorts 330. The idea was that we would help the development of these airlines and the commuter routes to provide more feed to intercontinental services. The British Caledonian Commuter plan involved

431

the airlines, the first of which was a company called Genair, painting their aircraft in BCAL colours to identify themselves as part of an international airline system in their markets. We also programmed their schedules into our computer reservations network and actively sold onward travel to the small UK regional cities overseas.

In Europe, we had at last won authority from the Bonn government to begin services to Frankfurt from Gatwick. The Germans did not, however, allow us to offer the lower fares we proposed for the twice-daily operation. The Geneva charter operation successfully evolved into a full scale scheduled operation, again at a frequency of two flights each day.

The North Atlantic routes were holding up well. We successfully saw off Pan American from the non-stop Houston route. After a period of direct competition Pan Am pulled away to revert to a one-stop service. Delta on the Atlanta route had given stiff competition on both price and flight frequencies. However, Alastair Pugh had earlier masterminded a marketing co-operation scheme with the major US carrier, Eastern Airlines. This effectively linked our two networks at the Atlanta gateway. It gave us a US domestic network to benefit from and Eastern gained a transatlantic service. It was the first such agreement of its kind and the thinking has subsequently been borrowed by other carriers. The effect of the BCAL/Eastern tie-up was to increase traffic between London and Atlanta by 32 per cent.

In summary, after the disappointments of the Falklands losses, in both route network and straight financial terms, the airline had picked itself up and its people and aircraft were working harder than ever before. Passenger numbers, at 2,692,572, were higher than they had ever been in a single year.

To a large extent, however, we were heading into the unknown, commercially and politically. There was little hope of any significant recovery from the world recession in 1983 and when economic factors force a decrease in the flow of international trade, air transport is affected immediately. The weakening of sterling against the dollar was one of the forces stacked against us. Many of the airline's costs were dollar related, the largest single item being fuel. The lower fuel prices which were emerging would not compensate fully for the continuing slide in the value of the pound. Travel on both scheduled services and charters would be

432

affected by constraints on disposable incomes and by the high levels of unemployment prevalent at the time. And, of course, there was the giant question mark formed by the British Airways privatisation policy hanging over the future of the civil aviation industry in the UK. But we were forecasting a return to profitability, realising that the going would be hard and that a maximum effort would be required in every aspect of the business.

# 75

In the spring and early summer of 1983, thoughts of politicians were hardly attuned to the problems of the airline business. They were fervently preoccupied with the impending General Election. The privatisation of state industries was, however, one of the main planks of the Conservatives' policies and in their election manifesto there appeared one paragraph which caught my eye and left me with a mixed feeling that this was either contemptuous irony, or heart-warming encouragement.

It read: 'Merely to replace state monopolies by private ones would be to waste an historic opportunity. So we will take steps to ensure that these new firms do not exploit their powerful positions to the detriment of consumers or their competitors.'

Precise decisions on the nature and the timing of the privatisation of British Airways had not yet been taken by the Cabinet. The problem of the corporation's balance sheet, deeper than most people had at first supposed, had put paid to plans for any earlier sale of shares. But legislative moves to sell off the state airline were announced by John Nott in 1979 and had passed into the Civil Aviation Act 1980.

The drive to prepare the business for a floating of its shares on the Stock Exchange had proceeded relentlessly under John King. His major move early in 1983 was to bring a new figure to stride through the corridors of Speedbird House and out into the industry. It was that of Colin Marshall, the new chief executive, replacing Roy Watts. Marshall, an Englishman, had spent most of his management career in the USA. He had worked extensively in the car rental business, with Hertz and with Avis. King's headhunters had attracted and recruited Marshall from his position as director and deputy chief executive of Sears Holdings plc. One of the first major problems that Marshall was to encounter at British Airways was one that he would share with us in BCAL for the next several years and which would have a profound effect on the progress of the state corporation from Whitehall to the City of London. It was the Laker Case.

Many months after the collapse of Laker Airways, in November 1982, the company's liquidator, Christopher Morris of the accountancy firm Touche Roche & Co., filed a law suit in Washington DC. It was an action put together by Laker's UK attorney, Robert Beckman, in the name of Laker Airways Limited (In Liquidation). The suit was filed under the US anti-trust, or anti-competition, laws as enshrined in legislation known as the Sherman Act. In short, the anti-trust laws prohibit commercial concerns from conspiring to fix prices or the supply of goods and services to the detriment of consumers or competitors. They are similar to the anti-competition rules of the Treaty of Rome which governs the European Economic Community. Under special agreement, airlines meeting under the auspices of IATA, or the US Civil Aeronautics Board, were exempt from the anti-trust laws.

Beckman's law suit named a number of airlines, McDonnell Douglas and McDonnell Douglas Finance Corporation, together with some individuals. It alleged that the airlines conspired together in a scheme to destroy charter airlines and the Laker Skytrain services by offering high cost services at low fares and that, to achieve their ends, high and secret sales commissions were paid to travel agents to divert business. A further allegation was that, towards the end of 1981, Lufthansa of Germany, Swissair and BCAL – all DC-10 operators – pressured lenders to deny support to Laker, thereby forcing the company out of business. The other airlines involved were Pan American, TWA and British Airways.

So far as we were concerned, BCAL had not competed directly with Laker on their transatlantic routes and therefore could not have undercut the airline in the New York and Los Angeles markets. The second allegation referred to my telex at the time it became known that McDonnell Douglas, our mutual aircraft supplier, was planning to help the financial rescue of Laker. I had told the manufacturer that if they were planning to invest in a competitive airline, then we would withdraw support for their products. The suit alleged that this, together with similar protests

435

from Lufthansa and Swissair, blocked the McDonnell Douglas funding of Laker and led directly to the airline's collapse. It was proven subsequently that this was not so. Our immediate reaction was that the Laker case against BCAL was frivolous and without foundation. It would be defended vigorously.

Beckman was claiming a total of $350 million in compensatory damages, plus $700 million in punitive damages. Further, under the US anti-trust law, a defendant found guilty could be ordered to pay triple damages. On the other side of the coin, however, if a not-guilty verdict was brought in, the defendant has no recourse to claim for costs.

The Laker case was to drag on in courts in England and the USA for the next two years, amid considerable publicity, with Leonard Bebchick competently taking care of the BCAL interest. For British Airways it was to prove to be the final delay factor in the struggle for privatisation.

One man who played a key role as Laker staggered towards its final collapse in February 1982 was Ray Colegate, group economic director for the CAA, and Britain's senior air transport regulator. Before the formation of the CAA, Colegate had been a senior civil servant, concerned with aviation, at the Department of Trade. Almost exactly a year after Laker, Colegate was invited by the Chartered Institute of Transport to deliver its annual Brancker Memorial Lecture, in memory of an early British aviation pioneer, Sir Sefton Brancker. This was the one key Institute lecture of the year devoted to aviation. For his address, Colegate chose the title 'British Air Transport in the Eighties'. His words would obviously not form a statement of official policy, but they would clearly give a firm indication of the CAA view of the industry for the future.

The small, balding figure of Colegate looked frail at the podium, surrounded by several crowded tiers of seats in the lecture theatre. His speech, however, was strong and reasoned. After going into the background of the 1969 Edwards Report and referring to the demise of Laker, he said:

Fortunately, we still have two intercontinental carriers and our duty is to support them both so that they can compete with foreign airlines as effectively as possible and with profit, in the interests of UK Ltd, as well as those of the travelling public and

436

of their own backers, whether they be the State or the private sector.

Despite its detractors, British Airways should emerge from its present agonies as a powerful competitor on the world scene. BCAL is an airline with many qualities that should enable it to look forward with confidence to a valuable role in the future. Not least of those qualities, as has been amply demonstrated over the last decade, is sheer staying power and I believe it would be contrary to the interests of UK Ltd to subject this to needless strains. I agreed with the Edwards Report that it is in the national interest, for all the reasons I have already referred to, that we should continue to have the services of these two airlines, each a centre of excellence in its own way. We should try to maximise the benefits of this and to avoid actions that put them at risk.

Colegate's feelings echoed my own. He then went on to correctly identify our fundamental problem of network strength, but came to a conclusion that was, for me, a drab one. Colegate said:

Nonetheless, I think it only right to acknowledge that BCAL, for all its evident worth, is not quite the second force that the Edwards Committee seems to have been looking for or, for that matter, that I personally had hoped.

The process of route transfer by which it was brought into being was traumatic for BOAC and BEA and not easy for Government to carry out. Nonetheless, I do sometimes wonder whether at that time the ship was not spoiled for a ha'p'orth of tar.

The network that had been created by 1972 was significantly smaller than the Edwards Committee had recommended and, recalling that the Committee's own forecasts of market growth turned out to be optimistic, the result was less strongly based than perhaps it should have been. It is also clear the BCAL's network is too dependent for comfort on a small number of routes. I do not know if the occasion will ever occur again where a further transfer of routes to BCAL might be justified. Certainly the best time to have got right was in 1971 and certainly now is not the time, nor is the immediately forseeable future, to take good routes away from British Airways, struggling as it is to put right the horrendously difficult problems that it faces.

It would in any case, be contrary to the Authority's declared policy for it to take from any airline a route that it was serving well in order to achieve a structural change in the industry.

Those words must have heartened those executives from British Airways in the lecture audience, as much as they depressed me. The only possible way to achieve a balanced and well structured industry was by a re-distribution of the route licence franchises – and that could only be carried out prior to any privatisation of British Airways.

Driving home from the lecture, across Albert Bridge and down through the South London suburbs to Gatwick and Crawley, I mused over Colegate's remarks. They furthered my resolve to get something done. If the Government was not going to put forward a comprehensive policy and neither, it appeared, would the CAA, then we would most definitely have to do something drastic ourselves. The one thing I had in my favour was time. It was clear, at this stage, that the Government could not consider a privatisation programme for British Airways until after the election.

In BCAL itself we were rapidly picking up the pieces from the operational and financial disruption of the previous year. The loss of the South American network not only had financial implications, it also left us with expensive, spare DC-10-30 capacity on our hands. Alastair Pugh and his marketing director, a man we had recruited from British Airways, David Coltman, together with Curly Walter's team in the aircraft trading company, were preoccupied with the task of finding work for the spare DC-10s.

We had no major new route opportunities and the only option was to seek work from other airlines, ideally on the basis of 'wet leases', where the aircraft, together with operating crews, is hired out. Eventually, we succeeded in winning two important contracts. The first was to operate scheduled services between London and Barbados on behalf of Caribbean Airways. Laker had previously carried out this contract and since its demise we had operated some services on an ad hoc basis for the Barbados company. With BCAL capacity available, this was turned into a firm, long-term contract.

The second contract was a similar arrangement for Air Seychelles, operating the route between London and Mahé, via Frankfurt. Air Seychelles was a small carrier operating inter-island services. It had no long-haul fleet, but such was the dependence of the country on tourism that its government wanted to ensure a regular air service from Europe. The conclusion of the agreement was a happy occasion for both sides. BCAL had operated to the Seychelles, as an extension of the Nairobi route, until 1976, when the then Labour Government's aviation review took away our East African network. Our relationship with the Seychelles government and the island people had been happy and productive.

Our drive to increase the BCAL competitive edge and to concentrate on aiming our product at the business traveller accelerated with the introduction of a new class of service on the intercontinental routes. This was Super Executive, a massively upgraded version of the former Executive class we had pioneered on the transatlantic route in 1978. Seats were bigger, with more recline and more legroom. Inflight service standards were upgraded. The new service matched the prime First Class standards of many other airlines. The business class that the major airlines offer today resembles the BCAL Super Executive we first placed on the market in 1982.

Similarly, our First Class service, already the subject of acclaim among passengers, was refined and brought to a standard that we felt very few of our competitors could match. One of our refinements in First Class was to do with the serving of dinner. We wanted it more like a fine restaurant and had the senior stewardess change into elegant evening wear – a full length tartan skirt and silk blouse – to serve our passengers dinner. It was a small touch, but a stark contrast to the sight of stewardesses in aprons, however well designed, that would be encountered on other airlines.

At the other end of the scale, we launched our own new tour firm, Chieftain Travel. Its purpose was to market holidays based on BCAL scheduled services and its first programme, 'American Adventure', offered tours to North America, ranging from a seven-day 'fly drive' arrangement for £305.

In the area of route development, we filed applications to serve Milan and Rome from Gatwick. In fleet development, we recognised the need to seek replacement for the BAC 1-11s which would soon be outside the aircraft noise legislation, unless the Rolls Royce

Spey engines were fitted with silencing systems, known as 'hush kits'. Our evaluations had focused on three possible aircraft types, the Boeing 737-300 which would become available in 1985, the McDonnell Douglas Super 90, ready a year later, and the planned European Airbus A.320 which would probably become available in 1988.

In June, our plans for the future of the airline were debated at an event which I called the major policy review. It was a series of meetings we held annually, over a weekend, away from the office. This year, the directors of the airline and a number of senior managers took ourselves off to Jersey. Inevitably, the meetings were unable to separate the straightforward commercial requirements from the political environment in which we operated and which at the time placed so much uncertainty over our heads.

We emerged with a thirteen-point manifesto. The first three items were strategic: to be the best airline in the world; develop customer service to the point of obsession; and take giant strides in people relations. The remaining ten were largely tactical and covered such areas as hush-kitting the 1-11s and developing blind landing capability at times of bad weather and poor visibility. We set ourselves targets of developing new routes in Europe and around the world; concentrating on being a businessman's airline; and developing marketing innovations to wholesale low-priced seats.

We also set ourselves a policy objective of trying to ensure that British Airways was 100 per cent privatised. The London airports congestion problems led us to the belief that charters should overflow from Gatwick to Stansted, allowing the space for more scheduled services at Gatwick. It was an additional objective that we should develop more partnership arrangements with other airlines, 'buddy relationships', we called them. In addition to the alliance we had forged with Eastern at Atlanta, we had recently concluded similar arrangements with Continental Airlines at Los Angeles and Ozark Air Lines (now US Air) at St Louis.

# 76

Margaret Thatcher swept back into power, stronger than before, with a landslide victory at the General Election of 9 June 1983. The Conservatives had secured a majority of 144 seats in the House of Commons, a degree of political power not seen since Clement Attlee's Labour Party defeated Winston Churchill's Conservatives at the end of the Second World War.

It was unthinkable that the Thatcher government could possibly fail to bring in whatever legislation they chose, under the terms they chose, including the procedures for privatising British Airways. The one interesting gap in the scheme was that left by Iain Sproat, the privatisation champion, who lost his seat.

One of the principal architects of the election success was Cecil Parkinson, chairman of the Conservative Party. Parkinson, amiable and approachable, was a good friend of ours from early days and continued to be so. I had maintained a regular liaison with him during his time as Minister of State at the Department of Trade and kept up the relationship when he moved to Central Office. In this new administration the existing Department of Trade, which governed aviation, and the Department of Industry were to be combined with Parkinson as Secretary of State. This I saw as a great move for us, had the airline industry remained with Trade. That, however, was not the case. We were being moved on to the Department of Transport, under Tom King, a man completely unknown to me.

There was, however, little time to waste in coming to terms with our new political master. I wrote to him just one week after the election. 'As you know,' I said, deferentially, in the certain knowledge that he knew very little about our business, 'the airline industry is going through the worst crisis in its history and

441

problems are not hard to find. At the same time we believe there are good opportunities for the British airline industry and these can be taken and turned into achievements if the right course is followed. Obviously, we have views on what is the "right course".'

The result of the correspondence was a visit to Gatwick by Tom King on 2 August 1983. After touring the BCAL operations, engineering and training facilities, the new Secretary of State was ushered into the boardroom, on the seventh floor of Caledonian House. There, lined up to meet him, was myself, Alastair Pugh, Trevor Boud, David Coltman, John Prothero-Thomas, Ian Ritchie, Colin Smith, the airline's financial director, and, our political 'big gun', Sir Peter Masefield.

King listened intently and responded intelligently to the presentation on where BCAL and the industry had come from, where it was now and where it might be going in the future. What he did not see, at this stage, was the detail of our proposals to get the industry on the 'right course'. Since Colegate's lecture in February and our own Jersey policy review in June, my thoughts had crystallised on how we were to tackle the problem of survival in the future against a privately-owned British Airways, vested with the monopoly on route licences from its history of state ownership.

I decided that, like the political parties, we should form our own policy unit and called together a group of key directors and managers. They included Masefield, Pugh, Ritchie, Boud, Mike Carter, Prothero-Thomas, Tony Cocklin, John de la Haye and our planning expert, Peter Smith. I also called in the lawyer, David Beety, and, when his visits to Gatwick coincided with meetings, Leonard Bebchick. The group was known as the Civil Air Transport Committee. Its notes and records were filed under the acronym, CATCOM. The work of CATCOM was necessarily conducted under a cloak of confidentiality. Minutes of the meetings, for instance, were marked 'Eyes of Addressee Only', not even long-standing, trusted personal secretaries should see what was going on.

Our objective was, in the absence of any government policy moves, to create an overall strategy for the future development of the airline industry in the UK, against the background of the privatisation of British Airways. It would be the last chance to cut through the chaos in which we had been left by a string of disparate, sometimes conflicting policies for Britain's airlines and airports and to fill the current policy vacuum with a cohesive plan for the future. It was, of course, prompted by a large degree of self-interest. All of us could see that an unshackled British Airways, seven times larger than ourselves, responsible only to shareholders seeking increasing profits and dividends, rather than to a minister who had the interests of the industry as a whole to consider, would have, as its first priority, to wipe out the competition. The main competition to British Airways in its home market was, of course, British Caledonian. Unless we were able to strengthen our business base, the route network, we were vulnerable to predatory and unmatchable competition from British Airways, impregnable at the UK's main airport, Heathrow, to which we were denied access, as a result of earlier government policy designed to contain congestion at that airport. The other part of that policy, to develop more scheduled services at Gatwick, had not worked effectively.

The task of detailed analysis of the industry and the job of translating those findings into a strategy that would stand up to commercial, financial and political scrutiny was daunting. The 'engine room' for the policy ship that we planned to drive down the Thames and anchor at the Houses of Parliament was the planning department. Their work was tough enough, but the tricky part would be piloting the policy through the largely unknown waters of political, press and public opinion.

As the planners got down to their work, therefore, Masefield, Ritchie, Pugh and I began to survey the journey and draw up charts. This involved a complete review of politicians – who did we know and were friendly with? Who didn't we know, but needed to? Who would be against us? Likewise we surveyed the scene for useful support lobbies, chambers of commerce, industrial and commercial organisations, our own institutional shareholders, local authorities and, of course, the Gatwick community which depended on jobs at and rates from Gatwick for its economy. There were also the consumer groups, especially the CAA-supported Air Transport Users' Committee, which could hardly be expected to back an argument which closed down the opportunity for more choice for the customer.

To draw up a picture of the shape of the industry in the UK, a standard gauge of measurement had to be used. This industry

443

gauge was – and still is – known as available tonne kilometres. That is the amount of passenger and cargo capacity operated over the distance of a route or route network. In 1983, on international scheduled services British Airways' share of Government franchised production amounted to 81.8 per cent of the total. BCAL's share was 17.2 per cent and the other independents, 1 per cent. On the basis of passengers carried on British-licensed international services, the BA share remained at 81.8 per cent. BCAL's was 11.1 per cent and the others combined held 7.1 per cent.

Unlike most other businesses – independent radio and television being the main ones that come to mind as anywhere near similar – airline growth, expansion and competition is directly related to government-held franchises for scheduled services. BA's franchise allowed it to operate to 135 destinations and deploy capacity to carry almost 11 million passengers. BCAL's operational licences gave us a network of 32 destinations, with capacity to accommodate just over two million scheduled passengers a year.

We analysed the airports situation and found that if the existing system discriminated against every airline, except British Airways, then so, too, did it discriminate against every airport, except Heathrow. As it does today, Heathrow represented, by far, not just the biggest international scheduled service market in Britain, but also the greatest international air service hub in the world. BA was the only UK airline allowed to operate international services from Heathrow. Of the total UK international scheduled traffic served at London area airports, Heathrow accounted for 79.1 per cent. Gatwick's share was 13.9 per cent.

At the two main regional airports in England, BA held a monopoly on international services operated from Manchester; and enjoyed a dominant position at Birmingham. Far from serving these markets well, the airline had actually reduced its direct services from the regions, preferring the more profitable but less customer-conscious course of feeding international passengers into its Heathrow hub, to the detriment of provincial markets and regional airport development.

There was, at the time, a legitimate demand, from both independent airlines and consumers, for an end to the stranglehold of Heathrow on the market and for a more equitable distribution of international services among the UK's airports. The consumers simply wanted the choice of service, the airlines simply sought the opportunity to provide that choice. The only way to achieve it was through a redistribution of the route franchises.

But it was the London area which formed the crux of the problem. Despite the policies of successive governments, Gatwick had failed to develop as a major international gateway alongside Heathrow. BA had paid only lip service to Gatwick scheduled service development and no foreign operator had been attracted to move its London base from Heathrow. A ceiling on the number of air transport movements allowed at Heathrow had been imposed and it was clear that a single airport was inadequate for scheduled services to and from London. Urgent development of scheduled services at Gatwick was required.

After weeks of analysis and debate, a plan steadily emerged. It was bold, in political terms, yet strategically and commercially logical. It centred on the creation of what we called 'British Heathrow Airlines' and 'British Gatwick Airlines', the one based on British Airways in private ownership, the other on BCAL. To achieve balance between the airlines and between the airports, we proposed that a number of routes were transferred from BA to BCAL and along with them the associated resources – aircraft, ground equipment and staff.

We studied routes most suitable for operation by the Gatwick airlines and identified examples. In addition to the eleven scheduled routes already operated at Gatwick by BA, we considered the transfer of services from Heathrow. Candidates were the Caribbean network; the North Pacific route to Japan, where BA was losing substantial market share to Japan Air Lines; low frequency European services, such as those to the Eastern Mediterranean; and the network to the Arabian Gulf. We were prepared to pay. Preliminary calculations of the asset value of aircraft used on the routes transferred to Gatwick, plus the ground equipment, suggested that somewhere between £200 million and £250 million might be raised by the Government through our plan. The strategy went further. To create opportunity and impetus in the development of regional services, we proposed that BA should divest itself of its operations in Scotland, the Highlands and Islands division, and its Manchester and Birmingham operations. These activities could be acquired by other UK airlines – not BCAL – with vested interests

445

in the respective areas and incentives to develop strong, competitive regional networks. Likewise, BA's Internal German Services, that remnant from the Second World War, would be acquired by another British airline. Under the terms of the allied occupation of Berlin, only British, French or US carriers were allowed to provide services to and from West Berlin. British Airtours, the Gatwick-based BA charter subsidiary, could also be taken over by other airlines.

It was a strategy that would bring revenue in to the Government through the sale of assets, uphold the BA position as the main British airline, confirmed in its dominant position at Heathrow, but also create unprecedented opportunity for existing independent airlines and bring shape and balance to the airports problem.

BA's balance sheet in 1983 showed that the airline had a deficiency of assets against liabilities of some £221 million, resulting from the enormous losses of the previous two years. The long-term financial debt at the balance sheet date, 31 March, totalled £1,053.2 million, £1,026.2 million of which had been guaranteed or lent by the Government. At the same time, the balance sheet revealed capital expenditure contracted or authorised, of £396.7 million, arising primarily from the acquisition of the new Boeing 757 aircraft for use on short and medium-range routes. A normal, commercial enterprise in BA's position would not be able to enter into capital expenditure commitments, as it was currently doing. It could only raise this finance because its bank borrowing was guaranteed by Government.

For the Government, our plan meant that the funding of a financial reconstruction of British Airways could be materially reduced and the privatisation process thereby advanced. British Airways would remain an attractive prospect for the private investor. The plan would have the effect of reducing the airline's existing share of UK-licensed production to 60 per cent. BCAL's share would grow from 15 to 30 per cent; and the other independents from two per cent to ten per cent.

For the consumer, it would create more competition and more choice, with a range of expanding centres of airline production in the UK, as opposed to the concentration on Heathrow.

The plan was formalised into a special document. We titled it 'A Strategy for British Civil Air Transport in Private Ownership'.

446

It ran to 169 pages of carefully-reasoned argument, supported by tables and graphs of statistics and illustrations of existing and proposed future route structures. It was contained in an azure-coloured cover and became known, within the airline, as the Blue Book.

The distribution of the Blue Book had to be very carefully planned. We printed just 100 copies and each was numbered and its recipient logged. We had to take care that its arguments and proposals were digested and understood by a central core of politicians and others of influence, before it could be generally released and exposed to attack by British Airways and the 'privatisation-at-any-cost' lobby. The list of those to whom we should send the Blue Book, under strictly confidential cover, was very carefully constructed around the boardroom table. The first, of course, should go to Tom King and the second to his Permanent Secretary, Peter Lazarus. Next came John Dent, CAA chairman, then members of our holding board.

We restricted the document to only a few politicians, the most prominent being Lord Whitelaw, who happened to be the father-in-law of our marketing director, David Coltman, and George Younger, Scottish Secretary. Two other important politicians whom we brought into our confidence were Lord Boyd-Carpenter, former chairman of the CAA and a solid spokesman for civil aviation in the House of Lords; and Nicholas Soames, who, that year, had become MP for Crawley, encompassing Gatwick.

I told Tom King, the Secretary of State, when sending him the Blue Book:

> If British Airways was a private airline at the moment, it would be bankrupt and its British private sector competitors would have excellent prospects for expansion domestically and internationally. Instead, British Airways is apparently to receive massive financial support which overnight will turn it into one of the strongest airlines in the world, rather than the failure it now is. This is particularly important at a time when the airline industry is going through the worst crisis in its history.
>
> British Caledonian believes that there is a better route for the privatisation of British Airways which will benefit the British airline industry as a whole, would make it a stronger competitor

internationally, thereby improving the British economy, will create regional sector airlines with all the benefits to the regions that entails, will ensure a financially successful Gatwick Airport and will partially privatise British Airways at a very early date and make a significant reduction in demand on Public Sector Borrowing Requirement.

I summarised the content of the Blue Book, before coming to our demand of last resort. If Government failed to respond to calls for a restructure of the industry, bringing balance and fair competition, our operation at Gatwick would be vulnerable and probably could not sustain unbridled competition from British Airways at Heathrow. Therefore, we believed that we must be allowed to exercise our commercial judgement and transfer our operations to Heathrow. The Blue Book strategy had already drawn up a plan whereby we could move lock, stock and barrel into the new Terminal 4 which was currently under construction and nearing completion. By operating from Heathrow, with its vastly superior traffic flows, our load factors and profits would improve dramatically. We estimated that a move to Heathrow would instantly give us an operating surplus of £20 million and we would enhance our ability to compete with a privatised British Airways.

# 77

Tom King replied to me in early October 1983. He was inevitably noncommittal. The Secretary of State said that he would want to consider my arguments carefully before he replied, adding that he was sure that I would understand that it might be a little while before he could reply substantively. His reply, in fact, never came. On 14 October the new Government was rocked by the resignation of Cecil Parkinson from the Cabinet and his job as Secretary of State for Trade and Industry over matters which have been well documented elsewhere and do not require reiteration here. In the subsequent reshuffle, King was moved on as Secretary of State for Employment and into the Department of Transport came the former Financial Secretary to the Treasury, Nicholas Ridley. Once more, I put pen to paper to address a Secretary of State and forwarded Ridley the Blue Book.

In the meanwhile, we had been carefully building up a fresh public relations platform, knowing that we could not possibly launch the Blue Book strategy from any other position than one of strength and favourable public opinion.

Against the background of British Airways' financial situation, BCAL had enjoyed a summer of substantial success and was on its way to making a good profit for the year. The transatlantic routes were attracting record business, as the new Super Executive and First Class service made their impact in the marketplace.

In September, our success was confirmed in the annual survey carried out among the readers of *Executive Travel* magazine to find out which airlines business travellers prefer most, and to give those who topped various categories special awards. The victor ludorum of the airline games received the 'Airline of the Year' award and this year it came to us, after being presented to British Airways,

449

for its improved performance, in 1982. The magazine's citation read: 'Polished service, both in the air and on the ground, cheerful efficient cabin staff, a good punctuality record and a genuine desire to satisfy the customer – all have doubtlessly contributed to the airline's success. The introduction, earlier this year, of BCAL's Super Executive Class, together with a comprehensive range of services geared to the business traveller, will also have influenced the voting.'

Such are the ups and downs of the six or so awards surveys that are carried out in the airline and the travel industry, that many executives believe that they do not count for much. Their value, it is said, is down to what the winner makes of them. Well, here was a chance for us to make mileage and we did so by featuring the award in advertising and in our own publications, and by a well-publicised gesture dreamed up by Alastair Pugh. In recognition of their achievements in winning the Airline of the Year award, every member of staff received in that month's pay packet vouchers to go and have a drink on the house at the airline's staff club, the Wingspan.

Normally, we would not reveal results of talk about profit levels until the time of the annual general meeting which, because of our November-October financial year, usually took place in the springtime. However, we had to take advantage of the good summer results and chose the venue of the 1983 IATA annual general meeting in New Delhi to release them. It might have seemed an incongruous occasion, but the IATA meetings attract a significant corps of aviation journalists, all hungry for stories to file back to their publications.

Thus, Ian Ritchie, Tony Cocklin and I and our Indian general sales agent found ourselves holding a press briefing in Delhi's Taj Hotel, being served drinks and exotic tit-bits of food by elaborately dressed, silent-footed waiters. I announced that BCAL would record a profit in the current financial year, following a record summer in which carryings were up by 21 per cent on certain routes. This increase was achieved on the Middle East and Far East routes. Traffic on transatlantic services had increased by 17 per cent.

My statement said: 'Our record summer results reflect the successful implementation of new routes, the introduction of improved products and the beginnings of an upturn in the economy.' I told the journalists that detailed financial information could not be confirmed until the year-end audits had been completed. 'At this stage, however, we know enough to be confident and place on the record the fact that BCAL and the Caledonian Aviation Group will earn a profit for the year which ends on 31 October,' I said.

The move gave us good results, not only in the UK press, but in publications around the world. Our hastily-convened press conference in Delhi was, however, a far cry from events earlier in October in the Churchill Room of the London Press Club. Throughout the year, an area of concentration had been the evaluation of aircraft types to replace the 1-11s. The fight among the three manufacturers, Boeing, McDonnell Douglas and Airbus Industrie, to gain the BCAL business had been fierce. Series after series of presentations had taken place and the race at last came down to a dash between the Boeing 737-300 and the planned Airbus A.320. At the end, the decision rested on the kind of financial package which each manufacturer could put forward – the aircraft were equally good.

The fact that Airbus Industrie was European and one of its consortium partners was British Aerospace, set to receive substantial contracts for building the wings of the A.320, placed a great deal of press and political interest in the way the BCAL order would go. If we chose the Airbus product, we would become a launch customer for the A.320 in which no airline had so far agreed to invest and this would give the company and its partner, British Aerospace, a significant boost. Such was the pressure of interest, that a team from the BBC television programme, Panorama, was virtually camped on our doorstep, as was a nervous Airbus executive, Arthur Howes, the salesman assigned to BCAL.

All of the manufacturers valued a BCAL order. Because we were privately-owned, with no government pressure on how or where we invested, our selection of aircraft was geared solely to the commercial and technical benefits of the equipment. BCAL's choice said a lot about an aeroplane, they felt – and no one felt this more than Airbus. It was a very close race to the finish between the A.320 and the 737-300, each extremely fine aircrafts.

In the final analysis, behind the closed doors of the Caledonian House boardroom, the A.320 won. It provided us with the best possible economic/operational formula through the 1990s and into the next century, with the most advanced technology yet proposed. It was the best option for the long term. The aircraft was geared to achieve exceptional productivity and fuel-efficiency, with costs per seat/mile 27 per cent lower than the 1-11s they would replace.

We signed with Airbus Industrie an order for seven of the A.320s, with options to acquire a further three. It was worth £150 million, to be financed by conventional bank funding secured against the aircraft. The first three would be delivered to Gatwick in the spring of 1988, with a further four coming in 1989. The A.320 was planned to enter scheduled service on European routes, carrying 150 passengers. On charter flights, the aircraft would accommodate 162 passengers. The following day, Roger Beteille, general manager and executive vice-president of Airbus Industrie, joined us in London to announce the order to the press.

Almost as important to us as the technical benefits of the aircraft, was the political kudos the order bestowed, although that did not come into the final reckoning. Nevertheless, I played on it at the press conference. 'By pinning our colours to the Airbus mast as a launch customer for the A.320, we are confident that BCAL will become the catalyst to bring the very latest European aircraft manufacturing venture into successful reality. With the A.300 and the A.310, Airbus has established beyond doubt that British and continental European industry can produce the type of aircraft to match the giant US manufacturers. We are confident that the A.320 will become, in turn, the success of its generation.'

The response was resounding. The order received massive press and broadcasting coverage and BCAL was contrasted with British Airways which had, so far, shown no interest in the British-backed product. Equally important for our political profile, the order prompted an Early Day Motion in the House of Commons, a device through which MPs can make their views known on or publicise specific subjects, although the motions are not debated in the Chamber. This one, initially sponsored by a mixed group of six Conservative, Labour and Liberal MPs, read: 'This House congratulates British Caledonian for its recent decision to buy the Airbus A.320, 25 per cent of which should be built in Great Britain, thereby creating and safeguarding British jobs and keeping the UK in the vanguard of civil aviation technology and calls upon

452

the Government to facilitate the participation of British firms in this collaborative project which is of such crucial importance to the long-term future of the civil aircraft manufacturing industry.' The Early Day Motion eventually came to be signed by scores of MPs.

In a quite separate move which did no harm to our desire to be seen as a thrusting, successful company, we negotiated the acquisition of the tour and travel firm, Jetsave, which specialised in bulk transatlantic travel from the Associated Communications Corporation of the Australian entrepreneur, Robert Holmes à Court. Its purpose was to provide high-volume traffic for the economy-class sections of the transatlantic routes.

We had achieved a great deal in the course of 1983. We had not only recovered from the effects of 1982 and the Falklands War, but were now sprinting into profit, with a good profile and a great deal of support. We were ready for battle.

# 78

From the autumn of 1983, the face of BCAL to the general public had been conveyed via the television screen through a parody of a song made famous by the legendary pop group, the Beach Boys. Instead of 'California girls', our commercial sang about 'Caledonian girls'. The commercial was created and produced by the advertising firm Abbott, Mead Vickers, which had replaced Saatchi & Saatchi after they had gone to take the British Airways account.

We had always used our uniformed air and ground staff promotionally, particularly the girls who epitomised the style of the airline in their bright and attractive tartan uniforms. The advertising agency persuaded us to go one stage further and make them our main advertising feature for a series of television commercials. I have to say that I was not sure if we were doing the right thing when I was played the first sample tapes, showing businessmen aboard the aircraft breaking out into song and dance. David Coltman and his marketing team persuaded me otherwise. They were right; the series worked to our advantage, showing that BCAL was a caring airline, geared to the needs of the business traveller, but was also prepared to enjoy itself and wanted its passengers to do so. Not only that, the commercial made our cabin and ground staff feel good about being the Caledonian girls – as seen on TV.

But while Abbott, Mead Vickers were enjoying the success of the lighthearted Caledonian girls commercials, they were called in for some sterner work. CATCOM, our special working group, was now preparing to take the Blue Book strategy out on the streets as a major campaign. We had converted the weighty and necessarily complicated document into a more readable brochure, called simply 'Airlines and Airports'.

454

Extensive mailing lists were drawn up, covering politics, commerce and industry. A briefing of our managers and shop stewards was scheduled for the morning of 3 November. It would be followed by a press conference at the London Press Club. Before we went public on the strategy, however, I sought a meeting with Nicholas Ridley. I explained our launch plan to him, giving him prior notice of the project and indicating that this was just the start of a major campaign.

Although several of us had, for some weeks, quietly and confidentially moved around Whitehall and Westminster giving details of the strategy – and received some surprisingly encouraging responses – the battle did not begin until 4 November 1983, the day the press came out with such headlines as BCAL OFFERS £200 MILLION FOR CUT OF BA ACTION' 'BCAL SEEKS BA SLICE' 'SHARE OUT BA OR WE QUIT GATWICK' 'BCAL MIGHT QUIT GATWICK'.

BA initially declined to comment. I assumed they were taken by surprise. But at a press conference later that day, John King, by now elevated to the peerage as Lord King of Wartnaby, did just the right thing for us. As expected, he attacked our plan vigorously and called it a 'smash and grab' raid, so heightening the profile and keeping the aviation headlines in front of the public.

The campaign was underpinned by a press advertisement, the first of a short series of political messages, prepared by Abbott, Mead Vickers. It was provocative and was intended to be so. It showed two boxers, preparing to go into the ring. One was of medium size, armed only with boxing gloves. On his shorts was the name of BCAL. The other fighter was a giant. In one hand he had an evil-looking machete, in the other a pistol. Around his body was a bullet-proof vest and on his head a protective guard. The headline ran: 'We relish the prospect of competing against a privately-owned British Airways. But shouldn't there be a change in the rules?' The body text ran through the arguments of the strategy.

Response to the campaign came immediately. Our own Crawley MP, Nicholas Soames, said: 'It is a constructive plan for the creation of a more powerfully competitive British civil air transport industry.' He said that he would be lobbying his colleagues, talking to the Secretary of State and raising the matter in debate. Bill Walker, MP, secretary to the Conservative Back Bench Aviation

Committee, took on the critics of the strategy by saying that nothing should be contemplated by the Government which could damage the position of either BCAL or BA. Robert McCrindle, MP, chairman of the All Party Parliamentary Aviation Group, made a statement insisting that the privatisation of British Airways should not be achieved 'in a manner detrimental to the current independent sector'. King had been all over the place with his 'smash and grab raid' statement.

At a meeting of the Conservative Aviation Committee, where we discussed our proposals with MPs, I said: 'I didn't propose throwing a brick through BA's window – we offered to buy some of their assets for about £200 million – and the fact is they will need this kind of money, unless there is to be some creative accountancy.'

We had great encouragement from the press. *The Guardian* stated: 'The proposal does highlight the present shambles which masquerades as a coherent and comprehensive policy for commercial aviation in Britain for the coming decade or longer.' Said the *Financial Times*, 'As far as BCAL is concerned, the privatisation of BA in its present form would lead to the creation of a powerful private sector monopoly – a monopoly which has been heavily subsidised by the taxpayer in order to reduce its debt burden before the sell off.' The *Daily Mail* commented: 'There is no reason why this huge enterprise should remain intact so as to create a private, instead of a state monopoly. The proposal of the thrusting and profitable British Caledonian is therefore one which the Government should take seriously.'

The campaign had got off to a good, fast start and the reactions were encouraging. But the one response which touched me most was a letter, in his own handwriting, from Bill Rodgers – the Rt Hon William Rodgers – Minister of State at the Board of Trade at the time of the Edwards Report and now out of front line politics. He wrote: 'Good luck with your bid for a slice of British Airways. If BA is to be privatised (I'm sure it will be), you certainly deserve a share of the routes. In the days of the Edwards Report, you were rightly seeking to establish yourself as the Second Carrier. You have done this magnificently and it would be wholly unfair if you failed to get the credit – and the opportunities . . .'

# 79

If the principles of our arguments and the logic of our strategy was accepted, there remained the quandary of how they might be implemented. In the Blue Book, we had made two proposals to put the plan into effect. The first was that resources associated with routes and activities to be sold off from British Airways to other airlines should be assessed by an independent valuer and traded on a fair commercial basis. The second was that the entire strategy should be analysed and final recommendations formulated for an industry restructure by a special committee comprising representatives from the CAA and the Department of Transport, assisted, where necessary, by British Airways and the other airlines involved.

Initial meetings with Nicholas Ridley and his senior civil servants, Peter Lazarus and William Knighton, turned out to be bland. I am certain they were intrigued by the Blue Book plan, but could not see immediately how they could proceed. We came back to the old argument that I should again meet John King to see what could be worked out, without Government intervention. That, I knew, would get us as far now as it had before – and that was precisely nowhere.

The political flak continued to fly in the days after the press conference to announce the 'Airlines and Airports' scheme. The British Airways lobby, which flew into furious action, enlisted the support of the Conservative MP for Surrey North West, Michael 'Micky' Grylls. As Chairman of the Tory Trade and Industry Committee, Grylls composed a letter of attack to Nicholas Ridley. It was made public by Chris Moncrieff, chief political correspondent of the Press Association. The letter urged Ridley to reject the BCAL proposals and to adhere to the privatisation timetable for

British Airways, although, as yet, no specific schedule had been set. 'It would be a grave error to asset-strip British Airways in the way proposed by BCAL and the result would be that it would be probably impossible, if you did this, to carry out the privatisation.'

Neither I, nor my colleagues, knew of any background or previous experience that Grylls had in the aviation industry. He must have been fed some extensive research, as he continued in attempting to rubbish our proposals: 'I understand BCAL already have licences to fly to Vienna, Stuttgart, Helsinki, Hanover and Cologne, as well as rights to New York. I gather none of these are being used. Therefore, if BCAL wish to expand, they can surely expand on routes for which they already have licences. The problem faced by Sir Adam Thomson is that he is alarmed at the competition he is now facing from a transformed and profitable BA. Understandably, he would rather compete with the lame duck British Airways of yesterday.'

He was on shaky ground. The European licences he referred to were the low fare 'Mini-Prix' routes awarded three years earlier. However, the Department of Trade, despite the zeal of Iain Sproat, had been unable to gain agreement from the foreign governments involved for us to operate. We had been ready to fly these services all along and were desperate to do so to increase Gatwick's scheduled network. Our Government was, however, unable to fix it for us. New York was similar. We held the original licence used in 1972, but, again, had no Government designation to operate.

Grylls failed to mention that British Airways actually held licences on forty-nine routes on which it did not operate services, mostly for economic reasons. The MPs who leapt to our defence did, however, bring up the point. Nicholas Soames released a statement in which he called Grylls' comments 'ill-judged and misleading accusations'. He went on:

Far from hindering the privatisation of British Airways, Sir Adam Thomson has proposed a plan which could speed up the process and make British Airways more commercially attractive, by transferring some routes to Gatwick and paying several hundreds of millions of pounds to the Government for the assets.

British Caledonian does hold licences for routes which it is

458

unable to serve because the Department of Transport has been unable to negotiate permits from the foreign governments involved. Let me ask, however, why British Airways holds licences for a total of forty-nine routes throughout the world which it does not operate.

I totally support Sir Adam and the management and workforce of BCAL in their proposals for a wholly privately-owned airline industry, achieved on a basis which is equable for the existing independent airlines, encourages the development of Gatwick and the regional airports and generates productive competition. We must avoid the creation of a private airline monopoly.'

Bill Walker, the open, honest Scot who was Tory Aviation Committee Secretary, was equally appalled by Grylls' attack. He hastily scribbled a press statement on House of Commons notepaper:

'I am deeply saddened,' he said, 'by the hostile reaction and by the statement of Michael Grylls to the press release by the chairman of British Caledonian Airways.

In my view, it is only right and proper for the UK's main private sector airline to express its fears and doubts about what may happen if the plans to privatise British Airways are not handled with great care and understanding.

Anyone who has followed the fortunes of both airlines will be aware that neither can operate in isolation. And whilst I believe it is right to congratulate British Airways on their splendid achievement during the last three years, it must also be remembered that the improvements and the previous losses were underwritten by the taxpayer. The opposite is the situation for a company like BCAL who, operating in the private sector, have been forced to sustain their enterprise by their own efforts.

The outburst by Grylls, and the response from other MPs unquestionably prompted by British Airways, was a foretaste of how bitter our battle was to become.

In addition to those in the House of Commons who favoured our case, we were also attracting powerful allies in the House of Lords, notably William Kinnoull and Lord Kings Norton, the former Sir Harold Roxbee Cox, Chancellor of the Cranfield Institute of

Technology and previous chairman of the Air Registration Board, who offered to take up the political cudgels on our behalf.

Away from Westminster, however, there was work to be done in the City, to prepare financial arrangements for the acquisition of aircraft and equipment from British Airways, if our plan succeeded. Trevor Boud and I had already had one meeting with Kleinwort Benson, our merchant bank and financial advisers. It took place over lunch in their offices in the City of London. The Kleinwort line-up was impressive, with Chairman Michael Hawkes and directors Andrew Caldecott and Tim Holland-Bosworth. With them was a young financier, Dr Michael Baker.

We described the strategy. The Kleinwort team showed a lively interest and fired question after question at us. I told them that, if we were successful, we would require between £200 million and £250 million, perhaps with £80 million in equity, raised through a new shares issue. They seemed to be more interested in this prospect than they had been earlier in the year in our outline proposals to raise an extra £20 million in equity as a hedge against the economic downturn. That capital turned out not to be necessary, as we traded our way out of our problems. In principle, the Kleinwort feeling we detected clearly was antagonism towards Government plans to pump in a great deal of money to British Airways to the disadvantage of the private sector. They indicated that they were not alone in that view.

The kind of political games we were playing in Whitehall and Westminster with ministers, MPs and civil servants were wonderfully satirised in the successful television programme, *Yes, Minister*, which humourously explored the relationship between a fictional Secretary of State, Jim Hacker, and his Permanent Secretary, Sir Humphrey Appleby. Adrian Vickers and David Abbott of our advertising agency, Abbott, Mead Vicers, came up with the idea of staging equally fictional dialogue between myself and Nicholas Ridley and presenting this in full-page advertisements in the main serious newspapers, such as *The Times, Financial Times, The Guardian* and the *Daily Telegraph*.

I started off with the words, 'You may have read of British Caledonian's plan for a more competitive British air transport industry. In summary, it proposes that we would pay to take over certain British Airways' routes and operate them from Gatwick.

The full plan is currently being considered by the Secretary of State for Transport. Doubtless it will raise a few questions in his mind.' The simple dialogue then followed:

'Will your proposals for the reduction of British Airways' virtual monopoly increase competition and therefore result in a better deal for the customer?'

'Yes, Minister.'

'Will the transfer of certain flights to Gatwick lessen the congestion travellers face at Heathrow and allow the Government's policy for the development of Gatwick to take off at last?'

'Yes, Minister.'

'Do I take it that your plan includes an early and substantial cash payment to British Airways?'

'Yes, Minister.'

'If your proposals are accepted, will British Airways continue to be the nation's largest airline, operating from the country's largest airport?'

'Yes, Minister.'

'Will your plan for a more competitive British air transport industry strengthen the potential for increased overseas earnings?'

'Yes, Minister.'

I was to wait until 30 November for the chance of a real and live dialogue with Ridley at the Marsham Street headquarters of the Department of Transport. I had requested the meeting with Ridley himself and on entering his office was surprised to see the 'Sir Humphrey' character of William Knighton sitting there with the Secretary of State. I felt that the political balance was shifting in our favour in the days prior to this discussion with Ridley. Only a week earlier, the man who had replaced Ridley at the Treasury, John Moore MP, had addressed a conference sponsored by the *Financial Times* on the subject of 'The Second Thatcher Government, the Economy, Privatisation, the City and Industry'. Moore was, in reality, publicising the forthcoming privatisation of British Telecom and pointed to those state corporations already denationalised: Britoil, Cable & Wireless and the National Freight Corporation.

461

But he did make one telling statement, as he addressed his audience of businessmen, bankers, economists and journalists in the plush surroundings of Park Lane's Intercontinental Hotel. 'So,' he exclaimed, 'I do not hesitate to put the elimination of monopoly and the promotion of air competition at the top of my list of motives for privatisation. Privatisation is often the byproduct of the Government's wish to see greater competition and greater benefits to the customer, not the other way round.' This was music to my ears, a policy statement which would give us additional political leverage in promoting the airlines and airports strategy.

I felt encouraged as I shook hands with Ridley and Knighton and we took our places around a coffee table at the opposite end of the room to the ministerial desk. Ridley told me at once that he had little to add to his previous comments, except to say that he had, as promised, approached John King and pressed him to consider constructively the BCAL proposal. He was hopeful, he said, of receiving a fairly positive response. Meanwhile, he said, looking over his glasses, it was important for us to maintain a low profile so as not to undermine his initiative. He felt, no doubt, that our public relations campaign might be coming on too strong for British Airways.

I acknowledged his point, but stated that we had an ongoing programme of political and PR activity with which we must continue. But we would endeavour to carry this out in a way which did not offend John King.

I took the opportunity to remind him of previous conversations with the politically ill-fated Iain Sproat and his attempts to conduct route rationalisation talks between BCAL and British Airways. Against the inconclusive result of Sproat's initiative, I ventured to suggest that if Ridley's move was to be anywhere near meaningful, a third party, such as John Dent of the CAA or a senior civil servant from the Department of Transport would have to sit in the middle. He seemd to like this idea.

I went further and suggested that Ridley should look into the possibility of asking the CAA to comment on policy concerning the airports and the position that might emerge from the British Airways privatisation. The Secretary of State did not appear to be aware that this was possible, but William Knighton intervened and confirmed that something along these lines could be done and explained how, through the various clauses in civil aviation legislation relating to the powers available to the responsible minister.

I told Ridley that we were getting a fair amount of support for our case, especially in the House of Commons. He responded with a dark warning that we also had strong political opponents, but refused to be drawn on identities.

Ridley told me that he would, in fact, be making an announcement shortly on the probable privatisation date for British Airways and indicated that this would take place in about a year's time. He reiterated his reluctance to legislate on our proposals and said that the lengthy Parliamentary process necessary would overrun the time of the planned privatisation. He felt the action he was taking with John King was the best hope for BCAL. As the three of us got up at the close of the meeting, Ridley told me that, by the way, he had been very amused by the *Yes, Minister* advetisement.

The one thing I had left on Ridley's desk was a copy of a letter I had written to Margaret Thatcher the previous day. There was nothing to lose, I believed, in going straight to the Prime Minister on the problem. The main objective in writing was to request a meeting at her earliest convenience. After a very short summary of the strategy, I said that I wanted a meeting and was prepared to lay on a BCAL helicopter to fly her from the centre of London to Gatwick for the meeting, so that she could see the BCAL organisation and get a feel for the spirit of our people.

One other appointment in Ridley's diary that day was with the MP Bob McCrindle, a good friend and supporter who eventually became BCAL's Parliamentary consultant. Bob telephoned me to tell me of his meeting and to compare notes. The only significant variance was that Ridley had expanded marginally on the identity of the source of the strong opposition to BCAL. McCrindle was told that it was from within the Government. We wanted to know more. I said that I would sound out Willie Whitelaw. Bob said he would endeavour to discuss the matter with the man who had replaced Cecil Parkinson at the Department of Trade and Industry, the former airline pilot and Aviation Committee Chairman, Norman Tebbit.

Curiously for one normally so prompt and punctilious, I was not to hear from Margaret Thatcher for virtually three weeks. Her reply was written on 19 December. In it she referred back to much earlier discussions with John Biffen and said, 'We cannot compel British Airways to do what you suggest and any redistribution now would only be possible by mutual agreement between the airlines concerned.' The Prime Minister said that she understood that the strategy had been discussed with Nicholas Ridley. She added: 'Meanwhile, you will have seen the statement that Nicholas Ridley made to Parliament on Monday and his answers to supplementary questions.'

Not only had I seen the statement, I was, once again, in the Strangers' Gallery of the House of Commons devouring every word and syllable. Ridley had given us the breakthrough we had been pushing, cajoling and lobbying for. Clearly, the wheels of Government had gone into overdrive on the air transport situation in those early days of December 1983 and, on hearing Ridley's announcement, the silence, so far, from the Prime Minister, became clear.

Ridley rose from the Government benches to make a statement about British Airways. It was about four o'clock in the afternoon of 12 December. He began his speech by going into the background behind the plans to privatise the State airline. He talked about the financial recovery of British Airways, bringing matters up to date by announcing that the corporation had paid back £100 million in borrowing since March and was expected to repay at least a further £160 million in 1984. 'Following this transformation of British Airways' financial prospects, I have decided to aim for privatisation as soon as possible, I hope in early 1985. To this end, I propose to establish British Airways as a public limited company, under Government ownership, in accordance with the 1980 Act.'

Ridley was arranging for the registration of a plc under the British Airways' name. 'British Airways plc' would take over the assets, liabilities and route licences of the corporation from the British Airways Board from 1 April 1984. The Government would, of course, remain the sole shareholder and be responsible for ultimate financial control until such time as shares were sold to private investors.

'From 1 April 1984 onwards, therefore, British Airways will be trading as a Companies Act company, wholly owned by the

Government. During this period, we shall exercise the degree of financial control appropriate to our role as sole shareholder. I shall inform the House early next year of the regime that will govern relations between the Government and British Airways in the period between vesting and the offer for sale but one element will be an assurance that . . . the Government continues to stand behind the company and will not allow it to default on its debts.'

Final decision on the timing of privatisation would, said Ridley, depend on the airline's financial performance, on the state of the stock market and on the general prospects for the airline industry. He responded to comments in the press and elsewhere that a capital reconstruction of the airline might be necessary. His aim, he said, was that, as far as possible, the necessary improvement to the airline's balance sheet should come from its own efforts. That, however, was far from denying that there could be a financial baling out by the Government.

Labour's new Transport spokesman was the tough and purposeful former railwayman from Hull, John Prescott. He straight away punched into the privatisation policy, confirming that the Labour Party would continue to oppose the policy as being detrimental to the maintenance of a major public flag carrier on domestic and international routes, many of which are guaranteed by Government agreements and not competition. Prescott moved to a point of interest to ask if the Government still foresaw just a part-privatisation, with the State retaining 40 per cent of 51 per cent of shares. He focused on the matter which was of vital concern. 'In view of the growing uncertainty in the civil aviation industry, and in view of the hopes expressed in the 1980 Act for greater competition through privatisation, the reality of Laker and its collapse and the prospect of British Caledonian, gravely concerned at a privatised competitor controlling 83 per cent of the scheduled markets, threatening to leave Gatwick, will he now consider a review of civil aviation policy while awaiting the sale?' he asked Ridley.

The Secretary of State first addressed the ownership question by saying that the Government had not finally decided whether to sell 100 per cent, but the probability was that they would when the time came to go to market. That was good news. The spectre of a part-private part-state British Airways with all the complications that provoked was receding. And there was even better news. Ridley said:

Finally the Honourable Gentleman asked about a review of civil aviation policy. I agree that the prospective privatisation of British Airways raises implications for competition and for the sound development of the British Airline industry. The Civil Aviation Act 1982 places certain responsibilities in this area on the Civil Aviation Authority. I have, therefore, asked the Chairman of the Authority for advice and will review these matters in consultation with the industry and representatives of users and make any desirable changes within the framework of the act in its statement of policies on air transport licensing or other recommendations. I welcome that.'

So Ridley had come up with the goods in deciding to act, as I had urged, in bringing the CAA into the middle of the debate.

One of the moves I had made, following his request for us to adopt a low PR profile, was to suppress a news release, already prepared. In this, we were calling for the intervention of the CAA, the body set up by Act of Parliament with responsibility for the regulation of the industry, yet whose voice had so far remained silent on what was undoubtedly the most important issue in UK civil aviation since the Second World War. We had also planned to announce that we had prepared applications to take over a series of British Airways licences for a range of routes to be transferred to BCAL at Gatwick. Such an announcement would have been a red rag to the British Airways' bull and escalated the political row to a new peak of frenzy. It was, however, not necessary.

The Commons debate ranged across the whole question of the British Airways' privatisation concentrating principally on the question of the airline's finances. In answer to a question from Bob McCrindle, Ridley went back to the problems of industry structure, revealing that the precise terms of the CAA review would be made soon. We were delighted with the news and said so publicly. It was the logical and honourable solution to a political conundrum.

British Airways, however, was digging in. In a statement issued the same day, the corporation said that its Chairman, Lord King,

466

and all the board were united in their opposition to any break up of British Airways as part of privatisation. 'Our publicly-stated belief is that privatisation and the assurance of future success can only be accomplished by keeping all of British Airways intact.'

In a Christmas message to his staff, John King told them, 'Now that we are successful, you will no doubt have noticed the opportunist attempts by others to demand a part of British Airways for themselves. My answer to that is: British Airways is staying as it is, united and complete. We believe in competition. We meet it every day of our lives against well over 190 airlines around the world.'

It was a theme we were to hear again and again from the Speedbird House camp over the next few years. Certainly there were many foreign airlines operating in the UK market, but apart from on the North Atlantic routes, most of the airlines were in partnership with British Airways, colluding on frequencies and capacities and sharing out the collective revenue. Whatever John King felt or said, it certainly was not competition and was certainly not in the interests of the customer.

# 80

The view through the window of the London office I now used more and more often as events dictated that I remained close to Government, Parliament and the City, looked out to the northwest corner of Trafalgar Square. To the right was the elegant façade of the National Gallery, ahead was stately St Martin's-in-the-Fields, shoulder to shoulder with South Africa House, invariably surrounded by anti-apartheid demonstrators. In the centre of the view was the square itself, lit, as it is every Christmas time by the giant Christmas tree sent over from Norway.

The office was part of a small suite on the first floor of the building which occupies the corner of Pall Mall East and Whitcombe Street. The Caledonian Aviation Group sign was the last indication that the building had been set up in 1978 as the Scottish Centre, a hub of Scottish interests in London. We had taken space there, along with the Scottish Tourist Board, the Scottish Council and the Scottish Development Agency. As recession pinched budgets harder and harder through the early 1980s, each of the Scottish organisations, except ourselves, had retrenched and closed down their Scottish Centre operations.

I glanced occasionally out at the crowds thronging the Trafalgar Square Christmas tree, but my mind was on the letter from the CAA. Ray Colegate of the CAA found himself in the driving seat in the restructuring of the airline industry. His was the signature on the letter announcing the details of the consultation on airline competition policy set in motion after Ridley's announcement in the House of Commons. It was dated 19 December. As the Transport Secretary had required, the CAA was initiating a programme of consultation with representatives of the civil air transport industry and its users.

468

'As the Authority sees it', said Colegate, and here I heard echoes of his Brancker Memorial lecture ten months earlier, 'the main underlying policy issue is one which goes back at least to the time of the Edwards Report on the future of British air transport.' Edwards, recalled Colegate, recommended, and all subsequent governments had accepted, that the country and the public were better served by having a number of profitable and keenly competitive airlines than by depending on a single monopoly carrier.

He wrote on about the evolution of the industry and opportunities for competition against the State corporation. 'As British Airways becomes keener and more efficient, these factors alone, quite apart from any further advantage that might accrue in the process of privatisation such as the strengthening of the British Airways' balance sheet, raises the question whether some action is needed and, if so, what that action should be. It is these underlying questions that need to be re-examined and this is not a review of the policy of privatisation as such.' Colegate went on to describe the parameters of the review, finally requesting that written submissions be lodged with the CAA no later than 31 January 1984. The shoppers and carol singers in Trafalgar Square were, no doubt, looking forward to the festivities and relaxation of the Christmas holidays. For us there would be little time to relax. We had to get the submission in to the CAA on time – and we had to get it right. We might get Christmas Day off with our families and perhaps the chance for festivities on New Year's Eve. Otherwise we would be hard at work. But at least we now had a proper framework in which to project our strategies and a firm target to aim for.

One of the tasks during that 'no-man's land' period after Christmas and before the New Year was the writing of my traditional New Year message to staff. I wrote that the translation of the CAA's philosophy into concrete policies and the laying down of strategies on which action could be taken required answers to a number of fundamental questions which the CAA had posed in its consultation letter, the most crucial of which was, 'Is there a case for redistribution of airline route networks, including the transfer of routes between airlines?' I wrote:

If the CAA was starting with a completely clean sheet of paper, it is inconceivable that it would draw up the blueprint for an industry where all airlines are privately owned, but one among them was endowed with an 83 per cent monopoly. Of course, the CAA does not have a clean sheet – it has to take account of the realities of an existing industry.

Nevertheless, the CAA and the Government have every right, the power – and, indeed, a responsibility – to consider the redeployment of air routes (assets which belong to the nation) in a way which is best for the consumer, best for the country and best for the industry overall . . . The CAA has a unique and dramatic opportunity to redesign and construct the shape of air transport in Britain and to ensure its deployment as the best in the world,' I wrote.

They were the last words I was to pen on the subject before the clock and the calendar pushed the world into a year already pre-conceived by H.G. Wells as one of dire politics: 1984.

# 81

Something infinitely more exciting than balance sheets was awaiting shareholders attending the annual general meeting at Gatwick in the middle of March 1984. We had arranged for the new Airbus A.310, shortly to be delivered, to make an appearance at Gatwick as part of the programme of pilot training from the Airbus head-quarters in Toulouse. It appeared in absolutely pristine condition, in BCAL colours, demonstrating the enormous leap forward in airframe and engine technology that the aircraft represented. But it was also more than that. The A.310's appearance at Gatwick, to be greeted by thousands of airline staff, many of our shareholders and invited press, was a demonstration of the strength of the airline, its commitment to the future and its dedication to the British and European aircraft manufacturing industries.

The A.310 was to enter service later in the month, replacing Boeing 707 equipment on routes to west, central and north Africa. Another of the aircraft was to be delivered later in 1984 and a third the following year.

The news we had to offer shareholders was as promising as we hoped the sight of the A.310 had been. The good results of the previous summer, when travel from North America boomed as the value of the pound slipped against the dollar, followed through to an end-of-year profit of £3.33 million, more than double that of the previous year. The airline's contribution to that result was £3.2 million, compared with the 1982-3 loss of £655,000. Although still far from providing a reasonable return on assets or on the £362 million turnover, it did reflect a healthier industry trend.

However, BCAL continued to experience serious problems in remitting locally earned revenues from South America and Africa. The greatest problem was – and continued to be – in Nigeria.

471

Nevertheless, profit was up, turnover had increased, passenger numbers had risen by three per cent, the passenger load factor was improving and production was on the increase.

Of the other group companies, only British Caledonian Helicopters, based in Aberdeen, incurred a loss due to a slowdown in demand for North Sea oil industry support services and the out break of an uneconomic price war among the helicopter companies which included British Airways Helicopters. The other subsidiaries, Blue Sky Holidays, Caledonian Hotels Holding, and Caledonian Airmotive up at Prestwick, were doing reasonably well. One of the highlights of the year for the hotel operation was the 100 per cent acquisition of the Copthorne Hotel at Gatwick.

The main issue I had to put before the shareholders, however, was to do with the civil aviation review and the possibility of having to raise £200 million, or more, to pay the Government for assets from British Airways. To raise such a large amount in share capital it would be necessary to go public, to seek a Stock Exchange quotation for the group. I revealed to our investors, both the institutions and the staff involved in the profit sharing scheme, that efforts were being made to go to the investment market before British Airways was, itself, privatised.

In the meanwhile, the political campaign rolled on. The supportive friendship with the MP, Bob McCrindle, was consolidated with his formal appointment as a consultant. Bob's involvement with BCAL would, quite rightly, become transparent through the need for him to register the affiliation in the House of Commons. Nevertheless, we valued his Parliamentary expertise and political guidance.

Submissions to the CAA flooded in from every quarter that was directly, or indirectly, concerned with the airline business. Our own views had not changed. The Blue Book strategy remained the course of action to which we were committed. Nevertheless, it was combed and recombed for consistency and every fact, statistic and calculation checked and rechecked. The document re-emerged under the title 'A Competitive Strategy for British Air Transport in Private Ownership'. The publication was similar in size and content to the earlier Blue Book, but its cover was printed in gold. It became the British Caledonian 'Gold Book' and was handed in to the CAA right on deadline, on the last day of January.

The contents of the British Airways submission were as predictable as our own. Essentially, John King was saying 'hands off', if not a similar phrase in a somewhat stronger vein.

At the CAA, Colegate set up his aviation review task force under the head of air service policy, Mike Overall. The extent of the task prompted him to nominate not one, but two joint secretaries, Des Brankin and Steve Hopper. Our own 'task force' was co-ordinated by Peter Smith and Mike Carter, an accountant-turned-strategy manager, who had recently returned to the airline after a period of secondment to the CAA.

In April 1984 Colegate issued his mid-term report, an interim assessment on the consultation. Its file number was CAP 489 and it ran to twenty-three pages as it discussed the UK air transport situation. In a section headed 'The need for changes in policy' it said:

The authority's analysis so far of the issues raised during the consultation suggests that there is a prima facie case in principle for moderating the present imbalances within the British airline industry, preferably in ways that will allow for a greater degree of competition, or at least for increasing the opportunities available to British airlines other than British Airways. The analysis also suggests that there is a case for licensing domestic services more freely and decontrolling domestic air fares. If the authority concludes after further consideration that such changes should be made, it envisages the need to make changes in its licensing policies that might be on the lines set out below. These affect mainly the authority's policies towards competition and substitution and on pricing, insofar as the latter affects domestic services. Consequential changes, mainly of emphasis, may also need to be made to other aspects of the authority's published policy.

The 'lines below' essentially explored possible ways of moving towards a liberal regime in terms of the contestability of route licences and pricing policies. Further gold was mined in a subsequent section in which the CAA discussed what it called 'The Competitive Balance'.

If it were possible to wipe the slate clean the structure of the UK civil air transport industry would undoubtedly look very different. It is most unlikely that present day regulatory philosophy and policy would allow an emergent industry wholly in private ownership to exhibit the competitive imbalances which currently exist. It is also unlikely that a single airline would have been allowed to establish a dominant position at the UK's principal airport.

The interim assessment was sent out to something approaching 100 organisations and individuals who had responded to the initial consultation invitation the previous December. They were, inevitably, varied in their views, but many were in support of our broad arguments.

One of the most powerful submissions in support came from Gatwick's own Member of Parliament, Nicholas Soames. Soames had warned the CAA that an intact, privately-owned British Airways, operating 83 per cent of the UK's schedules services from Heathrow, could have 'a devastating repercussion' on the Gatwick area. Nicholas Soames, son of the late Lord Soames, was in his first Parliamentary term as Member for the newly formed Crawley constituency. From the beginning he had taken an avid interest in his area's major industry, aviation, in particular in its single biggest employer, BCAL. At my invitation, he had made various trips on the flight deck of our aircraft to see, at first hand, how air transport worked. In those watershed days of 1984, Soames became the kind of political champion that Gatwick had never really had.

In his letter to Colegate, Soames naturally declared that he was in wholehearted support of the privatisation policies. 'I do not believe, however – and I have made my feelings known in the House of Commons and elsewhere – that to allow a privately-owned British Airways to harbour a disproportionately high share of UK-licensed services is in anybody's best interests, certainly not the consumer's and least of all that of Gatwick Airport and my constituency, in general,' he wrote. Soames warned that if we were forced to transfer to Heathrow the economy of his constituency would be little short of devastated. The fact was that about 13,500 people were employed in Gatwick's aviation at the time, a very high number in a largely rural area. All of those had dependents of one kind or another, families, local traders and local services.

Norman Payne, chairman of the British Airports Authority, was

474

also acutely aware of the long-term consequences for Gatwick of a 'do nothing' policy by the Government and supported moves to switch more traffic from Heathrow.

'In consequence', Soames told Colegate, 'I am bound to support the arguments and proposals put forward by British Caledonian and the BAA, insofar as they are vital to the development of Gatwick. With a wide range of scheduled services, Gatwick would become fulfilled in its politically-designated role as an international gateway for London, and the livelihood and security of my constituents would be assured.'

The ground for the final, telling, stage of the review was laid and as Mike Overall said in his letter sent out with CAP 489, the CAA aimed to reach its conclusions by mid-July. The review had two tasks. The first was to help the CAA respond to Nicholas Ridley's request for advice on the implications of the privatisation of British Airways for competition and the sound development of the industry. The second was to help the CAA consider whether, in the light of the consultation, its air transport policies should be revised, as the interim assessment had led it to believe that they might. Further comments were, therefore, sought, as any policy change proposed required consultation under the terms of the 1982 Civil Aviation Act. The deadline for responses was set at 15 May.

John King, Colin Marshall and their political supporters saw writing on the walls of Speedbird House that certainly didn't please them and gave rise to annoyance. The tone of the letter which John King circulated to politicians towards the end of May was, however, measured. 'We at British Airways,' he wrote, 'are in favour of competition where it benefits the consumer and strengthens the British civil aviation industry. We utterly reject, however, the suggestions made by certain of our competitors that they should be substituted for us on some routes. Substitution would do nothing to improve the competitive balance, nor would it benefit the consumer. It would merely enable other airlines to grow at the expense of British Airways.'

The BA stance was summed up in a political advertisement in which John King gave the pledge 'we welcome competition'. It was a glib argument to say in all apparent innocence and goodwill that British Airways welcomed any other British airline which wished to compete alongside it on any international route it chose. But, they said, BA should not be expected to give up any of its own route rights to allow competition.

On the face of it, that might have seemed to be a plausible proposition, but it disguised the reality. This was that with the exception of a very few areas of the world, air service rights were divided equally between the British side and the foreign airline. Protectionist policies in most overseas countries meant that the foreign airlines and their governments would not, under any circumstances, allow the British to have more than 50 per cent of the capacity and frequency between the two countries. Any aspiring new entrant was effectively blocked by the terms of the inter-governmental, bilateral agreements and British Airways, of course, knew it. John King's competition pledge was, therefore, an empty one.

There was only one way to increase competition and choice in British air transport to most areas of the world and that was to achieve a more even distribution of the international rights available to the UK among more airlines.

In the meanwhile, the financial clean-up at British Airways was continuing relentlessly. A few weeks later, King announced an operating surplus, or trading profit, of £268 million for the year which ended on 31 March 1984. But the news of this result for the airline was overshadowed in some news reports by King's remarks on the CAA review. He warned of a shattering financial backlash if the Government bowed to demands to reallocate routes before privatisation. He told a press conference that the arbitrary removal of routes and services was not in the public's interest. 'Furthermore,' he was reported as saying, 'any moves in this direction would have far-reaching consequences on the financial prospects of the company. There is also the effect that such moves would have on the morale of the staff and the potential for extensive redundancies with consequent considerable increase in costs.'

As well as the vibrations from the CAA, one other move by ourselves which had been exercising BA's patience in recent months was our winning of a licence to serve Riyadh, capital of Saudi Arabia, hitherto an exclusive BA province. An extension of the BCAL route network in the Middle East – so far we only had Dubai – was a strategic priority. In the constant process of combing the world for every glimmer of opportunity, we became aware that while the Saudi Arabian cities of Jeddah and Dhahran were well served by BA, there was no direct service to the capital. We bid for and won the licence, although Riyadh was not yet included as a point available for service in the agreement between the UK and the Saudi authorities. Nevertheless it was a way in, showing, at a crucial time in aviation politics, that another centre of aviation expertise could move to expand markets and increase choice.

The scheduled service between Gatwick and Tripoli was an important operation in many respects. It provided the link with Libya for the oil industry in the UK and also the USA. For us, it was a healthy and profitable route. Passengers were mainly oil industry workers, destined for tours of duty in the hot, dusty, highly disciplined and alcohol-free drilling rigs of the Libyan Sahara. Flights back from Tripoli became something special as a load of previously-deprived oil workers shovelled as much liquor down themselves as they possibly could during the journey to Gatwick. Our Caledonian girls had a way of dealing with them that never led to any real in-flight problems.

We were, however, warned on more than one occasion by local Gatwick hotels that they would consider refusing passengers from our Tripoli flights. It seemed the passengers would continue the liberty party started on the aircraft in the bars and lounges of the hotels, sometimes going on all night to the annoyance of the other hotel guests and the concern of the hotels' management and staff.

On 17 April 1984 the regular BAC 1-11 flight to Tripoli had left Gatwick and was heading across Europe on its regular route which took it to the Geneva reporting point, before heading down across Italy, Malta and into North Africa.

A thousand miles away, back in London, a demonstration against President Gadaffi's regime was moving, under police observance, around St James's Square to the Libyan Embassy offices. Amid the shouting of the demonstrators, a gun was fired from the window of the Libyan offices into the crowd. W.P.C. Yvonne Fletcher of the Metropolitan Police was fatally injured. As the news of the mayhem cut through radio and television news bulletins and St James's Square went under armed police siege, Ian Ritchie got in touch urgently with the Foreign Office.

We had no background to the situation in London or any idea

what the implications might be. We were concerned for the safety of our passengers and crew. Foreign Office officials told Ritchie that the aircraft should not land in Libya. Hurried radio messages were sent to the 1-11 ordering it to turn back.

At Tripoli, the BCAL airport manager, Doug Ledingham, was in the process of arranging alternative flights with other airlines for the northbound passengers who had arrived at the airport to be told that there would be no BCAL service that afternoon. Doug was sitting at a telex machine sending details of revised passenger itineraries to Gatwick when a Libyan told him he was required in a certain office. Unable to ascertain what the problem might be, Doug reluctantly went. It was the last we were to hear directly from him for four months. Ledingham was arrested and thrown into detention by one of Libya's revolutionary councils.

We subsequently learned of the deprivation he suffered as a hostage in the hands of the Libyans, but for the intervening period we had the fight for his release on our hands, one which Ian Ritchie, in particular, pursued relentlessly. The Doug Ledingham affair, including the care of his wife Veronica and four children, occupied a great deal of our attention at the time when the UK air transport battle was hotting up considerably. The concern for a colleague, however, overshadowed other considerations.

We maintained a constant pressure on the Foreign Office to press for Ledingham's release, or at least find out if any legitimate charges had been made against him. None ever were. I met the Foreign Secretary, Geoffrey Howe, on the subject. Ian Ritchie was in daily contact with Foreign Office officials. We ensured that Howe's Minister of State, Richard Luce, brought up the Ledingham question with King Hassan of Morocco and the Foreign Ministers of Algeria and Tunisia when he attended a meeting with the Arab League in Tunis. David Coltman, with extensive experience in the Arab world from his days with British Airways, invoked the help of influential contacts in Saudi Arabia and elsewhere in the cause of freeing the BCAL man held hostage in Tripoli.

The St James's Square incident led to the deportation, under tight security arrangements, of all those under siege inside the Libyan diplomatic offices and to the breaking of diplomatic relations between the two countries. The Foreign Office announced its intention to withdraw the Ambassador, Embassy officials, staff and families on 23 April. The move was to be effected by 29 April.

Had normal 'circumstances prevailed, Doug Ledingham would have been supervising the evacuation of British Embassy staff and families by way of our regular service to Gatwick on 17 April. No doubt he would have been as horrified to see at first hand as I was via television news, the jingoistic antics of some British ladies as they waved union jacks and sang 'Rule Britannia' as they walked from Libyan soil on to the waiting aircraft. I regarded this as a stupid and foolhardy display by people whose knowledge of our delicate relationship with Libya should have taught them better.

Such was the tension over the Libya situation that, after 29 April when diplomatic relations ended, some of our crews were reluctant to operate to Libya and the service was forced to continue by a system of volunteers.

The Italian Embassy took over responsibilities for representing British interests in Libya with one Consul, George Anderson, attached to it.

Doug Ledingham himself languished in extremely unpleasant conditions of detention until the following September, when he was unexpectedly released and flown to London on an aircraft of Libyan Arab Airlines. No charge had ever been made against him and we could all only reconfirm our earlier feelings that he had been seized as a hostage to protect the Libyans against possible reprisals from the British following the tragic gunning down of the policewoman in London.

After a period of rest and recovery with his relieved and overjoyed family, Doug announced he was fit to go back to work. There were a number of possible posts available, either at Gatwick, elsewhere in the UK or overseas. We felt sure that he would elect for a home posting after his ordeal. To our great surprise, he selected Sierra Leone in West Africa, running operations at the Lungi Airport in Freetown. He explained himself by saying that he held no grudge against Africa and was happy to go back.

If we wanted a better deal for Britain, we also wanted a better deal for Europe. We had done since 1979, when the low fare 'Mini Prix' scheme was conceived, promoted and approved by the CAA in London, only to be dashed by the protectionist policies of other European governments, manifested as they were by the 'pool' agreements between the respective state airlines.

The new Airbus A.310, a European product, provided a platform to promote a more liberal and more competitive airline regime in Europe. On a special route-proving flight at the end of April 1984, we invited press and politicians to travel with us to Geneva. At a lunch in a château on the shores of Lake Leman, I spoke on the subject. 'We want more competition,' I said. 'We want more opportunity, we want less regulation and we want simplified fares structures. We want these things, not through aeropolitical anarchy, but through a co-ordinated policy which is good for the countries of Europe, good for their airlines and airline workers and, of course, good for the consumer.'

I was speaking against the background of moves by the Commission of the European Community to unlock the restrictive system in European air transport. The Commission, in turn, had been motivated by a developing sense of dissatisfaction with airline service, particularly fares which were perceived as unnecessarily high – and especially when they were compared with prices on offer in the totally deregulated USA.

After the report by the Swedish MP, Anders Bjorck, in 1979, came a request from the Council of Transport Ministers to the Commission to conduct a study on air fares. The European Civil Aviation Conference, a body of regulators from both EEC and non-EEC countries, set out guidelines for increasing competition. The European Parliament declared in two resolutions that efforts should be made to bring about a real increase in competition.

In June 1980 the House of Lords Select Committee on Europe published a report on air fares, concluding that it appeared to many that governments and aviation administrations conspired to prevent advantageous air fares. In 1982, the Consumers in the European Community Group issued a pamphlet on air fares. Lord Bethell had formed his 'Freedom of the Skies' campaign and had resorted to litigation against European airlines over fares. In short, the pressure for liberalisation in Europe was becoming relentless. It resulted in the publication by the Commission in February 1984 of a document entitled, 'Progress Towards the Development of a Community Air Transport Policy'. It was the second such document published by the Commission and is known in aviation and regulatory circles as 'Memorandum 2'. It was, in fact, a consultation document and called for responses from interested parties.

Our response came in the form of another 'book', 'European Transport and the Consumer'. It was filed with the Commission in the early summer and coincided with a fight we were having with the Dutch Government, KLM and British Airways over a new low fare between London and Amsterdam. The old pool partners, KLM and BA, wanted the fare – £49 – to be hedged with restrictions. We wanted it made easily accessible to the consumer, or 'unbundled' as the industry jargon of the time would have it. Our insistence, ultimately backed by Nicholas Ridley, held up the fare's introduction for a while, but it also halted restrictive moves by BA and KLM.

It was a practical example of the problems in Europe put forward in our European document. We proposed a very simple fare structure on European routes. For business classes – executive class in our case, there would be a single, year round, unrestricted fare, close to existing business tariffs. But in economy class we would introduce a single, point-to-point fare whose price was determined by the time of travel. We gave examples – in the peak period the economy fare would be 75 per cent of the prime business class fare; in periods of medium demand, it would be 55 per cent; and in off peak periods, 45 per cent. Passengers would be able to choose the level of fare they required by selecting the time of day to travel.

The fares did come into operation, under the brand name of Time Flyers, but only on one route – UK-Netherlands, after air services between the two countries became totally deregulated.

European liberalisation was extremely important to us, it would open up new and comprehensive opportunities for entry into fresh markets. It was not, however, so pressingly important as the aviation debate at home.

The second stage of the CAA's consultation unfolded for BCAL as a non-stop series of meetings with Mike Overall and his team. Behind the scenes they had become more and more convinced of the need to create balance by reallocating British Airways routes and were more or less following the strategies we had proposed. Two of our planners were virtually seconded full time to the CAA, involved in the highly detailed route network and operational analysis that was taking place.

481

In summary, the CAA ended up asking BCAL for a schedule of routes it believed it could justifiably – in commercial and Gatwick policy terms – take over from British Airways. At the same time, the authority required in minute detail the investment and profit and loss projections associated with every single destination. Time was extremely tight. The final report was, after all, due to be submitted to Nicholas Ridley by mid-July.

In the Gold Book submission, we had detailed the routes we believed could, and should, be reassigned. However, we requested this to remain confidential. The Gold Books circulated to the wider audience did not contain this section on routes. The omission irritated British Airways considerably and they, in turn, sought to infer that our reticence to illustrate our proposals was a weakness.

The CAA, pressing on, asked for our final package of proposals in time for its Board Meeting on 11 June. The package had, in fact, been prepared but not formally discussed or ratified by the board. The policy review meeting that summer, although still scheduled to be away from the office, was planned to take place much nearer to Gatwick, in view of events surrounding us. Ron Lewis, the company secretary, decided on a place just a few miles east of Gatwick, Effingham Park, then a small meeting and banqueting centre, now a major hotel and conference venue.

We had distilled our requirements down to a set of categories – routes to be taken over completely; routes on which we would be permitted to gain licences to fly alongside BA; and routes which would go to other airlines from BA. Those we would take over and operate on a solus basis were Jedah and Dhahran, in Saudi Arabia; Harare, Zimbabwe; Abu Dhabi and Muscat, in the Gulf; Karachi and Rawlpindi (Islamabad), in Pakistan; Madrid; Bilbao; Barcelona; Lisbon; Nice; Helsinki; Vienna. The dual designation routes on which we would operate alongside BA were Sydney and Melbourne, in Australia, Singapore, Athens, Milan, Rome, Copenhagen and Dusseldorf. Routes which could go either to us or other airlines were Valencia, Malaga, Oporto and Gibraltar. We also proposed that we should be allowed an increased share of the market to Paris, Frankfurt and Geneva, where the BCAL capacity was restricted. Another proposal was that we should resume services to New York, for which we already held a licence, and that British Airways should come off the Hong Kong route.

To cope with this kind of expansion, it was estimated that BCAL would require four additional Boeing 747s, two additional DC-10s and three Boeing 737s. Total capital investment required to acquire the aircraft was calculated at £263.2 million.

The key to this potential – the single biggest opportunity we had ever had in prospect – was the ability to finance and sustain an operation which would effectively double the size of BCAL. Trevor Boud, his deputy Barry Firmin and I had been continuing our negotiations with 3i, Kleinworts and other finance institutions. Our plan was that we should first raise the money, in the form of loans, to acquire the additional assets – including staff transferred from British Airways – and then float shares on the Stock Exchange.

A five-year plan was drawn up which saw our profits going from £14 million to £170 million. Target date for floation – the offer for sale of shares to the public – was set at 28 February 1985. We would be in the investment market ahead of British Airways.

John Dent, the CAA chairman, and his board required the answer to a simple question. Can you finance this plan? I looked at the proposal with a mixture of euphoria and amazement. The plan the CAA had developed was to give us all the routes we had asked for. My words on the telephone to Stuart Young after I had stepped out of the doors of the CAA headquarters in Kingsway with Trevor Boud and Alastair Pugh were, 'We've got the lot!'

I called as many of the holding board members as could be contacted to a meeting in the Pall Mall office. All we had to do to unlock the plan and put it into action was to satisfy the CAA's financial advisers, County Bank, that we could raise the money. The Pall Mall meeting built on to the financial ground-work already achieved a very fast programme of presentations to financial institutions in Scotland and in London. We had to obtain guarantees good enough to satisfy both ourselves and the County Bank in just a few days.

The trawl around the banks and finance houses, particularly in Scotland, took me back to the earliest days of Caledonian. Then we sought just about £54,000. Now we were looking for in excess of £400 million, made up of new equity of some £150 million and asset-funding finance of about £250 million.

I simply could not believe the words that came from the CAA when we returned to Kingsway to confirm that indeed we could finance the route development programme. There was a new plan, I was told. A reduced proposal for transfers. We were to forget the previous plan and look instead at the amended version. Despite my protests, I was told that there was no argument against it – I would simply have to listen to what they were telling me. It was inconceivable that the CAA should have confided the previous proposal to us and sent us out talking to bankers, however confidentially, without the principle of what was being proposed having been cleared with Nicholas Ridley, or at least the very senior civil servants. I had, in fact, said the very same thing to a mildly sceptical Trevor Boud only a few days earlier. Yet that could not have been the case. The CAA could, to my mind, only have been turned from its planned course of action by a political word from the Department of Transport. We were required to study the new plan and again go through the fund-raising process. I demurred. If we could raise sufficient funds for a bigger programme of route expansion, surely it went without saying that we could finance a more modest scheme. But no, the process had to be gone through again.

The new proposal, we estimated, would require about £75 million of new equity and around a £100 million of loan finance and once more we went off the same institutions, with exactly the same story, on a somewhat different scale. Eventually, the feasibility of the financial plan was endorsed by Kleinwort Benson and the stockbrokers, Hoare Govett. Letters in support of our financial capacity were provided to the CAA by Hoare Govett, Kleinworts, Merrill Lynch, E.F. Hutton, National Westminster Bank, Bank of America and Citibank.

Our refinancing plan looked towards an initial placement among institutions. This was to be followed by a new issue, either through the introduction of the institutional shareholdings to the stock market, or an offer for sale to the general public. The new equity issue would occur in the spring or summer of 1985.

# 82

It was time, I felt, to launch a broadside. The war of words, carried
along by lobbying in Parliament and briefings in Fleet Street, was
becoming intense but had not yet risen to its peak. The battle
lines were fairly straightforward. John King at Heathrow and I
at Gatwick had moved the infantry of propaganda into the centre
of London, first to engage in Kingsway, headquarters of the CAA,
and after that skirmish to march on to Whitehall, to take the high
ground of Downing Street and Marsham Street, Nicholas Ridley's
citadel.

The main thrust of our attack was to ram home the message of
monopoly, to discredit the privatisation of BA if all that meant was
the turning of a state monopoly into a public one. John King's army
marched along to his 'we welcome competition' tune.

Both camps attracted their supporters. In our case, for instance,
three of the major charter airlines, Air Europe, Britannia Airways
and Orion Airways came out with a joint call for the CAA to have
the same powers over airlines as the Monopolies and Mergers
Commission did over commerce and industry in general. They
feared monopolistic practices in the fragile, low-margin, charter
market.

The high profile of the propoganda war hid from public view
the intense in-fighting that was taking place around the corridors
of Whitehall and in the lobbies of Westminster. The lobbying
programme was continuing at a rapid pace and one of our key
pieces of 'artillery' in this hidden war was Sir Peter Masefield,
whose vast array of contacts at extremely high levels was used to
its utmost.

Debates on aviation had taken place both in the Commons and
the Lords, but parliamentarians, at this stage, could only comment.

The real war was being fought in the consultation process of the CAA which was, by now, only weeks away from presenting its recommendations to Nicholas Ridley.

It was decided within our own 'war cabinet' at Gatwick that we should now support the war of words with a barrage of action in the field of airline competition. The only major new opportunity lay in New York. We still held the old licence for the route, but after the Laker collapse, the UK and USA government had agreed that a three-year moratorium against a new British airline coming on to the route should be imposed. The moratorium expired in the spring of 1985.

The London-New York market was not, however, as simple as it had been immediately following the Laker collapse. The airport at Newark, in New Jersey, had come into play with the introduction of a service linking it with Gatwick by a new US carrier, People Express, a low-cost, low-fare airline which was run as a sort of workers' co-operative. Their low fare was £113 one way between Gatwick and New York, but food and drinks were not complimentary although they were available for purchase on board.

The People Express service was matched by a new British airline headed by the unlikely figure of a young music industry tycoon, Richard Branson. In a curious sequence of financial moves, Branson's airline, Virgin Atlantic, had evolved from a company called British Atlantic Airways dreamed up by an American lawyer, Randolph Field. The airline actually came into Branson's control during the course of the hearing of its application for the Gatwick-Newark licence before the CAA, earlier in the year. In any event, Virgin Atlantic had recently begun operation, with one Boeing 747.

Nevertheless, we formulated plans for a return to the New York market – John F. Kennedy International, not Newark. The move was announced on 11 June 1984. BCAL would launch daily services between Gatwick and New York in the spring of 1985. Fares would be as low as £50 one-way. The New York announcement hit the headlines of the newspapers on 12 June and formed an extremely useful boost to the campaign, coming as it did on the eve of the CAA's pronouncement on the future of the industry.

# 83

It was our own version of 'D-Day', Monday 16 July 1984, the day when the CAA's report was to be presented to Nicholas Ridley and released publicly. From the to-ing and fro-ing of consultation, we had a good idea of what would lie inside the document, but in the shifting political sands we had seen over the previous weeks, we could not be sure until we had read every paragraph. I had already received the summons from John Dent and Ray Colegate to be present in their Kingsway headquarters and had arranged for Peter Masefield, Alastair Pugh and Ian Ritchie to accompany me. A press conference had already been called by the CAA for 4.30 p.m.

Our plan was to meet the CAA, receive the briefing they proposed to provide, take away the report to Ridley, analyse its content, then prepare an immediate response, following the CAA press conference.

The previous day, Sunday, had been spent in the offices at Caledonian House, preparing the broad outline of our response to the CAA from what we already knew. Pugh, Beety, Smith and I read and amended several drafts of a news release being prepared by Tony Cocklin. The objective was to achieve a more immediate and more comprehensive response to the CAA report than British Airways might be able to. Tactics were as important as strategy in this battle.

As the others left Caledonian House for their homes, mostly in the local Gatwick area, I heaved a suit carrier into the back of the Daimler to be driven to London where I would stay the night at the flat we had taken some years earlier in Ebury Street, close to Victoria Station. It was one of my small pleasures, when staying at the apartment, to step out of the world of power politics and

487

business drama, and undertake the simple chore of strolling to the open-all-hours grocery store, run by an Indian, to pick up a few basic provisions – bread, milk, coffee, butter – for breakfast the following day. Naturally, I could have had breakfast supplied, or gone to the Savoy Hotel, but the short and simple shopping interludes gave me a few moments to move from the centre of the arena and view things from a ground-level perspective. So, on that Saturday, as I carried the brown paper grocery bag in front of me, I mused over the drama that would unfold the following day.

I was still thinking of the visit to Kingsway as I made toast and poured coffee. Down at the front doors of Caledonian House, at the same time, a portable word processor was being gently loaded into one of the company vans. It was being taken, with public relations staff, to the Press Club, where a press office would be set up to cover the day's events from the heart of Fleet Street.

It was to be a fast-moving day, in every respect. The CAA's announcement would keep me in London until the early evening, the same evening in which I was scheduled to be in Brighton for a dinner at the University of Sussex, prior to receiving an honorary doctorate in law at a ceremony the following day. Also on the next day, we mapped out a detailed programme of briefings for managers, staff and union representatives on the outcome of the great civil aviation debate.

There were no surprises in store as I faced John Dent and Ray Colegate. They had in front of them copies of an A-4-sized booklet. It was bound in a blue cover. 'You've written a Blue Book,' I said, to break the obvious tension of the day. Colegate said nothing, but smiled across the table.

The CAA report was titled 'Airline Competition Policy'. Its file code was CAP 500. After studying submissions from 102 individuals and organisations and undertaking 38 separate consultative meetings over the previous 6 months, the CAA had delivered its verdict and was making policy recommendations to the Government. Its prime deduction upheld our own line that British Airways' dominance of the UK airline industry, in terms of scale, brought it firmly within the meaning of a monopoly, as defined in the Fair Trading Act of 1973.

Its answer to the question posed back in December by Nicholas Ridley was to recommend a judicious adjustment to the existing imbalance in the industry through a combination of methods: reallocation of a small number of route licences currently held by British Airways, and the opening up of other routes, where economically and politically feasible, to operation by more than one airline. The net effect of the proposals was to reduce British Airways in scale by seven per cent of its scheduled service revenue immediately and, as independent competition took bite over the years, BA's scheduled revenue might be further reduced by 4.5 per cent.

CAP 500 was the most comprehensive and definite review of civil aviation since the Edwards Report fifteen years earlier. The focus for us was, however, the ways and means proposed by the CAA of reducing the British Airways' monopoly and bringing balance to the industry.

The CAA told the Government that there was a need for an alternative 'world class' airline and only BCAL, among the independent carriers, was capable of fulfilling this role. Therefore, it recommended that we should be licensed, in place of BA, in conjunction with our existing route to Lusaka, and to serve Dhahran and Jeddah, in Saudi Arabia, in addition to Riyadh.

Curiously, despite the efforts with the financiers and the authority's own County Bank, the CAA said that before handing us these licences, it would need to be satisfied that we could raise the necessary additional resources required and that it would give us until early August to substantiate the feasibility of the proposed expansion plan. Other recommendations put to Ridley included the transfer of British Airways' services at Gatwick and at provincial airports to other airlines. It also proposed the deregulation of UK domestic services to allow open competition and a free fares policy.

The CAA summarised its main conclusion: 'There should be some reduction in the relative size of British Airways so that other airlines have adequate opportunity to develop and prosper, including at least one airline fit to replace British Airways on any major intercontinental route, should the need arise. Additional competition by British airlines on intercontinental routes should be licensed wherever possible.'

It was not easy for the journalists covering the announcement. First they had to attend the CAA conference and then race to meet us at the Press Club or British Airways at their response briefing. By the time the first journalists entered the Press Club's Churchill Room on the first floor of the International Press Centre, we had checked CAP 500, completed the writing of our response and produced the press release.

Our release headline read, 'BCAL Responds with Major Bid for More Competition.' I told the press, 'I had hoped for a bolder approach in restructuring the industry – but at least we have something of a fresh start.' The report, I said, was a manifesto which promised the progressive development of real competition, through previously-unavailable route licensing opportunities.

I reminded the journalists that our original plan – the Blue Book and the Gold Book strategies – was to reduce British Airways' 83 per cent near-monopoly on scheduled service output by about 20 per cent. The CAA's plan was more modest and was regarded by us as only the first stage of change. The routes to Saudi Arabia and Zimbabwe would be useful additions to the existing BCAL network. Our position as the major British carrier to Africa would be consolidated and the Saudi Arabian points would enhance the network serving oil industry centres. Then I revealed our real, competitive response. Under the provisions of the CAA recommendations, we were preparing immediate applications for twenty-five new routes to be operated from Gatwick – many of them in direct, head to head competition with BA services from Heathrow. The twenty-five new route applications called for new services from Gatwick to China, India, Singapore, Malaysia, the Arabian Gulf, the Iberian Peninsula, Greece, Italy, Germany and Scandinavia. Further bids, for later implementation included route expansion to Alaska, Japan, Sri Lanka, Australia and the addition of more points in Europe.

On the 'dual designation' routes, I said that we would be seeking the same share of capacity as BA, within the British entitlement in agreements with foreign governments. The whole expansion plan would require us to obtain more aircraft and other operational resources. The BCAL financial team would include merchant bankers, Kleinwort Benson, and stockbrokers, Hoare Govett.

We had all along envisaged that expansion for BCAL after the consultation could result in a requirement for some BA staff to join BCAL. I mentioned this and told the press that, in this case, there would be a close consultation with the trade unions to develop and implement a smooth transfer policy.

I was bullish as I wound up. 'We are ready to respond to the competitive challenge and we welcome the increased opportunity it will present. Now it is important for the industry – and for the refinancing plans of BCAL and BA – that the CAA plans are dealt with promptly and vigorously. No-one's interest would be served by a protracted period of uncertainty.'

Journalists who had been to collect the British Airways' response from the briefing session they were holding in a nearby hotel reported that John King was 'furious'. They quoted him as saying that the CAA proposals were 'disastrous and unacceptable'. He and his board would 'resist absolutely any arbitrary reduction' of the BA route network.

King called the proposals restrictive. They would, he said, mean potentially damaging further loss of BA jobs, not least in the regions, disturb and disrupt what he termed a highly successful enterprise, and if implemented would amount to a breach of faith by ministers. King was referring back to 1980 when John Nott, then Secretary of State for Trade, said that he did not propose that on privatisation any part of BA should be broken up or sold off – but that was before the privatisation proposals had crystallised and before the Government decided to seek the CAA's recommendations. In reality, Nott's statement was not just obsolete, it was dead and buried.

King raged on, protesting that the airline competition policy proposals would delay privatisation. He warned that BA would not voluntarily give up routes. It would rather await legislation.

A public admonishment came King's way very shortly after, when the CAA staged another press conference, this time to present its annual report. 'It seems to me that BA's reaction is having the effect of delaying privatisation and minimising the price the Treasury will get, rather than having the opposite effect,' commented John Dent. He went on, 'These are short-term problems and we need a long term solution. We need BA to behave responsibly and considerately to its other UK competitors and I would be happy if I saw some recognition of this at this time.'

At a meeting which concentrated more on the publication of the previous week, CAP 500, than on the annual report it was called to

491

discuss, Dent said of the airline competition policy report, 'There is nevertheless a general feeling of acceptance and a mood of "let's get on with it".' This was not sheer optimism. Dent was right; parliamentary and public opinion was, in the main, favouring the logic of the CAA's plans and proposals.

The leading article in the *Financial Times* the following day felt that the CAA might not have gone far enough, saying, 'the Government should not yield to demands to water down further the CAA's modest proposals . . . When BCAL was set up a decade ago, it lacked the resources to become a genuine second force airline. The same mistake may have been made this week.'

The *Daily Mail* commented: 'The CAA scheme is, of necessity, second best – but it is better than leaving things as they are. If anything, the privatisation of British Airways, by strengthening its commercial position only serves to underline the pressing case for a fairer share out of routes.'

Even the staunchly pro-privatisation, Thatcherite *Sun* turned its attention to aviation, saying, after being able to understand how John King felt, 'But it would be hard to justify allowing a public near-monopoly to be turned into a private near-monopoly.'

A further blow against British Airways came within days of CAP 500 and the comment and controversy which surrounded it. It came from Nicholas Ridley who on 24 July announced that he had thrown out BA's appeal against the CAA's grant to us of the licence to serve Riyadh, effectively breaking the monopoly held on British rights to serve Saudi Arabia by the state airline. Talks with the Saudi Arabian authorities on obtaining designation for BCAL were expected to take place shortly, Ridley announced.

When visiting London, Michael Bishop, the quiet-spoken, soberly suited and soberly mannered chairman of British Midland, stays in a suite at the Savoy Hotel. It was in Bishop's suite, one evening in late July, that the chiefs of eight independent airlines gathered round a table to consider a joint response to the BA objective of killing off the CAA proposals. Ian Ritchie had for some time been attempting to harness the existing independents into one cohesive lobby, but different priorities and commercial objectives – most were charter operators and some scheduled carriers – had prevented a true meeting of minds. But now, faced with the prospect of a window of major opportunity being closed to them in the face of the blast of political priority for the privatisation of British Airways, we had come together. Present, as well as Bishop and myself, were Alan Snudden of Monarch; Errol Cossey of Europe; Fred Newman of Dan Air; Stephen Hanscombe of Air UK; Bruce Tanner of Orion; and Derek Davison of Britannia.

Our purpose was to agree the quickest and most effective way to get the view of the independent airlines across to the highest reaches of Government. It was agreed that a letter should be written to Margaret Thatcher and her Cabinet members. Composition by committee is never an easy task, but during the course of the evening, the text of the letter was agreed. It was also agreed that we would stage a joint press conference at which we would all sit as a united group, at the top table. Between us, we represented some 17,000 jobs and carried almost 20 million passengers a year. We had, we felt, a strong voice.

The letter to Thatcher, made public at the press conference the following day, opened with a collective endorsement of the CAA report, saying that competition could not exist without effective competitors. To be effective, the independent airlines needed to be strengthened. 'Within the industry, British Airways is the only airline which stands against these conclusions and recommendations.'

We said that we refuted arguments brought by BA which had initiated a massive campaign to discredit the CAA's recommendations and went on to warn that jobs were at stake within the independent airlines as a consequence of the dominance of British Airways. 'We urge you to let this independent report determine the future of the air transport industry in this country and to implement its recommendations,' the letter concluded.

In the first week of August, the news came through that the Government had decided to delay its decision on the recommendations of the airline competition policy report. We came to understand that at a Cabinet meeting it was agreed that, in the face of the public debate, a special committee was to be formed to study the proposals and that no announcement of the Government's decision on CAP 500 was likely before September.

BA had indeed erupted in a fury of political, public and press campaigning as a counter to the CAA report and the lobbying and public relations activities undertaken by ourselves and the other

493

independents. They attempted to mobilise their entire workforce, their passengers, and travel agents against the CAA plan in general and against us in particular.

I began to collect a thick file on BA's campaign which must have been produced at substantial cost to the funds of its shareholder, the Government. Recipients of the propaganda forwarded it to BCAL in disgust at the state carrier's tactics. BA's line now was the catchphrase, 'British Airways is Winning for Britain – Let's Keep It That Way.' In a frenzy of activity, BA produced a million labels, 10,000 T-shirts, 45,000 badges, 90,000 car stickers and one million leaflets, which were distributed free to BA staff. Mailings were directed to all staff, cargo and travel agents and every regular passenger in the UK.

The fact was that British Airways was not winning for Britain. Figures in the CAA report showed that Britain enjoyed less than 50 per cent of revenue in the majority of the international markets that UK airlines served and British Airways enjoyed a smaller share of interline traffic at Heathrow that some of its main international competitors did at their home bases.

Action against this claim was never taken, but we did make protest at a dirty trick perpetrated in the Saudi Arabian market. The airline's sales manager in Jeddah had printed a letter to be handed to BA passengers on arrival in Saudi Arabia. It concluded with the sentence: 'British Airways, the leading British flag carrier, would be replaced by a secondary airline on these important routes and thereby risk diminution of Britain's prestige.'

Despite the gung-ho attitude in mobilising staff to fight the report, however, the BA moles did not give up. In a document circulated towards the end of July to the press and among MPs, the moles said that BA did not compete with hundreds of airlines daily, as Lord King had said. It collaborated with hundreds of airlines each day. 'The airlines,' said the BA moles, 'make Swiss bankers look like Brownies.'

For our part, we had organised, or encouraged staff to organise, their own campaigns. Employees were writing to their own local MPs and a delegation representing our Joint Shop Stewards' Committee, covering 6,300 staff in 13 unions, hand-delivered a petition to Margaret Thatcher and Nicholas Ridley. The delegation, including stewardesses in uniform, lobbied the Commons and attended a late night civil aviation debate in the House of Lords.

Their presence became immortalised in the Hansard official record, as Lord Kinnoull, speaking in support of our case, said: 'I recall that in 1974 [BCAL] had to dispose of 30 per cent of its staff right across the board. It survived without the comfort of the Government's overdraft facility. Today, Sir Adam Thomson and his colleagues – and I'm glad to see in the gallery a few tartan lassies to cheer us up – have a unique reputation for efficiency, warm service and pride in the company.'

We were truly in a period of fierce public debate, through newspapers and broadcasting; of campaign advertising; and of representation to Government Ministers and Members of Parliament of both Houses and all parties. In the busy public relations department, yet another booklet, 'Historic Opportunity' was published. It sought to demonstrate that denial of the CAA recommendations would go against the Conservative Party's 1983 Election Manifesto promise in respect of privatisation policies.

BCAL staff and union representatives launched their own campaign, 'Say Yes, Minister, to the CAA plan.' They conducted it through the medium of public demonstrations in the Gatwick area and in London. Their fear was that maintenance of the BA/Heathrow monopoly in private ownership would affect the development of BCAL and Gatwick and threaten their own jobs.

Many others had, of course, entered the fray, either supporting our case, British Airway's arguments, or proposing alternatives. One of these came from Roy Watts, the former chief executive of British Airways and now chairman of the Thames Water Authority, and the Secretary of State for Trade and Industry, Norman Tebbit. They wanted to see not a multiplicity of competing airlines in Britain, but the creation of one giant international airline for the UK, along the lines of the major national airlines in foreign countries. That, of course would mean a merger between BCAL and BA.

In the midst of the campaign furore, Ian Ritchie set up a Parliamentary lunch at which I would speak. Thirty-two Members were present, mostly from the Commons, but also some from the House of Lords. I talked through the familiar ground of the CAA report, on the way through refuting the arguments put up against it by British Airways. My conclusion started with the question of what would happen if British Airways was left as it was and privatised. There was no doubt, I said, that they could pick off the competition as and when they wished. With £2.5 billion (in revenue) this would be a fairly simple exercise and BCAL as the only other British intercontinental airline would and should be a prime target. In my opinion, there were only three alternatives:

The first and preferred course is that the review is adopted. British Caledonian expands and develops at Gatwick and is a significant competitor in the UK and international scene.

The second is, if the review is rejected, particularly the route transfer proposals, that BCAL should be permitted to compete in the main market place in the UK and allowed to move to Heathrow into the new Terminal 4 building. This way we have a much better possibility of survival.

The third alternative is for the government to adopt the Roy Watts/Norman Tebbit proposals and have one giant intercontinental and international airline. That would mean a merger of British Airways and BCAL. This, of course, is an option that is against everything for which we have been fighting for many years and surely against the Conservative Government's policy in general and their privatisation objectives, in particular.

# 84

I could not possibly count the number of times I had driven up and down Whitehall from one meeting to another. On every occasion, some sort of reflex would cause me to glance over towards the nondescript entrance to the most famous street in Britain, Downing Street. On the morning of 1 August 1984, it was different – this time the car turned into Downing Street. I was with Peter Masefield and he and I had succeeded in securing a meeting with Margaret Thatcher. Nicholas Ridley had been summoned to be present at the meeting with his Prime Minister and the four of us, in the presence of a stenographer, sat down to talk about the issues of civil aviation.

Margaret Thatcher was clearly well-briefed on the content of the current debate. As I had done so many times before, I began by outlining the background to our case and the arguments for it and brought the matter swiftly down to the question of finance and our ability to survive.

I told the Prime Minister that, far from holding up the BA privatisation, the CAA report had, in fact, deferred our own plans to go public. Before the privatisation of BA had been brought forward, we could have gone to the market for £30 million of new equity on the base of the present route structure and could have achieved that quite easily. If the CAA's recommendations were to be agreed by the Government, I said that I felt sure we could raise the £75 million required.

Her response was unsettling and it was clear that Thatcher had been briefed by someone, somewhere along the line, that BCAL's finances were not up to taking on the kind of expansion proposed in CAP 500. It seemed to her, she said, that finances were the crux of the matter. She had had a careful look at our balance sheet and remarked on how weak she thought it was and how out of line with normally accepted practice was the debt/equity ratio. What risks we took! How could we live so dangerously! How could we hope to finance the expansion we were now asking the Government to support?

Peter Masefield noted afterwards that someone had presented the Prime Minister with a very negative brief on the subject of our finances. She turned several times during the discussion to a folder of papers which appeared to contain a great many figures.

I jumped in to reaffirm that there was no doubt at all that we were able to finance the expansion. We had reported in convincing terms to the CAA and our forecasts and abilities had been endorsed by Kleinwort Benson and Hoare Govett – and also by a number of leading banks. We had, I said, come through a period of heavy recession when many airlines had returned severe losses, British Airways most notable among them. BCAL, on the other hand, had made profits in every year except one. On the subject of the debt/equity ratio, forecasts showed that if the Government accepted the CAA report, that would come down steadily to a one-for-one position. In any event, our present ratio was not out of step with a large part of the capital-intensive airline industry around the world.

Even so, there seemed little doubt that Margaret Thatcher remained concerned about financial aspects. I felt that a reassurance on these matters would go a long way towards inclining the Government towards a more favourable view of the CAA plan.

Peter Masefield, in his inimitable way, intervened with his recollection of what Viscount Swinton, whom he dubbed the arch-priest of Conservative political thought, had said in 1945 when he was the first Minister for Civil Aviation; 'No more monopolies in air transport – no more outdated concepts of a single chosen instrument.'

Finally, in a brief look at the repercussions of various possible Government decisions, the Prime Minister implied that she had understood that one of the options which BCAL would be ready to accept – if all else failed – would be a merger with British Airways. I was astonished. She must have been given a misinterpretation of my remarks at the Parliamentary lunch and I spoke quickly to put the comment in its context, emphasising that this turn of events would be against everything we stood for and would, surely, be opposed to Conservative policies.

We left with a warm farewell and the Prime Minister's thanks for putting the situation clearly. She remarked that John King had not asked to see her recently, but she expected that he would.

From Downing Street, we drove the short distance to Pall Mall, there to review the discussion with the Prime Minister, but most urgently to write a follow up letter to reassure her on the BCAL financial situation. In doing so, along with discussing debt/equity ratios and the plan to achieve a balance of 1.5 to 2 for the placement of shares for new equity among the institutions, I was forced to reveal our profit forecast of between £14 and £15 million for the current year, with now only three more months to run.

I also addressed the problem of overseas remittances which in the last annual report had shown an outstanding amount of £67.4 million. Since then, only 15 per cent was left outstanding.

The ominous aspect to the need for the follow up letter to Margaret Thatcher was that there was clearly some unpleasant work going on by some of those against us to undermine our financial ability. In fact, following its comment in the CAP 500 report, the CAA had already declared itself satisfied that we were able to raise sufficient finance, following yet another rerun of a financial presentation designed to satisfy the authority's advisers at the County Bank. It had issued a press release on the subject:

> In its report on Airline Competition Policy, the authority stated that before making a firm recommendation for the transfer to BCAL of the routes to Harare, Dhahran and Jeddah, it would need to be satisfied that BCAL could raise the necessary additional resources.
>
> Following discussions with BCAL and its financial advisors, the authority is now satisfied as to the prospect that BCAL will be able to raise the necessary finances to take over their routes and compete in intercontinental as well as European routes. The authority therefore reconfirms its recommendations to the Secretary of State.

We lost little time in circulating the text of the CAA statement to MPs and using it in briefings with the press, as we kept the PR campaign going ahead at full speed.

Despite the hyperbole of the 'Winning for Britain' theme, the BA campaign was beginning to rest on two key planks. One was the continuing attempt to discredit our financial position. The other was the 1980 'promise' of John Nott that the airline would be privatised intact. This, said BA, had been the basis on which they were able to achieve their massive staff cuts. Employees and unions were said to have been promised that there would be no more cut backs of the kind they had experienced.

As we had done the year before, in New Delhi, we took the course of issuing traffic statistics far in advance of the normal period of the annual general meeting. We promoted the fact that over the first six months of the year, passenger traffic had grown by seven per cent and freight loads by 25 per cent. It was an announcement to bolster confidence.

Back over at Speedbird House, John King was digging himself in. Reports came to the public attention, through the press, that he and his directors would refuse to implement any route transfers. The implication was that if the Government wanted to implement the CAA plan, then King would have to be sacked.

He and his shareholder, Nicholas Ridley, were facing an increasing barrage from the press. As the aviation correspondents and business writers kept their readers fully informed on every twist, turn, comment and counter-response in what they variously called 'dogfight in the air', or 'battle for the airways' the leader writers sat back to survey the scene.

After a short while, the *Financial Times* came out with its definitive leader, headed 'Monopoly in Civil Aviation'. It concluded: 'Even if, against logic, the CAA's proposals did substantially reduce the proceeds from BA's flotation, in theory this would matter very little . . . The Government's principal concern should be to increase efficiency and the scope for competition – this matters more than the change in ownership.'

The Government was in a dilemma. From the outside, I perceived that it did not want to deny its policies for competition. But to achieve the proposals put up by the CAA would require legislation, if John King and the BA board would not accede to carrying out route transfers at the Government's insistence voluntarily, but he had declared his hand and could not go back. The Government might have forced the BA hand back again had not King had powerful allies inside the Cabinet. For the Government to opt for legislation would have meant the passing of a Bill through Parliament and that would have put paid to the privatisation target date of spring 1985.

*The Times* leader of 11 August was published under the headline, 'Competition Versus Expediency'. It read:

> Lord King is playing a dangerous game. If British Airways were to agree to route transfers, no Bill would be needed and the practical damage could be minimised. There is thus a strong case for negotiating a settlement. The Government had plenty to offer Lord King in the way of a more favourable capital structure for British Airways, easing of limits on flight movements at Heathrow and even allowing a fifth terminal at Heathrow.
>
> In the end, however, the Government should not sacrifice the principle of competition to expediency, or water the CAA's minimal reforms down to a shabby compromise.

*The Times* was exceptionally well-informed and perceptive. We were, sadly, on our way towards that 'shabby compromise'.

# 85

Nicholas Ridley and five members of his department were lined up to meet Alastair Pugh, Trevor Boud and myself at his office in the Department of Transport's Marsham Street building one Thursday afternoon towards the end of September. His cohorts included his Parliamentary Under Secretary, the self-styled Minister for Aviation, Michael Spicer, his permanent secretary, Peter Lazarus, and three other civil servants, David Holmes, David Rowlands and Roger Clarke. This meeting was the one we had been waiting for. We were to be told the outcome of the Cabinet Committee meeting.

Ridley, in an apologetic manner, announced that he now had the bones of a civil aviation policy. He proceeded to talk from a document laid in front of him. He started by saying that it was intended to endorse the CAA proposals in respect of domestic deregulation. It was also in the Government's mind to increase intercontinental dual designation wherever possible and to increase services from Gatwick. So far as it was possible within his powers, every effort would be made to encourage applications for new dual designation services, particularly in Europe.

So far as the regions were concerned, the CAA's proposals to transfer services to independent airlines had proved difficult. British Airways, he said, had developed a modest counter proposal which would cost them £6.75 million over three years. He did not give details at the time, but this was, in fact, the buying off of smaller independents, providing financial assistance to develop regional services, in return for the Government backing down on the CAA proposals to take British Airways out of the provinces altogether.

He became extremely confidential at the next point which was that he planned to make it possible for UK airlines with domestic

502

slots at Heathrow to convert them for international use. Thus far, only British Airways was permitted to operate international scheduled services from Heathrow. It was this move that would eventually allow British Midland to begin its Heathrow-Amsterdam service. Although what Ridley was confiding was of great interest, it was nevertheless exasperating to wait until he came to key areas of interest for BCAL – route exchanges.

He had, he said, been consulting with 'colleagues' and arrangements were now pretty well in hand. He spelled out the detail. BA, revealed Ridley, would give up its twelve services each week to Jeddah and Dhahran for these to be taken over by BCAL. And, in turn, a number of routes would be given up by BCAL for operation by BA. They were the daily service to Atlanta; twice weekly operations to Brazil; the once weekly mid-Atlantic route. BA would also take our non-operated route to Morocco and we would not object to their planned applications to serve Orlando and Tampa.

Still digesting this news, I asked about the transfer of the Madrid, Lisbon and Barcelona services at Gatwick. This would probably be done, he replied curtly. The cost of these route exchanges to BA would be about £20 million a year and, therefore, equivalent to an £80 million – £100 million loss of taxpayers' money. This, he said, had been accepted by his 'colleagues' but they would not ask BA to give up any more, in the interests of privatisation. We all jibbed about our hard won Atlanta route. If BCAL wanted to secure that, we would have to ask John King ourselves, he said.

Ridley went on to say that peripheral developments around this package were possible and might emerge over the next few days, but the main points would be put to the Cabinet the following Thursday. An announcement would be made immediately afterwards. I made no further comment, except to say that the proposals would have to be put to the BCAL executive board and the Caledonian Aviation Group boards. I would, however, not be able to recommend them.

The proposals carried back from Downing Street by Ridley were certainly a shabby package. But they were not yet a compromise.

Peter Masefield had a separate meeting with the two civil servants, Lazarus and Holmes, that same day. His normally gentlemanly manner turned to anger as he heard the news. Against

Peter's attempts to fight back with suggestions that might get a little closer to what the CAA had in mind, he was told they would not be accepted by John King. Still in anger, Masefield told Lazarus that he ought to be made to accept, in the interests of Government policy.

In what Masefield described as an air of resignation to the situation, Lazarus told him that the real trouble was that if King was pushed too far, he and his board would probably resign, or have to be sacked, and this would put back the date of privatisation. If the government could get back £1 billion for BA early in 1985 that would be valuable against the cost of the coal strike which was taking place at the time.

Masefield told Lazarus that by no stretch of the imagination would £1 billion be coming to the Government from British Airways. It would probably be no more than one fifth of that sum. Every little would count, Lazarus replied.

The political expediency warned against by *The Times* had, indeed, come into play to undermine the careful and comprehensive report from the only body competent to analyse the industry and put forward logical and practical policy proposals: the CAA. Airline Competition Policy, CAP 500, was virtually wrecked; the Cabinet had made a mockery of Ridley's request for a review and recommendations for the future. Here we were, back to square one, horse trading with British Airways. The only difference was that this time, we had a Cabinet committee sitting in the middle as an arbiter, although not necessarily a totally impartial one.

The mood around the boardroom table at Caledonian House was sombre. Anger and frustration was vented by even the most mild mannered of the directors, but in the end it was agreed that we would have to accept some form of package. To press on promoting CAP 500 would be like flogging the proverbial dead horse. Everybody agreed, however, that we would not relinquish the Atlanta route. We would negotiate that out of the package. To give me firmer ground to stand on, I therefore requested and obtained a mandate – rather than an instruction – from the board to accept the deal outline, excluding Atlanta. It would include the rest of the package, with Orlando and Tampa going to British Airways.

It was those words, or similar, that formed my opening remarks to Ridley at our next meeting on 2 October, after he had said that the outcome of the civil aviation review and the whole controversy must now be finalised one way or the other. The uncertainty, said Ridley, was bad for all.

I asked Ridley to put our counter proposal to a full cabinet meeting and to stress that Atlanta was the only point of difference and British Airways' intransigence the only stumbling block.

The Minister replied that he could and would try once more with John King. But he had tried already and so far he had refused. He would, if we liked, put it also to his Cabinet colleagues. After some discussion, Ridley revealed that the BCAL case did have a small majority in the Cabinet who were sympathetic, but not if it came to a question of legislation. I fully believed him as a man of honesty and good will when he suddenly said that he had long ceased to argue on the merit of the BCAL case. That he was convinced of. But he had to be pragmatic about what could be delivered.

The deal was eventually done and enshrined in a flimsy, twelve-page White Paper, 'Airline Competition Policy', published in early October. The crucial outcome of virtually a year of acrimonious debate was tucked away in paragraph 23, page 8 of the White Paper. After talking about the CAA proposals, the White Paper said that instead of compulsory transfers, the Government favoured a reciprocal arrangement to strengthen British Caledonian financially, under which each airline would withdraw from routes which the other then might take up.

The two airlines have agreed to such an arrangement. British Airways has offered to withdraw from Jeddah and Dhahran in Saudi Arabia. The Government is ready, subject to the licensing processes, to designate British Caledonian as a British carrier in place of British Airways on these routes and to negotiate with the Saudi authorities to obtain the right for it to serve Riyadh.

For its part, British Caledonian has offered to withdraw from its South American routes. It will surrender its licences to Denver and Morocco which it currently does not use. In addition, British Caledonian will not oppose British Airways' licences applications to serve Orlando and Tampa in the USA. The Government is ready, again subject to the licensing process, to designate British Airways under the relevant Air Service Agreement. The

505

effect of these transfers would be to strengthen British Caledonian with increased annual pre-tax profits estimated at around £18 million. The reduction of British Airways' profits would be of the same order.

The White Paper summed up the new aviation policies it represented in four objectives:

* To encourage a sound competitive multi-airline industry with a variety of airlines of different characteristics serving the whole range of travellers' needs and strong enough to compete agressively against foreign airlines.

* To promote competition in all markets: internationally by working to reduce restrictions on services and by making it easier for new airlines to enter the market; and domestically, by cutting out controls on new services and on fares and capacity.

* To ensure adequate safeguards against anti-competitive or predatory behaviour by airlines, so as to protect the long-term interests of the public through the maintenance of a competitive industry.

* To put the ownership of British Airways into the hands of private investors including its employees, so as to remove from it both the restrictions and the protection of state ownership.

To me and the senior management of the airline, the whole thing was an apology, the shabby compromise into which we were marched with our hands behind our backs. The deal we had come out with was a far cry from what might have been and very nearly was. Yet it was still an improvement on the situation we had prior to Ridley's call for a review the previous December. Saudi Arabia, already profitable, would be an extremely valuable addition to our network and the White Paper did open the way for competitive opportunity. It was a win – but it was by no means the first prize we had sought.

In any event, it was important for our staff who had stood behind me so loyally over long months of struggle and our shareholders to use the White Paper outcome as a boost to morale and future prospects. 'The White Paper decisions,' I wrote in a staff message, 'will

506

bring about a new look BCAL, with a busier-than-ever long-haul route network, geared to the oil industry centres of the world. The Saudi Arabian routes – a market which BCAL has been seeking to enter for some time – will boost the airline's profitability and provide a sound and stable base for future development. The new route network will require the introduction of more long-range wide-body aircraft – DC-10-30 or Beoing 747 equipment. Analysis has already started and fleet expansion plans will be announced in the near future.'

It was left to the Sunday newspaper, *The Observer*, to have the final and most telling say on the saga of the 1984 civil aviation review. In its leading article, after the publication of the White Paper, the newspaper stated: 'In bowing to the realities of power, however, the Government has thrown away the opportunity to force long-overdue changes in a monopolistic industry. The Prime Minister, as she must know herself, has lost some of her claim to be the instinctive champion of consumer rights. The Chancellor, Mr Nigel Lawson, and the Trade Secretary, Mr Norman Tebbit, whose support so aided British Airways' position in Cabinet, now smell more of fudge and mudge than any genuine belief in free competition.'

My own final words were not intended for public ears, nor anybody outside the tight circle of our holding board. In a confidential memorandum, I wrote, 'For BCAL, the writing is now on the wall.'

507

# 86

The irony of 1984 was that while ideological politics prevented the airline from looking towards the great expansion envisaged by the CAA, BCAL had traded its way out of the problems of previous years and was earning more revenue, carrying more passengers and achieving bigger profits than at any time in its history. Our profit for the year was £15.4 million, an improvement of more than £12 million. Gains were recorded in all areas of performance, with passengers up by eight per cent and cargo by 20 per cent.

With the introduction of the two Airbus A.310 aircraft, the last of the Boeing 707s was sold, amid a great deal of emotion among crews and staff who had grown up with this trusty workhorse of the air.

Priorities for the coming year included the planning for the start of flights to Saudi Arabia and arrangements for the closing down of the South American network which included San Juan, Colombia, Venezuela and Brazil.

While Alastair Pugh was undertaking the sad task in the western hemisphere, David Coltman was busy in Saudi Arabia. Coltman had by then become deputy managing director and had been given a seat on the holding board. His post as marketing director had been filled by his deputy in that division, Alan Deller, another recruit from British Airways.

Early in the year, I was upset to hear of the death of Bill Richardson, the airline's long-serving engineering director who had retired in 1981. Bill had spent a lifetime dedicated to BCAL and its predecessor company, British United. He was a fine engineer who left a legacy of quality and professionalism behind him.

Another shock, however, was to come towards the end of January. Ian Ritchie had been troubled by heart and circulation problems for a number of years and had undergone several serious operations. Yet he continued to play an extremely full part in the airline as director of external affairs. His work on the civil aviation review political campaign had been tireless and at the same time he had fought relentlessly for the release of Doug Ledingham, the airport manager held hostage for several months in Libya. He had even volunteered to go down to Tripoli to negotiate with the Libyans; I had refused to allow this.

Ian was at work in his office, as usual. He and Tony Cocklin were grappling with the problem of an article in the magazine *Airport* which we considered to be commercially sensitive as it concerned our negotiations for the purchase of A.320 aircraft. I had just telephoned Ian from London when he suffered a heart attack at his desk. Cocklin rushed to the telephone to call for the chief medical officer, Dr Peter Chapman who, as luck would have it was at a meeting with flight operations director, John Fugl, in an adjacent office.

Dr Chapman controlled the situation and took Ian off to the general hospital in Crawley where he was put in intensive care. It was cause for relief. However, Ian suffered a further attack while in the hospital from which he never recovered.

Ian Ritchie's death was a blow for us all. But it was especially bitter for me. He was one of the few who had been with me in the Caledonian-BCAL venture almost from the very beginning. Although his sales and business talent attracted numerous attractive offers over the years, he remained absolutely loyal to the airline. He became a good friend and an almost indispensable colleague.

Ian's funeral in a local Gatwick crematorium was packed with friends and colleagues, as was the memorial service we staged later at the Church of Scotland in Pont Street, London. The best gesture we could make to his memory was, however, to name an aircraft after him, in line with our tradition of giving 747s and DC-10s the names of well known Scots. To the fleet which included 'Robbie Burns', 'Alexander Fleming', 'Mungo Park', 'John Logie Baird', and 'James S. Mcdonnell' was added 'Ian Ritchie'. His widow Jane came down to the airport to perform the naming ceremony with me. Ian, I know, would have been both amused and proud.

The one event that Ritchie had been looking forward to eagerly before the tragedy occurred was our return to New York, the key

509

piece in the jigsaw puzzle of the North Atlantic network. After the work he had carried out to lay the foundations for the earlier New York service in 1972, Ritchie was disappointed with the need to suspend the operation two years later and he, as much as anybody, wanted to see a triumphant return to the blue riband route.

Visitors to Inverary Castle, the ancestral home of the Dukes of Argyll, which sits at the head of Loch Fyne, are probably surprised to see a montage of photographs among the collections of family portraits and pictures of clan gatherings. It is a carefully laid out display of souvenir photographs taken during a programme of celebration for the inauguration of the New York route in May 1985. The current Duke of Argyll, the boyish Ian Campbell, was at the head of our list of guests who travelled on the special flight to mark the return of BCAL to the Big Apple.

It was a mixed bag of guests including Lord Kinnoull; MPs Sir Peter Emery and Bob McCrindle; financiers Andrew Caldecott of Kleinwort Benson and Michael Kennedy of the Edinburgh firm, Martin Currie; a clutch of editors, Sir John Junor of the *Sunday Express*, Sir David English of the *Daily Mail*, Arnold Kemp of the *Glasgow Herald* and Peter Cole of *The Guardian*; industrialists Sir (now Lord) Francis Tombs of Rolls Royce, and Sir Patrick Meaney of Rank. From the CAA came John Dent and Ray Colegate, from the Scottish Council Hamish Morrison, and from the Scottish Development Agency Robin Duthie. Trade Unions were represented by Mark Young of the British Airline Pilots Association and Lou Britz of the Electrical, Electronic, Telecommunications and Plumbing Union.

We had heralded the return to New York in as big a way as we could. In the UK we made the Frank Sinatra song, 'New York, New York' our own property in a series of television commercials. In the 'city that never sleeps' itself we created the biggest advertisement ever seen, even in that city of promotional excess. The BCAL team in New York, under the energetic John Ruzich, recruited from Eastern Airlines, negotiated to lease the outside wall of a building in Times Square and proceeded to have it hand-painted as a mammoth poster site. The 'British Caledonian Wall' caught the imagination of New Yorkers and it soon became something of a minor sightseeing attraction.

Based at the Pierre Hotel, facing Central Park, our guests from London took part in four days of activities which included meetings at City Hall, the New York Stock Exchange, a reception with Bankers Trust and a dinner with NatWest. It culminated in a gala banquet in the Pierre at which our guest speakers were William 'Bill' Brennen, New York's commissioner for international business development, and the US television personality Barbara Walters.

The one aspect of the trip which impressed the group from London was, however, our arrangements for moving them around the city from function to function. Ruzich had laid on a fleet of luxurious Mercedes limousines, ten in all. As one of our people said at one stage, 'When this lot sweeps down the street, everything stops – it looks like a Mafia convention!'

The limousines were, in fact, our way of emphasising a new kind of service we had introduced with the start of the New York route, 'door-to-door' service. Airline service on the ground, we believed, was as important as that in the air. The marketing men had, accordingly, come up with the plan that for first class and executive class passengers we would provide a limousine service, free of charge, to take them to the airport at one end, and deliver them to their homes, hotels or offices, at the other.

The New York start formed the culmination of several months of frenetic activity. It was like the early 1980s all over again when we seemed to be starting a new route each week, earning our reputation as Europe's fastest-growing airline.

Nicholas Ridley had given us and British Airways the deadline of 31 March to complete the route exchanges of the Airline Competition Policy White Paper. The infrastructure for Saudi Arabia had been very quickly set up under David Coltman's supervision, with our operations under the management of three separate general sales agencies in Jeddah, Riyadh and Dhahran. Like Nigeria before, we had a big job to do in Saudi Arabia with the British expatriate community, demonstrating that BCAL was far from the secondary airline that BA had alleged.

I made one tour of Saudi Arabia before we opened the route, meeting business groups in Jeddah and Dhahran and government ministers in Riyadh. Hospitality was lavish, as were the offices, palaces, airport and hotels we visited, especially the villa our group stayed in at Riyadh. I remember being in total awe at the magnificent Riyadh airport, complete with hanging gardens and its own integral mosque. It made Gatwick and Heathrow look like

511

bicycle sheds, in comparison. I recall thinking that when architects of future centuries came to uncover this edifice from the desert sands, they would identify it as some magnificent temple, rather than a simple transport terminal.

In addition to new cities, new people and new markets, the New York and Saudi Arabian routes also brought in new aircraft, two extra DC-10-30s and a Boeing 747-200 'Combi', a combined passenger/freight aircraft. The Combi joined us with the appropriate registration, G-HUGE, and was known as 'Huge' throughout its career in which it took over the operation of the New York route from DC-10 aircraft.

Inside the airline, I was wrestling with plans for the future which was now more uncertain than at any other time in our history.

At a luncheon earlier in the year of the Wings Club of New York, an eminent aviation forum, I had talked about the way airline competition was going and particularly pointed to the post-deregulation era in the USA, where airline combines were being formed through takeovers and mergers. I coined the phrase 'mega carriers', for that is what we were beginning to see – the emergence of formidably powerful airline groupings with the muscle to be able to wipe any competitor off the face of the route map.

At home, British Airways, now a public limited company, its finances cleaned up, was preparing to become private and free of the restraining hand of a responsible minister. Nothing had been done to reduce its monopoly grip on British-licensed scheduled services and it was allowed to operate from our network hub at Gatwick, while we were barred from competing at Heathrow.

BCAL was in a difficult situation, strategically. By now we were too big an airline to concentrate on specialist, niche activities, but too small to effectively compete on a comprehensive scale with the truly big airlines like BA, the US mega carriers and the expanding, lower cost operators in the Far East.

The most vital of our immediate requirements was to expand the capital base and towards the end of April, plans hardened to float the company on the Stock Exchange. With these plans came a restructure of the company. We required long-term strategy planning and Alastair Pugh moved from the airline to become executive vice-chairman and director of strategy for the group. Trevor Boud, responsible for overall financial strategy, also became an executive vice-chairman. Replacing Pugh as managing director of BCAL was David Coltman. In a subsidiary move, a new personnel director was appointed, a small, elfin-like Cornishman, Jack Roach. Roach had been a consultant on industrial relations matters for some while, bringing to our industry his experience with the English China Clay company, where in the face of economic ruin, he had brought management and workers together to share problems, doing away with demarcation lines and wasteful practices to increase efficiency, profitability and the prospects for job security. Roach called his theory 'The Way Ahead', and it was such a scheme that we needed to take BCAL into its next phase of development.

Relationships with industrial workers – the engineers, loaders and drivers – had traditionally been good. BCAL and Caledonian before it had always run as a team, almost a family, in a business where interdependence between different areas of responsibility is vital. Pugh, Coltman and I were as used to discussing business development with the staff union representatives as we were with board colleagues. It was a mutual and natural, not contrived, arrangement where the union representatives were free to walk through my office door at any time, as I was to go to the shop floor areas and discuss problems openly and frankly. Yet, probably because of our concentration on political events in 1984, a situation had been allowed to develop where dissent between workforce and management developed and successive pay awards had pushed our labour costs far too high.

Jack Roach was charged with negotiating and implementing The Way Ahead policy with each of the five key union areas of the airline. The Way Ahead required a complex programme of negotiation, education, discussion and agreement with every staff union panel. Essentially, the scheme was designed to do away with traditional union demarcation lines and working methods. We would offer employees a higher basic wage, eliminating the awkward, sometimes shaky structure of a low basic, topped up by overtime and shift payments. In return, employees would agree to flexible working methods – a plumber would undertake a piece of carpentry, if that meant finishing the job efficiently – and flexible working hours. If a job required a man to stay on over normal hours, he would do so as a matter of course, without expecting, or receiving, overtime pay.

513

Roach had laid down five principles for the conduct of The Way Ahead: security, mutual trust, that people matter, involvement and cooperation. The principles had to be agreed by both managers and the managed for the scheme to work. They certainly formed the basis of the way I wanted to see the company develop. The traditional, regular confrontations over pay claims between unions and management were wasteful, tedious for both sides and should become a thing of the past.

We were also vitally concerned with training and had developed a comprehensive training centre close to Gatwick where the many skills involved in an airline were taught and practised, whether this was the way a stewardess should be groomed for inflight duties, the essential safety and survival techniques, the workings of computer reservations systems or the duties of a flight engineer.

In September 1985 the opportunity came to expand the training capability with the acquisition of a flight training centre at Gatwick, previously operated and owned by American Airlines. The centre provided training for pilots and flight engineers, using advanced simulators for DC-10s and Boeing 737 aircraft. A separate company, British Caledonian Flight Training Ltd, was formed and the unit began to take care of our own DC-10 training needs, as well as undertaking profitable training contracts from other airlines. The simulators themselves were manufactured by the Rediffusion company, located nearby. They were eventually to come into BCAL Flight Training as a partner.

The same month, Peter Smith was dispatched for a one-day visit to Riyadh, travelling aboard the first service into the Saudi capital. Although the Jeddah and Dhahran services had been launched earlier in the year, protracted negotiations delayed the implementation of flights to Riyadh. Once the permit was received from the Saudi President of Civil Aviation, no time at all was wasted – the service was opened within just five days, with our Dubai-based manager for the Gulf, Mike Turley, being sent to Riyadh to set up arrangements.

A frequent visitor to my office in the summer of 1985 was Chris Smart, chief executive of our tour operating and travel activities, now known as Caledonian Leisure Holdings. The Leisure offices were in a quiet, residential part of East Grinstead, an archetypal English market town which went about its business in a gentle and

514

refined way. This was in stark contrast to the atmosphere inside Smart's offices as he and his team grappled with the problems of the ever-volatile travel business.

Caledonian Leisure included the chain of Blue Sky Travel agencies, a total of thirty shops in London and around the South East. Although it was a profitable part of the business, the growth of major travel agency multiples, the likes of Hogg Robinson, Pickfords Travel, Lunn-Poly and Thomas Cook, meant that we would have had to expand Blue Sky Travel substantially in order to remain competitive. Like the airline, Blue Sky Travel was too big to be small and too small to be big. In July we negotiated with Thomas Cook to sell off the travel agency chain and withdraw from retailing.

On the tour operating side, where our brand was Blue Sky Holidays, the market was suffering through the kind of 'numbers game' we had experienced years earlier. The market leaders, Thomson Holidays and Intersun, were placing excess capacity in the market, resulting in substantial discounting and drops in load factors. Blue Sky was especially vulnerable, as with carryings of just under 200,000, the company was unable to exercise the economies of scale and benefits of bulk purchasing enjoyed by the market leaders. To try and achieve a competitive position, we purchased the northern tour firm, Arrowsmith Holidays, from its present owners, Greenall Whitley, the brewery. The plan was to integrate the two operations to achieve increased market penetration for 1986, at realistic pricing levels. In October, however, Thomson Holidays, in a move for market dominance, placed 2.2 million holidays on the market at rates substantially below existing levels. Other tour operators followed suit and destabilised the entire European inclusive tour market for 1986. For our part, we had had enough. The Leisure company was already in a loss situation, although a large part of that had been alleviated by the travel agency sale. It was decided to get out of the European tour business and a hurried deal was struck with Rank Travel, our partners in the charter airline, to take Blue Sky off our hands.

Jetsave, our travel company specialising in travel to North America, was also suffering as the pound weakened against the dollar. But, in a smooth change of strategy, Smart organised the opening up of a sales office in Orlando, Florida, to exploit the

515

sudden demand in travel to Europe, brought about by the strong dollar. Jetsave's US operation carried 16,000 passengers in that first summer of operation.

Smart had also taken over responsibility for the British Caledonian charter operation, as the group's 50 per cent shareholding was transferred from BCAL to Caledonian Leisure Holdings. We had experienced identity problems between the charter operator and BCAL itself. Frankly, we were concerned that passengers travelling in a high-density DC-10 charter, carrying our name, might believe that this was the standard of seating and catering on the main scheduled services. Frank Hope, who ran the charter side, was commissioned to come up with a new name and identity. He eventually chose and we eventually agreed on the name Cal-Air, with a red, white and blue livery, featuring the lion symbol in red.

# 87

I found myself sitting on the floor, alongside a group of men, singing folk songs and being plied liberally with liquor by exotically-clad ladies. This was no bawdy pub or club, but the most prestigious traditional restaurant in Tokyo. My companions were senior members of the Japanese banking community, the ladies were the resident geishas of the city's famous Happo-En restaurant, the liquor they were serving was sake and the songs were in Japanese.

The evening was the brainchild of Toshi Gonda, a general manager with the Nissho-Iwai Corporation, with whom we had had dealings in the finance of aircraft, and was laid on to welcome a BCAL team to Japan. With me was Peter Smith and our general manager, based in Hong Kong, Ranald Noel-Paton.

The background to the visit was a new plan for route expansion into the Far East with services to Tokyo and Seoul. Earlier in the year, Peter Smith had realised the opportunity which was emerging politically in the Soviet Union and Japan, for the opening up of a new route to Tokyo across Siberia. It would enable the first-ever non-stop air service between London and Tokyo, cutting hours off the existing transpolar route which operated via Anchorage in Alaska.

British Airways had failed to spot the opportunity and after presentations on the plan to the board, the airline received the go-ahead to place an application with the CAA. At the same time, we decided to bid for the licence to serve Seoul, held by BA but not used. Under the competitive regime of the new Ridley policy, we had no qualms about snatching away the BA licence on the basis of 'use it or lose it'.

The application was before the CAA and an outcome was expected in early 1986 as I made the ground-preparing visit to

517

Japan. In fact it was part of an extensive tour which had included Dubai and Hong King and was to take in Seoul.

I was fascinated to learn from Japan's director general of international transport, Toyoichiro Nakada, that the country, for so long a nation cautionary on policies in aviation, was moving towards the kind of liberal and competitive environment which had emerged in the UK. In visits to the Japanese domestic airlines, All Nippon Airways and Toa Domestic Airlines, I learned that they were both sizing up opportunities for expanding international operations, alongside the national carrier, Japan Air Lines.

If the sushi dishes of raw fish eaten with a soy and horseradish sauce, with chopsticks of course, were a new culinary experience, the kimchee of Korea, hot-spiced pickled cabbage, was even more so. Seoul was a fascinating city, nestling in the mountains and only a short way from the border with North Korea from which, locals would say, you could occasionally hear the sound of artillery fire. Commercially the place was booming, exporting almost any commodity or service that could be humanly provided. I had learned a new expression in Saudi Arabia through the road and building contracts being carried out for the Saudi government by the Korean construction company, Hanyang. The usual excuse in Riyadh, Jeddah or Dhahran for being held up on the way to a meeting because of roadwork diversions, was simply, 'Sorry, I've been Hanyanged.'

The serious side of this was that our proposed new services were welcomed warmly by the business communities. In Japan, they wanted more choice and competition to the existing monopoly of BA and Japan Airlines. In Korea they were delighted at the thought of getting any direct service to London at all. Assuming we received the approval from the CAA, and the Department of Transport secured rights from the Japanese and Korean authorities, the start date for the new services were set for summer 1987.

Despite the hopes and plans raised in Downing Street and at Heathrow for the privatisation of British Airways in 1985, the airline remained firmly in the public sector. Its programme had been irretrievably delayed by the Laker case which rumbled on through 1984 and into 1985.

The airlines involved finally decided to go for an out of court settlement and our contribution was agreed at £3,034,000. We were clear of a major irritation. British Airways was cleared to proceed with privatisation.

Our own flotation plans were being moved ahead, under the supervision of Kleinwort Benson and Hoare Govett. By the end of 1985, we had invested £588,000 in professional fees, expenses and other costs in the process of carrying out studies for a share issue and the creation of an investment market. Bankers, lawyers and stockbrokers were pressing ahead and we had gone so far as to plot out the associated PR and promotional campaign, calling in the assistance of one of the specialist companies in this field. Tony Cocklin and I had laid the ground with a series of interviews with financial journalists. 'BCAL FOR EARLY £86 QUOTE,' said the headline on one front page article in *The Observer* business section on 6 October.

At the time, BA's probable launch date for privatisation was May or June of 1986. That left us with the choice of going public very early in the New Year or in the autumn. I was keen to get to the market ahead of BA and that was the reason for the very fast and expensive programme we were involved in.

As the year was closing in on us, so, too, was the financial climate. At the time of the route transfers, great play was made of the fact that the Saudi Arabian routes would bring us £20 million in additional profit. The reality, however, was falling very far short of the promise. Although the Saudi routes provided high-frequency services strengthening the network and developing the Gatwick hub, the down turn in the petro-chemical industry had meant a downturn in business traffic to and from Saudi Arabia. The value of the network was diminished, from the figures originally assessed, although the results produced were still much better than the loss-making South American operation. New York was proving very successful, but we were still swallowing the heavy development costs.

Currencies were moving against us, most notably in the weakening of the US dollar and the Nigerian Naira. With thirty-five flights across the Atlantic and ten flights to Nigeria, these were our two key revenue currencies and the fall in value was bound to make an impact on the overall financial performance.

We were, at the same time, facing increases in the charges for aviation fuel which would add a very significant extra burden on to costs, already accounting for more than 20 per cent of operating expenses. Planned expansion in Europe was affected by the difficulty in obtaining rights to serve Milan. Negotiations to expand the Middle East network to Muscat and San'a, South Yemen, remain inconclusive.

Conspiring with each of those items was the overall slowdown in the rate of worldwide traffic growth. Knut Hammarskjold at IATA had already reported that traffic growth in 1986 was likely to be around six per cent, compared with ten per cent in 1985. Increasing airline competition, on the other hand, would ensure that capacity was likely to grow by more than seven per cent. The consequent fight for market share would mean that yields, contribution to profit for fares and cargo rates, would stay at the same level, if not decrease.

Hammarskjold had told the airlines that the financial result for the industry was expected to fall into deficit again and warned everybody to attack costs as a matter of urgency.

For us the threat of increased competition was more pronounced than for many other carriers. BA was closer to going out of government control and we could expect rough and tough tactics in the market place we shared with a competitor many times our size. We were also extremely exposed on the North Atlantic, our single most important route network, where we predicted that the mega carriers would dump capacity to acquire market share. Against this background it was very difficult to make specific predictions about 1986 and to justify our financial expectations to the market.

It was in November that I painted this gloomy picture over dinner at the Copthorne Hotel with members of the group board which included representatives of major shareholders. It had become a useful tradition that we would meet for a meal in the hotel's Caledonian Suite on the eve of each board meeting, as a means of talking informally and bringing each other up to date on various issues in order to save time at the formal meeting the following day.

My recommendation was that we should, reluctantly, shelve plans for a public flotation. Larry Tindale, Stuart Young, David Beety and Leonard Bebchick nodded their assent. The decision was taken formally around the Caledonian House Board Room table the following day.

As it was, the 1985 financial year closed with a profit of £21.7 million on a revenue which had risen to £602 million. Passenger numbers had gone up by 8.5 per cent and cargo carryings by 10 per cent. The staff share scheme was boosted by an allocation of £900,000 and a dividend of 15 pence declared. It was the best result ever achieved. Prospects, however, were not so promising as the figures might have made out.

# 88

To be stared at for any length of time, across the seats of a train or the cabin of an aircraft, for instance, is an uncomfortable experience. But to have a person sitting, staring and catching your every move as you work from your desk for hours on end would, I thought, be completely intolerable. It was with a great deal of trepidation, therefore, that I agreed to be the subject of a portrait commissioned by the Scottish National Portrait Gallery and its keeper, Duncan Thomson – no relation, by the way. I was flattered as Thomson said that he wanted to hang it in their collection of eminent Scots.

The artist he had selected was John Wonnacott, based at Southend in Essex and who was more renowned for his landscapes of the Thames Estuary. Wonnacott is a bright and breezy person with a laugh permanently waiting to break out from his ruddy, open air face. I never saw him wear a tie – his shirt collar was worn flattened back against the lapels of his jacket in that typically British seaside style. It follows that I took to Wonnacott and my worries about being a sitting target for a nit-picking, highly-strung portrait painter diminished the moment I first met him.

Wonnacott's commission was to produce a massive, more than life-size oil painting. The first thing he did was to bring some of his work down to the office at Caledonian House and hang the pictures on the walls, after taking down some of the paintings I had collected or been given, dismissing them as 'rubbish'. The pictures, he emphasised, were only on loan, but they would help me to get a feel for his style and he certainly could not have worked with the existing paintings in front of him.

John had surveyed the airport scene minutely for his preferred setting and eventually decided that he would paint me in a hangar scene, amid the busy process of overhauling and maintaining the aircraft fleet. He made his arrangements with the engineers and set up a studio on a gantry in the main DC-10 hangar. His first job, however, was to carry out a series of pencil drawings of me to catch, as he said, the full range of expressions on my face. To do this, he parked himself in a corner of the office and quietly stared and sketched as I went about my normal business. Visitors were invariably startled to attend meetings with Wonnacott, gnome-like in the corner, saying nothing at all, but variously looking intently at me and sketching furiously on his pad.

Throughout 1986, the artist would have caught all the expressions in my emotional repertoire, ranging from absolute delight to severe despondency. Wonnacott was painting his way into a year which would see BCAL's fortunes plunge from record profit to record losses.

The good news, as always, came first. This was the winning of the Tokyo and Korea licences from the CAA. We wanted to begin the services in the summer of 1986, but complications in air service negotiations, largely brought about by British Airways seeking to jump on the trans-Siberia bandwagon, were to delay the start of the operation for a full year.

1986 was the year of the Chernobyl atomic power station disaster in the Soviet Union and of a spate of terrorism in Europe which led ultimately to the US bombing raid on Libya. These events conspired to cause a crippling downturn in tourist and leisure traffic from North America. This was an especially bitter blow as transatlantic traffic accounted for no less than 37 per cent of the business. So serious was the decline in US traffic for both BCAL and British Airways that major promotional programmes were hastily put into place, including a visit to the USA by aviation minister, Michael Spicer, to rally confidence among Americans in the safety and security of a trip to Britain.

Two separate terrorist trials in London had the consequent effect of bringing operations to Tripoli to a halt, as the Government tore up the air services agreement with Libya and banned Libyan Arab Airlines from flying to London. Syrian airspace was closed to British airlines, causing expensive reroutings to flights going east.

The new Saudi routes which we were preparing to extend to Muscat and San'a were operating below budget still. Costs had to be tackled as a matter of urgency and a series of hard negotiations succeeded in obtaining an agreement among all of our staff to a wages freeze. It was to prove insufficient. In May, David Coltman fronted a press conference in London at which he announced a scheme of voluntary severance and early retirement, designed to prune staff numbers by 1000.

In the same month, Nicholas Ridley departed from the Department of Transport to go to the Department of the Environment. In his place came John Moore, until now Financial Secretary to the Treasury. Ridley marked his departure from the aviation industry with a blow that was to add further to our financial problems. He rejected our bid to renew the licence for the Airlink Helicopter operation between Gatwick and Heathrow which was so important to the generation of 'interline' traffic. The cost of Ridley's decision, taken in the face of protest from environmental groups in the Surrey stockbroker belt over which the Sikorsky flew, would be £4 million.

Alastair Pugh, Trevor Boud, David Coltman and I knew that BCAL was in a squeeze from which it would be difficult to recover. We could have recovered from events outside our control on certain areas of the network, if our business base had been stronger and more widespread as it might have been in 1984. Now, the only method of expansion was by merger, by linking up with another airline to create strength and flexibility. We began to think of who we might approach to begin discussions.

One of our recurring problems was the depressed economics of the shorthaul European routes and with the Airbus A.320 fleet due for delivery in 1988, inventive strategies were required. At the same time, the prospects of liberalisation in Europe promised an immense amount of opportunity in the longer term, if we could create the right kind of vehicle to exploit the scope for expansion which would inevitably come.

A sequence of analyses and confidential contact led to the formation in February of a joint working group between BCAL and the International Leisure Group, parent company for the predominantly charter airline, Air Europe. Its chairman was the flamboyant travel entrepreneur, Harry Goodman. The working group was headed from our side by Alastair Pugh and, for ILG, by Robert Smart.

The idea was to merge the shorthaul operations of BCAL and Air

Europe into what was called in confidential reports, 'An airline for Europe'. The bankers, Kleinwort Benson, were consulted privately and asked to provide their financial criteria for the proposed venture. The working group met in a series of secret sessions, away from either company's base, at an obscure hotel in Haslemere, Surrey. Their report was produced in April.

Essentially the proposal was for the formation of a completely new airline company which would take over the European activities of BCAL and Air Europe, operating both scheduled and charter services with the same aircraft fleet to maximise aircraft utilisation, the eternal problem on networks involving short flying sectors.

It would have to achieve cost levels up to 25 per cent below traditional European scheduled operations to cut the price of fares below a level which carriers like British Airways could afford to go to. Its fleet would comprise nineteen aircraft, the BCAL A.320s and two BAC1-11s, plus the Air Europe's Boeing 737s. The possibility of rolling Cal Air into the new airline was discussed to bring in the big DC-10 capacity.

Detailed plans were proposed for the 'Airline for Europe' to commence operation in the spring of 1987 on the existing scheduled routes of BCAL and the two scheduled services of Air Europe. These points would be boosted with the introduction of a completely new set of services to Barcelona, Dusseldorf, Hamburg, Milan, Munich and Nice. The fares scheme for the new carrier was taken from our own pricing structure proposed in 1984 to the European Commission.

It was a bold plan to form an airline that would create the very manifestation of liberalisation policies demanded by consumer which were beginning to emerge in Brussels and for which Michael Spicer at the Department of Transport was pressing as part of the Conservatives' competition ideology. It was not until I had gone away on a trip to the USA that Goodman saw his chance to make a bid for the whole of BCAL. He chose this moment to make an offer of a paltry £36 million . . . The ever loyal and straightforward Larry Tindale told Goodman that he would do no other business involving the BCAL shareholding without my knowledge.

On my return, the board conferred and agreed that negotiations with ILG would be broken off forthwith. However secret the talks with ILG were kept, there nevertheless occurred some leak, especially with the travel trade press. Denials that talks were taking place inevitably led to speculation and rumours with some undermining consequence for BCAL became prevalent.

It was a question I had to address in the July at a meeting in the Houses of Parliament of the Parliamentary Aviation Group. After explaining the background to our cutbacks and redundancies, I told the MPs that we had, at the same time, mounting speculation in the press and within industry circles on discussions between BCAL and ILG. 'Fuelled by semi-informed comment, the two developments became intertwined, with the result that some interpretations implied that BCAL was in financial trouble, ILG was ready to come to the rescue, but the deal hinged upon the airline being required to prune its costs, overheads and staff in advance. They also implied that our major shareholders wanted to sell stock in BCAL. This was very far from the truth, and would have been laughable if the rumour had not put unnecessary pressure on us, our shareholders and our staff, at a particularly crucial time.' In fact, although the talks with Harry Goodman and his team started in complete confidence, once they became public knowledge we made no secret of the fact that they were based on the possible cross-utilisation of the large shorthaul aircraft both groups had on order.

'It made sense to study the possibilities of operational and commercial collaboration. The talks did extend into other areas, as we said publicly. The talks were friendly throughout, but they ultimately entered a number of difficult areas on which agreement could not be found. They were, therefore, ended towards the end of May', I said.

If the ILG cooperation venture failed, we were able to achieve another notable liaison, to the immense annoyance of British Airways. To improve efficiency and release aircraft capacity, David Coltman made approaches to Sabena, the Belgian National Airline, to see if there was any room for jointly serving the Atlanta route. We wanted Boeing 747 capacity on the service to meet the competition from Delta Air Lines, Sabena had the 747 and was already serving Atlanta at a minimal frequency. The Belgians were interested and between us we eventually evolved the plan for a joint operation. The route would be operated by Sabena's aircraft starting from Brussels and coming to Gatwick before the transatlantic crossing. Technically, the scheme was a blocked space agreement, under which

Sabena operated our service which, naturally, carried the BCAL flight number. In the passenger cabins, BCAL staff would work alongside Sabena crews. The idea formed an extremely interesting and forward looking experiment in international aviation and was certainly well ahead of its time.

British Airways turned its jingoistic attention towards this move, claiming that we had given over British rights to a foreign airline. It was, of course, nonsense, but that did not stop BA from lodging a bid with the CAA to revoke our licence and take over the Atlanta route – a service they had coveted in 1984 – for themselves. Their bid failed and the Sabena 747, operating on our behalf, became a familiar addition to the Gatwick fleet.

# 89

The intercom in my office sounded its strident tone, summoning my attention from the sheaf of board papers and management accounts I was studying. It had to be important, as I was usually interrupted with a direct call only if the matter was urgent. Otherwise, a message would be left with Margaret Trett, in her small side office.

It was Tony Cocklin. 'Sir Adam,' he said, 'The *Sunday Telegraph*'s got the story.' He went on to relate how the chief press officer, Bob Millichap, had received a call from *Telegraph* business correspondent, Jeff Randall. It turned out that his city editor had picked up the tip that British Caledonian was in negotiation to sell the company to British Airways.

Randall was a good, reliable, solid journalist who knew a great deal about the airline industry. He was as incredulous about receiving the tip as Millichap was to pick up the query. He of course knew absolutely nothing about what had been going on behind the scenes and the proposal before him was as daft a thing as he had ever heard. Millichap went back to Randall and poured scorn on the story. It was a load of rubbish. Randall in trust of a good professional relationship over many years, said something like he thought it was and promptly went back to the city editor and told him to forget it. Millichap reported the call to Cocklin who made no comment, but promptly went to his office, closed the door for privacy and called me.

He told me what had happened, but warned that if the *Sunday Telegraph* source was strong enough, the newspaper might still run a non-attributable story, or 'fly a kite', as they say in the news business.

We were about a week away from finalising a deal that would rock the industry, not just in Britain, but around the world. A leak at this stage could be damaging, if not disastrous. There were enough people out there like Michael Bishop of British Midland and Harry Goodman of Air Europe who might attempt to use political muscle to stop, or at least, baulk a deal from which would emerge a giant airline which, in their minds, could adversely affect their own businesses and their future prospects.

Randall went off on a business trip to New York. The following Sunday came and went. There was no mention of us in the *Sunday Telegraph*. The journalist did not know that he was within a grasp of getting a scoop on the biggest business story of the year until he returned to London on 16 July. As his taxi from Heathrow drew up to drop off a colleague before taking him on to his own office in Docklands, he caught sight of an *Evening Standard* billboard. Randall was aghast. The heavy, black, handwritten characters spelled out a headline which proclaimed that British Airways had taken over British Caledonian in a multi-million deal.

I received a furious letter of complaint from the *Sunday Telegraph* city editor. His anger was understandable. His newspaper could have beaten the whole of Fleet Street to what was an astounding story. I explained in my reply that the press officer, Millichap, genuinely did not know about the deal. Had I or Cocklin received the call, as well we might have done from a close contact like Randall, I said that we would simply have had to use the time-honoured phrase, 'no comment', leaving the *Sunday Telegraph* free to use its own journalistic instincts in the matter. As it was, our press officer's innocence of any detail whatsoever, coupled with Randall's mild disbelief at the news he had, saved our secrets.

In fact, only a handful of people inside either British Caledonian or British Airways knew of the takeover talks. Most of the BCAL directors had no clue of what was going on, never mind managers and staff. Despite the setback, the relationship with Randall did not deteriorate and he went on to cover subsequent events with great accuracy and reliability.

The story he had stumbled across began not in London, but in Seattle at the home of a senior executive of the giant Boeing aircraft company. Along with our own John Prothero-Thomas, visiting Boeing for product briefings, was the British Airways planning director, Keith Wilkins. In the course of conversation between the two of them, the subject of airline mergers came up. After some discussion, Wilkins turned to Prothero-Thomas and said that he did not suppose that Adam Thomson would consider talking to British Airways. The BCAL man replied that he thought I would be prepared to talk to anybody and if Wilkins was serious, he would talk to me. Wilkins nodded his assent.

This was at the end of May 1987. Prothero-Thomas duly reported the conversation to me behind the closed door of my office on his return. A few days later, I received a call from the British Airways chief executive, Colin Marshall. Although he had received his Knighthood earlier in the year, he seemed to prefer to be called, by all and sundry, just plain Colin. The words of our conversation were cryptic. We both knew what we were talking about, without having to spell it out over a telephone line. We agreed to meet, each with other colleagues, at my office in Pall Mall on 16 June 1987. We put in place a plan for drastic cost cuts, including the reduction in numbers through a scheme of voluntary severance and early retirements. A total of 900 jobs were eliminated. Airline revenues dropped by £15.5 million and earnings by the tour operating companies by almost £30 million. The airline load factor, the amount of revenue load carried against the capacity deployed, dropped a crucial three points.

By end of October 1986, our previous year's pre-tax profit of £21.7 million had slumped to a loss of £19.3 million, the worst in our history. Drastic measures over and above the redundancies involved the selling of Blue Sky Holidays to Rank Travel, Arrowsmith Holidays to Owners Abroad and the hotels in the Balearic Islands to the Spanish company, Sol Hotels. The artificial ski slope at Hillingdon, owned and operated by Blue Sky, went to a French ski equipment manufacturer.

Curly Walter was instructed to dispose of the two Airbus A.310 aircraft. He did so in a deal which was to become a major saga of intrigue and landed us in trouble with the US Department of Trade, the UK Inland Revenue and in legal action in France. It turned out that the Hong Kong company with whom Curly had struck a deal for the aircraft had, in turn, sold them on. A series of deals later, they ended up in Libya, in breach of US regulations which forbade the sale of US technology, which the A.310s featured, in their systems and engines to President Gaddafi's regime. We had carefully monitored the process of the sale and truly believed that the aircraft were finally destined for a French operator.

For the Hong Kong company, the aircraft were delivered to Dubai, where they sat for some time as the speculation about their true destination emerged. The A.310s were eventually moved to Jordan before, indeed, they found their way to Libya.

Bolstered by the strong foundation of the kind of route network the CAA had sought fruitlessly to grant us two years previously, we could have weathered the economic storms of 1986 with some, but not too much, discomfort. If we were blocked from strengthening the network through the fact that there were simply no opportunities available in the UK, with British Airways holding a virtual monopoly of route franchises, we would have to find other ways to expand the airline. In the US the mega carriers had evolved through a series of takeovers and mergers. We would achieve a similar solution for BCAL.

Ownership regulations, the same ones we had encountered on the formation of Caledonian back in 1961, meant that we could only sell up to about 25 per cent of our shareholding to a foreign carrier. The important thing, however, was not so much the cross shareholding as the merging of our route network into that of another airline by linking our respective hubs. A list of possibilities was drawn up and respective directors assigned to the task of pursuing talks with the selected carriers.

At a meeting in the board room of Caledonian House on 16 June 1987, progress reports came in, as they did regularly each week. Mike Carter, Alastair Pugh's strategy specialist, reported that he would provide the research and development director of Alitalia with financial data at the end of the month. A further meeting had been arranged for July. I informed the group that Sergio Orlandini, chairman of KLM, had been invited to meetings at Gatwick. A response was still awaited. David Coltman told us that in his dealing with Air France, positive indications had been given and a meeting would be arranged.

An anticipated meeting with the President of Texas Air, owners of Continental and Eastern, in the USA, had not taken place and it was felt that we would not pursue this area. American Airlines was discussed, but Peter Masefield said he had difficulty in seeing what major benefits there could be in collaborating with the Dallas/Fort Worth-based airline. David Coltman reported that he and Alastair Pugh would be meeting Roger Hauge, the vice-president, Atlantic division, for Northwest Airlines, at Gatwick three days later, following the airline's declared interest in a closer relationship with BCAL.

I reported on a non-airline involvement, my talks with the Australian Bell group, headed by the entrepreneur, Robert Holmes à Court. I had met him in London several times and he had indicated positive interest in investing in BCAL. The latest news came from one of his associates in London who had told me at a recent meeting that Holmes à Court was still interested in investment in our company and would be happy to meet when I was ready to proceed.

Discussions which had made more progress than any others were with the French independent airline, Union de Transports Aeriens (UTA) which, although locked into a strict spheres of influence policy and separated from direct competition with the larger Air France, felt they might, in the future, find themselves constrained of opportunity for growth, just like ourselves. A working group comprising executives from the two airlines had been set up to study proposals to bring the two airlines together as a combined force in world air transport.

Things had gone so far with UTA that a draft press release had been written in secret, ready to go out if the news leaked as the talks went on and became more and more apparent. In it, Alastair Pugh was quoted as saying: 'If our studies and discussions are conclusive we would create the first, pan-European, intercontinental gateway, by linking Gatwick and Charles de Gaulle as a joint hub for the combines networks of BCAL and UTA.' The release concluded that both airlines were confident that the talks would result in positive developments within the next few months.

But there were two other airlines in our sights, Sabena of Belgium and SAS, Scandinavian Airlines System. They had themselves been involved in highly-publicised merger talks. Sabena, like us, needed strength in the new competitive environment evolving in international air transport. SAS, based primarily at Copenhagen, with other hubs at Stockholm and Oslo, needed to develop a hub much closer to the heart of Europe and the major air travel markets.

532

It was reported to the meeting that both companies had indicated they would be interested in exploring possible collaboration with BCAL. We were already running a joint operation linking Brussels and London with Atlanta, in conjunction with Sabena. It was agreed, however, to put both these approaches on the 'back burner' in order to concentrate on issues of greater priority.

Unbeknown to most of our colleagues sitting round that table, David Coltman and I had, earlier in the day, had another meeting. This time it was in London, at my office in Pall Mall. Our visitor was Colin Marshall of BA. Marshall is a courteous and pleasant man, always extremely well-groomed, in a way that veers towards neatness and sobriety, rather than flamboyance. Before I could greet him and usher him into my private room, he insisted on going over to Margaret Trett, sitting at a typewriter, and introducing himself and shaking her hand.

He sat in the middle of the sofa. Coltman sat at the other end, I positioned myself between them, facing them in an armchair. Pleasantries were exchanged. In particular, Marshall asked about our new route to Tokyo, opened just days before at the beginning of June. In getting down to the real business, he came straight out and said that he was interested in buying BCAL and merging the two airlines. I responded by confirming to him that we, in turn, were interested in talking with British Airways. Subject to satisfactory conditions, we were interested in a deal. We agreed that we would meet again as soon as possible, this time with a full team and our respective financial advisers.

Through the years, our financial advisers had been Kleinwort Benson. They had, indeed, been plotting our own aborted plan for a Stock Exchange listing. However, through a series of aircraft financing deals, Trevor Boud had brought us into contact with the London branch of the US investment bank, Goldman Sachs. We had both been immensely impressed with the professionalism and drive of the Goldman's people and each wanted them to take on the British Airways project. Boud brought John Thornton and Paul Deighton, two of Goldman Sachs' brightest merchant bankers, into the scheme. I first met them at Caledonian House. Neither of them, to my mild surprise, was out of their thirties, yet both had immense reputations in the City of London. Thornton, an American, was also rated highly on Wall Street. Their first task, in conjunction with Boud, was to undertake a full evaluation of BCAL. Before any negotiation could take place, they had to know what the company and its assets were worth to set the best price. At the end of their considerable studies and analyses, Thornton and Deighton came up with guideline figures. They told us that we should be looking for a price somewhere in the bracket between £220 million and £250 million, going, of course, hard for the upper figure.

Lord King of Wartnaby, in addition to his estate in the Midlands, keeps an apartment in London's Eaton Square. It was to this address that Les Smith the driver took me with Trevor Boud, Alastair Pugh and David Coltman. We were ushered into a large lounge. There, alongside John King, was Colin Marshall, Gordon Dunlop and a figure I had last met in New York where he was the British Consul-General, Sir Francis Kennedy. Kennedy, on retiring from the diplomatic service, had been recruited by King to be his special adviser and to join the board of British Airways.

It was around midday. Drinks were offered around as we began to talk. The purpose of the gathering was more of a get to know you session, rather than a negotiation. The hard bargaining would be left to the bankers. As the chat went on, us talking about BCAL, the routes and the aircraft, them telling us about developments since the privatisation in February, King suddenly interjected. He said that if nobody else was going to talk about money, he was. He looked at me, as I puffed gently at one of his Havana cigars, and told me he would give me £5 a share. Whether he was joking, or not, I don't know. Perhaps he meant it as a joke, but hoped he might catch me out by revealing the price we were looking for. I simply roared with laughter back at him to cut the conversation on the subject of money dead.

# 90

I was talking to Trevour Boud on a non-too-clear ship-to-shore telephone line, from the new yacht I had recently purchased, a Moody 41, the *Lazy Lion*. She was moored in the marina at Alicante, southern Spain, having just completed the passage from Gibraltar. The next morning we were due to set sail for the Balearic islands of Ibiza and Majorca, where *Lazy Lion* would be based permanently.

Talks between BCAL and British Airways had begun in London through the medium of our respective bankers, Goldman Sachs, and Lazard Brothers for British Airways, the same firm which had conducted the sale in February to at last achieve privatisation for the airline. Negotiations were going very slowly indeed, with the Lazards team, led by Ned Dawnay, picking its tortuous way through the evaluation of BCAL prepared by Goldmans. Assigned to the bankers were senior executives from the two airlines, Trevor Boud, Alastair Pugh and David Coltman for BCAL, backed as necessary by experts in finance, planning and legal affairs. As well as the bankers, we had each appointed our own firm of lawyers to the negotiations.

In the midst of the affairs of the airline, I had devoted some time to one of my relaxations, sailing, in particular to the purchase of a new yacht. I had for some years kept a Moody 39 in the Club de Mar at Palma, in Majorca. It had, coincidentally, been moored close to Freddie Laker's motor cruiser *Tutinelle*. But now I had found and bought the boat I wanted. She had been taken to the Marina at Brighton, where an old friend and former Caledonian colleague, Frank Legge, was fitting her out with the latest in navigation and radio systems. Frank and I had planned the sail down to Majorca for some time. I was looking forward to playing with this new toy, as much as I was to enjoying the break of a week's sailing.

With the new events developing, I reluctantly told the delivery skipper to go ahead without me. It was possible, I told him, that I might be able to join the yacht in Gibraltar to complete the last two legs. With the talks appearing to get nowhere, I decided to go to Gibraltar, after first setting up a complex arrangement of telephone communication through the ship-to-shore radio service. I would keep in touch with a regular series of calls.

'How's it going?' I asked Boud from Alicante.

'Nothing's happening,' he replied, 'you might as well go ahead with the voyage.'

The sailing across the Mediterranean was magnificent. *Lazy Lion* handled well, I was enjoying setting up and testing the navigation systems and felt extremely relaxed. By the time we reached Ibiza, however, things had changed. An urgent message was waiting at the harbour. I was wanted back in London and an executive jet aircraft, an HS 125, was waiting at the airport, to leave as soon as I could be ready. I wasted no time, scrambling my few items of clothing and personal effects together to rush for the car laid on to take me to the airport. I was unshaven, in slacks and shirt and must have looked an unlikely figure to climb out of the jet at Gatwick, scramble through the small immigration and customs shed which served the private aircraft on the north side of the airport and climb into the Daimler as Les Smith held open the door for me. At home, Dawn had a clean shirt, suit, shoes, socks and tie laid out for me. I changed on the run after a shower and shave, jumped back in the car to be driven to the railway station at Gatwick, where David Coltman and Tony Cocklin were waiting for me.

There seemed to be little air of urgency as we entered the Fetter Lane offices of Goldman Sachs, to be ushered into a conference room, joining Trevor Boud and our team of bankers and lawyers. Each side in the talks had its own conference room as a base and people shuffled to and fro with new points for discussion or confirmation. The middle ground was the giant Goldman's boardroom on the floor below us.

Tea was served, followed by drinks and dinner brought in from outside caterers as the negotiation went on. I was brought up to date by Trevor Boud and John Thornton of Goldman's. They said that they were getting near to a deal which would be acceptable. I gave instruction to try for more cash and immediately called Leonard Bebchick in Washington to brief him on the latest turn in events.

It was close to midnight when Thornton came back with the latest offer from Lazards and British Airways. The deal was for Lazards to acquire on behalf of BA the whole of our issued share capital for a total of £237 million. It valued our ordinary shares at £10.71 each. Before the sale could proceed with recommendations to shareholders, Lazards required an irrevocable undertaking from 3is to sell its 40.1 per cent stake in the company. Larry Tindale agreed.

The deal was struck and the process of putting together the announcement to be posted at the Stock Exchange at the opening of business the following morning was started. It was a ten-page document, trawling through the financial minutiae of the sale and included comments from John King and myself.

'The merger of BA and BCAL,' said King, 'gives British aviation an unrepeatable opportunity to create a British airline capable of taking on the world.'

I was quoted as saying: 'The merger is a source of satisfaction to me. The new combine will provide Britain with its own mega carrier, operating a route network unrivalled in the world, with the inherent strength to challenge and beat the most aggressive competition.'

In the early hours of 16 July 1987, BCAL came to rest. The deal was done, the announcement on its way to the Stock Exchange and the press. It was about 1.30 a.m. that I came through the door of Goldman's offices to the taxi that had been ordered. I was going to the flat for the night. As the cab door closed and I sat exhausted into the seat, I said two words to myself: 'Oh, shit!'

Alastair Pugh and David Coltman had the unenviable task of informing BCAL managers and staff of the sale of the company to British Airways in a series of briefing meetings which began at 7 a.m. the next morning, 16 July.

The news broke to amazement and almost disbelief on the part of the press and the industry. BCAL and BA were seen as bitter enemies and the thought of the two of them coming together in

537

business harmony was perceived as almost impossible. Apart from that the legend our PR campaign had perpetuated all through had come up with the wrong ending. Goliath had swallowed David.

John King was sitting in his corner office in St James's Square. As I walked in he greeted me warmly and ordered some champagne to be brought in. We discussed the tactic we would take with the press waiting to meet the two of us at the adjacent British Airways offices on the other side of the square, curiously in the same block that the Libyans had occupied and from where the policewoman, Yvonne Fletcher, had been shot and killed in 1984. It was equally curious and slightly unreal that here was I with John King, a British Airways stewardess on my arm, a Caledonian girl on his, being photographed in St James's Square.

The television and radio reporters were all over us, cameras and microphones being thrust in all directions. It was at a quieter moment, inside the BA offices with some of the Fleet Street press that King, asked about the future of BCAL, said that he intended to 'cherish the best of BCAL' and that we would retain our own identity.

And what, the press said, was the plan for Adam Thomson? I was not sure what I wanted to do, but there was the general idea from the BA side that I would stay to be chairman of the merged company at Gatwick and this is what the journalists were told.

# 91

Lunch on 25 August 1987 was served at a table in my office by Margaret Trett and our seventh floor kitchen supervisor, Edith Barry. I had a single guest, one Dr Haldor Topsoe, chairman of Scandinavian Airlines Systems, SAS. He had contacted me by telephone the previous day to ask if a meeting could be arranged to discuss the possibility of some form of co-operation between his airline and ours. He wanted to meet the following day, no later. Topsoe had timed his call perfectly and had clearly been watching events in Britain extremely closely.

Following the agreement for the merger between BA and BCAL – in reality it was a takeover – the proposition had gone, as a matter of course, to Sir Gordon Borrie, director of the Office of Fair Trading. It was up to Borrie to recommend, not to our own Secretary of State, Paul Channon, but to the Secretary of State for Trade and Industry, Lord Young, whether the deal should be referred to the Monopolies and Mergers Commission.

A referral, if not disastrous, would be extremely unhelpful. These affairs usually took many months to complete and during that time the effect of uncertainty over the future of BCAL could do untold damage to our business, to say nothing of the morale of staff. Equally, Colin Marshall at BA did not want a protracted wrangle. He wanted the deal completed quickly and the merger effected as soon as it could be. We therefore set up a lobbying programme among MPs and Ministers.

Marshall and I made joint presentations to MPs, the main plank of our case being that against the threat of competition from the US mega carriers, Britain required one strong overseas airline and that could only be achieved by merging BA and BCAL together. I had to turn our previous arguments on their head by affirming that the joint BA-BCAL would not be a monopoly and adopting the BA stance that between us we fought competition from more than 100 foreign airlines every day of our commercial lives and therefore it was better to join forces in a way which was good for the British airline industry, good for the staffs of the companies and good for the consumer.

But at no time did I feel that I was betraying our previous principles. Rather, we had been betrayed in 1984 by political expediency. In any event, I had told MPs quite firmly in 1984 that if the Government was not prepared to implement the CAA report and was not prepared to let us transfer to Heathrow, then their only possible option was to create one giant airline for Britain. Well, they had chosen which option they wanted and here it was.

Nevertheless, David Young saw fit to take the cautious path and ordered the matter to be referred to the Monopolies and Mergers Commission, under its chairman, Sir Godfray LeQuesne, a lawyer originally from the Channel Islands. The referral had the effect of making the BA bid null and void. The game was halted. If the bid was approved by LeQuesne and his panel, a fresh deal would have to be negotiated; and if he turned it down, we were on our own. Young, however, in an acknowledgement of the problems caused by months of uncertainty, ordered that the inquiry should be a 'quickie' affair and be completed in three months.

We had the option of withdrawing from the deal there and then, by refusing to enter into an inquiry. But at a board meeting at Caledonian House on 8 August, two days after David Young's announcement, we agreed unanimously to proceed, swayed by the three-month deadline. An open-ended enquiry would have left BCAL in an uncertain period for too long and it is unlikely that we would have accepted the usual unrestricted arrangement.

Alastair Pugh took responsibility for coordination of the preparation of the BCAL submission to the MMC. Teams of managers, secretaries and the internal print room worked long into the night, day after day, to complete the submission which came in two separate sections. We were totally frank in the confidential report. We told Sir Godfray that BCAL's financial position was now both serious and urgent, due to the collapse of important markets and the disadvantage of being based at Gatwick. Only a merger with BA offered the immediate and tangible prospect of preserving the future of BCAL's business in substantially its present form, while at the same time strengthening BA's ability to compete with major foreign carriers. Of course, there were many who took advantage of the MMC referral to fight against the planned merger, most notably the other independent airlines. The submission to the MMC was handed in on 21 August and, three days later, I was in talks with the chairman of SAS.

Topsoe said that the company was interested in a deal with BCAL if the MMC result went against the BA deal. He envisaged share participation from SAS but acknowledged that more than 24 per cent might be difficult to achieve. But, he confided, British – particularly Scottish – associates might form part of the deal.

I had to advise him that BA was our favoured partner. However, if the deal were to fall through, then a number of US and European airlines had already approached us regarding possible areas of cooperation and investment. I would be pleased to add SAS to the list. I thought to myself that my earlier thinking about SAS as a possible partner had indicated little synergy between us. However, if Dr Topsoe were to come back with a reconfirmation of his interest, we should look into the matter further. I asked Alastair Pugh to take on the SAS project, in consultation with David Coltman and John Prothero-Thomas.

Three months after the lunch meeting with Haldor Topsoe at Gatwick, I was back in the offices of Goldman Sachs, undertaking a negotiation for the sale, or partial sale, of BCAL. This time, instead of facing the negotiating team from Lazards, our financial advisers were talking with the Morgan Guaranty Company, merchant bank to SAS. It was 9 December 1987.

Sir Godfray LeQuesne had presented his report to David Young. His commission panel had approved the BA-BCAL merger, but there were concessions made by BA, without our knowledge, to get the deal through. Colin Marshall had thrown in some carrots of competition, in the form of an offer to relinquish the Gatwick-based domestic routes and for these to be given to other independent airlines. The MMC's findings were made public early in November and British Airways confirmed that, within three weeks, they would resume negotiations with us. In the meanwhile, my early discussion with Haldor Topsoe had flowed into a full scale review of the possibilities for a cooperation deal. The chief executive of SAS is

Jan Carlzon, a young and charismatic leader who had turned SAS into an envied airline. He had assigned his deputy to work with us, an elegant Norwegian with immense experience in aviation, Helge Linberg. Alastair Pugh and Linberg had been locked in talks for several weeks and the prospects for a positive conclusion looked good.

We had made no secret of the fact that we were in contact with other interested parties throughout the period of the MMC inquiry, although we did not name SAS. I am certain that BA and Lazards did not believe a word of this and felt that they had BCAL where they wanted it: in the palm of their hand. Notwithstanding the fact that the stock market crash a short while earlier had decreased the value of the BA shares, I am sure it was BA's confidence in believing that we had nowhere else to go that prompted their next offer for BCAL, at a price vastly reduced from the July offer. Their bid went out to our shareholders on 20 November with a cash offer of £5.75 for each ordinary share. It valued us at £147 million, compared with the £237 million of four months earlier.

My own feelings were very clear. In no way would we place BCAL up for grabs at such a ridiculous price. We had drifted apart from British Airways and those photographs of John King and myself back in the summer now looked decidedly contrived. They were clearly seeking a bargain basement price for our airline and I now regarded their bid as hostile. I was supported in my view by Larry Tindale of 3is and the other board members, although a formal board meeting was not due immediately. Nevertheless, Goldman Sachs were requested to write to shareholders to tell them that, in the meantime, they should take no action on the BA offer.

All of us were now on the more familiar ground of opposing the old enemy and I sensed within the airline, at all levels, that a renewed sense of commitment had replaced the air of resignation which had descended after the news of the deal with British Airways. The staff must have been affected at the thought of seeing all they had worked to achieve over the years – the aircraft fleet, the route network, styles and standards which set the pace for other airlines, including the national carrier, and sheer independent pride – being swallowed up by British Airways, despite John King's promise to 'cherish the best' of BCAL.

Some journalists had articulated thoughts that many employees harboured but did not express openly, when they wrote back in July that Sir Adam had 'thrown in the towel'. Yet, only a few months later, we all had the chance to be ourselves again after the derisory new offer from BA. John King's reasoning for his lower offer might have been plausible for his shareholders and staff. It certainly was not for mine. The Stock Market crash and BA's reduced share price was not our problem. The view that I expressed publicly was that the deal focused squarely on the value of BCAL to BA and nothing had changed in our affairs to diminish that from £237 million to £147 million.

For the press, the events at BCAL had moved from a sensational new story in July into a long-running saga of high drama through the autumn and winter. The media, in fact, were for us another form of negotiating table and our campaign was designed to flesh out the very bare facts that we were allowed to place on the record under the terms of Stock Exchange rules, laid down in what is known as the 'Yellow Book' by the Takeover Panel.

We attracted our own press corps, either financial writers or aviation correspondents, or in some cases, both. The telephone traffic between Caledonian House or Pall Mall and the press was non-stop, as was the to-ing and fro-ing between our headquarters and the offices, restaurants and pubs of Fleet Street. At one stage, Tony Cocklin and I would travel around in the Daimler with three mobile telephones in action.

Our key objective in November was solely to fight against the BA offer and get the price up. We let loose, unattributably, a target price of £200 million plus. In August, during the MMC referral period, we had put out figures to show the airline was buoyant – North Atlantic traffic up 25 per cent, European business up 18 per cent, long-haul sales up 32 per cent and 655,000 forward bookings held in the reservations computer. The statistics, all accurate, were designed to hold the business together during a time of confusion and uncertainty.

Now, we continued to press the figures home. They were given more impetus by the fact that we let it be known that, in the financial year which ended on 31 October, the BCAL group would show a profit.

The uncertainty caused by the MMC inquiry was heightened

even further by the emergence of commercial vultures in the form of our fellow independent airlines. They wanted to dismember the body of British Caledonian before it died. A number of independents had already got together to form a lobby against the merger with British Airways, fearing that the end of BCAL as a separate and autonomous carrier would also herald their own demise as the combined airline threw its considerable weight around in the market place, closing out opportunity for others. A number of them, Virgin, Air UK, and Loganair, moved to place bids with the CAA to take over those bits and pieces of BCAL's route network they thought might be useful to themselves. Harry Goodman's ILG company, owners of Air Europe, announced that they intended to make a bid to buy the BCAL short-haul European network for they continued to harbour aspirations to create the 'Airline for Europe' we had plotted together to create a year previously.

The independents need not have worried unduly. As it happened a deal between Lord King and Godfray LeQuesne opened up fresh opportunity for the other airlines. The British Airways/British Caledonian merger was cleared by the MMC on the proviso that a number of conditions were met. The offer put up by BA and accepted by the commission was that within a month of acquiring a controlling interest in our company, BA would return to the CAA all of the BCAL licences to operate domestic routes and the licences to serve Paris, Brussels, Nice, Athens, Copenhagen, Hamburg, Oslo, Rome, Stuttgart and Stockholm. The last seven of these licences had not yet been implemented by us.

BA also agreed to withdraw the BCAL appeals against the recent CAA grant of eight European licences, most duplicating our network, to Air Europe. In addition they agreed to give up a minimum of 5000 aircraft 'slots' (aircraft departure and arrival times) at Gatwick.

To live up to John King's promise in July, BA said that it would merge the charter activities of its own British Airtours with the very small number of charters operated by BCAL and run these activities under the BCAL name. In their submission to the MMC, BA said that they expected these concessions to cause 2000 redundancies.

The shape of the deal I had amicably, if reluctantly, agreed with John King in the sunny days of July, had changed significantly from the one that emerged in the chill and gloom of November.

It was this, as much as anything, which prompted us to seek new partners, so that our business could remain intact and the jobs of as many of our staff as possible remain secure.

I had organised contingency plans to carry on our own if a suitable deal with British Airways became impossible or a new partner remained elusive. As in 1974, the file was labelled 'S-plan' 'S' for survival. It would involve cut backs in non-economic activities and extensive cost-cutting. Its success would hinge on the continued support of our majority shareholders, 3is, represented by the affable Larry Tindale.

The business for the future would involve only airline activities as we had pursued relentlessly a policy of selling off group companies in order to turn assets into additional profit and capital. On the last day of the financial year, 31 October, the hotel chain which earlier had taken the name of the flagship property to become Copthorne Hotels Ltd was sold to the Aer Lingus company, London Tara Hotel Ltd. All that remained, aside from the 50 per cent stake in Cal Air, was BCAL Helicopters, struggling and loss-making in the turbulent economic waters of the North Sea. After talks with a number of helicopter companies, our concern was sold on 27 November to United Helicopters, part of the group owned by Alan Bristow, the managing director of British United Airways at the time we took that airline over to form BCAL. Sadly, I watched Trevor Boud's pet helicopter project and the hotel group in which I had taken great personal interest, go the way of the tour and travel firms and Caledonian Airmotive, out of the group and into the unknown arms of new owners.

On the main front, talks with SAS were stepping up into top gear. Helge Lindberg and a small team were now establishing in London, at the Portman Hotel. The initial four main players in the talks between BCAL and SAS were Lindberg, Alastair Pugh, John Thornton of Goldman Sachs and Fred Vinton, the jocular UK head of Morgan Guaranty, SAS's American bankers.

The outline deal proposed would involve our existing shareholders retaining 40 per cent of the equity of BCAL. SAS would put up an equivalent 40 per cent. The remaining 20 per cent would come from new shareholders. Presentations on the plan had been made by Lindberg and Vinton to a range of institutional investors such as Standard Life, Prudential and Legal and General.

The attraction to SAS of an investment in BCAL was evident. The prime long-term strategy of its president, Jan Carlzon, was to achieve a series of airline mergers around the world to create what he called a 'constellation' of airlines – a global carrier. SAS was already in discussion with Belgium's Sabena, had renewed its links with Thai International and was talking with Qantas of Australia. It was close to achieving financial links with a US airline and a subsequent agreement was reached with the Texas Air Corporation, the parent company of Continental Airlines.

At a board meeting at Caledonian House on 17 November we hammered out the pros and cons of the deal with SAS. BCAL, we agreed, would have an airline partner committed to a strategy of developing a multi-national airline. BCAL would retain its route network, name and identity and our products and style would move closer to those of SAS. Instead of losing 2000 jobs from the combined BA/BCAL, employment in the UK would be increased as a result of the proposal that SAS would move its DC-10 maintenance to Gatwick from Switzerland, where it was currently undertaken by Swissair. The benefits of traffic and revenue feed from the SAS networks to BCAL and vice-versa were calculated to be worth £45 million and the deal itself would give BCAL an equity injection of £50 million. Politically, many of the complaints about monopolisation and reduction of competition snapping around the edges of the BA/BCAL merger would be answered. We went further and proposed that other independents could be offered participation in the new combine. We though particularly of the Gatwick-based scheduled service division of Dan Air. So far as running BCAL was concerned, it would be autonomous but with three SAS nominated directors on its board.

Around the table, Masefield, Tindale, Bebchick, Pugh, Coltman, Marshall Gibson, Beety and I agreed. The BCAL/SAS proposal was attractive because it enabled, potentially, BCAL to continue as an airline, rather than being absorbed or dismembered as it would be with a successful BA offer. While price negotiations might in the end determine whether we chose BA or SAS, there appeared enough in the SAS deal at present to merit full consideration being given to it. SAS was undoubtedly completely serious and determined in its pursuit of BCAL as a partner.

While we were delighted to have found a viable alternative to the British Airways offer we had not overlooked the one major obstacle. In our attempts to get the SAS deal off the ground we would be going straight back to square one and to the very point of formation of the original Caledonian Airways. This involved the question of foreign participation in a British airline and the CAA's interpretation of whether or not a licensed airline was substantially British-owned.

The other possible obstacle was a referral of the SAS deal to the MMC. Although the route networks of BCAL and SAS barely overlapped and the question of diminishing competition hardly arose, it was a possibility. In any event, the proposed deal would have to go before Sir Gordon Borrie at the Office of Fair Trading. We could also be sure that the British Airways lobby would direct every piece of propaganda it could conceive at the competing offer.

Our strategy to harden up the story of an alternative offer to BA took shape shortly after the approval of the BA bid, with its concessions, by the MMC. I agreed with the proposal that I should offer myself for an interview on the Sunday afternoon *Business Programme* on Channel Four. In the programme's Docklands studio, after a Sunday lunch of a pint of bitter and a sandwich in an East London pub, I appeared with presenter John Plender. As a polished professional, Plender obviously tried to draw out of me much more than I was prepared to say, but I did confirm we were talking seriously with others.

'But what has happened over the last few weeks is that the European airlines we have been negotiating with seriously have come forward with more practical propositions and the time scale looks as if it has been shortened,' I told Plender, the viewing business community and those in British Airways who were unquestionably watching.

SAS was specifically identified in the press in mid-November, before the second bid by British Airways was made on 20 November. How the news had not leaked earlier was a mystery as the 'Scandihoovians' as Helge Lindberg referred to his team, and their bankers sought informal and confidential information and guidance from officials at the Office of Fair Trading, the Department of Transport and the Civil Aviation Authority. The background work continued with increased guided speculation in

547

the press up to 23 November, the day of our own board meeting at which we formally took the decision to recommend shareholders against the new BA bid. The same day, newspapers carried the story that SAS was poised to make a bid that would value BCAL at up to £200 million and that it was being advised by Morgan Guaranty and the stockbrokers, Cazenove. The following day, the *Financial Times* attributed the news to 'whispers in the market'.

The whisper turned to a shout later on 24 November, when at last SAS came out in the open, with the issue of a statement authorised by Jan Carlzon. It read:

SAS is evaluating the feasibility of making a partial offer to the shareholders of British Caledonian and of entering into a close co-operation to establish a competitive worldwide traffic system.

It is still too early to indicate if and when a possible offer could be made, or to outline how it would be formulated.

SAS's interest in British Caledonian reflects the strategy pursued by the Scandinavian carrier to create a constellation of medium-sized European airlines to provide efficient intercontinental transportation in competition with Asian and American mega carriers.

# 92

Bob McCrindle was nervous. Nicholas Soames was angry. The reactions of the two MPs, the former our own Parliamentary consultant, the latter our Gatwick constituency Member came as we began to mount a political campaign, alongside the PR programme, to gain understanding and support for the proposed link with SAS.

The first base of our proposition was that the SAS move to make a partial offer should be allowed to come to fruition and go forward to shareholders so that they could study a viable alternative to the British Airways offer and make an informed choice.

Initial rumblings of excitement among the BCAL staff at the prospect of the SAS deal had accelerated to a wave of overwhelming support, especially from the industrial workers, the engineering and maintenance people. Their feelings were articulated by two union representatives, Wally Harding and Mick Alleway, who put out of statement in the name of BCAL Joint Shop Stewards Committee:

> Many BCAL staff would wish to see, if at all possible and viable, the very special British Caledonian image and innovative style remain. For these and other reasons, the staff of BCAL believe that any alternative proposal that could allow us to continue functioning as the alternative independent airline, offering a secure future, should, subject to present legislation, not only be fully analysed, but judged on its merits without undue political, or any other, interference which could lead to suppression of fair opportunity. If one of these alternatives should happen to be a partial shareholding by a foreign interest, we must remember that British Airways has a significant foreign investment and

further, almost all so-called British carriers are to a greater or lesser extent supported by overseas finance. Above all, we believe that staff and shareholders have the right to consider any serious alternative to the BA offer and that Members of Parliament representing the Gatwick area constituencies should support us in that view.

On the day of the SAS announcement of its intention to make a partial offer, David Coltman and David Richardson, our government affairs manager, met Soames to brief him on developments. Coltman reported to me that Soames was 'very angry' with us. We had written to and lobbied almost everybody in the Houses of Parliament to gain support for the merger with British Airways, now we decided to do something else. Coltman explained to Soames how different the original BA merger plan was from the one which now existed. He showed him some detail of the SAS plan. Soames was apparently more settled towards the end of the meeting, but insisted that he would not support one plan against the other and he was not going to be pushed into supporting the SAS proposal.

After a meeting with McCrindle the same day, Richardson reported the MP's anxieties. Bob thought that the massive Parliamentary campaign against it might not be beatable. He foresaw John King making an emotional argument based on nationalistic, anti-European feeling. These would be simple to get across, against our own complex explanations in favour of the SAS deal.

Even if clearance for the investment was given by the Office of Fair Trading and the CAA, McCrindle felt that the issue would still get into Parliament, because 'people' would make sure it would. He pointed out that the lowest point of Margaret Thatcher's reign occurred during the earlier Westland Helicopters and Land Rover affairs, involving issues of foreign ownership. They could, he said, have been because British interest appeared to be being sold to foreigners. The Westland affair, of course, had gone so far as to force the resignation of my friend, Michael Heseltine.

In fact, we had foreseen the probability that artificial, jingoistic, political barriers might be erected against the SAS investment and undertook some preventative work. Jan Carlzon had slipped quietly into London to link up with Helge Lindberg and Fred Vinton and for liaison with me. Carlzon was young, in his early forties, and dynamic. He had taken control of a rather staid airline at SAS and injected that attitude of motivation, competition and customer care which Americans sum up in a neat phrase as 'can do'. Colin Marshall had been using similar techniques to lift British Airways out of the doldrums, to the extent of using the same Scandinavian staff training company as SAS had done. Despite his energy and competitive spirit, Carlzon, blond and immaculately groomed, looked more like an actor than the tough boss of an international airline. His manner was quiet and courteous, not at all aggressive or overpowering. It went down well with the two members of the No 10 Policy Unit, Margaret Thatcher's political advisers, whom we met on 23 November for lunch in a private corner of Locket's Restaurant, an eating place in Westminster favoured by politicians and senior civil servants.

Professor Brian Griffiths, the Policy Unit's head, and his colleague, John Wybrew, listened carefully as Carlzon and I outlined the details of the SAS proposal to invest in BCAL. Their reaction was one of support, on the grounds of competition. Wybrew wanted to know what clearances would be necessary and, after being briefed, gave the view that they could not see a problem with the OFT, as there were no major competitive issues, but realised there could be problems with the CAA over foreign ownership. Wybrew told us they were grateful for the briefing, so as to be well prepared in case the issue should come up in the House of Commons during Prime Minister's Question Time.

Similarly, we had prepared the ground with the Foreign and Commonwealth Office. At a meeting with FCO official, Roger Beetham, David Richardson was told that there was some negative feeling around in the Department of Transport towards the SAS deal, especially among people who felt that future bilateral air service negotiations with foreign governments could be more difficult. However, Richardson was told that the Foreign Office believed that this was insufficient to create a policy objection. Beetham said that he would be prepared to say that the current view at the Foreign Office was that there were no foreign policy objections to the proposal. He went further to say that the prospect of a European tie up was attractive and he would anticipate difficulties with the governments of Denmark, Sweden and Norway if Britain appeared

551

to block the proposals on the grounds of the new investor in BCAL being foreign.

As a company under offer, through the revised British Airways bid, we were constrained by the City takeover code in the amount and extent of information we could release publicly. PR and lobbying activities had to be, of necessity, covert and guided at all times by John Thornton and Paul Deighton of Goldman Sachs, our financial advisers.

Nevertheless, the need to get across the philosophy and practicality of the proposed SAS deal prompted the preparation and publication of a booklet. It was headed 'World Class Enterprise for Britain', and sub-titled 'British Caledonian . . . with SAS'. We argued that the purpose of the plan was to enable the smaller but efficient quality carrier to compete and prosper in a mega carrier world, by using new thinking to loosen air transport's historic nationalistic bonds.

The BCAL/SAS link would, we said, preserve intact and enhance the long-term policy of every government since 1969 to have a strong second force as the spearhead of a multi-airline industry and would allow the UK to retain two airlines of world class. Further, the UK would be able to take a strategic initiative in a new phase of air transport development, the supra-national airline.

The two networks would be linked through Gatwick, so putting muscular flesh on to the bones of the Government's policy for the development of the airport as a major scheduled service hub, alongside the crowded Heathrow. BCAL and SAS would combine resources in marketing, computerised reservations systems, engineering and maitenance, purchasing, aircraft catering and in the running of overseas stations where both airlines served the same point. Emotively, we said the BCAL brand of service, identity and route network would be retained – and 'The Caledonian girls live on!'

As in 1961, we had wrestled with the old Air Transport Licensing Board on the ownership question of Caledonian, so in 1987, we struggled to get clearance for a restructured BCAL from its successor, the CAA. Ray Colegate remained in office as the fulltime regulator, but Sir John Dent – he was knighted, to my great pleasure, in 1986 – had retired to be replaced by one Christopher Tugendhat, a former Member of Parliament and vice president of the EEC.

Discussions with the CAA were tortuous. There is no precise definition of what constitutes substantial British ownership within the Civil Aviation Act and the CAA, like the ATLB before it, would give no guidance. All Tugendhat and Colegate could do was to look at a proposal and say whether it was acceptable within the terms of section 66 of the Act, or not. SAS and ourselves, notably Alastair Pugh and Helge Lindberg, who were now closeted every day and most nights on the project, were trying to find our way in the dark. Some illumination was provided by specialist lawyers hired to give opinions on the interpretation of the Act, but it was a mere glimmer. The situation was well know to us, but to Helge Lindberg it was a source of acute frustration. 'We don't know what they want and they won't tell us. What are we supposed to do?' he exclaimed in an uncharacteristic burst of anger at one meeting in Fred Vinton's office.

The first, key meeting with the CAA, on 24 November, was disappointing. During the discussion, it was accepted that the original proposal for three SAS directors to look after its investment in BCAL would have to be dropped, in order to meet the requirement for 'British control'. If the CAA was not satisfied with any proposal, the process was to refer the matter to the Secretary of State for Transport. We could not, under any circumstances, allow the decision to rest with Paul Channon, sensing from all we had heard that he would wield a political knife and kill the project.

I wrote back to Tugendhat on the revisions we had made, confirming that SAS's voting rights would not increase even though the would make an offer to acquire between 50 and 60 per cent of our existing ordinary shares. I confirmed that all of the BCAL directors, including the chairman and managing director, would be British with the exception of one non-executive director from SAS. I said that, under these circumstances, the question of a referral to Channon should not arise.

Tugendhat's reply was depressing. He could not, he said, give me confirmation of that. I had argued with Channon over the foreign ownership and funding of other British airlines, like Monarch with its Swiss involvement, Britannia with Canadian interest, Air Europe with New Zealand investment through its parent company ILG, and Air UK which was 15 per cent owned by the Dutch airline, KLM. Especially, there was British Airways with 18 per cent of its shares sold by the Government itself to foreign investors, with plans to increase overseas shareholdings to 25 per cent. There was no moving of the Secretary of State.

I was now, metaphorically, sitting in a game of poker which had become dangerous, with very high stakes. The stake on the table was BCAL, its assets, shareholders' funds and the jobs of around 7000 employees. I did not know how well I might be able to build my hand, but Paul Channon had clearly demonstrated the strength in his cards.

The only offer we had on the table for BCAL was the miserly revised bid from John King, risen in value to £156 million as the BA share price improved. Channon actually stated, 'I must advise you that if this case comes before me I shall be minded to reject it.' It looked as though we were in a cul-de-sac.

BBC Radio 2's morning *Jimmy Young Programme* offers easy music and light-hearted banter, as a rule. On the morning of 3 December, however, its first interviewee was none other than Norman Tebbit. He was discussing the future of British air transport, not in the Commons chamber or before a select committee, but with the show's eponymous presenter, a pop singer turned disc jockey, and his audience of housewifes and motorway drivers. Tebbit's presence in the studios of Broadcasting House was to wind up a campaign against the SAS deal into a state of near hysteria. The fact was that BA had been nationalised intact, back in February. A few months later, it was on the brink of sweeping up the main competitive thorn in its side, BCAL. Events had now turned, and BA and the Government, which had sold shares to private investors, saw the legitimate prospect of an even stronger competitor emerging in its home market and around the world in the form of a BCAL/SAS combine. British Airways had improved considerably, after more than £800 million of taxpayers' money had been injected to make it fit for sale, but it was not good enough to be totally confident at winning hands down against this new and different choice for the consumer.

That same morning, David Young at the Department of Trade and Industry dropped a bombshell on BA when he released his verdict on the BCAL/SAS merger proposal, following the report from Sir Gordon Borrie at the Office of Fair Trading. So far as Young was concerned, it could go ahead. He would not, he decided,

554

refer the proposal to the Monopolies and Mergers Commission – it caused no competition or other public interest issues which merited an investigation. 'In reaching his final decision not to refer,' read the official communique, 'he [Lord Young] took into account all relevant factors, including the powers available to the Secretary of State for Transport to decide whether to direct the revocation of licences of an airline in the circumstances described in the Civil Aviation Act.'

SAS, 3is and I jumped for joy, each of us issuing press statements. 'This is an important first step. At least one important hurdle has been overcome,' said Helge Lindberg. SAS, he added, was looking forward to BCAL as a partner able to go forward into the future as an independent, British-controlled airline flying its own flag.

The 3is statement announced its pleasure at Young's decision: 'This means that the SAS bid can be prepared and that 3is, along with the other BCAL shareholders, will have the legitimate opportunity to consider a serious alternative to the offer from British Airways.'

Coinciding with David Young's statement was a letter from Paul Channon to me covering the meeting the day before. He released the text to the press, broadcasting the fact that he had set his face against us. Channon cited among his reasons possible difficulties with other governments in negotiating rights for a British airline which they could perceive as having some foreign control, and the fact that SAS, unlike British Airways, was state owned. I believed these reasons while technically sound, were based on archaic principles that were far from the reality of the industry as it was then, never mind the furious rate of the development of cross shareholdings that have since taken place. SAS, in fact, was 50 per cent privately-owned, with the other 50 per cent of shares held by the three Scandinavian governments. They operated to the same ownership formula as the Thatcher government had originally envisaged for BA.

Tebbit who, back in 1969 and 1970 had been so supportive in our fight to create BCAL through the combination of Caledonian and BUA, was now set on halting the further evolution of the 'second force'. 'It's a nationalised industry,' said Tebbit, telling Jimmy Young about SAS. 'It's controlled by the foreign governments and they have sitting on the board of their company a representative of their governments, at the moment it's a Danish civil servant. And his job is to make sure that all the goodies get back to them – fair enough, that's what he should be doing. They would nominate a chap onto the BCAL board and his job would obviously be to make sure that the deal was to the benefit of SAS – after all they are not putting money into BCAL out of charity, they're putting it in because they think it would be a good deal for them. And if it's a good deal for them, it's very unlikely to be a good deal for us ... My judgement is that a 40 per cent shareholding in the company and the way that this is rigged up, would amount to control.'

In the course of this interview, Tebbit rewrote the style of international air services negotiations, usually conducted in a serious, academic and gentlemanly fashion. Quoting the hypothetical response of a foreign negotiator to a British official seeking rights for a BCAL with SAS investment, Tebbit said: 'Oi, we've done a deal with the Scandinavians and they've got their share – we're not gonna give 'em another share.'

Nicholas Soames also had joined the Heathrow bandwagon, proclaiming in a guest article in *The Times* that a BCAL/SAS merger might hurt British interests. In a spate of uncharacteristic lyricism, Soames wrote that a SAS bird in the hand for BCAL now might well be a 'cuckoo in Britain's nest in years to come'.

But the most sinister political turn was that, however carefully he had worded his public letter to me, Paul Channon had effectively and purposefully prejudged a case which had not yet been fully considered by the CAA with whom we were still talking.

The Shadow Transport Minister, Peter Snape, was waiting for Channon in the Chamber of the House of Commons later in that eventful day of 3 December. Snape asked for a statement on policy in light of the latest developments in the negotiations between BCAL and SAS. Channon replied coldly that the policy remained as set out in the 1984 Airline Competition Policy White Paper.

Snape, pressing Channon, went on to say, if the question of shareholding in BCAL was the problem, what percentage SAS shareholding he would find acceptable. And what percentage of British Airways shares were sold on foreign stock exchanges at the time the airline was 'unwisely' privatised? 'Will Mr Channon assure the House,' said Snape, 'that any final decision on this matter will be made in the interests of air travellers and those employed in the industry and will not be based on the apparently endless ambition of Lord King or the rambling xenophobia of Norman Tebbit?'

Paul Channon responded by telling Snape that the matter was for the CAA to decide under the airline ownership clauses of the Civil Aviation Act and referring to the fact that the CAA had turned down the original investment proposal. He chose to ignore the fact that terms were altered and could be altering further. 'Again,' he declared, 'I cannot take a final decision about this matter. I can only say what I am minded to do. And I think it is strongly in the public interest that I should say what I would be minded to do.'

Norman Tebbit stepped in with a gratuitous welcome for the way the matter had been handled. 'Equally there will be a wide welcome for the fact that he [Paul Channon] has made it clear that he would not tolerate ownership or control by a foreign airline of a British flag carrier.'

David Steel, the Liberal leader, asked Channon to make it clear that there was a difference between 'control' and a minority stake and to confirm that SAS was not wholly government owned. Channon again deferred his response to the CAA.

In what sounded like a set piece, Nicholas Soames asked Channon to confirm that it would be 'a very serious matter indeed' for British aviation if air service agreements were lost because BCAL was to lose its UK interest. This enabled Channon to ramble on about a hypothetical and highly unlikely situation involving the trading of air service rights between governments.

Tam Dalyell, the Labour MP, articulated the thought that had been on many minds. 'Can we be sure that Mr Channon is also representing the views of Lord Young?' he asked. Channon denied categorically that there was a rift between himself and this counterpart at the Department of Trade and Industry. Young acted under certain powers and Channon acted under the Civil Aviation Act.

We were by now in the midst of a full-blown political and public relations battle of the kind we had been embroiled in many times in the past. For us, it was par for the course of commercial aviation in Britain. But to the SAS men, the scene was unbelievable. They were incredulous at the force of opinion and invective being thrown at us. Especially, they watched in amazement as British Airways, their friendly pool partner for many years, go into hysterical rages against them and their ownership structure, and accusing them of commercial protectionism. Executives even flew to Scandinavia to hold press conferences to denounce SAS in their home countries.

The *Daily Express*, prompted by the pressure of Norman Tebbit, succumbed to joining the anti-SAS campaign, launching a 'Keep Caledonian British' campaign. Their front-page banner promoting a page five story on 4 December, after the publication of Channon's letter, read: 'Maggie puts block on SAS.'

The story itself opened with the hysterically puerile words: 'Mrs Thatcher has decided to repel the Viking invasion of British Caledonian. After weeks of controversy, Ministers moved yesterday to block the proposed deal with SAS on the grounds it would hand a scheduled British airline into control by foreign governments – Norway, Sweden and Denmark.'

There was no doubt about how the *Daily Express* interpreted the intent of Channon's letter as it went on to denigrate Jan Carlzon as SAS's 'glamorous, playboy' president.

The battle was far from one-sided, however. We had some solid support in the Houses of Parliament and in the press.

Two separate Early Day Motions were set down in the House of Commons in support. A leading article in the *Financial Times*, a few days later, stated: 'The SAS-BCAL link appears to offer the twin benefits of fostering competition and strengthening the European airline industry. The Government's reaction to it is depressingly narrow-minded.'

We had, in fact, successfully dispelled the myth perpetrated by Paul Channon and Tebbit that the SAS investment would affect air service relations with foreign governments. Reaction in the USA had been cited. We asked Leonard Bebchick to contact the US Transportation Department for their view and he obtained a statement from the head of its international aviation division assuring us that if the British authorities (the CAA) was happy about the issue of control, then it would not be questioned by the Americans. Officials at the US Embassy in London told the Foreign Office that they had no wish to be dragged into a British domestic issue.

Similarly, we were studying the Channon stance against the background of Europe and the Treaty of Rome and were taking legal advice. We were advised that any attempt to take away BCAL licences in the grounds of an investment from SAS which counted as an EEC airline through its Danish shareholding, was certain to be a breach of the Treaty and therefore illegal.

As the month of December began to creep on towards the Christmas holidays, time was beginning to run out for ourselves and SAS. Talks with the CAA were continuing in an attempt to obtain an indication of the right kind of package. The revised British Airways deal remained on the table, but the first closing date was coming up fast. We had to get the SAS alternative offer out to shareholders before the BA offer closed to keep the BCAL options alive.

The action now centred in the City of London, moving between the offices of Morgan Guaranty, the SAS bankers, and Goldman Sachs, our advisers. Alastair Pugh and Helge Lindberg were working relentlessly on interpretations of the Civil Aviation Act and permutations of structure which might satisfy the inconclusive Section 66 and avoid our plans going on to certain death on the political gallows of Marsham Street.

Although SAS had reduced its voting shares down to 24 per cent, the 40 per cent investment still posed a problem. The importance of 3is in the BCAL story had never been more important than now and in addition to the redoubtable Larry Tindale, we had as 3is chairman, Sir John Cuckney, who had earlier crossed swords with the government over another foreign investment controversy as chairman of Westland.

The problem that the financial experts pondered was how to achieve the recapitalisation of BCAL, but dilute the SAS stake to meet the CAA's requirements. One key aspect of the development was the wholehearted support for the BCAL/SAS proposal from the BCAL workforce and the unions. It was Mark Young of the British Airline Pilots' Association who, in the course of regular consultation, suggested we talk to the trade union bank, Unity Trust. Eventually arrangements were outlined between Unity Trust and Goldman Sachs for the creation of a special Employee Share Ownership Trust, allowing employees to have an additional 7.19 per cent voting stake in the company.

With that in place, in principle, John Cuckney and Larry Tindale conferred to consider the 3is position. Tindale came back with the news that he would raise the limit of his earlier level of shareholding in the BCAL structure. But the key to a new financial package which would get past the CAA was carefully cut in the expert financial mind of John Thornton of Goldman Sachs. Thornton, knew, as we all did, that with the emergence of a single European market with no national protectionism in the 1990s, the ownership rules would be a thing of the past. He therefore hit on the idea of splitting the SAS investment into two parts – one that would provide voting rights immediately and the other maturing in a set number of years' time.

Thornton had invented what we came to call 'the exploding share'. Over long hours, deep into the night, at either the Morgan Guarnaty headquarters or in the Goldman Sachs building, Thornton led the negotiations among bankers, lawyers, stockbrokers, ourselves and SAS to piece together a viable new structure.

A deal began to emerge on 8 December. SAS indicated that it would make an offer to acquire 26.14 per cent of existing BCAL Ordinary Shares at a price of £20.44 each of £110 million in aggregate. If this was accepted by shareholders, the airline would then undergo a capital restructure. It was a complex financial manoeuvre. After the initial SAS purchase of shares, BCAL would call an extraordinary general meeting of shareholders to authorise an increase in capital of £50 million through two means – a rights issue of 'Convertible Participating Cumulative Preference Shares'; and a rights issue of 'Convertible Ordinary Shares.'

The rights issue of the cumulative preference shares would raise about £50 million and be underwritten by the stockbrokers Cazenove & Co., with UK institutional investors and an Employee Trust. The total would represent about 20 per cent of the voting rights of the recapitalised company. It was through this rights issue that 3is would increase its investment, to the sum of £1.25 million. SAS would not be a part of it.

The rights issue of convertible ordinary shares was designed to raise about £20 million and would be underwritten by SAS. However, they would represent only 3.5 per cent of the voting rights attached to the issued share capital so long as the UK Civil Aviation Act continued to constrain the level of overseas ownership in British airlines. As and when regulatory circumstances changed – when the single market was formed with the EEC – SAS's 'Convertible A Ordinary' shares would convert into ordinary shares to give

Carlzon's organisation a total of not more than 40 per cent of the expanded voting rights.

Protection would be given to the investors in the first rights issue against dilution on the conversion of the SAS shares to maintain their 20 per cent of the expanded voting rights.

It was an extremely clever, but complex, formula. It depended as much on 3is as it did on SAS. Cuckney and Tindale wanted to reduce their shareholding in BCAL, but agreed to stay with the deal until such time as SAS could increase its voting share and they could reduce their stake. It was an offer of immense goodwill and determination on the part of Larry Tindale whose investment in BCAL had, so far, yielded comparatively little.

After the capital reconstructions, BCAL would have 26,904,512 shares of which SAS would hold 23.5 per cent, new investors 19.17 per cent, 3is 23.53 per cent, and existing shareholders 33.8 per cent. After deregulation in Europe, shares would move in a formula which gave 73 Ordinary shares for Convertible Ordinary 'As', 113 Ordinary shares for Convertible Ordinary 'Bs', and one Convertible Ordinary 'B' for one Preferential share. This would create a total shareholding of 38,002,624 shares, of which SAS would hold 40 per cent, the new investors 19.17 per cent, 3is 16.9 per cent, and existing shareholders 23.93 per cent.

A further part of the structure was that Larry Tindale would be appointed deputy chairman to emphasise the British control of the airline. Only Jan Carlzon from SAS would be invited to join the board, as a non-executive director.

The amount of work which went into the creation of this reconstruction was staggering, as was the number of individuals and organisations involved. Details were refined during the day of 9 December and the work was carried on in Goldman Sachs' Fetter Lane offices. The comings and goings of financiers, investors, lawyers and stockbrokers was under the tight scrutiny of Goldman's security guards. I based myself in the first floor board room of the Fetter Lane building, as Thornton, Vinton, their teams and the lawyers painstakingly negotiated to bring the restructure into the reality of an offer.

Jan Carlzon had returned to London, quietly installing himself in a suite at the Portman Hotel, in Portman Square, several miles west of Fetter Lane from where Helge Lindberg kept him informed of progress. Carlzon did not want to attract any publicity and controversy and had organised his reservation under an assumed name. To my knowledge, he did not leave the hotel, but remained in the suite conducting business by telephone with his base in Stockholm and ordering meals from the hotel's room service menu.

Anticipating that the deal could come about at any time, we had planned a joint press conference and booked a room at the Waldorf Hotel in the Aldwych for three o'clock. Journalists were telephoned to be advised that there could be an announcement and to be prepared to come to meet us at the Waldorf at short notice. Three o'clock came and went with still no firm agreement emerging. But the signs that were relayed from time to time to myself and Larry Tindale in the Goldman's board room were positive. Leonard Bebchick who had, to his annoyance, been stuck in Washington at the time of the agreement with British Airways in the summer, had flown to London and joined me at Goldmans. It was now just a matter of waiting and waiting until the financial and legal 'Is' had been dotted and 'Ts' crossed on the deal.

At around seven o'clock I was told by an emissary from the room in which Thornton was working that it could be another hour or so before the deal was agreed and written up. I had been in the room for most of the day and felt in need of a breath of fresh air. I turned to Bebchick. 'I'm going out for a beer – coming?' After a moment of hesitation, Bebchick grabbed his raincoat and walked with me towards the door.

The quiet, unreal atmosphere of the Goldman's inner sanctum gave way to the noise of buses and taxis in Fetter Lane. The pavement was slippery from a dismal winter drizzle that was falling as Bebchick and I walked past a bus-stop, crowded with a queue of homegoing office workers. The illuminated sign of a pub became apparent a few yards along, on the opposite side of the road. The White Hart, it read, shining its faint light into the dismal street by the side of the building containing Robert Maxwell's Mirror Group empire.

We pushed our way into the pub, alive with a full crowd of people enjoying after-work drinks. There were groups of women and loudly-laughing men, probably *Mirror* journalists. Bebchick and I pushed through to a back bar, quieter than the other, to order a glass of bitter each. As we relaxed we talked about our personal lives, he telling me about his wife, Gabriella, and the children back in Washington; and me giving him the latest news of Dawn and the two boys, Scott and Anthony. He asked about the new boat and told me about the new stereo system he had constructed in the basement of his home in Maryland. There were photograhs on the wall – news pictures of sportsmen and celebrities, obviously from the *Mirror*'s picture desk. We studied them, and I told Bebchick who most of the British personalities were. I thought of the irony of me being here, in this ordinary pub at a time when I had found myself catapulted into the biggest business news story of the year and surrounded by newspaper people.

The greater irony of the situation came when Bebchick and I had dodged taxis across the rain-sodden street to rejoin those in the board room at Goldman's. After explaining where we had been, Tony Cocklin, returned from a regular spell of updating the press by telephone, told me the story of the pub. It was, he said, the *Mirror*'s 'office' pub and was known universally, not by the name on the sign, but as 'The Stab in the Back'. When I looked at him quizzically, he explained that in the volatile newspaper business, you were as likely as not to find your job gone after an absence in the pub.

The break came at about nine o'clock. The deal was agreed. From the silent tediousness of waiting, the Goldman's offices erupted into a fury of action. The negotiating teams came out of their conference rooms into the main boardroom. Signatures were required on the series of documents laid before us and a press release had to be written and produced.

Helge Lindberg telephoned Jan Carlzon to leave the hotel and come to Fetter Lane. Cocklin telephoned the press – an impromptu press conference would be set up in the lobby area.

The headline on the news release read, 'Recapitalisation for British Caledonian – SAS to Make Minority Investment.' Details of the offer were spelt out: 'British Caledonian Group and its financial advisers, Goldman Sachs International Corp., announce arrangements for a capital reconstructure, involving a minority investment by SAS and the injection of new capital from UK institutional investors and a BCAL Employee Trust.'

We had conducted a board meeting around the Goldman table

to accept the offer and to recommend to shareholders that we unanimously recommended them to accept the SAS partial offer. In the letter I had prepared for shareholders and which would go out the following day, I wrote: 'The SAS offer is more attractive financially. The SAS offer is £110 million in cash for 26.14 per cent of your holding. By comparison, British Airways' cash alternative is £119 million for 100 per cent of your holding and their share offer values BCAL at £148 million.'

I said that the SAS partial offer would be posted to shareholders shortly and should be completed by the end of January, 1988. I had advised shareholders, however, to delay their acceptance of the SAS offer until SAS had indicated that it was satisfied or waived the condition of its offer that the CAA gave assurance that BCAL's licences would not be affected by the proposed investment.

By the time Carlzon appeared at Goldman's and was ushered into the room in which I was waiting, the place was mayhem with telephones ringing non-stop and calls being put out, mainly dealing with the press. He was wearing a raincoat, and as he came into the room and walked towards me he pulled from each of the inside pockets a bottle of champagne.

News of the deal caught the tail end of that night's television news bulletins. The coverage showed Carlzon and myself together, shaking hands, toasting our deal with his champagne. It was repeated in a number of the following morning's newspapers and as I scanned the press in the Pall Mall office I thought of the immense distance, philosphically, we had come from those other pictures of myself with John King, back in the summer.

The photograph with Carlzon, however, represented a real celebration – we were a minute distance away from succeeding in keeping BCAL intact and competing under its own momentum.

# 93

On the day that deal was momentously struck with SAS, Helge Lindberg and I, together with John Thornton, had taken the new structure around to Ray Colegate at the CAA. He had made no judgement at the time, simply asking for some more information on a couple of points. He wanted, chiefly, to be assured that the reduced SAS shareholding was unconditional.

Over at British Airways and at their financial adviser, Lazard Brothers, our actions had been monitored as closely as it was possible. They took a full twenty-four hours to make any kind of formal response. It came on 10 December, with the announcement that they were planning to up their offer to buy BCAL to a cash deal of £200 million. Details would be announced later.

At ten o'clock in the morning of Friday, 11 December 1987, the entire BCAL board gathered once again in Fetter Lane to convene a formal meeting, to consider the BA intended new offer. We called John Thornton in to outline the scene for us. He said we were now in a straightforward auction and that BA's actions had a clear implication that they assumed that the CAA would clear the partial offer.

The board confirmed its preference for the SAS deal, but Larry Tindale warned that 3is needed to take a commercial, dispassionate view of the situation. Larry emphasised the urgent requirement for us to produce audited accounts, as assessment of the ongoing value of the airline and the adequacy of the capital planned to be injected. 3is, he said, would not consider putting in any further cash.

Alastair Pugh had left the room to telephone Ray Colegate to see where they were with their crucial views. He returned saying that the CAA response was anticipated that same afternoon and that whatever they had to say, they would make public. We agreed that the latest day for announcing our decision on which direction we would move towards would have to be after Christmas, on 29 December.

A telephone call in the afternoon told Alastair Pugh that Colegate's letter of response was awaiting collection. It must have been the most eagerly-awaited document in London that day. It eventually arrived, to be torn from its envelope. It was a long, two-page document. After recapitulating the question we had asked and the considerations he had taken into account, Colegate gave us his answer in a sentence buried in the middle of page two. 'Nonetheless,' he wrote, 'on the information now before us, we have formed the tentative view that we could not, under Section 66 of the Act, refer BCAL to the Secretary of State on the grounds that ownership or control, on the date of implementation of this proposal, passed into the hands of foreign nationals.' The 'exploding share' scheme had worked. The deal with SAS was complete and safe.

John King and Colin Marshall were clearly beside themselves with anger and frustration. No doubt Paul Channon and Norman Tebbit felt similar. For BA, the manoeuvres with SAS had cost them a potential £81 million more than they believed they could get away with at the end of November.

'A move of absolute petulance,' was how I described the next move against us by BA. What they did on 11 December, the day of the CAA announcement, was to file an application to revoke every single one of BCAL's route licences. I saw this as no more than a spoiling tactic, designed to create uncertainty and, indeed, to question the CAA's own considered judgement in the matter of BCAL and SAS, though Colin Marshall said that he wanted the whole matter aired in a public hearing. I did not see any reason for us to be unduly concerned by this latest BA tactic. I told Colegate: 'If, after acceptance of the SAS offer, British Airways wishes to apply for the revocation of BCAL's licences, they can do so at that time. We are wholly confident that they would fail.'

The mood in the private dining room of the St James's Court Hotel, close to Victoria and not far from the Marsham Street office of the Department of Transport, was festive and jolly. It belied the air of uncertainty which still existed over the future of BCAL.

The occasion was a dinner organised a few weeks before Christmas by Alastair Pugh for the teams of SAS, BCAL, Goldman Sachs and

Morgan Guaranty executives who had been involved in the saga. Helge Lindberg, allowing himself the relaxation of a glass of Scotch whisky after many long days and late nights, told everybody he could not wait to get home for Christmas. We all felt the same as we celebrated in an air of mutual congratulation at pulling off a plan which had been always extremely difficult and, at times, had seemed impossible.

If there was one thing that had kept me motivated, it was the response of the staff at BCAL to the prospect of keeping their airline intact through the deal with SAS. They were all good, honest, dedicated people, not looking for the easy way out or a soft living for little effort. That was impossible in the airline business, in any event. They all simply wanted to keep their airline up there flying and competing with the rest and in meetings and conversations with them, I had to accept, humbly, that they trusted me to deliver the airline back to them.

As much as I wanted to do that, there and then, I could not. John King was pushing his £200 million offer as hard as he and his team could. It was posted to shareholders on 18 December, together with the news that they had already acquired a small percentage of share in BCAL, mainly through a deal with Kleinwort Benson, one of our shareholders. It was estimated to be nine per cent and King was reported to have approached John Cuckney at 3is with a view to short-cutting the process. By combining the 3is holding of 41 per cent with the newly acquired British Airways nine per cent, King's thinking was that these could be combined to form a controlling interest and the future could be decided quickly and simply.

Cuckney, however, stayed firm, if, indeed, those reports were absolutely true. But 3is did want to see how far SAS and Morgan Guaranty could go in order to have a deal on the table over which there could be no argument.

The paradox of the situation was that while we were negotiating for sale, partial or otherwise, of the company, the airline had enjoyed its best ever year in passengers carried. Over the twelve months to 31 October, BCAL welcomed a total of 2,676,970 passengers on to its scheduled services – 12.25 per cent more than in the previous year. Cargo at 82,893 tonnes was up by 8.26 per cent. Performance, measured in the amount of revenue tonnage of passengers and freight multiplied by the number of kilometres flown, increased by 16.3 per cent and our revenue load factor, the amount of space filled against capacity available, increased by 4.1 percentage points to 60.2 per cent. We had sold two DC-10s, replacing them with two further Boeing 747s. An additional 747, our fifth, came into the fleet in October.

Apart from the new Tokyo service, opened to great acclaim, with a full-scale inaugural in June, just weeks before we began talking with British Airways, new routes were developed to Nice, Milan and Gaborone, Botswana. The Gaborone licence came after an unsightly tussle with British Airways which tried to block the twice-weekly service via Lusaka, on the grounds that we were trying to get through the back door to South Africa, in anticipation of their own services to Johannesburg and Capetown being axed as part of a programme of sanctions against the Pretoria government.

The new Saudi Arabian routes continued to suffer, however, from the depression in the oil industry. The biggest single financial blow came from the important West African routes, as a result of the further deteriorating economic climate in Nigeria. Traffic on the routes fell by a third and revenue by £31 million. Deterioration in the Nigerian currency, the naira, meant that the value of sales within Nigeria fell by some £48 million. Although traffic was increasing across the North Atlantic – figures were up by 23.6 per cent – revenue remained depressed from 1986, the year the Americans turned their backs on Europe, when fares were discounted heavily to attract any kind of business at all.

The overall effect was a reduction in turnover and an operating loss of £10.8 million. The sales of assets – chiefly other group companies – netted £47.5 million and, after interest payments, BCAL's last full financial year ended with a profit, before tax, of £9.94 million.

The months of uncertainty, however, were beginning to take their toll on business for the new financial year we entered in November, especially the bulk tour business for the summer months of 1988. The major travel wholesalers on whom all airlines depend for a significant bulk of traffic, simply were not booking with BCAL because the airline's future was so uncertain.

In the face of this, I proposed that a continuing drama of bid and counter bid and the time the process could take to reach a conclusion was so damaging that it had to be halted. We must, I told the board and Goldman Sachs, place a deadline on offers. What I wanted was a sealed bid system to take place on an allocated day. Both SAS and British Airways would be asked to place their best bids in envelopes to be placed before the BCAL board. We would then choose the one which best met the interests of the shareholders. John Thornton was asked to relay the information to the other two financial advisers and conduct the process.

The SAS team were striving hard to raise additional money among UK institutions to raise the level of their bid – £220 million would have done it – when John Thornton, with 3is' agreement, proposed to the takeover panel the course of action to curtail the auction process that had developed.

With the agreement of the takeover panel, 3is had written to Morgan Guaranty, for SAS, and Lazard Brothers, for BA, waiving the undertakings given to them not to irrevocably commit to their party's offer, with effect from nine o'clock on Monday, 21 December. Thornton told Morgan Guaranty and Lazards that the BCAL board would meet at noon on 21 December to consider offers on the table and make recommendations to shareholders.

The business pages of the Sunday newspapers of 20 December were full of the heightening drama. We encouraged the stories that SAS and Morgan Guaranty were locked all weekend putting together an improved deal which would handsomely top the BA £200 million. BA's shareholding in BCAL had now reached 8.4 per cent, as some smaller institutional shareholders opted for the bird in the hand. The key to the whole deal was now 3is, with its 41.7 per cent. Cuckney and Tindale had a choice between £82 million straight from BA or £45 million plus a continuing 23.5 per cent stake with the SAS deal.

In response to reports of the impending increased offer from SAS, Colin Marshall was reported as saying 'This lends further credibility to our assertions that SAS is seeking control of Caledonian.' British Airways appeared to be rattled and nervous. They had failed to halt the SAS offer so far, in both political and financial terms. The proud Helge Lindberg, however, stayed cool. 'I am not moving out of here until I have won. BA has promised a

569

battle on all legal fronts and this doesn't scare me at all,' he told *The Times* the previous Friday.

I had written to shareholders urging them to hold firm until the increased offer from SAS emerged and news leaked that Jan Carlzon was due to fly into London imminently to unveil a new deal. Press speculation put the new SAS deal at between £20 to £30 million on top of its original partial offer.

In the meanwhile, John Thornton was in the middle of events, dealing with the bidders. Numerous telephone conversations had taken place with Morgan Guaranty and Lazards. An executive from Lazards, at the instigation of BA, had broken ranks and visited Larry Tindale in an effort to pull off a deal with 3is. Larry simply referred him back to Goldman Sachs.

Thornton had met Lindberg and the Morgan Guaranty team earlier in the morning of 21 December to be advised of a possible revised offer, but no details emerged.

The dramatic news was, however, that British Airways had responded to the reported bigger bid from SAS. In their anxiety, King and Marshall put together a shut-out bid. It was the final hand in the game of poker being played for the jackpot of BCAL. Their move came in the form of a sealed bid: a letter from Peter Grant of Lazards. On behalf of BA, he was offering the new price of £250 million for the entire shareholding of BCAL. This was £50 million more than the bid already on the table and £13 million more than the sum agreed back in July. The proviso was that the offer had to be accepted that day.

Each of the directors, David Beety, Leonard Bebchick, Trevor Boud, David Coltman, Marshall Gibson, Peter Masefield, Alastair Pugh and Larry Tindale, made their various ways across London to Goldman Sachs. This time we were in the bank's offices at Old Bailey, a mile or so away from the Fetter Lane scene of triumph with Jan Carlzon twelve days earlier. With the famous Central Criminal Court alongside the Goldman building, here we were sitting in judgement on the future of 7000 people. My responsibilities in the matter had, by law, to be dispassionately deployed in the interests of our shareholders and them alone.

It did not take long, after a presentation on the choices before us by John Thornton, to come to a verdict. The minutes of that meeting record that we agreed, in view of the unconditional nature of the offer by British Airways which was clearly superior to the position with SAS, that shareholders be recommended to accept the new BA offer. It was agreed to request 3is to sell their shareholding to British Airways plc, as requested by Lazards, and further to make it clear in announcements that the board was relying on the numerous public statements made by Colin Marshall about the job security of employees.

As I stepped out of the Daimler on to the pavement of Fetter Lane, once again to meet with the BA team and its bankers, Lazards, I glanced across the road. The Stab in the Back was disgorging its customers from the lunchtime session and one of the staff was busy bolting one side of the door, before he disappeared inside finally to slam the place shut.

It was all matter of fact, as we set about the arrangements for the announcement of the conclusion of the deal. My overnight feelings were as mixed as the two separate stories in the following morning's *Times*. On the front page of the main paper, the story started with the words, 'British Airways last night won the battle for British Caledonian with a £250 million offer which knocked out its Scandinavian opponent.' A photograph of a buoyant John King ran alongside the article. The headline on the main story on the front page of the business section read, 'Deal triumph for BCAL,' referring to comments from City analysts that the £250 million deal was a triumph for my own negotiating skills.

I felt a pang of remorse as I read further down in the article that Helge Lindberg had confirmed that SAS was prepared to increase its offer, but to match British Airways was out of the question. 'Such a price is too high for BCAL,' he was quoted as saying. 'It makes it clear to us that BA is paying the price for keeping its monopoly.' It made no sense to try to compete.

Of course, I was pleased with the deal we had eventually pulled off. The cash offer stood at £12.15 for each BCAL share. 3is would net £100 million, an enormous yield from the £12 million they had invested originally. All the shareholders, especially staff, would receive good rewards. I stood to gain a personal fortune, as did a number of the other board members who had put up substantial sums of money all those years ago.

But I did not want, at that moment, a weary Helge Lindberg to drag his files onto an SAS aircraft at Heathrow on his way back

571

home believing that the SAS deal was all part of a hard negotiating game to get the BA offer price up. I had desperately wanted the deal with SAS to come off. I wanted the chance to continue with BCAL more than I wanted any amount of cash for myself.

I was reading *The Times* and all of the other newspapers from my desk at Caledonian House. I knew that this office, with its familiar furniture, the books and souvenirs I had collected over the years, the gifts I had been given on numerous overseas visits, would shortly be closed down. The battle for BCAL was over. I looked across out of the north-facing window, to the runway at Gatwick and to the passenger terminals where BCAL aircraft, the golden lion on the tail, continued to go about their daily business on the routes of the network we had so carefully pieced together over the years. In a drawer of the desk, I reached for a small plastic file, placed it on the desk in front of me and took out the two sheets of paper it contained. I started to read, over again, the words I had composed in that heady and exciting day after the completion of the arrangement with SAS. It was a message to staff, ready to be used in the very near future of which, at the time, I had little doubt. It read:

Our battle to keep our airline independent and intact has been won. The victory is heightened by the fact that we have emerged stronger, with great competitive potential, through the association with SAS. The SAS financial investment is just the tip of the iceberg . . . We have battled against odds, which, at times, have appeared to be overwhelming. The development we have embarked on this week is not just a major phase in the evolution of BCAL. It is a momentous milestone in the history of British and European air transport . . .'

Margaret Trett interrupted my thoughts as she came through on the inter-office telephone. 'Sir Colin Marshall is here.'

# Postscript

The story of my aviation career is strewn with ironies. But there is none so rich as the one which manifests itself many times over, every day, in the view from my present office close to Gatwick Airport. From there, I can see the aircraft coming and going. Especially, I look out for the old BCAL DC-10s and 747s, now painted in the colours of British Airways, flying the old BCAL routes, operated by former BCAL pilots and cabin staff – the Caledonian girls – also in BA uniform. I also see a more familiar looking livery, the golden lion of BCAL adorning the tails of the old British Airtours fleet, operating charter services to the holiday spots of Europe, North America and further afield.

John King and Colin Marshall said, at the time the Monopolies and Mergers Commission was considering the takeover plan, that they would keep the BCAL name and identity for charter activities. It was the gesture towards King's promise to 'cherish the best of BCAL'. Yet the British Airtours operation carrying the name of 'Caledonian Airways' is a pretence. Apart from the cosmetic of the name, symbol, and the tartan uniforms of its female cabin staff, the airline contains nothing of British Caledonian or the original Caledonian Airways (Prestwick) Ltd.

Today's 'Caledonian' is simply the old charter operation set up in the 1970s by the state-owned British Airways against which the real British Caledonian and the other independents protested so vehemently, on the ground of unfair competition. That it now flies under the banner of the enterprise I and a few friends founded in 1961 and took to the heights of international air transport over three decades is cause for a wry smile.

The task of merging British Caledonian into British Airways began on 4 January 1988 and was formally completed by 14 April.

573

The period was one of emotion and uncertainty at Caledonian House and at the former BCAL stations around the scheduled service network, as staff waited to find out whether or not they had jobs with British Airways.

So far as I was concerned, there was no question, after the events of November and December 1987, that I would stay, as earlier indicated, to run the Gatwick end of the business. It was not, in any event, something I had seriously considered. At Caledonian House, the work of tidying up the affairs of BCAL and conducting the sale of shares to Lazard Brothers fell to the company secretary Peter Atkin and his staff. They became the proverbial sweepers up after the Lord Mayor's Show. Alastair Pugh, Trevor Boud, David Coltman and I resigned, under agreement with British Airways, on 1 February, with arrangements that we could stay in our offices until the end of April. None of us did, but moved out as soon as it was convenient and, in my case, as soon as I was sure that the best care, under the circumstances, was being extended to the staff of BCAL.

It was an emotional and confusing time, as the British Airways men moved in to implement the process of integration. Caledonian House, which just a short time earlier had been a hive of industry, gradually slowed down to a halt as departments were emptied out and work transferred to the corresponding units at Heathrow, central London or other parts of Gatwick.

There were, of course, individuals who felt hard done by in the process of takeover, and some sections of the press tried to exaggerate the emotion associated with the demise of BCAL as we knew it. Overall, however, Colin Marshall has to be given credit for the caring way in which our managers and staff were treated. Those who were invited to stay on were, I was assured, welcomed into British Airways. Others, for whom there were no suitable posts, went on their way with generous severance packages.

The task of implementing the merger was given by Marshall to the British Airways operations director, Peter Owen, with whom I was in close consultation in the early period. I have nothing but praise for the human and professional way he went about a complex and emotive task. To many former BCAL staff Owen became their 'champion' in dealings with headquarters at Heathrow.

One of the saddest parts of the merger was the sale of BCAL

paraphernalia – inflight catering equipment, blankets, aircraft models and the like – at the Gatwick distribution centre. There is many a small restaurant where guests may find their cocktail served in a BCAL first class cut-glass goblet, complete with the Lion Rampant symbol.

The bitter-sweet nature of the whole affair came home at a dinner given at London's Ritz Hotel by John Cuckney and Larry Tindale. Ostensibly it was a celebration of the £250 million deal and the his guest list comprised all of those in BCAL, Goldman Sachs, the law firms and stockbrokers who had played a central part in the deal. For some of us – the BCAL people – it was also a wake. I decided to attend in my full Highland dress and spoke, not about the financial coup we had dramatically pulled off, but about the airline, its people and our joint achievements. We had gone further, far further, than any independent British airline had ever gone, I told the guests, just in case they thought BCAL was simply a set of figures on an offer for sale document.

Goldman Sachs sent me an engraved silver cigar case, filled with my favourite Havanas, as a memento of the great deal of 1987. I wrote a letter of thanks to John Thornton, saying that I hoped the cigars were not as explosive as the share scheme we had invented to get the SAS offer past the CAA.

As I can see the aircraft of British Airways and 'Caledonian' at Gatwick, so I can also view the expanding fleets of the likes of Air Europe, Dan Air and Air UK plying the old BCAL routes that John King and Colin Marshall sacrificed to achieve the vote of approval from Sir Godfray LeQuesne and his Monopolies and Mergers Commission – the routes to Paris, Brussels, Nice, Glasgow, Edinburgh and Manchester. Each of these airlines, particularly Air Europe, have taken on the spirit and, indeed, many of the management and staff of BCAL. Richard Branson's Virgin Atlantic fought its way to take the BCAL place as the second UK airline on the trans-Siberian route to Japan, as well as boosting its transatlantic operations.

A special invitation came my way from Jean Pierson, the burly and genial president of Airbus Industrie. Quietly and with no fuss, he invited me to Toulouse to travel on a test flight of the A.320, the European aircraft for which BCAL was launch customer and which was now being repainted in British Airways' livery. It was

575

a private and genuine gesture on the part of Pierson. For myself, it was a nostalgic trip, reflecting the drama of the sales battle between Airbus, Boeing and McDonnell Douglas and the political kudos that selection of the A.320 had generated. John King and Paul Channon were later to preside over a hand-over ceremony in Toulouse to take the delivery of the first A.320, receiving accolades established for them by BCAL.

John King's own gesture was to host a reception to mark my 'retirement' from aviation at the Institute of Directors in Pall Mall. The guest list was of my choosing and consisted of a string of old friends of BCAL, political, commercial, personal and media. Ray Colegate was there. So, too, was William Kinnoull and Bob McCrindle. Peter Masefield mixed with Pat Meaney and no less than six cabinet ministers, past and present, gave their time to attend. I had been apprehensive about the occasion, but John King was a gentleman, keeping out of the limelight and allowing me to take the centre stage. He refused to speak, I recall, saying simply: 'No, it's Adam's party.'

Jan Carlzon and Helge Lindberg retired back to Stockholm, but Norman Tebbit's 'Vikings' would return to the UK later. They had lost the chance to link with BCAL, but they learned lessons about British politics they would never forget. Helge had taken some time off for Christmas and after. On 14 January, on his return to his office at Stockholm's Bromma Airport, he wrote me a letter. He referred to the events at the end of 1987 as 'our exciting venture'. Said Helge: 'I cannot remember having had such an exciting time in my forty-one years in the airline business – and I doubt that I will ever experience such a situation again, when so many people worked so concentrated, day and night.'

In reading Helge's letter my mind went back to November and December. I thought of the to-ing and fro-ing between Gatwick, Pall Mall, and the banker's City offices where intrigue and high finance was our staple diet. I remembered repeated visits to the Houses of Parliament, to the ugly utilitarian offices of the Department of Transport and to the curious, threepenny piece shaped headquarters of the CAA in Kingsway. Coming into recall was the paradox between sumptuous lunches with political and press contacts in the River Restaurant at the Savoy, and snatched snacks of sandwiches at the desk of the Pall Mall office, fetched from a local café by my driver, Les Smith. My thoughts went to the journeys home, after long hours in the City, through the drowsy late night streets of the South London suburbs, to the amplified sound of Beethoven on the Daimler's stereo system.

The sound of the every-busy fax machines, radio pagers and telephones came back to me. They manifested the constantly-alert intelligence system we had to maintain for the press activities, the political dialogues and the negotiations over the battle for BCAL itself. Margaret Trett, operating a mobile office wherever I might need it, and Janet Manning, the mainstay at Gatwick, were at its centre.

Lindberg also wrote to Larry Tindale and a paragraph of his letter is worth quoting. 'I must admit,' wrote Helge, 'that I also felt very sorry and rather empty when leaving London just before Christmas. However, we in SAS have not given up to find suitable partners in Europe and I guess that within short [sic] I will be involved in another opportunity . . .'

SAS went on to complete a deal to acquire a stake in Mike Bishop's Airlines of Britain Group whose best known company is British Midland, and then to complete a partnership deal with Swissair. The deal with British Midland, negotiated under the noses of the Government and British Airways, must have brought a taste of sweet revenge to the palates of Carlzon and Lindberg. There was no way, by now, that the Monopolies and Mergers Commission or the EEC Competition directorate would allow British Airways to swallow up any further British airlines. Their field was clear and they now knew the UK political rules.

A whole new concept of cross-border mergers and groupings among airlines has now been accepted as a matter of course, politically and commercially. Lufthansa, the German national airline, has linked with Air France, SAS with Swissair, Air New Zealand with Qantas. U.T.A., the proud independent French airline with whom we were so closely linked, had now been bought by Air France. In the Far East, there are well-founded rumours that the likes of Japan Air Lines and Singapore Airlines are seeking partners. The mega carrier combines in the USA have taken in more small airlines and tightened their grip on their base markets.

I watch with special interest the recapitalisation of Belgium's Sabena which has attracted investments of 20 per cent each from

KLM of Holland and British Airways. Sabena became 40 per cent foreign-owned even before the single European market rolled away the sovereignty barriers with the EEC. It was the same level of shareholding that SAS planned to hold in BCAL, in the longer, deregulated term.

The crucible for the future moulding of airline competition is now the computerised reservation systems, or CRSs, as an aviation person would say. Here the internationalisation of the airline business is more pronounced than anywhere else. The rival systems, each with an evocative name like Galileo, Amadeus, Fantasia, Abacus, Sabre, are ventures of consortia, formed by groups of airlines.

Their purpose is to achieve global distribution advantages through an electronic catalogue of products and prices incorporating a transaction system which will confirm the booking and the fare and then print the passenger's ticket.

'Globalisation' is the buzz word in contemporary air transport. It represents simply the major airlines' strategies to break out of the old system of nationalism and spread themselves around a world which has become one global air travel market. The notion of having one major international airline for each country is obsolete. For the future of Europe, look towards the USA. Within a short space of time, Europe will have but three or four, perhaps five, gigantic airline combines operating intercontinental routes. Many small countries in the so-called third world, who had no commercial right to be in the airline business in the first place, will ultimately withdraw from major, overseas air transport, instead selling their national route rights on a franchise basis to the mega carriers of Europe, North America and the Pacific.

The developed airlines have the capability; all that halts true globalisation is politics, or rather aeropolitics, one of the last remaining constraints in an industry which has broken through the frontiers of technology and economics. But there will be a place for the small and inventive airlines to create niche markets for themselves, especially in the development of inter-regional services within Europe, or in low fare alternative airlines on the main international trunk routes which should emerge as the distinction between scheduled carriers operating under negotiated route rights and charter airlines flying in a deregulated environment fade away, or change with the times.

The other great constraint to the industry is its infrastructure of airports and controlled airspace, under monopoly suppliers, mainly government agencies. More terminals and more runways are needed desperately in most parts of the world, especially in the southeast of England. Congested airports and airways are the single biggest source of customer frustration and dissatisfaction with airline services. Governments need to take a giant philosophical leap forward to realise that there needs to be sensible balance between the demands of environmentalists and the requirement to provide an efficient and safe air transport infrastructure, for the benefit of international trade and commerce and the individual leisure traveller. It is a fair bet that many of the people who fume at delays to their holiday flights to the trendy Greek Islands are the same ones who petition to halt night flying and airport construction. Governments must also invest in the system. Air transport needs ministers of vision and enterprise, not penny-pinching bookkeepers, jealously guarding the national petty cash boxes. It needs, also, administrators to create a co-ordinated air traffic control system for Europe, and to open up more airspace for civil use by releasing areas devoted to the military but rarely used for exercises.

The infrastructure is by no means at its limit, there is plenty of space for growth if the political will is applied. Short-term strategies for the putting up of slots at Heathrow and Gatwick for auction to the highest bidder, for instance, are stupid in the extreme. Those who prepare them are creating policies for stagnation, not growth. In the end, I believe that airlines will themselves take over the running of airports and airways, in the same way that railways run their own tracks and termini. But that will take a long process of evolution.

Over BCAL's latter years the sinister and cowardly arm of terrorism came to affect air transport with many mindless, tragic results. There is no easy answer to the question of when the need for high security will end: probably never, as air transport has proved to be a soft target. But governments must resolve never to allow such horrors as the Pan Am 747 incident at Lockerbie to happen again. And the British government must take responsibility for and finance airline and airport security, rather than pass the job on to airport authorities who pass the cost to airlines, who, in turn, pass the charges to passengers. Security at airports is a national responsibility in just the same way as the policing of the streets. Until the contemporary, blinkered view is dropped, airlines and passengers will suffer delay and frustration, while paying for the privilege in the cost of their air tickets.

Politicians and others who believe that air transport is at its zenith need only to look back over the last twenty or thirty years. Did those who travelled in a DC-7C ever imagine an aircraft like the Boeing 747-400, carrying more than 400 people non-stop from London to Tokyo?

There is continued high growth in the industry, and although the rates of increase are not what they were in the so-called boom years after the War, in absolute terms they are enormous and there seems to be general agreement that demand for air transport will approximately double its current level by the end of the century, giving an average growth per year equal to the total size of the world air transport product at the beginning of the turbine era. This growth is expected to require between 5000 and 6000 major new aircraft units by the turn of the century and some forecasters are even more optimistic.

I have been asked many times if I plan to return to the airline business. The answer is an emphatic 'No!' I will always remain close to an industry I helped to create, but I have handed on my control column to others, in circumstances which were financially rewarding but politically distasteful. BCAL could – and would – have been part of the free-enterprise future of civil aviation into the next century. Our appetite for bustling expansion, innovation and the creation of style, sharpened by a constant set of forces stacked against us, would have served the customer well in a climate of free and fair competition, whether we were linked with SAS or another carrier or, indeed, standing on our own, as we did for so many years.

It needed only a government honest enough to stand by the recommendations it had itself sought from its only competent authority on the subject of airline competition. I refer, of course, to the events of 1984 and the cynical crushing of the Civil Aviation Authority's Airline Competition Policy proposals – the famous, or infamous, file CAP 500.

BCAL lived on to fight and compete for a further three years and very nearly regained its full strength through a plan for restructure which was sadly too advanced for its time. The 'second force' airline and the serious competition it represented for UK air transport was, however, grievously wounded by the stab in the back administered by a conniving Cabinet in the latter months of 1984. The coup de grâce was delivered as it tried to lift itself up to stand, free, on its own two feet, by the same politicians at the end of 1987.

Some might say that BCAL was its own worst enemy. It nourished itself on the politics which brought forth its creation and might have predicted that political intent in 1970 would not stand the test of time in the face of shifting ideology. The airline might exist, in years to come, simply as an historical footnote, as 'an interesting experiment'. However, so long as former BCAL people are employed in aviation and hand down their legacy to others, so long as our former customers demand the level of personal service and value for money we strove to provide and so long as aspiring airlines battle to open new markets, BCAL lives on.

The story I have recounted cannot, in any way, include every single person, event and place who, or which, played a part in my career. I could not have described, for reasons of length, every single trip I made, each of which was momentous to one degree or another. I had not the space to mention all those I met in a web of journeys around the world, many of whom became firm friends. The description of warm African nights, crisp New York winters, long and lonely night flights, the bustle of Hong Kong, the lazy leisure of California, the homely face of Glasgow and the pace of an international meeting in Geneva will have to be imagined.

Latter stages of the story concentrate on the business, rather than my home life, for that is the way it was. Dawn stood by in support of the enterprise she had helped conceive and give birth to as a young married woman. She made for me a home that was a haven of comfort and privacy. My son Scott slipped quietly and anonymously into BCAL as an operations officer, latterly ending up as an airport manager in Paris, after duty in North America. He kept away from the centre of things, not wanting accusations of nepotism, preferring to stand on his own feet. My other son, Anthony, steered his own path, into a career in horticulture. After a sad marriage and divorce, Scott came back to the UK and the two boys share a house in Brighton.

581

My mother, Jemima, so strong a figure in my early days, remained an influence throughout. She became frail in body, but not in mind, and I arranged for her to move from Glasgow to Sussex, to be close to Dawn and me in 1986. She reached her hundredth birthday in 1988 and, as I write in 1989, remains as vital a part of my life as she did in my formative years.

Her Scottish pragmatism cut through all of the emotions associated with the end of the airline which I had dreamed of creating years before in Glasgow. After telling her of the events leading to the sale of BCAL, she thought for one or two moments, leaned forward in her chair and asked, 'Well, are you a millionaire, then?'

# Index

Borrie, Sir Gordon, 539, 547
Boud, Trevor, 151, 159, 166, 170, 218, 220, 241, 245, 246, 256, 265, 287, 294, 308, 320, 323, 324, 352, 361, 442, 460, 483, 484, 502, 512–13, 533–4, 535, 536–7, 570, 574
Boyd, Alan, 329, 332
Boyd-Carpenter, John (Lord), 275–6, 286–7, 291, 293, 300, 301, 318, 326, 447
Bradley, Fred, 267
Braniff Airlines, 343, 344–5, 346–7
Branson, Richard, 486, 575
Brilliant, Hugh, 175, 199, 265, 291, 304
Bristol 170, 70–1, 74
Bristol Britannia, 144, 146, 158
Bristow, Alan, 197, 212, 213, 220, 232, 240, 258, 261, 545
Britannia Airways, 202, 215, 275, 368, 371, 485, 493
Britavia, 74, 75–6, 77, 81, 82, 97, 131
British Aircraft Corp.: BAC1-11/500, 169–70, 185, 190, 191; Concorde, 174, 317; Super VC-10, 153, 160, 161–2
British Airlines Ball, 189–90, 218
British Airports Authority, 171, 474
British Air Services, 201
British Airways, 290; and BCAL's attempts at route rationalization, 290–4, 298–9, 301, 304, 307–8, 310; financial losses, 310, 406–7, 419; privatization of, 375, 407–15, 434, 463–7, 474, 475, 512, 518–19; and Hong Kong route, 378–83, 385; BCAL campaign against, 455, 500; 'welcomes competition', 475–6; financial clean–up of, 476; response to CAP 500, 491, 493–4; takeover of BCAL, 528–30, 533–41, 542–4, 547, 554, 565, 567, 569, 570–1, 573; anti-SAS campaign, 557–8
British American Club, 164, 188, 228
British and Commonwealth Shipping Co., 97, 154, 213, 214; see Cayzer, Anthony
British Aviation Services, 74
British Caledonian Airways (see also Caledonian Airways (Prestwick) Ltd): West African services, 267, 271–2, 295; inaugural scheduled flights to New York, 270–1, 280–3; 'Moonjet' flights, 273–4; finances, 276, 289, 303, 313, 319, 340–1, 365, 385, 521, 530; North Atlantic charters, 276–8, 295; management reorganization, 278–9; publicity campaigns, 284–5, 454, 455, 460–1; and fuel crisis, 285, 289, 290; route expansion, 285–8, 292; route rationalization, 290–4, 298–9, 308; and Horizon collapse, 294–5; fleet size, 294, 319, 321, 324, 325, 341, 352–3, 359, 430; 'Expo 74', 297; survival ('S') plan, 297, 298, 301–2,

304–7, 308–9; management reorganization, 308–9; and Shore review, 308, 309–10, 313–15; and 'Bermuda II', 327–33; applications to serve Dallas/Fort Worth, 333, 344, 357–9; participation in IATA, 337–9; and Houston route, 341, 344, 346, 350, 358, 360; and Los Angeles route, 347–50; Airlink service, 355–6; 'Mini-Prix' plan, 367–8, 369, 371; Hong Kong routes, 378–88, 391; Nigerian route, 398–9, 471–2, 519, 568; South American services, 399–400, 415, 431; effect of Falklands War on, 400, 411, 415, 418, 430; and Papal visit, 402–5; and privatization of BA, 409–15, 417–18, 440, 442–3, 447–8; British Caledonian Commuter plan, 431–2; contracts with Caribbean Airway, 438, and Air Seychelles, 439; planning and analysis of air industry, 442–6; 'Blue Book', 446, 447, 448, 454, 457; 'Airline of the Year' award, 449–50; orders Airbus 320, 451–2; campaign against BA, 455, 493; 'Airline and Airports' scheme, 454–5, 457–8; 'Gold Book', 472, 482; Saudi Arabian routes, 476–7, 492, 511–12, 514, 519, 523; service to Tripoli, 477–9, 523; 'European Transport and the Consumer', 481; CAA press release on, 499; route exchanges with BA, 503–7, 511–12; 'Way Ahead' policy, 513–14; Far East services, 517, 523; public flotation plans, 519, 520; proposed merger with Air Europe, 524–6; BA takeover, 528–30, 533–41, 542–4, 547, 554, 565, 567, 569, 570–1, 573; proposed merger with SAS, 532, 539, 541–2, 545–64, 565, 566–7, 569–72
*British Caledonian and Gatwick Airport in the Eighties*, 363–4
British Caledonian (Charter) Ltd, 397
British Caledonian Commuter, 31–2
British Caledonian Flight Training Ltd, 514
British Caledonian Helicopters, 472, 545
British Eagle International Airlines, 147, 167, 173, 175, 176, 177, 179, 180, 182, 189, 190, 196
British European Airways, 64, 65, 147, 173, 196; Highlands and Islands network, 66, 67; Edwards' report on, 200, 202, 205–6, 209; industrial unrest in, 205; merger with BOAC, 285
British Island Airways, 257
British Midland Airways, 202, 415, 431, 492, 503, 577
British Overseas Airways Corp., 96, 124, 133, 136, 144, 189; protectionist policies, 138, 139–40, 147, 167–8, 173, 176–80; and

Cocklin, Tony, 129, 166–7, 168, 176, 187, 218, 224, 243, 244, 347, 369, 378, 442, 450, 487, 509, 528, 536, 543, 563
Colegate, Ray, 192, 219, 225, 251, 277, 290–1, 293, 369, 371, 436–8, 468–9, 473–5, 487, 488, 510, 552, 553, 565–6, 576
Colker, Sol, 138
Coltman, David, 438, 442, 447, 454, 533, 534, 535, 536–7, 541, 546, 550, 570, 574
Colvin, Michael, 413, 420–1
Compania Hotelera del Mediterraneo, 247, 248–9
Continental Express, 163, 186, 251
Cooper, 'Duff', 43, 44
Copthorne Hotels Ltd, 278, 472, 520, 545
Corfield, Fred (Sir Frederick), 198, 217, 226, 229–33, 251, 252
Council of British Societies, 186–7, 227
Court Line, 202, 249, 275, 295, 299
Cowes, I. of W., 37–48
Cox, H.W. ('Rocky'), 341–2, 357, 360, 400
Crosbie, Leonard, 304
Crosland, Anthony, 192, 199–200, 205, 214, 215
Cuckney, Sir John, 559, 561, 567, 575
Cumming, R.L., 256, 258
Cunard Eagle Airways, 83, 122, 123, 147

Damon, Captain Barry, 133–4
Dan Air, 275, 308, 369, 493
Davies, John, 263, 274
Dawnay, Ned, 535
Daymon, Phil, 76, 82, 90–1
Deane, Peter, 111
Deighton, Paul, 533–4, 552
de la Haye, Barbara, 83
de la Haye, John, 83–4, 85–90, 93, 94, 95, 97, 98, 99, 101, 102–3, 108, 111, 112–13, 116, 117, 117, 118, 119, 133, 139, 141–4, 148, 153, 160, 166, 169, 175–6, 184, 191, 196, 199, 209, 218, 219, 222, 224–5, 228, 238, 241, 243, 244, 247, 251, 255, 256, 257, 265, 266, 267, 269, 271, 277, 278–9, 289, 291, 347, 442
Dell, Edmund, 327, 331, 333, 334, 336, 344, 345–7, 350
Deller, Alan, 508
Delta Air Lines, 344, 354, 390, 432
Dennison, Captain Hugh, 145
Dent, John, 398, 414–15, 447, 483, 487, 488, 491–2, 510, 552
Dibbs, Alex, 407
Dobson, Ray, 214–15, 217, 229, 251, 252, 255–6, 260, 265, 291, 300, 308, 309
Donachy, John, 17
Donaldson, Alex, 91

Donaldson Airways, 207, 275
Donaldson Line, 137, 138, 148, 149, 160, 166
Donne, Michael, 203
Donovan, Len, 139
Douala Airport, Cameroon: air crash, 111–15, 116
Douglas Aircraft Co., 115; DC-3, 66; DC-6B, 133; DC-7C, 84–5, 95, 96–7, 115, 144, 152, 166; see also McDonnell Douglas
Dourleys, the, 46–7, 55, 60, 61, 73
Draper, Gerry, 207, 415
Drewery, Ted, 129
Dunlop, Gordon, 411, 415, 416, 417, 418, 534
Dykes, 'Gabe', 19

Eagle Airways, 77, 83, 122, 123, 147
Eagle Aviation Ltd, 122–3
Edwards, Professor Ronald, 174, 214, 218
Edwards' Committee of Inquiry, 174–5, 182, 192, 194, 195–207, 294, 436, 437
El Al, 127, 178, 194

Fajemirokum, Henry, 272, 350–1
Falcon Airways, 100
Farrell, Reg, 183
Field, Peter, 184
Field, Randolph, 486
Finlay, Alec, 310
Fisher, Bernard, 93, 95, 98, 99
Fitzpatrick, George, 187
Fleet Air Arm, 16–36, 63, 64–5
Forrest, Bob, 177
Forsyth, Charlie, 320, 322–3, 324–5
Fraser, Sir Hugh, 98
Frost, Alan, 111
Fuller, Don, 144–5

Garland Compton, 284–5
Garrity, Tom, 90, 119, 125, 151, 153, 155
Gatwick Airport, 155, 160, 171, 184, 334, 340, 353, 354–5, 360–1, 363, 366, 375, 376, 445, 474–5
Geekie, Tom, 207
General Electric, 325, 341
Gerrard, David, 183
Gibson, Richard Marshall, 98, 137, 151, 153, 155, 159, 190, 218, 269, 546, 570
Glasgow Royal Technical College, 15, 17
Glasgow University Naval Division, 17, 18, 98
Global of London (Global Tours), 190–1, 247, 248
Golden Lion Travel, 246, 277
Goldman Sachs International Corp., vi, vii, 533, 535, 536–7, 541, 542, 559–62, 563–4, 569, 575

Kleinwort Benson, 241–2, 252, 253, 256, 258, 268, 460, 483, 484, 490, 498, 519, 525, 533, 567
KLM, 531, 553, 577
Knighton, William, 409, 457, 461, 462–463
Kollek, Teddy, 129
Koven, Len, 294

Lagos, Nigeria, 88–73
Laker, (Sir) F.A. (Freddie), 97, 167, 184–5, 192–3, 222, 232, 236, 237, 308, 317–18, 353, 368, 369, 380, 381, 382, 383, 394–6, 535
Laker Airways, 185, 274, 331, 332, 368–9, 371, 394, 395–7, 435–6
Lang, Sir John, 147
Lathière, Bernard, 369–70
Laverick, Judy, 243
Lazard Brothers, vi, 535, 537, 541, 542, 565, 569, 570
Lazarus, Peter, 457, 502, 503–4
Ledingham, Doug, 478, 479
Legg, George, 111
Legge, Frank, 535
Le Goy, Ray, 193
Lemon, A.E., 220, 256, 258
LeQuesne, Sir Godfray, vi, 540, 541, 544
Levine, Mike, 345
Limbert, Captain Alan, 128
Lindberg, Helge, 542, 545, 547, 550, 553, 555, 559, 561, 562, 565, 567, 569–70, 571, 576, 577
Lloyds International, 84, 202, 275, 276
Lockett, Jim, 172
Lockhart, Captain, 107
Logan, Bobby, 187
Lossiemouth, RNAS, 84–5
Loughlin, Charles, 275
Lubbock, Eric (Lord Avebury), 230, 237, 291
Lyle Shipping, 166, 190, 268, 304
Lympne airport, 74–5

MacArthur, 'Mac', 34, 36, 37, 111
McCrindle, Robert, 413, 463, 472, 510, 549, 550, 576
McDonald's School, 4, 7, 323–4
McDonnell Douglas, 320–1, 322–5, 359, 373–4, 394, 401, 435–6, 451; DC-10, 319, 321, 322, 372–3, 374
Mackay McIntosh, 91, 92
Mackenzie, P.A. ('Mac'), 309
McLeod, Duncan, 137
Macpherson, Ruth, 107, 111
McWilliam, Jimmy, 92, 108, 324

Magowan, Derek, 183
Maitland, 'Jock', 129
Manzie, Gordon, 197
Marking, Henry, 310
Marshall, Colin, 434–5, 475, 530, 533, 534, 539, 541, 551, 566, 569, 570, 571, 572, 573, 574
Marten, Neil, MP, 199, 200
Martin, George, 90, 108
Masefield, Sir Peter, 171–2, 305, 323, 324, 327, 336, 352, 408, 411, 442, 443, 485, 487, 497, 498, 503–4, 531, 546, 570, 576
Mason, Gordon, 183, 187, 244
Mason, Ken, 113
Mason, Roy, 215–16, 222, 229, 230, 233–6, 238, 240, 242, 251, 254, 260, 261
Meaney, Sir Patrick, 510, 576
Millichap, Bob, 528, 529
Milward, Sir Anthony, 196
Moncton, New Brunswick, 22, 31
Monopolies and Mergers Commission inquiry, 539, 540–2, 543–4, 547, 577
Moore, John, 461–2, 524
Morant, Sylvia, 243
Morgan, Audrey, 53, 54, 55, 61
Morgan Aviation Ltd, 53–4, 55–61
Morgan Guaranty, 541, 545, 548, 559, 567, 569, 570
Mountbatten, Lord Louis, 270, 280, 281–3
Mulley, Fred, 158
Murdoch, 'Purdie', 19

NAS Airport Services (Gatwick), 247
National Commercial and Schroeders, 160, 190
National Joint Council of Civil Aviation, 206, 260
Newman Airways 62–3
Nickalls, Frank, 220
Noble, Michael, 251, 253, 262, 263, 264
Noel–Paton, Ranald, 273, 350, 351, 387, 517
Nordio, Umberto, 338
Nott, John, 333, 363, 369, 374–7, 384, 385–7, 406, 416, 434, 491, 500
Novak, John, 114

Office of Fair Trading (OFT), 539, 547, 550, 551
Ogilvy, Hon. Angus, 300, 400
Onslow, Cranley, 200, 237–8
Orientours, 127–9
Orion Airways, 100, 485, 493
Overall, Mike, 473, 475, 481
Overseas Aviation, 84, 100, 102
Overseas Visitors' Club, 99, 102, 109
Owen, Peter, 574